terra australis 48

Terra Australis reports the results of archaeological and related research within the south and east of Asia, though mainly Australia, New Guinea and Island Melanesia — lands that remained terra australis incognita to generations of prehistorians. Its subject is the settlement of the diverse environments in this isolated quarter of the globe by peoples who have maintained their discrete and traditional ways of life into the recent recorded or remembered past and at times into the observable present.

List of volumes in Terra Australis

terra australis 48

The Archaeology of Sulawesi

Current Research on the Pleistocene to the Historic Period

**Edited by Sue O'Connor,
David Bulbeck and Juliet Meyer**

Australian
National
University

PRESS

ANU PRESS

Published by ANU Press
The Australian National University
Acton ACT 2601, Australia
Email: anupress@anu.edu.au

Available to download for free at press.anu.edu.au

A catalogue record for this book is available from the National Library of Australia

ISBN (print): 9781760462567
ISBN (online): 9781760462574

WorldCat (print): 1062353902
WorldCat (online): 1062354017

DOI: 10.22459/TA48.11.2018

Editorial board: Sue O'Connor, Sally Brockwell, Ursula Frederick, Tristen Jones and Ceri Shipton
Series Editor: Sue O'Connor

Cover design and layout by ANU Press.

Cover photograph: Dr Ben Marwick and Dr Rose Whitau (standing at base of the excavation) recording the stratigraphy at Gua Talimbue in Southeastern Sulawesi. (Photo by Sue O'Connor.)

Contents

List of figures

List of tables

Preface

Sue O'Connor, David Bulbeck and Juliet Mayer

Sulawesi has a unique place in the archaeology of Island Southeast Asia (ISEA). During the Pleistocene, when lower sea levels created a continuous land mass from Sumatra to Borneo, Sulawesi remained isolated by sea, but its long coastline, rich ecology and proximity to Borneo made it a promising destination for colonists and an ideal way station for onward seaborne travel to the east. When sea levels rose during the Holocene, producing the current geographical configuration of ISEA, Sulawesi's central location placed it at the crossroads of the maritime migrations that spread new languages and technological skills across this island realm. Numerous Sulawesi communities began to convert to Islam and Christianity in the 17th century, but even in the 20th century European explorers ventured upon remote communities who practised ancestor worship unaffected by influences from world religions. These attributes of Sulawesi inspired the successful application by Sue O'Connor, Jack Fenner, Janelle Stevenson and Ben Marwick for an Australian Research Council Discovery Grant ('The archaeology of Sulawesi: A strategic island for understanding modern human colonization and interactions across our region', ARC DP110101357), with the aim of documenting cultural change in Sulawesi within the parameters of local and regional environmental change.

The first step was to consult the Makassar Archaeology Office whose jurisdiction for archaeological research included the location earmarked for the project's fieldwork. Muh. Husni, the then director of the Makassar Archaeology Office, and project personnel subsequently met with National Research Centre for Archaeology staff in Jakarta to establish a formal agreement for implementing the project. Site survey, excavation and analysis proceeded with the participation of numerous archaeologists from the Makassar Archaeology Office, the National Research Centre for Archaeology and The Australian National University, as well as the project's nominated investigators. In keeping with the project's aim, and related advances in archaeological research on Sulawesi, the occasion seemed opportune to stage a symposium on current knowledge on Sulawesi's archaeology. Accordingly, between 31 January and 3 February 2016, under the joint auspices of the ARC project and the Makassar Archaeology Office, the symposium 'The Archaeology of Sulawesi – An Update' was held in Makassar.

As described in the chapter by Irfan Mahmud, who was promoted to directorship of the Makassar Archaeology Office in late 2015, 30 papers were presented at the symposium with a geographical coverage that extended from the Talaud Islands at the far north of Sulawesi to Muna Island, which lies off Sulawesi's southeastern arm. Not all of the presented papers were subsequently prepared for inclusion in this volume, in some cases because their content was published in journal articles shortly before or after the symposium. This volume's chapters nonetheless provide a taste of current archaeological research in Sulawesi, including contributions by Indonesian researchers (translated from the original Indonesian) that may not otherwise reach an international audience. The chapters also include two site reports on the archaeology of the Walandawe District, in Southeast Sulawesi, where the ARC project focused its fieldwork.

The ARC project would not have been possible without the assistance of its numerous Indonesian collaborators, and we particularly acknowledge the support of Made Sudarmika, who was director of the Makassar Archaeology Office during the main period of fieldwork and laboratory analysis. Funding for the editing and publication of this volume included two sources other than the ARC DP110101357 project, namely an ARC Laureate Fellowship FL120100156 to Sue O'Connor and a publication subsidy from ANU Press. This volume was double-blind peer reviewed and we thank the reviewers who put their time into reading and improving the chapters. We also acknowledge the services of Sally Brockwell and Katie Hayne in preparing the volume for publication.

1

The archaeology of Sulawesi: An update, 2016

Muhammad Irfan Mahmud

Symposium overview

The symposium on 'The Archaeology of Sulawesi – An Update' was held in Makassar between 31 January (registration day) and 3 February 2016 (field-trip day) as a joint initiative between the Balai Arkeologi Makassar (Balar Makassar, Makassar Archaeology Office) and The Australian National University (ANU). The main organisers were Sue O'Connor, David Bulbeck and Juliet Meyer from ANU, who are also the editors of this volume, and Budianto Hakim from Balar Makassar. Funding for the symposium was provided by an Australian Research Council Discovery Grant (DP110101357) to Sue O'Connor, Jack Fenner, Janelle Stevenson (ANU) and Ben Marwick (University of Washington) for the project 'The archaeology of Sulawesi: A strategic island for understanding modern human colonization and interactions across our region'.

Between 1 and 2 February, 30 papers were presented by contributors representing ANU, Balar Makassar, the National Research Centre for Archaeology (Jakarta), Balai Makassar Manado, Hasanuddin University (Makassar), Gadjah Mada University (Yogyakarta), Bandung Institute of Technology, Geology Museum in Bandung, Griffith University and James Cook University (Queensland), University of Wollongong and University of New England (New South Wales), University of Göttingen and Christian-Albrechts-Universität zu Kiel (Germany), the University of Leeds (United Kingdom), Brown University (United States of America) and Tokai University (Japan). Not all of the presenters were able to prepare their contribution for inclusion in this volume; fortunately, a summary of the presentations has been published by Macknight (2017). As detailed there, the presentations ranged in time depth from more than 100,000 years ago to less than 300 years ago, and covered five of Sulawesi's six provinces including the Talaud Islands, which lie approximately halfway between the Sulawesi mainland and Mindanao in the Philippines, with topics as diverse as initial settlement by archaic hominins, occupation by early modern humans as registered by their rock art and tool technologies, Holocene developments including the transition to the Neolithic and Early Metal Phase, the renowned megaliths of Central Sulawesi, early Bugis-Makasar history (South Sulawesi), early Islamic graves in South and West Sulawesi, and relevant palaeoenvironmental correlates.

Quite a few of the presentations focused on results from cave sites in Kabupaten (District) Maros, a short distance north of Makassar, which was the destination for the 3 February field trip. The visited sites included Leang Burung 1 and Leang Karassaq, both of which had been excavated during the 1969 Australian–Indonesian Archaeological Expedition to Sulawesi (Mulvaney and

Soejono 1970); Leang Timpuseng, with its painting in ochre of a babirusa 'pig deer' dated to at least 35,000 years ago (Hayes and van den Bergh, this volume); and Leang Burung 2, where excavations led by Adam Brumm (currently Griffith University) recovered faint traces of an early human or archaic hominin presence deep beneath the ~30,000 BP habitation layer documented by Glover (1981).[1]

Early scientific research into Sulawesi's past

The English naturalist Alfred Russel Wallace, who can be considered the founder of zoogeography, visited Sulawesi three times between 1856 and 1859 during his travels across the islands of Indonesia and Malaysia from 1854 to 1862 (Baker 2001). He took the map of Island Southeast Asia and drew a line (now known as Wallace's line) between Borneo with its fully Asian mammalian fauna, as also found on islands to the west, and Sulawesi with its peculiar representation of related mammals that shared their habitat with some species similar to those of New Guinea and Australia. In 1947, the colonial Dutch archaeologist Robert van Heekeren began a series of discoveries of Sulawesi mammalian fossils on the Walennae river terraces in South Sulawesi province. These included very archaic forms with no living relatives such as stegodons, primitive elephants and *Celebochoerus* suids as well as the similarly archaic *Babyrousa* suids and Anoa water buffaloes, which have survived on Sulawesi to this day (Hooijer 1975). Van Heekeren, and later R.P. Soejono, also collected stone artefacts from the same terraces including point picks and thick points, a range of scrapers (end-, crude concave, keeled and small-core scrapers) and chopping tools. Van Heekeren (1972) felt confident in dating the artefacts to the Pleistocene from the supposed faunal associations, and estimated a late Middle Pleistocene antiquity. Later research disassociated the mammalian fossils and the stone artefacts, dating the former to the Upper Pliocene and the latter to the Upper Pleistocene (Bartstra 1997), although the most recent investigations have vindicated van Heekeren's views (see below).

A different approach to Sulawesi's past, launched from an ethnographic perspective, was initiated by the Swiss second cousins Fritz and Paul Sarasin at the turn of the 20th century. Seeking evidence of the eastward migration of the ancestors of the Veddas, who the Sarasins had investigated in Sri Lanka, they ventured to the Lamoncong highlands of South Sulawesi on the basis of reports of *Toale* (forest people) who continued to dwell there in caves. They excavated one inhabited cave and three other caves at Lamoncong, and recovered bone points, distinctive stone points with a hollowed base and denticulate outline, and a variety of other stone artefacts (Sarasin and Sarasin 1905). Similar assemblages were excavated by Dutch colonial archaeologists near Lamoncong, along South Sulawesi's south coast and in the Maros District during the 1930s and 1940s, and were assigned to a Mesolithic 'Toalean culture' based on their similarities to the assemblages recorded by the Sarasins (van Heekeren 1972). The Maros sites proved to be of particular interest for their rock art, including hand stencils and *Babyroussa* paintings, which van Heekeren (1972) assumed to be Mesolithic but whose origins can now be traced back to much earlier times (see below).

Similarities between the South Sulawesi Toalean and the 'small tool tradition' of late Holocene Australia caught the attention of Australian archaeologists, leading to the Australian–Indonesian Archaeological Expedition to Sulawesi led by D.J. Mulvaney and R.P. Soejono (1970; Macknight, this volume). The goals of the expedition were, first, to excavate stratified assemblages that would allow investigation of Toalean cultural change—in particular, to test van Heekeren's (1972) sequence of a progression from an initial proto-Toalean to a middle Toalean characterised by geometric microliths and an upper Toalean marked by denticulated arrowheads and bone

---

1   Recently published by Brumm et al. (2017) during the period of preparation of the current volume.

points—and, second, to obtain radiocarbon dates for the Toalean. A then junior member of the expedition team, Ian Glover, continued work in the Maros karsts, including further survey along with excavation of early to late Holocene, Toalean materials at Ulu Leang 1 and Late Pleistocene, pre-Toalean materials at Leang Burung 2 (Glover 1978, 1981). Subsequent analysis of the materials excavated during the Australian–Indonesian Archaeological Expedition to Sulawesi, and synthesis with the Ulu Leang 1 reported results, indicated that both bone points and geometric microliths were longstanding characteristics of the Toalean, up to the late Holocene appearance of pottery, and the main chronological marker was the production of denticulated arrowheads restricted to the middle Holocene (Bulbeck 2004).

Recent revelations on Sulawesi's early past

Recent investigations relevant to Sulawesi's early prehistory have involved teams of Indonesian and international experts who have applied modern scientific dating techniques as part of an interdisciplinary approach to strategic sites, as per the examples below.

The potential antiquity of the earliest colonisation of Sulawesi was turned completely open with the demonstration of very early colonisation of Flores, an island that (like Sulawesi) is one of the non-continental islands of Wallacea to the east of Wallace's line. Stone artefacts of hominin manufacture associated with extinct fauna in the Soa basin have been dated to as early as 1 million years ago (Brumm et al. 2010), and linked to the occupation of the Liang Bua cave by the primitive *Homo floresiensis* species between c. 190,000 and 40,000 years ago (Sutikna et al. 2016). Mike Morwood, who instigated the scientific investigation of an archaic hominin presence on Flores, promoted Sulawesi as a likely source for the Pleistocene colonisation of Flores (Morwood and van Oosterzee 2007), which directed attention back to Sulawesi in archaeologists' hunt for evidence of archaic hominins in Wallacea.

A self-evident location for investigation was the Walennae river terraces, which had lapsed into obscurity as a result of Barstra's recensions noted above. At the site of Talepu, a predominantly Australian–Indonesian team identified a stratified sequence of 4.2 metres depth with *in situ* stone artefacts and vertebrate fossils, and which could be dated through optical luminescence dating of the deposits and uranium-series dating of the fossils. One of the excavation pits (T2) produced the majority of the stone artefacts — comparable to those described by van Heekeren (1972) — in deposits dated to around 126,000 years ago (in assocation with an Anoa-like fossil) and later. The other excavation pit (T4) produced a small number (four) of stratigraphically older stone artefacts bracketed between an overlying stegodon fossil and eight underlying *Celebochoerus* fossils. The latter have a minimum age of 200,000 years ago but are younger than 780,000 years ago (from palaeomagnetism evidence). The results accordingly date the colonisation of Sulawesi by *Homo* to at least 126,000 years ago and perhaps as early as 200,000 years ago, an antiquity indicative of an archaic hominin, even if it is not as early as in Flores (van den Bergh et al. 2016).

Fossil skulls in Africa assigned to very early representatives of modern humans have been dated to between c. 200,000 and 300,000 years ago (Gibbons 2017), but the earliest evidence for Island Southeast Asia (ISEA) relies on isolated teeth, assigned on morphological and metrical grounds to *Homo sapiens*, recovered as a minor component of Late Pleistocene rainforest faunal assemblages. Storm et al. (2005) identified a modern human premolar in the Punung fauna of East Java, which they dated to between 81,000 and 126,000 years ago based on consideration of the time period when East Java would have supported tropical rainforest. Westaway et al. (2017) demonstrate the modern human affinity of a molar and an incisor from Lida Ajer, West Sumatra, associated with a rich tropical rainforest faunal assemblage, which is firmly dated to between 63,000 and 73,000 years ago from luminescence dates on the deposit, uranium-series dates on speleothems and electron spin resonance dating on the mammalian fossils.

For evidence of substantive occupation by anatomically modern humans in ISEA, we need to refer to a later interval from about 45,000 years ago. A spectacular example is the uranium-series dating of 14 of the Maros cave paintings to the Late Pleistocene. Expressed in terms of rounded two standard-error age intervals, the minimum ages include 38,000–50,000 years ago for an undetermined animal figure, as well as 35,500–38,500 years ago for a *Babyroussa* figure, and 38,500–43,000 to 17,500–18,100 for hand stencils (Aubert et al. 2014). The older of these artworks are approximately contemporary with early habitation records from countries neighbouring Indonesia, including the deepest deposits at the Niah Caves in Sarawak, dated to between 35,000 and 50,000 years ago, and the basal deposits at Jerimalai and Laili Cave in East Timor, 40,000–45,000 years ago. The deep Niah deposits include a *H. sapiens* cranium and femur, generally considered to be of 'Australo-Melanesid' racial affinity, along with food refuse and more than 50 specimens of stone tools (identified from use wear and residues) and flaking debitage (Krigbaum and Datan 2005; Reynolds et al. 2013). The early East Timor deposits include marine and terrestrial fauna debris associated with flaked stone artefacts (Marwick et al. 2016; Hawkins et al. 2017).

Recent work has also extended the outreach of archaeological research in Sulawesi. Excavations at Gua Talimbue in Southeast Sulawesi, undertaken as part of 'The archaeology of Sulawesi: A strategic island for understanding modern human colonization and interactions across our region' project, have obtained the first Late Pleistocene dates for human habitation on the Sulawesi mainland outside of South Sulawesi (Suryatman et al. 2016). And a program of survey and excavation in the Bontocani area in Bone, along the Walennae valley downstream from Lamoncong where the Sarasins undertook their foundational research, has recovered evidence of rock art, haematite in a stratified context and local Toalean habitation (Sardi 2016).

Origins and early history of Sulawesi's major ethnolinguistic groups

Austronesian languages, and more specifically Malayo-Polynesian languages, are spoken universally as the indigenous languages throughout Sulawesi as they are across Indonesia west of the Moluccas. Simanjuntak (2006) emphasises the importance of the dispersal of Malayo-Polynesian speakers from the Philippines, associated with a Neolithic material culture (marked by polished adzes and pottery) for understanding the deep history of the indigenous ethnolinguistic societies of Sulawesi and Indonesia's other islands. The Karama River of West Sulawesi is particularly relevant for this topic of research, notably the open-air hamlet sites of Kamassi and Minanga Sipakko. These sites were initially excavated by Dutch colonial archaeologists (van Heekeren 1972), but their significance for understanding the early Neolithic of Sulawesi was not apparent until Carbon-14 dating could be applied. It is now clear that Neolithic occupation at these sites commenced at some point between 3500 and 3000 years ago, and that the diet included domestic pigs (*Sus scrofa*) introduced from overseas as well as the endemic suids hunted by local foragers from time immemorial, and that rice (wild or domesticated) was probably harvested (Anggraeni et al. 2012).

Statistical analysis of the lexicons of Malayo-Polynesian languages (Gray et al. 2009) has arrived at the following scenario. A lengthy period intervened between the initial rapid dispersal of proto-Malayo-Polynesian from the Philippines to western Indonesia and to Melanesia, between approximately 4000 and 3500 years ago, and the diversification of languages into the main

Malayo-Polynesian language groups that are recognisable today. In Sulawesi, for instance, the groups of languages in the Sangihe-Talaud Islands and in Central/Southeast Sulawesi can be traced back to ancestral languages dated to around 2500 years ago, and to 2000 years ago in the case of the languages of South and West Sulawesi, while the ancestor of the present-day languages of Sulawesi's northern arm may be no older than 1500 years ago. As a further complication, the Sulawesi northern arm languages are more closely related to Philippine languages than to other Sulawesi languages, suggestive of a Philippine-to-Sulawesi language dispersal much later in time than the one associated with the Neolithic colonisation of the Karama River. In summary, the reconstructible origins and history of Sulawesi's present-day Malayo-Polynesian speakers may date to the Early Metal Phase (Bellwood 2017) rather than the Neolithic.

In western Indonesia, the Early Metal Phase is associated with early Hindu/Buddhist influences from India, leading into the period of classic archaeology, but the situation for Sulawesi is far less clear. The most tantalising hint is a bronze Amaravati Buddha statue found in 1921 at Sikendeng near the mouth of the Karama River and dated by Bosch (1933) to between the 2nd and 7th centuries AD. This discovery prompted the excavation by A.A. Cense of Neolithic habitation traces at Sikendeng and the subsequent excavations further upstream at Kamassi and Minanga Sipakko, noted above, but no traces of Hindu/Buddhist influence (van Heekeren 1972). The classic period in Java continued through to the Majapahit empire dating to around the 14th century AD, by which time Java and South Sulawesi had maintained regular contact for several centuries, but with little indication of a Hindu/Buddhist influence on ideological systems in Sulawesi (Caldwell and Bougas 2004).

An alternative approach towards understanding early history is available for the Bugis of South Sulawesi, with their rich traditional literature that includes the La Galigo epic cycle as well as *lontaraq* texts on the origins and early history of the Bugis kingdoms. From his study of these sources as well as Bugis ethnography, Christian Pelras (1996), who first came to South Sulawesi in 1967, developed a scenario whereby their ethnic character changed over time from a focus on maritime travel to intensive farming (along with the trade of surplus produce as far east as Papua). Pelras (1996) also drew upon local traditions that ships formerly sailed from the Strait of Makassar through Lake Tempe to the mouth of the Walennae—effectively, that South Sulawesi south of Lake Tempe was geographically an island—partially supported by evidence that a continuous network of channels, rivers and lakes may have connected the west and east coasts of South Sulawesi during the elevated sea levels of Neolithic and Early Metal Phase times (Caldwell and Lillie 2004).

To conclude these introductory remarks, I would like to emphasise the importance of the public use of research and scholarship. The results of novel research should be presented in a social arena, starting with publication, which can greatly help our community. Schmidt (2004) observed that the integrity of a nation can be weakened in three ways: first, through submergence of its history; second, through fragmentation of the evidence of its history until it can no longer be detected and demonstrated; and third, through sundering the nation's relations with its ancestral antecedents. Archaeological research can help to overcome these setbacks and accordingly illuminate and celebrate the history of the Indonesian people and Indonesian society over the long term. This observation applies not just to scholarly research on topics that would be broadly familiar to members of the lay public—topics such as Islamic archaeology and the early development of the Bugis-Makasar kingdoms—but also to research on much earlier times when the material culture and belief systems of Sulawesi's inhabitants were very different from today's. In all, it is important that a volume of the nature presented here covers a wide-ranging chronological and geographic sweep.

Author biography

Muhammad Irfan Mahmud Director, Makassar Archaeology Office, Makassar, Indonesia

References

Anggraeni, T. Simanjuntak, P. Bellwood and P. Piper. 2014. Neolithic foundations in the Karama valley, West Sulawesi, Indonesia. *Antiquity* 88(341):740–756. doi.org/10.1017/S0003598X00050663 (accessed 5 June 2018).

Aubert, M., A. Brumm, M. Ramli, T. Sutnika, E.W. Saptomo, B. Hakim, M.J. Morwood, G.D. van den Bergh, L. Kinsley and A. Dosseto. 2014. Pleistocene cave art from Sulawesi, Indonesia. *Nature* 514:223–227. doi.org/10.1038/nature13422 (accessed 5 June 2018).

Baker, D.B. 2001. Alfred Russel Wallace's records of his consignments to Samuel Stevens, 1854–1861. *Zoologische Mededelingen Leiden* 75(16):251–341. www.repository.naturalis.nl/document/45070 (accessed 5 June 2018).

Bartstra, G.-J. 1997. A fifty year commemoration: fossil vertebrates and stone tools in the Walanae valley, South Sulawesi, Indonesia. *Quärtär* 47/48:29–50.

Bellwood, P. 2017. *First Islanders*. Hoboken: Wiley Blackwell. doi.org/10.1002/9781119251583 (accessed 5 June 2018).

Bosch, F.D.K. 1933. Het bronzen Buddha-beeld van Celebes' Westkust. *Tijdschrift voor Indische Taal-, Land- en Volkenkunde* 73:495–513.

Brumm, A., G.M. Jensen, G.D. van den Bergh, M.J. Morwood, I. Kurniawan, F. Aziz and M. Storey. 2010. Hominins on Flores, Indonesia, by one million years ago. *Nature* 464:748–752. doi.org/10.1038/nature08844 (accessed 5 June 2018).

Brumm, A., B. Hakim, M. Ramli, M. Aubert, G.D. van den Bergh, B. Li, B. Burhan, A.M. Saiful, L. Siagan, R. Sardi, A. Jusdi, Abdullah, A.P. Mubarak, M.W. Moore, R.G. Roberts, J.-x. Zhao, D. McGahan, B.G. Jones, Y. Person, K. Szabó, M.I. Mahmud, K. Westaway, Jatmiko, E.W. Saptomo, S. van der Kaars, R. Grün, R. Wood, J. Dodson and M.J. Morwood. 2017. A reassessment of the early archaeological record at Leang Burung 2, a Late Pleistocene rock-shelter site on the Indonesian island of Sulawesi. *PLOS One.* doi.org/10.1371/journal.pone.0193025 (accessed 5 June 2018).

Bulbeck, D. 2004. Divided in space, united in time: The Holocene prehistory of South Sulawesi. In S.G. Keates and J.M. Pasveer (eds), *Quaternary Research in Indonesia*, pp. 129–166. Modern Quaternary Research in Southeast Asia, Volume 18. Leiden: A.A. Balkema.

Caldwell, I. and W. Bougas. 2004. The early history of Binamu and Bangkala, South Sulawesi. *Bijdragen tot de Taal-, Land- en Volkenkunde* 160:456–510.

Caldwell, I. and M. Lillie. 2004. Manuel Pinto's inland sea: Using palaeoenvironmental techniques to assess historical evidence from southwest Sulawesi. In S.G. Keates and J.M. Pasveer (ed.), *Quaternary Research in Indonesia*, pp. 259–271. Modern Quaternary Research in Southeast Asia, Volume 18. Leiden: A.A. Balkema.

Gibbons, A. 2017 (7 June). World's oldest *Homo sapiens* fossils found in Morocco. *Science.* doi.org/10.1126/science.aan6934 (accessed 5 June 2018).

Glover, I.C. 1978. Survery and excavaton in the Maros district, South Sulawesi, Indonesia: The 1975 field season. *Bulletin of the Indo-Pacific Prehistory Association* 1:60–103.

Glover, I.C. 1981. Leang Burung 2: An upper Palaeolithic rockshelter in South Sulawesi, Indonesia. In G.-J. Bartstra and W.A. Casparie (eds), *Modern Quaternary Research in Southeast Asia*, pp. 1–38. Modern Quaternary Research in Southeast Asia, Volume 6. Rotterdam: A.A. Balkema.

Gray, R.D., A.J. Drummond and S.J. Greenhill. 2009. Language phylogenies reveal expansion pulses and pauses in Pacific settlement. *Science* 323:479–483.

Hawkins, S., S. O'Connor, T.R, Maloney, M. Litster, S. Kealy, J.N. Fenner, K. Aplin, C. Boulanger, S. Brockwell, R. Willan, E. Piotto and J. Louys. 2017. Oldest human occupation of Wallacea at Laili Cave, Timor-Leste, shows broad-spectrum foraging response to late Pleistocene environments. *Quaternary Science Reviews* 171:58–72.

Hayes, S. and G. van den Bergh. 2018. Cave art, art and geometric morphometrics: Shape changes and the babirusa of Sulawesi. In S. O'Connor, D. Bulbeck and J. Meyer (eds), *The Archaeology of Sulawesi: Current Research on the Pleistocene to the Historic Period*, pp. 43–60. Canberra: ANU Press.

Hooijer, D.A. 1975. Quaternary mammals west and east of Wallace's line. In G.-J. Barstra and W.A. Casparie (ed.), *Modern Quaternary Research in Southeast Asia*, pp. 37–46. Modern Quaternary Research in Southeast Asia, Volume 2. Rotterdam: A.A. Balkema.

Krigbaum, J. and I. Datan. 2005. The Deep Skull and associated human remains from Niah Cave. In Z. Majid (ed.), *The Perak Man and other Prehistoric Skeletons of Malaysia*, pp. 1–31. Penang: Penerbit Universiti Sains Malaysia.

Macknight, C.C. 2017. Symposium on 'The Archaeology of Sulawesi – An Update', held in Makassar, Indonesia, from 31 January to 3 February 2016. *Archipel* 93:3–7.

Macknight, C.C. 2018. The joint Australian–Indonesian archaeological expedition to South Sulawesi in 1969 in context. In S. O'Connor, D. Bulbeck and J. Meyer (eds), *The Archaeology of Sulawesi: Current Research on the Pleistocene to the Historic Period*, pp. 9–16. Canberra: ANU Press.

Marwick, B., C. Clarkson, S. O'Connor and S. Collins. 2016. Early modern human lithic technology from Jerimalai, East Timor. *Journal of Human Evolution* 101:45–64. doi.org/10.1016/j.jhevol.2016.09.004 (accessed 5 June 2018).

Morwood, M. and P. van Oosterzee. 2007. *The Discovery of the Hobbit*. Sydney: Random House Australia.

Mulvaney, D.J. and R.P. Soejono. 1970. The Australian-Indonesian Archaeological Expedition to Sulawesi. *Asian Perspectives* 13:163–176.

Pelras, C. 1996. *The Bugis*. London: Blackwell Publishers.

Reynolds, T., G. Barker, H. Barton, G. Cranbrook, L. Farr, C. Hunt, L. Kealhofer, V. Paz, A. Pike, P.J. Piper, R.J. Rabett, G. Rushworth, C. Stimpson and K. Szabó. 2013. The first modern humans at Niah, c. 50,000–35,000 years ago. In G. Barker (ed.), *Rainforest Foraging and Farming in Island Southeast Asia*, pp. 135–172. Cambridge: McDonald Institute for Archaeological Research.

Sarasin, P. and F. Sarasin. 1905. *Die Toála-hoehlen von Lamontjong. Versuch einer Anthopologie der Insel Celebes. Erster Teil: Die Toála-höhlen von Lamontjong.* (Materialien zur Naturgeschichte der insel Celebes, V Band, 1 Teil). Wiesbaden: C.W. Kriedel's Verlag.

Sardi M., R. 2016. Eksistensi budaya Mesolitik di situs prasejarah Bontocani Sulawesi Selatan: The existence of pre-Neolithic culture in Bontocani prehistoric sites South Sulawesi. *Walennae* 14(2):69–80.

Schmidt, F.W. 2004. *The Secret History of Freemasonry: Its Origins and Connections to the Knights Templar*. San Francisco: Harper.

Simanjuntak, T. 2006. Advancement of research on the Austronesian in Sulawesi. In T. Simanjuntak, M. Hisyam, B. Prasetyo and T.S. Nastiti (eds), *Archaeology: Indonesian Perspective, R.P. Soejono's Festschrift*, pp. 223–231. Jakarta: Indonesian Institute of Sciences.

Storm, P., F. Aziz, J. de Vos, D. Kosasih, S. Baskoro, Ngaliman and L.W. van den Hoek Ostende. 2005. Late Pleistocene *Homo sapiens* in a tropical rainforest fauna in East Java. *Journal of Human Evolution* 49:536–545.

Suryatman, S. O'Connor, D. Bulbeck, B. Marwick, A.A. Oktaviana and U.P. Wibowo. 2016. Teknologi litik di situs Talimbue, Sulawesi Tenggara: Teknologi berlanjut dari masa Pleistosen akhir hingga Holosen. *Amerta* 34(2):81–98. doi.org/10.24832/amt.v34i2.146 (accessed 26 October 2018).

Sutikna, T., M.W. Tocheri, M.J. Morwood, E.W. Saptomo, Jatmiko, R.D. Awe, S. Wasisto, K.E. Westaway, M. Aubert, B. Li, J.-x. Zhao, M. Storey, B.V. Alloway, M.W. Morley, H.J.M. Meijer, G.D. van den Bergh, R. Grün, A. Dosseto, A. Brumm, W.L. Jungers, and R.G. Roberts. 2016. Revised stratigraphy and chronology for *Homo floresiensis* at Liang Bua in Indonesia. *Nature* 532:366–369. doi.org/10.1038/nature17179 (accessed 5 June 2018).

van den Bergh, G.D., B. Li, A. Brumm, R. Grün, D. Yurnaldi, M.W. Moore, I. Kurniawan, R. Setiawan, F. Azi, R.G. Roberts, Suyono, M. Storey, E. Setiabudi and M.J. Morwood. 2016. Earliest hominin occupation of Sulawesi, Indonesia. *Nature* 529(7585):208–211. doi.org/10.1038/nature16448 (accessed 5 June 2018).

van Heekeren, H.R. 1972. *The Stone Age of Indonesia*. Revised edition. Verhandelingen van het Koninklijk Instituut voor Taal-, Land- en Volkenkunde 61. The Hague: Martinus Nijhoff.

Westaway, K.E., J. Louys, R. Due Awe, M.J. Morwood, G.J. Price, J.-x. Zhao, M. Aubert, R. Joannes-Boyau, T.M. Smith, M.M. Skinner, T. Compton, R.M. Bailey, G.D. van den Bergh, J. de Vos, A.W.G. Pike, C. Stringer, E.W. Saptomo, Y. Rizal, J. Zaim, W.D. Santoso, A. Trihascaryo, L. Kinsely and B. Sulistyanto. 2017. An early modern human presence in Sumatra 73,000–63,000 years ago. *Nature* 548:322–325. doi.org/10.1038/nature23452 (accessed 5 June 2018).

2

The joint Australian–Indonesian archaeological expedition to South Sulawesi in 1969 in context

Campbell Macknight

Abstract

The original impetus for the joint Australian–Indonesian archaeological expedition that visited South Sulawesi in July and August 1969 can be traced to the beginning of the 20th century, but its more immediate background lay in a particular conjunction of personal, intellectual, political and security factors in both Indonesia and Australia. The opportunity to apply radiocarbon dating and an interest in stone tool typology were important aspects of the archaeological work itself. The expedition was highly successful in terms of its objectives and the archaeological data it recovered has continued to attract attention even as research interests have shifted to new questions. Participation in the work of the expedition also opened up opportunities in unexpected areas, which some of those associated with the expedition's activities have followed up in subsequent years. The conduct of the expedition established a precedent for collaboration between local, national and foreign researchers, which has been particularly happy and productive.

Keywords: Sulawesi archaeology, Australian–Indonesian collaborations, Sulawesi history

Pre-1969 context

The oldest continuous area of research collaboration between Indonesians and Australians is associated with the prehistoric archaeology of Sulawesi. Of course, scholars from other countries have also been involved, but the Australian connection goes back to 1937 with a continuing web of interaction down the decades.

The story really begins, however, as a small element in the obsessive collecting of the enigmatic Swiss second cousins, Paul and Fritz Sarasin of Basel: Paul the tall and dreamy one; Fritz the organiser and master of public relations. They met as students of zoology and their natural history interests were always central, but in the late 19th-century enthusiasm for Darwinian thought and colonial expansion, this scientific vision easily encompassed specimens of humanity.

This investigation of 'anthropology', as they understood it, led them, when they were already in Sulawesi, to seek out the groups they knew as Toála (literally bushmen and its equivalents in many languages).[1]

In 1902 in the hills of south Bone, the Sarasins found people apparently living in caves and they recovered from the caves a collection of artefacts, including finely worked stone tools and points. They assumed that the current inhabitants and the makers of the stone tools were directly connected, though they lacked any means of directly dating the tools. In his discussion, Paul Sarasin draws a fateful comparison:

> This apparent mixture [of stone tool types], which at first glance just gives the impression of being Magdalenian, appears in a still greater measure to relate to actual present-day tribes which maintain a stone age culture, such as, in particular, the Australians among whom the absolutely crudest tools are found alongside good Neolithic work (translated by author from Sarasin and Sarasin 1905a:25).[2]

Right from the beginning, connections with Australia were in the air.[3]

Almost exactly 30 years later, a chain of events began that led to further discoveries. In December 1932, Abdul Maula, a school inspector, reported that on a tour of inspection he had come across a bronze statue in a government guest house near the mouth of the Karama River in West Sulawesi. It just so happened that Abdul Maula's brother was Nuruddin Daeng Magassing, the assistant, colleague and very good friend of A.A. Cense, the government linguist and well-known to L.J.J. Caron, then Governor of Celebes and a considerable scholar in his own right. Things moved with lightning speed; since the governor was visiting the area anyway, he collected the statue and sent it off to the museum in Batavia, where it still is. On 20 May 1933, Cense was dispatched to make field investigations and a week or so later was excavating stone axes and earthenware on the site of Sikendeng. He also heard that similar artefacts had been found at Kalumpang, up the Karama River. In August, the governor was touring again and visited the sites. He decided to call in P.V. van Stein Callenfels, then the leading prehistoric archaeologist in the Indies. The archaeological discovery of the Karama valley had begun, but still had a long way to go.[4]

---

1   The name deserves some comment. In the German text, the name is consistently written with an acute accent on the middle syllable; this is probably intended to mark the stress. Matthes in his Bugis dictionary (1874:872) gives a form that in modern orthography is rendered *Tau-ale'* for the Dutch *een boschmensch*, and he goes on to note that the term is also used for its counterpart in Malay, *orang-utan*. The standard modern Bugis form would be *Toaleq*. I can find no Bugis form of the word for bush or forest ending in /-a'/ or /-a/, though Cense in his Makasar dictionary (1979:7) gives *ala'* as a dialect form influenced by the Bugis *ale'*. Specifically, in relation to the stone tools, Paul Sarasin uses *Toalien* as an adjective. Van Heekeren, in Dutch, writes *Toale* for the people and *Toaliaan* for the stone tools (van Heekeren 1969:112–113) and, in English, Toale and Toalean (van Heekeren 1972:109). The widespread reliance on this later work of van Heekeren seems to have established the usage Toalean in English. I use the Bugis form, Toaleq, here for the people.

2   This is not the only comparison with Australian material to be found in the Sarasins' work. In his discussion of the knotted string bags found in the caves, Paul refers to Brough Smyth's description of rather simpler examples from Victoria (Sarasin and Sarasin 1905a:21–22; referring to Smyth 1878:343). A few weeks later, at Kantissang, southeast of Pangkajene, Paul is comparing the sticks used to throw at birds in the rice fields to Australian boomerangs and quotes the then Governor of Celebes, G.W.W.C. Baron von Hoévell, who had already made the same observation in an ethnographic article (Sarasin and Sarasin 1905b:229–230).

3   For a detailed record of the Sarasin collections from the Toalean sites, see Bulbeck (2006). Simon (2015) provides a very thorough recent account of the lives, work and intellectual background of the Sarasins. Schär (2015a, 2015b) relates the lives and work of the Sarasins to the wider scientific, political and cultural themes of the time. As this recent explosion of scholarly interest shows, from the time of Alfred Russel Wallace's travels in the middle of the 19th century, research in Sulawesi has played an important role in European thought about the 'deep history' of the world.

4   See Anggraeni (2012). This paragraph is based on the Cense papers in the Koninklijk Instituut voor Taal-, Land- en Volkenkunde in Leiden. The most relevant for this matter are translated in Anggraeni (2012:371–373).

Once in Sulawesi, however, Callenfels also followed up other archaeological prospects.[5] He began by revisiting the area where the Sarasins had found the Toaleq, and towards the end of 1933 was excavating sites there with the assistance of Cense and H.D. Noone from Malaya. Van Heekeren (1972:110) says that Nuruddin had been to the area with the Sarasins and I strongly suspect that Nuruddin played a critical role in guiding the new researchers.

Van Heekeren (1972:106–125) provides a detailed account of excavations and discoveries over the next few years. A striking feature of this period is the way in which various people were drawn in and worked together. The leadership of Cense and Nuruddin seems to have been important in this. For example, in 1933, Cense had noticed a Toalean site at Ara in the southeast, but when in 1936 he and Nuruddin returned there with van Heekeren, who was not yet formally employed as an archaeologist, an over-enthusiastic district officer had already seriously disturbed the site. After Ara, van Heekeren moved on to Leang Karassak, which seems to have been the first cave near Maros to have been excavated. This spectacular karst area, and especially the Bantimurung waterfall, had been admired by visitors since, at least, the middle of the 18th century;[6] a century later, Alfred Russel Wallace rhapsodised over its wealth of butterflies. The Sarasins too had visited the Leang Leang valley, but did not notice the cave deposits.

The following year, 1937, saw major campaigns. Van Heekeren continued digging in the Maros karst sites and, under Callenfels's overall direction, two cave sites further north were dug, as well as Batu Ejayya and Panganreang Tudea near Bantaeng. Callenfels had recruited to help him—in addition to his loyal assistant, Munaf, who actually did the work—two younger men. Dr W.J.A. Willems was a young archaeologist whom Callenfels had met in Groningen in 1932 and whom he had invited to succeed him as prehistorian in the Archaeological Service from the beginning of 1938. This fieldwork in Sulawesi was intended to introduce Willems to the realities of working in Southeast Asia.[7] The second young man was F.D. McCarthy from the Australian Museum in Sydney, who was also meant to be learning how to dig.

It is possible to reconstruct the chain of connections that led McCarthy to come to Sulawesi. On his home visit to the Netherlands in 1932, Callenfels had also met Professor J.L. Shellshear, a physical anthropologist then from Hong Kong. In 1935, Shellshear retired to Sydney where, in settling into the local scene, he soon met McCarthy, then an assistant ethnologist at the museum. About this time, McCarthy also took a course in physical anthropology from Professor A.N.StG. Burkitt. McCarthy credits Shellshear and Burkitt with 'arranging' his trip (McCarthy 1984:74). Another possible contact was through H.V.V. Noone, who was helping McCarthy with his work classifying Australian stone tools and was the father of H.D. Noone, who had dug with Callenfels in 1933. In 1938, McCarthy went on to visit H.D. Noone in the Malayan jungle.[8] McCarthy seems to have been the source for some Australian ideas in Sulawesi archaeology, such as the term *muduk* for the double-ended bone point, and he was probably the first to recognise geometric microliths.[9]

Callenfels died in 1938 and World War II put a stop to further work for almost a decade. Van Heekeren, however, now officially attached to the Archaeological Service, was active again in Sulawesi between 1947 and 1950, until the troubles of that time made fieldwork impossible until

---

5   Callenfels was not entirely unprepared for this. On his way back to the Indies at the end of 1932, he visited Fritz Sarasin who was still living in Basel (Swanenburg 1951:213).

6   See de Roever and Brommer (2008) for various maps and drawings from the 18th century.

7   Swanenburg (1951:212 and Plate 29) provides information on who Callenfels met at this time. See also van Stein Callenfels (1938).

8   In addition to the references in the previous note, see McCarthy (1984). There is more work to be done on McCarthy's papers about his visit to Southeast Asia in 1937 and 1938. McCarthy also mentions meeting Willems in Sydney in the early 1940s, but Willems gave up his career in archaeology. Bulbeck (2000) also discusses McCarthy's visit and other matters relevant to this discussion.

9   Willems was back in the field in 1939, though only to show the restricted geographic range of the Toalean.

the late 1960s. He then went on to other interests. Indonesia was not forgotten, however, and, in 1957, the first edition of his invaluable synthesis, *The Stone Age of Indonesia*, was published. This provides an account of all this earlier work.[10] He also had various Australian visitors in the Netherlands; in particular, John Mulvaney visited him in 1961 (Mulvaney 2011:149). In March 1968, van Heekeren returned to Indonesia in connection with preparing the second edition of *The Stone Age of Indonesia*, and this trip included revisiting the Maros and Cabengnge sites with his protégé, friend and successor as prehistorian in the Archaeological Service, R.P. Soejono.[11]

Another visitor to van Heekeren in the Netherlands in 1961 was Jack Golson, who had just been appointed to a position in the Research School of Pacific Studies at The Australian National University in Canberra. In the course of a long return trip to Australia, Golson also met Soejono in Bali in 1962 and established a strong connection. In 1966, Mulvaney met Soejono for the first time at the Pacific Science Congress in Tokyo (Mulvaney 2011:142).[12]

It is not clear who first had the idea of a joint team to continue research in Sulawesi in 1969, but circumstances on both sides were favourable.[13] Soejono had moved from Bali to Jakarta and was keen to continue work on the sites in Sulawesi he had recently inspected with van Heekeren. Although Golson had shifted his interest to New Guinea, Mulvaney had been working in north Australia for some years and, in looking for external origins or linkages, it was natural to gaze northwards. He was, of course, well aware of McCarthy's ideas (1940) and McCarthy himself was by now in Canberra as founding principal of the Australian Institute of Aboriginal Studies, as it was then known. Among Mulvaney's PhD students, Ian Glover was excavating sites in then Portuguese Timor and I was investigating trepangers from Makassar in Arnhem Land. I had also visited Jakarta in early 1966 and had been allowed to study the museum's holdings of materials from excavations in Sulawesi. In late 1968, Soejono came to Canberra to help plan a combined expedition.

The 1969 expedition and its aftermath

R.P. Soejono and John Mulvaney were the joint leaders of the Australian–Indonesian archaeological expedition to Sulawesi.[14] The other members on the Indonesian side were Basuki, who served as draftsman, and Teguh Asmar, later director of Indonesia's National Museum (in Jakarta). On the Australian side were Ian and Emily Glover and myself. We worked in two areas. The first was around Callenfels's site of Batu Ejayya near Bantaeng, where we re-excavated the main cave and another shelter nearby, as well as exploring the area for further sites. Conditions were rough; it took four hours in a large truck to reach Bantaeng on the main road from Makassar, while the side road up to Campagaloe near the sites was even worse. My most enduring memory is the constant surveillance by a crowd of onlookers—on the site, out in the fields or on the street outside the village house where we ate and slept. This was compensated for, to some extent, by the companionship of several young assistants—among them, Mukhlis Paeni was still an undergraduate at Universitas Hasanuddin, while Darmawan Mas'ud Rahman and Harun Kadir were already graduates. It was quite a team, given all our future careers (Figure 2.1). The assistants did not follow us to the Maros area where conditions were much easier and we employed several

---

10   Hooijer (1950) also offers a useful commentary on earlier excavations.

11   van Heekeren (1969) is an important source on this trip and his earlier work.

12   I wish to thank both John Mulvaney and Jack Golson for conversations about these contacts.

13   The end of *gerombolan* (bandit) control of much of the interior was also critical. At least travel was now safe, though researchers were subject to careful oversight and the infrastructure of roads and accommodation was in a very poor state.

14   See Mulvaney (2011) for an account of Mulvaney's career; Simanjuntak et al. (2006) give a picture of Soejono's remarkable contributions to Indonesian archaeology.

local men to help with excavation. We dug in Leang Burung 1, Ulu Leang 1 and Leang Karassak, and recovered broken burial earthenware from Ulu Leang 2 and Ulu Wae. We also explored various other sites with deposit and, in many cases, hand stencils and other rock art.

Figure 2.1: Dinner at Campagaloe, near Batu Ejayya in 1969.
From the left: Harun Kadir, Basuki, Ian Glover, Campbell Macknight (just visible behind), Emily Glover, John Mulvaney and R.P. Soejono.
Source: Photograph by Teguh Asmar.

This is not the place to discuss the archaeological results of this work in detail. Two brief articles were published very promptly (Mulvaney and Soejono 1970, 1971). These reported the first radiocarbon dates for Sulawesi and, not unexpectedly, dated the Toalean stone industry well back into the Holocene. In due course, Chapman (1986) produced more detailed analysis of the stone tools, while Bulbeck and his students followed up with studies of a wider range of materials.[15] What is most remarkable, however, is the variety of arrangements, projects, friendships and interests that can be traced back to this 1969 expedition.

Most obviously, Ian Glover returned and dug further in the Maros caves, obtaining the first Pleistocene dates from Leang Burung 2 (Glover 1981). One of Soejono's objectives in 1969 had been to investigate the possibility of setting up a branch of the then Lembaga Purbakala dan Peninggalan Nasional in Makassar. Its first head, Hadimuljono, visited Canberra before taking up his post. One of the continuing interests of this branch and its successors has been research into the art and archaeology of the Maros caves, as this volume demonstrates so well.

Our interests were not just prehistoric. Soejono with, I think, Teguh Asmar, took the opportunity to inspect Islamic sites in Soppeng, and the Glovers endured a very rough trip up to Tana Toraja to see some standing stones, as well as the usual sights.

---

15   See, especially, Bulbeck et al. (2000) for a comprehensive study of the Toalean culture. The suggested links with Australian stone technology, which still feature in Mulvaney and Soejono's articles, receive less attention in more recent work. Bulbeck (2000:48) helpfully lists the work of his students and others on the ceramic and faunal materials.

In the local government office in Bantaeng, we saw a table laid out with Chinese and other ceramic pieces recovered from pre-Islamic graves. This revealed the potential for systematic study of the material. One of Hadimuljono's great achievements was to bring this business—since there were considerable financial interests involved—under control. A few weeks later in Leang-Leang, I was shown a steel rod for probing the ground in the search for ceramics. In 1970, Uka Tjandrasasmita and Abu Ridho conducted the first careful excavation of burial sites from this period in Takalar and near Pangkajene (Purbakala 1970).[16] Later, Hadimuljono and I published an article together that provided a base line for so much further work (Macknight and Hadimuljono 1983).

Even more important for my future—through the good offices of Andi Abubakar Punagi, Abdurrahim and La Side, all board members of the Yayasan Kebudayaan Sulawesi Selatan dan Tenggara—I was able to view the collection of Bugis and Makasar manuscripts, most of which had been assembled by Cense in the 1930s. It was then that I dimly glimpsed the potential for investigating the early history of South Sulawesi by combining ceramic and textual sources.[17] There is no room here to trace the development of this vision, especially through the work of Ian Caldwell, David Bulbeck and Steve Druce, but one of its great pleasures has been working with so many Indonesian friends and colleagues. Let me here just acknowledge the scholarship and friendship of two so that they do not get forgotten among the archaeologists: Professor Andi Zainal Abidin and the inimitable Muhammad Salim.

Lastly, through Abdurrahim, Nuruddin's successor as Cense's assistant and, indeed, Cense's successor as the indispensable contact for visiting scholars, I met Mangngellai Daeng Maro who had twice sailed to Arnhem Land with his father in search of trepang.[18] This was a contact later followed up by Peter Spillett. Even more evocative, I spent a day sailing with the *bupati* (district head) of Maros on a *pajala* to Barrang Lompo.[19] We ended up well after dark on the beach in front of Fort Rotterdam; an aide was sent to find a vehicle and the *bupati* drove us back to Maros in the local ambulance. Someone was deputed to drop me off last of all in the middle of the night—and I had to get up to continue digging Leang Burung in the morning. A few days later, together with Teguh Asmar and Daud Limbungan, the only assistant from Batu Ejayya brave enough to take to the water, I sailed out to Barrang Lompo on a *soppe'* for further enquiry about trepang and to collect a sample of sherds that littered the shallows.[20]

Conclusion

The world the Sarasins found when they came to Sulawesi well over a century ago is now barely imaginable, and even the late colonial arrangements within which McCarthy was a welcome visitor are long gone. While, as the career of Nuruddin Daeng Magassing demonstrates, Indonesians were active participants in early research too, the 1969 expedition, under the joint leadership of Mulvaney and Soejono, set a precedent for collaboration and friendship

---

16   Projek Penggalian di Sulawesi Selatan/The South Sulawesi Excavation Project in 1970 was funded by a most distinguished list of sponsors, with a committee chaired by Adam Malik, then minister for foreign affairs. The strong diplomatic interest in this project contrasts with the official Australian disinterest in the 1969 expedition as described by Mulvaney (2011:149–150).

17   See Macknight (1975) for an early exploration of this potential. It should also be noted that the chair of the Yayasan board was Andi Pangerang Petta Rani who graciously took an interest in later work.

18   In the 1960s, I corresponded with Cense, who had written a classic article on the trepangers in northern Australia, and had the very great pleasure of meeting him in the Netherlands in 1975. On trepanging, see Macknight (1976) and, most recently, Clark and May (2013).

19   A *pajala* is a fishing boat with a tripod mast and large rectangular sail.

20   A *soppe'* is an outrigger canoe with a single mast and smaller sail.

between Indonesian and, especially, Australian researchers in Sulawesi that endures to this day. This volume is testament to the spectacular results of this collaboration; the friendship should also be celebrated.

Author biography

Campbell Macknight College of Asia and the Pacific, The Australian National University, Canberra, Australia

References

Anggraeni. 2012. The Austronesian migration hypothesis as seen from prehistoric settlements on the Karama River, Mamuju, West Sulawesi. Unpublished PhD thesis, School of Archaeology and Anthropology, The Australian National University, Canberra.

Bulbeck, D. 2000. A historical perspective on the Australian contribution to the practice of archaeology in Southeast Asia. *Australian Archaeology* 50:45–53. doi.org/10.1080/03122417.2000.11681665 (accessed 5 June 2018).

Bulbeck, D. 2006. Economic and technological change during the middle and late Holocene in the Lamoncong highlands, South Sulawesi, Indonesia. In E.A. Bacus and I. Glover (eds), *Uncovering Southeast Asia's Past: Selected Papers from the 10th International Conference of the European Association of Southeast Asian Archaeologists*, pp. 393–410. Singapore: NUS Press.

Bulbeck, D., M. Pasqua and A. Di Lello. 2000. Culture history of the Toalean of South Sulawesi, Indonesia. *Asian Perspectives* 39(1–2):71–108. doi.org/10.1353/asi.2000.0004.

Cense, A.A. 1979. *Makassaars-Nederlands Woordenboek*. The Hague: Martinus Nijhoff. doi.org/10.1002/j.1834-4453.1986.tb00127.x (accessed 5 June 2018).

Chapman, V. 1986. Inter-site variability in southwest Sulawesi: Results of the 1969 Australian–Indonesian Archaeological Expedition. *Archaeology in Oceania* 21(1):76–84.

Clark, M. and S.K. May (eds). 2013. *Macassan History and Heritage: Journeys, Encounters and Influences*. Canberra: ANU E Press.

de Roever, A. and B. Brommer. 2008. *Grote Atlas van de Verenigde Oost-Indische Compagnie/Comprehensive Atlas of the Dutch United East India Company, III Indische Archipel en Oceanië/Malay Archipelago and Oceania*. Voorburg: Asia Maior/Atlas Maior.

Glover, I.C. 1981. Leang Burung 2: An upper Palaeolithic rock shelter in South Sulawesi, Indonesia. In G.-J. Bartstra and W.A. Casparie (eds), *Quaternary Research in Southeast Asia*, pp. 1–38. Modern Quaternary Research in Southeast Asia, Volume 6. Rotterdam: A.A. Balkema.

Hooijer, D.A. 1950. *Man and other Mammals from Toalian Sites in south-western Celebes*. Verhandelingen der Koninklijke Nederlandse Akademie van Wetenschappen, Afd. Natuurkunde. Amsterdam: North-Holland Publishing Company.

Macknight, C.C. 1975. The emergence of civilisation in South Celebes and elsewhere. In A. Reid and L. Castles (eds), *Pre-colonial State Systems in Southeast Asia*. (Monographs of the Malaysian Branch of the Royal Asiatic Society No 6), pp. 126–135. Kuala Lumpur: Perchetakan.

Macknight, C.C. 1976. *The Voyage to Marege': Macassan Trepangers in northern Australia*. Melbourne: Melbourne University Press.

Macknight, C.C. and Hadimuljono. 1983. Imported ceramics in South Sulawesi. *Review of Indonesian and Malaysian Affairs* 17:66–91.

Matthes, B.F. 1874. *Boegineesch-Hollandsch Woordenboek*. The Hague: Martinus Nijhoff.

McCarthy, F.D. 1940. A comparison of the prehistory of Australia with that of Indo-China, the Malay Peninsula and the Netherlands East Indies. In F.N. Chasen and M. Tweedie (eds), *Proceedings of the Third Congress of Prehistorians of the Far East: Singapore, 24th January – 30th January, 1938*, pp. 30–50. Singapore: Government Printing Office.

McCarthy, F.D. 1984. A coat of paint. *Australian Aboriginal Studies* 2(1984):72–81.

Mulvaney, D.J. 2011. *Digging Up A Past*. Sydney: UNSW Press.

Mulvaney, D.J. and R.P. Soejono. 1970. The Australian–Indonesian Archaeological Expedition to Sulawesi. *Asian Perspectives* 13:163–177.

Mulvaney, D.J. and R.P. Soejono. 1971. Archaeology in Sulawesi, Indonesia. *Antiquity* 45(177):26–33. doi.org/10.1017/S0003598X00069015 (accessed 5 June 2018).

Purbakala, J. 1970. *The South Sulawesi Excavation: Final Report*. Jakarta: Jajasan Purbakala.

Sarasin, P. and F. Sarasin. 1905a. *Versuch einer Anthopologie der Insel Celebes. Erster Teil: Die Toála-höhlen von Lamontjong*. (Materialien zur Naturgeschichte der insel Celebes, V Band, 1 Teil). Wiesbaden: C.W. Kriedel's Verlag.

Sarasin, P. and F. Sarasin. 1905b. *Reisen in Celebes: Ausgeführt in den Jahren 1893–1896 und 1902–1903*. Wiesbaden: C.W. Kriedel's Verlag.

Schär, B.C. 2015a. Earth scientists as time travelers and agents of colonial conquest: Swiss naturalists in the Dutch East Indies. *Historical Social Research/Historische Sozialforschung* 40(2):67–80.

Schär, B.C. 2015b. *Tropenliebe: Schweizer Naturforscher und niederländischer Imperialismus in Südostasien um 1900*. Frankfurt: Campus Verlag.

Simanjuntak, T., M. Hisyam, B. Prasetyo and T.S. Nastiti (eds). 2006. *Archaeology: Indonesian Perspective, R.P. Soejono's Festschrift*. Jakarta: LIPI Press.

Simon, C. 2015. *Reisen, Sammeln und Forschen: Die Basler naturhistoriker Paul und Fritz Sarasin*. Basel: Schwabe.

Smyth, R.B. 1878. *The Aborigines of Victoria: With Notes relating to the Habits of the Natives of other Parts of Australia and Tasmania, compiled from various Sources for the Government of Victoria*. Melbourne: Government Printer.

Swanenburg, B.D. 1951. *Iwan de verschrikkelijke. Leven en werken van Dr. P. V. van Stein Callenfels*. Maastricht: Leiter-Nypels.

van Heekeren, H.R. 1957. *The Stone Age of Indonesia*. Verhandelingen van het Koninklijk Instituut voor Taal-, Land- en Volkenkunde 21. The Hague: Martinus Nijhoff.

van Heekeren, H.R. 1969. *De onderste steen boven: Belevenissen van een globetrotter*. Assen: Van Gorcum.

van Heekeren, H.R. 1972. *The Stone Age of Indonesia*. Revised edition. Verhandelingen van het Koninklijk Instituut voor Taal-, Land- en Volkenkunde 61. The Hague: Nijhoff. doi.org/10.26530/OAPEN_613383.

van Stein Callenfels, P.V. 1938. Archeologisch onderzoek in Celebes. *Tijdschrift van het Nederlandsch Aardrijkskundig Genootschap* 55:138–142.

3

Vegetation and climate of the Last Glacial Maximum in Sulawesi

Janelle Stevenson

Abstract

Lake Towuti, a large lowland tectonic lake situated within the Indo-Pacific Warm Pool, is perfectly situated to evaluate how large-scale changes in climate have manifested themselves in the Asian tropics. High-resolution geochemical data serving as proxies of surface runoff and vegetation for the last 60,000 years suggest that the Last Glacial Maximum (LGM) was extremely dry, bracketed by the much wetter conditions of marine isotope stage 3 (MIS3) and the Holocene. Existing pollen-based records for Sulawesi also suggest that the LGM was drier than present; however, these records are short and discontinuous over this time period. A pollen record, still being refined for Lake Towuti, also shows a sudden and profound response in the vegetation over the LGM period; however, the expected increase in grassland, in line with the enriched $\delta^{13}C$ of terrestrial leaf wax in the geochemistry record, is not apparent. Instead, there is a loss of high-altitude taxa and the expansion of several lowland dicots that remain taxonomically unresolved. An expanded research program under the auspices of Towuti Drilling Program has begun to improve our insight and understanding of this globally important region, enabling a better assessment of the potential threats that projected climate change and human activities pose for one of the most diverse rainforest ecosystems on Earth. While numerous questions of fine detail remain concerning LGM climate and its impact on these tropical forests, in the context of this monograph, palaeoenvironmental research, and in particular the palaeovegetation record, provides an important environmental backdrop to trajectories of human occupation in Sulawesi and the subsequent cultural changes and interactions that took place across the region.

Keywords: Sulawesi, Lake Towuti, palaeovegetation record, pollen record, human environmental impacts

Introduction

The geographic position of Sulawesi, within the heart of the 'Maritime Continent' (Ramage 1968), is an important setting for exploring how the tropics have responded to global climate change. The Maritime Continent, also known as the Indo-Pacific Warm Pool, has the highest sea surface temperatures on earth and, as a consequence, is an area of deep atmospheric convection and a significant driver of the Earth's climate through its interactions with the El Niño-Southern Oscillation (ENSO), the Austral-Asian monsoons and the Intertropical Convergence Zone (ITCZ) (Cane 2005; Chiang 2009). Despite all this, we do not completely understand how the climate system in this region operates today, how it will respond to future change, nor what environmental conditions were like in the past (Meehl et al. 2007; Kumar et al. 2013). In addition, Sulawesi is recognised as a 'hotspot' of Southeast Asian biodiversity (Whitten et al. 1987; Cannon et al. 2009), yet we know very little about the modern vegetation of the island, how resilient it has been in the past and what threats future change may pose for its numerous species.

The region

The Last Glacial Maximum (LGM) is the most recent significant deviation from current climatic conditions. From around 27,000 to 21,000 years ago, global temperatures were significantly cooler and global sea level was lower by around 120 m due to the extensive growth of ice-sheets in the northern hemisphere and thickening of the Antarctic ice sheet (Lambeck and Chappell 2001). The dramatic impact the LGM had on plants, animals and dependent human populations in the northern hemisphere is well documented (Gamble et al. 2004); however, much less is known about its impact in the tropics. It is clear though that the tropical regions did not go unaffected, with the most unequivocal evidence for change in this region observed in records from the larger mountain ranges of New Guinea. Here, for example, tropical glaciers expanded and montane forest zones shifted to lower elevations (Hope and Peterson 1975; Hope 2005). Similarly, faunal evidence from archaeological sites at 350 metres above sea level (m asl) on the Bird's Head of Papua reveal montane forest mammals present during LGM times at an elevation that today supports lowland rainforest with its distinctive mammal species (Pasveer and Aplin 1998). Other lowland records, such as the fauna recovered from the caves of Liang Lemdubu and Nabulei Lisa, in the Aru Islands, point to increasingly drier conditions during the LGM with a peak in open grassland species and a corresponding decline in forest species between 20,000 and 16,000 years BP (O'Connor et al. 2005).

Palaeovegetation records based on the fossil content of lake and swamp sediments are some of the most powerful descriptors of terrestrial landscape change at our disposal. The available evidence from the broader region are locally variable, but overall demonstrate a similar timing and direction of change over crucial time periods from locations such as Sumatra (Stuijts et al. 1988; Flenley and Butler 2001), Java (van der Kaars and Dam 1995, 1997) and Papua (Hope and Tulip 1994; Haberle 1998), as well as two records from Sulawesi (Dam et al. 2001; Hope 2001) (Figure 3.1). While many of these records are low in resolution and sometimes poorly dated, generally they document responses to the glacial cycle; cool and wet conditions over much of Indonesia c. 30,000 years ago, universally cooler and dryer conditions during the LGM, replaced by warmer and wetter conditions during the Holocene (see reviews by De Deckker et al. 2003; Hope et al. 2004; Reeves et al. 2013).

The longest published palaeovegetation record from a terrestrial location in the region is the 135,000-year-old record from the Bandung Basin, in Java (van der Kaars and Dam 1995, 1997) (Figure 3.1). This lowland record indicates that the last inter-glacial (approximately 125,000 years ago) was warm and humid, and that drier conditions had their onset around 81,000 years ago, thought to be in response to lower sea levels and the consequent changes to monsoon flows. The period from 47,000 to 20,000 years BP is interpreted as the driest and coolest in the record, once again suggesting the strong influence of the glacial cycle on vegetation structure.

The records that underpin much of our understanding of long-term Quaternary vegetation change in the region, however, come from marine cores (van der Kaars 1991; van der Kaars and Dam 1995; van der Kaars et al. 2000, 2010) (Figure 3.1). The two longest marine records, spanning 300,000 and 180,000 years, also suggest significant reorganisation of vegetation in line with glacial–interglacial cycles and infer drier and cooler conditions during glacial periods and warmer and wetter conditions during interglacials. A drawback of marine pollen records, however, is their complexity, incorporating pollen from vast source areas that often represent several biogeographic zones and, as a consequence, they are not sensitive indicators of change at any one location (e.g. van der Kaars et al. 2000). They can also be influenced by changes in land–ocean distributions that 'mimic' orbitally forced precipitation.

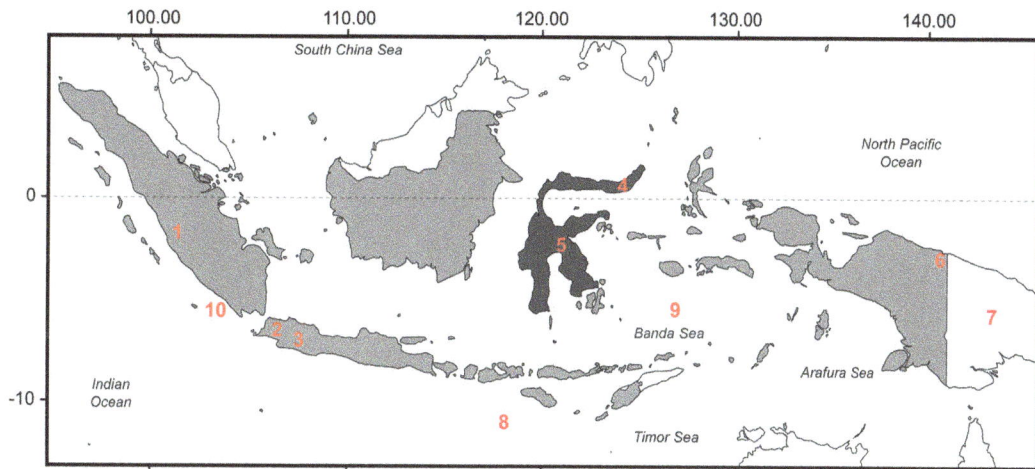

Figure 3.1: Sites mentioned in text.

Terrestrial Pollen Sites: 1. Danau di Atas, Sumatra (Newsome and Flenley 1988; Stuijts et al. 1988); 2. Rawa Danau, Java (van der Kaars et al. 2000); 3. Bandung Basin, Java (van der Kaars and Dam 1995, 1997); 4. Lake Tondano, Sulawesi (Dam et al. 2001); 5. Wanda mire, Sulawesi (Hope 2001); 6. Lake Hordorli, Irian Jaya (Hope and Tulip 1994); 7. Tari Basin, Papua New Guinea (Haberle 1998). Marine Cores: 8. Lombok Ridge (van der Kaars 1991); 9. Banda Sea (van der Kaars et al. 2000); 10. core BAR94-42, Sumatra (van der Kaars et al. 2010).

Source: CartoGIS, College of Asia and the Pacific, The Australian National University.

Sulawesi

The two published palaeovegetation records for Sulawesi that extend beyond the LGM are from Lake Tondano in the north of Sulawesi (Dam et al. 2001) and Wanda mire from South Sulawesi (Hope 2001) (Figure 3.2). Both are lowland/submontane records (i.e. below 800 m) and both are from near-shore shallow water settings, making them highly sensitive to shoreline fluctuations. Consequently, both are discontinuous from around 30,000 years ago through to the late glacial/early Holocene, with the absence of record interpreted as signifying lower lake levels and therefore a much drier LGM (Figures 3.3 and 3.4).

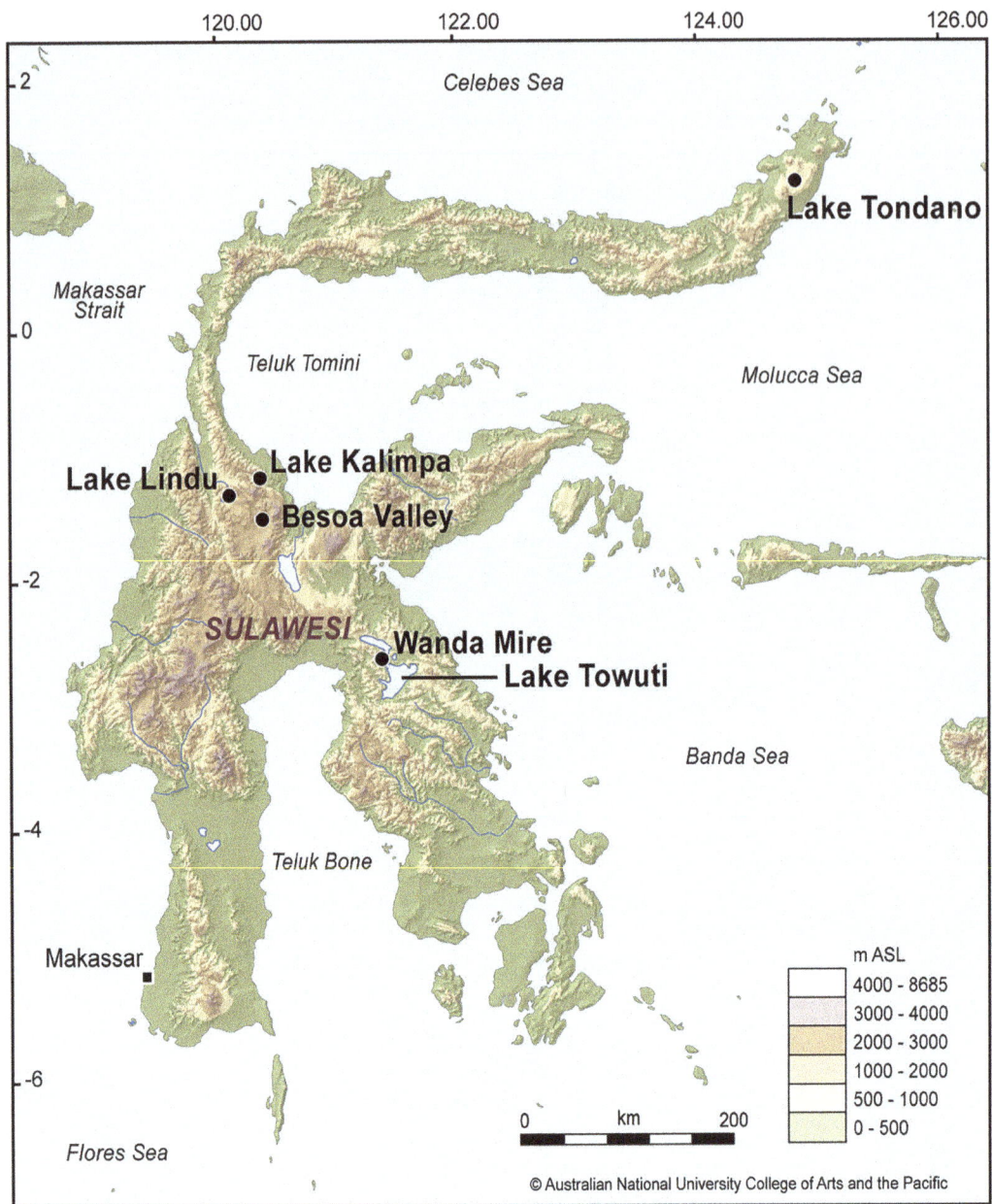

Figure 3.2: Location of pollen sites mentioned in text for Sulawesi.

Source: CartoGIS, College of Asia and the Pacific, The Australian National University.

Although discontinuous over the LGM time period, pollen assemblages of these two records have many similarities including the greater abundance of submontane taxa around 30,000 BP (Figures 3.3 and 3.4). In particular, both records have a greater representation of *Castanopsis–Lithocarpus* (Fagaceae) forest, today found at higher altitudes (i.e. above 850 m). This suggested, to all authors, cooler and wetter conditions during the late Pleistocene, becoming drier during the LGM; in other words, the movement downslope of temperature and moisture conditions only found above 800 m today. The degree of altitudinal lowering, however, remains uncertain. Also of note during the LGM is an expansion of grasses and an increase in fire frequency in the lowland environment (Figures 3.3 and 3.4). Hope (2001) interpreted the increase in grass as representing small forest openings or the growth of swamp vegetation on a drying swamp floor, with the charcoal record possibly suggesting onsite fires as a result of burnable vegetation. Dam et al. (2001) came to similar conclusions for the increase in burning during the late Pleistocene for the Lake Tondano record.

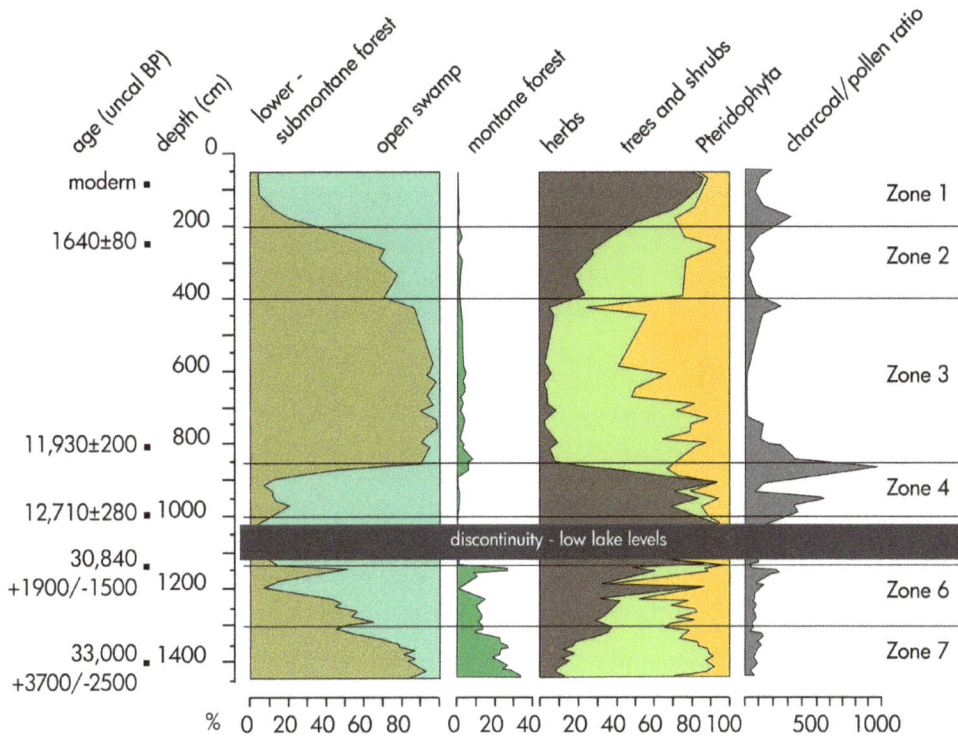

Figure 3.3: Lake Tondano pollen record.

Source: Adapted from Dam et al. (2001).

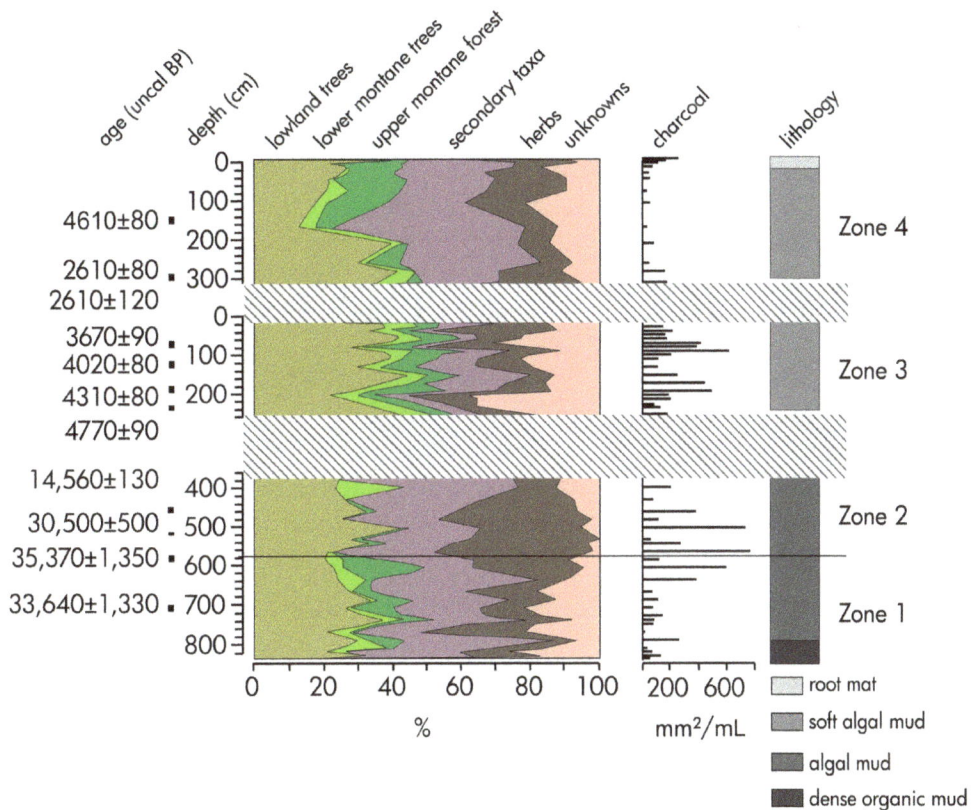

Figure 3.4: Wanda mire pollen record.

Source: Adapted from Hope (2001).

The Lake Tondano diatom record (Dam et al. 2001) also suggests that conditions were wet in the period immediately preceding the LGM, with the relative water level of the lake 4–6 m higher than present levels, then dropping significantly from 31,000 to 13,000 years ago, before rising above present levels until the mid-Holocene when they once again began to fall. Possibly not surprisingly, the combined pollen and diatom data from Lake Tondano attributes a greater magnitude of temperature and precipitation change for the region during the LGM than is commonly concluded from the marine records alone.

The composition of both records, Wanda and Tondano, during the Holocene is substantially different to the pre-LGM record, with Hope (2001) suggesting rapid turnover at the Wanda site associated with ongoing disturbance. However, the dating of the two Holocene sections at Wanda is wildly inconsistent, and it is hard to reconcile whether these segments are truly representative of the site for last 5,000 years.

In the far north of Sulawesi, at Lake Tondano, the landscape becomes more open from around the mid–late Holocene onward, in association with an increase in burning (Figure 3.3; Dam et al. 2001). The potential that these changes are associated with human activity need greater exploration, but they do overlap temporally with known archaeological record, such as the Mansiri site that contains dentate stamped pottery (Azis et al., this volume).

The only continuous palaeoenvironmental record stretching back beyond the LGM is from Lake Towuti, in South Sulawesi (Figure 3.2). Formed in the mid-Pleistocene (Brooks 1950), Lake Towuti is one of three lakes known as the Malili lake system. It is also Indonesia's largest tectonic lake with a surface area of around 560 km^2, a catchment area of around 1500 km^2 and a maximum water depth of just over 200 metres.

In 2010, Russell and Bijaksana (2012) collected nine piston cores across Lake Towuti, concentrating their palaeoenvironmental analyses on a 12 m core from the northern basin (Figure 3.2). The high-resolution geochemical records from the lake suggest reduced terrigenous runoff and strong drying from 33,000 to 16,000 years ago, in keeping with interpretations from the discontinuous records of Wanda mire and Lake Tondano (Russell et al. 2014) (Figures 3.4 and 3.5). The strong signal of drying is derived primarily from the stable isotope measurements of terrestrial leaf waxes ($\delta^{13}C_{wax}$), which exhibit an enrichment of 15‰ over the LGM from ~–40‰ to ~–25‰, suggesting to the authors a more open forest canopy, potentially with an expanded grass understorey (Russell et al. 2014) (Figure 3.5). The interpretation of grassland expansion is based on the premise that vegetation utilising the C_3 photosynthetic pathway (the bulk of herbaceous and woody plant life) has $\delta^{13}C$ values between –29‰ to –31‰, whereas plants utilising the C_4 pathway (primarily tropical and warm season grasses) have $\delta^{13}C$ values of –14‰ to –26‰ (Chikaraishi and Naraoka 2003; Bi et al. 2005). However, while the $\delta^{13}C_{wax}$ signal can vary with these two different photosynthetic pathways, it can also be influenced by water availability and temperature as well as vegetation structure (e.g. closed-canopy verses open-canopy forest), with closed-canopy forest often producing more depleted signals (i.e. more negative) due to microclimate cycling (Cowling 2007; Marshall et al. 2007; Vogts et al. 2009).

Shifts to more enriched values of $\delta^{13}C_{wax}$ over the LGM are also seen in a record from neighbouring Lake Matano (from –38‰ to –35‰) (Wicaksono et al. 2015) and again in a record from Mandar Bay off the southwest coast of Sulawesi (from –28‰ to –25‰) (Wicaksono et al. 2017). In each of these records, enrichments over the LGM is more muted than the Lake Towuti record, with the differences in magnitude of change attributed to catchment size and catchment morphology.

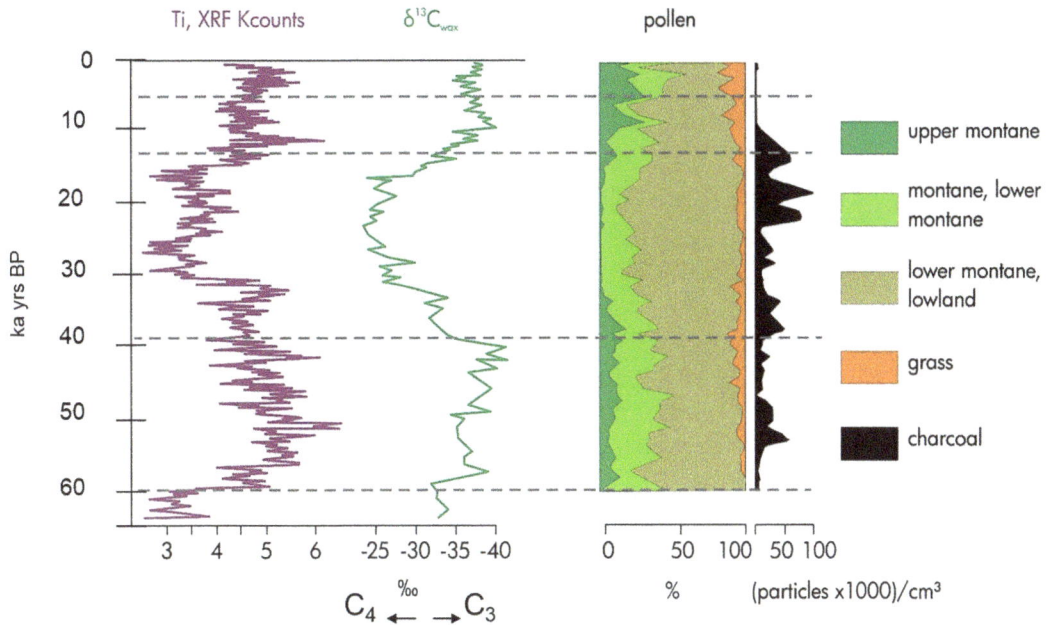

Figure 3.5: Geochemical and pollen data for Lake Towuti (TOW-10-9). Ti counts – proxy for terrestrial erosion. δ13Cwax – proxy for C_3/C_4 vegetation.

Source: Adapted from Russell et al. (2014).

Liu et al. (2005) have cautioned, however, that the interpretation of LGM C_4 grass expansion globally could be over-estimated, as drought-stressed C_3 grasses can give similar shifts in $\delta^{13}C$ values. In addition, a more open canopy alone will produce a quite different sub-canopy microclimate and a more enriched signal. All three records from Sulawesi, however, suggest some degree of forest canopy change during the LGM for the island.

While the pollen data from Lake Towuti exhibits similar large-scale changes in vegetation over the late Pleistocene, it does not immediately support a more open forest or the expansion of grassland. On the contrary, the amount of grass pollen changes little over this period (Figure 3.5) (Stevenson, unpublished data). Complicating this picture is the fact that grass pollen cannot usually be resolved beyond the family level, leaving the possibility open that while the coverage of grasses in the landscape may not have changed, the grasses growing around Lake Towuti during the LGM may have undergone a compositional shift with a greater dominance of C_4 species. Sedge pollen (Cyperaceae), another potential source of C_4 leaf waxes, also increase during this period, possibly expanding in extent on exposed shoreline sediments, suggesting that the $\delta^{13}C_{wax}$ signal could be reflecting quite local changes and not broader-scale landscape change.

Instead, the most profound changes in the Lake Towuti pollen record supporting drier than present conditions are the reduced quantities of montane gymnosperms (*Agathis, Dacrydium, Phyllocladus, Podocarpus*) from around 35,000 to 12,000 years BP, species that are sensitive to both temperature and moisture availability (Figure 3.5) (Stevenson, unpublished data). The Wanda and Lake Tondano pollen records both have an increase in Fagaceae forest prior to the LGM. What the Lake Towuti record reveals, however, is that this forest type declines over the LGM, a finding not in keeping with marine records of the region, and that these forest elements are instead replaced by other submontane taxa that tend to grow within a much broader climatic envelope such as the Cunoniaceae/Elaeocarpaceae and *Triadica* (Euphorbiaceae), a small deciduous lowland tree of primary and secondary forest.

The Wanda mire and Lake Tondano records hint at the likelihood that fire is more prevalent over the LGM. The Lake Towuti record bears this out, with the greatest fire activity occurring during the LGM and lowest during the Holocene (Figure 3.5). Overall this probably suggests that seasonality increased during the late Pleistocene, providing both sufficient rainfall for growth and fuel, and a season dry enough for ignition and fire.

What is known so far from the only long and continuous pollen record for Sulawesi is that higher altitude elements declined during the LGM, suggesting that lower temperatures were not the only aspect of the climate that changed, and that rainfall and seasonality in particular must also have changed significantly. While the composition of the lowland vegetation around Lake Towuti appears not to have altered significantly during the LGM, the structure of the vegetation—that is, how closed or open the canopy structure was—remains unknown at this point.

Holocene records and human impact

There are more records covering various periods within the Holocene for Sulawesi, with the biggest disturbance factors interpreted as a result of human activity, in particular the use of fire with the arrival of the metal age and later with European contact. The most profound impact on all ecosystems appears related to late 20th-century forest clearance associated with logging and other land use pressures (Kirleis et al. 2011, 2012; Biagioni et al. 2015, 2016).

The mountain regions of the Lore Lindu National Park in Central Sulawesi today have an ever-wet climate and little seasonality in precipitation. The Lake Kalimpa record at 1600 m asl reveals that Fagaceae forest has dominated this landscape for the last 1500 years, and although several episodes of increased fire activity are detected in the record (thought to be associated with increasing El Niño intensity), this forest type has overall been resilient to both drought and fire (Biagioni et al. 2015). A different trend is apparent starting from the second half of the 20th century, however, as a consequence of increasing human activities around the lake. In particular, *Agathis*, an emergent conifer in these montane forests, although able to respond to long-term rainfall variability and fire in the past, has not re-established after the years of intensive selective logging in the second half of the 20th century. Other records from this region but from lower elevations show similar responses to late Holocene climate variability, but overwhelmingly the changes correspond to human activity with, for example, the conversion of forest to grassland as early at 2000 years ago (Kirleis et al. 2011) and the effects of late 20th-century deforestation (Biagioni et al. 2016). While the impact of people in Wanda mire record is equivocal, the expansion of grassland and the increase of fire in the Lake Tondano record since the late Holocene is possibly related to human activity and has many similarities with the work from Lore Lindu region.

Possibly the most important development in palaeoenvironmental research for Sulawesi, however, has been the establishment of the Towuti Drilling Project (TDP) (Russell et al. 2016). The overarching goal of this project is to generate multi-proxy palaeoclimate and palaeoenvironmental data to better understand long-term environmental and climatic change in the tropical western Pacific over multiple glacial–interglacial cycles. Geophysical work associated with the project has established that the lake contains a well-stratified sequence up to 150 m thick (Russell and Bijaksana 2012), potentially representing the longest and most continuous terrestrial record in the tropical western Pacific. In 2015, with the assistance of the International Continental Scientific Drilling Program (ICDP), the TDP carried out a drilling program at Lake Towuti, resulting in the collection of approximately 1000 m of sediment from 11 boreholes centred on three drilling locations. The maximum core depth recovered was 175 m below the lake floor, capturing the entire sedimentary infill of the basin and estimated to cover the last 600,000 years (Russell et al. 2016). While the analysis of these cores has only just begun, initial data from core and borehole logging reveals the evolution of a highly dynamic system.

Summary

Numerous reviews have concluded that temperature is the major variable influencing vegetation change at high altitudes in this region during the LGM, and that moisture availability had the greatest effect on lowland vegetation (De Deckker et al. 2003; Hope et al. 2004; Kershaw et al. 2007; Reeves et al. 2013). In particular, they highlight the influence on rainfall and its seasonality by the alternate drowning and exposure of the extensive continental shelves as a result of sea level fluctuations over glacial cycles.

The pollen records from Sulawesi reveal a significant vegetation shift in response to glacial climate. If climatic conditions in central/southern Sulawesi during the LGM were not only cooler but also remained wet with reasonable cloud cover, then we could expect montane gymnosperm forest taxa and ferns to increase in abundance in the lowland records, as they do in the lower montane site of Lake Hordorli, Irian Jaya (Hope and Tulip 1994). The various pollen records, however, as well as the Lake Towuti geochemistry record, instead suggest that conditions were in fact drier or more seasonal during the LGM in Sulawesi (Dam et al. 2001; Hope 2001; Russell et al. 2014).

As Hope (2001) noted, the lowland Sulawesi landscape during the LGM seems to reflect conditions midway between those observed in Java to the west and those seen in Irian Jaya to the east. In the Bandung record from Java, van der Kaars and Dam (1995, 1997) saw only minor evidence of cooling in this lowland record but significant evidence for much drier conditions, keeping in mind that due to lowered sea level this site occupied a much more continental position during the LGM than it does today. By contrast, Hope and Tulip (1994) concluded that LGM climate at Lake Hordorli in Irian Jaya was cool enough and, importantly, cloudy enough to produce an altitudinal lowering of montane forest with an absence of fire. The combined Sulawesi records have some evidence for cooling leading up to the LGM, but overwhelmingly the data suggests a significantly drier or more seasonal climate over the LGM associated with greater natural fire activity than present.

Given the size and volume of Lake Towuti, the water body would have remained a viable water resource for humans throughout the LGM. What impact the significantly drier or more seasonal climate had on the other smaller river systems in the area, however, remains uncertain. The degree to which the forest opened up during the LGM at Lake Towuti is also still equivocal, but faunal evidence from archaeological excavations in the region may give some clues similar to those for the Aru Islands and Bird's Head Peninsula (Pasveer and Aplin 1998; O'Connor et al. 2005). Post LGM, the nutrient poor ultramafic soils of the Towuti catchment (Brooks 1987) are a factor limiting the attractiveness of this region for human activities. This contrasts with the more fertile regions of Lore Lindu and Lake Tondano, where pollen records appear to capture the impact of late Holocene forest clearance and the use of fire (Dam et al. 2001; Kirleis et al. 2011, 2012; Biagioni et al. 2015, 2016).

Throughout the region, but for Sulawesi in particular, numerous questions of fine detail remain. Through the expanded research program of the TDP, improved insight and understanding will be gained of climate and environmental change in this globally important region, with the findings contributing to a better assessment of the potential threats that projected climate change and human activities pose for one of the most diverse rainforest ecosystems on Earth.

Author biography

Janelle Stevenson Department of Archaeology and Natural History, School of Culture, History and Language, College of Asia and the Pacific, The Australian National University, Canberra, Australia; and ARC Centre of Excellence for Australian Biodiversity and Heritage, The Australian National University, Canberra, Australia

References

Azis, N., C. Reepmeyer, G. Clark, Sriwigati and D.A. Tanudirjo. 2018. Mansiri in North Sulawesi: A new dentate-stamped pottery site in Island Southeast Asia. In S. O'Connor, D. Bulbeck and J. Meyer (eds), *The Archaeology of Sulawesi: Current Research on the Pleistocene to the Historic Period*, pp. 191–206. Canberra: ANU Press.

Bi, X., G. Sheng, X. Liu, C. Li and J. Fu. 2005. Molecular and carbon and hydrogen isotopic composition of n-alkanes in plant leaf waxes. *Organic Geochemistry* 36(10):1405–1417. doi.org/10.1016/j.orggeochem.2005.06.001 (accessed 5 June 2018).

Biagioni, S., T. Haberzettl, L.-C. Wang, G. St-Onge and H. Behling. 2016. Unravelling the past 1,000 years of history of human–climate–landscape interactions at the Lindu plain, Sulawesi, Indonesia. *Vegetation History and Archaeobotany* 25(1):1–17. doi.org/10.1007/s00334-015-0523-1 (accessed 5 June 2018).

Biagioni, S., M. Wündsch, T. Haberzettl and H. Behling. 2015. Assessing resilience/sensitivity of tropical mountain rainforests towards climate variability of the last 1500 years: The long-term perspective at Lake Kalimpaa (Sulawesi, Indonesia). *Review of Palaeobotany and Palynology* 213:42–53. doi.org/10.1016/j.revpalbo.2014.11.005 (accessed 5 June 2018).

Brooks, J.L. 1950. Speciation in ancient lakes. *Quarterly Review of Biology* 25(2):131–176. doi.org/10.1086/397539 (accessed 5 June 2018).

Brooks, R.R. 1987. *Serpentine and its Vegetation: A Multidisciplinary Approach*. Portland, Oregon: Dioscorides Press.

Cane, M.A. 2005. The evolution of El Niño, past and future. *Earth and Planetary Science Letters* 230(3–4):227–240. doi.org/10.1016/j.epsl.2004.12.003 (accessed 5 June 2018).

Cannon, C.H., R.J. Morley and A.B.G. Bush. 2009. The current refugial rainforests of Sundaland are unrepresentative of their biogeographic past and highly vulnerable to disturbance. *Proceedings of the National Academy of Sciences* 106(27):11188–11193. doi.org/10.1073/pnas.0809865106 (accessed 5 June 2018).

Chiang, J.C.H. 2009. The tropics in paleoclimate. *Annual Review of Earth and Planetary Sciences* 37(1):263–297. doi.org/10.1146/annurev.earth.031208.100217 (accessed 5 June 2018).

Chikaraishi, Y. and H. Naraoka. 2003. Compound-specific δD–$\delta 13C$ analyses of n-alkanes extracted from terrestrial and aquatic plants. *Phytochemistry* 63(3):361–371. doi.org/10.1016/S0031-9422(02)00749-5 (accessed 5 June 2018).

Cowling, S.A. 2007. Ecophysiological response of lowland plants to Pleistocene climate. In M.B. Bush and J.R. Flenley (eds), *Tropical Rainforest Responses to Climatic Change*, pp. 333–349. Heidelberg, Germany: Springer Berlin Heidelberg. doi.org/10.1007/978-3-540-48842-2_13 (accessed 5 June 2018).

Dam, R.A.C., J. Fluin, P. Suparan and S. van der Kaars. 2001. Palaeoenvironmental developments in the Lake Tondano area (N. Sulawesi, Indonesia) since 33,000 yr B.P. *Palaeogeography, Palaeoclimatology, Palaeoecology* 171(3–4):147–183. doi.org/10.1016/S0031-0182(01)00244-9 (accessed 5 June 2018).

De Deckker, P., N.J. Tapper and S. van der Kaars. 2003. The status of the Indo-Pacific Warm Pool and adjacent land at the Last Glacial Maximum. *Global and Planetary Change* 35(1–2):25–35. doi.org/10.1016/S0921-8181(02)00089-9 (accessed 5 June 2018).

Flenley, J.R. and K. Butler. 2001. Evidence for continued disturbance of upland rain forest in Sumatra for the last 7000 years of an 11,000 year record. *Palaeogeography, Palaeoclimatology, Palaeoecology* 171(3–4):289–305. doi.org/10.1016/S0031-0182(01)00250-4 (accessed 5 June 2018).

Gamble, C., W. Davies, P. Pettitt and M. Richards. 2004. Climate change and evolving human diversity in Europe during the last glacial. *Philosophical Transactions of the Royal Society of London. Series B: Biological Sciences* 359(1442):243–254. doi.org/10.1098/rstb.2003.1396 (accessed 5 June 2018).

Haberle, S.G. 1998. Late Quaternary vegetation change in the Tari Basin, Papua New Guinea. *Palaeogeography, Palaeoclimatology, Palaeoecology* 137(1–2):1–24. doi.org/10.1016/S0031-0182(97)00097-7 (accessed 5 June 2018).

Hope, G. 2001. Environmental change in the Late Pleistocene and later Holocene at Wanda site, Soroako, South Sulawesi, Indonesia. *Palaeogeography, Palaeoclimatology, Palaeoecology* 171(3–4):129–145. doi.org/10.1016/S0031-0182(01)00243-7 (accessed 5 June 2018).

Hope, G. 2005. The Quaternary in Southeast Asia. In A. Gupta (ed.), *The Physical Geography of Southeast Asia*, pp. 24–37. Oxford: Oxford University Press.

Hope, G., A.P. Kershaw, S. van der Kaars, S. Xiangjun, P.-M. Liew, L.E. Heusser, H. Takahara, M. McGlone, N. Miyoshi and P.T. Moss. 2004. History of vegetation and habitat change in the Austral-Asian region. *Quaternary International* 118–119:103–126. doi.org/10.1016/S1040-6182(03)00133-2 (accessed 5 June 2018).

Hope, G. and J.A. Peterson. 1975. Glaciation and vegetation in high New Guinea mountains. *Royal Society of New Zealand Bulletin* 13:155–162.

Hope, G. and J. Tulip. 1994. A long vegetation history from lowland Irian Jaya, Indonesia. *Palaeogeography, Palaeoclimatology, Palaeoecology* 109(2):385–398. doi.org/10.1016/0031-0182(94)90187-2 (accessed 5 June 2018).

Kershaw, A.P., S. van der Kaars and J.R. Flenley. 2007. The Quaternary history of far eastern rainforests. In M.B. Bush and J.R. Flenley (eds), *Tropical Rainforest Responses to Climatic Change*, pp. 77–115. Heidelberg, Germany: Springer Berlin Heidelberg. doi.org/10.1007/978-3-540-48842-2_4 (accessed 5 June 2018).

Kirleis, W., J. Müller, C. Kortemeier, H. Behling and S. Soeghondo. 2012. The megalithic landscape of central Sulawesi, Indonesia: Combining archaeological and palynological investigations. In M.L. Tjoa-Bonatz, A. Reinecke and D. Bonatz (eds), *Crossing Borders in Southeast Asian Archaeology: Selected Papers from the 13th International Conference of the European Association of Southeast Asian Archaeologists, Berlin, 2010,* pp. 199–220. Singapore: NUS Press.

Kirleis, W., V.D. Pillar and H. Behling. 2011. Human–environment interactions in mountain rainforests: Archaeobotanical evidence from Central Sulawesi, Indonesia. *Vegetation History and Archaeobotany* 20(3):165–179. doi.org/10.1007/s00334-010-0272-0 (accessed 5 June 2018).

Kumar, S., V. Merwade, J.L. Kinter III and D. Niyogi. 2013. Evaluation of temperature and precipitation trends and long-term persistence in CMIP5 twentieth-century climate simulations. *Journal of Climate* 26(12):4168–4185. doi.org/10.1175/jcli-d-12-00259.1 (accessed 5 June 2018).

Lambeck, K. and J. Chappell. 2001. Sea level change through the last glacial cycle. *Science* 292(5517):679–686. doi.org/10.1126/science.1059549 (accessed 5 June 2018).

Liu, W., X. Feng, Y. Ning, Q. Zhang, Y. Cao and Z. An. 2005. δ13C variation of C3 and C4 plants across an Asian monsoon rainfall gradient in arid northwestern China. *Global Change Biology* 11(7):1094–1100. doi.org/10.1111/j.1365-2486.2005.00969.x (accessed 5 June 2018).

Marshall, J.D., J.R. Brooks and K. Lajtha. 2007. Sources of variation in the stable isotopic composition of plants. In R. Michener and K. Lajtha (eds), *Stable isotopes in ecology and environmental science*, pp. 22–60. Malden, MA: Blackwell Publishing. doi.org/10.1002/9780470691854.ch2 (accessed 5 June 2018).

Meehl, G.A., T.F. Stocker, W.D. Collins, P. Friedlingstein, A.T. Gaye, J.M. Gregory, A. Kitoh, R. Knutti, J.M. Murphy, A. Noda, S.C.B. Raper, I.G. Watterson, A.J. Weaver and Z.-C. Zhao. 2007. Global climate projections. In S. Solomon, D. Qin, M. Manning, Z. Chen, M. Marquis, K.B. Averyt, M. Tignor and H.L. Miller (eds), *Climate Change 2007: The Physical Science Basis. Contribution of Working Group I to the Fourth Assessment Report of the Intergovernmental Panel on Climate Change*. Cambridge, United Kingdom, and New York, NY, USA: Cambridge University Press.

Newsome, J. and J.R. Flenley. 1988. Late Quaternary vegetational history of the central highlands of Sumatra. II. Palaeopalynology and Vegetational History. *Journal of Biogeography* 15(4):555–578. doi.org/10.2307/2845436 (accessed 5 June 2018).

O'Connor, S., M. Spriggs and P. Veth. 2005. *The Archaeology of the Aru Islands, Eastern Indonesia*. Canberra, ACT: Pandanus Books.

Pasveer, J.M. and K.P. Aplin. 1998. Late Pleistocene to Recent faunal succession from the Bird's Head of Irian Jaya, Indonesia. In J. Miedema, C. Odé and M.A.C. Dam (eds), *Perspectives on the Bird's Head Peninsula of Irian Jaya, Indonesia*, pp. 891–930. Leiden: Rodopi.

Ramage, C.S. 1968. Role of the tropical 'maritime continent' in the atmospheric circulation. *Monthly Weather Review* 96(6):365–370. doi.org/10.1175/1520-0493(1968)096<0365:roatmc>2.0.co;2 (accessed 5 June 2018).

Reeves, J.M., H.C. Bostock, L.K. Ayliffe, T.T. Barrows, P. De Deckker, L.S. Devriendt, G.B. Dunbar, R.N. Drysdale, K.E. Fitzsimmons, M.K. Gagan, M.L. Griffiths, S.G. Haberle, J.D. Jansen, C. Krause, S. Lewis, H.V. McGregor, S.D. Mooney, P. Moss, G.C. Nanson, A. Purcell and S. van der Kaars. 2013. Palaeoenvironmental change in tropical Australasia over the last 30,000 years – a synthesis by the OZ-INTIMATE group. *Quaternary Science Reviews* 74:97–114. doi.org/10.1016/j.quascirev.2012.11.027 (accessed 5 June 2018).

Russell, J.M. and S. Bijaksana. 2012. The Towuti Drilling Project: Paleoenvironments, biological evolution, and geomicrobiology of a tropical Pacific lake. *Scientific Drilling* 14:68–71. doi.org/10.2204/iodp.sd.14.11.2012 (accessed 5 June 2018).

Russell, J.M., S. Bijaksana, H. Vogel, M. Melles, J. Kallmeyer, D. Ariztegui, S. Crowe, S. Fajar, A. Hafidz, D. Haffner, A. Hasberg, S. Ivory, C. Kelly, J. King, K. Kirana, M. Morlock, A. Noren, R. O'Grady, L. Ordonez, J. Stevenson, T. von Rintelen, A. Vuillemin, I. Watkinson, N. Wattrus, S. Wicaksono, T. Wonik, K. Bauer, A. Deino, A. Friese, C. Henny, Imran, R. Marwoto, L.O. Ngkoimani, S. Nomosatryo, L.O. Safiuddin, R. Simister and G. Tamuntuan. 2016. The Towuti Drilling Project: Paleoenvironments, biological evolution, and geomicrobiology of a tropical Pacific lake. *Scientific Drilling* 21:29–40. doi.org/10.5194/sd-21-29-2016 (accessed 5 June 2018).

Russell, J.M., H. Vogel, B.L. Konecky, S. Bijaksana, Y. Huang, M. Melles, N. Wattrus, K. Costa and J.W. King. 2014. Glacial forcing of central Indonesian hydroclimate since 60,000 y B.P. *Proceedings of the National Academy of Sciences* 111(14):5100–5105. doi.org/10.1073/pnas.1402373111 (accessed 5 June 2018).

Stuijts, I., J.C. Newsome and J.R. Flenley. 1988. Evidence for late quaternary vegetational change in the Sumatran and Javan highlands. *Review of Palaeobotany and Palynology* 55(1):207–216. doi.org/10.1016/0034-6667(88)90086-3 (accessed 5 June 2018).

van der Kaars, S. 1991. Palynology of eastern Indonesian marine piston-cores: A Late Quaternary vegetational and climatic record for Australasia. *Palaeogeography, Palaeoclimatology, Palaeoecology* 85(3):239–302. doi.org/10.1016/0031-0182(91)90163-L (accessed 5 June 2018).

van der Kaars, S., F. Bassinot, P. De Deckker and F. Guichard. 2010. Changes in monsoon and ocean circulation and the vegetation cover of southwest Sumatra through the last 83,000 years: The record from marine core BAR94-42. *Palaeogeography, Palaeoclimatology, Palaeoecology* 296(1–2):52–78. doi.org/10.1016/j.palaeo.2010.06.015 (accessed 5 June 2018).

van der Kaars, S. and R. Dam. 1995. A 135,000-year record of vegetational and climatic change from the Bandung area, West-Java, Indonesia. *Palaeogeography, Palaeoclimatology, Palaeoecology* 117(1):55–72. doi.org/10.1016/0031-0182(94)00121-N (accessed 5 June 2018).

van der Kaars, S. and R. Dam. 1997. Vegetation and climate change in West-Java, Indonesia during the last 135,000 years. *Quaternary International* 37:67–71. doi.org/10.1016/1040-6182(96)00002-X (accessed 5 June 2018).

van der Kaars, S., X. Wang, P. Kershaw, F. Guichard and D.A. Setiabudi. 2000. A Late Quaternary palaeoecological record from the Banda Sea, Indonesia: Patterns of vegetation, climate and biomass burning in Indonesia and northern Australia. *Palaeogeography, Palaeoclimatology, Palaeoecology* 155(1–2):135–153. doi.org/10.1016/S0031-0182(99)00098-X (accessed 5 June 2018).

Vogts, A., H. Moossen, F. Rommerskirchen and J. Rullkötter. 2009. Distribution patterns and stable carbon isotopic composition of alkanes and alkan-1-ols from plant waxes of African rain forest and savanna C3 species. *Organic Geochemistry* 40(10):1037–1054. doi.org/10.1016/j.orggeochem.2009.07.011 (accessed 5 June 2018).

Whitten, T., M. Mustafa and G.S. Henderson. 1987. *The Ecology of Sulawesi*. Yogyakarta: Gadjah Mada University Press.

Wicaksono, S.A., J.M. Russell and S. Bijaksana. 2015. Compound-specific carbon isotope records of vegetation and hydrologic change in central Sulawesi, Indonesia, since 53,000 yr BP. *Palaeogeography, Palaeoclimatology, Palaeoecology* 430:47–56. doi.org/10.1016/j.palaeo.2015.04.016 (accessed 5 June 2018).

Wicaksono, S.A., J.M. Russell, A. Holbourn and W. Kuhnt. 2017. Hydrological and vegetation shifts in the Wallacean region of central Indonesia since the Last Glacial Maximum. *Quaternary Science Reviews* 157:152–163. doi.org/10.1016/j.quascirev.2016.12.006 (accessed 5 June 2018).

4

The contemporary importance and future of Sulawesi's ancient rock art

Paul S.C. Taçon, Muhammad Ramli, Budianto Hakim,
Adam Brumm and Maxime Aubert

Abstract

In October 2014, the world learned that the oldest surviving hand stencils and rock paintings of animals were located in southern Sulawesi rather than in Europe. These results, produced using uranium-series dating methods, were the first reported Pleistocene ages for figurative rock art imagery in Island Southeast Asia. We summarise this discovery and its significance in relation to associated research on the oldest rock art of Europe before discussing future research priorities including contemporary concerns about the rock art's conservation that resulted from discussions between the authors and others in 2015. This review is relevant for rock art research not only for the greater Sulawesi region but also many other parts of the world.

Keywords: rock art, dating, conservation, Toalean, Austronesian Painting Tradition

Introduction

Sulawesi has produced exciting archaeological discoveries of global significance for over 60 years, as this volume attests. From van Heekeren's (1952, 1957) early reports on intriguing stone tools and rock art to the recent publication of what may well be the world's oldest rock art, at least 40,000 years old (Aubert et al. 2014), to the more recent publications about stone tools dated to between 118,000 and 194,000 years BP (van den Bergh et al. 2016) and unique Pleistocene portable symbolic material culture (Brumm et al. 2017), Sulawesi has been at the forefront of our understanding of the long-term human history of Island Southeast Asia (ISEA), Sunda and even Sahul. In this paper, we focus on the rock art of Southwest Sulawesi, particularly paintings (Figure 4.1), stencils and drawings, and outline seven future research priorities in order to better understand the rock art imagery as well as the relationship between the artists and other peoples of nearby Borneo and even northern Australia. Furthermore, we argue that Sulawesi's significant rock art heritage is threatened by a range of natural and human threats necessitating conservation and management plans to be revisited (Taçon et al. 2014).

Figure 4.1: Early painting of a possible babirusa similar to one dated to over 35,000 years ago.
Source: Photograph by Paul S.C. Taçon.

Early rock art

Research in Sulawesi is changing the traditional view that sophisticated 'cave art'—long seen as one of the paragons of early human creativity and innovation—originated in Europe. For instance, uranium-series dating has provided minimum and maximum ages for 12 hand stencils and two naturalistic animal paintings from seven sites in the limestone karsts of Maros, on the southern peninsula of Sulawesi. The earliest minimum age for a hand stencil is 39,900 years BP at Leang Timpuseng. The oldest animal painting, apparently depicting a female babirusa 'pig-deer' (see Hayes and van den Burgh, this volume), also at Leang Timpuseng, was made at least 35,400 years BP. A second animal painting (probably a pig) at another site has a minimum age of 35,700 years BP (Aubert et al. 2014). Other minimum and maximum ages of Maros District hand stencils indicate they were made over at least a 12,000-year period.

This challenges the view that figurative rock paintings and stencils first emerged in Europe as a red disc design from El Castillo, Spain (the oldest directly dated European rock art image; see Pike et al. 2012), and the Leang Timpuseng hand stencil are both at least 40,000 years of age. Furthermore, even if depictions of two 'fighting' rhinoceroses in France's Chauvet Cave are 32,410±720 radiocarbon years BP (about 35,000 calendar years BP) based on ^{14}C dating of charcoal pigment (see e.g. Quiles et al. 2016; Valladas et al. 2001, 2004), some Sulawesi paintings of animals are the same age or older. However, the animal paintings of Chauvet may be no more than 26,000 years BP according to Pettitt and Bahn (2015) (see also Combier and Jouve 2012, 2014). Carved ivory figurines from the Swabian Alps of Germany may actually be the oldest surviving animal depictions in Europe, some estimated to be 35,000 years old based on dated excavated material nearby (Conard 2003, 2007, 2009), but they are also younger than the Sulawesi paintings.

Importantly, the hand stencils and animal paintings of Sulawesi closely resemble those of nearby eastern Kalimantan (Indonesian Borneo; e.g. Fage and Chazine 2009; Plagnes et al. 2003) and the two areas may well be part of a very early regional tradition, despite the large expanse of water separating them. Indeed, early rock art consisting of naturalistic animals and sometimes hand stencils can be found in many parts of Southeast Asia (Taçon, Tan et al. 2014) and northern Australia (Chaloupka 1993), and some examples may be equally old. However, we caution against arguing that they represent the work of closely related peoples, emphasising instead that 'humans have a shared rock-making legacy that includes the production of naturalistic depictions of animals and that motifs of these kinds should not be viewed as evidence of particular ethnicities' (Taçon, Tan et al. 2014:1062).

This recent dating of cave paintings in Maros has altered our understanding of the origins and spread of the first painting traditions, suggesting that rock art developed independently in Europe and Southeast Asia at about the same time, or that our species invented this trait prior to its initial expansion from Africa. Gibbons (2014:1447) reports for *Science* that 'The finding could rewrite the history of a key stage in the development of the human mind'. In this regard, she is referring to the fact that the Sulawesi rock art dates strongly indicate that a 'symbolic explosion' in Europe did not bring about the modern human mind but rather it has its origins much earlier in Africa (Aubert et al. 2014; Taçon, Tan et al. 2014).

Future research priorities

Given this significance and the resulting international attention Sulawesi rock art is receiving, we suggest seven future research priorities. In various ways, some of these priorities apply for parietal art in other regions of Southeast Asia, as well as other parts of the world.

Survey and recording

Until recently, there were 127 known sites in the Maros-Pangkep karst region (Said et al. 2007; Tim Penelitian 2011) but each year new discoveries are made. For instance, with Indonesian colleague Adhi Agus Oktaviana, dozens more sites were found in mid-2017. However, most sites have not been recorded in great detail due to time and budget constraints and other logistical issues. Detailed recording and survey across southern Sulawesi will give us a comprehensive database of information for conservation, interpretation and comparison to other regions. Some important sites should be recorded in high-resolution 3D for public replications in museums and interpretation centres, and for rock art conservation (see below). Of course, more survey and recording are important in any region, but there are significant portions of the Maros-Pangkep landscape that have not been assessed archaeologically that have huge potential. Furthermore, because of the age of paintings and stencils that have been scientifically dated, there is likely much more very early rock art that, when described and dated, will flesh out our understanding of this aspect of Pleistocene symbolic behaviour. Unfortunately, due to industrial development across southern Sulawesi that needs limestone for cement and other products, there is an urgency to locate and document rock art throughout the karst region before sites are lost forever.

Scientific rock art dating

As noted above, ancient hand stencils and some paintings of animals are also common at what are argued to be the oldest Kalimantan rock art sites (Plagnes et al. 2003; Fage and Chazine 2009). New dates from both types of Kalimantan rock art as part of a project led by Maxime Aubert and Pindi Sttiawan (ARCHE 2016) will be published soon. More dating of these forms of Sulawesi and Kalimantan rock art needs to be undertaken. Various forms of Holocene rock art also need to be directly dated (Figure 4.2, and see below).

Figure 4.2: Mubarak Andi Pampang and Maxime Aubert sampling for rock art dating.
Source: Photograph by Paul S.C. Taçon.

Pleistocene connections

Importantly, Sulawesi rock art is about the same age as the Deep Skull found in the Great Cave of Niah in Sarawak, Malaysian Borneo. The Deep Skull was recently redated to about 39,000–45,000 years BP, although it is more likely around 37,000 years old (Barker et al. 2013; Hunt and Barker 2014). The relationship between people who inhabited Niah Cave 37,000 years ago and the artists who made animal paintings and hand stencils in the Maros region of Sulawesi and eastern Kalimantan at this time would be important to explore but would depend on the recovery of fossil human material of this age in southern Sulawesi or eastern Kalimantan, DNA extraction, further rock art dating and further Pleistocene rock art discoveries between Niah and the eastern Kalimantan rock art sites.

In northern Australia, there are archaeological sites as old or older (e.g. see Clarkson et al. 2017), and the earliest art also consists of stencils and large naturalistic animals, including extinct species, based on the superimposition of different styles (Chaloupka 1993; Taçon, Langley et al. 2010; Taçon, Tan et al. 2014), as in ISEA and Western Europe. Some Australian rock art may be just as old but not yet dated. And some Kalimantan human-like figures (Fage and Chazine 2009) resemble Australian Dynamic Figures of Arnhem Land, Australia (Chaloupka 1993) and

Elegant Action Figures of the Kimberley (Walsh 2000). Perhaps there were ancient Pleistocene connections across the region or shared cultural practices that first peoples brought with them— this needs further scientific investigation.

The relationship between Pleistocene parietal art and portable symbolic material culture also needs better exploration as a recent publication by Brumm et al. (2017) highlights. They found 'an unusually rich and unique symbolic complex' in archaeological deposits dated to between 30,000 to 22,000 years ago (Brumm et al. 2017:4105) consisting of disc-shaped beads from a *Babyrousa* sp. lower incisor, a perforated *Ailurops ursinus phalanx* 'pendant', five stone artefacts with incised lines, as well as pigmented artefacts. This suggests that there was a rich array of symbolic behaviour practised in Pleistocene Sulawesi manifest in many ways, including rock art and portable material culture, just as in Pleistocene Europe.

Toalean rock art?

But what of more recent rock art in Sulawesi? Was there a Holocene Toalean rock art tradition? Bulbeck et al. (2000) have described a prehistoric hunter-gatherer culture traditionally glossed as 'Mesolithic' in nature, which occupied South Sulawesi; this so-named Toalean culture is specifically 'applied to microlithic assemblages in South Sulawesi with an age range between c. 8000 and 1500 B.P.' (Bulbeck et al. 2000:71). These hunter-gatherers were able to travel distances of up to 30 km to offshore islands (Bulbeck et al. 2000:94). Could they have also made rock art?

For instance, at some Maros sites there are rare small paintings of humans and animals in red outline that are very different to the earliest red rock art referred to above and late Holocene charcoal designs. A number of these can be found at the Maros area site Leang Jing (see Figure 4.3). Our initial impression, based on superimpositions and other field observations, is that they appear to be more recent than the old, large animal paintings and stencils. Were these 'intermediate' images made by the Toaleans? We do not have direct dates, so this art needs to be dated and further investigated.

Figure 4.3: Intermediate red painting of a human figure from Leang Jing.
Source: Photograph by Paul S. C. Taçon.

Charcoal rock art

As noted above, there may be connections between the old red Pleistocene rock art of Sulawesi and Borneo in terms of hand stencils and naturalistic animal depictions. Is there a relationship for the recent Holocene charcoal-based rock art as well? For instance, many charcoal drawings and recent engravings of human figures, animals and abstract designs in Borneo, Sulawesi and other parts of ISEA are stylistically similar, including rare Sabah engravings and charcoal rock art, found by the Malaysian archaeologist Mokhtar Saidin in a remote part of Sabah in 2007 (Mokhtar 2008; Mokhtar et al. 2008).

Did Austronesian farming culture and rock art—the so-named 'Austronesian Painting Tradition'—emerge in Sulawesi and nearby parts of Indonesia rather than come from Taiwan? The situation is likely complex and not quite an either/or scenario, as Bulbeck (2008), Taçon, Aubert and Brumm (2014), O'Connor (2015), Hoerman (2016) and others point out. Thus we need to better describe and compare Sulawesi charcoal drawings to similar designs across the region (e.g. compare Figures 4.4 and 4.5). These designs also need to be directly dated. An initial result from samples obtained from a site in Maros as part of an ongoing rock art dating research program will be available soon.

Figure 4.4: Charcoal human figure from Sampeang 1, Maros region, Sulawesi.

Source: Photograph by Paul S.C. Taçon.

Figure 4.5: Charcoal human figure from Gua Sireh, Sarawak, Malaysia.

Source: Photograph by Paul S.C. Taçon.

Holocene Sulawesi: Northern Australia connections

Traditional Owners of northern Australia, such as Ronald Lamilami and his son Patrick, Mawng men of the Namunidjbuk clan, refer to their Wellington Range rock art sites in northwest Arnhem Land as their history books, their libraries (Agnew et al. 2015:15). Sulawesi rock art sites can be viewed similarly in that they provide a rich visual record of some periods of the past. The Namunindjbuk Estate was visited by people from Macassar[1] for hundreds of years (Macknight 1976; Taçon, May et al. 2010; Wesley et al. 2016) and records of this can be found at rock art sites.

---

1   The Dutch colonial spelling for the city prior to Indonesia's independence when the Indonesian spelling of Makassar came into use.

For instance, the Malarrak rock art site has paintings of a *perahu* sailing boat, a *badi'* (a type of iron dagger from Southwest Sulawesi; Figure 4.6) and possibly a monkey in a tree (Taçon and May 2013; but also see May et al. 2013 for interpretation that a quoll might have been depicted). A second site, Djulirri, has a white *perahu* with a minimum age between AD 1644 and 1802 (median age of 1777)[2] as well as a large yellow painting of a *perahu* that is older. The *perahu* painting is under a beeswax snake that was radiocarbon dated. The beeswax snake has been Carbon-14 dated to AD 1624–1674 (94% accuracy; using OxCal4.1) or 1517–1664 with a median age of 1577 (99% accuracy using IntCal09) (Taçon, May et al. 2010).[3] This sits comfortably with results from recent excavations at a Macassan trepang processing site on the nearby coast that indicates people from Macassar were visiting as early as AD 1637 (Wesley et al. 2016).

Figure 4.6: Rock painting of a *badi'* (a type of iron dagger from Southwest Sulawesi) at the Malarrak site, Wellington Range, northwest Arnhem Land.

Source: Photograph by Paul S.C. Taçon.

Future research could look for earlier rock art and other connections between Sulawesi, Borneo and northern Australia as canine DNA and other evidence suggests some group of people from the Borneo–Sulawesi region probably brought the dog (dingo) to Australia about 4000 years ago (see review in Fillios and Taçon 2016).

Rock art conservation

World rock art is disappearing at an increasing rate and Southeast Asia is particularly vulnerable. Sulawesi's rock art, like that of most countries, faces a wide range of natural and human threats (Agnew et al. 2015; Lambert 2007; Taçon 2013; Taçon and Marshall 2014). Natural threats, such as general weathering, water washing over surfaces, changes in exposure to sunlight, vegetation, deterioration of rock surfaces, damage by animals such as termites and mud wasps that build nests over rock art panels and other environmental forces are difficult, if not impossible, to fully protect against. However, human impacts, such as development, feral animals, road dust, unauthorised visitation, graffiti, theft, vandalism and so forth can be better controlled against. Although various forms of legislation in many countries make it an offence to disturb a rock art site, this has not stopped a rise in graffiti, vandalism and damage from development. Furthermore, sites open to the public often do not have appropriate infrastructure and are not monitored effectively. Graffiti, vandalism, development and even tourism threaten sites across the world.

---

2   Between 306 and 148 years BP, with a median age of 173 years BP.

3   Respectively, 326–276 years BP, and 433–286 with a median age of 373 years BP.

In Australia and Indonesia, we need to find new ways to look after our rock art before it is gone forever and to continue to pass on our knowledge to younger generations and each other. Key issues for Sulawesi include:

(a) Graffiti (Figure 4.7) is an increasing problem in parts of Sulawesi that could be addressed through education, increased site monitoring and new forms of access restrictions.

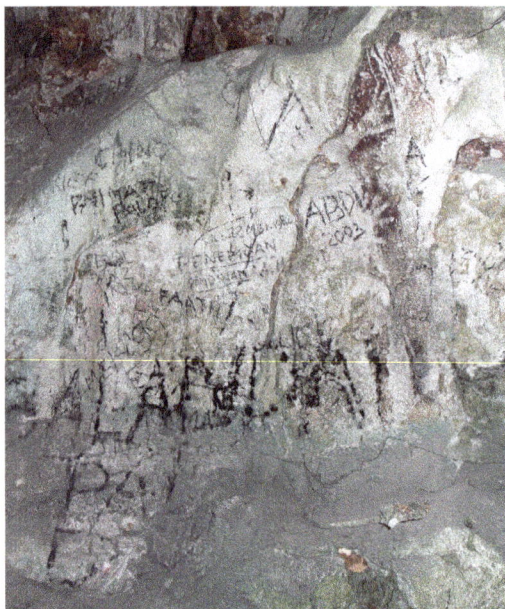

Figure 4.7: Graffiti is a growing threat to Maros rock art sites and to rock art globally.

Source: Photograph by Paul S.C. Taçon.

(b) Various forms of development, including cement processing, marble quarrying and resulting new dusty roads is another growing risk for rock art.

(c) One of us (Muhammad Ramli) and others have noticed that many stencils and old animal paintings have been lost or damaged since the early 1980s due to a rapid increase in flaking of limestone surfaces (Figure 4.8).

(d) There are local people who look after rock art sites and some sites have signs and locked gates but future tourist pressure will require revised management and conservation plans. This could include a 3D scanning program of the more important sites so that should something catastrophic happen to them a detailed permanent record would be available for replication.

Figure 4.8: There appears to have been an increase in flaking of limestone surfaces since the 1980s, damaging paintings, stencils and drawings in the process.

Source: Photograph by Paul S.C. Taçon.

Summary and conclusion

After ongoing discussions between the authors and many other people that began in June 2015, we conclude that new research on Sulawesi rock art should focus on six priorities. The first consists of survey in areas not yet considered and detailed recording at sites deemed significant and/or under threat. The second priority is more rock art dating, which will assist with the third of exploring the nature of Pleistocene connections between Sulawesi, Borneo and possibly northern Australia. We also need to better understand the Holocene rock art with a study of red outline paintings such as at Leang Jing and by describing and comparing Sulawesi charcoal rock art to that of Borneo and other parts of ISEA. This will then allow us to better explore the nature of mid to late Holocene connections between Sulawesi and Borneo, and very recent connections with northern Australia. The sixth priority would involve research on new ways to conserve Sulawesi rock art for future generations, focusing especially on (a) graffiti, (b) development pressures, (c) changes to cave environments and (d) tourism. Through future collaborations between us and other colleagues in both Indonesia and Australia, we hope to address these priorities and, indeed, two new projects commenced in 2017.

By studying rock art, we can learn about ancient cultures, their spirituality, history and relationships to land. The art also informs us about past periods of environmental change, what long-extinct animals looked like, reactions to the arrival of outsiders from various places and many other things. Rock art sites are museums and art galleries embedded in natural landscapes with ongoing cultural connection for contemporary peoples. Unlike built museums/galleries rock art sites do not have high security, protection from the elements or the financial support required to conserve them into the future. This is why it is important to develop a comprehensive and fully funded conservation and management program for Sulawesi's rock art—so that the world's oldest surviving rock art continues to be available to future generations.

Acknowledgements

We thank Griffith University, Balai Pelestarian Cagar Budaya Makassar and Balai Arkeologi Makassar for supporting this research and allowing us to participate in 'The Archaeology of Sulawesi' symposium. The symposium organisers are thanked for inviting us to contribute to this volume. Two anonymous referees provided comments on an earlier version of this paper.

Author biographies

Paul S.C. Taçon Evolution and Rock Art Heritage Unit, Griffith Centre for Social and Cultural Research, Australian Research Centre of Human Evolution and School of Humanities, Languages and Social Science, Gold Coast campus, Griffith University, Queensland, Australia

Muhammad Ramli Balai Pelestarian Cagar Budaya Makassar, South Sulawesi, Indonesia

Budianto Hakim Makassar Archaeology Office, Makassar, South Sulawesi, Indonesia

Adam Brumm Australian Research Centre of Human Evolution, Environmental Futures Research Institute, Nathan campus, Griffith University, Queensland, Australia

Maxime Aubert Evolution and Rock Art Heritage Unit, Griffith Centre for Social and Cultural Research, Australian Research Centre of Human Evolution and School of Humanities, Languages and Social Science, Gold Coast campus, Griffith University, Queensland, Australia

References

Agnew, N., J. Deacon, N. Hall, T. Little, S. Sullivan and P.S.C. Taçon. 2015. *Rock Art: A Cultural Treasure at Risk*. Los Angeles: Getty Conservation Institute.

ARCHE (Australian Research Centre of Human Evolution). 2016. Rock art research. www.griffith.edu.au/environmental-futures-research-institute/research-centre-human-evolution (accessed 27 October 2018).

Aubert, M., A. Brumm, M. Ramli, T. Sutikna, E.W. Saptomo, B. Hakim, M.J. Morwood, G.D. van den Bergh, L. Kinsley and A. Dosseto. 2014. Pleistocene cave art from Sulawesi, Indonesia. *Nature* 514(7521):223–227, doi.org/10.1038/nature13422 (accessed 5 June 2018).

Barker, G., H. Barton, F. Cole, C. Doherty, D. Gilbertson, C. Hunt, L. Lloyd-Smith, P. Piper, R. Rabett, T. Reynolds and K. Szabó. 2013. The Niah Caves, the 'human revolution', and foraging/farming transitions in island Southeast Asia. In G. Barker (ed.), *Rainforest Foraging and Farming in Island Southeast Asia: The Archaeology of the Niah Caves, Sarawak*, Vol. 1, pp. 341–366. Cambridge: McDonald Institute for Archaeological Research.

Brumm, A., M.C. Langley, M.W. Moore, B. Hakim, M. Ramli, I. Sumantri, B. Burhan, Andi M. Saiful, L. Siagian, Suryatmane, R. Sardi, A. Jusdi, Abdullahj, A. Pampan Mubarakj, Haslianae, Hasriantie, A. A. Oktaviana, S. Adhityatamak, G. D. van den Bergh, M. Aubert, J. Zhao, J. Huntley, B. Lil, R.G. Roberts, E. Wahyu Saptomok, Y. Perstond and R. Grün. 2017. Early human symbolic behavior in the Late Pleistocene of Wallacea. *PNAS* 114(16):4105–4110, available at www.pnas.org/content/114/16/4105 (accessed 5 June 2018).

Bulbeck, D. 2008. An integrated perspective on the Austronesian diaspora: The switch from cereal agriculture to maritime foraging in the colonisation of Island Southeast Asia. *Australian Archaeology* 67(Dec. 2008):31–52. doi.org/10.1353/asi.2000.0004 (accessed 5 June 2018).

Bulbeck, D., M. Pasqua and A. Di Lello. 2000. Culture history of the Toalean of South Sulawesi, Indonesia. *Asian Perspectives* 39(1–2):71–108.

Chaloupka, G. 1993. *Journey in Time. The World's Longest Continuing Art Tradition: The 50,000 Year Story of the Australian Aboriginal Rock Art of Arnhem Land*. Chatswood: Reed Books.

Clarkson, C., Z. Jacobs, B. Marwick, R. Fullagar, L. Wallis, M. Smith, R.G. Roberts, E. Hayes, K. Lowe, X. Carah, S.A. Florin, J. McNeil, D. Cox, L.J. Arnold, Q. Hua, J. Huntley, H.E.A. Brand, T. Manne, A. Fairbairn, J. Shulmeister, L. Lyle, M. Salinas, M. Page, K. Connell, G. Park, K. Norman, T. Murphy and C. Pardoe. 2017. Human occupation of Australia by 65,000 years. *Nature* 547(7663):306–310. doi.org/10.1038/nature22968 (accessed 5 June 2018).

Combier, J. and G. Jouve. 2012. Chauvet cave's art is not Aurignacian: a new examination of the archaeological evidence and dating procedures. *Quartär* 59(1):131–152.

Combier, J. and G. Jouve. 2014. Nouvelles recherches sur l'identité culturelle et stylistique de la grotte Chauvet et sur sa datation par la méthode du 14C. *L'Anthropologie* 118(2):115–151. doi.org/10.1016/j.anthro.2013.12.001 (accessed 5 June 2018).

Conard, N.J. 2003. Palaeolithic ivory sculptures from southwestern Germany and the origins of figurative art. *Nature* 426(6968):830–832. doi.org/10.1038/nature02186 (accessed 5 June 2018).

Conard, N.J. 2007. De nouvelles sculptures en ivoire aurignaciennes du Jura Souabe et la naissance de l'art figurative. In H. Floss and N. Rouquerol (eds), *Les chemins de l'art Aurignacien en Europe. Das Aurignacien und die Anfänge der Kunst in Europa*, pp. 317–330. Aurignac: Éditions Musée-forum Aurignac.

Conard, N.J. 2009. A female figurine from the basal Aurignacian of Hohle Fels Cave in southwestern Germany. *Nature* 459(7244):248–252. doi.org/10.1038/nature07995 (accessed 5 June 2018).

Fage, L.-H. and J.-M. Chazine (eds). 2009. *Bornéo: la mémoire des grottes.* Lyon: Fage editions.

Fillios, M.A. and P.S.C. Taçon. 2016. Who let the dogs in? A review of the recent genetic evidence for the introduction of the dingo to Australia and implications for the movement of people. *Journal of Archaeological Science: Reports* 7:782–792. doi.org/10.1016/j.jasrep.2016.03.001 (accessed 5 June 2018).

Gibbons, A. 2014 (8 October). Indonesian cave art may be the world's oldest. *Science Magazine* 346:1447.

Hayes, S. and G. van den Bergh. 2018. Cave art, art and geometric morphometrics: Shape changes and the babirusa of Sulawesi. In S. O'Connor, D. Bulbeck and J. Meyer (eds), *The Archaeology of Sulawesi: Current Research on the Pleistocene to the Historic Period*, pp. 43–60. Canberra: ANU Press.

Hoerman, R. 2016. Utilizing Rock Art to Trace Human Migration: Case Studies from Sarawak, Malaysian Borneo. Unpublished PhD thesis. Honolulu: University of Hawai'i.

Hunt, C. and G. Barker. 2014. Missing links, cultural modernity and the dead: Anatomically modern humans in the Great Cave of Niah (Sarawak, Borneo). In R. Dennell and M. Porr (eds), *Southern Asia, Australia, and the Search for Human Origins*, pp. 90–107. Cambridge: Cambridge University Press. doi.org/10.1017/CBO9781139084741.008 (accessed 5 June 2018).

Lambert, D. 2007. *Rock Art Conservation Guidelines.* Sydney: NSW Office of Environment & Heritage.

Macknight, C.C. 1976. *The Voyage to Marege': Macassan Trepangers in Northern Australia.* Melbourne: Melbourne University Press.

May, S.K., P.S.C. Taçon, A. Paterson and M. Travers. 2013. The world from Malarrak: Depictions of South-East Asian and European subjects in rock art from the Wellington Range, Australia. *Australian Aboriginal Studies* 1(2013):45–56.

Mokhtar, S. 2008. Malaysian prehistoric works of art. In N.A.D. Mohamed (ed.), *Susurmasa/Timelines. Seni Lukis Malaysia Bersama 50 Tahun Balai Seni Lukis Negara/Malaysian Art with 50 years National Art Gallery*, pp. 32–39. Kuala Lumpur: National Art Gallery Malaysia.

Mokhtar, S., P.S.C. Taçon, D. Yang, G. Nash, S.K. May and B. Lewis. 2008. Illustrating the past: The rock art of Southeast Asia. *Current World Archaeology* 29:40–48.

O'Connor, S. 2015. Rethinking the Neolithic in Island Southeast Asia, with particular reference to the archaeology of Timor-Leste and Sulawesi. *Archipel* 90:15–48. doi.org/10.4000/archipel.362 (accessed 5 June 2018).

Pettitt, P. and P. Bahn. 2015. An alternative chronology for the art of Chauvet cave. *Antiquity* 89(345):542–553. doi.org/10.15184/aqy.2015.21 (accessed 5 June 2018).

Pike, A.W.G., D.L. Hoffmann, M. García-Diez, P.B. Pettitt, J. Alcolea, R. De Balbín, C. González-Sainz, C. de las Heras, J.A. Lasheras, R. Montes and J. Zilhão. 2012. U-Series Dating of Paleolithic Art in 11 Caves in Spain. *Science* 336(6087):1409–1413. doi.org/10.1126/science.1219957 (accessed 5 June 2018).

Plagnes, V., C. Causse, M. Fontugne, H. Valladas, J.-M. Chazine and L.-H. Fage. 2003. Cross dating (Th/U-14C) of calcite covering prehistoric paintings in Borneo. *Quaternary Research* 60(2):172–179.

Quiles, A., H. Valladas, H. Bocherens, E. Delqué-Količ, E. Kaltnecker, J. van der Plicht, J.-J. Delannoy, V. Feruglio, C. Fritz, J. Monney, M. Philippe, G. Tosello, J. Clottes and J.-M. Geneste. 2016. A high-precision chronological model for the decorated Upper Paleolithic cave of Chauvet-Pont d'Arc, Ardèche, France. *Proceedings of the National Academy of Sciences* 113(17):4670–4675. doi.org/10.1073/pnas.1523158113 (accessed 5 June 2018).

Said, M.A., M. Hum, M. Ramli and I. Sumantri (eds). 2007. *Directory of Cultural Potency at Maros-Pangkep Karst Area South Sulawesi Indonesia.* Makassar: Balai Pelestarian Peninggalan Purbakala Makassar.

Taçon, P.S.C. 2013. Australia's rock art heritage: Past knowledge for a richer future. *The Sarawak Museum Journal* LXXI(92):49–79.

Taçon, P.S.C., M. Aubert and A. Brumm. 2014 (9 October). 40,000 year old rock art found in Indonesia. *The Conversation.* theconversation.com/40-000-year-old-rock-art-found-in-indonesia-32674 (accessed 5 June 2018).

Taçon, P.S.C. and M. Marshall. 2014. Conservation or crisis? The future of rock art management in Australia. In Y. Zhang (ed.), *A Monograph of Rock Art Research and Protection*, pp. 119–141. Beijing: Zhong Guo Zang Xue Chu Ban She/China Tibetology Publishing House.

Taçon, P.S.C., S.K. May, S.J. Fallon, M. Travers, D. Wesley and R. Lamilami. 2010. A minimum age for early depictions of Southeast Asian praus in the rock art of Arnhem Land, Northern Territory. *Australian Archaeology* 71:1–10. doi.org/10.1080/03122417.2010.11689379 (accessed 5 June 2018).

Taçon, P.S.C. and S.K. May. 2013. Rock art evidence for Macassan-Aboriginal contact in northwestern Arnhem Land. In M. Clark and S.K. May (eds), *Macassan History and Heritage: Journeys, Encounters and Influences*, pp. 127–139. Canberra: ANU E Press. doi.org/10.22459/MHH.06.2013.08 (accessed 5 June 2018).

Taçon, P.S.C., M. Langley, S.K., May, R. Lamilami, W. Brennan and D. Guse. 2010. Ancient bird stencils in Arnhem Land, Northern Territory, Australia. *Antiquity* 84(324):416-27. doi.org/10.1017/S0003598X00066679 (accessed 5 June 2018).

Taçon, P.S.C., N.H. Tan, S. O'Connor, J. Xueping, L. Gang, D. Curnoe, D. Bulbeck, B. Hakim, I. Sumantri, H. Than, I. Sokrithy, S. Chia, K. Khun-Neay and S. Kong. 2014. The global implications of the early surviving rock art of greater Southeast Asia. *Antiquity* 88(342):1050–1064. doi.org/10.1017/S0003598X00115315 (accessed 5 June 2018).

Tim Penelitian. 2011. Delineasi Kawasan Cagar Budaya Gua Prasejarah Kars Maros Pangkep. Unpublished report. Makassar: Balai Pelestarian Peninggalan Purbakala.

Valladas, H., J. Clottes and J.-M. Geneste. 2004. Chauvet, la grotte ornée la mieux datée du monde. *Pour La Science* 42(Temps et Datations special issue):82–87.

Valladas, H., N. Tisnerat, M. Arnold, J. Évin and C. Oberlin. 2001. Les dates des fréquentations. In J. Clottes (ed.), *La Grotte Chauvet, les origines del'art*, pp. 32–34. Paris: Le Seuil.

van den Bergh, G.D., B. Li, A. Brumm, R. Grün, D. Yurnaldi, M.W. Moore, I. Kurniawan, R. Setiawan, F. Aziz, R.G. Roberts, Suyono, M. Storey, E. Setiabudi and M.J. Morwood. 2016. Earliest hominin occupation of Sulawesi, Indonesia. *Nature* 529(7585):208–211, doi.org/10.1038/nature16448 (accessed 5 June 2018).

van Heekeren, H.R. 1952. Rock-paintings and other prehistoric discoveries near Maros (South West Celebes). *Laporan Tahunan Dinas Purbakala* 1950:22–35.

van Heekeren, H.R. 1957. *The Stone Age of Indonesia.* Verhandelingen van het Koninklijk Instituut voor Taal-, Land- en Volkenkunde 21. The Hague: Martinus Nijhoff.

Walsh, G.L. 2000. *Bradshaw Art of the Kimberley.* Toowong, Qld.: Takarakka Nowan Kas Publications.

Wesley, D., S. O'Connor and J.N. Fenner. 2016. Re-evaluating the timing of the Indonesian trepang industry in north-west Arnhem Land: Chronological investigations at Malara (Anuru Bay A). *Archaeology in Oceania* 51(3):169–195. doi.org/10.1002/arco.5091 (accessed 5 June 2018).

5

Cave art, art and geometric morphometrics: Shape changes and the babirusa of Sulawesi

Susan Hayes and Gert van den Bergh

Abstract

There is considerable evidence that the babirusa of Sulawesi and its neighbouring islands has long attracted human attention. This is probably in part due to the male babirusa appearing as a bizarre compound of two familiar ungulates (*babi* = 'pig', *rusa* = 'deer') in that the male's upper canines resemble deer antlers. In October 2014, Aubert et al. announced in *Nature* that a cave art depiction in Leang Timpuseng, Maros, interpreted by the authors to depict a female babirusa, was created at least 35,400 years ago and is therefore of comparable antiquity to the oldest recorded Late Pleistocene cave art of Europe. Using geometric morphometrics, we compare the Leang Timpuseng cave art to profile photographs and illustrations depicting the babirusa and the endemic Sulawesi warty pig, including historical illustrations produced by Europeans during the period ~AD 1740–1860. Our analysis indicates that geometric morphometrics can be applied to meaningfully analyse naturalistic cave art. However, because of the relatively small sample size and that the male babirusa dominates both historical and contemporary illustrations, the results are only indicative. These are that the Leang Timpuseng cave art is more likely to be depicting a female, and that this depiction differs markedly from historical and contemporary illustrations in that it shows a morphologically female suid as independently active. With regards to which animal is depicted, the results suggest the Leang Timpuseng cave art is possibly either an illustration of a female hairy/golden babirusa, which has not yet been proven to have a range extending to Sulawesi, or the extinct *Babyrousa bolabatuensis*, which is part of the existing Sulawesi fossil record and has been noted to be similar in tooth size to the hairy/golden babirusa.

Keywords: cave art, Maros, Sulawesi, babirusa, geometric morphometrics

Introduction

Within the Maros cave site of Leang Timpuseng (Leang = 'cave'; Timpuseng = 'tapering') in the southwestern peninsula of Sulawesi, a profile illustration of an animal has recently been dated using the uranium-thorium (UTh) method. The results show that this animal was depicted ~35,400 years ago, and is therefore one of the oldest naturalistic representations in the world (Aubert et al. 2014). The authors of this paper provisionally interpret the animal to be a representation of a female babirusa (see Figure 5.1), but allow the possibility that it could also be an illustration of the Sulawesi warty pig, both of which are endemic suids of Sulawesi and both are present in the Late Pleistocene fossil record of this Indonesian island. Frantz et al. (2016), however, in their review of the evolution of Suidae, state that the Leang Timpuseng cave art is 'clearly picturing a *Babyrousa* female' (n.p., text box insert 'The Enigmatic Babyrousa').

Traditional morphometrics has been applied to analyse human hand and crocodile claw stencils (e.g. Galeta et al. 2014; Honoré et al. 2016) and naturalistic cave art depictions of horses and bison (Cheyne et al. 2009). The advantage of using geometric morphometrics over traditional morphometrics is that more complex patterns of 3D and 2D shape variance can be measured and their statistical values expressed (O'Higgins and Jones 2006; Rohlf 2015), though because of the number of 'measures' used in geometric morphometrics, studies that are limited in sample sizes are of necessity exploratory rather than conclusive (Cardini and Elton 2007). We appear to be the first to apply geometric morphometrics to cave art depictions, and the first to compare cave art depictions with historical and contemporary illustrations. Our inclusion of artistic illustrations as well as photographs is justifiable as it results in an exploratory analysis that compares like with like. The Leang Timpuseng representation is an artistic rendering, and therefore some of the ways that it may differ from photographs may be due to those features that are characteristic of how humans tend to depict real world objects. These include the influence of the materials and the medium in shaping a depiction (Gombrich 1977), as well as the role of human visual perception, memory, recall and recognition (e.g. Arnheim 1974; Gombrich 1977; Ramachandran and Hirstein 1999; Cavanagh 2005; Vogt and Magnussen 2007).

Figure 5.1: Leang Timpuseng cave art, Maros, Sulawesi.

Source: Image reproduced with permission from Adam Brumm.

The babirusa of Sulawesi and its neighbouring oceanic islands have fascinated Europeans for centuries, and continue to do so today, primarily because of the adult male babirusa upper and lower canines, which take the shape of distinctive upward and posteriorly curved tusks (see Figure 5.2). It is for this reason that the animals have the Malay name of *babirusa*, or deer-pig (*babi* = 'pig', *rusa* = 'deer', with the Malay syntax noun + adjective). The size and curvature of these tusks varies between the known species of babirusa. The largest and most notably curved canines belong to the male Sulawesi babirusa (*Babyrousa celebensis*), which is thought to be currently extinct in the southwest peninsula of Sulawesi (Meijaard and Groves 2002) where the Leang Timpuseng cave art is located. This animal is also distinctive in that both the males and females display sparse or absent body hair, and both have a nearly hairless tail tuft. Comparatively little is known about the extinct *B. bolabatuensis*, though its Late Pleistocene fossil remains are noted to be similar in tooth size to that of the extant Moluccan hairy/golden babirusa (*B. babyrussa*) from the Sula Islands and Buru (Hooijer 1950; Groves 1980). Although there are no fossil remains that have been identified as being hairy/golden babirusa in Sulawesi, it is possible that its past habitat included the southwestern peninsula (Meijaard and Groves 2002). The extant hairy/golden babirusa differs from the Sulawesi babirusa in that it is smaller, the males have shorter tusks, both sexes have a coat of long, relatively thick body hair, and both display a tail tuft that is well developed.

SKULL OF BABIRUSA. (From Guillemard's *Cruise of the Marchesa.*)

Figure 5.2: Historical drawing of the male babirusa skull.

Source: Image from Guillemard's *Cruise of the Marchesa*, reproduced in Lydekker and Sclater (1893:145). wiki.edu.vn/wiki/index.php?title=File:BabirusaSkullLyd2.png.

THE BABIROUSSA,

(*Sus Babyrouſſa,* Lin.—*Le Babirouſſa,* Buff.)

Figure 5.3: Historical illustration of a male hairy/golden babirusa.

Source: Beilby et al. (1790).

Figure 5.4: Historical illustration of a male Sulawesi babirusa.

Source: Werner (1835, 1830). fr.wikipedia.org/wiki/Fichier:Babiroussa_1.jpg.

Compared to the babirusa, the Sulawesi warty pig (*Sus celebensis*) appears to have attracted very little European interest. This animal has a short mane, a coat of body hair that is often dark with a dark dorsal stripe, and its tail is long and simply tufted (Groves 1980, 1981). Where the Sulawesi warty pig differs from the babirusa is that while the adult males have similarly large canine-tusks, these are only weakly curved and the upper canines project laterally and occlude with the lower canines, and male warty pigs also possess three pairs of facial warts (Groves and Grubb 2011). The females of both the babirusa and the Sulawesi warty pig have small canines, which do not have the appearance of tusks, and it is likely for this reason that the females of both species are minimally represented in both photographs and illustrations.

Animals described variously as babirusa, babirussa, babiroussa, babyrousa, babyroussa and babiruza have appeared in English texts since 1673 (Scott 1896). Internet image searches conducted between 2013–2016 indicate that historical illustrations (c. 1740–1860) depict both the hairy/golden babirusa (e.g. Beilby et al. 1790) (see Figure 5.3) and the Sulawesi babirusa (e.g. Werner 1835, 1830) (see Figure 5.4). The Sulawesi babirusa appears to predominate after about 1820, which is following the first living pair to be housed in a European zoo (*Jardin des Plantes*, Paris) (Renshaw 1907). No illustrations of the female hairy/golden babirusa, and just one historical profile illustration of the female Sulawesi babirusa, could be found during our internet searches (2013–2016). Only one contemporary image of a hairy/golden babirusa could be sourced (Naish 2010), and this is a stuffed exhibit housed in the Raffles Museum of Biodiversity Research (Singapore). Similarly, only one artistic illustration of the Sulawesi warty pig was able to be found, which is a scientific illustration dated to the mid-1800s (Reichenbach 1845), and while there are very few photographs of this animal published on the internet, we were able to source profile photographs of one male and one female.

As with the historical illustrations, there are not many contemporary illustrations (c. 1950 to present day) of the female babirusa. Furthermore, contemporary illustrations appear to only depict the Sulawesi babirusa, which include 3D sculptures accomplished in a variety of media (e.g. clay, cloth, metal, paper, wool), as well as 2D drawings and paintings. Where both the photographs and contemporary illustrations differ from historical illustrations is that the contemporary images show the babirusa in a wide variety of body orientations and from a range of different perspectives. Nearly all of the pre-photography illustrations, however, show the hairy/golden babirusa, Sulawesi babirusa and Sulawesi warty pig in a profile view, a characteristic that is also a global feature of Late Pleistocene cave art.

The Late Pleistocene preference for profile views may suggest this is evidence of an ancient pattern of global cultural exchange that has been sustained well into the late Holocene. This preference, however, is thought to be far more likely the result of how anatomically modern humans have evolved to visually process animals (e.g. Hodgson 2008, 2013, 2014; Dobrez and Dobrez 2013; Hodgson and Watson 2015). Profiles can more easily show the visually diagnostic characteristics of a particular animal (i.e. body shape, body proportions and salient anatomical features), and as a consequence profile depictions are more rapidly recognised (Dobrez and Dobrez 2013; Hodgson 2013). A further characteristic of artistic depiction is a tendency for exaggeration of what are perceived to be salient features. This occurs across all artistic media and regardless of the degree of abstraction or verisimilitude, though what is considered salient will vary according to time, place, what animal is being depicted and by whom (Bedaux 1996; Ramachandran and Hirstein 1999). In cave art, the more salient features are understood to be those that are more attended to during actual human–animal interactions, and are therefore recalled with greater clarity. Studies suggest that the sequence and extent of detail in the drawing process follows this order of salience: neck and body, head, legs, and tail (Cheyne et al. 2009; Hodgson 2008).

To summarise, there are four possible candidates for which animal was selected for depiction in Leang Timpuseng some 35,400 years ago. These are the Sulawesi babirusa, the hairy/golden babirusa, the extinct *Babyrousa bolabatuensis* and the Sulawesi warty pig. Only the extant candidates are able to be tested, and we include illustrations as well as photographs to carry out our analyses. This is because, due to human visual processing regarding how an animal is perceived, recalled and represented, no artistic illustrations, including naturalistic cave art depictions and scientific illustrations, are likely to be anatomically accurate renderings of an animal in profile. Instead, the illustrations will likely contain elements of emphasis and exaggeration, which are related to both what are perceived to be the diagnostic characteristics of an animal, and which aspects of the animal are seen to have the greater salience. Our 2D geometric morphometric exploratory analysis of the Leang Timpuseng cave art is therefore an estimation of:

(i)   the extent to which the illustration accords with the body morphology of extant babirusa and the Sulawesi warty pig as depicted in profile photographs

(ii)   how this Late Pleistocene cave art compares to historical and contemporary illustrations of the hairy/golden babirusa, Sulawesi babirusa and Sulawesi warty pig.

Materials and methods

Image data

All images (n=36) used in this analysis are profile depictions selected from over 200 images sourced from the internet over three periods (September 2013; August–September 2015; January 2016). As is discussed above, the Sulawesi warty pig, hairy/golden babirusa and females generally are unavoidably under-represented in the database. The image types and references to the image sources are as follows:

(i)   photograph of the Leang Timpuseng cave art (Aubert et al. 2014)

(ii)   photographs of male (n=5) and female (n=4) Sulawesi babirusa (see References, under Babirusa Photographs c. 2000)

(iii)   photograph of a stuffed hairy/golden babirusa Museum exhibit (n=1) (Naish 2010), which for this analysis is taken to be equivalent to both a photograph of a living animal and an artistic illustration

(iv)   photographs of male (n=1) and female (n=1) Sulawesi warty pig (see References, under Warty Pig Photographs c. 2000)

(v)   historical and contemporary illustrations of male (n=18) and female (n=3) babirusa (see References, under Babirusa Art ~300 BP to present) and a historical illustration (n=1) of the Sulawesi warty pig (Reichenbach 1845). The selected historical representations are those that have an associated date of publication, which in most cases is likely later than the actual date of artistic production.

Landmark coordinates

Those images displaying a right profile were mirrored to the left and, using Adobe Photoshop CS2, all were rotated to best fit with the body orientation of the Leang Timpuseng cave art, referencing the hindquarters and start of the hind limbs. Because the Leang Timpuseng cave art can be interpreted as displaying a mane, two versions were entered into the analyses—one without and one with a mane. The landmarks (x, y coordinates) were digitised using tpsDig2, v.2.17, 2013 (Rohlf 2008). Anchor points consisting of 17 homologous landmarks were first identified following the anatomical features able to be identified in the Leang Timpuseng cave art. Because the cave art depicts the limbs as narrow 'sticks', which is a common feature of cave art animal profiles and possibly due to being low in the order of salience (Cheyne et al. 2009; Hodgson 2008), we do not include the shape of the fore or hind limbs, but only where the left lateral limbs intersect with the hindquarters, abdomen, trunk and chest. The anchor points were subsequently referenced to calculate 10 semi-landmark curves by length. Initial analyses indicated that variance in tail length and curvature exceeded all other variance, and because this was a significant difference between animals of the same genus, species and sex, only the anchor points for the base of the tail were included in the analyses.

The resulting 38 landmarks (16 homologous anchor landmarks and 9 curves comprising 22 semi-landmarks) are shown in Figure 5.5 and defined in Table 5.1. The lighter wireframe in Figure 5.5 shows the Leang Timpuseng cave art with a mane. In all other respects, the landmark sets (with and without a mane) are identical. Dark circles are the homologous landmarks, while the lighter, unnumbered circles are the semi-landmarks.

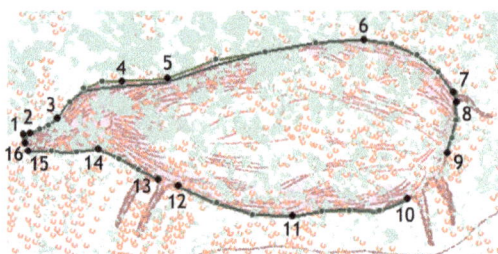

Figure 5.5: Landmarks used in the geometric morphometric analyses.

Source: Authors' adaptation of Figure 5.1.

Table 5.1: Homologous landmark definitions.

Number	Definition
1	Anterior top of nose
2	Posterior end of the nose disc/posterior edge of the rhinarium[1]
3	Proximal termination of the muzzle, at the point where the frontal starts to rise
4	Back of the head at the point where the occipital crest merges into the neck
5	Proximal onset of the neck, showing as a depression in front of the spine of the first thoracic vertebra or dorsal tip of the shoulder blade.
6	Most superior point of the back. Depending on sex, species and medium of depiction, this point can be at the rump, the loin or the anterior back region
7	Superior onset of the tail
8	Inferior onset of the tail
9	Posterior projected intersection of the left hind leg and hindquarter. This is the receding point where the biceps femoris crosses the gastrocnemius muscle
10	Anterior projected intersection of the left hind leg and the abdomen
11	Midway point between landmarks 10 and 12
12	Posterior projected intersection of the left front limb with the chest
13	Anterior projected intersection of the left front limb with the chest
14	Angle of neck where the neck merges into the lower jaw
15	Most anterior and inferior projecting point of the lower lip
16	Base of nose/upper lip

[1] Although *Babyrousa* differs from *Sus* in the lack of a bony nose disc, the posterior dorsal termination of the rhinarium (wet snout in most mammals) can be clearly distinguished in the pictures of members of both genera.

Source: Authors' analysis.

Geometric morphometric analyses

The landmark and semi-landmark coordinate data were uploaded into the statistical shape analysis software morphologika2, v.2.5 (O'Higgins and Jones 2006), which outputs the statistical variance arising from multivariate regression and Principle Components (PC) analyses as dynamic wireframes and Thin Plate Spline (TPS) deformation grids. In order to overcome the confounding variable of differences in size due to image type and resolution, all images were first Procrustes registered, which rotates and scales the landmark coordinates to best overall comparable fit. This also enables calculation of the Procrustes Distances (PD), which is the degree of overall morphological similarity between each of the images. The morphologika2 Procrustes registered coordinate data were also analysed using the palaeontological statistics software PAST, v.3.11, 2016 (Hammer et al. 2001). The PAST principle components analysis (relative warps) (PCA) replicates the PC results of morphologika2 and, in addition to the output being of a higher image resolution than morphologika2 in the PC scatter plots, PAST includes minimal spanning trees (morphological distances between the shapes within individual PC pairings) and 95% confidence ellipses (a bootstrap value of 100 was used for all analyses).

The image datasets with which the two versions (with and without the appearance of a mane) of the Leang Timpuseng cave art were compared are listed below, together with the independent variables applied for the morphologika2 multivariate regression analyses:

(i)   photographs of the babirusa and the Sulawesi warty pig (independent variables = image type; sex)

(ii) historical and contemporary illustrations of the hairy/golden babirusa, Sulawesi babirusa and the Sulawesi warty pig (~1740–1860; c. 2000) (independent variables = year, sex)

(iii) all representations of the babirusa and the Sulawesi warty pig (photographs, historical illustrations, contemporary illustrations) (independent variable = image type).

Results

Because the number of landmarks (n=38) is greater than the total number of images (n=36) and exceeds the number of individuals in all of the multivariate regression analyses, the results are constrained to the significant correlation coefficients that include the largest variance (i.e. PC1 and PC2), and in these instances only the adjusted r^2 results are reported (r^2 expresses the size of the variance under the assumption that every independent variable explains the variance, whereas adjusted r^2 expresses only the variables that affect the dependent variables). However, the statistical significance of all of the results, regardless of size and power, need to be interpreted as indicative of trends that may, or may not, sustain with a larger and more representative database of images.

(i) Photographs of babirusa and the Sulawesi warty pig (n=14)

A multivariate regression by image type (cave art 1, photograph 3) accounts for 30% of the overall variance, which is significant ($p = 0.02$) and there are two significant partial regression coefficients, PC1 (adjusted $r^2 = 0.39$, $p = 0.01$) and PC2 (adjusted $r^2 = 0.23$, $p = 0.046$). The wireframe and TPS deformation grids resulting from this multivariate regression are shown in Figure 5.6, and indicate that the Leang Timpuseng cave art differs from the photographs in displaying a smaller and narrower head and neck, and a larger and more rounded shape to the hindquarters. When the photographs of the babirusa and Sulawesi warty pigs and the Leang Timpuseng cave art are analysed by sex, sexual dimorphism is insignificant. Sexual dimorphism accounts for 9.7% of the overall variance when the cave art is coded as indeterminate sex (the wireframes and TPS deformation grid arising from the multivariate regression analysis is shown in Figure 5.8). When the cave art is coded as female, the overall sexual dimorphism increases to 17.2%, but the multivariate regression remains statistically insignificant ($p = 0.08$).

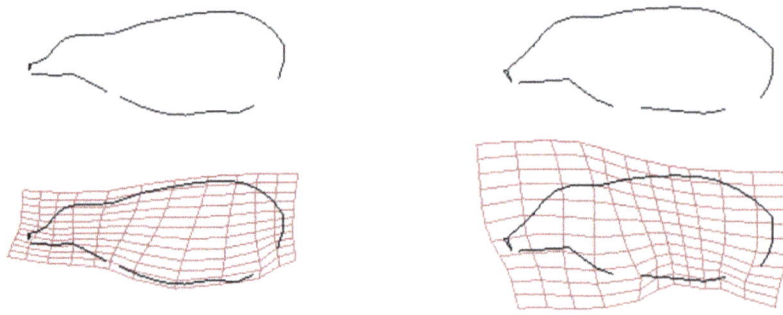

Figure 5.6: Leang Timpuseng cave art compared to photographs.

Wireframes and Thin Plate Spline deformation grids of how the cave art differs from the photographs (left), and how the photographs differ from the Leang Timpuseng cave art (right) following a multivariate regression with image type (cave art, photograph) as the independent variable.

Source: Authors' adaptations of Figure 5.5.

PCA (relative warps) of the Procrustes registered landmark coordinates in PAST shows the Leang Timpuseng cave art falls well within the 95% confidence ellipsis, and the minimal spanning tree indicates the cave art is most similar to a photograph depicting a young adult female Sulawesi babirusa. Within morphologika2, the PD between the Leang Timpuseng cave art and the photographs (range 0.011–0.226) replicates the results of the PAST minimal spanning tree, with the Leang Timpuseng cave art having greatest morphological similarity to (lowest PD from) the same young adult female Sulawesi babirusa (PD = 0.128). This is followed by a photograph of a mid-adult female Sulawesi babirusa (PD = 0.142) and, third, the male hairy/golden babirusa Museum exhibit (PD = 0.158).

Overall, these results indicate that the Sulawesi babirusa, which dominate the group, may have a low level of sexual dimorphism in body shape. The morphology of the Leang Timpuseng cave art, however, is most similar to that of a young Sulawesi babirusa female, and given that coding of the cave art as female nearly doubles the variance due to sexual dimorphism, it is possible that the Leang Timpuseng cave art may be depicting a female body morphology in a more exaggerated form.

(ii) Artistic depictions of babirusa and the Sulawesi warty pig (n=28)

The multivariate regression analysis by chronology shows there is a significant shape variance according to when the artistic depictions were published (overall variance 20.7%, $p = 0.001$). This analysis results in the first two PCs being significant correlation coefficients (PC1 adjusted $r^2 = 0.48$, $p = 0.0001$; PC2 adjusted $r^2 = 0.24$, $p = 0.008$), which are shown in Figure 5.7. The scatter plot of PC1 (horizontal x axis) and PC2 (vertical y axis) shows the clustering of the Leang Timpuseng cave art (black dots: LTCA, LTCAm, where m = with mane), historical illustrations (numbers are year of publication) and contemporary illustrations (Mod, ModF, where F = female). The hairy/golden babirusa illustrations are enclosed in a rectangle in the negative values of PC1; the filled square (HGB) is the photograph of the hairy/golden babirusa museum exhibit. Historical illustrations of the Sulawesi babirusa and warty pig (the warty pig is shown as a triangle) are nearly all enclosed in the adjacent rectangle. Modern illustrations are nearly all enclosed in the largest rectangle within the high positive values of PC1. The wireframes show the statistical trend of each PC axis and are taken from the maximum values for individuals on each axis. See the Legend for more detail regarding coding of the symbols.

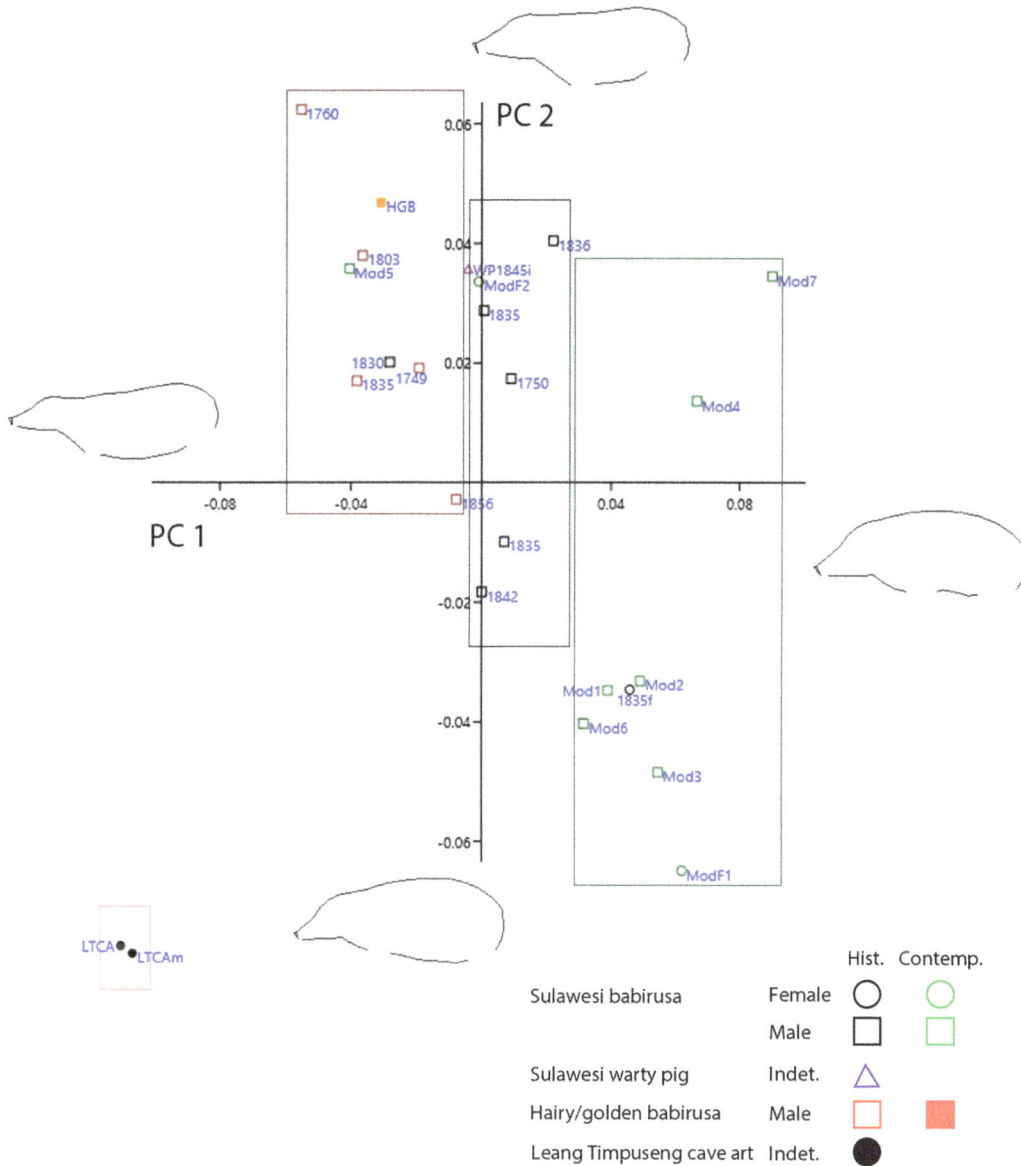

Figure 5.7: Changes to babirusa illustrations over time.
Source: Authors' data.

As can be seen, PC1 is separating the depictions by species as well as by chronology. The Leang Timpuseng cave art has the most negative values on PC1, followed by the historical illustrations of the male hairy/golden babirusa. The historical illustrations of the Sulawesi babirusa tend to have close to the mean and positive values, while the contemporary artistic illustrations of the Sulawesi babirusa have the highest positive values on PC1 because they display a larger neck and body shape. The hairy/golden babirusa museum exhibit clusters with the historical illustrations of this species, while the historical illustration of the Sulawesi warty pig is located between the historical illustrations of the hairy/golden babirusa and the historical illustrations of the Sulawesi babirusa.

Although female babirusa and the Sulawesi warty pig are under-represented in the historical and contemporary illustrations, when sexual dimorphism is examined the multivariate regression attains significance, and this significance is sustained whether the Leang Timpuseng cave art is coded male (7.1% overall variance, $p = 0.03$), indeterminate (6.9% overall variance, $p = 0.03$) or female (9.3% overall variance, $p = 0.02$). For all analyses, the sexual dimorphism manifests as the females displaying a smaller head, narrower neck, broader mid-section and larger, higher and more rounded hindquarters, which is similar to how the Leang Timpuseng cave art is morphologically differentiated from the dataset of photographs (see Figure 5.6). How these sexually dimorphic features are more exaggerated in the artistic depictions than the statistically insignificant sexual dimorphism of the photographs is shown in Figure 5.8 (for both of these multivariate regressions the sex of the Leang Timpuseng cave art is coded as indeterminate).

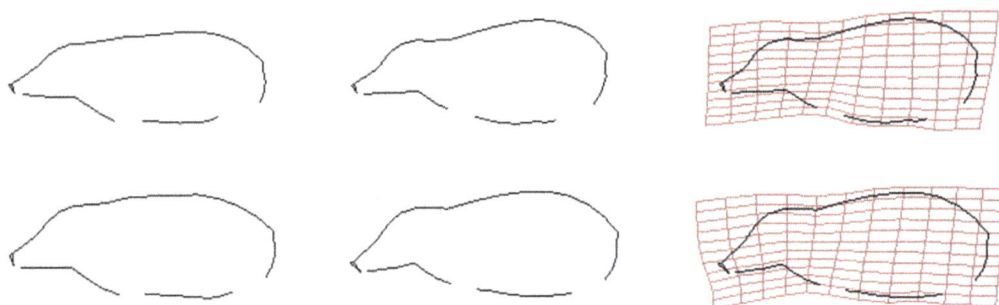

Figure 5.8: Sexual dimorphism in illustrations and photographs.

Wireframes showing how male (far left) and female (centre) depictions differ following a multivariate regression with sex as the independent variable. The upper row is the degree of sexual dimorphism in the illustrations (historical and contemporary) and the lower row is the sexual dimorphism as displayed in the photographs. The Thin Plate Spline deformation grids indicate how the females differ in morphology from the males.

Source: Authors' adaptations of Figure 5.5.

PCA (relative warps) of the Procrustes registered landmark coordinate data in PAST shows the Leang Timpuseng cave art pairs fall outside the 95% confidence ellipsis for the artistic illustrations. Within the minimal spanning tree for PC1/PC2, the closest individual to the Leang Timpuseng cave art is a male hairy/golden babirusa illustration that was published in 1835. When the PD output of morphologika2 is examined (range 0.011–0.232), a historical depiction of the hairy/golden babirusa illustration published in 1856 is closest in overall morphology to the cave art (PD = 0.133 to the version with a mane, PD = 0.135 to the version without a mane), followed by the same 1835 hairy/golden babirusa illustration that was linked to the cave art within the PCA (relative warps) minimal spanning tree.

What this analysis of the artistic illustrations shows is that sexual dimorphism tends to be exaggerated in the historical and contemporary illustrations, with this sexual dimorphism increasing only slightly when the Leang Timpuseng cave art is coded as female. However, despite the Leang Timpuseng cave art displaying a more female body morphology, within the group of illustrations the cave art is most similar, morphologically, to the historical illustrations of the hairy/golden babirusa—all of which are depicted bearing distinctively curved tusks and therefore all of which can be assumed to be male.

(iii) Photographs and artistic depictions of babirusa and the Sulawesi warty pig (n=36)

Figure 5.9 is a scatter plot of PC1 (horizontal x axis) and PC2 (vertical y axis) showing the Leang Timpuseng cave art (black dots), illustrations (open shapes), the hairy/golden babirusa museum exhibit (filled orange square), and photographs (other filled shapes). Most of the photographs and contemporary illustrations are in the positive values of PC1 and enclosed in an ellipse. The historical illustrations are enclosed in an ellipse within the negative values of PC1. The wireframes show the statistical trend of each PC axis, and are taken from the maximum values for individuals on each axis. Thus, when the photographs and illustrations of the babirusa and Sulawesi warty pigs are analysed together, it can be seen that they cluster together, and are morphologically distinct from both the Leang Timpuseng cave art and the historical illustrations of the hairy/golden babirusa, Sulawesi babirusa and Sulawesi warty pig. Also, the dynamic wireframes extracted from PC1 and PC2 indicate that both the photographs and the contemporary illustrations of the Sulawesi babirusa display an animal with a more downwards head orientation and a fatter neck and body than the historical illustrations and the Leang Timpuseng cave art.

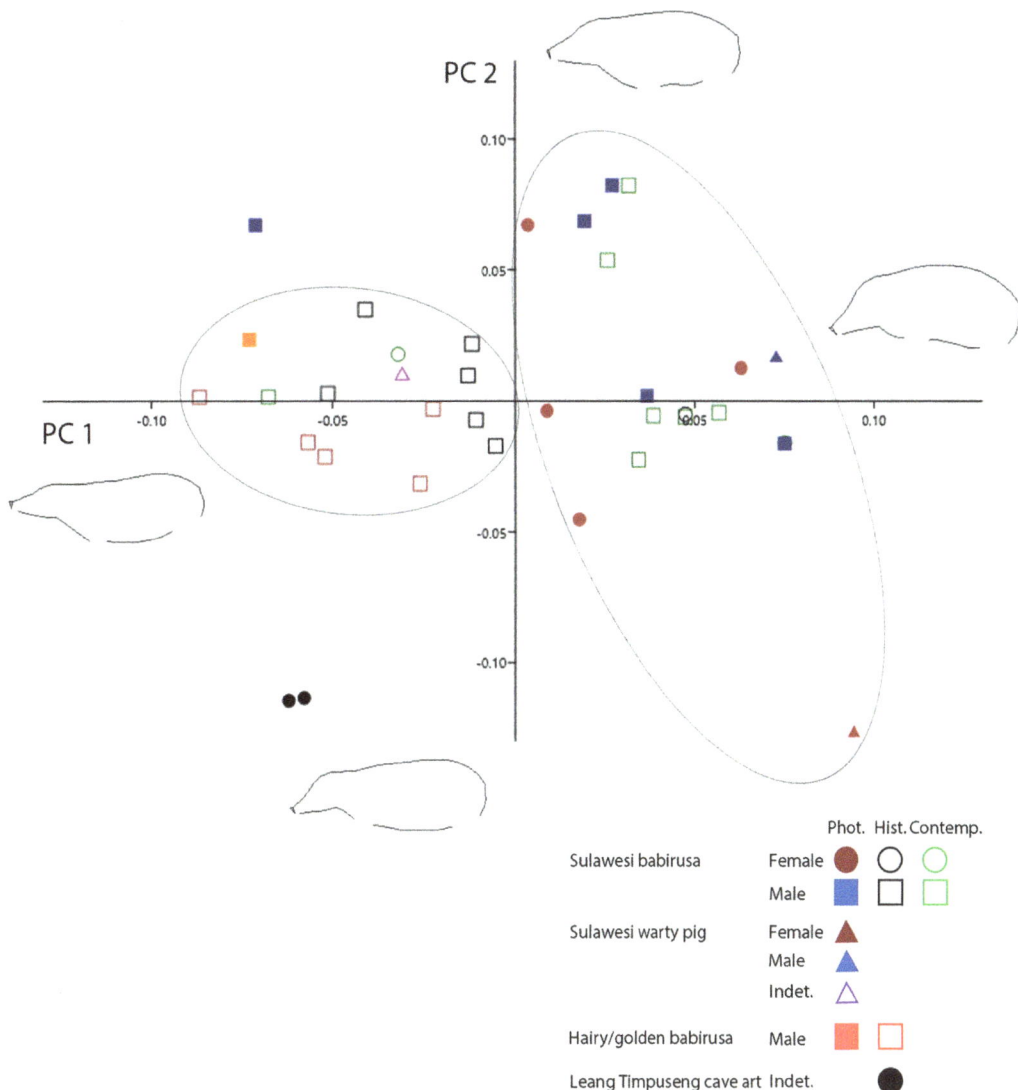

Figure 5.9: Babirusa illustrations compared to photographs.

Source: Authors' data.

The overall variance of the photographs and illustrations is sexually dimorphic when the Leang Timpuseng cave art is coded as being of indeterminate sex (overall variance due to sex 6.7%, $p = 0.01$). This overall dimorphism rises slightly (8%, $p = 0.001$) and PC2 is a significant correlation coefficient for sexual dimorphism when the Leang Timpuseng cave art is coded as female (PC2 adjusted $r^2 = 0.154$, $p = 0.01$). It is the negative values that are associated with female body morphology on PC2 and, as can be seen in Figure 5.9, the Leang Timpuseng cave art is located with the photograph of a female Sulawesi warty pig at the extreme of the negative PC2 values (< –0.10).

Within the PCA (relative warps) minimal spanning tree for PC1/PC2, the Leang Timpuseng cave art is closest to a hairy/golden babirusa with a publication date of 1749. The morphologika2 PD pattern (range 0.011–0.232) repeats the previous analyses and shows the Leang Timpuseng cave art to be closest in overall morphology to the same photograph of a young adult female Sulawesi babirusa (PD = 0.128). This is followed by the same two historical images of hairy/golden babirusa (illustration from 1856, PD = 0.135; illustration from 1835, PD = 0.137), with the Leang Timpuseng cave art 'with mane' version being closest to the 1856 hairy/golden babirusa illustration (PD = 0.133).

To summarise, what these analyses of the complete dataset (Leang Timpuseng cave art, historical illustrations, contemporary illustrations and photographs) suggest is that the Leang Timpuseng cave art is most similar, morphologically, to the golden/hairy babirusa (all of which are illustrations of males), but shares morphological affinity with the female form, at least in so far as this is represented in a photograph of a young adult female Sulawesi babirusa. The Leang Timpuseng is not, however, morphologically similar to either the relatively slender historical illustrations of male and female Sulawesi babirusa, or the somewhat fatter contemporary illustrations of these animals.

Discussion

The geometric morphometric analyses, while not conclusive due to the ratio of landmarks to images, do suggest that the Leang Timpuseng cave art is morphologically similar to young adult female Sulawesi babirusa, and that the sexual dimorphism of the dataset is more evident in the illustrations than the photographs. However, despite the Leang Timpuseng cave art displaying female characteristics that include (in addition to the lack of clearly visible tusks) a comparatively small head, narrow neck, rounded and higher hindquarters and a wider mid-section, the Leang Timpuseng cave art does not cluster with any of the historical or contemporary illustrations of male and female Sulawesi babirusa. Instead the Leang Timpuseng cave art shows a closer morphological affinity to historical illustrations of the male hairy/golden babirusa.

A summary of the findings indicated by these analyses are that:

(i) Both the photographs and the contemporary illustrations depict an animal that is fatter and displays a more downwards head pose than the historical illustrations. This is possibly because the contemporary photographs are predominantly of grazing zoo babirusa, which may tend towards obesity. It is also likely that many, if not all, of the contemporary illustrations are sourced from photographs of zoo babirusa and/or living zoo babirusa. In contrast, nearly all of the historical illustrations depict an animal with an upright head pose and a relatively slender body. A noted exception to this trend is the downwards head pose of the only historical illustration that was able to be sourced of a female babirusa.

(ii) Photographed Sulawesi babirusa tend to display a limited level of sexual dimorphism. This, however, may be in part due to the obesity levels displayed by most of the babirusa photographed. Two notable exceptions are the photographs of a young adult female Sulawesi babirusa and a female warty pig, both of which were photographed in the wild. It is the young adult female Sulawesi babirusa that, when it is included in the analyses, bears the highest morphological similarity (lowest PD) to the Leang Timpuseng cave art.

(iii) Allowing for the compounding variable of zoo babirusa obesity, both the contemporary and historical illustrations of the babirusa appear to exaggerate sexual dimorphism, and this characteristic may also be a feature of the Leang Timpuseng cave art. However, the cave art does not cluster with any of the illustrations of female Sulawesi babirusa. This may be because two depict the female babirusa with a more downwards head orientation—in one (c. 1835) the female babirusa is nurturing an infant, while in the other (c. 1950) the female is shown with a lower head orientation than the male that accompanies her. Somewhat in contrast, although comparatively slender and displaying an upwards head pose, the third illustration of a female babirusa (c. 2000) is similar in head size and hindquarter morphology to the males. In effect, this illustration has the head and body of a male babirusa lacking tusks, and this may explain why this artwork clusters with the male historical illustrations in all of the analyses that include it. Therefore, the Leang Timpuseng cave art would appear to be the only illustration of a morphologically female suid displaying a comparatively active body pose.

On balance, the evidence, limited as it is, suggests the Leang Timpuseng cave art does depict a female suid. This is not just because of the absence of canine-tusks in the image, which could have been depicted using a less resilient material and therefore may have disappeared with the passage of time, but because the body morphology is more clearly female than male. The evidence is also that the Leang Timpuseng cave art may depict a babirusa, but not necessarily a Sulawesi babirusa. The analyses repeatedly link the cave art's overall morphology to historical illustrations of the hairy/golden babirusa, and never to any illustrations of the Sulawesi babirusa (females and males) or the illustration of the Sulawesi warty pig (sex indeterminate).

Two features of the Leang Timpuseng cave art that were not captured by the geometric morphometric analyses, but that also suggest the cave art may not be of the Sulawesi babirusa, are (i) the inscription of what appear to be relatively horizontal lines within the body of the animal, and (ii) the shape of the tail tuft. As noted, the Sulawesi babirusa has scarce body hair and is distinctive in displaying vertical skin folds, which are described by Renshaw (1907:171) as 'wrinkled tranversely [sic] like a maggot's'. The golden/hairy babirusa is, as its name suggests, hairy and, as with the Leang Timpuseng cave art, in all of the historical illustrations of this animal the coat is depicted with short lines running horizontally across the body and converging beneath the tail. The Leang Timpuseng cave art, however, differs from both the Sulawesi babirusa and the hairy/golden babirusa in the depiction of the tail. The hairy/golden babirusa has a distinctive tail tuft, and an early description is that the tail is both long and twisted (Beilby et al. 1790), while the Sulawesi babirusa has a relatively straight and minimally tufted tail. The tail of the Leang Timpuseng cave art is not long, does not appear to be tufted, but it is twisted. This may be due to the depicted animal not having a tail tuft, having this detail lost through weathering and time, and/or this aspect of the animal having, like the legs, less salience for the artist. Another possibility that cannot be ruled out given the composition of the images in this analysis is that the Leang Timpuseng cave art is a depiction of a Sulawesi warty pig. The Sulawesi warty pig is also hairy, has a long and simply tufted tail, and has a mane, which may or may not be present in the Leang Timpuseng cave art (and thus two versions were used for the analyses). However, while Aubert et al. (2014) allow for this possibility, Frantz et al. (2016) state that it is clear that the Leang Timpuseng cave art depicts a female babirusa, and not a warty pig.

Overall, this study suggests that the Leang Timpuseng cave art is a depiction of a female hairy/golden babirusa, which to date does not appear in the published fossil record of Sulawesi. The fossil record of the southwestern peninsula does, however, contain the remains of an extinct babirusa, *Babyrousa bolabatuensis*, which is similar in tooth size to the hairy/golden babirusa (Hooijer 1950; Groves 1980), and it is possible that the hairy/golden babirusa once inhabited this part of Sulawesi. However, until more images of the Sulawesi warty pig, the hairy/golden babirusa and females of both animals can be sourced, the only relative certainty is that this analysis shows that:

(a)   geometric morphometrics can be used to meaningfully analyse the anatomical characteristics of cave art depictions

(b)   sexual dimorphism is more apparent or exaggerated in both the Leang Timpuseng cave art and the illustrations than photographic depictions

(c)   the Leang Timpuseng cave art differs from both historical and contemporary European depictions in that it shows a morphologically female suid in an active pose.

Conclusion

Due to the limitations of the sample size, the limited representation of the Sulawesi warty pig in both photography and art, the absence of hairy/golden babirusa in photographs and the absence of any photographs or illustrations depicting a female hairy/golden babirusa, the results of the analyses conducted here are at best indicative. What the results do seem to suggest is that the Leang Timpuseng cave art is most likely female, and is most similar to later, historical depictions of the hairy/golden babirusa. If this is the case, then the Leang Timpuseng cave art would appear to be not just the oldest, or amongst the oldest, naturalistic cave art depiction (Aubert et al. 2014), but is possibly also a depiction of a female hairy/golden babirusa (which is not currently known to occur on the island of Sulawesi) or a female of the extinct *Babyrousa bolabatuensis*, whose fossilised remains have been noted as being somewhat similar to that of the hairy/golden babirusa (Hooijer 1950; Groves 1980).

Author biographies

Susan Hayes Centre for Archaeological Science, School of Earth and Environmental Sciences, Faculty of Science, Medicine and Health, University of Wollongong, New South Wales, Australia; and Vertebrate Collection, Bandung Geology Museum, West Java, Indonesia

Gert van den Bergh Centre for Archaeological Science, School of Earth and Environmental Sciences, Faculty of Science, Medicine and Health, University of Wollongong, New South Wales, Australia

References

Arnheim, R. 1974. *Art and Visual Perception: A Psychology of the Creative Eye*. Berkley and Los Angeles: University of California Press.

Aubert, M., A. Brumm, M. Ramli, T. Sutikna, E.W. Saptomo, B. Hakim, M. Morwood, G.D. van den Bergh, L. Kinsley and A. Dosseto. 2014. Pleistocene cave art from Sulawesi, Indonesia. *Nature* 514(7521):223–227, doi.org/10.1038/nature13422 (accessed 5 June 2018).

Babirusa Art ~300 BP to present. Historical (images 3–14) and Contemporary (images 15–23) Babirusa Depictions. 3: www.zvab.com/servlet/FrameBase?content=/de/imagegallery/imagegallery.shtml?images =pictures.abebooks.com/ANTIQUARIATMURRBAMBERG/16117456525.jpg; 4: img0.etsystatic. com/001/1/5842899/il_570xN.388485840_27i9.jpg; 5: www.wpclipart.com/animals/B/babirusa/ Babirusa_vintage.png; 6: www.ebay.ca/itm/Babirusa-Pig-Deer-Rare-Antique-Engraving-Print-from-1803-200-Yrs-Old-/172039166278?hash=item280e555946; 7: img0.etsystatic.com/008/0/5663576/ il_214x170.377133020_8euh.jpg; 8: ecx.images-amazon.com/images/I/71lcLnWllML._SX425_.jpg; 9: a407.idata.over-blog.com/0/04/43/94/Gravures-de-mammiferes/Babiroussa-male.jpg; 10: i.ebayimg. com/images/g/sTsAAOSw-W5UuT1b/s-l1600.jpg; 11: www.ebay.ca/itm/Babirusa-Pig-Deer-Antique-1842-Engraving-Print-170-Years-Old-/172039166268?hash=item280e55593c; 12: h7.alamy.com/ comp/BDWTEE/sus-domesticus-domestic-dog-porcus-babyrussa-asiatic-hog-sus-scropha-BDWTEE. jpg; 13: a141.idata.over-blog.com/0/04/43/94/Gravures-de-mammiferes/Babiroussa-male--age-de-7-mois.jpg; 14: www.french-engravings.com/images/artworks/ART-13629/MQ.jpg; 15: www.ebay.ca/ itm/N-69-Babiroussa-Babyrousas-Suide-Babi-Porc-Rusa-Cerf-Babirusa-Pig-Deer-CHROMO-/16183 9520797?hash=item25ae631c1d; 16: www.ebay.ca/itm/Babirusas-also-called-Wild-pig-deer-Babyrousa-celebensis-Porc-IMAGE-CARD-1985-/161836466859?hash=item25ae3482ab; 17: annemiekebunjes. nl/Zoogdieren.htm; 18: www.flatpyramid.com/uploads/imagecache/3d/3d-models/images/animals_3d_ models/babirusa-3d-model-30168-173421.jpg; 19: www.collecta.biz/collecta_files/products/88727 -small.jpg; 20: i344.photobucket.com/albums/p323/Bokichops/Bokichops026/DSCN1181_zps5fa 7c0cc.jpg; 21: i344.photobucket.com/albums/p323/Bokichops/Bokichops052/DSCN2071_zpsd bmhieoz.jpg; 22: mttmuzeum.blog.hu/2014/06/30/szarvas_diszno; 23: davidlomaxsculpture.com/wp-content/uploads/lomax-sculpture-18-image-2.jpg (accessed 2013–2016).

Babirusa Photographs c. 2000. Babirusa Profile Photographs (M: 1–5, F: 6–9). 1: fuzfeed.com/wp-content/uploads/2014/08/513_1babirusa_boars-1024x682.jpg; 2: i902.photobucket.com/albums/ ac228/jesselton88/Babi%20Guling%20Ibu%20Oka/P1240102_zpsuyq4sm2v.jpg; 3: thumb1. shutterstock.com/display_pic_with_logo/732580/276498950/stock-photo-babirusa-in-a-zoo-buru-babirusa-babyrousa-babyrussa-276498950.jpg; 4: previews.123rf.com/images/leungchopan/leung chopan1208/leungchopan120800132/14749046-Wild-boar-or-babirusa-Stock-Photo.jpg; 5: cdn1. arkive.org/media/11/118B3B2C-AE47-4B99-8DC0-873F8D7A1340/Presentation.Large/Male-Sulawesi-babirusa-walking.jpg; 6: farm6.static.flickr.com/5476/14184496246_c60c797128_m. jpg; 7: thumbs.dreamstime.com/thumblarge_2109/21090536.jpg; 8: Gert van den Bergh, personal collection; 9: www.pbase.com/cokesmith/image/148426075 (accessed 2013–2016).

Bedaux, J.B. 1996. From normal to supranormal: Observations on realism and idealism from a biological perspective. In R. Woodfield (ed.), *Gombrich On Art and Psychology*, pp. 171–195. Manchester: Manchester University Press.

Beilby, R., T. Bewick and S. Hodgson. 1790. *A General History of Quadrupeds*. S. Hodgson, R. Beilby, and T. Bewick, Newcastle: sold by them, by GGJ and J. Robinson, and C. Dilly, London.

Cardini, A. and S. Elton. 2007. Sample size and sampling error in geometric morphometric studies of size and shape. *Zoomorphology* 126(2):121–134. doi.org/10.1007/s00435-007-0036-2 (accessed 5 June 2018).

Cavanagh, P. 2005. The artist as neuroscientist. *Nature* 434:301–307. doi.org/10.1038/434301a (accessed 5 June 2018).

Cheyne, J.A., L. Meschino and D. Smilek. 2009. Caricature and contrast in the Upper Palaeolithic: Morphometric evidence from cave art. *Perception* 38(1):100–108. doi.org/10.1068/p6079 (accessed 5 June 2018).

Dobrez, L. and P. Dobrez. 2013. Rock art animals in profile: Visual recognition and the principles of canonical form. *Rock Art Research* 30(1):75–90.

Frantz, L., E. Meijaard, J. Gongora, J. Haile, M.A.M. Groenen and G. Larson. 2016. The evolution of Suidae. *Annual Review of Animal Biosciences* 4(1):61–85. doi.org/10.1146/annurev-animal-021815-111155 (accessed 5 June 2018).

Galeta, P., J. Bruzek and M. Lázničková-Galetová. 2014. Is sex estimation from handprints in prehistoric cave art reliable? A view from biological and forensic anthropology. *Journal of Archaeological Science* 45:141–149. doi.org/10.1016/j.jas.2014.01.028 (accessed 5 June 2018).

Gombrich, E.H. 1977. *Art and Illusion: A Study in the Psychology of Pictorial Representation.* Oxford: Phaidon Press.

Groves, C.P. 1980. Notes on the systematics of Babyrousa (Artiodactyla, Suidae). *Zoologische Mededelingen* 55(3):29–46.

Groves, C.P. 1981. *Ancestors for the Pigs: Taxonomy and Phylogeny of the Genus Sus.* Department of Prehistory Technical Bulletin No. 3. Canberra: The Australian National University.

Groves, C.P. and P. Grubb. 2011. *Ungulate Taxonomy.* Baltimore: Johns Hopkins University Press.

Hammer, Ø., D. Harper and P. Ryan. 2001. PAST: Palaeontological statistics software package for education and data analysis. *Palaeontologica Electronica* 4(1). palaeo-electronica.org/2001_1/past/issue1_01.htm (accessed 5 June 2018).

Hodgson, D. 2008. The visual dynamics of Upper Palaeolithic cave art. *Cambridge Archaeological Journal* 18(03):341–353. doi.org/10.1017/S0959774308000401 (accessed 5 June 2018).

Hodgson, D. 2013. The visual brain, perception, and depiction of animals in rock art. *Journal of Archaeology* 2013:1–6. doi.org/10.1155/2013/342801 (accessed 5 June 2018).

Hodgson, D. 2014. Commentary on Turing instabilities and symbolic material culture by Froese, Woodward and Ikegami. *Adaptive Behavior* 22(1):86–88. doi.org/10.1177/1059712313509653 (accessed 5 June 2018).

Hodgson, D. and B. Watson. 2015. The visual brain and the early depiction of animals in Europe and Southeast Asia. *World Archaeology* 47(5):776–791. doi.org/10.1080/00438243.2015.1074871 (accessed 5 June 2018).

Honoré, E., T. Rakza, B. Senut, P. Deruelle and E. Pouydebat. 2016. First identification of non-human stencil hands at Wadi Sūra II (Egypt): A morphometric study for new insights into rock art symbolism. *Journal of Archaeological Science: Reports* 6:242–247. doi.org/10.1016/j.jasrep.2016.02.014 (accessed 5 June 2018).

Hooijer, D.A. 1950. *Man and Other Mammals from Toalian Sites in South-Western Celebes.* Amsterdam: North-Holland Publishing Company.

Lydekker, R. and P.L. Sclater. 1893. *The Royal Natural History.* London: Frederick Warne & Co. doi.org/10.5962/bhl.title.126325 (accessed 5 June 2018).

Meijaard, E. and C. Groves. 2002. Upgrading three subspecies of babirusa (*Babyrousa* sp.) to full species level. *Asian Wild Pig News* 2(2):33–39.

Naish, D. 2010. A close-up look at a Hairy babirusa. *ScienceBlogs*, scienceblogs.com/tetrapodzoology/2010/05/22/better-look-hairy-babirusa/ (accessed 20 July 2016).

O'Higgins, P. and N. Jones. 2006. *Tools for Statistical Shape Analysis*. Hull York Medical School. hyms.fme. googlepages.com/resources (accessed 5 June 2018).

Ramachandran, V.S. and W. Hirstein. 1999. The science of art: A neurological theory of aesthetic experience. *Journal of Consciousness Studies* 6(6–7):15–51.

Reichenbach, H.G.L. 1845. *Die vollständigste Naturgeschichte des In- und Auslandes*, Plate 34. Dresden and Leipzig: Expedition der vollständigste Naturgeschichte. commons.wikimedia.org/wiki/File:Sus_celebensis (accessed 20 July 2016).

Renshaw, G. 1907. *Final Natural History Essays*. London: Sherratt & Hughes. doi.org/10.5962/bhl. title.18262.

Rohlf, F.J. 2008. tpsDig. Stony Brook: Department of Ecology and Evolution, State University of New York at Stony Brook.

Rohlf, F.J. 2015. The tps series of software. *Hystrix, the Italian Journal of Mammalogy* 26(1):9–12.

Scott, C.P.G. 1896. The Malayan words in English. *Journal of the American Oriental Society* 17:93–144. doi.org/10.2307/592501 (accessed 5 June 2018).

Vogt, S. and S. Magnussen. 2007. Expertise in pictorial representation: Eye-movement patterns and visual memory in artists and laymen. *Perception* 36:91–100. doi.org/10.1068/p5262 (accessed 5 June 2018).

Warty Pig Photographs c. 2000. Sulawesi Warty Pig Photographs (1M, 1F) M: www.wildborneo.com. my/images/cld09040760.jpg; F: www.pbase.com/cokesmith/image/148425743 (accessed 2013 and 2016).

Werner, J.-C. 1835, 1830. *Babyrousa, Babiroussa male, Babyrousa babyrussa*. www.oldantiqueprints.com/ product_info.php?products_id=13632; upload.wikimedia.org/wikipedia/commons/thumb/b/b6/Babi roussa_1.jpg/1280px-Babiroussa_1.jpg; environnement.ecole.free.fr/2bgal/disp_img.php?id_img= 3214&titreimg=Babiroussa%20male.jpg&titrealb=Gravures%20anciennes%20de%20mammiferes; www.french-engravings.com/images/artworks/ART-13632/details/01.jpg (accessed 20 July 2016).

6

Hand stencils and boats in the painted rock art of the karst region of Muna Island, Southeast Sulawesi

Adhi Agus Oktaviana

Abstract

The rock paintings of Muna Island first became the subject of research by Indonesia's National Research Centre of Archaeology in Jakarta, Indonesia, almost 40 years ago. Since then, a large assortment of images has been documented, the majority of which are done using brown pigment. The rock art includes figurative motifs such as anthropomorphs, zoomorphs, sun and boat imagery, sometimes in active scenes like hunting and sailing, as well as non-figurative motifs. In 2005, the first observations of negative hand stencils on Muna Island were made at Gua Pominsa by the Makassar Archaeology Office. In 2015, more negative hand stencils were recorded at two further Muna Island sites (Gua Mentanduno and Gua Kabori) by the Directorate of Cultural Property Preservation and Museums, and in 2016 a new site with parietal art (Gua Lakan Taghu) was discovered. Analysis of the Muna Island boat imagery documents the depiction of five propulsion methods, providing an insight into the navigation technology of Muna Island's Austronesian inhabitants. These new developments in rock art research on Muna Island are described here, expanding the catalogue and contributing to a wider understanding of Island Southeast Asian rock art.

Keywords: rock art, hand stencils, boat images, Austronesian Painting Tradition, Muna Island karsts

Introduction

Visual art is a physical representation of human creativity that has been practised since ancient times, including some of the oldest examples from Island Southeast Asia (ISEA) as revealed in two recent publications in *Nature* (Aubert et al. 2014, Joordens et al. 2015). Joordens et al. (2015), after revisiting deposits first collected in 1891 by the Dutch scientist, Eugene Dubois, from the open-air site at Trinil in East Java, found zigzag-patterned incisions on a freshwater bivalve that was dated to around 500,000 years ago, thereby attributing their production to *Homo erectus*. Aubert et al. (2014) dated hand stencils and large animal motifs on the walls and ceilings of caves and rockshelters in the Maros karst system of South Sulawesi using the uranium-thorium (UTh) method, with minimum ages achieved of 40,700 and 36,900 BP, respectively, and younger ages for one stencil of 17,770 BP. The youngest of the dated stencils had additional pigment applied between the fingers to produce a narrowed or sharpened shape referred to here as narrowed fingers, while the older hand stencils do not show any alterations to the fingers' morphology and are referred to here as normal fingers (Table 6.1).

Table 6.1: Early dates for hand stencils in Island Southeast Asia.

Site	Region	Hand stencils type	Minimum dates	Reference
Leang Timpuseng	Maros, South Sulawesi	Hand stencil with normal fingers	40,700+870/≤ 840 BP	Aubert et al. 2014
Leang Jarie	Maros, South Sulawesi	Hand stencils with normal fingers	39,670±320 BP and 34,980±410 BP	Aubert et al. 2014
Leang Sampeang	Maros, South Sulawesi	Hand stencil with normal fingers	32,600±760 BP	Aubert et al. 2014
Gua Jing	Maros, South Sulawesi	Hand stencils with normal fingers	30,900+1700/≤1800 and 24,000±1100 BP	Aubert et al. 2014
Leang Barugayya	Maros, South Sulawesi	Hand stencils with normal fingers	29,100+3200/≤3100 BP, 24,000+3100/≤3000 BP, and 19,700±1000 BP	Aubert et al. 2014
Leang (Tapuang) Lompoa	Maros, South Sulawesi	Hand stencil with normal fingers; hand stencil with narrowed fingers	29,300+1200/≤1100 BP; 17,770±420 BP, respectively	Aubert et al. 2014
Gua Jeriji Saleh	East Kalimantan	Hand stencil with normal fingers	~9900 BP	Plagnes et al. 2003

Note: Two standard dating error ranges are presented for the Maros dates.

Source: Adapted from Oktaviana, Bulbeck et al. (2016).

In Timor Leste, calcite bracketing red pigment in Lene Hara Cave has been dated using the UTh technique to between 29,000 and 24,000 years ago, raising the possibility of equally old painted art in Timor (Aubert et al. 2007). In the Sangkulirang-Mangkalihat karsts of East Kalimantan (Indonesian Borneo), there are hand stencils of probable Pleistocene age: one of these is covered by a stalactite flow dated to around 10,000 years ago (see Table 6.1; Plagnes et al. 2003). These products of human creativity are millennia older than the Neolithic phase of ISEA, which is associated with the southward incursion of early speakers of Malayo-Polynesian (a branch of the Austronesian language family) recorded widely across ISEA in ethnographic times.

Improved technologies for recording and analysing rock art have been more recently implemented in ISEA research to bolster the documentation and understanding of these images. This includes the use of portable 3D scanners with a DStretch plug-in that uses colours to sharply expose subtle contrasts and textures in rock paintings otherwise missed by the observer; an example of this technique was used for the art at Gua Harimau in Sumatra (Oktaviana 2015b). These 3D scanners have also been used for mapping various painted caves in the Maros-Pangkep and Sangkulirang-Mangkalihat karst systems performed under the auspices of the Directorate for Cultural Property Preservation and Museums (Direktorat Cagar Budaya dan Permuseuman).

Most of the recorded rock paintings of Indonesia and Timor Leste are contained within caves (*gua*), caverns (*ceruk*) and sea cliffs (Figure 6.1). The most easterly of these have been recorded in West Papua in the karst districts of the Berau Gulf, Kaimana, the Baliem Valley (Arifin and Delanghe 2004), Triton Bay (Gonthier et al. 2013), and Misool (Sulistyarto et al. 2014). Others have been recorded in the Matgugul Kakun karsts on Buru Island (Ririmasse 2007) and at the Tala River in Seleman Bay on Seram (Oktaviana, Lape et al. 2016). Other sites occur on the Kei Islands to the east of Seram (Ballard 1988; Setiawan 1994) and near Kupang in West Timor

(O'Connor et al. 2015), and in Timor Leste various sites with rock paintings near Tutuala and Baucau (O'Connor 2003), Baguia (O'Connor and Oliveira 2007) and the island of Atauro (Galipaud et al. 2016) .

In the karst regions of Kalimantan, rock art has been recorded since 1995 including sites in the Sangkulirang-Mangkalihat karsts of East Kalimantan (Fage et al. 2010) as well as the sites of Batu Cap (Yondri 1996) and Liang Kaung (Chazine 1999) in West Kalimantan. Recent discoveries include rock art on Sumatra, specifically the Gua Harimau site in the Padang Bindu karsts of South Sumatra (Oktaviana, Setiawan et al. 2016) and Bukit Bulan in the Sarolungan karsts of Jambi (Fauzi et al. 2015). Painted rock art sites on Sulawesi occur in the karsts of Maros-Pangkep (Permana 2005; Aubert et al. 2014), Bone (Oktaviana, Bulbeck et al. 2016), Morowali and Matarombeo (Fage 2015), as well as Muna Island, which is the focus of this contribution.

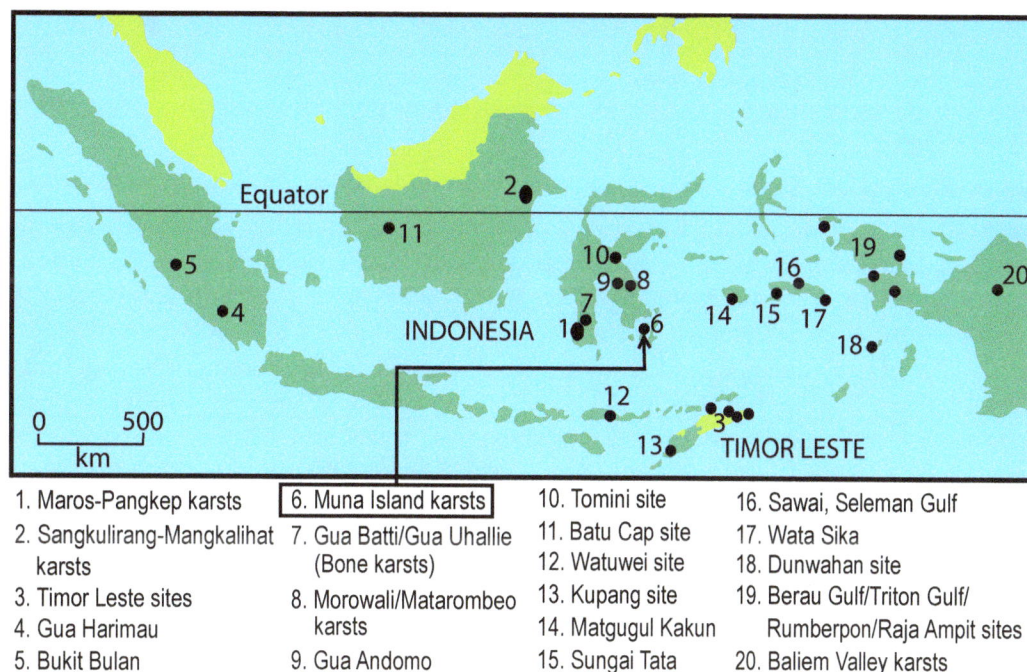

1. Maros-Pangkep karsts	6. Muna Island karsts	10. Tomini site	16. Sawai, Seleman Gulf
2. Sangkulirang-Mangkalihat karsts	7. Gua Batti/Gua Uhallie (Bone karsts)	11. Batu Cap site	17. Wata Sika
		12. Watuwei site	18. Dunwahan site
3. Timor Leste sites	8. Morowali/Matarombeo karsts	13. Kupang site	19. Berau Gulf/Triton Gulf/ Rumberpon/Raja Ampit sites
4. Gua Harimau		14. Matgugul Kakun	
5. Bukit Bulan	9. Gua Andomo	15. Sungai Tata	20. Baliem Valley karsts

Figure 6.1: The distribution of painted rock art in Indonesia and Timor Leste.

Source: Adapted from Oktaviana (2016).

Fieldwork area

The general fieldwork area for this study is the Muna Island karsts (Figure 6.1), which are part of the Muna District in Southeast Sulawesi Province. The rock art contained within this region was first documented by Indonesia's National Research Centre for Archaeology in 1977, with further studies in 1984 and 1986 (Kosasih 1985, 1989, 1995). The 10 sites of Gua Metanduno, Gua Kabori, Gua Wa Bose, Gua Toko, Gua La Kolumbu, Ceruk Ida Malangi, Ceruk Lasabo A, Ceruk Lasabo B, Ceruk La Nsafora and Ceruk Tangga Ara were recorded for a variety of motifs including anthropomorphs, zoomorphs, sun and boat motifs, and warfare and hunting weapons that were possibly made from metal. These motifs were painted on cave walls and ceilings and on cavern walls. Most of the images were produced using brown pigments, though some are black and a small number are red.[1] Kosasih (1995) wrote that the diversity of these paintings reflects the lifestyle and daily realities of the past communities that produced them, characterised by dynamic activities such as hunting, combat and warfare.

One main focus of this contribution is the recent discovery of hand stencils from the Liang Kabori village, Lohia Subdistrict, Muna District. Rock art research has been conducted for around 40 years across the island, yet it was not until 2005 that reports surfaced of negative hand stencils, which are a common motif throughout the Sulawesi karst systems (for example, those at Maros-Pangkep, Bone and Lake Towuti in South Sulawesi, and Matarombeo in Southeast Sulawesi) (Oktaviana, Bulbeck et al. 2016). Archaeologists from the Makassar Archaeology Office recorded hand stencils at Gua Pominsa, with further hand stencils later found at Gua Metanduno and Gua Kabori where their presence had been overlooked during previous studies of these sites' rock paintings (e.g. Aksa (1991) for Gua Kabori; Kosasih (1995) for Gua Metanduno and Gua Kabori; and Alamsyah (2014) for Gua Metanduno).

Methods

Direct observations of the art were undertaken in 2015 by the Directorate of Cultural Property Preservation and Museums, the Ministry of Education and Culture (during its preparation of the Muna Island chapter for an illustrated edition of the rock art of Indonesia), the author as a representative of the National Research Centre of Archaeology and Pindi Setiawan from the Bandung Institute of Technology. These observations documented the parietal art of various caves and caverns, including Gua Metanduno, Gua Kabori, Ceruk Ida Malangi, Gua Sugi Patani, Ceruk La Podo, Gua Pominsa and Ceruk Lakan Taghu (Figure 6.2). A review of the literature was done to contextualise these observations with those from earlier texts relating to the prehistoric art in the Muna Island karsts, including Kosasih (1987, 1989, 1995) and BCPBM (2015).

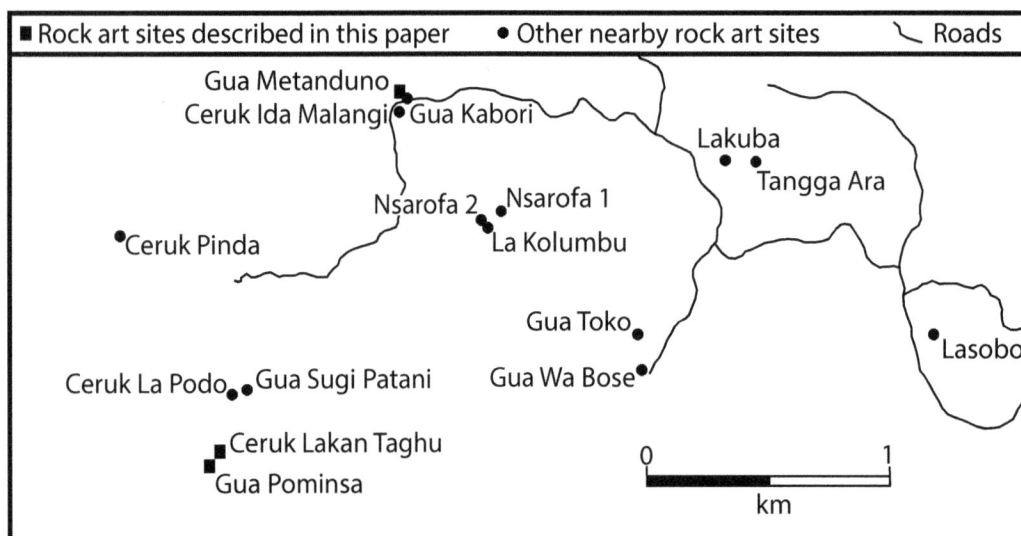

Figure 6.2: Rock art sites in the study area.
Source: Adapted from Oktaviana (2016).

---

1   See Marschall and Wäfler (2012) for site maps, photographs and sketches of the rock art from Gua Metanduno, Gua Kabori, Gua Wa Bose, Gua Toko, Gua La Kolumbu and Ceruk Lasabo.

Several phases of work were implemented to systematically record and analyse the rock art at all of the relevant sites (Oktaviana, Bulbeck et al. 2016; Oktaviana, Setiawan et al. 2016). The first step was to describe the geographic locality of the site and the positioning of the art at the site. Observations were then made to identify if there was any apparent directionality or implicit movement of the images across the panel(s) and whether it went to the left, right or swivelled around. The rock paintings were described and their dimensions, colour, type, creation technique, position in the panels and condition were documented (Maynard 1977; Arifin 1992). Once the type, location and directionality of the imagery across the site were determined, photographs were taken of each panel that captured the context of the depictions in their panels. A handheld digital camera with LED lighting was used to record the art, including use of an International Federation of Rock Art Organizations (IFRAO) standard scale (where possible). The panels and their motif compositions were sketched in the field in an effort to minimise error from parallax in the photographs. The next phase involved downloading the files from the camera to a laptop computer. Metadata for the photographs was created during fieldwork for the photographic records.

The photographs of the Muna Island karst rock paintings were processed with the ImageJ application and a decorrelation stretch (DStretch) plug-in. This plug-in was used to clarify motifs (including false-colour enhancement) as they are often faded or obscured by dirt, or by other superimposed images (Harman 2008; Le Quellec et al. 2015; Oktaviana 2015b). Finally, analysis was performed on the hand stencils and boats from the Gua Metanduno, Gua Pominsa, Gua Kabori and Ceruk Lakan Taghu sites.

Gua Pominsa

In 2005, the Makassar Archaeology Office undertook the first study of Gua Pominsa and reported two hand stencils at the site. This finding was queried by the Indonesian rock art community on the basis that there were no prior records of hand stencils found on Muna Island during previous years of archaeological inspection. In 2014, BCPBM sent a team to Gua Pominsa who confirmed that the hand stencils were, in fact, present. Additional hand stencils at this site were recorded by the Directorate for Cultural Property Preservation and Museums in 2015.

The geographic coordinates of Gua Pominsa are 4°54'38.0"S 122°40'13.9"E and the altitude is 277 metres above sea level (m asl). The site is reached by driving along a 4WD track for about 300 m, then walking for about 1 km through hilly terrain on a maintained trail (see Figure 6.2 for the location of the site in the survey area). The walking trail is bordered by stone walls marking local farmers' garden plots. Access to the site is via a 6 m high wooden footbridge. Gua Pominsa has two separate galleries, each involving multiple panels. The first gallery is encountered at the exit of the footbridge when entering the site, and the other is to the east in a more external position.

This exterior gallery contains hand stencils (Figure 6.3), as well as human, animal, flying and geometric figures. The interior gallery (Figures 6.4–6.6) has various human figures (often holding weapons) in an upright stance, riding horseback or in a boat; the panel also contains geometric figures. The figurative designs are generally positioned between 30 cm and 200 cm above the cave floor and were produced mostly through the direct application of brown pigment to the walls of the cave. There are also some black drawings whose pigment was derived from charcoal. The hand stencils were created by spraying pigment onto the wall where a hand was placed. One of the human figures is covered by calcite (Figure 6.7), allowing the potential for future UTh dating at the site (Oktaviana 2015a).

Figure 6.3: Pair of negative hand stencils at Gua Pominsa.
Source: Oktaviana (2016).

Figure 6.4: Human figures bearing weapons including three on a boat at Gua Pominsa.
Source: Oktaviana (2016).

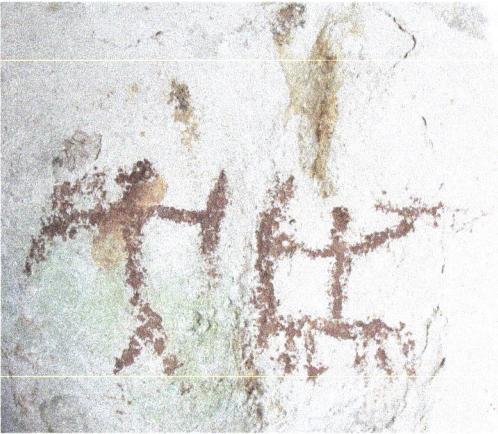

Figure 6.5: Human figures bearing weapons including one riding horseback at Gua Pominsa.
Source: Oktaviana (2016).

Figure 6.6: Human figure with digits outstretched at Gua Pominsa.
Source: Oktaviana (2016).

Figure 6.7: Human figure with calcite coating at Gua Pominsa.
Source: Oktaviana (2016).

Gua Metanduno

Gua Metanduno is a prime tourist destination on Muna Island and is easily reached along the tourist route to the site. Its geographic coordinates are 4°53'54.5"S and 122°39'33.7"E. The name of the site in the Muna language means to clash horns (bovids implied). The cave is shaped like a dome with a northwesterly orientation, and measures 21 m across its mouth, 23 m from the entrance to the rear, 25 m at its greatest width and 8 m high (Figure 6.8, centre). The interior cave is full of collapsed rubble from the walls and roof, and in various places stalactites and stalagmites are actively forming. A rudimentary staircase has been built at the front of the cave to create an easy access point for visitors.

The rock paintings are generally still visible, notwithstanding some vandalism on the left wall and inside the cave. Some of the paintings are covered with green lichen and some of the images are peeling away from the wall. Most of the paintings are in the cave's well-lit zone. Kosasih (1985) originally recorded 316 paintings at this site. The painted motifs include a wide variety of human figures, horses, deer, pigs, dogs, chickens, snakes, centipedes, boats, sun figures, hand stencils, and unidentifiable motifs (Figure 6.8). The large corpus of work was created mainly using brown and red ochre, along with charcoal for the black figures. The painting techniques used at the site consisted of applying pigment directly to the walls producing solid stick figures, outlines and solid infill depictions of humans and animals, except for the hand stencils, which were made with sprayed pigment. One of the hand stencils can be found on the inside of the cave and another five at the right of the entrance, all of which were found later during the 2015 survey at the site.

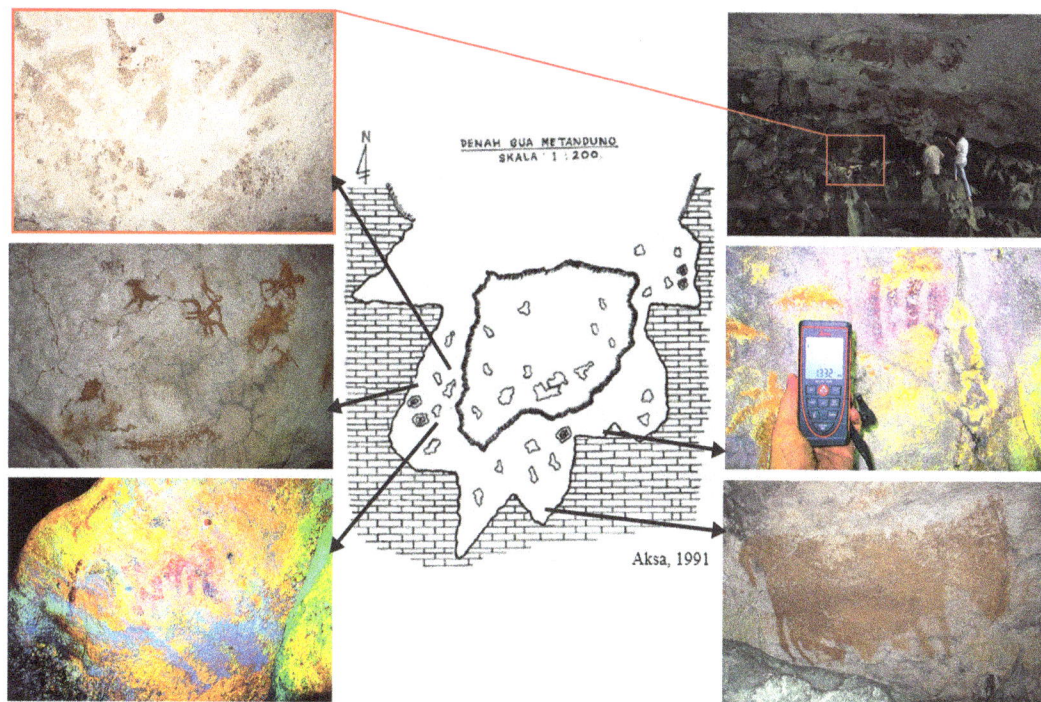

Figure 6.8: Mosaic of Gua Metanduno rock art.

Clockwise from top left: hand stencils; interior site plan with rubble and location rock art; site inspection with location of hand stencil in red; example of false-colour image enhancing; possible bullock figure; false-colour image enhancing of hand stencil within cave's interior; Figure 6.11 panel.

Source: Oktaviana (2016).

The greatest variety of the Gua Metanduno rock art is positioned to the left of the cave mouth, with rock art extending to the interior of the cave as well as to the right of the cave mouth. The left wall contains human figures, mounted warriors, flying humans, boats with passengers, sun figures and geometric designs; all of them in miniature and located between 1 m and 2 m above the floor. The cave interior has mostly miniature designs dominated by a variety of human figures, deer, horses, boats with passengers (some of the boats with covered decking), sun symbols, a hand stencil and unidentified motifs. The largest figure resembles a bullock. It is facing to the right and its back legs overlie a portion of an adjacent boat motif (Figures 6.9 and 6.10). The main motifs on the right and left sides of the cave are boats with more than one passenger. The hand stencil within the cave's interior has just three fingers stretched out and is located at 1.3 m above the cave floor near an anthropomorphic figure.

Figure 6.9: Male zoomorph within Gua Metanduno interior panel.

Source: Adhi Agus Oktaviana.

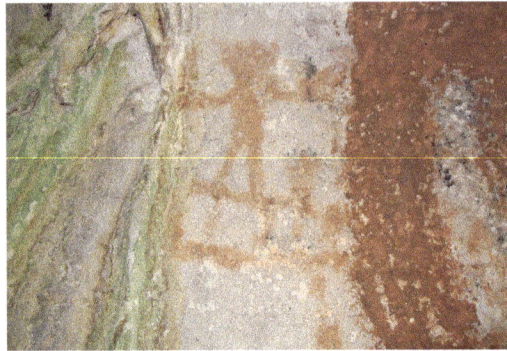

Figure 6.10: Detail of human figure standing on 'boat', superimposed by back legs of male zoomorph, Gua Metanduno cave.

Source: Adhi Agus Oktaviana.

The right-hand side of the cave is painted with many scenes of horse riders and their dogs hunting deer and pig. Several of the horses have large dimensions but their riders are depicted as disproportionately small. There is also a painting of a hunter spearing a deer. Horses are more dominant on this wall compared with the interior or left wall of the cave. This wall also has a stencil of a hand with sharpened or narrowed fingers underneath (and older than) a painting of a chicken (Figure 6.11, top right). There is also a hand stencil with normal fingers near the head of the chicken (Figure 6.11, top left), covered in part by coralloid speleothems, which could be used for dating (Aubert et al. 2014). Nearby are three other hand stencils. Two of these hand stencils were identified on a boulder turned toward the outside of the cave (Figure 6.8, top left), while the third was found in a section of the ceiling somewhat hidden by obtruding rocks (Oktaviana 2015a).

The Gua Metanduno human figures are depicted in a multitude of activities and dynamic actions, including mounted and unmounted hunters, humans in combat, humans with hands on their waist, flying humans, and apparently unfinished paintings. The cave paintings overall are dominated by horses, which probably arrived in Muna within the last 500 years or so (see Discussion). The rock art often features boats with passengers, perhaps suggesting inter-island voyaging for trade and/or combat.

Figure 6.11: Gua Metanduno panel.

Top left: ochre hand stencil with normal fingers near chicken head; top right: hand stencil with sharpened fingers beneath chicken; bottom: human figures (one riding a horse) and faunal figures, charcoal drawings of a sun motif (superimposed by a boat motif) and human figure.

Source: Oktaviana (2016).

The belated discovery of hand stencils at Gua Metanduno supports the need for further inspections of known cave art sites on Muna Island. While most of the hand stencils at this site have normal digits, one of them had the fingers modified to appear sharpened or narrowed. This stencil possibly reflects a tradition that originated in the Maros-Pangkep karsts before spreading to the Southeast Sulawesi including Muna Island (Oktaviana, Bulbeck et al. 2016). At least one stencil underlies the red-brown pigment art and its faded condition suggests greater antiquity (Figure 6.11).

Gua Kabori

Gua Kabori is located 25 m southeast from the Gua Metanduno site. The cave is dome-shaped with ledges along the wall. Its mouth faces west, and there is an ongoing process of stalactite and stalagmite formation. The term *kabori* translates to a cave with writing (or drawings). As originally recorded by Kosasih (1985, 1995), the cave paintings include numerous anthropomorphs and zoomorphs as well as the sun motif. The scenes of human activity include hunting scenes, horse riders, passengers on boats and flying humans. The animal figures include horse, deer, dog, crocodile, monitor lizard and centipede. There is also a poorly preserved hand stencil at around 3 m height on the right side of the cave wall, with three fingers remaining (Figure 6.12).

Figure 6.12: Three-fingered hand stencil at right wall, Gua Kabori.

Source: Adhi Agus Oktaviana.

A new site: Ceruk Lakan Taghu

Ceruk Lakan Taghu (Figure 6.13) is located in the same part of the Muna karsts as Ceruk Sugi Patani and Gua Pominsa (Figure 6.2), at 4°54'35.9"S 122°40'12.6"E. This rockshelter was discovered by the author in 2015 after faded paintings were seen on the Lakan Taghu hill during the survey trip for Gua Pominsa rock art.

The rockshelter has two terraces that are linked by a passage that is 1 m high and 40 cm in breadth. When first approaching the site, it is possible to see multiple rock paintings including boats with their sail unfurled, two human figures, and a human figure gazing out. Underneath the human figures, there are geometric motifs and an image resembling a comb or faunal emblem. The external surface of the cave on a lower wall has a human figure that is oriented to the right.

Access to the left-side terrace involves climbing over a steep rock pile. The outer part has a standing human figure with one arm pushed away from the waist and to the left, and two bandy legs. The interior has at least 27 figures on the wall (Figure 6.13, lower right), including humans riding horses, figures in an upright pose (one with his arm extended from his waist to the right, others with extended arms and hands stretched up with fingers joined together facing out) and various triangular designs facing out (though it could be that these are unfinished parts of other figures). Quadruped mammals are also present. Within the interior section of this terrace that connects to the right-side terrace of the site is a boulder that carries the design of a flying human with the head directed downwards, and adjacent to it is a horse rider facing right. Another boulder has two boats with sail unfurled. The boat on the right is shown as though being held by a figure in upright pose. All of these figures are in brown pigment and appear to have been created by using fingers to apply the pigment. Unfortunately, this terrace has been vandalised by people writing their name and the year, along with some recent human figures drawn in charcoal.

Figure 6.13: Ceruk Lakan Taghu (top) and some of its rock paintings (below).

Source: Oktaviana (2016).

The right-side terrace is a 2 m high corridor that penetrates the karst at this point. Various paintings can be found here, including an external ceiling panel with brown finger-painted figures. This panel features two figures in upright pose who are disproportionately large compared with the animals below them in the panel. There is a beast with a disproportionately large head, and beneath its right legs, a human figure with only half of a body and an elongated right arm. This panel contains about 14 figures, mainly human, painted with a brown pigment. The interior panel has a human figure lacking its head and

with an unnaturally long left arm (Figure 6.13, upper right). There are also four human figures with headbands and their arms extended from their waist holding weapons. There are several more human figures either upright or riding horses as well as animal images. Unfortunately, the paintings here are covered with lichen, owing to the orientation of the walls facing the cave opening and, therefore, the external environment (Oktaviana 2015a).

Discussion

The animals represented in the Muna panels are potentially instructive in terms of the age of the paintings. There is indirect evidence for the introduction of the chicken to ISEA in the Neolithic when pottery and other domestic animals such as dogs and pigs were also introduced (Bellwood 2017), so scenes containing these animals would have been painted sometime in the last 3500 years. In Indonesia, as in other parts of Southeast Asia, cock fighting has been argued to have a ritual or symbolic function, being closely associated with male blood-letting, and having replaced various forms of traditional warfare and headhunting (Maxwell 1990:150), so it is possible that the chickens in the painted panels represent more than just subsistence scenes. However, a shallow time depth for many of the chicken and other brown and red pigment motifs is supported by the prominence of horses and horses and riders in the panels. Although there is no archaeological evidence for the date of introduction of the horse into Sulawesi, or for that matter into other islands in Indonesia, it is likely to have been in the late historic period. By 1650 BP, one king in southeastern Sumatra had imported horses from India (Hall 1992:194), another king in Borneo had performed horse sacrifices, but the earliest record for horses in Southeast Sulawesi (or anywhere in Sulawesi) dates to the 4th century BP (Whitten et al. 1987:76). Accordingly, the panels in Muna showing horses being used for hunting and combat are unlikely to be older than c. 500 years ago.

The presence and implications of the boat images and hand stencils on Muna Island are important for discussion, despite being less common than the zoomorphic images such as deer, horses and dogs. Setiawan (2010) proposed that the boat imagery is associated with the influence of Austronesian (Malayo-Polynesian) speakers. Hand stencils were clearly present prior to the immigration of Austronesian speakers who nonetheless may have continued the tradition.

There has been extensive research done on hand stencils across Indonesia from the karsts of East Kalimantan to West Papua. Special designs have been observed in several regions, such as the points and lines painted inside more than 30 of the 40-plus normal-fingered, red hand stencils in one cluster of hills in the Sangkulirang-Mangkalihat karsts (Fage et al. 2010; Setiawan 2010). A variety of hand stencils largely restricted to the karst regions of southwest and northeast South Sulawesi has narrowed fingers made by adding pigment to fill in space between fingers or, sometimes, from two superimposed hands (Oktaviana, Bulbeck et al. 2016). The southern Misool region (Raja Ampat) also has an unusual design feature where hand stencil variations are produced with two hands clasped together (Chazine 2011; Sulistyarto et al. 2014).

The Leang-Leang karsts of Maros have the greatest number of hand stencils in a single Sulawesi location, and have some of the oldest associated dates of between 40,000 and 18,000 years ago (Table 6.1). One stencil dating to 18,000 years ago at Leang-Leang has narrowed fingers, which is a variant that has also been recorded in the Bone karsts, the Lake Towuti karsts and the Matarombeo karsts near Kendari, and now at Gua Metanduno (Oktaviana, Bulbeck et al. 2016). The documentation of hand stencils at Gua Kabori, Gua Pominsa and Gua Metanduno carries considerable significance because it demonstrates that the tradition of creating stencils did, in fact, include Muna Island. The stencils at these three sites are relatively plain, lacking the infill of geometric designs noted for certain stencils from Kalimantan sites, and the majority of them have normal fingers. All of them are faded, many of them are covered by flowstone, and the narrow-fingered stencil at Gua Metanduno is overlain by a brown painting of a chicken. These last three observations suggest that at least some of the Muna Island hand stencils are older than the Muna Island zoomorphs.

The hand stencils found in the Muna karsts suggest the possibility of a local variant of pre-Austronesian culture. Dates are needed to confirm this claim, and the coralloid speleothems that cover one of the Gua Metanduno stencils may prove suitable for dating.

Table 6.2: Recorded prau motifs in the Muna karsts.

Site	Number of prau motifs	Source
Gua Mentanduno	17	Kosasih 1995
	13	BCPBM 2015
Gua Kabori	16	Kosasih 1995
	9	BCPBM 2015
Gua Pominsa	14	BCPBM 2015
La Kolumba	2	Kosasih 1995
Lasobo A	2	Kosasih 1995
Lakuba	1	BCPBM 2015
Ceruk Lakan Taghu	2	Oktaviana 2016

Source: Oktaviana (2016).

The *prau* (boat) images from the Ceruk Lakan Taghu site are a recurring maritime motif in the Muna karsts with a minimum of 43 recorded from seven sites (Table 6.2). Boat images are widespread across ISEA including the Kain Hitam 'Painted Cave' at the Niah Caves in Sarawak (Szabó et al. 2009), Gua Mardua in the Sangkulirang karsts of East Kalimantan (Setiawan 2004),

Gua Sumpangbita and Gua Bulu Sipong in South Sulawesi (Kosasih 1995; Suprapta 1996), at a number of caves in Tutuala in Timor Leste (Lape et al. 2007), at Dunwahan in the Kei Islands (Ballard 1988) and the Berau Gulf in West Papua (Arifin and Delanghe 2004).

Five methods for propelling the boats are depicted in the Muna karst sites (Oktaviana 2009, 2012; see Figure 6.14): (1) paddling by a single person who is seated and holding oars, seen at Gua Pominsa and Gua Mentanduno; (2) paddling by multiple oarsmen, at Gua Pominsa and Gua Mentanduno; (3) single-masted sails, at Gua Pominsa and Ceruk Lakan Taghu; (4) sailing by a person with a combined sail and banner, at Gua Kabori; and (5) sailing by a person with a two-masted sail, at Gua Kabori. These images have not been dated in either relative or absolute terms, and so it is not possible to determine whether they reflect a progression of increasing technological complexity or whether they document the variety of watercraft that would been available to Muna's Austronesian-speaking inhabitants, at least in historic times. Nonetheless, they indicate that human inventiveness was well-developed during earlier times and that the region's traditional knowledge included mastery of sailing technology, thus adding greatly to the cultural heritage at Muna Island.

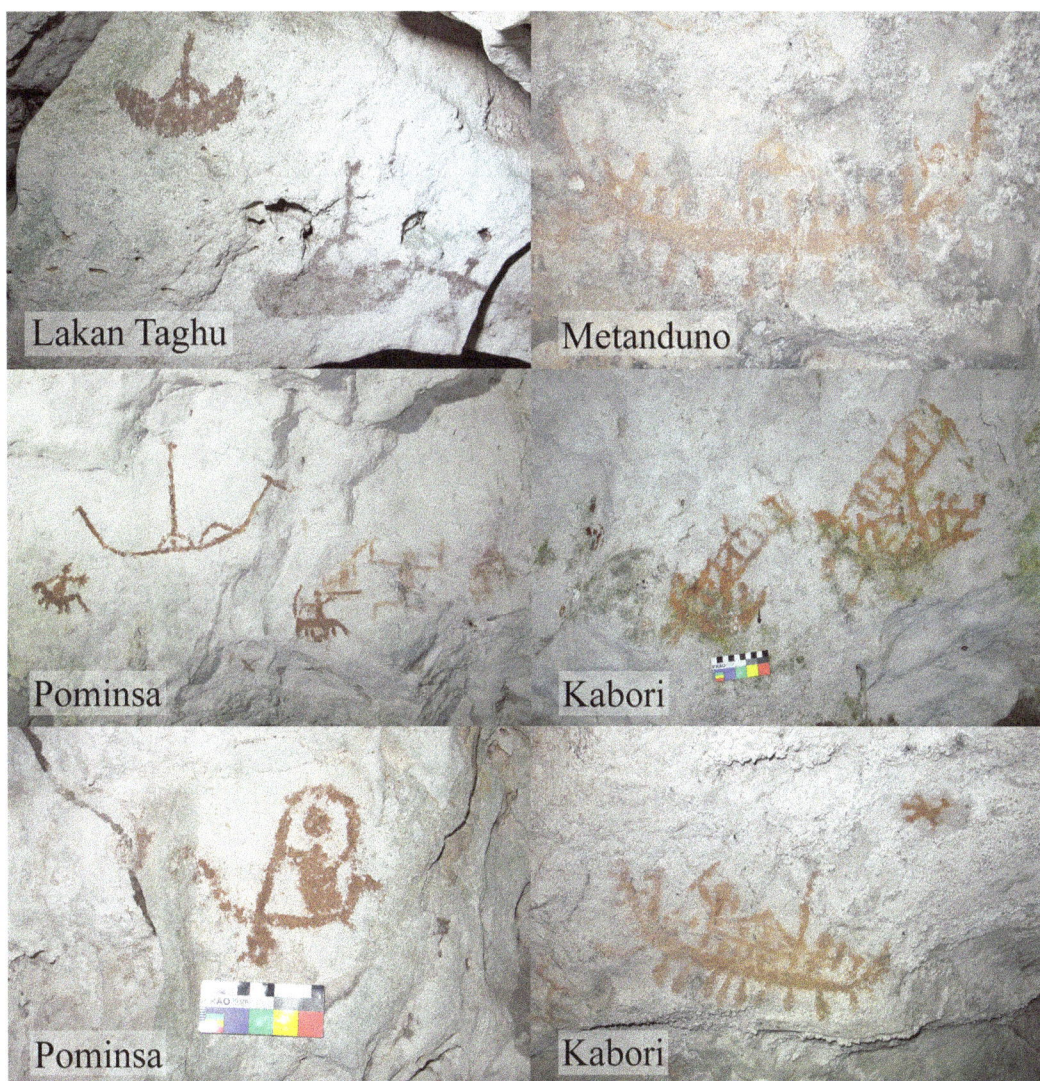

Figure 6.14: Examples of *prau* motifs from sites in the Muna karsts.
Source: Oktaviana (2016).

Conclusions

The archaeological potential of the Muna Island karsts has been investigated for 40 years, leading to the documentation of figurative paintings of hunting scenes, sailing and other activities as well as non-figurative paintings. The absolute chronology of the Muna art motifs is not known, but the observation of superimpositions at Gua Mentanduno suggests a relative chronology that would be consistent with the following order for the motifs' inceptions: (1) hand stencils, (2) sun symbols, (3) boat images and (4) zoomorphs. Human figures occur in compositions with introduced domestic animals such as horses, dogs and deer; in hunting scenes, in boats, individually and in groups. The paintings of birds that appear to represent chickens probably reflect a painting event in the last 3500 years. The same is likely to apply to the bovids, which may represent cattle or buffalo, both introduced after this time (Bellwood 2017). The paintings that include horses may be amongst the more recent and probably date to the historic period.

Comparing the distribution of the painted caves and caverns with the distribution of the karst belt within Muna Island, we can see that archaeological survey should continue so as to appreciate the full potential of Muna's parietal art. The recent discovery in 2016 of paintings on a sea cliff near the port of Raha by the Directorate for Cultural Property Preservation and Museums exemplifies the potential for finding more art on the island. In addition, as a first step towards ascertaining an absolute chronology for the Muna parietal art, UTh dates could be obtained from the calcite covering a Gua Pominsa anthropomorph (Figure 6.7) and the coralloid speleothems formed above one of the Gua Mentanduno hand stencils (Figure 6.11). Similarly, Accelerator Mass Spectrometry (AMS) dating on the charcoal images would provide direct dates on one component of the Muna Island rock art, even if the black images may be generally younger than the paintings in red or brown pigment. The results would assist in placing the Muna rock paintings in a temporal context with rock art recorded elsewhere in Indonesia and add to the understanding on possible migration routes of the people who introduced rock art across Indonesia. It is also vital that rock art conservation is paid more attention by stakeholders who have authority over the Muna Island karst sites. The BCPBM and the local tourism office should implement ways to monitor activity at the sites and deter acts of vandalism by tourists and other visitors.

Acknowledgements

The author gratefully acknowledges the valuable comments of two anonymous referees.

Author biography

Adhi Agus Oktaviana The National Research Centre of Archaeology, Research and Development Agency, Ministry of Education and Culture, Jakarta, Indonesia

References

Aksa, M.L. 1991. Lukisan Dinding Gua Metanduno dan Gua Kabori di Pulau Muna, Sulawesi Tenggara (Suatu Analisa Arkeologi). Unpublished Bachelor of Arts (Drs) thesis, Jurusan Sejarah dan Arkeologi, Hasanuddin University, Ujung Pandang [Makassar].

Alamsyah, N. 2014. Bentuk dan Letak Motif Kuda pada Gua Metanduno, Pulau Muna Sulawesi Tenggara. Unpublished Bachelor of Arts (Drs) thesis, Program Studi Arkeologi, University of Indonesia, Jakarta.

Arifin, K. 1992. *Lukisan Batu Karang di Indonesia: Suatu Evaluasi Hasil Penelitian*. Depok: Lembaga Penelitian-Universitas Indonesia.

Arifin, K. and P. Delanghe. 2004. *Rock Art in West Papua*. Paris: UNESCO Publishing.

Aubert, M., A. Brumm, M. Ramli, T. Sutikna, E.W. Saptomo, B. Hakim, M.J. Morwood, G.D. van den Bergh, L. Kinsley and A. Dosseto. 2014. Pleistocene cave art from Sulawesi, Indonesia. *Nature* 514(7521):223–227. doi.org/10.1038/nature13422 (accessed 5 June 2018).

Aubert, M., S. O'Connor, M. McCulloch, G. Mortimer, A. Watchman and M. Richer-LaFlèche. 2007. Uranium-series dating rock art in East Timor. *Journal of Archaeological Science* 34(6):991–996. doi.org/10.1016/j.jas.2006.09.017 (accessed 5 June 2018).

Ballard, C. 1988. Dudumahan: A rock art site on Kai Kecil, SE Moluccas. *Bulletin of The Indo-Pacific Prehistory Association* 8:139–161. doi.org/10.7152/bippa.v8i0.11274 (accessed 5 June 2018).

BCPBM (Balai Pelestarian Cagar Budaya Makassar). 2015. *Pendataan Cagar Budaya di Kabupaten Muna Provinsi Sulawesi Tenggara*, Makassar.

Bellwood, P. 2017. *First Islanders: Prehistory and Human Migration in Island Southeast Asia*. Hoboken, NJ: John Wiley & Sons. doi.org/10.1002/9781119251583 (accessed 5 June 2018).

Chazine, J.-M. 1999. Unraveling and reading the past in Borneo: An archaeological outline of Kalimantan. In J.-C. Galipaud and I. Lilley (eds), *Le Pacifique de 5000 à 2000 avant le Présent : Suppléments à l'Histoire d'une Colonisation* [*The Pacific from 5000 to 2000 BP: Colonisation and Transformations*]. Paris: Colloques et séminaires.

Chazine, J.-M. 2011. *New survey of painted panels off North West Papua: A precise identification of their location parameters and some insight into their function*, pp. 106–114. XXIV Valcamonica Symposium, June. Capo di Ponte, Italy: Centro Camunio di Prehistoria and Pr. Anati Emmanuel.

Fage, L.-H. 2015. *Rapport préliminaire: Prospection archéologique, massif de Matarombeo* Sulawesi Central, octobre 2014, NaturEvolution. doi.org/10.13140/RG.2.1.1934.3205 (accessed 5 June 2018).

Fage, L.-H., J.-M. Chazine and P. Setiawan. 2010. *Borneo, Menyingkap Gua Prasejarah*. Jakarta: Le Kalimanthrope.

Fauzi, M.R., S.E. Prasetyo, F.S. Intan, W. Andhifani and A.O. Hendrata. 2015. *Survei Arkeologis Potensi Gua di Provinsi Jambi Tahap II*. Laporan Penelitian Arkeologi. Palembang: Balai Arkeologi Palembang.

Galipaud, J.-C., R. Kinaston and D. Guillaud. 2016. Aleti Tunu Bibi: Contextualizing a new rock art site in East Timor and the wider Asia-Pacific region. *Asian Perspectives* 55(2):128–147. doi.org/10.1353/asi.2016.0016 (accessed 5 June 2018).

Gonthier, E., Budiman, E.N.I. Djami and T. Simanjuntak. 2013. Art pariétal dan le baie de Triton, sud-ouest de la Papua-Barat: Études sémiologiques des tracés pariétaux archéologiques. *Les Amis du Muséum National d'Histoire Naturelle* 256:54–57.

Hall, K.R. 1992. Economic history of early Southeast Asia. In N. Tarling (ed.), *The Cambridge History of Southeast Asia*, pp. 183–275. Cambridge: Cambridge University Press.

Harman, J. 2008. *Using decorrelation stretch to enhance rock art images*. www.dstretch.com/Algorithm Description.html. (Paper originally presented American Rock Art Research Association Annual Meeting 2005.)

Joordens, J.C.A., F. d'Errico, F.P. Wesselingh, S. Munro, J. de Vos, J. Wallinga, C. Ankjaergaard, T. Reimann, J.R. Wijbrans, K.F. Kuiper, H.J. Mucher, H. Coqueugniot, V. Prie, I. Joosten, B. van Os, A.S. Schulp, M. Panuel, V. van der Haas, W. Lustenhouwer, J.J.G. Reijmer and W. Roebroeks. 2015. *Homo erectus* at Trinil on Java used shells for tool production and engraving. *Nature* 518(7538):228-231. doi.org/10.1038/nature13962 (accessed 5 June 2018).

Kosasih, E.A. 1985. Hasil penelitian lukisan-lukisan pada beberapa gua dan ceruk di Pulau Muna (Sulawesi Tenggara). In R.P. Soejono, S. Suleiman, S. Satari, N.A. Subagus and R. Indraningsih (eds), *Rapat Evaluasi Hasil Penelitian Arkeologi II, Cisarua, 5–10 Maret 1984*, pp. 55–66. Jakarta: Pusat Penelitian Arkeologi Nasional.

Kosasih, E.A. 1987. *Lukisan Gua Prasejarah: Bentangan Tema dan Wilayahnya*. Diskusi Ilmiah Arkeologi II. Jakarta: Pusat Penelitian Arkeologi Nasional.

Kosasih, E.A. 1989. *Sumbangan data seni lukis bagi perkembangan arkeologi di kawasan Asia Tenggara*. Pertemuan Ilmiah Arkeologi V. Jakarta: Ikatan Ahli Arkeologi Indonesia.

Kosasih, E.A. 1995. Lukisan Gua di Sulawesi Bagian Selatan: Refleksi Kehidupan Masyarakat Pendukungnya. Unpublished PhD thesis, Department of Archaeology, University of Indonesia, Jakarta.

Lape, P.V., S. O'Connor and N. Burningham. 2007. Rock art: A potential source of information about past maritime technology in the south-east Asia-Pacific region. *International Journal of Nautical Archaeology* 36(2):238–253. doi.org/10.1111/j.1095-9270.2006.00135.x (accessed 5 June 2018).

Le Quellec, J.-L., F. Duquesnoy and C. Defrasne. 2015. Digital image enhancement with DStretch®: Is complexity always necessary for efficiency? *Digital Applications in Archaeology and Cultural Heritage* 2(2):55–67. doi.org/10.1016/j.daach.2015.01.003 (accessed 5 June 2018).

Marschall, W. and M. Wäfler. 2012. *Felsmalereien Indonesiens. Band 1: Pulau Muna*. Borsdorf: Edition Winterwork.

Maxwell, R.J. 1990. *Textiles of Southeast Asia: Tradition, Trade, and Transformation*. Oxford: Oxford University Press.

Maynard, L. 1977. Classification and terminology in Australian rock art. In P.J. Ucko (ed.), *Form in Indigenous Art: Schematisation in the Art of Aboriginal Australia and Prehistoric Europe*, pp. 387–403. Canberra: Australian Institute of Aboriginal and Torres Strait Islander Studies.

O'Connor, S. 2003. Nine new painted rock art sites from East Timor in the context of the Western Pacific region. *Asian Perspectives* 42(1):96–128. doi.org/10.1353/asi.2003.0028 (accessed 5 June 2018).

O'Connor, S., J. Louys, S. Kealy and Mahirta. 2015. First record of painted rock art in Kupang, West Timor, Indonesia and the origins and distribution of the Austronesian Painting Tradition. *Rock Art Research* 32(2):193–201.

O'Connor, S. and N.V. Oliveira. 2007. Inter-and intraregional variation in the Austronesian painting tradition: A view from East Timor. *Asian Perspectives* 46(2):389–403. doi.org/10.1353/asi.2007.0014 (accessed 5 June 2018).

Oktaviana, A.A. 2009. Penggambaran Motif Perahu pada Seni Cadas di Indonesia. Unpublished MA thesis, Program Studi Arkeologi, University of Indonesia, Jakarta.

Oktaviana, A.A. 2012. Teknik menggerakkan perahu yang terekam dalam seni cadas sebagai kekayaan seni dan maritim di Indonesia. In S. Rahardjo (ed.), *Arkeologi untuk Publik*, pp. 537–549. Jakarta: Ikatan Ahli Arkeologi Indonesia.

Oktaviana, A.A. 2015a. Kawasan Pula Muna, Sulawesi Tenggara. In R.C.E. Permana (ed.), *Gambar Cadas Prasejarah di Indonesia*, pp. 144–169. Jakarta: Direktorat Pelestarian Cagar Budaya dan Permuseuman.

Oktaviana, A.A. 2015b. Pengaplikasikan DStretch pada perekaman gambar cadas di Indonesia. In S.N. Titi and R. Handini (eds), *Prosiding Diskusi Ilmiah Arkeologi (DIA) Tahun 2015 Perkembangan Penelitian Arkeologi Indonesia*, pp. 72–90. Jakarta: Ikatan Ahli Arkeologi KOMDA Jabotabek.

Oktaviana, A.A. 2016. Eksistensi gambar tangan negatif pada gambar cadas di Kawasan karst Pulau Muna, Sulawesi Tenggara. In H. Widianto (ed.), *Jejak Austronesia di Indonesia*, pp. 96–120. Yogyakarta: Gadjah Mada University Press.

Oktaviana, A.A., D. Bulbeck, S. O'Connor, B. Hakim, Suryatman, U.P. Wibowo, E. St Pierre and Fakhri. 2016. Hand stencils with and without narrowed fingers at two new rock art sites in Sulawesi, Indonesia. *Rock Art Research* 33(1):32–48.

Oktaviana, A.A., P. Lape and M.N. Ririmasse. 2016. *Recent rock art research on East Seram, Maluku: A key site in the rock art of West Papua and South East Maluku*. 2nd SEAMEO SPAFA International Conference on Southeast Asian Archaeology, Bangkok, 30 May – 2 June.

Oktaviana, A.A., P. Setiawan and E.W. Saptomo. 2016. Rock art pattern in Harimau cave site in South Sumatra. In T. Simanjuntak (ed.), *Harimau Cave and the long Journey of OKU Civilization*, pp. 267–286. Yogyakarta: Gadjah Mada University Press.

Permana, R.C.E. 2005. Bentuk gambar telapak tangan pada gua-gua prasejarah di Kabupaten Pangkajene Kepulauan, Sulawesi Selatan. *Wacana* 7(2):161–174. doi.org/10.17510/wjhi.v7i2.304 (accessed 5 June 2018).

Plagnes, V., C. Causse, M. Fontugne, H. Valladas, J.-M. Chazine and L.-H. Fage. 2003. Cross dating (Th/U-14C) of calcite covering prehistoric paintings in Borneo. *Quaternary Research* 60(2):172–179. doi.org/10.1016/S0033-5894(03)00064-4 (accessed 5 June 2018).

Ririmasse, M.N. 2007. Tinjauan kembali seni cadas di Maluku. *Kapata Arkeologi* 3(4):1–21.

Setiawan, P. 1994. Gambar Cadas Dunwahan, Tinjauan awal Isi-Wimba Berdasarkan Posisi Sebenarnya di Cadas. Unpublished Graphic Arts thesis, Fakultas Seni Rupa dan Desain, Bandung Institute of Technology, Bandung.

Setiawan, P. 2004. *Pesan dari jaman yang hilang: Gambar cadas Kalimantan*. Seminar Penelitian Perancis di Indonesia, National Museum, Jakarta.

Setiawan, P. 2010. Gambar Cadas Kutai Prasejarah: Kajian Pemenuhan Kebutuhan Terpadu dan Komunikasi Rupa. Unpublished PhD thesis, Fakulta Seni Rupa dan Desain, Bandung Institute of Technology, Bandung.

Sulistyarto, P.H., A.A. Oktaviana, S. Adhityatama, A.S. Ramadhan, A.P. Ariadi, I. Mahmud and Y. Prameswari. 2014. *Penelitian Arkeologi: Maritim Hunian Prasejarah dan Lukisan Cadas di Kepulauan Misool, Kabupaten Raja Ampit, Provinsi Papua Barat*. Jakarta: Laporan Penelitian Arkeologi.

Suprapta, B. 1996. Lukisan Dinding Gua di Daerah Pangkep: Suatu Kajian tentang Makna Lukisan dalam Kehidupan Mesolitik. Unpublished MA thesis, Program Studi Arkeologi, University of Indonesia, Jakarta.

Szabó, K., P.J. Piper and G.W. Barker. 2009. Sailing between worlds: The symbolism of death in northwest Borneo. In G. Clark, F. Leach and S. O'Connor (eds), *Islands of Enquiry: Colonisation, Seafaring and the Archaeology of Maritime Landscapes*, pp. 149–170. Terra Australis 29. Canberra: ANU E Press.

Whitten, A.J., M. Mustafa and G.S. Henderson. 1987. *The Ecology of Sulawesi*. Yogyakarta: Gadjah Mada University Press.

Yondri, L. 1996. Batucap: Temuan awal tinggalan seni lukis gua/ceruk di wilayah Indonesia Barat. *Jurnal Penelitian Balai Arkeologi Bandung* 3:57–66.

7

Black drawings at the cave site of Gua Pondoa, Southeast Sulawesi: The motifs and a comparison with pigment art elsewhere in Sulawesi and the broader Western Pacific region

Budianto Hakim, Sue O'Connor and David Bulbeck

Abstract

Drawing on cave surfaces constitutes a human production that involved depicting objects, events or symbolic notions. With this perspective, we can gain an insight into both mundane and ritual aspects of the life of earlier communities. Here we look at the art of Gua Pondoa in the Matarombeo Massif of Southeast Sulawesi and discuss its commonalities with other pigment art in Sulawesi and that found elsewhere in the Western Pacific region referred to under the umbrella term the 'Austronesian Painting Tradition', and find both similarities and differences.

Keywords: Gua Pondoa, Matarombeo Massif, Southeast Sulawesi, cave drawings, Austronesian Painting Tradition

Background

Sulawesi has many regions of limestone karsts where numerous caves and rockshelters have formed along cliff margins as a result of long-term erosion. These caverns and overhangs provide natural protection from the elements and so have long attracted human habitation, notably during the Palaeolithic and Mesolithic, prior to the establishment of permanent village settlements. Of particular appeal were roomy caverns with an open floor area, providing adequate light and comfortable space for maintenance and subsistence activities and large enough for group dwelling (Hakim 2006). In Southwest Sulawesi, the oldest known habitation deposits date to at least 40,000 years ago, and the use of caverns for ceremonial purposes evidently has an equal time depth (Brumm et al. 2017). This is demonstrated by uranium-thorium (UTh) dates of between c. 40,000 and 18,000 years ago obtained on calcite deposits overlying hand stencils and naturalistic ungulate depictions painted on the walls of Maros limestone caverns (Aubert et al. 2014). Despite the lack of direct dating evidence, cave paintings are also likely to have been produced in Sulawesi during the early and middle Holocene (Oktaviana et al. 2016; Taçon et al., this volume). Then in the last several thousand years a distinctive rock art tradition arose, the so-called 'Austronesian Painting Tradition' (APT) (Ballard 1992), often in concert with the specialised use of caves for burial and ceremonial rites during the Neolithic and Metal Phase (Bulbeck, this volume).

Within Sulawesi, hand stencils are sometimes regarded as a marker of pre-APT art production, but they are also often found at the same sites as APT motifs. Oktaviana et al. (2016) found that the 52 documented rock art sites from South Sulawesi Province included 29 with hand stencils only, a 30th pre-APT site with a probable suid (dated to around 40,000 years ago), 18 sites with hand stencils and APT motifs, and a remainder of four entirely APT sites. In Southeast Sulawesi Province, hand stencils have been encountered only occasionally, specifically at the Gua Anawai site in the Matarombeo Massif (Oktaviana et al. 2016), and at three sites (all of them dominated by APT paintings) on Muna Island (Oktaviana, this volume). Gua Pondoa, one of the three Matarombeo Massif APT sites referred to by Oktaviana et al. (2016), is the focus of this contribution.

This paper describes the black charcoal drawings recorded by the first author on the rock surfaces of the inner chamber of the Gua Pondoa limestone cave. The subject and style of the motifs suggest that the drawings fit within the APT, as originally defined by Ballard (1988, 1992). The Gua Pondoa motifs are compared with other APT repertoires, with a focus on Sulawesi examples. The resulting comparisons are included in a consideration of the possible symbolic associations represented by the Gua Pondoa drawings and the implications for understanding prehistoric Malayo-Polynesian (Austronesian) lifeways in the vicinity of Gua Pondoa.

The Austronesian Painting Tradition

The APT is characterised by the positioning of some paintings in 'inaccessible but highly visible locations, most commonly sea cliffs' (Ballard 1992:98). Boats, anthropomorphs and 'sun symbols' are prominent and hand stencils are also often found associated with early APT art (Ballard 1988). It has been suggested that the placement of the paintings may have had significance in terms of visual signalling of rites/beliefs, and also that there may be a co-association of painted art with human burials, including boat/canoe burials (Ballard et al. 2004). For example, Röder (1938:88) notes that in the Arguni cliff sites in Papua, sun symbols similar to those found in the painted art were also painted on the prows of boats and boat-shaped coffins (see also Ballard 1992; Ballard et al. 2004). APT art is thought to postdate the movement of Austronesian-speaking communities into eastern Indonesia but to be possibly as late as 2000 BP (Ballard 1992:98; Ballard et al. 2004:98), and may have been an innovation linking island communities in a shared symbolic tradition (O'Connor et al. 2015).

In terms of colour, the earliest examples of the APT are red pigment; however, areas where black art dominates are known. For instance, in Vanuatu, and to a lesser extent in New Caledonia and Fiji, a painted assemblage is produced that observes many of the same conventions in terms of the placement of art (despite a shift from cliff to cave sites in some locations), but a much higher proportion of the art is black pigment. Detailed studies in a few regions have shown that the APT style develops and changes over time, whilst retaining some of its characteristic motifs (Wilson 2002:225). Although in the APT red pigment art is usually thought to be older than black pigment art, this is not always the case; on the basis of superimposition of motifs, the earliest phase of Vanuatu's art sequence has both black and red paintings and stencils, similar to painted art assemblages in New Ireland and New Caledonia. The latter's painted art is almost exclusively black, and includes stencils and linear motifs, while the painted motifs include leaf shapes, anthropomorphs and symmetrical linear geometric forms (Wilson 2002).

Gua Pondoa in the context of the geography and geology of North Konawe District

Gua Pondoa falls within Desa (Village) Pondoa, Kecamatan (Subdistrict) Wiwirano, Kabupaten (District) Konawe Utara, Southeast Sulawesi Province. The administrative centre of North Konawe is Asera, which lies about 174 km from Kendari, the capital of Southeast Sulawesi. Geographically, Konawe Utara lies slightly to the south of the equator, between 03°00' and 04°15'S, and extends 121°44' to 123°9'E west to east. Land surface area is around 510,000 hectares (BPK RI 2009).

The physical environment of North Konawe consists of lowlands and highlands, including coastal beach at the east, rivers and extensive swamp, and mountains to the west. Tropical forest is found everywhere. The hinterland can be accessed from the swamps and lowlands by river courses, which were the major traffic routes before land was cleared for roads (Budianto Hakim, pers. observations).

In terms of lithology (Nurhasan et al. 2013), North Konawe consists of ophiolites at its east near Lasolo Gulf, stretching to the west and widening to the north at the Tangeboruwaki range. These ophiolites include periodite, harzburgite, dunite, gabbro and serpentinite minerals. In various places, the ophiolitic rocks are interspersed with alluvial sediments such as river pebbles and gravels, sand and clay. There are also non-ophiolitic rocks, notably calcilutite with shale and chert intercalations, extending along the middle of North Konawe from Matanakasi Mountain to Wiwirano at the west, producing the Matarombeo Massif. These rocks are part of the Matano Formation. In certain places, such as the Samandete and Tetewatu locales, the calcilutite is interspersed with alluvial sediments (river pebbles and gravels, sand and clay).

The Matarombeo Massif is characterised by karstic towers. The streams lacing the karsts join up along the Solo Lawe River, which flows east to debouch at the Lasolo Gulf. At the karst bases there are many caves, rockshelters and tunnels such as the Rukuo tunnel produced by underground streams (Intan 2005).

Gua Pondoa site description

The geographic coordinates of Gua Pondoa are 3°24'20"S 122°3'28"E, and it lies 247 metres above sea level (m asl). The cave is an underground cavern with two entrances inside a limestone hill. The interior of the cave is damp with wall drips in some places that foster the growth of fungi and lichen. It includes a connecting passageway between the front chamber, which is partially lit, and the larger rear chamber, which is poorly lit and houses a bat colony. Human habitation at the site appears to have been desultory at best based on the scarcity of subsistence refuse (animal bones and shell fragments) or artefacts (some earthenware fragments but no lithics) recorded on the cave surface. However, various human remains including a skull, mixed with earthenware pottery fragments, were observed in the front chamber, demonstrating that the site was used for mortuary disposal. The rear chamber, which measures approximately 15 m x 15 m in area and 5 m in height, contains the art gallery.

Both the walls and the ceiling of the rear chamber contain artwork. All the recorded art on the walls has been drawn on an old flowstone surface, which provides an even and regular 'canvas' compared with the uneven limestone surface that the flowstone covers. The majority of the artwork is concentrated together in what may be considered the 'main panel'. Within that panel, some drawings appear to cluster in groups, which allows for the possibility that the groups each represent a single story or message envisioned by the artist(s). All of the paintings were created using charcoal and the forms that can be recognised include boats, people including some in elaborate headdress, animals, sun symbols and a variety of geometric forms (Figure 7.1).

Gua Pondoa: Interpretation of the motifs

Four definite, and probably more, examples of boats can be recognised. Two are located towards the top of the main panel (Figure 7.1), well above head height. Although in highly schematised form, one of them (Figure 7.2) appears to include a sail—although based on its size and positioning, this may be a ceremonial standard or banner, rather than a sail. Inside the boat are five upright human figures. The figures at the ends of the boat may be navigators. Interestingly, this boat has neither upswept prow or stern or a steering oar as is common in boat depictions elsewhere in Indonesia (O'Connor 2003; Lape et al. 2007; Marschall and Wäfler 2012). The second boat (Figure 7.3) looks like a long boat with a line of standing passengers from the stern to near the bow, where another figure separated from the passengers may be the boatman who is navigating the boat. The curvilinear designs above the passengers' heads may be symbolically related to the boat design or signify the movement of the craft. A third craft is depicted at centre far right of the main panel. This motif group shows two highly abstracted human figures with elaborate headdresses standing on what may be either the prow or stern of a boat. A fourth craft, to the left central area of the panel appears to have one human central figure, a possible steering oar and an upright decorative 'standard' like that seen on the first craft. Other horizontal lines with human figures shown standing on or just above them also likely represent watercraft in highly schematised form. An example can be seen close to the base of the main panel to the left of an internally speckled 'sun symbol' (Figure 7.1).

Stick figure human depictions, with the arms and legs splayed, are common (Figure 7.1). Some of them lack digits or headdresses/adornments (Figure 7.2), while others distinctly show the head with one or two headdresses (Figures 7.4 and 7.5). Two similarly depicted humans with arms outstretched and touching, as in Figures 7.2 and 7.5, appear to be deliberately juxtaposed, suggesting some connection between them. The highly schematised nature of many of the figurative motifs, and incorporation of curvilinear and linear motifs into figurative motifs, makes it difficult in some cases to determine whether anthropomorphic or geometric motifs are represented (Figure 7.6).

There are some readily recognisable depictions of mammals shown with four limbs, head, body and tail. The four clearest examples, towards the upper right of the main panel, are shown enlarged in Figure 7.3, including the two lower zoomorphs, which (from left to right) might represent a horned water buffalo and a dog facing each other. If the water buffalo interpretation is correct, this could be either the wild endemic Anoa or the introduced, domestic form (*Bubalus bubalis*). Other possible candidates for the horned quadruped are a goat or deer. All of the five mammals referred to here have been documented in the prehistoric faunal record for South Sulawesi (Simons 1997; Simons and Bulbeck 2004), and so would probably have been familiar to the Gua Pondoa inhabitants either as domesticates or forest game at the presumed time of production of APT art in Sulawesi.

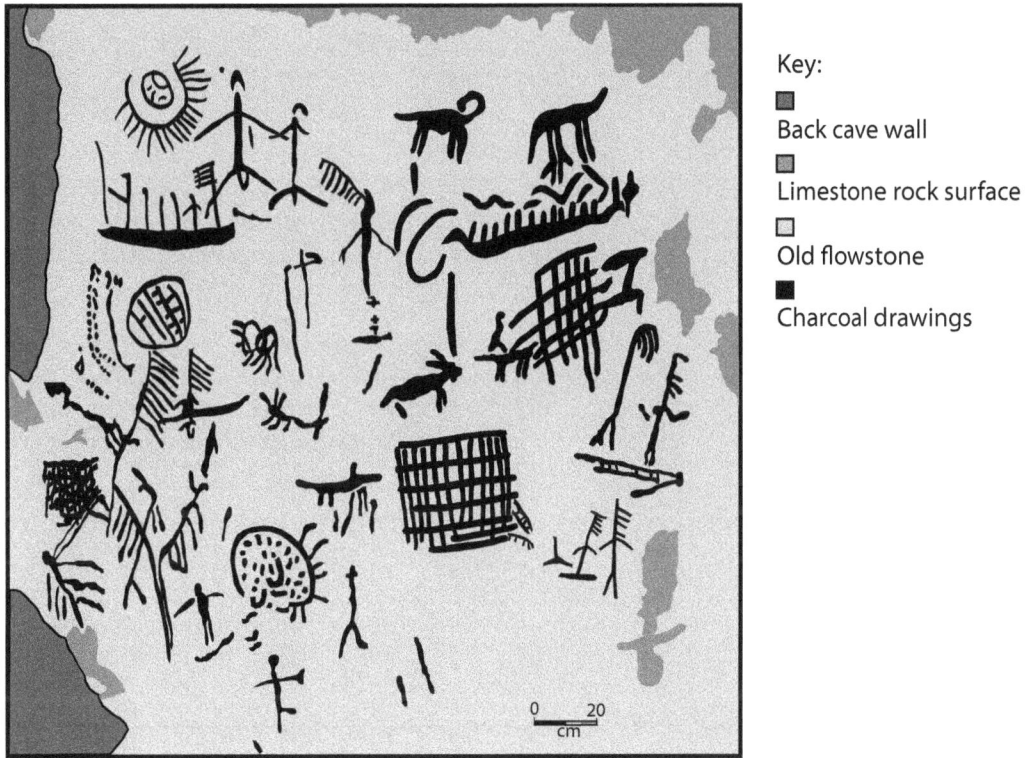

Figure 7.1: Gua Pondoa main panel.

Source: Drawing by David Bulbeck from photograph by Budianto Hakim.

Figure 7.2: Motifs of boat with passengers (lower left), sun symbol (upper left) and two anthropomorphs (right).

Source: Drawing by David Bulbeck from photograph by Budianto Hakim.

Figure 7.3: Motifs of boat with schematised human figures (upper centre), quadrupeds (top and bottom centre) and geometric grid pattern (lower centre).

Source: Drawing by David Bulbeck from photograph by Budianto Hakim.

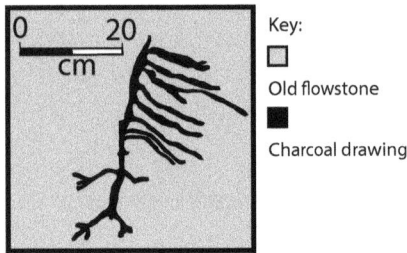

Figure 7.4: Motif of anthropomorph with frond-like headdress.
Source: Drawing by David Bulbeck from photograph by Budianto Hakim.

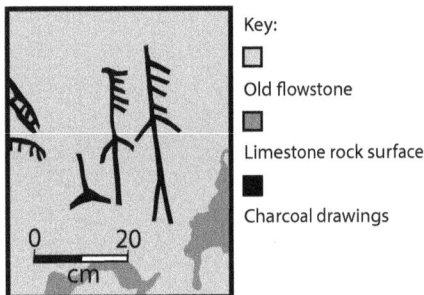

Figure 7.5: Two anthropomorphs with headdresses.
Source: Drawing by David Bulbeck from photograph by Budianto Hakim.

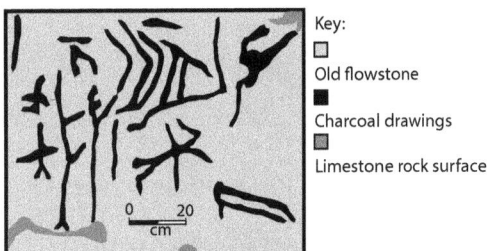

Figure 7.6: Possible anthropomorphs associated with geometric motifs.
Source: Drawing by David Bulbeck from photograph by Budianto Hakim.

Curvilinear and linear geometric motifs are also abundant in Gua Pondoa (Figures 7.7 to 7.10). While it is not possible to interpret these motifs, the fact that the headdresses on the anthropomorphs and the uprights on the boats are similar might suggest that they represent ritual or ceremonial regalia, such as feather or palm frond head or body decorations (e.g. Figures 7.4 and 7.5). In addition, towards the bottom left of the main panel are two

intersecting lines with shorter lines sprouting at right angles, in what may be an abstract representation of palm fronds (Figure 7.9). Palm fronds are still used in Indonesia during ceremonial occasions as free-standing uprights or standards, much as they are in many religions around the world. The motif in Figure 7.9 is reminiscent of these decorations used during ceremony.

Two definite sun symbols have been identified, based on their exterior rays or spokes radiating out from a circular form at the centre (see definition in O'Connor 2003). One is located at the top left of the main panel (see Figure 7.2 for detail) and the second is positioned beneath the main panel (Figure 7.11). A third possible sun symbol appears central left near the base of the main panel; however, the radiating spokes are irregularly represented (Figure 7.1).

Geometric designs along with depictions of humans and boats, are the dominant motifs at Gua Pondoa. Spread widely across the main panel, geometrics include crescents, circles infilled with lines or dots, checkerboard grates, lattices, linear frond-like motifs and dotted and continuous lines (Figure 7.1). Similar forms are also present beneath the main panel (see Figures 7.6 and 7.10), and include a design with rhomboids drawn along a central line (Figure 7.12). Some of them may be based on decorative craftwork, hand-held implements or natural phenomena, but any specific interpretation would be speculative.

In summary, the Gua Pondoa drawings constitute a diverse body of art, including passengers in boats, other anthropomorphs wearing elaborate head decorations, quadruped animals including possible dogs and water buffalo, sun symbols, and a variety of linear and curvilinear designs. There are many instances of designs touching or overlapping with each other (Figure 7.1), but the nature of any intended associations is unclear. As explored in more detail below, the Gua Pondoa repertoire includes signature APT motifs (Ballard 1988).

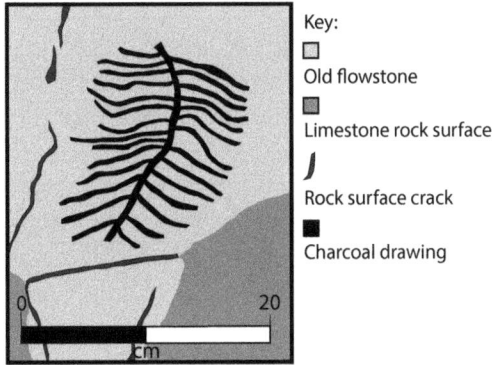

Figure 7.7: Linear frond-shaped motif.

Source: Drawing by David Bulbeck from photograph by Budianto Hakim.

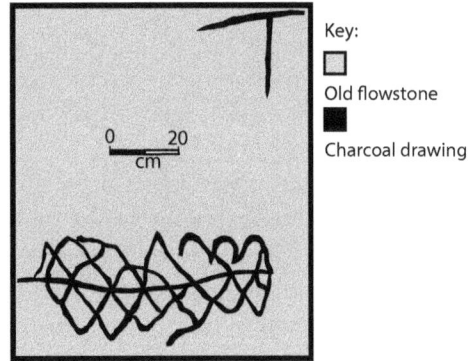

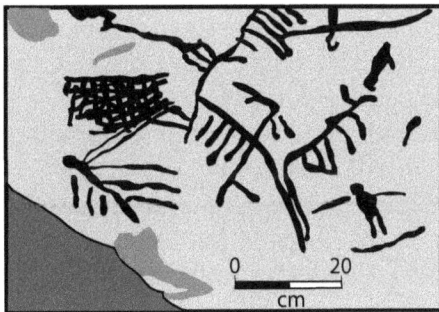

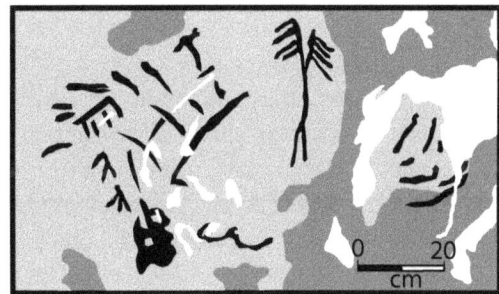

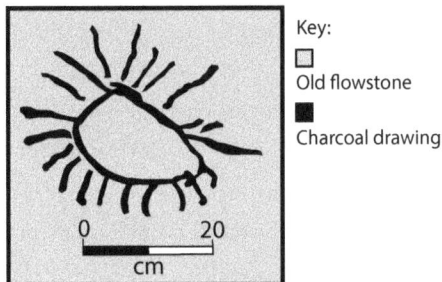

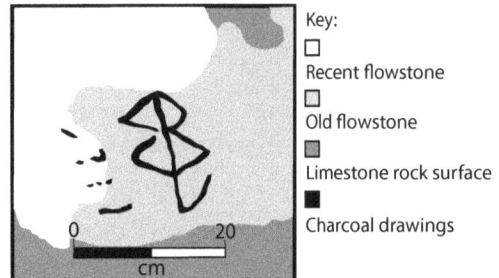

Figure 7.8: Curvilinear geometric motif.

Source: Drawing by David Bulbeck from photograph by Budianto Hakim.

Figure 7.9: Linear motifs (left and centre), cross-hatched motif (left) and anthropomorph on schematised boat (right).

Source: Drawing by David Bulbeck from photograph by Budianto Hakim.

Figure 7.10: Indeterminate geometric motifs (left), stylised anthropomorph with headdress (centre) and abstract curvilinear motifs (right).

Source: Drawing by David Bulbeck from photograph by Budianto Hakim.

Figure 7.11: 'Sun symbol' motif positioned beneath the main panel.

Source: Drawing by David Bulbeck from photograph by Budianto Hakim.

Figure 7.12: Curvilinear kite-shaped motif.

Source: Drawing by David Bulbeck from photograph by Budianto Hakim.

Sulawesi comparisons

The geographically closest sites of relevance may be the caverns of the Towuti-Routa region, approximately 25 km to the west of Gua Pondoa. The comparison lies not in the rock art, which consists almost entirely of hand stencils at Towuti-Routa (Oktaviana et al. 2016), but in the mortuary assemblages (Bulbeck et al. 2016). Curvilinear designs shared between the decorated mortuary pottery at Gua Talimbue (1st millennium AD) and Gua Pondoa include semi-circles arranged in compositions, frond designs, compositions of dots in lines or fields, and lattices of lines. The Gua Pondoa boat designs evoke the boat-shaped coffins placed in various Towuti-Routa caverns. Although in the Towuti-Routa case the coffins' time range was evidently restricted to the second half of the 2nd millennium AD, coffin interment has greater antiquity in Indonesia probably stretching back into the Neolithic or beyond (Ballard et al. 2004).

The largest body of rock art in Southeast Sulawesi is found in the karsts of Muna Island, approximately 220 km to the south of Gua Pondoa. As described by Kosasih (1983) and Oktaviana (this volume), and extensively illustrated by Marschall and Wäfler (2012), the Muna Island rock art sites have a preponderance of human figures, quadruped mammals including horses, boats and sun symbols, but other figurative motifs and linear and abstract designs also occur. The Muna Island artwork can (like the Gua Pondoa art) be classified within the APT, but it is very different from Gua Pondoa in its execution and colour. Most of the designs in the Muna sites were painted in solid red ochre rather than drawn in charcoal, giving them a filled-in appearance. The Muna rock art also includes (very faded) red hand stencils, a recurrent feature of APT painted art assemblages in eastern Indonesia and East Timor, but no hand stencils were recorded in Gua Pondoa. A recurring Muna motif is horses with riders, and the human figures often appear to be holding weapons and sometimes in apparent hand-to-hand combat (e.g. Metanduno 14 in Marschall and Wäfler 2012:148–149), but representation of humans with headdresses is absent or minimal on the Muna anthropomorphs.

Mammals are abundant in the Muna sites and often identifiable as to their type, including cattle, deer, pigs and dogs. Horned ungulates similar to the Gua Pondoa 'water buffalo' are also seen in the Muna art at Lasabo 1, as are quadrupeds with back curving horns at Lasabo 5 (Marschall and Wäfler 2012:89, 97). The Muna animal paintings include hunting scenes such as the panel at Metanduno 13, which shows a human figure spearing a stag with large antlers (Marschall and Wäfler 2012:146). Horses and riders are also found in the rock art of Timor Leste at the site of Ile Kere Kere (O'Connor et al. 2018). Although both the Muna and Timor Leste art assemblages fit comfortably within Ballard's description of the art of the APT on the basis of colour, motif location and motif composition, the inclusion of definite horses and riders indicates a continuation of tradition into the Indonesian Metal Age or historic period. Horses are not endemic to Indonesia and do not occur in the prehistoric layers of archaeological sites. They are thought to have been introduced into eastern Indonesia, probably as pack animals, by Indian or Chinese traders.

Most of the boats figured in the Muna site have steeply raked prows and sterns. Most also include human rowers with the oars shown extending below the boat (e.g. Metanduno 10 in Marschall and Wäfler 2012:127). Some of the Muna boats show the sun symbols intercepting the prow of the boat, indicating a relationship between these motifs (e.g. Metanduno 8 and 20 in Marschall and Wäfler 2012:121–122, 127–128). None of these features are evident at Gua Pondoa.

A closer similarity to Gua Pondoa than the Muna artwork is the APT art from Southwest Sulawesi. For instance, Aubert et al. (2014) depict black drawings at the Leang Bulu Bettue site (Maros) that include human figures with outstretched limbs, lattice structures and series of parallel lines. Sumantri (1996) documents the variety of black paintings and drawings in the Biraeng karsts a short distance to the north of Maros. Similarities with Gua Pondoa include motifs of boats, one with six passengers linked arm to arm, other human figures in dynamic pose and/or arrayed in processing troupes, a quadruped mammal, a motif similar to our Figure 7.8, cross-hatching and lattice structures, squiggles and complex curvilinear designs. However, differences in detail from Gua Pondoa are again evident, such as the oval bodies of the Biraeng anthropomorphs and their lack of headdress, and the presence of fish motifs combined with a lack of sun symbols.

Comparisons with other sites in eastern Indonesia and the broader Western Pacific

The activity of creating art would not have been undertaken for the idle pursuit of 'art for art's sake', but instead as a cost-effective use of time and energy (Kosasih 1983; McDonald and Veth 2012). Also, although works of 'primitive art' are based on objects or experiences from the artists' life at the time, they incorporate cultural themes for purposes such as social solidarity and the inculcation of traditional knowledge (Kelly 2016). In the specific case of Gua Pondoa, the burial of mortuary remains towards the front of the cave, and the rear location of the artwork in a dark, moist chamber creating a sacred and magical, indeed inscrutable, impression, suggest that the execution of the art was related to the afterworld of the deceased. Thus, the drawings produced by the Gua Pondoa artists provide a visual representation of facets of their society, but probably not ones related to mundane aspects of day-to-day life.

Subsistence and economy

Evidence from the Gua Pondoa motifs informing on subsistence and economy is ambivalent. The possible depictions of a dog and an ungulate that may be a buffalo, goat or cattle would suggest a settled village lifestyle and economy. However, dogs could be kept by foragers for hunting and campsite purposes (as with Australia's dingo or 'native dog') or could be fully domestic. Similarly, the representation of ungulates with or without horns could portray either wild or domestic animals.

Indirect evidence may be more valuable for establishing an agricultural component in the subsistence economy. First, the use of caverns for mortuary purposes in Sulawesi appears to have been a specific development of low-intensity farming, as argued by Bulbeck (2010) for South Sulawesi and Bulbeck et al. (2016) for the Towuti-Routa region. Second, the dispersal of Malayo-Polynesian languages across their range including Sulawesi probably involved the propagation of cultigens even if this involved a shift over time from cereal crops to tree and root crops (O'Connor 2015). There is indeed evidence for prehistoric habitation by Malayo-Polynesian speakers in Kecamatan Wiwirano, North Konawe, based on the finds of polished stone axes and earthenware pottery sherds from the 2009–11 Makassar Archaeology Office excavations (led by the first author) at the Gua Tengkorak site. On the other hand, Gua Pondoa is in a part of Sulawesi inhabited in ethnographic times at low population densities by hamlet-based communities (Mead 1999) and so intensive agriculture here at any time in the past appears unlikely.

As just discussed, the society that included the Gua Pondoa artists probably carved out swiddens and/or other small fields within their broader environment, which in the case of North Konawe would have been equatorial rainforest of rich ecological diversity (Whitten et al. 1987). That said, Gua Pondoa is a cultural statement of rights to occupation bequeathed by the ancestors (cf. Bulbeck et al. 2016) rather than a journalistic depiction of how society adapted to the specific challenges and opportunities of its environment. This perspective can accommodate themes that would be puzzling from the viewpoint of vulgar materialism, such as the depictions in a hinterland location of sizeable boats ferrying passengers.

APT cultural foundations and comparison with other sites in Indonesia and the wider Western Pacific region

The Gua Pondoa art has some features in common with APT art in other parts of eastern Indonesia and the Western Pacific, but also exhibits some distinctive features. In terms of location, the Gua Pondoa art is executed in a cave away from the sea, albeit sharing the frequently recorded feature of a locational context that would be regarded as inaccessible. The motifs are drawn in charcoal rather than painted in red pigment. Features shared with the APT are motif dominance of small anthropomorphs, boats and sun symbols. Gua Pondoa lacks hand and arm stencils, which are thought to be a prominent feature of the early APT and which are found in APT sites in Kei Kecil, Timor Leste and Papua (Röder 1956; O'Connor 2003), and the figurative motifs such as boats and anthropomorphs are so highly schematised as to be little more than suggestive of form. The Gua Pondoa humans are depicted as simple stick figures and lack the detailed features and dynamism of the small red figures seen in the Timor Leste, Kei Kecil and Kisar Island. Gua Pondoa also lacks the hand stencils found in these sites.

Boats with human figures are a common theme in APT art, as noted previously and are often interpreted as closely tied to mortuary aspects (Ballard et al. 2004). At the Niah Caves in Borneo, they are specifically interpreted as ships of the dead (Szabó et al. 2009), which would also appear relevant to Gua Pondoa with its mortuary associations. Boat-shaped coffins were widely built throughout the islands of Indonesia. Specifically, they are found across Sulawesi, not only in the Towuti-Routa region (as noted above) but also in the Enrekang and Tana Toraja hinterland of South Sulawesi (Duli 2013). Duli (2013:133) concludes that the Enrekang coffins symbolised the transport of the deceased to the spirit world where they could maintain a watch over the welfare of their descendants occupying the same social landscape.

Anthropomorphs with headdresses/head adornments constitute another common APT subject. The frequent depictions of headdresses at Gua Pondoa suggest a specific representation of ceremonies or rituals. If so, based on Sulawesi ethnography the ceremonies could have been agricultural festivities, 'shamanistic gatherings' (McCall 2017) or concerned with mortuary rites. As noted, the last of these possibilities may be of most relevance to Gua Pondoa. Although it is possible that some of these scenes were painted in the Neolithic, O'Connor et al. (2015, 2018) have recently noted the similarity of some of the anthropomorphs shown in the Kisar and Timor Leste panels to scenes figured on Dong Son drums. Thus, the production of rock art may be referencing images seen on other types of material culture. If Dong Son drums, the images must have been produced in the Indonesian Metal Age (the last 2000 years).

Sun symbols, a common APT motif, may have particular relevance for Sulawesi societies. As discussed by Bougas (2007), various groups in South Sulawesi traditionally associate the sun with the life force, and one group, the *patuntung* with their core of non-Islamic beliefs sheltered beneath an Islamic veneer, associate the rising sun with the resurrection of the spirits to return to the world of the living. The sun would certainly appear to have been a potent symbol for Gua Pondoa residents throughout time even if interpretation of exactly what it symbolised may be speculative.

Finally, abstract curvilinear motifs also commonly feature in APT bodies of art, similar to their frequent occurrence in the 'Sa Huynh-Kalanay' decorated pottery of Neolithic to Metal Age antiquity across coastal Vietnam and insular Southeast Asia (e.g. Solheim 1967). In the specific case of Gua Pondoa, there appear to be particular similarities with the mortuary pottery decorations at the nearby site of Gua Talimbue (noted above), a point that forms a bridge to consideration of APT motifs at Gua Pondoa shared with just a small number of other sites.

Gua Pondoa also has parallels with other APT sites in Sulawesi in the representation of quadruped animals. This may partly reflect the variety of Sulawesi's forest fauna, which includes species descended from crossings by placentals from Borneo to Sulawesi at various times during the late Tertiary and Quaternary, and Java deer (apparently introduced by human agency during the Holocene), not to mention two endemic cuscus species (Whitten et al. 1987; Rozzi 2017). The variety of forest fauna may have promoted the assignment of shades of symbolic associations with the different encountered species. On the other hand, the likely identification of a dog in Figure 7.3 hints at a specific role for this domesticated human companion, whose importance for Island Southeast Asian village communities is suggested by a c. 3000-year-old dog burial in East Timor (Gonzalez et al. 2013). Dogs also occur in the painted art of Kisar Island, to the east of Timor, in association with a variety of other motifs and scenes that suggest a Metal Age rather than a Neolithic antiquity (O'Connor et al. 2018).

As the largest and the most ecologically diverse island in Wallacea, located close to the sub-continental island of Borneo and creating a bridge between the tropical regimes of the Philippines to the north and Nusatenggara to the south, Sulawesi occupies a strategic position as a crossroad for cultural influences reaching across ISEA. Wherever the APT might have started—and the location of its single or multiple origins is far from ascertained (O'Connor 2015)—Sulawesi likely had a central role in its transmission, no doubt enriching the tradition rather than standing as a passive intermediary.

Conclusion

The Gua Pondoa drawings present an iconography quite distinct from that of the earliest tradition of parietal art in Sulawesi, which was based on hand stencils and naturalistic depictions of ungulates, and which has a Late Pleistocene time depth. Hand stencils are absent from Gua Pondoa. And while there are some quadruped depictions at Gua Pondoa, their naturalistic status is debatable, added to which is the point that the earliest parietal art in Sulawesi's southeast arm appears to have been limited to hand stencils. Instead, the Gua Pondoa drawings can be assigned to the so-called 'Austronesian Painting Tradition' with its presumed maximum time depth of several thousand years in ISEA. Having said this, the Gua Pondoa art does not share all the characteristics typically assigned to APT rock art elsewhere in eastern Indonesia or in East Timor. Gua Pondoa rock art is produced in black pigment rather than red and is highly schematised. The anthropomorphs are shown with headdress but are static in pose rather than dynamic. This may indicate regional variation in the APT in Sulawesi such as is found with the black art in Vanuatu, or it may be that Gua Pondoa dates more recently in time than the red painted assemblages. The presence of scenes with horses and riders in the red painted art of Muna Island allows for either possibility.

Although the research program at Gua Pondoa has not been completed, for the time being it can be proposed that the cave was probably not a habitation site, but instead used for rituals, notably burials. The mortuary associations of the artwork strongly contextualise its limitations for attempts to reconstruct the lifeways of the society that produced the Gua Pondoa art. Instead, it should be interpreted as symbolic of the perceptions the people had of the mortuary belief systems. This point is well represented by the depictions of boats carrying passengers, which are unlikely to reflect the material culture and transport means of the hinterland habitants living in the environs of Gua Pondoa, but instead the passage of the souls of the deceased, as noted widely amongst the Malayo-Polynesian speakers of Sulawesi and other islands.

The Gua Pondoa iconography may have limited applicability as a direct source of evidence on the lifeways of its associated society, the establishment of a cave for community mortuary practices, combined with the observation of a settlement pattern of low-density hamlets in ethnographic times, suggests that Gua Pondoa may have been connected to a subsistence system based on garden plots carved out of the local equatorial forests. In summary, the Gua Pondoa charcoal-drawn art adds to our knowledge of the diversity of the pigment art corpus in Sulawesi, and contributes to a perspective in which localised expressions of the APT shared common roots at some level but were also tuned to divergent trajectories and a diversity of local world views.

Author biographies

Budianto Hakim Makassar Archaeology Office, Makassar, South Sulawesi, Indonesia

Sue O'Connor Department of Archaeology and Natural History, School of Culture, History and Language, College of Asia and the Pacific, The Australian National University, Canberra, Australia; and ARC Centre of Excellence for Australian Biodiversity and Heritage, The Australian National University, Canberra, Australia

David Bulbeck Department of Archaeology and Natural History, School of Culture, History and Language, College of Asia and the Pacific, The Australian National University, Canberra, Australia

References

Aubert, M., A. Brumm, M. Ramli, T. Sutikna, E.W. Saptomo, B. Hakim, M.J. Morwood, G.D. van den Bergh, L. Kinsley and A. Dosseto. 2014. Pleistocene cave art from Sulawesi, Indonesia. *Nature* 514(7521):223–227. doi.org/10.1038/nature13422 (accessed 5 June 2018).

Ballard, C. 1988. Dudumahan: a rock art site on Kai Kecil, SE Moluccas. *Bulletin of The Indo-Pacific Prehistory Association* 8:139–161. doi.org/10.7152/bippa.v8i0.11274 (accessed 5 June 2018).

Ballard, C. 1992. Painted rock art sites in western Melanesia: Locational evidence for an 'Austronesian'tradition. In J. McDonald and I. Haskovec (eds), *State of the Art: Regional Rock Art Studies in Australia and Melanesia*, pp. 94–106. Occasional AURA Publication 6. Melbourne: Australian Rock Art Research Association.

Ballard, C., R. Bradley, L.N. Myhre and M. Wilson. 2004. The ship as symbol in the prehistory of Scandinavia and Southeast Asia. *World Archaeology* 35(3):385–403. doi.org/10.1080/0043824042000185784 (accessed 5 June 2018).

Bougas, W.A. 2007. Gold looted and excavated from late (1300 AD–1600 AD) pre-Islamic Makasar graves. *Archipel* 73(1):111–166. doi.org/10.3406/arch.2007.3877 (accessed 5 June 2018).

BPK RI (Badan Pemeriksa Keuangan Republik Indonesia). 2009. *Profil Kabupaten Konawe Utara*. kendari. bpk.go.id/?page_id=392 (accessed 5 February 2017).

Brumm, A., M.C. Langley, M.W. Moore, B. Hakim, M. Ramli, I. Sumantri, B. Burhan, Andi M. Saiful, L. Siagian, Suryatmane, R. Sardi, A. Jusdi, Abdullahj, A. Pampan Mubarakj, Haslianae, Hasriantie, A. A. Oktaviana, S. Adhityatamak, G.D. van den Bergh, M. Aubert, J. Zhao, J. Huntley, B. Lil, R.G. Roberts, E. Wahyu Saptomok, Y. Perstond and R. Grün. 2017. Early human symbolic behavior in the Late Pleistocene of Wallacea. *PNAS* 114(16):4105–4110. www.pnas.org/content/114/16/4105 (accessed 5 June 2018).

Bulbeck, D. 2010. Uneven development in Southwest Sulawesi, Indonesia during the Early Metal Phase. In B. Bellina, E.A. Bacus, T.O. Pryce and J.W. Christie (eds), *50 Years of Archaeology in Southeast Asia: Essays in Honour of Ian Glover*, pp. 153–169. Bangkok: River Books.

Bulbeck, D. 2018. Holocene site occupancy in Sulawesi. In S. O'Connor, D. Bulbeck and J. Meyer (eds), *The Archaeology of Sulawesi: Current Research on the Pleistocene to the Historic Period*, pp. 93–116. Canberra: ANU Press.

Bulbeck, D., F.A. Aziz, S. O'Connor, A. Calo, J.N. Fenner, B. Marwick, J. Feathers, R. Wood and D. Prastiningtyas. 2016. Mortuary caves and the dammar trade in the Towuti-Routa region, Sulawesi, in an Island Southeast Asian context. *Asian Perspectives* 55(2):148–183. doi.org/10.1353/asi.2016.0017 (accessed 5 June 2018).

Duli, A. 2013. The mandu coffin: A boat symbol of ancestral spirits among the Enrekang people of South Sulawesi. *Review of Indonesian and Malaysian Affairs* 47(1):115–138.

Gonzalez, A., G. Clark, S. O'Connor and L. Matisoo-Smith. 2013. A 3000 year old dog burial in Timor-Leste. *Australian Archaeology* 76(1):13–20. doi.org/10.1080/03122417.2013.11681961 (accessed 5 June 2018).

Hakim, B. 2006. Interpretasi lukisan hasil survei di Gua Pominsa dan Sugi Patani, Kabupaten Raha, Sulawesi Tenggara: Lukisan masa prasejarah atau bukan? *Walennae* 9(2):51–61.

Intan, M.S.F. 2005. Geologi situs-situs gua (Pinda, Paminsa, Lansifora 2, Lakuba) Kabupaten Muna, Provinsi Suawesi Tenggara. In D.W. Utomo, Hasanuddin, B. Hakim and A.F. Umar (eds), *Menguak Tabir Kehidupan Masa lalu dan kini*, pp. 85–102. Makassar: Balai Arkeologi Makassar/Hasanuddin University Press.

Kelly, L. 2016. *The Memory Code*. New York: Pegasus Books.

Kosasih, E.E. 1983. *Tradisi Berburu pada Lukisan Gua di Pulau Muna (Sulawesi Tenggara)*. Cisarua: REHPA I.

Lape, P.V., S. O'Connor and N. Burningham. 2007. Rock art: A potential source of information about past maritime technology in the south-east Asia-Pacific region. *International Journal of Nautical Archaeology* 36(2):238–253. doi.org/10.1111/j.1095-9270.2006.00135.x (accessed 5 June 2018).

Marschall, W. and M. Wäfler. 2012. *Fels-male reien Indoensiens. Band 1: Pulau Muna*. Borsdorf: Edition Winterwork.

McCall, G.S. 2017. Add shamanism and stir? A critical review of the shamanism model of forager rock art production. *Journal of Anthropological Archaeology* 26:224–233. doi.org/10.1016/j.jaa.2006.09.001 (accessed 5 June 2018).

McDonald, J. and P. Veth (eds). 2012. *A Companion to Rock Art*. Hoboken, NJ: Blackwell.

Mead, D.E. 1999. *The Bungku-Tolaki Languages of South-Eastern Sulawesi, Indonesia*. Pacific Linguistics Series D, Volume 91. Canberra: The Australian National University.

Nurhasan, I., V. Isnaniawardhani and N. Sulaksana. 2013. Penentuan kawasan pertambangan berbasis sektor komoditas unggulan sumberdaya nikel Kabupaten Konawe dan Konawe Utara Provinsi Sulawesi Tenggara. *Buletin Sumber Daya Geologi* 8(2):41–53.

O'Connor, S. 2003. Nine new painted rock art sites from East Timor in the context of the Western Pacific region. *Asian Perspectives* 42(1):96–128. doi.org/10.1353/asi.2003.0028 (accessed 5 June 2018).

O'Connor, S. 2015. Rethinking the Neolithic in island Southeast Asia, with particular reference to the archaeology of Timor-Leste and Sulawesi. *Archipel* 90:15–48. doi.org/10.4000/archipel.362 (accessed 5 June 2018).

O'Connor, S., J. Louys, S. Kealy and Mahirta. 2015. First record of painted rock art in Kupang, West Timor, Indonesia and the origins and distribution of the Austronesian Painting Tradition. *Rock Art Research* 32(2):193–201.

O'Connor, S., Mahirta, D. Tanudirjo, M. Ririmasse, H. Mohammad, S. Kealy, S. Hawkins and Alifah. 2018. Ideology, ritual performance and its manifestations in the rock art of Timor-Leste and Kisar Island, Island South East Asia. *Cambridge Archaeology Journal* 28(2):225–241. doi.org/10.1017/S095977431700816 (accessed 5 June 2018).

Oktaviana, A.A. 2018. Hand stencils and boats in the painted rock art of the karst region of Muna Island, Southeast Sulawesi. In S. O'Connor, D. Bulbeck and J. Meyer (eds), *The Archaeology of Sulawesi: Current Research on the Pleistocene to the Historic Period*, pp. 61–78. Canberra: ANU Press.

Oktaviana, A.A., D. Bulbeck, S. O'Connor, B. Hakim, Suryatman, U.P. Wibowo, E. St Pierre and Fakhri. 2016. Hand stencils with and without narrowed fingers at two new rock art sites in Sulawesi, Indonesia. *Rock Art Research* 33(1):32–48.

Röder, J. 1938. Felsbildforschung auf West-Neuguinea. *Paideuma* 1(2):75–88.

Röder, J. 1956. The rock paintings of the MacCluer Bay. *Antiquity and Survival* 1:387–400.

Rozzi, R. 2017. A new extinct dwarfed buffalo from Sulawesi and the evolution of the subgenus Anoa: An interdisciplinary perspective. *Quaternary Science Reviews* 157:188–205. doi.org/10.1016/j.quascirev.2016.12.011 (accessed 5 June 2018).

Simons, A.C. 1997. The Whole Hog. The Indigenous Response to the Introduction of Farming to South Sulawesi: A Faunal Analysis. Bachelor of Arts (Hons) dissertation. Perth: University of Western Australia Centre for Archaeology.

Simons, A.G. and D. Bulbeck. 2004. Late Quaternary faunal successions in South Sulawesi, Indonesia. In S.G. Keates and J.M. Pasveer (eds), *Quaternary Research in Indonesia*, pp. 167–189. Modern Quaternary Research in Southeast Asia, Volume 18. Leiden: A.A. Balkema.

Solheim, W.G. II. 1967. The Sa-huynh-Kalanay pottery tradition: Past and future research. In M.D. Zemora (ed.), *Studies in Philippine Anthropology*, pp. 151–174. Quezon City: Alemar-Phoenix Publishing House.

Sumantri, I. 1996. Pola Pemukiman Gua-Gua Prasejarah di Biraeng Pangkep, Sulaswesi Selatan. Unpublished MA thesis, Program Studi Arkeologi, University of Indonesia, Jakarta.

Szabó, K., P.J. Piper and G.W. Barker. 2009. Sailing between worlds: The symbolism of death in northwest Borneo. In G. Clark, F. Leach and S. O'Connor (eds), *Islands of Enquiry: Colonisation, Seafaring and the Archaeology of Maritime Landscapes*, pp. 149–170. Terra Australis 29. Canberra: ANU E Press.

Taçon, P., M. Ramli, B. Hakim, A. Brumm and M. Aubert. 2018. The contemporary importance and future of Sulawesi's rock art. In S. O'Connor, D. Bulbeck and J. Meyer (eds), *The Archaeology of Sulawesi: Current Research on the Pleistocene to the Historic Period*, pp. 31–42. Canberra: ANU Press.

Whitten, T., M. Mustafa and G.S. Henderson. 1987. *The Ecology of Sulawesi*. Yogyakarta: Gadjah Mada University Press.

Wilson, M. 2002. Picturing Pacific Prehistory: The Rock Art of Vanuatu in a Western Pacific Context. Unpublished PhD thesis, Department of Archaeology and Natural History, The Australian National University, Canberra.

8

Holocene site occupancy in Sulawesi

David Bulbeck

Abstract

This contribution presents an analysis of the number of Sulawesi sites (summed probability) occupied per 500-year interval between 10,000 and 0 BP, based on radiometric dates. The number of occupied sites was low between 10,000 and 4500 BP, ranging between 1 to 4 per half-millennium. There were subsequent increases in the number of occupied sites per half-millennium to 5–8 between 4500 and 2000 BP, 9–13 between 2000 and 1000 BP, and over 30 between 1000 and 0 BP. These figures would be consistent with a scenario of substantial population increases at around 4500, 2000 and 1000 BP. However, care should be exercised in making a literal interpretation of these figures. For instance, with respect to the 4500–2500 BP period, the number of closed sites was highest during 4500–3500 BP and the number of open-air sites highest during 3500–2000 BP. Also, the large number of documented sites dating to the last millennium BP reflects a particular focus of Sulawesi archaeological research on sites related ethnohistorically to the Bugis and other major ethno-linguistic divisions in South Sulawesi.

Keywords: Sulawesi Holocene, site occupancy, summed probabilities, closed sites, open-air sites

Introduction

The increased availability of radiometric determinations from archaeological sites has encouraged archaeologists to use these dates as a proxy measure for population levels in times past. Peros et al. (2010) and Williams (2012) outline the history and growing popularity of this approach, and its respective application to North America and Australia—two continents for which there are large numbers of radiocarbon dates from archaeological sites. The statistical basis for their analysis is to calibrate the dates, distribute the resulting calibrated probabilities across brief intervals and to sum the probabilities for each of the analytical intervals, followed by correction of the calculated numbers for factors such as the increasing probability of taphonomic loss of archaeological deposits with age and the perturbations inherent in the calibration curve (Peros et al. 2010; Williams 2012). While these two studies used the results to construct a scenario of continent-level changes in population size following initial colonisation, the same basic approach has been applied to more targeted research questions, such as the nature of the demographic transition in Europe following the early to mid-Holocene introduction of agriculture (Downey et al. 2014).

One pointed criticism of this approach is the possibility of a particularly intensive program of obtaining radiometric dates from certain sites compared with others, resulting in a biased representation of the periods of site occupancy represented by the intensively studied sites

(Hiscock and Attenbrow 2016). Examples of Sulawesi sites represented by large numbers of radiometric determinations include the Gua Talimbue cave site in Southeast Sulawesi and the Minanga Sipakko open site in West Sulawesi. A solution to this objection is to employ the determinations to estimate the probabilities of site occupancy per specified interval (here, half-millennium intervals BP), and to sum these probabilities as an estimate of the number of occupied sites per interval. Then, in fact, there would arguably be a reversal in the bias; specifically, that a certain interval at a given site represented by a single unsupported date may be as prominent (up to 100% occupancy probability) as another interval at the same site represented by multiple confirmatory dates (see Discussion). Also, there remains the potential objection of bias in the types of sites focused on, although this issue can be addressed by examining the research programs covered by the radiometric determinations and is open to correction in the future as novel research programs are initiated.

A particularly thorny issue is which determinations to accept for analysis. My general approach here is to include dates if clearly from an archaeological context, and to reject dates only if there are positive reasons for their rejection. The justifications for this approach include: (1) to allow the inclusion of dates back to the 1970s for sites that have not since been re-excavated; (2) to incorporate dates processed in Indonesia for excavations undertaken by Indonesian archaeologists without foreign collaboration; and (3) to avoid subjective decisions of dates' acceptability—for instance, whether they 'fit' the excavator's expectations based on dates obtained from other sites or even the same site. In accord with this last point, when a date is rejected the decision is made whether or not the date is compatible with the *a priori* expectation of the dated material's radiometric determination. For instance, the median Carbon-14 date of 7170 BP from basal Ulu Leang 2 (ANU 1606, Table A8.1) is entirely compatible with the Carbon-14 dates obtained from higher in the site's deposit, but the large standard error of 600 years makes the determination useless for pinning down the probabilities of the 'real age' by half-millennium intervals BP (cf. Spriggs 2003).

Table A8.1 in Appendix A lists the radiometric dates from Sulawesi rejected for the purposes of the present analysis and the reasons for their rejection. In the future, when the archaeology of Sulawesi is better documented, it may be feasible to impose stricter criteria on the acceptance of radiometric determinations—for instance, to exclude any Carbon-14 dates that are not Accelerator Mass Spectrometry (AMS) dates—and to still have a sufficiently large sample of dated sites to produce a robust scenario of Holocene site occupancy patterns. For present purposes, analytical time intervals of 500 years (Bulbeck 2014) are employed to accommodate the motley assemblage of accepted determinations with alternatively wide and tightly defined standard errors (Tables A8.2–A8.6).

Note that Sulawesi in this contribution is defined to include the main body of the island and any immediately offshore islands (Figure 8.1). The Sangihe and Talaud island chains, while politically part of Sulawesi, lie approximately halfway from North Sulawesi to Mindanao in the Philippines and so are not considered here to be geographically part of Sulawesi.

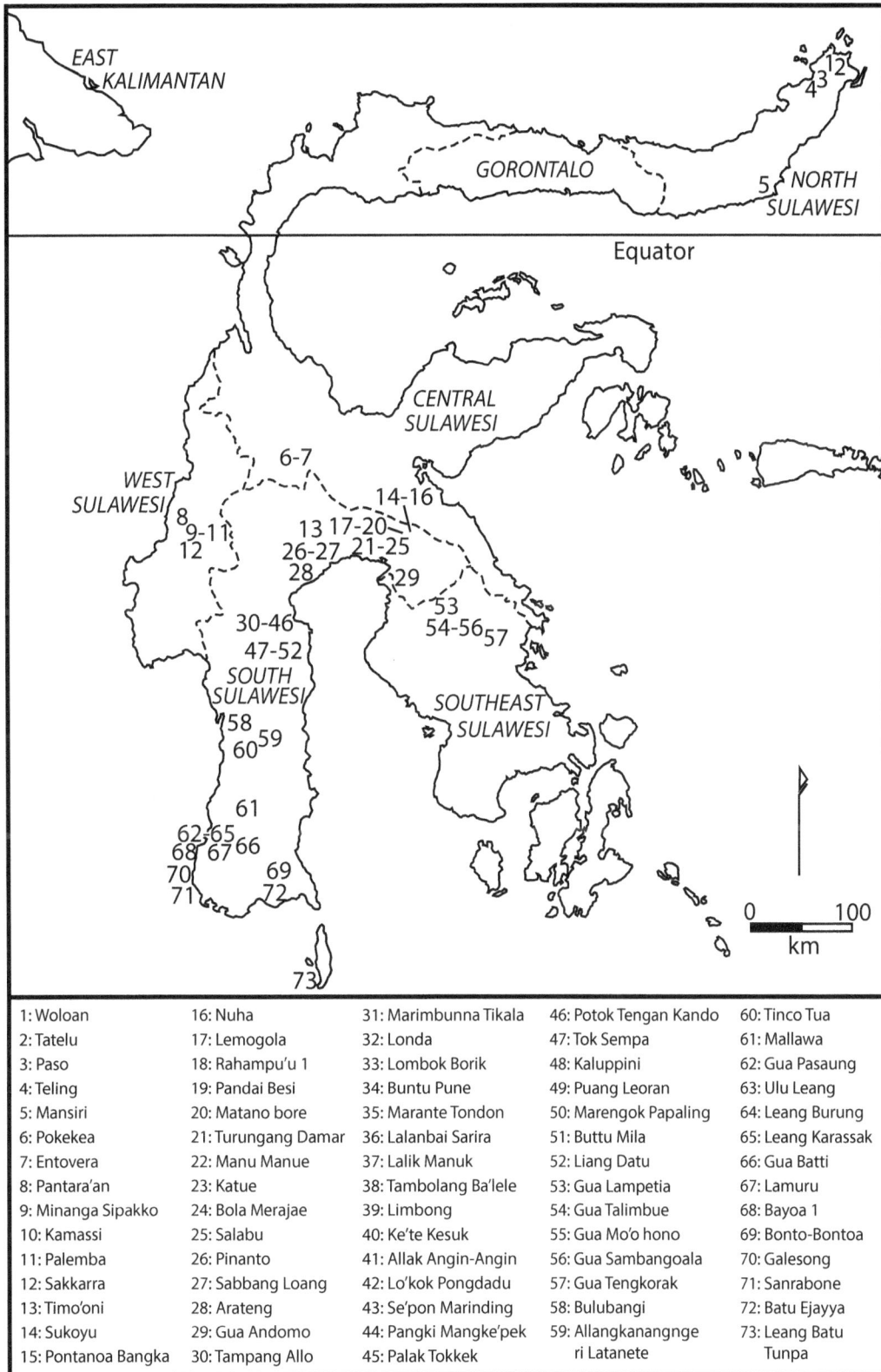

Figure 8.1: Sites in Sulawesi that have yielded accepted radiometric determinations.
Source: Tables A8.2–A8.7.

1: Woloan	16: Nuha	31: Marimbunna Tikala	46: Potok Tengan Kando	60: Tinco Tua
2: Tatelu	17: Lemogola	32: Londa	47: Tok Sempa	61: Mallawa
3: Paso	18: Rahampu'u 1	33: Lombok Borik	48: Kaluppini	62: Gua Pasaung
4: Teling	19: Pandai Besi	34: Buntu Pune	49: Puang Leoran	63: Ulu Leang
5: Mansiri	20: Matano bore	35: Marante Tondon	50: Marengok Papaling	64: Leang Burung
6: Pokekea	21: Turungang Damar	36: Lalanbai Sarira	51: Buttu Mila	65: Leang Karassak
7: Entovera	22: Manu Manue	37: Lalik Manuk	52: Liang Datu	66: Gua Batti
8: Pantara'an	23: Katue	38: Tambolang Ba'lele	53: Gua Lampetia	67: Lamuru
9: Minanga Sipakko	24: Bola Merajae	39: Limbong	54: Gua Talimbue	68: Bayoa 1
10: Kamassi	25: Salabu	40: Ke'te Kesuk	55: Gua Mo'o hono	69: Bonto-Bontoa
11: Palemba	26: Pinanto	41: Allak Angin-Angin	56: Gua Sambangoala	70: Galesong
12: Sakkarra	27: Sabbang Loang	42: Lo'kok Pongdadu	57: Gua Tengkorak	71: Sanrabone
13: Timo'oni	28: Arateng	43: Se'pon Marinding	58: Bulubangi	72: Batu Ejayya
14: Sukoyu	29: Gua Andomo	44: Pangki Mangke'pek	59: Allangkanangnge ri Latanete	73: Leang Batu Tunpa
15: Pontanoa Bangka	30: Tampang Allo	45: Palak Tokkek		

Hypotheses on changes in Sulawesi past population sizes

An overall scenario of population size increases in ISEA is posited by Brandão et al. (2016) from their analysis of mitochondrial DNA haplogroups found in recent ISEA populations. They infer low population sizes during the Pleistocene, followed by a 19-fold increment, which commenced around 10,500–8000 years ago, and a further 70-fold increment starting at around 4000 years ago. They relate the first of the inferred population expansions to the early Holocene stabilisation of sea levels in ISEA following the drastic rises of sea levels during the terminal Pleistocene. The second population expansion is related to the immigration of Austronesian speakers from Taiwan into ISEA (where the great majority of indigenous languages are Austronesian) commencing at around 4500 BP, and probably involved increasing numbers of both the genes introduced by immigrant Austronesians and the autochthonous genes established in ISEA prior to the Austronesian incursion.

The first of the inferred population expansions is not directly tested in this study but one reason for starting the analysis at 10,000 BP is the scarcity of ISEA radiometric dates relating to the terminal Pleistocene—for instance, to my knowledge there are just two radiometric determinations for Sulawesi with a median age between 20,000 and 10,000 BP, both from the single site of Gua Talimbue (O'Connor et al. 2014). In contrast, as we shall see, the millennia after 10,000 BP are consistently represented by radiometric determinations, compatible with the persistence of sustainable population sizes.

The second of the inferences by Brandão et al. (2016) would predict an increase in occupied sites starting at around 4000 BP. However, as explicitly noted by the authors, this would not rule out major steps in population size (and numbers of occupied sites) at later times. For instance, my research into the early historical archaeology of Southwest Sulawesi has led me to postulate watersheds in population size growth at approximately 2000 BP and 750 BP (Bulbeck 2010).

Materials and methods

This study accepts radiometric determinations of Holocene age (Tables A8.2 to A8.6) from 73 archaeological sites in Sulawesi. As shown in Figure 8.1, large swathes of Sulawesi remain undocumented for their archaeological chronology, including all of Gorontalo Province, almost all of Central Sulawesi Province and the southern four-fifths of Southeast Sulawesi Province. Even in South Sulawesi, which is the province with by far the best documented archaeology, there are large gaps in the geographic coverage. Accordingly, there is ample scope for future archaeological research to test the scenario of Holocene site occupancy generated here from the currently available data.

The available radiometric determinations are characterised in terms of the class of dated material, site aspect and site use (detailed in Bulbeck 2014, 2016). The seven dated material classes in order of precedence are 'Ceramic' (including dates from charcoal extracted from ceramic objects), 'Boat' (including boat-shaped coffins), 'Human bone', 'Marine shell', 'Charcoal', 'Animal matter' and 'Plant matter'. The 'Ceramic' and 'Boat' classes are of particular interest for dating these important developments in Sulawesi's prehistoric technology. The site aspect categories in order of precedence are 'Closed', 'Monumental' (megalithic sites in the context of this study), 'Maritime' (no examples for Sulawesi), 'Marine shell midden', 'Freshwater shell midden' and 'Open' (where none of the preceding applies). The site usage categories in order of precedence are 'Mortuary', 'Ceremonial' (for ritual contexts lacking strong evidence of a mortuary association), 'Industrial', 'Transport' (no examples for Sulawesi), 'Gardening' (especially charcoal probably related to forest clearance) and 'Habitation' (where none of the preceding applies).

Site occupancy is analysed in terms of the probability of occupation during any 500-year interval between 10,000 and 0 cal BP. The Carbon-14 (including AMS) dates were calibrated using the OxCal 13 internet program (Bronk Ramsey 2013). The program includes a capacity to distribute the 100% probability of the date's antiquity across five-year intervals, allowing these probabilities to be summed to 500-year intervals cal BP. The calibration of these dates did not include any correction factor for southern hemisphere determinations, in view of the proximity (within 6°) of all of the dated sites to the equator (Figure 8.1). The small number of accepted determinations that required a marine reservoir correction factor or that were a luminescence date were modelled as normal distributions in order to be assigned to 500-year intervals (cal) BP. (Note that in the Results and Discussion sections, the terminology 'BP' is used instead of 'cal BP', so as to incorporate luminescence dates, which do not require calibration.)

For the sake of explanation, we can use the Mallawa determinations, which are all dates on 'Charcoal' from 'Habitation' usage in an 'Open' site aspect (Table A8.6). The calibrated date probabilities span the 10 half-millennia between 5000–4500 cal BP and 500–0 cal BP. As these are the probabilities of occupation, their complements equate to the probabilities that the date does not document any occupation during the half-millennium in question. The product of the complements equates to the probability that none of the dates document occupation during the said half-millennium, and so the complement of the product equates to the joint probability of occupation at the site during the said half-millennium. This mathematical procedure (grounded in classical probability theory) caps the probability of occupation during any half-millennium to 1 (100%), whilst allowing multiple dates that relate to a half-millennium to be used in consort to increase the overall probability of site occupation, up to a maximum of 1 (Table 8.1).

Table 8.1: Occupation probabilities of Mallawa by half-millennium cal BP.

Date	5–4.5 k BP	4.5–4 k BP	4–3.5 k BP	3.5–3 k BP	3–2.5 k BP	2.5–2 k BP	2–1.5 k BP	1.5–1 k BP	1–0.5 k BP	0.5–0 k BP	Sum
P3G-06	0.001	0.273	0.718	0.008							1.0
P3G-06			0.001	0.137	0.704	0.158					1.0
ANU 11276				0.054	0.535	0.395	0.016				1.0
Wk-20380					0.016	0.971	0.013				1.0
ANU 11274						0.004	0.968	0.028			1.0
ANU 11275									0.973	0.027	1.0
Joint probability	0.001 (1)	0.273 (2)	0.718 (3)	0.190 (4)	0.865 (5)	0.985 (6)	0.969 (7)	0.028 (8)	0.973 (9)	0.027 (10)	—

(1) 1–(1-0.001). (2) 1–(1-0.273). (3) 1–((1-0.718)*(1-0.001)). (4) 1–((1-0.008)*(1-0.137) *(1-0.054)). (5) 1–((1-0.704)*(1-0.535)*(1-0.016)). (6) 1–((1-0.158)*(1-0.395)*(1-0.971) *(1-0.004)). (7) 1–((1-0.016)*(1-0.013)*(1-0.968)). (8) 1–(1-0.028). (9) 1–(1-0.973). (10) 1–(1-0.027).

Source: Authors' analysis.

Figure 8.2 presents a graphical view of the Mallawa example, using the 95.4% (two standard error) probability curves generated using Bronk Ramsey (2013). These curves do not cover the 100% probabilities captured in Table 8.1, and so the chronological ranges they cover are narrower (compare, for instance, the Wk-20380 results in Figure 8.2 and Table 8.1), but they are still useful for illustrating the computation procedure. Now, the 500-year period between 2500 and 2000 BP covers the entire 95.4% probability (in fact, 97.1%) for the Wk-20380 determination, but there are three other determinations (P3G-06 (second), ANU 11276, ANU 11274) whose true calendrical date may also fall between 2500–2000 BP. Do these other determinations substantially increase the probability, compared with relying just on Wk-20380, for occupation at Mallawa during 2500–2000 BP? Simply summing the probabilities for the four determinations (Table 8.1) would produce a probability greater than 100%, which is a mathematical impossibility. Instead, following the statistically correct method outlined above, we find that the four determinations together do indeed produce a somewhat greater probability (98.5%) of Mallawa's occupation during 2500–2000 BP compared with just relying on Wk-20380 on its own.

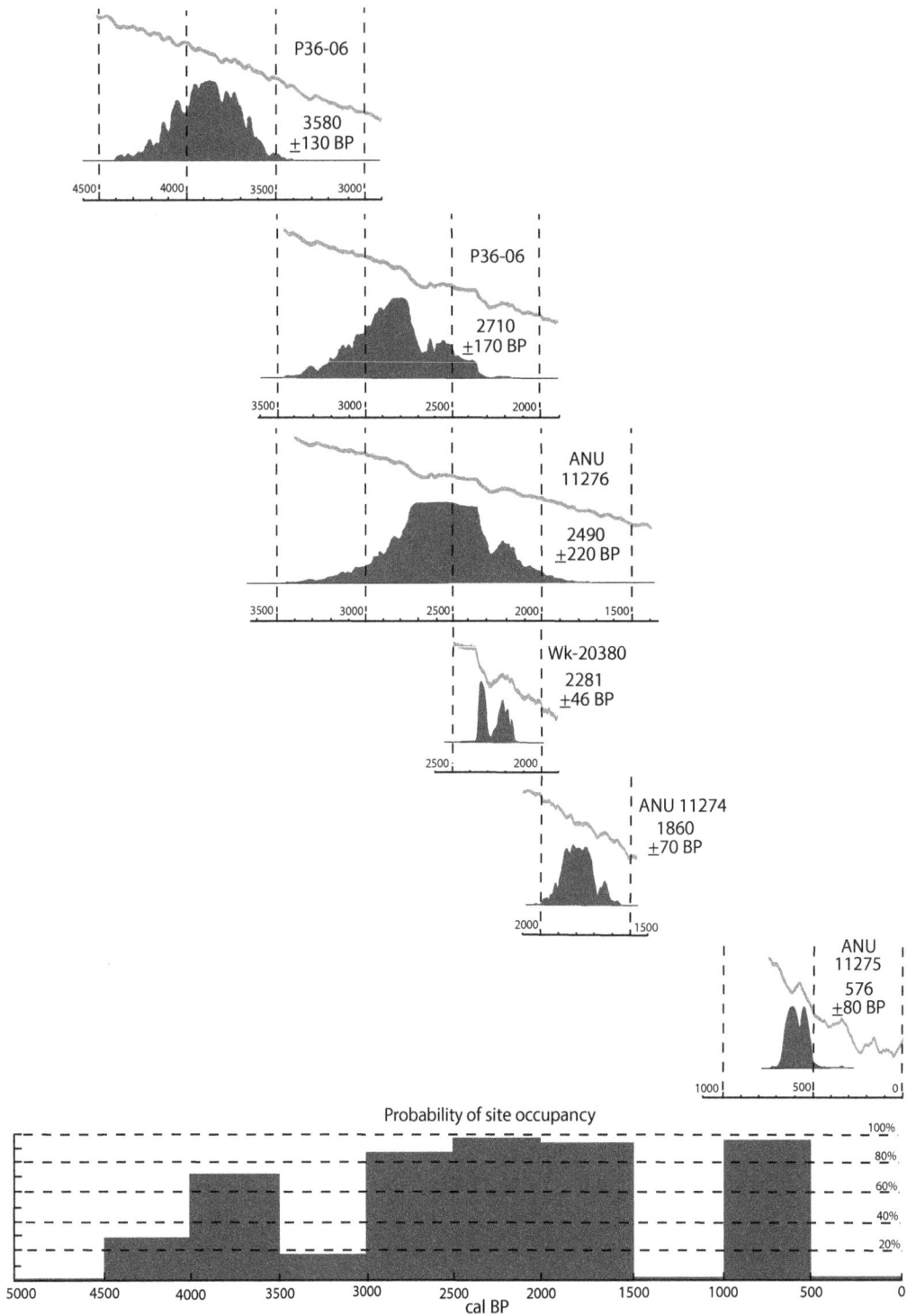

Figure 8.2: Mallawa radiocarbon dates' 95.4% probability distributions and related calibration curves related to the probability of site occupancy by 500-year cal BP intervals.

Sources: Bronk Ramsey (2013) output histograms (redrawn); Table 8.1.

Figure 8.2 illustrates an additional benefit of using 500-year intervals compared with attempting to generate granular curves of radiometric dating incidences (as done by Peros et al. (2010) and Williams (2012)). The peaks and troughs in the radiocarbon calibration curve often fall comfortably inside a 500-year interval, and so have minimal impact on the probability that a determination would relate to a given interval compared with the adjacent intervals. For instance, the trough at around 2300 BP is clearly reflected in bimodal calibration curves for ANU 11276 and Wk-20380 during the 2500–2000 BP interval (Figure 8.2), but the two modes are aggregated when the probability of 2500–2000 BP occupation at Mallawa is calculated (Table 8.1). Accordingly, the risk is neutralised of producing apparent patterns of occupation intensity that are a product of the radiocarbon calibration curve (as discussed by Bamforth and Grund 2012), and any need to accommodate for this effect is minimised.

The 73 sites with accepted determinations are independent entities, and so their joint probabilities of occupancy by half-millennium can be summed to estimate the probable number of Sulawesi sites occupied for each half-millennium. Take the example of four sites each with a 0.25 probability of occupancy during a given half-millennium, producing a summed probability of one occupied site. In reality, the number of occupied sites could be between zero and four, with the following probabilities:

0 sites: $1 * (0.75*0.75*0.75*0.75) = 0.316$
1 site: $4 * (0.25*0.75*0.75*0.75) = 0.422$
2 sites: $6 * (0.25*0.25*0.75*0.75) = 0.211$
3 sites: $4 * (0.25*0.25*0.25*0.75) = 0.047$
4 sites: $1 * (0.25*0.25*0.25*0.25) = 0.004$

The modal probability is one occupied site. Also, while there is a greater probability of zero than two–four occupied sites, this is offset by the possibility of several sites more than 1 occupied site as represented by the probabilities for three and for four occupied sites.

The procedure outlined above can also be undertaken as separate exercises for the site aspect categories, site usage categories and dated material classes (see Results).

Because the site occupancy levels are modest in scale, reaching a maximum of 33 occupied sites for any 500-year interval (see below), no attempt is made to formally correct the calculated site numbers for potential biases such as site taphonomic loss. Instead, these potential biases will be considered at an intuitive level in the Discussion.

Results

The clearest introductory overview of Sulawesi Holocene site occupancy is provided by considering site aspect. All of the sites have a single aspect except for the large Tinco Tua site (Kallupa et al. 1989), which has 'Monumental' and 'Open' aspects (Table A8.6), computed separately. Also, in view of the hierarchy of site aspect categories, the two overarching aspects are **closed** sites and **open-air** sites (covering all sites that are not closed).

The site aspect graph (Figure 8.3) shows continuous use of closed sites in Sulawesi covering the last 10,000 years BP, including a mid-Holocene spike for the 4500–3500 BP period, followed by a second, more pronounced spike after 2000 BP. This second spike predominantly reflects the use of closed sites for depositing human remains over the last couple of millennia BP, as will become evident when the site usage categories are considered.

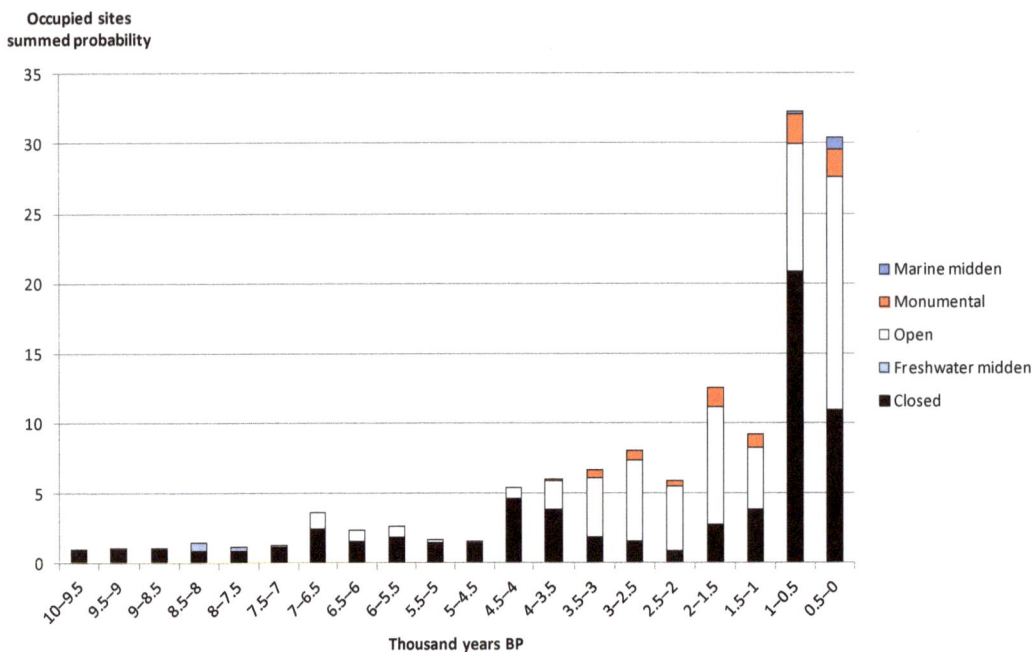

Figure 8.3: Sulawesi sites summed probabilities by site aspect.
Source: Author's data.

Shell middens make just a miniscule contribution to Sulawesi's archaeological chronometry, even though the Paso freshwater shell midden (3 in Figure 8.1) is the oldest open-air site in Sulawesi. The single dated marine shell midden, named Salabu (25 in Figure 8.1), has a very high probability of dating to the <500 years BP interval. 'Open' sites make a detectable contribution to Sulawesi site occupancy levels during the 7000–5500 BP interval and then with increasing impact from 4500 BP onwards. They are joined by 'Monumental' (megalithic) sites from 2500 BP onwards, present with sufficient regularity to propose 2500 BP as an approximate inception date for Sulawesi's widespread megalithic tradition(s).

When site usage is considered, we see that the 'Habitation' category accounts for all of the radiometric determinations up to 3500 BP, and the great majority of radiometric determinations till as recently as 2500 BP (Figure 8.4). The 'Ceremonial' category (notably for open-air sites) is consistently represented for the period between approximately 3000 BP and the present, along with the 'Mortuary' category (for both closed and open-air sites) after 2500 BP. The late Holocene dating for these site usage categories reflects the availability of accepted radiometric determinations rather than the limitations of Sulawesi's early to middle Holocene inhabitants for a symbolic capacity. Uranium-series dates obtained for parietal paintings in the Maros karsts document an age range of c. 40,000–18,000 years BP for a symbolic propensity in Sulawesi *Homo sapiens*; unfortunately, direct dates are yet to be published for the very large body of Sulawesi rock paintings that are not covered by the collaroid speleothems that allowed the above-mentioned late Pleistocene dates to be obtained (Oktaviana et al. 2016). Similarly, the mid-Holocene date for a burial from Leang Burung 1 (ANU 6175 in Table A8.1) is fully consistent with the burial's preceramic stratigraphic context, but the determination was obtained from the human bone apatite fraction and so is sadly not reliable enough for inclusion in the present study.

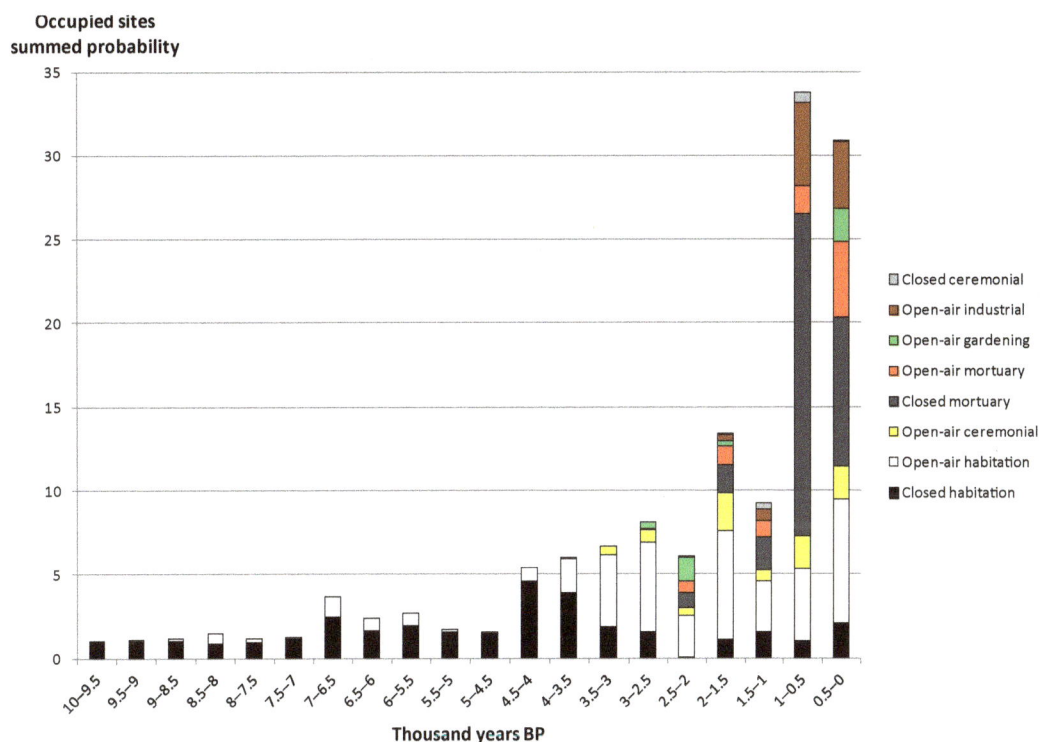

Figure 8.4: Sulawesi sites summed probabilities by site usage.
Source: Author's data.

However, there are two examples of site usage categories whose late Holocene representation is more reasonably taken at face value. One is the 'Gardening' category, convincingly documented for 2500–2000 BP, which can be interpreted as a minimum estimate for when farming activities allowed the establishment of permanent kampong settlements in Sulawesi (e.g. Anggraeni et al. 2014). The second is the 'Industrial' category, in particular ironworking for which Sulawesi (*sula besi* = 'island of iron') received its name. The industry appears to have originated by around 1500 BP and to have been in full operation throughout the last millennium BP (Figure 8.4).

Until approximately 2500 BP, the available radiometric determinations reflect the exclusive or predominant of closed sites for habitation rather than mortuary disposals, but this relationship switches after 2500 BP, especially during the last millennium BP when dates on mortuary disposals in closed sites make up the single largest site usage category.

The graph for dating material (Figure 8.5) shows the exclusive reliance on charcoal both for closed and open-air sites until c. 5000 BP. Animal matter as a dating material appeared in closed sites during the 5th millennium BP and in open-air sites from around 3500 BP to the present. The ceramic category is convincingly represented in open-air sites during 3000–2500 BP and in open-air and closed sites (in combination) during 2000–500 BP. This is direct evidence for a minimum date of 3000 BP for the appearance of pottery in Sulawesi.

Occupied sites
summed probability

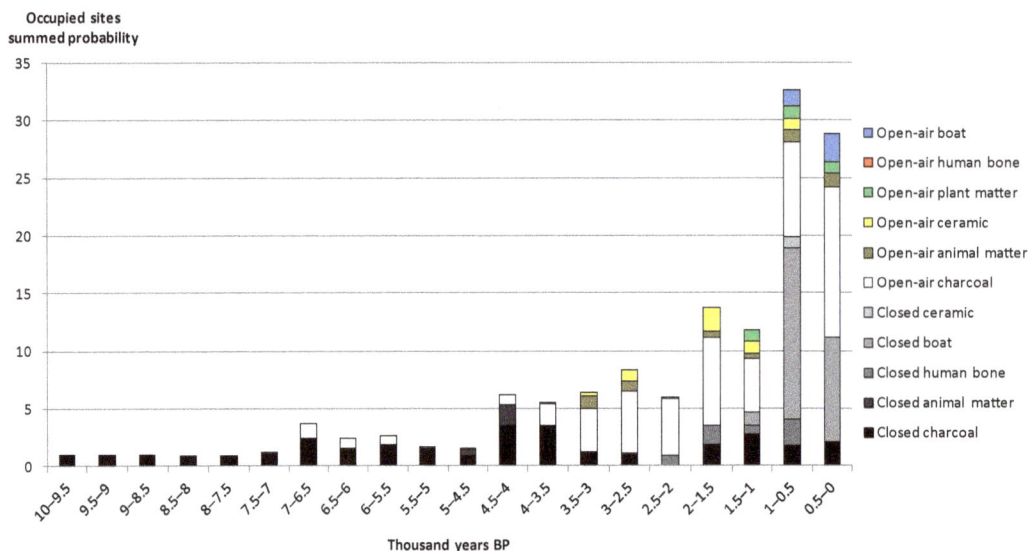

Figure 8.5: Sulawesi sites summed probabilities by dating material.
Source: Author's data.

The three dating materials restricted to the last 2000 years BP on current documentation are the 'Human bone', 'Plant matter' and 'Boat' categories. The boat category, constituted by dates on boat-shaped coffins, is represented at a modest number of closed sites for the 1500–1000 BP interval and then a large number of closed sites and moderate number of open-air sites for the last millennium BP. These boat dates are maximum estimates of antiquity because the samples generally derive from the bark and/or outer tree-rings, and so more closely reflect the date when the tree was a sapling rather than when it was felled for making into a coffin. For instance, in his discussion of the dates from the Enrekang coffins (47–52 in Figure 8.1), Duli (2013) noted that the dates on *Elmerillia celebica* (Dandy) wood were systematically several centuries older than the dates on *Vitex cofassus* (Reinwald) wood, and so proposed that the c. 600 to 700 cal BP dates on *E. celebica* wood should be interpreted as maximally 500 to 550 cal BP in terms of the Enrekang coffins' age.

Accordingly, although it is not possible to formally accommodate the 'old wood effect' impacting on the boat-shaped coffins' age, it is fully possible that all of these coffins would correctly date to the last millennium BP, and that the number of them that are <500 BP in age is at least equal to the number with a true antiquity of 1000–500 BP. The implied effects on the overall pattern of site occupancy over time would be to increase the degree to which the 1500–1000 BP interval is less well represented than the 2000–1500 BP interval, but also to even up the 1000–500 BP and 500–0 BP histogram heights.

Discussion

Taphonomic effects may have had some impact on the results. For instance, the slightly lower site occupancy recorded between 10,000–7000 BP compared with 7000–4500 BP, and the fact that the only open-air site for the former period is a freshwater shell midden, may reflect greater taphonomic loss or burial of early Holocene sites. Also, the greater variability of late Holocene dating materials compared with early to mid-Holocene materials may partly reflect disintegration of older samples to the status of 'Charcoal', although two of the late Holocene material categories (the 'Ceramic' and 'Boat' categories) would appear to reflect late Holocene technological innovations. Overall, a generally increased visibility of open-air sites between the 4500–4000 and 500–0 BP intervals (Figure 8.3) would have had some impact on site occupancy levels, even if difficult to quantify.

On the other hand, any impact of calibration effects would be debatable. For instance, these effects should exaggerate the 2500–2000 BP occupancy level compared with 3000–2500 BP (Williams 2012:582), but the results actually suggest a slight dip during 2500–2000 BP. As observed in the earlier discussion for Figure 8.2, late Holocene dips and troughs in the calibration curve appear to be accommodated by this study's 500-year BP intervals and, as for the early Holocene, site numbers by 500-year interval are uniformly small.

Overall, the proposition by Brandão et al. (2016) of a 70-fold population increase in ISEA commencing at around 4000 years ago appears to be broadly confirmed by the sustained increase in Sulawesi site occupancy levels documented to have begun at around 4500 BP. Yet the interpretation is complicated by the observation that the increased site occupancy levels initially spiked for closed habitation sites, but these levels declined after 4000 BP as occupancy levels of open-air sites and closed mortuary sites came to the fore (Figure 8.4). This increased occupancy of sites other than closed habitation sites may be a more fitting counterpart to the population increase posited by Brandão et al. (2016).

The transition from mainly closed habitation sites to mainly open-air sites between 4500 and 2000 BP, during a period when overall site occupancy levels appear to have remained stable, is intriguing but difficult to explain. Explanation is difficult because the sites concerned are located in mutually exclusive areas. The critical closed sites are located in South and Southeast Sulawesi (specifically, 54–56, 62–65 and 72 in Figure 8.1), compared with the critical open-air sites in North and West Sulawesi plus a single South Sulawesi site (Mallawa, lying to the north of the South Sulawesi closed habitation sites). A simplistic explanation would entertain a desertion of the closed sites whose former occupants migrated to the locations where open-air sites have been documented. But the distances involved are large, and most authorities today would link the growth of open-air sites to the incursion of Austronesian speakers from the Philippines (e.g. Simanjuntak 2008; Anggraeni et al. 2014). In addition, even if the increase in open-air sites after 3500 BP can be linked to the greater visibility of Austronesian settlements compared with pre-Austronesian forager campsites, this would not explain the apparent decline in closed habitation sites after 4000 BP.

Accordingly, it may seem more reasonable to propose that the Malayo-Polynesian (Austronesian) incursion led to disturbances to the environment or transformations of the social landscape that diminished the attractiveness of habitation of closed sites. However, to test this proposition, relevant data would be required from open-air sites in the locations where we have the closed sites and closed sites where we have the open-air sites. This may be a strategic priority for future research on Sulawesi's late Holocene archaeology, which may also test whether the currently recorded 4500–4000 BP peak in closed habitation sites (Figure 8.4) is an artefact of sampling or a firm result to be reckoned with.

The author's proposition of a population increase with the advent of the Early Metal Phase at around 2000 BP, based on my review of the archaeological evidence from South and West Sulawesi (Bulbeck 2010), is confirmed for Sulawesi generally in terms of site occupancy levels. Documented occupancy levels were higher throughout the 2nd millennium BP than at any earlier stage. Also, the site usage categories were variable, including the evident addition of local industrial (ironworking) sites at some point during the millennium. However, there is no sign of increased site occupancy levels during the millennium, whether or not we literally interpret the apparent dip in these levels during the 1500–1000 BP interval compared with the 2000–1500 BP interval.

The author's proposition of a population increase at around 750 BP (Bulbeck 2010) is also confirmed by the high site occupancy levels, in excess of 30 per 500-year interval, throughout the 1st millennium BP. In this case, the majority of the avalanche of site dates were obtained through projects that aimed to elucidate the early history of specific ethnographic-cum-historical situations as recorded for South Sulawesi: Bulbeck's (1992) study of the origins of the Macassar empire; Bulbeck and Caldwell's (2000) investigation into the origins of ironworking associated with the rise of the Bugis kingdom of Luwu; and the projects by Duli (2012, 2013) to date the coffins stored in caves by the Tana Toraja and Enrekang ethnic groups. This point raises the possibility that the observed leap in site occupancy levels reflects a c. 1000-year time depth for most of the archaeological sites that can be encountered from following up on ethnohistorical reports (oral and/or written).

However, it is also the case that most of South Sulawesi and the lowland stretches of West Sulawesi were well populated as of c. 500 BP (e.g. Andaya 1981), and in the case of Macassar and its immediate hinterland, the number of archaeological sites combined with historical records suggests a population increase from around 60,000 people in the 14th century AD to 170,000 in the 17th century AD (Bulbeck 1992). The urban and dense rural populations recorded for much of southwestern Sulawesi at this time reflects the combination of widespread wet-rice agriculture, cultivation of numerous ancillary crops on generally fertile soils and intensive trade (Bulbeck 1992; Bulbeck et al., this volume), which may not have applied generally across Sulawesi. The significant number of Indian cotton *patola* traded to Central Sulawesi, with AMS dates of c. 600 BP and later (Table A8.1), possibly suggests similar developments there to those documented for southwestern Sulawesi; unfortunately, these *patola* lack any archaeological context. In short, the documented peak in site occupancy levels during the last millennium BP relates specifically to South Sulawesi, and the extent to which it could be generalised across Sulawesi would be a matter for future research.

One topic for discussion is the impact of radiometric determinations that fall outside of the main concentration of dates, which can be addressed by considering these determinations for the Minanga Sipakko and Kamassi sites (9 and 10 in Figure 8.1). At both sites, multiple dates refer to the 3500–2500 BP 'Neolithic' period, resulting in a probability of occupancy of 100% for 3500–3000 BP and over 75% for 3000–2500 BP. However, the accepted determinations also point to probable earlier occupancy, as early as 7000–6500 BP (80% probability for Kamassi), 4500–4000 BP (56% probability for Minanga Sipakko) and 4000–3500 BP (100% probability for Minanga Sipakko). No suggestion is being made here that the Neolithic in Sulawesi necessarily dates to earlier than 3500 BP; instead, that the excavation of these sites recovered evidence for pre-Neolithic occupancy at riverside locations ideal for habitation.[1]

The Kamassi site contributes to the intriguing suggestion of a minor, isolated peak in occupancy levels of open sites (and therefore sites overall) between 7000–5500 BP (Figure 8.3). But the apparent 5500–4500 BP dip probably reflects sampling error, as suggested by the significant number of 'Maros points' recorded as surface finds in Southwest Sulawesi. A Toalean type (see footnote 1), these hollow-based, denticulated projectile points are dated from closed sites to 5000–3500 BP (Bulbeck 2004). Accordingly, if they could be dated, the open sites with Maros points may counteract any 5500–4500 BP dip in occupancy levels. A case in point is Pammangkulang Batua, on the bank of a major river (the Je'ne'berang, just south of the Lamuru site; 67 in Figure 8.1), where 422 stone artefacts including two Maros points were collected. Unfortunately, the site would be unsuitable for excavation, not only because the stone artefacts'

---

1 The decision by Anggraeni et al. (2014) to reject these early dates, based on the lack of 'Toalean' tool types in the excavated deposits, is without foundation, because the Toalean was restricted to the Southwest Sulawesi peninsula, as documented by Bulbeck (2004:154; see also the papers in this volume by Hasanuddin and by O'Connor et al.).

original context was apparently a thin soil covering the local conglomerates, but also because they were subsequently disturbed to the surface through quarrying of the site's conglomerates (Pasqua 1995).

In general, the recovery of open-air pre-Neolithic sites in stratified context is a confronting task for archaeologists in the face of the 'twin taphonomic terrors' of wholesale erosion of the site or its burial deep beneath overburden deposit. Certainly, pre-Neolithic open habitation are drastically under-represented by their small number of available dates, even after acceptance of the examples from Minanga Sipakko and Kamassi.

Conclusion

The radiometric dates from Sulawesi sites accepted for this study suggest persistent but low levels of site occupancy between 10,000 and 4500 BP, followed by dynamic change during the late Holocene. Site occupancy levels stepped up during the 4500–2000 BP period, and again during the 2000–1000 and 1000–0 BP periods. Habitation occupancy of closed sites peaked during the 4500–4000 BP interval, but declined in later times as the occupancy of open-air sites for habitation and other purposes, and (after 2000 BP) the use of closed sites for mortuary purposes, became increasingly evident. Dating material analysis indicates a minimum age of 3000 BP for the presence of ceramics in Sulawesi, while site aspect analysis and site usage analysis suggest a minimum age of 2500 BP for gardening activities and the inception of megalithic practices in Sulawesi, respectively. Other important developments in Sulawesi for which dating evidence is available include ironworking by 1500 BP and the production of boat-shaped coffins (after allowing for the potential 'old wood effect' in these coffins) by 1000 BP.

Remembering that the synopsis presented here is based on just 73 sites, and that the accepted dates include many that were obtained before AMS dating became standard practice, we should treat the results of this study as a hypothesis for future testing as archaeological outreach across Sulawesi is extended and the recovery of strongly rigorous radiometric determinations becomes more entrenched.

Acknowledgements

The author thanks two anonymous referees for their valuable comments on the originally submitted version of this manuscript.

Author biography

David Bulbeck Department of Archaeology and Natural History, School of Culture, History and Language, College of Asia and the Pacific, The Australian National University, Canberra, Australia

References

Andaya, L.Y. 1981. *The Heritage of Arung Palakka: A History of South Sulawesi (Celebes) in the Seventeenth Century*. Verhandelingen van het Koninklijk Instituut voor Taal-, Land- en Volkenkunde 91. The Hague: Martinus Nijhoff.

Anggraeni. 2012. The Austronesian Migration Hypothesis as seen from Prehistoric Settlements on the Karama River, Mamuju, West Sulawesi. Unpublished PhD thesis, School of Archaeology and Anthropology, The Australian National University, Canberra.

Anggraeni. 2016. *The development of Neolithic-Palaeometallic pottery with a special reference to the Karama Valley, West Sulawesi*. Presentation at 'The Archaeology of Sulawesi – An Update', Makassar, Sulawesi, 31 January – 2 February.

Anggraeni, T. Simanjuntak, P. Bellwood and P. Piper. 2014. Neolithic foundations in the Karama valley, West Sulawesi, Indonesia. *Antiquity* 88(341):740–756. doi.org/10.1017/S0003598X00050663 (accessed 5 June 2018).

Azis, N., C. Reepmeyer, G. Clark, Sriwigati and D.A. Tanudirjo. 2018. Mansiri in North Sulawesi: A new dentate-stamped pottery site in Island Southeast Asia. In S. O'Connor, D. Bulbeck and J. Meyer (eds), *The Archaeology of Sulawesi: Current Research on the Pleistocene to the Historic Period*, pp. 191–206. Canberra: ANU Press.

Bamforth, D.B. and B. Grund. 2012. Radiocarbon calibration curves, summed probability distributions, and early Paleoindian population trends in North America. *Journal of Archaeological Science* 39(6):1768–1774. doi.org/10.1016/j.jas.2012.01.017 (accessed 5 June 2018).

Barnes, R. and M.H. Kahlenberg (eds). 2010. *Five Centuries of Indonesian Textiles: The Mary Hunt Kahlenberg Collection*. Munich: Delmonico Books.

Bellwood, P. 1976. Archaeological research in Minahasa and the Talaud Islands, Northeastern Indonesia. *Asian Perspectives* 19(2):240–288.

Brandão, A., K.K. Eng, T. Rito, B. Cavadas, D. Bulbeck, F. Gandini, M. Pala, M. Mormina, B. Hudson, J. White, T.-M. Ko, M. Saidin, Z. Zafarina, S. Oppenheimer, M.B. Richards, L. Pereira and P. Soares. 2016. Quantifying the legacy of the Chinese Neolithic on the maternal genetic heritage of Taiwan and Island Southeast Asia. *Human Genetics* 135(4):363–376. doi.org/10.1007/s00439-016-1640-3 (accessed 5 June 2018).

Bronk Ramsey, C. 2013. *OxCal 4.2 manual*. RC.arch.ox.ac.uk/oxcal/Oxcal.html (accessed 3 November 2016).

Bronson, B. and I. Glover. 1984. Archaeological radiocarbon dates from Indonesia: A first list. *Indonesia Circle* 12(34):37–44. doi.org/10.1080/03062848408729585 (accessed 5 June 2018).

Bulbeck, F.D. 1992. A Tale of Two Kingdoms: The Historical Archaeology of Gowa and Tallok, South Sulawesi, Indonesia. Unpublished PhD thesis, School of Archaeology and Anthropology, The Australian National University, Canberra. www.oxis.org/theses/bulbeck-1992.pdf (accessed 5 June 2018).

Bulbeck, D. 2004. Divided in space, united in time: The Holocene prehistory of South Sulawesi. In S.G. Keates and J.M. Pasveer (eds), *Quaternary Research in Indonesia*, pp. 129–166. Modern Quaternary Research in Southeast Asia, Volume 18. Leiden: A.A. Balkema.

Bulbeck, D. 2010. Uneven development in Southwest Sulawesi, Indonesia during the Early Metal Phase. In B. Bellina, E.A. Bacus, T.O. Pryce and J.W. Christie (eds), *50 Years of Archaeology in Southeast Asia: Essays in Honour of Ian Glover*, pp. 153–169. Bangkok: River Books.

Bulbeck, D. 2014. The chronometric Holocene archaeological record of the southern Thai-Malay Peninsula. *International Journal of Asia Pacific Studies* 10(1):112–162.

Bulbeck, D. 2016. The Neolithic Gap in the Southern Thai-Malay Peninsula and its implications for Orang Asli prehistory. In K. Endicott (ed.), *Malaysia's Original People: Past, Present and Future of the Orang Asli*, pp. 123–152. Singapore: NUS Press.

Bulbeck, D., F.A. Aziz, S. O'Connor, A. Calo, J.N. Fenner, B. Marwick, J. Feathers, R. Wood and D. Prastiningtyas. 2016. Mortuary caves and the dammar trade in the Towuti-Routa region, Sulawesi, in an Island Southeast Asian context. *Asian Perspectives* 55(2):148–183. doi.org/10.1353/asi.2016.0017 (accessed 5 June 2018).

Bulbeck, D. and I. Caldwell. 2000. *Land of Iron: The Historical Archaeology of Luwu and the Cenrana Valley. Results of the Origin of Complex Society in South Sulawesi Project (OXIS).* Hull: Centre for South-East Asian Studies, University of Hull. www.oxis.org/books/land-of-iron.pdf (accessed 5 June 2018).

Bulbeck, D. and I. Caldwell. 2008. *Oryza sativa* and the origins of kingdoms in South Sulawesi, Indonesia: Evidence from rice husk phytoliths. *Indonesia and the Malay World* 36(104):1–20. doi.org/10.1080/13639810802016117 (accessed 5 June 2018).

Bulbeck, D., I. Caldwell, S. Druce, B. Hakim and C. Macknight. 2018. Imported tradeware ceramics and their relevance for dating socio-political developments in South Sulawesi, with special reference to the Allangkanangnge ri Latanete site. In S. O'Connor, D. Bulbeck and J. Meyer (eds), *The Archaeology of Sulawesi: Current Research on the Pleistocene to the Historic Period*, pp. 269–286. Canberra: ANU Press.

Bulbeck, D. and M.A. Fadillah. 2000. The context of the carnelian beads from Bonto-Bontoa, Bantaeng, South Sulawesi. *Walennae* 3(1):44–48.

Bulbeck, D. and B. Hakim. 2005. The human fossil cranium from Leang Batu Tunpa, Selayar, Sulawesi Selatan. In D.W. Utomo, Hasanuddin, B. Hakim and A.F. Uma (eds), *Menguak Tabir Kehidupan Masa lalu dan kini*, pp. 71–84. Makassar: Balai Arkeologi Makassar.

Bulbeck, D. and Nasruddin. 2002. Recent insights on the chronology and ceramics of the Kalumpang site complex, South Sulawesi, Indonesia. *Bulletin of The Indo-Pacific Prehistory Association* 22:83–100.

Bulbeck, D., M. Pasqua and A. Di Lello. 2000. Culture history of the Toalean of South Sulawesi, Indonesia. *Asian Perspectives* 39(1–2):71–108. doi.org/10.1353/asi.2000.0004.

Downey, S.S., E. Bocaege, T. Kerig, K. Edinborough and S. Shennan. 2014. The neolithic demographic transition in Europe: Correlation with juvenility index supports interpretation of the summed calibrated radiocarbon date probability distribution (SCDPD) as a valid demographic proxy. *PLoS ONE* 9(8):e105730. doi.org/10.1371/journal.pone.0105730 (accessed 5 June 2018).

Druce, S., D. Bulbeck and I. Mahmud. 2005. A transitional Islamic Bugis cremation in Bulubangi, South Sulawesi: Its historical and archaeological context. *Review of Indonesian and Malaysian Affairs* 39(1):1–22.

Duli, A. 2012. Budaya Keranda Erang di Tana Toraja. Unpublished PhD thesis, Centre for Archaeological Research Malaysia, Universiti Sains Malaysia, Kuala Lumpur.

Duli, A. 2013. The mandu coffin: A boat symbol of ancestral spirits among the Enrekang people of South Sulawesi. *Review of Indonesian and Malaysian Affairs* 47(1):115–138.

Fakhri. 2016. Situs Rampi: Masa persebaran arca batu dan hubungannya dengan di wilayah situs terdekat (Rampi sites: The dispersion age of stone statue and the connection between nearest site areas). *Walennae* 14(1):23–36. walennae.kemdikbud.go.id/index.php/walennae/article/view/38 (accessed 27 October 2018).

Fakhri. 2018. Vertebrate fauna from Gua Sambangoala, Southeast Sulawesi. In S. O'Connor, D. Bulbeck and J. Meyer (eds), *The Archaeology of Sulawesi: Current Research on the Pleistocene to the Historic Period*, pp. 153–170. Canberra: ANU Press.

Fakhri, Suryatman, B. Hakim and R. Sardi. 2015. Exploration of prehistoric sites in the Karama watershed, West Sulawesi, Indonesia. *Journal of Indo-Pacific Archaeology* 39:18–25. journals.lib.washington.edu/index.php/JIPA/article/view/14786/12489 (accessed 5 June 2018).

Glover, I. 1978. Survey and excavation in the Maros district, south Sulawesi, Indonesia: The 1975 field season. *Bulletin of The Indo-Pacific Prehistory Association* 1:60–103.

Glover, I.C. 1981. Leang Burung 2: An upper Palaeolithic rock shelter in South Sulawesi, Indonesia. In G.-J. Bartstra and W.A. Casparie (eds), *Modern Quaternary Research in Southeast Asia*, pp. 1–38. Modern Quaternary Research in Southeast Asia, Volume 6. Rotterdam: A.A. Balkema.

Glover, I. 1997. Southeast Asia. In S. Hooper (ed.), *Robert and Lisa Sainsbury Collection*, pp. 214–217. Ipswich: University of East Anglia.

Guy, J. 1998. *Woven Cargoes: Indian Textiles in the East*. London: Thames and Hudson.

Hakim, B., M. Nur and Rustam. 2009. The sites of Gua Pasaung (Rammang-Rammang) and Mallawa: Indicators of cultural contact between the Toalian and Neolithic complexes in South Sulawesi. *Bulletin of The Indo-Pacific Prehistory Association* 29:45–52. doi.org/10.7152/bippa.v29i0.9476 (accessed 5 June 2018).

Hasanuddin. 2015. Kebudayaan Megalitik di Sulawesi Selatan dan Hubungannya dengan Asia Tenggara. Unpublished PhD thesis, Centre for Archaeological Research Malaysia, Universiti Sains Malaysia, Kuala Lumpur. www.oxis.org/theses/hasanuddin-2015.pdf (accessed 5 June 2018).

Hasanuddin. 2018. Prehistoric sites in Enrekang Kabupaten, South Sulawesi. In S. O'Connor, D. Bulbeck and J. Meyer (eds), *The Archaeology of Sulawesi: Current Research on the Pleistocene to the Historic Period*, pp. 171–190. Canberra: ANU Press.

Higham, T., C. Bronk Ramsey, F. Brock, D. Baker and P. Ditchfield. 2007. Radiocarbon dates from the Oxford AMS system: Archaeometry datelist 32. *Archaeometry* 49(Supplement s1):S1–S60. doi.org/10.1111/j.1475-4754.2007.00363.x (accessed 5 June 2018).

Hiscock, P. and V. Attenbrow. 2016. Dates and demography? The need for caution in using radiometric dates as a robust proxy for prehistoric population change. *Archaeology in Oceania* 51(3):218–219. doi.org/10.1002/arco.5096 (accessed 5 June 2018).

Kallupa, B., D. Bulbeck, I. Caldwell, I. Sumantri and K. Demmanari. 1989. *Survey Pusat Kerajaan Soppeng 1100–1986 [Survey of the Capital of Soppeng Kingdom 1100–1986]*. Final Report to the Australian Myer Foundation, Privately published in Canberra, ACT. www.oxis.org/books/soppeng-1986.pdf (accessed 5 June 2018).

Kirleis, W., J. Müller, C. Kortemeier, H. Behling and S. Soeghondo. 2012. The megalithic landscape of Central Sulawesi, Indonesia: combining archaeological and palynological investigations. In M.L. Tjoa-Bonatz, A. Reinecke and D. Bonatz (eds), *Crossing Borders in Southeast Asian Archaeology: Selected Papers from the 13th International Conference of the European Association of Southeast Asian Archaeologists, Berlin, 2010*, pp. 199–220. Singapore: NUS Press.

O'Connor, S., F.A. Aziz, B. Marwick, J. Fenner, B. Prasetyo, D. Bulbeck, T. Maloney, E.S. Pierre, R. Whitau, U.P. Wibowo, B. Hakim, A. Calo, Fakhri, M. Husni, Hasanuddin, A.A. Oktaviana, D. Prastiningtyas, F.Z. Campos, and P.J. Piper with an appendix by A.A. Oktaviana and Suryatman. 2014. *The Archaeology of Sulawesi: A Strategic Island for Understanding Modern Human Colonization and Interactions Across our Region*. Final Report to Indonesia's Bureau of Research and Technology, Department of Archaeology and Natural History, The Australian National University, Canberra and Department of Prehistory, Indonesia's National Centre for Archaeological Research and Development, Jakarta.

O'Connor, S., D. Bulbeck, P.J. Piper, F. Aziz, B. Marwick, F. Campos, J. Fenner, K. Aplin, Fakhri, Suryatman, T. Maloney, B. Hakim and R. Wood. 2018. The human occupation record of Gua Mo'o hono shelter, Towuti-Routa region of Southeastern Sulawesi. In S. O'Connor, D. Bulbeck and J. Meyer (eds), *The Archaeology of Sulawesi: Current Research on the Pleistocene to the Historic Period*, pp. 117–152. Canberra: ANU Press.

Oktaviana, A.A., D. Bulbeck, S. O'Connor, B. Hakim, Suryatman, U.P. Wibowo, E. St Pierre and Fakhri. 2016. Hand stencils with and without narrowed fingers at two new rock art sites in Sulawesi, Indonesia. *Rock Art Research* 33(1):32–48.

Pasqua, M. 1995. Mid–Late Holocene Toalean Sites in South Sulawesi: A Technological Analysis. Unpublished BSc Honours thesis, Centre for Archaeology, University of Western Australia, Perth.

Peros, M.C., S.E. Munoz, K. Gajewski and A.E. Viau. 2010. Prehistoric demography of North America inferred from radiocarbon data. *Journal of Archaeological Science* 37(3):656–664. doi.org/10.1016/j/jas.2009.10.029 (accessed 5 June 2018).

Simanjuntak, T. 2008. Austronesian in Sulawesi: Its origin, diaspora, and living tradition. In T. Simanjuntak (ed.), *Austronesian in Sulawesi*, pp. 215–251. Jakarta: Center for Prehistoric and Austronesian Studies.

Simanjuntak, T. 2010. Penutur dan budaya Austronesia. In N. Harkantiningsih, T. Simanjuntak and E.S. Hardiati (eds), *Arkeologi Indonesia Dalam Lintasan Zaman*, pp. 41–71. Jakarta: Pusat Penelitian dan Pengamban Arkeologi Nasional.

Simanjuntak, T., M.J. Morwood, F.S. Intan, I. Mahmud, K. Grant, N. Somba, B. Akw and D.W. Utomo. 2008. Minanga Sipakko and the Neolithic of the Karama River. In T. Simanjuntak (ed.), *Austronesian in Sulawesi*, pp. 57–75. Jakarta: Center for Prehistoric and Austronesian Studies.

Spriggs, M. 2003. Chronology of the Neolithic transition in Island Southeast Asia and the Western Pacific: A view from 2003. *The Review of Archaeology* 24(2):57–80.

Storm, P., R. Wood, C. Stringer, A. Bartsiokas, J. de Vos, M. Aubert, L. Kinsley and R. Grün. 2013. U-series and radiocarbon analyses of human and faunal remains from Wajak, Indonesia. *Journal of Human Evolution* 64(5):356–365. doi.org/10.1016/j.jhevol.2012.11.002 (accessed 5 June 2018).

Williams, A. 2012. The use of summed radiocarbon probability distributions in archaeology: A review of methods. *Journal of Archaeological Science* 39(3):578–589. doi.org/10.1016/j.jas.2011.07.014 (accessed 5 June 2018).

Yuniawati, D.Y. 2006. *Kubur Batu Waruga di Sub-Etnis Tou' Mbulu Sulawesi Utara*. Jakarta: Pusat Penelitian dan Pengembangan Arkeologi Nasional.

Appendix A: Sulawesi radiometric determinations

Table A8.1: Rejected Sulawesi Holocene radiometric determinations (oldest to youngest determinations): Radiocarbon dates unless otherwise specified.

Site/ Location	Date	Dating material	Laboratory code	Reference	Reason for rejection
Ulu Leang 2	8995±50 BP	Freshwater shell	GRN-8647	Bronson and Glover 1984	Freshwater shell date in karstic environment
Ulu Leang 2	8785±45 BP	Freshwater shell	GRN-8291	Bronson and Glover 1984	Freshwater shell date in karstic environment
Paso	7530±450 BP	Charcoal	ANU 1517	Bellwood 1976	Standard error in excess of 400 years
Ulu Leang 2	7170±600 BP	Charcoal	ANU 606	Glover 1978	Standard error in excess of 400 years
Gua Mo'o hono	6855±32 BP (AMS)	Freshwater shell	D-AMS 001620	O'Connor et al. this volume	Freshwater shell date in karstic environment
Gua Mo'o hono	6808±28 BP (AMS)	Freshwater shell	D-AMS 001618	O'Connor et al. this volume	Freshwater shell date in karstic environment
Gua Mo'o hono	6531±28 BP (AMS)	Freshwater shell	D-AMS 001619a	O'Connor et al. this volume	Freshwater shell date in karstic environment

Site/ Location	Date	Dating material	Laboratory code	Reference	Reason for rejection
Kamassi	6498±25 BP (AMS)	Phytoliths	NZA 34860	Anggraeni 2012	Experimental dating material
Leang Burung 1	4880±480 BP	Charcoal	ANU 1264	Bulbeck et al. 2000	Standard error in excess of 400 years
Gua Mo'o hono	4730±36 BP (AMS)	Freshwater shell	D-AMS 001616a	O'Connor et al. this volume	Freshwater shell date in karstic environment
Gua Mo'o hono	4718±26 BP (AMS)	Freshwater shell	D-AMS 001624a	O'Connor et al. this volume	Freshwater shell date in karstic environment
Gua Mo'o hono	4702±29 BP (AMS)	Freshwater shell	D-AMS 001617	O'Connor et al. this volume	Freshwater shell date in karstic environment
Leang Burung 1	4610±220 BP	Human bone apatite	ANU 6175	Bulbeck et al. 2000	Bone apatite fraction
Kamassi	4282±25 BP (AMS)	Phytoliths	NZA 34861	Anggraeni 2012	Experimental dating material
Kamassi	4282±20 BP (AMS)	Phytoliths	NZA 34896	Anggraeni 2012	Experimental dating material
Gua Mo'o hono	4202±31 BP (AMS)	Freshwater shell	D-AMS 001615	O'Connor et al. this volume	Freshwater shell date in karstic environment
Ulu Leang 2	4000–3000 years ago	Pottery (thermo-remnant magnetism)	Not stated	Glover 1978	Date's probability by half-millennium BP can't be estimated
Mansiri	414±380 BC	Sediment (OSL)	X6841	Azis et al. this volume	Suspected incomplete bleaching/no cultural association
Gua Mo'o hono	1690±25 BP (AMS)	Freshwater shell	D-AMS 001614	O'Connor et al. this volume	Freshwater shell date in karstic environment
Gua Mo'o hono	1568±21 BP (AMS)	Freshwater shell	D-AMS 001622a	O'Connor et al. this volume	Freshwater shell date in karstic environment
Mansiri	AD 725±195	Sediment (OSL)	X6839	Azis et al. this volume	Suspected incomplete bleaching
Gua Mo'o hono	1103±21 BP (AMS)	Freshwater shell	D-AMS 001612	O'Connor et al. this volume	Freshwater shell date in karstic environment
Gua Lampetia	AD 900±120	Burial jar cover (OSL)	UW2871	Bulbeck et al. 2016	Older of two dates for same object
Talaborong	920±170 BP	Human bone apatite	ANU 5924	Bulbeck 1992	Bone apatite fraction
Leang Burung 1	660±200 BP	Human bone apatite	ANU 6173	Bulbeck et al. 2000	Bone apatite fraction
Leang Burung 1	640±240 BP	Human bone apatite	ANU 6174	Bulbeck et al. 2000	Bone apatite fraction
Toraja region	650±40 BP (AMS)	Cotton patola	OxA-6482	Guy 1998	Ethnographic object
Toraja region	580±40 BP (AMS)	Cotton patola	OxA-6481	Guy 1998	Ethnographic object
Bulubangi	570±60 BP	Human bone	ANU 11852	Druce et al. 2005	Dating facilities not set up for human bone
Poso	630–470 cal BP	Cotton patola	Not stated	Barnes and Kahlenberg 2010	Ethnographic object
Sulawesi	550±40 BP (AMS)	Cotton patola	OxA-5769	Guy 1998	Ethnographic object
Toraja region	539±64 BP (AMS)	Cotton patola	NZA-8090	Guy 1998	Ethnographic object
Saukang Boe	450±220 BP	Human bone apatite	ANU 5923	Bulbeck 1992	Bone apatite fraction
Poso	531–323 cal BP	Cotton patola	Not stated	Barnes and Kahlenberg 2010	Ethnographic object
Minahasa	510–310 cal BP	Cotton patola	Not stated	Barnes and Kahlenberg 2010	Ethnographic object

Site/ Location	Date	Dating material	Laboratory code	Reference	Reason for rejection
Sulawesi	410±23 BP (AMS)	Cotton patola	OxA-13343	Higham et al. 2007	Ethnographic object
Palu	466–287 cal BP	Cotton patola	Not stated	Barnes and Kahlenberg 2010	Ethnographic object
Sulawesi	384±24 BP (AMS)	Cotton patola	OxA-13297	Higham et al. 2007	Ethnographic object
Sulawesi	355±40 BP (AMS)	Cotton patola	OxA-6484	Guy 1998	Ethnographic object
Sulawesi	295±55 BP (AMS)	Cotton patola	OxA-6587	Guy 1998	Ethnographic object
Tana Toraja	346– ~170 cal BP	Cotton patola	Not stated	Barnes and Kahlenberg 2010	Ethnographic object
Central Sulawesi	230±40 BP (AMS)	Cotton patola	OxA-6483	Guy 1998	Ethnographic object
Pontanoa Bangka	50±60 BP (AMS)	Cotton	OZE644	Bulbeck and Caldwell 2000	Larger standard error than Oxford Laboratory redating for same sample
Rahampu'u 1	Modern	Charcoal	ANU 11075	Bulbeck and Caldwell 2000	No reason to suspect pre-1950 antiquity
Katue	Modern	Charcoal (AMS)	OZD846	Bulbeck and Caldwell 2000	No reason to suspect pre-1950 antiquity
Sabbang Loang	Modern	Charcoal (AMS)	OZE129	Bulbeck and Caldwell 2000	No reason to suspect pre-1950 antiquity
Marante Tondon	Modern	Boat (coffin)	Beta-274723	Duli 2012	No reason to suspect pre-1950 antiquity
Allangkan-anangnge ri Latanete	Modern	Charcoal (AMS)	Wk-17743	Bulbeck et al. this volume	No reason to suspect pre-1950 antiquity
Petta Balubue	Modern	Burnt cranial bone	ANU 5928	Kallupa et al. 1989	No reason to suspect pre-1950 antiquity
Bayoa 1	Modern	Boat (coffin)	ANU 5926	Bulbeck 1992	No reason to suspect pre-1950 antiquity
Batu Ejjaya 2	Modern	Charcoal	ANU 606	Bronson and Glover 1984	No reason to suspect pre-1950 antiquity

Note: Reasons for dates' rejection explained in Bulbeck (2014), except for 'experimental dating material' (Anggraeni 2012), bone apatite fraction (Storm et al. 2013), 'incomplete bleaching of dated sediment' (Azis et al., this volume) and 'ethnographic object' (rather than archaeological status of dated object), which are added here.

Table A8.2: Accepted Holocene radiometric determinations from North and Central Sulawesi (all Carbon-14).

Site	Date BP	Laboratory code	Dated material	Site aspect	Site use	Reference
Woloan	1540±140	Not stated	Charcoal	Monumental	Mortuary	Yuniawati 2006
Woloan	1260±80	Not stated	Human bone	Monumental	Mortuary	Yuniawati 2006
Woloan	1180±80	Not stated	Human bone	Monumental	Mortuary	Yuniawati 2006
Tatelu	2070±140	Not stated	Animal bone	Monumental	Mortuary	Yuniawati 2006
Tatelu	850±140	Not stated	Charcoal	Monumental	Mortuary	Yuniawati 2006
Paso	7360±310	ANU 1518	Charcoal	Freshwater shell midden	Habitation	Bellwood 1976
Teling	3100±210	Not stated	Charcoal	Open	Habitation	Simanjuntak et al. 2008
Teling	2770±120	Not stated	Charcoal	Open	Habitation	Simanjuntak 2010
Mansiri	3035±35 (AMS)	S-ANU 40031	Charcoal	Open	Habitation	Azis et al. this volume
Mansiri	2494±20 (AMS)	Wk-44605	Charcoal	Open	Habitation	Azis et al. this volume

Site	Date BP	Laboratory code	Dated material	Site aspect	Site use	Reference
Mansiri	2469±20 (AMS)	Wk-44610	Charcoal	Open	Habitation	Azis et al. this volume
Pokekea	1251±31 (AMS)	ErL-10584	Plant matter	Monumental	Ceremonial	Kirleis et al. 2012
Pokekea	1197±30 (AMS)	ErL-10585	Plant matter	Monumental	Ceremonial	Kirleis et al. 2012
Pokekea	949±45 (AMS)	ErL-10584	Plant matter	Monumental	Ceremonial	Kirleis et al. 2012
Pokekea	890±30 (AMS)	ErL-10584	Plant matter	Monumental	Ceremonial	Kirleis et al. 2012
Entovera	2890±120	Not stated	Charcoal	Monumental	Ceremonial	Simanjuntak 2010
Entovera	2460±120	Not stated	Charcoal	Monumental	Ceremonial	Simanjuntak 2010

Table A8.3: Accepted Holocene radiometric determinations from West Sulawesi (all Carbon-14).

Site	Date BP	Laboratory code	Dated material	Site aspect	Site use	Reference
Pantara'an 1	2850±50 (AMS)	ANU 9707	Ceramic	Open	Habitation	Anggraeni et al. 2014
Pantara'an 1	2505±25 (AMS)	ANU 9438	Ceramic	Open	Habitation	Anggraeni et al. 2014
Pantara'an 1	277±30 (AMS)	Wk-25697	Charcoal	Open	Gardening	Anggraeni 2012
Minangka Sipakko	2810±50 (AMS)	OZE-132	Animal matter (bone)	Open	Habitation	Bulbeck and Nasruddin 2002
Minangka Sipakko	2570±110	P3G-97	Charcoal	Open	Habitation	Simanjuntak 2008
Minangka Sipakko	4950±180	P3G-05	Charcoal	Open	Habitation	Simanjuntak et al. 2008
Minangka Sipakko	3690±160	P3G-05	Charcoal	Open	Habitation	Simanjuntak et al. 2008
Minangka Sipakko	3446±51 (AMS)	Wk-14561	Charcoal	Open	Habitation	Anggraeni et al. 2014
Minangka Sipakko	3343±46 (AMS)	Wk-17981	Charcoal	Open	Habitation	Anggraeni et al. 2014
Minangka Sipakko	3082±50 (AMS)	Wk-14562	Charcoal	Open	Habitation	Anggraeni et al. 2014
Minangka Sipakko	2996±41 (AMS)	Wk-14564	Charcoal	Open	Habitation	Anggraeni et al. 2014
Minangka Sipakko	2881±46 (AMS)	Wk-14563	Charcoal	Open	Habitation	Anggraeni et al. 2014
Kamassi	5830±140	P3G	Charcoal	Open	Habitation	Anggraeni 2012
Kamassi	3345±40 (AMS)	ANU 36406	Marine shell*	Open	Habitation	Anggraeni et al. 2014
Kamassi	3225±40 (AMS)	ANU 36406	Animal matter (freshwater shell)	Open	Habitation	Anggraeni et al. 2014
Kamassi	3140±30 (AMS)	ANU 35128	Animal matter (freshwater shell)	Open	Habitation	Anggraeni et al. 2014
Kamassi	2700±150 (AMS)	Geolabs-411	Charcoal	Open	Habitation	Anggraeni et al. 2014
Kamassi	1620±30 (AMS)	ANU 35126	Animal matter (freshwater shell)	Open	Habitation	Anggraeni et al. 2014
Palemba	1720±30 (AMS)	Beta-360430	Ceramic	Open	Habitation	Anggraeni 2016
Sakkarra	2047±40 (AMS) #	S-ANU 39336-2	Charcoal	Open	Habitation	Fakhri et al. 2015
Sakkarra	2000±40 (AMS) #	S-ANU 39336-1	Charcoal	Open	Habitation	Fakhri et al. 2015

*Calibrated using Marine 0.914c, applied correction factor for marine reservoir effect delta R 89±70 (Borneo), assuming 50% marine contribution.

#Standard error back-calculated from median age BP and 95% calibrated range provided by Fakhri et al. (2015).

Table A8.4: Accepted Holocene radiometric determinations from South Sulawesi north and east of the southwest peninsula (all Carbon-14).

Site	Date BP	Laboratory code	Dated material	Site aspect	Site use	Reference
Timo'oni	1854±25 (AMS)	Wk-39675	Charcoal	Monumental	Ceremonial	Fakhri 2016
Timo'oni	1850±25 (AMS)	Wk-39676	Charcoal	Monumental	Ceremonial	Fakhri 2016
Timo'oni	1823±25 (AMS)	Wk-39677	Charcoal	Monumental	Ceremonial	Fakhri 2016
Sukoyu	2070±50	ANU 11271	Charcoal	Open	Gardening	Bulbeck and Caldwell 2000
Sukoyu	830±70	ANU 11272	Charcoal	Open	Industrial	As above
Pontanoa Bangka	1520±70	ANU 11107	Charcoal	Open	Industrial	As above
Pontanoa Bangka	1010±60	ANU 11108	Charcoal	Open	Industrial	As above
Pontanoa Bangka	152±33 (AMS)	OxA-10457	Plant matter (cotton)	Open	Mortuary	Higham et al. 2007
Nuha	960±70	ANU 11105	Charcoal	Open	Industrial	Bulbeck and Caldwell 2000
Nuha	130±50	ANU 11278	Charcoal	Open	Industrial	As above
Lemogola	120±70	ANU 11277	Charcoal	Open	Industrial	As above
Rahampu'u 1	5680± 130	ANU 11802	Charcoal	Open	Habitation	As above
Rahampu'u 1	1400± 110	ANU 11801	Charcoal	Open	Habitation	As above
Rahampu'u 1	1000±40 (AMS)	OZE646	Ceramic	Open	Habitation	As above
Rahampu'u 1	430±120	ANU 11077	Charcoal	Open	Industrial	As above
Rahampu'u 1	400±60	ANU 11080	Charcoal	Open	Industrial	As above
Rahampu'u 1	350±70	ANU 11074	Charcoal	Open	Industrial	As above
Rahampu'u 1	310±90	ANU 11076	Charcoal	Open	Industrial	As above
Rahampu'u 1	310±90	ANU 11079	Charcoal	Open	Industrial	As above
Pandai Besi	480±130	ANU 11083	Charcoal	Open	Industrial	As above
Pandai Besi	410±70	ANU 11084	Charcoal	Open	Industrial	As above
Matano bore	2350± 140	ANU 11104	Charcoal	Open	Gardening	As above
Turungang Damar	350±70	ANU 11353	Charcoal	Open	Habitation	As above
Manu Manue	170±70 (AMS)	OZD848	Charcoal	Open	Habitation	As above
Katue	1850±40 (AMS)	OZE581	Charcoal	Open	Habitation	As above
Katue	1810±40 (AMS)	OZD847	Charcoal	Open	Habitation	As above
Katue	1100±50 (AMS)	OZD845	Charcoal (carbonised shell)	Open	Habitation	As above
Katue	370±35 (AMS)	OZE580	Charcoal	Open	Gardening	As above
Bola Merajae	1980±90 (AMS)	OZD843	Charcoal	Open	Habitation	As above
Bola Merajae	1870±40 (AMS)	OZE579	Charcoal	Open	Habitation	As above
Bola Merajae	1260±60 (AMS)	OZD844	Charcoal	Open	Habitation	As above
Bola Merajae	660±70	ANU 11356	Charcoal	Open	Habitation	As above
Bola Merajae	310±40 (AMS)	OZE578	Charcoal	Open	Habitation	As above
Salabu	400±60 (AMS)	Wk-7336	Animal (dentine)	Marine shell midden	Habitation	As above
Pinanto	390±90	ANU 11355	Charcoal	Open	Habitation	As above
Sabbang Loang	2020± 140	ANU 11106	Charcoal	Open	Mortuary	As above
Sabbang Loang	1990± 200	ANU 11273	Charcoal	Open	Mortuary	As above
Sabbang Loang	1910±70 (AMS)	OZD850	Ceramic	Open	Habitation	As above
Sabbang Loang	1780±50 (AMS)	OZD851	Ceramic	Open	Habitation	As above
Sabbang Loang	1750±50 (AMS)	OZD852	Ceramic	Open	Habitation	As above
Arateng	450±60	ANU 11109	Boat (coffin)	Open	Mortuary	As above

Site	Date BP	Laboratory code	Dated material	Site aspect	Site use	Reference
Gua Andomo	1000±25 (AMS)	SANU 34619	Human bone	Closed	Mortuary	Bulbeck et al. 2016
Tampang Allo	1070±50	Beta-281928	Boat (coffin)	Closed	Mortuary	Duli 2012
Marimbunna Tikala	1130±50	Beta-287186	Boat (coffin)	Closed	Mortuary	Duli 2012
Londa	1000±40	Beta-274728	Boat (coffin)	Closed	Mortuary	Duli 2012
Lombok Borik	930±40	Beta-274725	Boat (coffin)	Closed	Mortuary	Duli 2012
Buntu Pune	810±50	Beta-281927	Boat (coffin)	Closed	Mortuary	Duli 2012
Marante Tondon	800±50	Beta-287188	Boat (coffin)	Closed	Mortuary	Duli 2012
Lalanbai Sarira	780±60	Beta-294688	Boat (coffin)	Closed	Mortuary	Duli 2012
Lalik Manuk	710±40	Beta-294684	Boat (coffin)	Closed	Mortuary	Duli 2012
Tambolang Ba'lele	660±40	Beta-294687	Boat (coffin)	Closed	Mortuary	Duli 2012
Lalik Manuk	640±50	Beta-287183	Boat (coffin)	Closed	Mortuary	Duli 2012
Limbong	570±50	Beta-287189	Boat (coffin)	Closed	Mortuary	Duli 2012
Allak Angin-Angin	510±50	Beta-287187	Boat (coffin)	Closed	Mortuary	Duli 2012
Lombok Borik	400±50	Beta-274726	Boat (coffin)	Closed	Mortuary	Duli 2012
Ke'te Kesuk	400±50	Beta-274726	Boat (coffin)	Closed	Mortuary	Duli 2012
Marimbunna Tikala	390±50	Beta-287185	Boat (coffin)	Closed	Mortuary	Duli 2012
Lo'kok Pongdadu	360±50	Beta-294686	Boat (coffin)	Closed	Mortuary	Duli 2012
Lombok Borik	360±50	Beta-281929	Boat (coffin)	Closed	Mortuary	Duli 2012
Se'pon Marinding	360±40	Beta-294685	Boat (coffin)	Closed	Mortuary	Duli 2012
Pangki Mangke'pek	350±60	Beta-294689	Boat (coffin)	Closed	Mortuary	Duli 2012
Tampang Allo	310±40	Beta-274727	Boat (coffin)	Closed	Mortuary	Duli 2012
Palak Tokkek	280±40	Beta-274724	Boat (coffin)	Closed	Mortuary	Duli 2012
Potok Tengan Kando	240±40	Beta-287184	Boat (coffin)	Closed	Mortuary	Duli 2012
Tok Sempa	790±50	Beta-274731	Boat (coffin)	Closed	Mortuary	Duli 2013
Kaluppini	790±50	Beta-274732	Boat (coffin)	Closed	Mortuary	Duli 2013
Marengok Papaling	700±40	Beta-274729	Boat (coffin)	Closed	Mortuary	Duli 2013
Puang Leoran	700±40	Beta-274730	Boat (coffin)	Closed	Mortuary	Duli 2013
Buttu Mila	570±40	Beta-274733	Boat (coffin)	Closed	Mortuary	Duli 2013
Liang Datu	470±40	Beta-274734	Boat (coffin)	Closed	Mortuary	Duli 2013

Table A8.5: Accepted Holocene radiometric determinations from Southeast Sulawesi (all Carbon-14 unless otherwise stated).

Site	Date BP	Laboratory code	Dated material	Site aspect	Site use	Reference
Gua Lampetia	890±100	UW2870 (OSL)	Ceramic	Closed	Mortuary	Bulbeck et al. 2016
Gua Talimbue	8735±38	D-AMS 004042	Charcoal	Closed	Habitation	O'Connor et al. 2014
Gua Talimbue	8526±42	D-AMS 004040	Charcoal	Closed	Habitation	O'Connor et al. 2014
Gua Talimbue	8191±33	D-AMS 004039	Charcoal	Closed	Habitation	O'Connor et al. 2014
Gua Talimbue	7961±39	D-AMS 004038	Charcoal	Closed	Habitation	O'Connor et al. 2014
Gua Talimbue	6506±38	D-AMS 004037	Charcoal	Closed	Habitation	O'Connor et al. 2014
Gua Talimbue	6127±31	D-AMS 004036	Charcoal	Closed	Habitation	O'Connor et al. 2014
Gua Talimbue	5973±30	D-AMS 004035	Charcoal	Closed	Habitation	O'Connor et al. 2014

Site	Date BP	Laboratory code	Dated material	Site aspect	Site use	Reference
Gua Talimbue	5740±36	D-AMS 004034	Charcoal	Closed	Habitation	O'Connor et al. 2014
Gua Talimbue	3923±30	D-AMS 004032	Charcoal	Closed	Habitation	O'Connor et al. 2014
Gua Talimbue	3843±29	D-AMS 004031	Charcoal	Closed	Habitation	O'Connor et al. 2014
Gua Talimbue	3800±28	D-AMS 004033	Charcoal	Closed	Habitation	O'Connor et al. 2014
Gua Talimbue	3767±29	D-AMS 004029	Charcoal	Closed	Habitation	O'Connor et al. 2014
Gua Talimbue	3733±29	D-AMS 004030	Charcoal	Closed	Habitation	O'Connor et al. 2014
Gua Talimbue	3726±33	D-AMS 004041	Charcoal	Closed	Habitation	O'Connor et al. 2014
Gua Talimbue	3372±27	D-AMS 004028	Charcoal	Closed	Habitation	Bulbeck et al. 2016
Gua Talimbue	1710±20	SANU 40418	Human bone	Closed	Mortuary	Bulbeck et al. 2016
Gua Talimbue	347±26	D-AMS 004027	Charcoal	Closed	Habitation	Bulbeck et al. 2016
Gua Mo'o hono	5618±29	D-AMS 001627	Charcoal	Closed	Habitation	O'Connor et al. this volume
Gua Mo'o hono	5461±29	D-AMS 001625	Charcoal	Closed	Habitation	O'Connor et al. this volume
Gua Mo'o hono	5460±32	D-AMS 001621	Charcoal	Closed	Habitation	O'Connor et al. this volume
Gua Mo'o hono	5371±28	D-AMS 001619	Charcoal	Closed	Habitation	O'Connor et al. this volume
Gua Mo'o hono	5214±32	D-AMS 001626	Charcoal	Closed	Habitation	O'Connor et al. this volume
Gua Mo'o hono	3905±26	D-AMS 001616	Charcoal	Closed	Habitation	O'Connor et al. this volume
Gua Mo'o hono	3870±40	SANU 10573	Animal matter (tooth)	Closed	Habitation	O'Connor et al. this volume
Gua Mo'o hono	3865±29	D-AMS 001624	Charcoal	Closed	Habitation	O'Connor et al. this volume
Gua Mo'o hono	3452±26	D-AMS 001623	Charcoal	Closed	Habitation	Bulbeck et al. 2016
Gua Mo'o hono	450±24	D-AMS 001622	Charcoal	Closed	Habitation	Bulbeck et al. 2016
Gua Sambangoala	4923±30	D-AMS 001993	Charcoal	Closed	Habitation	Fakhri this volume
Gua Sambangoala	4802±26	D-AMS 001994	Charcoal	Closed	Habitation	Fakhri this volume
Gua Sambangoala	4766±31	D-AMS 001991	Charcoal	Closed	Habitation	Fakhri this volume
Gua Sambangoala	4482±28	D-AMS 001992	Charcoal	Closed	Habitation	Fakhri this volume
Gua Sambangoala	3925±29	D-AMS 001989	Charcoal	Closed	Habitation	Fakhri this volume
Gua Sambangoala	3883±29	D-AMS 001990	Charcoal	Closed	Habitation	Fakhri this volume
Gua Sambangoala	3297±29	D-AMS 001988	Charcoal	Closed	Habitation	Fakhri this volume
Gua Tengkorak	7239±36	D-AMS 009676	Charcoal	Closed	Habitation	Ugo Zoppi pers. comm.
Gua Tengkorak	7139±35	D-AMS 009675	Charcoal	Closed	Habitation	Ugo Zoppi pers. comm.

Table A8.6: Accepted Holocene radiometric determinations from the South Sulawesi southwest peninsula (all Carbon-14).

Site	Date BP	Laboratory code	Dated material	Site aspect	Site use	Reference
Bulubangi	270±140 BP	ANU-11853	Charcoal	Open	Mortuary	Druce et al. 2005
Allangkan-anangnge ri Latanete	955±30 (AMS)	Wk-19966	Animal matter (marine shell)*	Open	Habitation	Bulbeck et al. this volume
Allangkan-anangnge ri Latanete	820±60	ANU 11352	Animal matter (marine shell)*	Open	Habitation	Bulbeck and Caldwell 2008
Allangkan-anangnge ri Latanete	752±34 (AMS)	Wk-17818	Charcoal	Open	Industrial	Bulbeck et al. this volume
Allangkan-anangnge ri Latanete	364±25 (AMS)	Wk-29737	Charcoal	Open	Mortuary	Bulbeck et al. this volume
Tinco Tua	762±30 (AMS)	Beta-324215	Charcoal	Monumental	Ceremonial	Hasanuddin 2015
Tinco Tua	380±30 (AMS)	Beta-324216	Charcoal	Open	Habitation	Hasanuddin 2015
Tinco Tua	320±30 (AMS)	Beta-324217	Charcoal	Monumental	Ceremonial	Hasanuddin 2015
Mallawa	3580± 130	P3G-06	Charcoal	Open	Habitation	Simanjuntak 2008
Mallawa	2710± 170	P3G-06	Charcoal	Open	Habitation	Simanjuntak 2008
Mallawa	2490± 220	ANU 11276	Charcoal	Open	Habitation	Bulbeck 2004

Site	Date BP	Laboratory code	Dated material	Site aspect	Site use	Reference
Mallawa	2281±46	Wk-20380	Charcoal	Open	Habitation	Hakim et al. 2009
Mallawa	1860±70	ANU 11274	Charcoal	Open	Habitation	Bulbeck 2004
Mallawa	576±80	ANU 11275	Charcoal	Open	Habitation	Bulbeck 2004
Gua Pasaung	6026±70 (AMS)	Wk-20381	Charcoal	Closed	Habitation	Hakim et al. 2009
Ulu Leang 1	5740± 230	ANU 394	Charcoal	Closed	Habitation	Bulbeck et al. 2000
Ulu Leang 1	4390± 110	PRL-231	Charcoal	Closed	Habitation	Bulbeck et al. 2000
Ulu Leang 1	4050±90	HAR-1734	Charcoal	Closed	Habitation	Bulbeck et al. 2000
Ulu Leang 1	3550± 130	PRL-230	Charcoal	Closed	Habitation	Bulbeck et al. 2000
Ulu Leang 1	1490± 210	SUA-1080	Charcoal	Closed	Habitation	Bulbeck et al. 2000
Leang Burung 1	3420± 400	ANU 390	Charcoal	Closed	Habitation	Bulbeck et al. 2000
Leang Burung 1	2820± 210	ANU 391	Charcoal	Closed	Habitation	Bulbeck et al. 2000
Leang Burung 1	2260±90	ANU 6173	Human bone collagen	Closed	Mortuary	Bulbeck et al. 2000
Leang Burung 1	1660± 190	ANU 6174	Human bone collagen	Closed	Mortuary	Bulbeck et al. 2000
Leang Burung 1	1160± 200	ANU 6172	Human bone collagen	Closed	Mortuary	Bulbeck et al. 2000
Leang Burung 2	1665±80	T-9096	Charcoal	Closed	Habitation	Glover 1981
Leang Burung 2	1275± 5	Not stated	Charcoal	Closed	Habitation	Glover 1981
Leang Karassak	2690±60 (AMS)	Wk-3823	Charcoal	Closed	Habitation	Bulbeck et al. 2000
Leang Karassak	370±50 (AMS)	Wk-3824	Charcoal	Closed	Habitation	Bulbeck et al. 2000
Gua Batti	2928±26 (AMS)	Wk-30264	Charcoal	Closed	Habitation	Oktaviana et al. 2016
Lamuru	340±70	ANU 5922	Boat (coffin)	Open	Mortuary	Bulbeck 1992
Bayoa	270±120	ANU 5927	Boat (coffin)	Open	Mortuary	Bulbeck 1992
Bonto-Bontoa	170±55	OZE-130	Charcoal	Open	Gardening	Bulbeck and Fadillah 2000
Galesong	1910±90 (AMS)	Oxford	Ceramic	Open	Ceremonial	Glover 1997
Near Galesong	1640±70 (AMS)	Not stated	Ceramic	Open	Ceremonial	Glover 1997
Bayoa, Sanrabone	780±80	ANU 5564	Boat (coffin)#	Open	Mortuary	Bulbeck 1992
Batu Ejayya 1	4430±50 (AMS)	Wk-5464	Marine shell*	Closed	Habitation	Bulbeck et al. 2000
Batu Ejayya 1	4370±70 (AMS)	Wk-5465	Marine shell*	Closed	Habitation	Bulbeck et al. 2000
Batu Ejayya 1	920±275	ANU 392	Charcoal	Closed	Ceremonial	Bulbeck et al. 2000
Leang Batu Tunpa	500±33 (AMS)	Wk-15438	Human bone (dentine)	Closed	Mortuary	Bulbeck and Hakim 2005

*Calibrated using Marine 0.914c, applied correction factor for marine reservoir effect delta R 89±70 (Borneo), assuming 50% marine contribution.

#80 years subtracted from calibrated date to allow for 80 countable tree rings ('old wood effect') between radiocarbon-dated wood sample and tree heart.

9

The human occupation record of Gua Mo'o hono shelter, Towuti-Routa region of Southeastern Sulawesi

Sue O'Connor, David Bulbeck, Philip J. Piper, Fadhila Aziz, Ben Marwick, Fredeliza Campos, Jack Fenner, Ken Aplin, Fakhri, Suryatman, Tim Maloney, Budianto Hakim and Rachel Wood

Abstract

Here we describe the excavation, chronology and assemblage from Gua Mo'o hono, a rockshelter in the Lake Towuti region in Southeast Sulawesi. The excavation produced glass, ceramics and pottery, dense faunal and lithic assemblages and a diversity of bone tools. The Gua Mo'o hono sequence demonstrates that humans were active in and around the rockshelter from at least 6500 cal BP, and informs on early to late Holocene subsistence and technology in this region. Although the occupants of Gua Mo'o hono exploited a diverse range of fauna from a variety of habitats around the site, there appears to have been a particular focus on suids, both the babirusa and the Sulawesi warty pig.

Keywords: Gua Mo'o hono, Southeast Sulawesi, Holocene prehistory, pottery, stone artefacts, human remains, faunal remains, bone artefacts

Introduction

Excavation in caves and shelters in Sulawesi has largely been focused on the limestone karst region near Maros, which has a long history of investigation and has recently revealed some surprisingly early evidence for occupation as well as painted rock art dating back to the Pleistocene (Aubert et al. 2014). In 2012, we initiated a project to explore the Lake Towuti region in the southeastern arm of Sulawesi. As no previous research had been undertaken here, the project was designed with a broad brushstroke to encompass the human occupation record of this region from the Late Pleistocene to the Metal Age. During the course of the three-year project, five shelter and cave sites were tested with small excavations and new rock art was recorded in two of them (Bulbeck et al. 2016; Oktaviana et al. 2016). Three of the excavated sites were southeast of Lake Towuti near the small village of Walandawe: Gua Sambangoala, Gua Mo'o hono and Gua Talimbue (Figure 9.1). Here, we focus on the results of the excavation of Gua Mo'o hono, located about 90 km southeast of Lake Towuti. The excavation produced glass, ceramics and pottery, dense faunal and lithic assemblages and a diversity of bone tools.

Figure 9.1: Map showing location of excavated sites in Walandawe area, and inset showing location of Lake Towuti and Maros region.

Source: CartoGIS, College of Asia and the Pacific, The Australian National University.

Gua Mo'o hono excavation results

Site context and excavation methods

Gua Mo'o hono is a limestone rockshelter in Desa (Village) Walandawe, Kecamatan (Subdistrict) Routa, Kabupaten (District) Konawe Utara at coordinates 3°1'40.0"S 121°43'12.9"E (Figure 9.1). It is located at the edge of the Sungai Wiwirano river flats approximately 344 metres above sea level (m asl) (Figure 9.2). The floor area of the shelter runs approximately 20 m from northwest to southeast and has a maximum width of up to c. 5 m from the back wall to the drip line (Figures 9.3 and 9.4). The excavation was carried out in the central area of the shelter where the floor was highest. Towards the southeast, the floor slopes at about 10° to a slump zone where sediment is being actively eroded and lost through a fissure in the back wall into a deep cave below (Figure 9.4).

Figure 9.2: View of landscape on edge of the Sungai Wiwirano river flats.

Source: Photograph by Sue O'Connor.

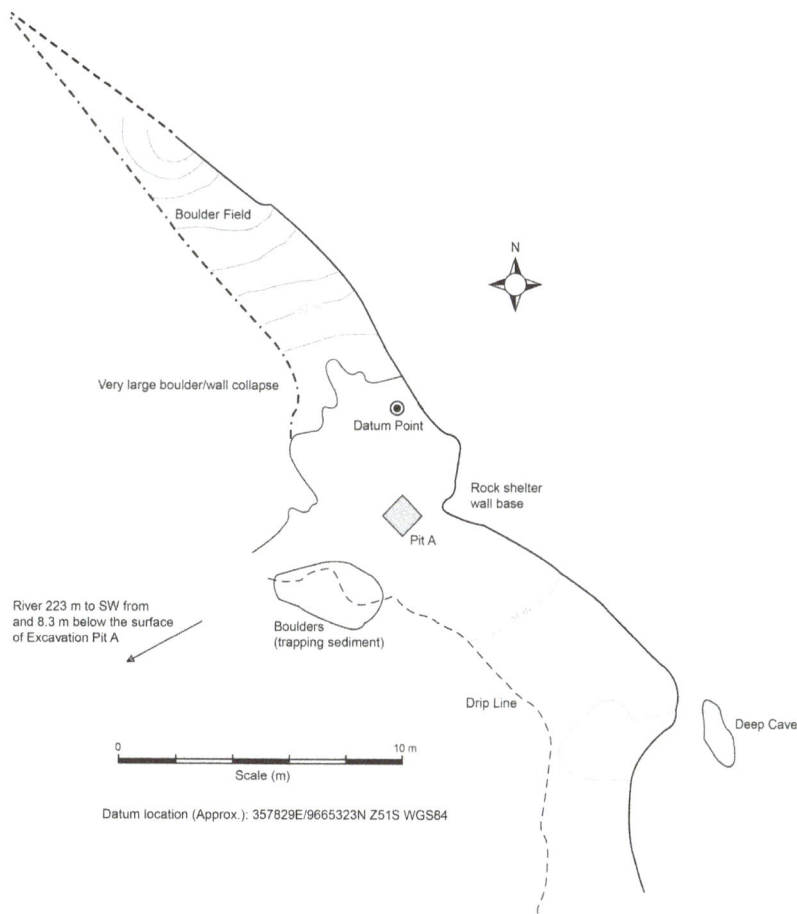

Figure 9.3: Plan of Gua Mo'o hono showing location of test pit and area of deep cavern.

Source: Plan prepared by Jack Fenner.

Figure 9.4: Gua Mo'o hono viewed from the northwest showing the location of the test pit and team member.

Source: Photograph by Sue O'Connor.

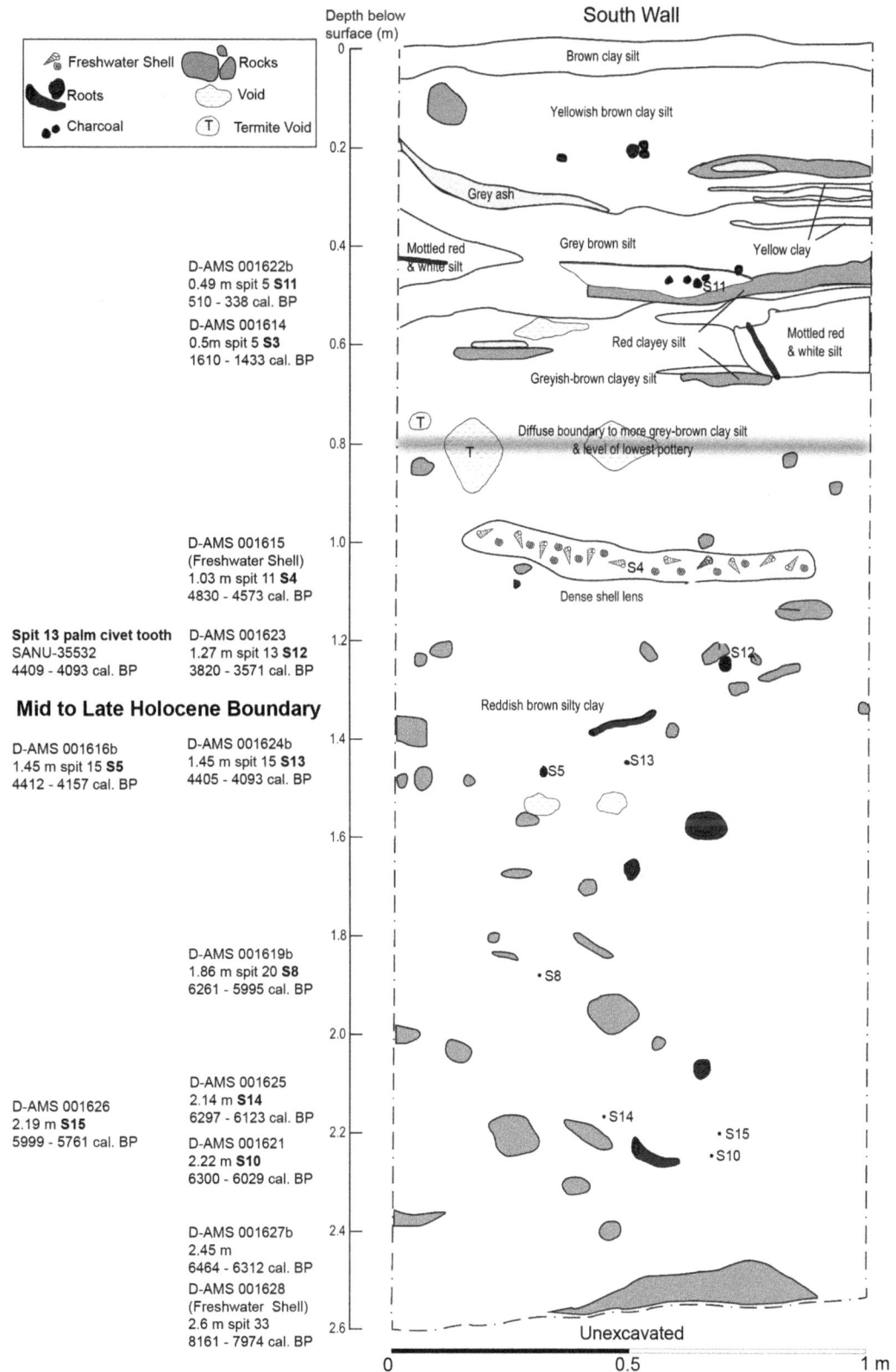

Figure 9.5: South section of Mo'o hono showing shell lenses, bioturbation features and location of dating samples.

Source: Section prepared by Ben Marwick.

In October 2012, a single 1 x 1 m² test pit (Test Pit A) was excavated in 33 spits to a depth of about 2.7 m (Figures 9.5 and 9.6). Spits of approximately 10 cm were excavated in the upper 1.5 m (Spits 1–18) (Figure 9.5). Below this, spits were approximately 5 cm in depth. Figure 9.7 shows this reflected in the weight of total deposit excavated per spit, including finds, loose sediment and rock. The lowest spits were even smaller in terms of volume of sediment excavated owing to the large rocks encountered in plan that could not be removed. The upper metre of the deposit consisted of compact, well-sorted sandy silt with several distinct lenses of ash, charcoal and reddened sediment and abundant freshwater gastropods. Below these the deposit graded into increasingly clayey silt with an increase in weathered igneous rock and limestone cobbles. Excavation stopped when large limestone boulders filled the square at 270 cm depth (Spit 33). It seems likely that the archaeological deposit continues below this, but further investigation would require extension of the excavation area.

Figure 9.6: Photo of south section of Gua Mo'o hono showing ash lenses and burnt earth features.

Source: Photograph by Sue O'Connor.

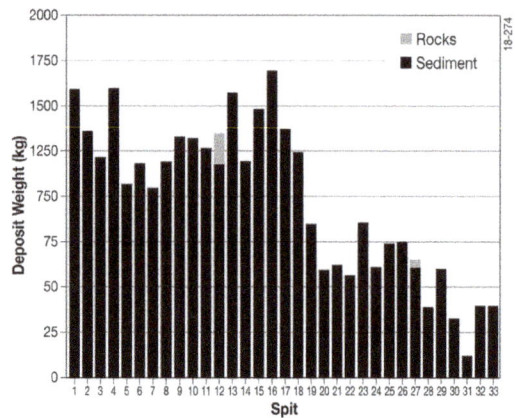

Figure 9.7: Weight of excavated deposit in Gua Mo'o hono by spit.

Source: Authors' data.

Chronology

The Gua Mo'o hono stratigraphy is anchored by a series of 22 radiocarbon dates, on charcoal and freshwater shell and one bone date (Table 9.1). The purpose of dating both freshwater shell and charcoal from the same test pit (and equivalent spits) was to determine if there is a standard difference in the calibrated ages that could be used as a correction factor for the shell ages. The difference between the intercepts of linear models computed for the ages determined from shell dates and those determined from charcoal is 933 years, indicating that the shell ages overestimate the true ages of deposit formation by about 1000 years.[1] As a result, the charcoal dates are taken here to provide the more reliable age estimate for the excavation sequence at Gua Mo'o hono (Table 9.1, in bold).

---

1   This is because during life the gastropods likely ingested radiometrically 'old' carbon from the surrounding karst limestone, dissolved in the stream water they inhabited (Spriggs 1989).

Table 9.1: Charcoal, freshwater shell and bone radiocarbon dates showing distribution of ceramics from Gua Mo'o hono Test Pit A excavation.

Lab. code	Depth below surface (m)	Excavation unit (spit)	Measured fraction	d(13C) per mil	pMC	1s error	14C age	Calibrated radiocarbon age 95.4%	Earthenware pottery
—	—	1	—	—	—	—	—	—	41 sherds, 51 grams
—	—	—	—	—	—	—	—	—	23 sherds, 27 grams
D-AMS 001612	0.23	3	Freshwater Shell	-8.6	87.17	0.23	1103±21	1047-1028 (6.4%) 982-926 (89.0%)	47 sherds, 32 grams
—	—	4	—	—	—	—	—	—	91 sherds, 146 grams
D-AMS 001622a	0.49	5	Freshwater Shell	-14.2	82.27	0.22	1568±21	1506-1500 (0.7%) 1484-1353 (94.7%)	
D-AMS 001622b	0.49	5	Charcoal	-15.9	94.55	0.28	450±24	510-449 (88.4%) 355-338 (7.0%)	118 sherds, 136 grams
D-AMS 001614	0.5	5	Freshwater Shell	-12.2	81.03	0.25	1690±25	1610-1417 (94.8%) 1440-1433 (0.6%)	
—	—	6	—	—	—	—	—	—	206 sherds, 255 grams
—	—	7	—	—	—	—	—	—	174 sherds, 159 grams
—	—	8	—	—	—	—	—	—	46 sherds, 75 grams
—	—	9	—	—	—	—	—	—	2 sherds, 8 grams
D-AMS 001615	1.03	11	Freshwater Shell	-12.6	59.27	0.23	4202±31	4830-4573	—
SANU-35532		13	Sulawesi Palm Civet Tooth				3870±40	4409-4142 (88.7%) 4127-4093 (6.7%)	
D-AMS 001623	1.27	13	Charcoal	-26.4	65.07	0.21	3452±26	3820-3794 (4.1%) 3761-3752 (0.9%) 3725-3571 (90.4%)	
D-AMS 001616a	1.45	15	Freshwater Shell	-0.6	55.5	0.25	4730±36	5580-5528 (14.5%) 5483-5315 (80.9%)	
D-AMS 001616b	1.45	15	Charcoal	-14.4	61.5	0.2	3905±26	4412-4223 (82.9%) 4205-4157 (12.5%)	
D-AMS 001624a	1.45	15	Freshwater Shell	-11.1	55.58	0.18	4718±26	5574-5550 (5.7%) 5474-5315 (89.7%)	

Lab. code	Depth below surface (m)	Excavation unit (spit)	Measured fraction	d(13C) per mil	pMC	1s error	^{14}C age	Calibrated radiocarbon age 95.4%	Earthenware pottery
D-AMS 001624b	**1.45**	**15**	**Charcoal**	**-26.5**	**61.81**	**0.22**	**3865±29**	4405-4367 (5.3%) 4357-4324 (5.9%) 4317-4142 (77.7%) 4126-4093 (6.5%)	—
D-AMS 001617	1.51	17	Freshwater Shell	-9.1	55.69	0.2	4702±29	5570-5558 (2.2%) 5471-5311 (93.2%)	—
D-AMS 001618	1.68	18	Freshwater Shell	-14.6	42.85	0.15	6808±28	7671-7575	—
D-AMS 001619a	1.86	20	Freshwater Shell	-9	44.35	0.15	6531±27	7464-7320	—
D-AMS 001619b	**1.86**	**20**	**Charcoal**	**-13.5**	**51.24**	**0.18**	**5371±28**	6261-6252 (1.3%) 6210-5995 (94.1%)	—
D-AMS 001625	**2.14**	**25**	**Charcoal**	**-21.9**	**50.67**	**0.18**	**5461±29**	6297-6178 (92.3%) 6145-6123 (3.1%)	—
D-AMS 001626	**2.19**	**27**	**Charcoal**	**-25.3**	**52.25**	**0.21**	**5214±32**	5999-5885 (87.8%) 5821-5761 (7.6%)	—
D-AMS 001620	2.22	27	Freshwater Shell	-15.8	42.6	0.17	6855±32	7703 - 7582	—
D-AMS 001621	**2.22**	**27**	**Charcoal**	**-20.6**	**50.68**	**0.2**	**5460±32**	6300-6176 (89.8%) 6150-6118 (4.7%) 6040-6029 (0.9%)	—
D-AMS 001627a	2.45	31	Freshwater Shell	-13.6	43.33	0.21	6718±39	7619-7461	—
D-AMS 001627b	**2.45**	**31**	**Organics**	**-19.9**	**49.69**	**0.18**	**5618±29**	6464-6312	—
D-AMS 001628	2.6	33	Freshwater Shell	-22	40.42	0.17	7277±34	8161-7974	—

Note: Excludes spits without corresponding radiocarbon dates or pottery. Dates were calibrated using OxCal version 4.2 (Bronk Ramsey et al. 2009) with the ShCal13 calibration curve (Hogg et al. 2013).

Source: Authors' data.

Based on radiometric dating and the material culture, the archaeological stratigraphy from Gua Mo'o hono can be split into three chronological phases, which permits the identification of changes in the archaeological record through time (Figure 9.5; Table 9.1). The upper eight spits (80 cm) can be distinguished from the rest of the stratigraphic sequence by the presence of pottery. This marks a distinctive change in material culture and perhaps human activity within the last 2000 years of occupation at the site. The sequence is also divided into those deposits below Spit 15 (125 cm) that can be confidently assigned to a mid-Holocene age beyond 4500 cal BP; and Spits 9–5 that were deposited in the later Holocene after 4500 cal BP, but before the introduction of pottery.

Sediments

Field observations and geoarchaeological analysis of the sediments at Gua Mo'o hono indicates that the deposit can be divided into three major depositional units (Appendices A and B; see also Figure 9.6). The upper unit is a crusty yellow-brown surface deposit of silt, probably formed by recent cattle trampling. This unit has high concentrations of soluble salts and organic matter, probably due to the contribution of animal waste and the limited exposure to weathering. The second unit contains several well-preserved hearth features with characteristic sequences of white ash, small lenses of black charcoal and red baked clay. This unit is also distinguished by higher pH values and concentrations of carbonate minerals and lower concentrations of soluble salts and organic matter. Shells were present in some of the hearths, often broken and burnt. This second unit is interpreted as a result of frequent human activity at the site, especially related to cooking and food preparation. Surrounding the hearths were yellow-brown to red silts and clayey silts. Below this unit was a massive red-brown clayey silt deposit with sparse limestone angular cobbles and rare river cobbles. This unit has higher concentrations of organic matter, lower pH values and concentrations of soluble salts. This lower unit probably formed by low energy surface water flow transporting fine sediments into the site. The undifferentiated structure of this deposit suggests that substantial bioturbation has occurred, most likely due to the growth of plant roots and termite burrowing.

Comparison of the dates with depth of deposit (Table 9.2) indicates that most of the excavated deposit accumulated during short intervals. The top 55 cm accumulated within 500 years, the 45 cm just below 1 m accumulated within 600 years, and the bottom metre within a millennium. There are two periods whose chronology is poorly documented, corresponding to Spits 6–10 and 15–16. These may reflect periods of slow deposition or, alternatively, they may bracket gaps of up to two millennia in the depositional sequence.

Table 9.2: Summary of the Gua Mo'o hono sedimentary sequence.

Spits	Depth	Approximate age span	Summary description of sediments
1-5	0-55 cm	0-500 BP	Compacted upper topsoil, hearth features
6-10	55 cm – 1.05 m	>500 BP, <3400 BP	Hearth features in brown sediment
11-14	1.05-1.5 m	3400-4500 BP	Massive red-brown clayey silt
15-16	1.5-1.65 m	>4500 BP, <6000 BP	Massive red-brown clayey silt
17-33	1.65-2.60 m	6000-6500/7000 BP	Massive red-brown clayey silt

Source: Authors' analysis.

Imported ceramics and glass

A rim sherd from a European creamware bowl of about 150 years antiquity was recovered in Spit 1. The stoneware body is white and the crackled glaze is pale yellow. Spit 2 produced a curved sherd of greenish-black bottle glass, weighing around 0.4 g. It would be of a similar age to the European creamware sherd. Spit 6 produced a very small sherd from a Chinese blue-and-white porcelain. A dash of greyish-blue decoration is visible both exteriorly and interiorly, beneath the light greenish-grey glaze. The fabric where freshly exposed is pinkish white. This sherd is too small to be firmly diagnostic but may be of Ming antiquity.

Earthenware

A total of 748 earthenware sherds weighing 889 g were recovered from Gua Mo'o hono (Table 9.1). Only 111 of these sherds were recovered from Spits 1 to 3, which may reflect occasional use of the shelter in recent centuries by villagers within the site's vicinity.[2] The majority of the pottery spanned Spits 4 to 8, and the two small sherds from Spit 9 almost certainly reflect vertical displacement from the pottery concentrations higher in the profile. Even the lowest sherds are 40 cm above the 4th millennium cal BP date, which corresponded to Spit 13 (Table 9.1). Most of the identifiable vessel forms are jars, but a box rim was observed in Spit 5. As described below, the earthenware assemblage is variable, but there are few clear differences between the sherds in the uppermost and the lower pottery-bearing spits. In summary, it would appear to be a 'Metal Phase' assemblage dating to within the last 2000 years.

Approximately half of the sherds have no macroscopically visible inclusions in their fabric, except perhaps a sparse presence of white, sand-sized particles ('No inclusions' in Table 9.3). Where these white particles (presumably limestone grit) were more prominent, the fabric can be classified as 'white sandy' (18% of sherds), and where the white inclusions were larger, the fabric can be classified as 'white granular' (14% of sherds). A 'grey ware' fabric was also recognised on the basis of a cream to light greyish fabric colour, a relatively rough texture and occasional dark-red to black inclusions (11%). These four fabric varieties occurred essentially throughout the pottery sequence. A small number of sherds with conspicuous red grains in their fabric were also recorded in Spits 5 and 6.

Table 9.3: Fabric varieties recorded for Gua Mo'o hono Test Pit A earthenware pottery (sherds).

Spit	Fabric variety					Decorated sherds
	No inclusions	White sandy	White granular	Grey ware (rough texture, sparse dark inclusions)	Red grained	
1	16 (39%)	5 (12%)	20 (49%)	—	—	7 (17%)
2	9 (39%)	6 (26%)	7 (30%)	1 (4%)	—	1 (4%)
3	34 (72%)	1 (1%)	11 (23%)	1 (4%)	—	1 (2%)
4	57 (63%)	13 (14%)	15 (16%)	6 (7%)	—	5 (5%)
5	74 (63%)	10 (8%)	25 (22%)	1 (1%)	8 (6%)	14 (12%)
6	118 (58%)	10 (4%)	7 (3%)	67 (33%)	4 (2%)	10 (5%)
7	72 (41%)	80 (46%)	14 (8%)	8 (5%)	—	15 (9%)
8	32 (70%)	6 (13%)	7 (15%)	1 (2%)	—	1 (2%)
9	—	2 (100%)	—	—	—	—
Total	412 (55%)	133 (18%)	106 (14%)	85 (11%)	12 (1%)	54 (7%)

Note: Fabric variety percentages (summed across) may not exactly sum to 100% due to rounding.

Source: David Bulbeck's laboratory data.

2   Gua Mo'o hono was first recorded by the anthropologists McWilliam and Lorenzen (2009) during their survey of the heritage resources of the Routa and Walandawe districts. They noted that the site had been occupied temporarily by the villagers of Walandawe while they were setting up their houses.

With both the 'no inclusions' sherds, and the assemblage in total, the exterior colour is brown for around 40%, dark brown to very dark brown for about 40%, reddish-brown for about 10%, and dark grey to very dark grey for about 10% (Table 9.4). The external surface of the white sandy sherds is more often brown (56%) than dark to very dark brown (20%), whereas the external surface of the white granular sherds is more often brown (59%) than dark to very dark brown (25%). 'Grey ware' sherds include a high proportion with a dark to very dark brown exterior surface (84%). Finally, the small collection of red-grained sherds includes 25% with a reddish-brown exterior surface and 17% with a red exterior surface.

Table 9.4: External colour of Gua Mo'o hono Test Pit A earthenware pottery (sherds).

Munsell colour (external surface)	Fabric variety					Total
	No inclusions	White sandy	White granular	Grey ware	Red grained	
Brown	152 (37%)	75 (56%)	62 (59%)	24 (28%)	4 (33%)	317 (42%)
Dark to very dark brown	171 (42%)	27 (20%)	26 (25%)	54 (84%)	2 (17%)	280 (37%)
Reddish-brown	44 (11%)	17 (13%)	7 (7%)	5 (6%)	3 (25%)	76 (10%)
Red	1 (<1%)	1 (1%)	1 (1%)	—	2 (17%)	5 (1%)
Greyish to dark greyish-brown	—	2 (2%)	3 (3%)	—	—	5 (1%)
Dark to very dark grey	41 (10%)	11 (8%)	6 (6%)	2 (2%)	1 (8%)	61 (8%)
Black	3 (1%)	—	1 (1%)	—	—	4 (1%)
Total	412 (100%)	133 (100%)	106 (100%)	85 (100%)	12 (100%)	748 (100%)

Note: Percentages may not sum vertically to exactly 100% due to rounding.
Source: David Bulbeck's laboratory data.

The Gua Mo'o hono assemblage shows sufficient variety for more than one production centre to have been involved. Whether there were multiple production centres, and whether there were changes over time in terms of the contribution of these centres to the Gua Mo'o hono assemblage, would require chemical analysis of the sherds to determine. However, there is firm evidence for chronological change in the surface treatment of the pottery (Table 9.5). Around 13% of the sherds had a lustrous external finish that would seem to have resulted from application of dammar resin (Figure 9.8B) (Bulbeck et al. 2016). The proportion of sherds treated this way was 17–39% in the uppermost and bottom spits, contrasting with 0–9% in Spits 3 to 6. The middle of the pottery sequence included the only sherds with definite or possible red slipping on their external surface. This was particularly pronounced in Spit 5 (Figure 9.8E–H) where 18% of the sherds were clearly or possibly red-slipped. Dammar coating and red slipping were recorded for all fabric varieties, with the single exception that none of the small assemblage of red-grained sherds presented signs of dammar coating. Finally, there is also some indication of a trend to increased burnishing of the pottery's external surface over time.

Table 9.5: External surface treatment of Gua Mo'o hono Test Pit A earthenware sherds.

Spit	Dammar coated	Red slipped	Possibly red-slipped	Burnished	No special treatment	Total
1	16 (39%)*	—	—	10 (24%)	15 (37%)*	41 (100%)
2	7 (30%)	—	—	1 (4%)	15 (65%)*	23 (100%)
3	—	—	—	2 (4%)	45 (96%)*	47 (100%)
4	8 (9%)*	—	1 (1%)	4 (4%)	78 (86%)*	91 (100%)
5	2 (2%)	14 (12%)*	6 (5%)	1 (1%)	95 (80%)	118 (100%)
6	9 (4%)	1 (1%)	1 (1%)	1 (1%)	194 (94%)*	206 (100%)
7	49 (28%)*	—	2 (1%)	—	123 (71%)*	174 (100%)
8	8 (17%)	—	—	—	38 (83%)*	46 (100%)
9	—	—	—	—	2 (100%)*	2 (100%)
Total	99 (13%)	15 (2%)	10 (1%)	19 (3%)	605 (81%)	748 (100%)

* Recorded for at least one sherd from every fabric variety in the spit.

Note: Percentages may not sum horizontally to exactly 100% due to rounding.

Source: David Bulbeck's laboratory data.

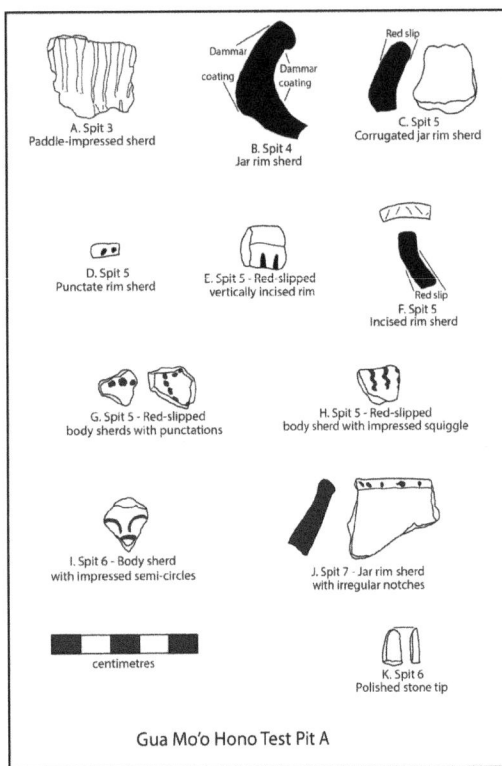

Figure 9.8: Gua Mo'o hono decorated pottery and rims (A-J) and polished stone tip (K).

Source: David Bulbeck's laboratory notes.

As for forming techniques, approximately 20% of the sherds were recorded as having traces of internal dimpling and/or external paddle-impressed designs (Figure 9.8A), which would appear to reflect use of a paddle and anvil in forming or at least finishing the vessels. Sherds with these characteristics were recorded for every spit, and also for 17–33% of all fabric varieties (Table 9.6). Wheel lines were observed on nine sherds, including the only identified sherd from a cover, and otherwise a small proportion of the rim, neck, shoulder and body sherds. These wheel lines appear to reflect the occasional use of a slow wheel to finish vessels prior to being fired. Of particular interest are 16 sherds with a ribbed rim, or diamond or quadrilateral designs on the body, that appear to have been achieved by pressing the clay into a mould, such as a basketry casing, although they could possibly be produced by the use of a stamp (Figure 9.9). Sherds from these vessels were recorded in Spits 1, 6, 7 and 8. Finally, the majority of the sherds did not present a clear indication of how they were formed (Table 9.6), but it probably involved some use of a paddle in a way that did not leave obvious traces of the manufacturing method involved.

Table 9.6: Forming techniques observed on Gua Mo'o hono Test Pit A earthenware pottery (sherds).

Production technique	Fabric variety					Total
	No inclusions	White sandy	White granular	Grey ware	Red grained	
Paddle and anvil	72 (18%)	22 (17%)	35 (33%)	25 (29%)	2 (17%)	156 (21%)
Slow wheel	6 (2%)	—	2 (2%)	—	1 (8%)	9 (1%)
Moulded/stamped	4 (1%)	9 (7%)	3 (3%)	—	—	16 (2%)
No observations	330 (80%)	102 (77%)	66 (62%)	60 (71%)	9 (75%)	567 (76%)
Total	412 (100%)	133 (100%)	106 (100%)	85 (100%)	12 (100%)	748 (100%)

Note: Percentages may not sum vertically to exactly 100% due to rounding.

Source: David Bulbeck's laboratory data.

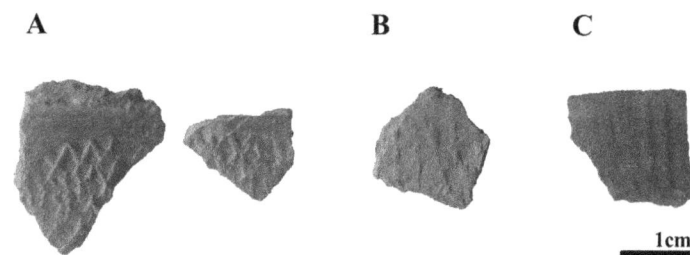

Figure 9.9: Gua Mo'o hono decorated pottery.

A) White sandy earthenware shoulder sherds with mould or stamp produced diamond designs, Spit 7. B) White sandy earthenware body sherd with mould or stamp produced quadrilateral design, Spit 8. C) High-fired, white granular earthenware rim sherd with mould-produced external ribbing, Spit 6.

Source: Photograph by David Bulbeck.

Around 7% of the sherds were decorated, with a variety of techniques. In addition to the moulded/stamped designs recorded from Spits 1 to 8, paddle-impressed designs (Figure 9.8A) were recorded from Spits 1 to 7. This was the most common decoration technique, recorded on 20 of the 54 decorated sherds (37%). Other recorded techniques include incised horizontal, vertical and slanting lines (Figure 9.8E–F), recorded in Spits 5 and 6; impressed diamonds, squiggles and semi-circles, recorded in Spits 4 to 6 (Figure 9.8H–I); punctate circles in Spit 5 (Figure 9.8D and 9.8G); notches, recorded in Spits 5 and 7 (Figure 9.8J); vertical gouges, recorded in Spit 1; a corrugated rim in Spit 5; and a bossed rim in Spit 7.

Polished stone artefacts

Spit 6 produced a polished stone tip, 11 mm long, 5 mm wide and 3 mm thick (Figure 9.8K). The stone is fine and siliceous, and dark brown with traces of banding. Spit 6 also produced a rim fragment to a polished stone container, weighing 22 g (Figure 9.10). The extant shape is more consistent with a square box than a curved jar. Rim thickness is approximately 12 cm, although thickness increased beneath the rim up to 17 mm.

Figure 9.10: Gua Mo'o hono stone box rim fragment, internal view Spit 6.

Source: Photograph by David Bulbeck.

Flaked stone artefacts

Approximately 13,506 flaked stone artefacts were recovered from Gua Mo'o hono (Figure 9.11; Table 9.7). The artefacts are almost entirely manufactured from nodules of high-quality chert, typical of other assemblages in Sulawesi. Very small amounts of white quartz and chalcedony are also present. The flake assemblage reflects extensive reduction with little to no cortex remaining on most pieces. The median mass of complete flakes is 1 g and shows no significant changes between spits. The median mass of cores is 13 g and also shows no significant change over time. There are two broken cobbles of coarse-grained igneous material with pitting on their flat surface, indicating use as anvils. A further two cobbles have been bifacially flaked, one with extensive polish, indicating the use of grinding to sharpen the working edge (Spit 11).

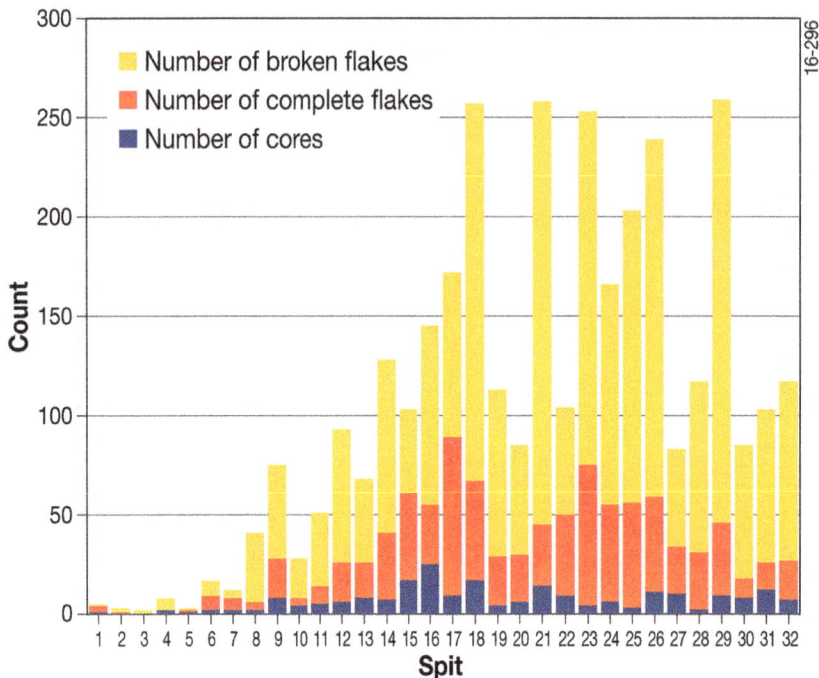

Figure 9.11: Number of cores, flakes and broken flakes in Gua Mo'o hono by spit.

Source: Ben Marwick's laboratory data.

Table 9.7: Counts of flaked stone artefacts in each spit.

Spit	Number of complete flakes	Number of broken flakes	Number of cores
1	3	1	1
2	1	2	0
3	0	2	0
4	0	6	2
5	1	1	1
6	7	8	2
7	6	4	2
8	4	35	2
9	20	47	8
10	4	20	4
11	9	37	5
12	20	67	6
13	18	42	8

Spit	Number of complete flakes	Number of broken flakes	Number of cores
14	34	87	7
15	44	42	17
16	30	90	25
17	80	83	9
18	50	190	17
19	25	84	4
20	24	55	6
21	31	213	14
22	41	54	9
23	71	178	4
24	49	111	6
25	53	147	3
26	48	180	11
27	24	49	10
28	29	86	2
29	37	213	9
30	10	67	8
31	14	77	12
32	20	90	7

Source: Ben Marwick's laboratory data.

Bayesian change point analysis indicates that the majority of artefacts were discarded between Spits 18 to 29, with very few in the pottery-bearing spits (1–8). The low level of lithic discard in the more recent spits is probably because of the appearance of other technologies such as metal and ceramics. The interval of highest discard corresponds to calibrated dates of around 6000–6300 cal BP (Table 9.1), indicating a relatively short period for the deposition of most of the artefacts at this site. Curiously, this period overlaps with the peak of Maros points in Ulu Leang site in South Sulawesi (Glover and Presland 1985), suggesting this was a time when stone artefact production was high across Sulawesi.

Retouched stone artefacts

Retouched tools are rare, comprising <1% of the assemblage (n = 31) and show no recurring formal types. Retouching is most frequently found around the distal region of flakes. Notches and beak-like retouch are present on scrapers but rare. Notable absences from the Gua Mo'o hono assemblage are the geometric microliths and other backed artefacts that characterise the Toalean assemblages of South Sulawesi (Bulbeck et al. 2000). Maros points, with their distinctive isosceles triangular shape, denticulate or biface edges and hollow base (Glover and Presland 1985) were not found in the Gua Mo'o hono assemblage. The absence of these forms of stone artefacts from this site lends some support to the claim by Bulbeck et al. (2000) that the Toalean assemblages may have been made only by a group localised to the southwest of the South Sulawesi peninsula and perhaps culturally and linguistically distant from communities occupying other parts of Sulawesi including the occupants of Gua Mo'o hono.

Figure 9.12 shows a representative selection of retouched stone artefacts from Gua Mo'o hono. Artefact 12(a) from Spit 9 is retouched around the entire perimeter of the piece. The retouch is steep, multiple-layered, feather-terminated scars, overlain by small crushing fractures in many parts of the margin. These traces are consistent with deliberate shaping and resharpening of the artefact combined with probable use-wear damage on some parts of the margin. It features an unusual tang or waist geometry formed by two asymmetric notches. Small crushing fractures are visible in the notches, suggesting they were edges used to perform work, such as shaving wood. In light of this use-wear in the notches, the asymmetric relationship of the notches, and the thickness of the artefact, the tang-like appearance of this artefact is probably coincidental and does not indicate that the piece was a hafted point. Artefact 12(b) shows the same combination of retouch and use-wear as Artefact 12(a), with small, steep, overlapping feather-terminated scars overlain by crushing use-wear, but the retouch is limited to part of one margin.

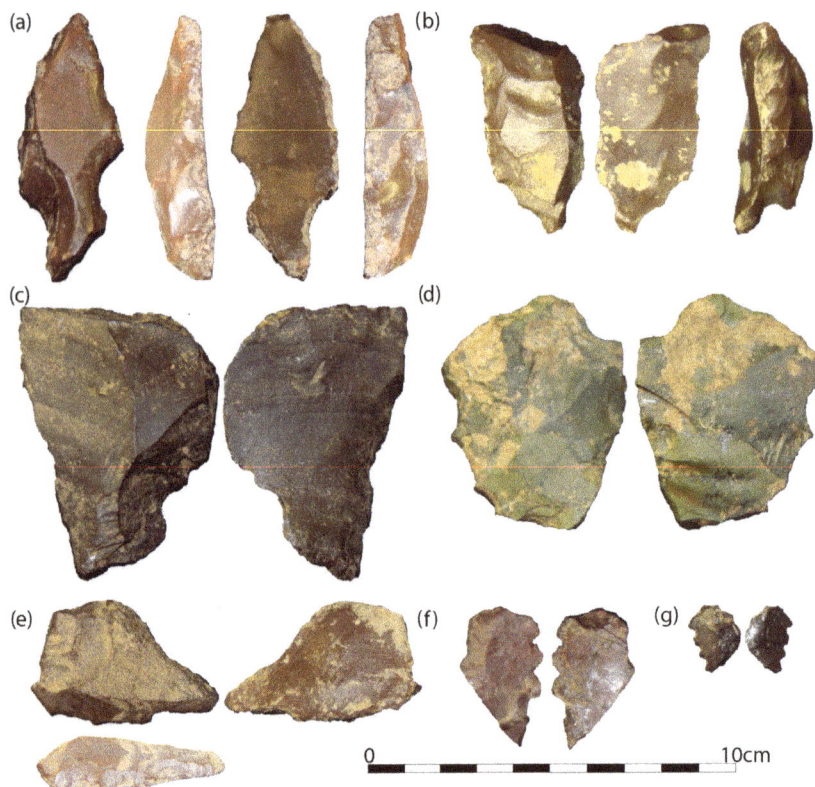

Figure 9.12: Selection of retouched artefacts from Gua Mo'o hono.
(a) Spit 9 (5005); (b) Spit 10 (5009); (c) Spit 27 (2111); (d) Spit 11 (0035); (e) Spit 9 (5004); (f) Spit 9 (5009); (g) Spit 8 (5003).
Source: Photograph by Ben Marwick.

Artefacts 12(a), (b) and (e) were recovered from Spits 9 and 10, the two spits that contained the most retouched pieces. Artefact 12(e) shows a pattern of retouch similar to 12(a) and (b), but is an end-scraper, with the retouched edge located on the distal margin of the flake, which is the longest margin on this flake. Artefact 12(c) was found in Spit 27, and is among the earliest retouched pieces at Gua Mo'o hono (the earliest appeared in Spit 32). Artefact 12(c) shows a slightly different approach to retouch with retouch flakes removed off the ventral and dorsal surfaces of the artefact, rather than only the dorsal surface, as seen on Artefacts 12(a) and (b). Artefact 12(c) has a small notch on the dorsal surface, and on the opposite margin a short length of retouch following the same pattern as the other artefacts. The raw material is a siliceous bedded sedimentary rock, and a small area of cortex is present, unlike the majority of retouched pieces, which are highly siliceous chert with no cortex. This piece illustrates some of the diversity among the retouched pieces, suggesting that the selection of nodules for flaking and retouching was not tightly constrained. Artefact 12(d) from Spit 11 further demonstrates this diversity with a series of shallow notches along one margin. Artefacts 12(f) and (g), from Spits 8 and 9, also show notching on a single margin similar to Artefact 12(d). The notches on Artefacts 12(f) and 12(g) are deeper and more concave, suggesting the edges of these artefacts were serrated to use as a saw-like tool.

Cores

Most cores are made from chert, and all show signs of extensive reduction, with an average 10% cortex. They are typically very small, with an average mass around 24 g, and most appear to be broken, with truncated scars on many pieces. Most cores have single or multiple platforms, with a small number of radial and prismatic cores. Bipolar anvil-rested reduction techniques are evident in the form of flake scars with opposing initiations and crushing at both ends. The overall impression we have from the cores discarded at the site is that raw material nodules were probably small when they were acquired, sourced from small fragmented seams and outcrops near the site, and flaking continued until the cores were too small to easily manage. The use of bipolar techniques represents efforts by the knappers to extend the useful life of the cores beyond what can be easily managed by freehand direct percussion (Hiscock 2015).

Figure 9.13 shows a sample of cores from Gua Mo'o hono. Artefacts 13(a), 13(b), and 13(e) show flake scars of small blade-like removals, but 13(a) and 13(c) also show aberrant terminations, suggesting that the core was at a stage where the knapper found it difficult to remove complete flakes. Artefacts 13(b) and 13(e) display bipolar traces, with flake removals initiated from the top and bottom of the core. Artefact 13(e) also has a third platform orthogonal to the bipolar axis. Artefact 13(d) shows a truncated ventral surface, where a relatively large flake was broken and then the ventral surface used as a platform for flake removals. This technique is rare in this assemblage, but has been documented elsewhere in Indonesia, such as Jerimalai (Marwick, pers. observation) and Liang Bua (Moore et al. 2009). Artefact 13(f) is similarly a flake fragment that has subsequently had some small flakes removed. Taken together, the signs of extensive reduction on these cores indicate that raw material conservation was a high priority in using stone at this location.

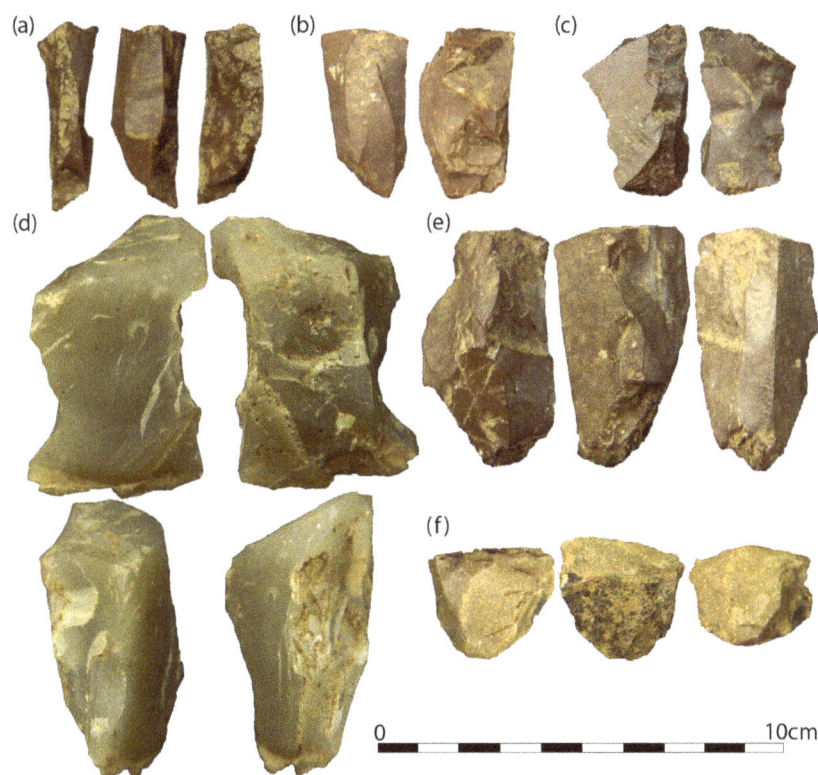

Figure 9.13: Selection of cores from Gua Mo'o hono.
(a) Spit 32 (5026); (b) Spit 15 (1031; (c) Sit 9 (1009); (d) Spit 11 (1016); (e) Spit 18 (1021); (f) Spit 18 (1025).
Source: Photograph by Ben Marwick.

Human remains

Of considerable interest are the fragmentary human remains from Spits 19, 23 and 26, at a stratigraphic level corresponding to around 6000 cal BP (Table 9.1). Including a deciduous first molar from Spit 14, a minimum number of three individuals are represented. An attempt to directly date the mandible from Spit 19 was abandoned when an assay by Rachel Wood determined that the carbon content would probably be too low to produce a reliable determination.

Two joining fragments from an adult human mandible were recovered from Spit 19 (Figure 9.14). The extant mandible is small, as can be seen by comparing its available measurements with those of other Sulawesi mandibles (Table 9.8), and so is probably female. The mandible is gracile in terms of the anatomical features described by Larnach and Macintosh (1971). The mental trigone, submental notch, *fossa mentalis*, basal trigone, anterior marginal tubercle and superior transverse torus are all slight. Additional features recorded in the chin region include medium anterior incurvature, a slightly declined alveolar plane, small genial spines and the absence of a genial pit.

Figure 9.14: Gua Mo'o hono mandible fragment with Spit 19 first left lower molar fitted into place.
Source: Photograph by David Bulbeck.

Table 9.8: Measurements on the Gua Mo'o hono mandible fragment.

Measurement[a]	Gua Mo'o hono	Toaleans[b]	Sulawesi males[c]	Sulawesi females[c]
Chin height (h1)	27	32	30.0 (22–36)	28
Symphysis height	28	—	31.1 (23–37)	31.1 (28.5–34.5)
Symphysis thickness	12	—	14.2 (12–15.5)	13.6 (11–16.5)
Height at first premolar (p1h)	28	31	31.9 (29–35)	27.3 (24.5, 30)
Corpus height at mental foramen (M69(1))	~29	30.5–31.5	28.9 (25–33)	26.3 (24–29)
Corpus thickness at mental foramen (M69(3))	12	11–14	12.5 (9–17)	11.0 (9.5–13)
Bimental breadth (zz)	~40	48	47.8 (44.5–55)	41.7 (38–45)

(a) Definitions: h1, p1h, zz (Morant 1923); symphysis height and thickness (Brown 1989); M69(1) and M69(3) (Bräuer 1988).

(b) Two mid-Holocene mandibles from Southwest Sulawesi (Bulbeck 2004).

(c) Ethnographic museum specimens and archaeological sites less than 1500 years old—maximum sample size 16 ♂, 5 ♀, Bulbeck (unpublished).

Source: David Bulbeck's laboratory data.

The alveoli are present for all of the incisors, both canines and the left first premolar, which had evidently been lost prior to the individual's death. The left second premolar appears to have been recently sheared off, but no trace of it was found in the excavated material. However, a left mandibular first molar from Spit 19, whose moderate tooth wear corresponds to Smith's stage 4 (Hillson 1996:Figure 11.1), can be fitted back onto the mandible.

The teeth from Spits 23 and 26 represent a minimum of two individuals. Eight of the nine teeth from Spit 23, and the tooth from Spit 26, are extremely worn, with degrees of occlusal wear between Smith's stages 5 and 7 (Hillson 1996:Figure 11.1). They would appear to represent an adult of moderate to advanced age, depending on the rate of occlusion experienced by this mid-Holocene forager. Accordingly, in most cases tooth size could be gauged only by taking the diameters at the cemento-enamel junction (Table 9.10). Fortunately, the ethnohistorical Gua Andomo and Gua Lampetia burials (Bulbeck et al. 2016) were also recorded for their tooth diameters at the cemento-enamel junction, allowing a comparison to be made. There was also a right second premolar tooth bud recovered from Spit 23, corresponding to a child of about five years of age (cf. Hillson 1996).

The available metrical data do not allow for a clear distinction in tooth size between the study region's mid-Holocene and ethnohistorical inhabitants (Tables 9.9 and 9.10). In some cases, the mid-Holocene tooth diameter lies above the ethnohistorical range, as in the P^2 length and the cemento-enamel junction diameters for the lower incisors and the M^1 length. However, there are also cases where the mid-Holocene tooth diameter falls below the ethnohistorical range, as in the M^2 cemento-enamel junction breadth.

Table 9.9: Gua Mo'o hono occlusal diameters (mm) compared with the Gua Lampetia/Gua Andomo means and ranges.

Tooth	Diameter	Gua Mo'o hono spits			Gua Lampetia/Gua Andomo		
		19	23	26	Sample size	Mean	Range
P^2	Mesio-distal length		8.5		8	7.0	6.5–7.6
	Bucco-lingual breadth		9.3		8	9.5	9.1–10.5
M_2	Mesio-distal length	11.0			12	11.2	10.0–11.7
	Bucco-lingual breadth	11.0		9.3	12	10.3	9.7–10.6

Source: David Bulbeck's laboratory data.

Table 9.10: Gua Mo'o hono diameters at the cemento-enamel junction (mm) compared with the Gua Lampetia/Gua Andomo means and ranges.

Tooth	Diameter	Gua Mo'o hono spits			Gua Lampetia/Gua Andomo		
		19	23	26	Sample size	Mean	Range
I_1	Mesio-distal length		5.4		8	4.3	3.8–4.8
	Bucco-lingual breadth		7.8		7	6.3	5.9–7.6
$I_2^{(a)}$	Mesio-distal length		5.1		10	4.4	3.5–5.1
	Bucco-lingual breadth		7.4		10	5.9	5.5–6.6
M_1	Mesio-distal length		9.5		8	10.4	9.5–10.9
	Bucco-lingual breadth		9.1		8	9.8	9.1–10.6
M_2	Mesio-distal length	10.0	9.7		11	9.9	9.2–10.7
	Bucco-lingual breadth	9.6	8.8	8.5	11	9.6	8.5–10.5
M_3	Mesio-distal length		9.4		2	9.5	8.9–10.1
M^1	Mesio-distal length		9.6		8	8.6	8.0–9.5
	Bucco-lingual breadth		10.4		8	11.3	10.3–12.4
M^2	Mesio-distal length		9.5		9	8.3	7.0–9.6
	Bucco-lingual breadth		9.7		9	11.0	10.0–13.0

(a) Both right and left lower second incisors are present, with identical measurements.

Source: David Bulbeck's laboratory data.

Fauna: Freshwater gastropods

Freshwater gastropods were found throughout the Gua Mo'o hono sequence and in places occurred in dense lenses (Figure 9.5 south section). Shell was most abundant in the upper units and decreased in the red-brown clayey silt no doubt due to poor preservation with depth (Figure 9.15).

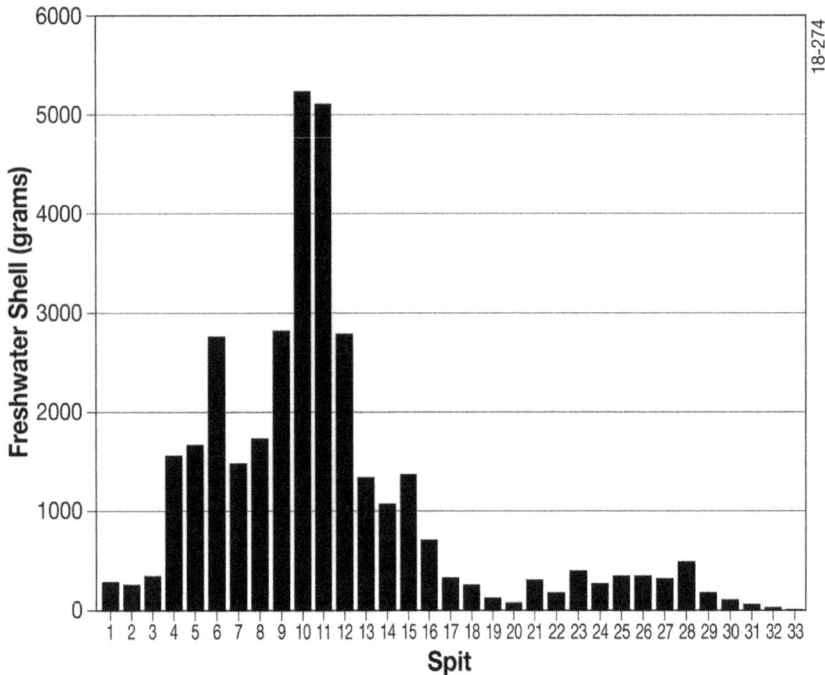

Figure 9.15: Gua Mo'o hono freshwater shell (weight shown by spit).
Source: Authors' data.

A component of the recovered shell was heavily burnt, making identification to species difficult. Shell quantities decreased with depth in layers where the bone appeared heavily burnt and some of the shell associated with presumed hearths contained fragments of burnt shell. The process of burning is likely to be incidental rather than from cooking the gastropods as the shell is so heavily burnt that the process has clearly been destructive. Most of the shell exhibits broken or fractured apices. This pattern may be the result of detaching the apex to extract the meat for consumption.

Two species were identified as dominating the samples (99.9%). Both of these species probably occur in pools in the river adjacent to the site. One is a species of *Tylomelania* (*Tylomelania* sp.). There are both smooth- and ribbed-shelled specimens in this variable species (Thomas von Rintelen, pers. comm., 2014). The other species is *Melanoides tuberculata*. This species is less abundant than *Tylomelania*; however, it was not possible to completely separate the two species as *Melanoides* specimens can be confused with smaller specimens of *Tylomelania* if the shells are incomplete, as many in the deposit are (Thomas von Rintelen, pers. comm., 2014).

Vertebrate fauna

The bone assemblage was analysed at the Department of Archaeology and Natural History, The Australian National University, Canberra, between May and July 2013, and has since been returned to Balai Arkeologi Makassar, Makassar, where it has been curated for long-term preservation. The thorough recovery strategy that included sieving sediments through 1.5 mm mesh has resulted in the recovery and analysis of approximately 70,000 animal bones at Gua Mo'o hono, weighing almost 16 kg (Figure 9.16). The majority of these (over 98%) consisted of very small fragments of bone measuring less than 20 mm in length. The very small size of most bone fragments has strongly influenced the numbers of identifiable bones recorded in the assemblage with just 1.5% of the total assemblage (Number of Individual Specimens, NISP = 1223) identifiable to class or lower taxonomic level (Table 9.11). The rest were determined as ungulates (n=76) or intermediate/large mammals (n=29), and other small and unidentified vertebrates (n=28), while approximately 68,000 were categorised as indeterminate small fragments of animal bone.

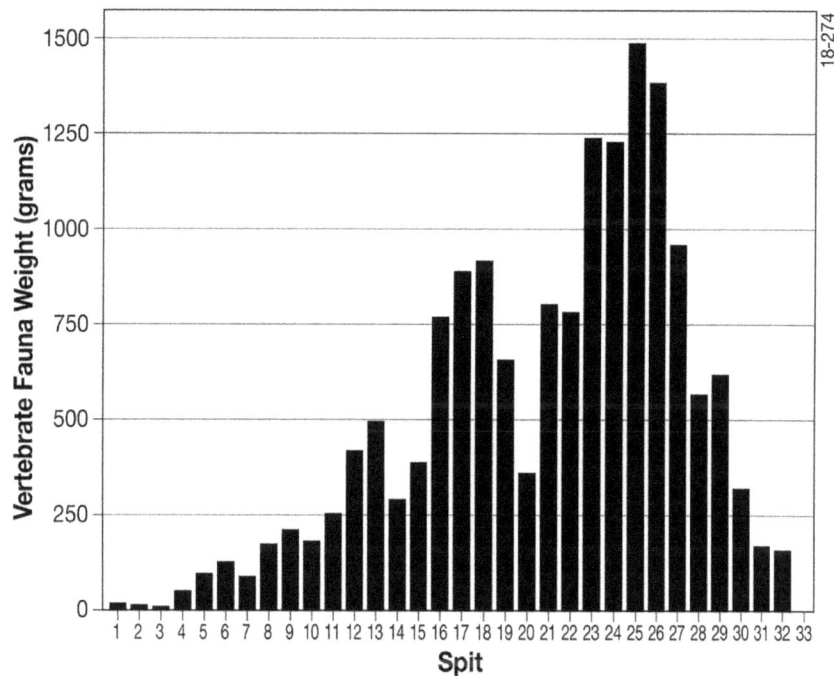

Figure 9.16: Gua Mo'o hono vertebrate fauna (weight shown by spit).

Source: Philip Piper's laboratory data.

Within the upper 80 cm (Spits 1–8, last c. 2000 years), bone fragments were typically light to dark brown in colour as a consequence of uptake of pigmentation from the surrounding dark soil matrices. Below this, there was an increased density of bone fragments, with increasing numbers of charred dark red/black (burnt) and blue/white-coloured (calcined) bones resulting from their exposure to heat at varying temperatures (see Lyman 1994). Below Spit 14, many bone fragments had been moderately or severely eroded, resulting in partial or complete loss of distinctive morphology. In the lower levels of excavation, in particular from Spit 27 down, only small burnt fragments of bone and teeth were recovered. This implies differential preservation of burnt and calcined bone fragments with depth at Gua Mo'o hono. Other common modifications that indicate some of the complex taphonomic processes involved in the preservation and destruction of bone on the site included longitudinal hairline surface cracking resulting from subsurface exposure to weathering prior to 'deep' burial, and rounding, polishing and loss of morphology. These latter types of modification are characteristic of bones either being transported by water, or by sediments suspended in flowing water passing over them and eroding surfaces (Behrensmeyer et al. 2000).

Butchery was rare in the highly fragmented and modified bone assemblage but evidence of extensive burning and the presence of shell and stone artefacts throughout, coupled with the degree of incidental burning on site indicate that people were the primary accumulators of the majority of large mammal remains. This interpretation is strengthened by the absence of any other large bone accumulators and/or scavengers on Sulawesi until the late Holocene introduction of the dog and Sunda porcupine (*Hystrix javanica*), and the lack of traces of gnawing on the fragments. The processes of accumulation of small vertebrate remains is a little more enigmatic; they could have resulted through natural accumulations of inhabitants of the rockshelter (bats), introduction of denizens of the local environment from in and around Gua Mo'o hono (mammals, reptiles and birds) by predators (e.g. Sulawesi civet cat), and/or human predation. The high proportion of murids within the late Holocene sequences might indicate a higher input of bones through natural processes of accumulation than in the mid-Holocene, where proportionately more large game was identified (Table 9.11).

Table 9.11: A provisional list of the different taxa identified in the zooarchaeological record of Gua Mo'o hono.

Class	Order	Family	Taxon	English Vernacular	Mid-Holocene	Later Holocene	Last c. 2000 years	Total
Osteichthyes	Anguilliformes	Anguillidae		Eels			4	4
				Bony fishes		4	18	22
Amphibia	Anura			Frogs and toads	20	12	10	42
Reptilia	Squamata	Gekkonidae		Geckos	1	1		2
		Varanidae	*Varanus* sp(p).	Monitor lizards	5	3	3	11
	Serpentes (suborder)	Pythonidae	*Python* sp.	Python		1		1
				Snakes[1]	91	73	33	197
Aves				Unidentified birds		2	12	14
Mammalia	Diprotodontia	Phalangeridae	*Ailurops ursinus*	Sulawesi bear cuscus	5	2		7
			Strigocuscus celebensis	Sulawesi dwarf cuscus	4			4
				Sulawesi marsupials[2]	4	7	5	16
	Megachiroptera (suborder)			Old world fruit bats		4		4
	Microchiroptera (suborder)			Insectivorous bats		4	1	5
	Chiroptera			Unidentified Bats	1	2		3
	Primates	Tarsiidae	*Tarsius* sp.	Tarsier	1			1
		Cercopithecidae	*Macaca* sp(p).	Sulawesi macaques	31	13	2	46
	Rodentia	Muridae	*Rattus hoffmanni*	Hoffmann's rat	4	3		7
			Rattus facetus	Elegant xanthurus rat		1	1	2
			Bunomys chrysocomus	Common Bunomys		1		1
			Bunomys andrewsi	Andrew's Bunomys		3	1	4
			Bunomys sp.	*Bunomys* species		1		1
			Lenomys meyeri	Meyer's Lenomys	2			2

Class	Order	Family	Taxon	English Vernacular	Mid-Holocene	Later Holocene	Last c. 2000 years	Total
			Paruromys dominator	Giant Sulawesi rat	3	1		4
			Taeromys celebensis	Long-tailed Taeromys		2		2
			Taeromys punicans	Sulawesi forest rat	1	1		2
			Maxomys musschenbroekii	Musschenbroek's Sulawesi Maxomys	2	2		4
			Maxomys hellwaldii	Hellwald's Sulawesi Maxomys		1		1
			Muridae	Rat-sized murids[3]	62	102	24	188
		Sciuridae		Squirrels			1	1
	Carnivora	Viverridae	*Macrogalidia musschenbroekii*	Sulawesi palm civet	2	1	1	4
				Unidentified viverrid		1	1	2
				Unidentified carnivore	1			1
	Artiodactyla	Suidae	*Babyrousa celebensis*	Sulawesi Babirusa	43	2	1	46
			Sus cf. *celebensis*	Celebes warty pig	28	3	1	32
			Suidae	Barbirusa/ Celebes warty pig	363	95	22	480
		Cervidae/ Bovinae		Undifferentiated deer or cattle	13	5		18
		Bovinae	*Bubalus* cf. *depressicornis*	Lowland Anoa	29	12	2	43
				TOTAL NISP	716	365	143	1224

1. Probably includes numerous specimens of python.

2. As yet undifferentiated into *Ailurops ursinus* (Sulawesi bear cuscus) and *Strigocuscus celebensis* (small Sulawesi cuscus).

3. Several species of rats are present but not yet fully studied—this includes *Rattus hoffmanni* (Hoffmann's rat) and *R. xanthurus* (yellow-tailed rat).

Source: Philip Piper's laboratory data.

By far the most common taxon represented in the zooarchaeological record from Gua Mo'o hono is Suidae (NISP = 561). Pigs are present throughout the archaeological sequence from the earliest phases to the subsurface levels. The endemic suid taxa, the babirusa (*Babyrousa celebensis*; NISP = 50) (Figure 9.17A) and the Celebes warty pig (*Sus celebensis*; NISP = 33) (Figure 9.17B) are present (easily separable on the shape and morphology of the canines and premolars). Provisional biometric analyses of the upper and lower molars suggest that these are the only two pig taxa represented. Notably we have found no firm evidence of the remains of any introduced domestic pigs (*S. scrofa*) in the site.

A

5mm

B

5mm

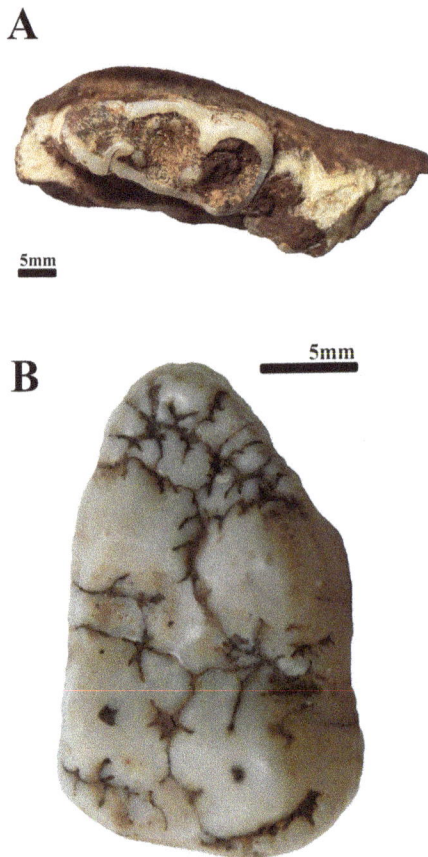

Figure 9.17: A – Babirusa (*Babyrousa celebensis*) right maxillary M3 from Spit 21; B – Fragment of Suidae right maxilla with broken M2 and heavily worn M3 from Spit 18.

Source: Photographs by Philip Piper.

Another large endemic mammal, the Anoa (*Bubalus depressicornis*; NISP = 47), was recorded throughout the archaeological sequences in small numbers between Spits 4 and 30, indicating the presence of the species in the local environments of Gua Mo'o hono through to the late Holocene (Table 9.11; Figure 9.18A). The remains of both the Sulawesi bear cuscus (*Ailurops ursinus)* and Sulawesi dwarf cuscus (*Strigocuscus celebensis*) (Figure 9.18B) have also been recorded from the mid (Spit 32) to the late Holocene (Spit 4). Forty-six Sulawesi macaque (*Macaca* sp(p).) remains, mostly teeth, were recorded in the assemblage. With reference to the known biogeographic distributions of the macaque species of Sulawesi, the likely candidates in the archaeological record of Gua Mo'o hono are the Tonkean macaque (*Macaca tonkeana*)

and/or booted macaque (*M. ochreata ochreata*) (Supriatna 2008; Supriatna and Richardson 2008). Six fragments, including four teeth of a civet cat (Viverridae) were also recorded. The maxillary right and left P4s from Spits 12 and 28 respectively, as well as the maxillary M1 from Spit 29 are all allocated to the brown palm civet (*Macrogalidia musschenbroekii*). This Sulawesi endemic has recently been recorded in the central and southeastern regions of the island at Rawa Aopa National Park, Tanjung Peropa Wildlife Reserve and Mangolo Recreation Forest (Tasirin et al. 2008). A maxillary canine from Spit 7 could potentially be from the endemic brown palm civet or the common palm civet (*Paradoxurus hermaphroditus*), a late Holocene introduction to Sulawesi (Heinsohn 2002).

Of the smaller mammals, a single right maxilla of a squirrel (Sciuridae) and several fragments of old world fruit bats (Megachiroptera) and insectivorous bats (Microchiroptera) were recorded throughout the archaeological sequences. But by far the most common small mammal skeletal elements were the cranial and postcranial elements of rats (Muridae; NISP = 203). Guy Musser of the American Museum of Natural History kindly assisted identification. In total, 10 species of endemic rat have so far been recorded including the giant Sulawesi rat (*Paruromys dominator*; Figure 9.18D), Sulawesi forest rat (*Taeromys punicans*) and the elegant xanthurus rat (*Rattus facetus*). Research continues and the murids will be reported in greater detail elsewhere. In addition to mammals, numerous reptile skeletal elements were recorded. These included 215 snake vertebrae, many of which were likely to be from pythons, based on their large size. Also represented were several specimens of monitor lizard (*Varanus* sp(p).), two fragments of Gecko (Gekkonidae) premaxillae, 42 pieces of frog and/or toad and 14 fragments of unidentified bird bone. Fish vertebrae were recorded from the surface to Spit 12, but the clear majority (21/26 (81%)) were identified in the subsurface layers (Spit 1). These included the characteristic dentaries and ceratohyals of freshwater eels (Anguillidae).

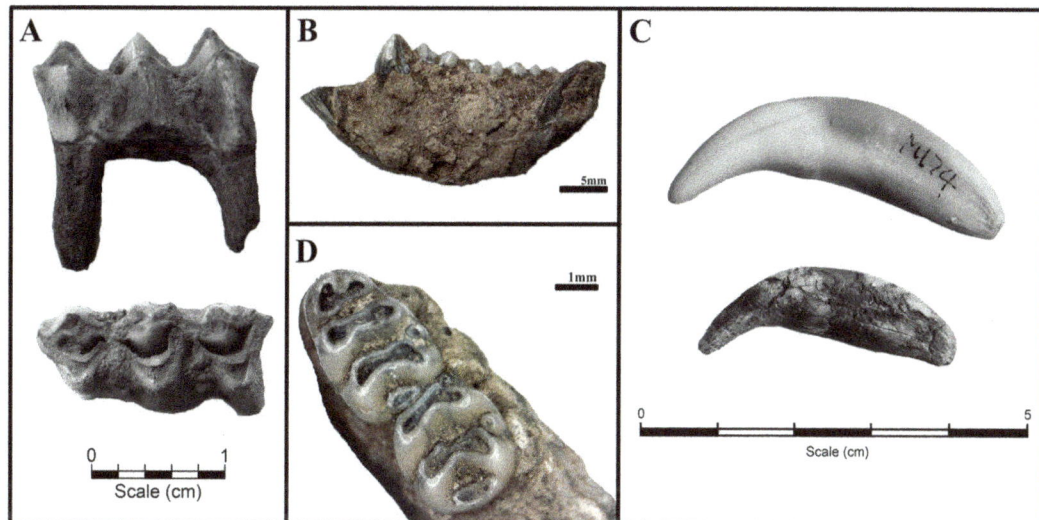

Figure 9.18: A – The labial (above) and occlusal (below) aspects of the left mandibular dp4 provisionally recorded as the Javan deer (*Rusa timorensis*) and subsequently reallocated to Anoa (*Bubalus depressicornis*). B – *Strigocuscus celebensis* left mandibular body from Spit 17. C – (below) The left mandibular canine from Spit 13 originally attributed to a dog and subsequently reallocated to the Sulawesi brown civet cat (*Macrogalidia musschenbroekii*). D – Fragment of giant Sulawesi rat (*Paruromys dominator*) right mandible with M1 and M2 from Spit 19.

Source: Photographs by Philip Piper.

During preliminary analysis, two species of terrestrial vertebrate introduced to Sulawesi were provisionally identified: the dog (*Canis lupus familiaris*) and deer (*Rusa timorensis*). Continued analysis and access to more comprehensive comparative collections of Sulawesi's endemic fauna and supporting biometric data have questioned both these identifications.

A single mandibular left canine recovered from Spit 13 was initially considered to be that of domestic dog (Figure 9.18C). A sample of dentine from the tooth returned a direct date of 3870±40 BP (SANU-35532), calibrating to 4467–4274 (84.5%) or 4256–4208 (10.9%) cal BP (Table 9.1). The stable isotope ratios are typical of a carnivore feeding on terrestrial resources and are considered reliable ($\delta^{13}C$ –19.4‰, $\delta^{15}N$ –8.7‰). The direct date is supported by two charcoal samples: one from Spit 13 dated 3820–3571 cal BP (D-AMS 001623) and another from the underlying Spit 15 of 4405–4093 cal BP (D-AMS 001624b) (Table 9.1). The evidence clearly indicates that the canine was from an animal present on the island in the mid to late 5th millennium BP. If correctly identified, this would have represented the oldest securely dated introduction for domestic dog anywhere in ISEA. However, closer morphometric examination of maxillary and mandibular canines of the endemic brown palm civet indicates that they are considerably larger than expected for a moderately sized civet cat, and overlap in size with small Southeast Asian dogs. Although the maxillary canines can be easily differentiated between dogs and brown civet on morphology, the mandibular canines are considerably more difficult to distinguish. To increase confidence in species identification, the specimen was sent to the ancient DNA laboratory at the University of Oxford for sequencing. Unfortunately, the analysis proved inconclusive. Further suspicion was raised when an opportunity arose to study the much better preserved bone assemblage from the rockshelter site of Gua Talimbue, just a short distance from Gua Mo'o hono. Here, several well-preserved examples of brown palm civet were identified, including maxillary and mandibular canines. Thus, the Gua Mo'o hono canine is in all likelihood from the brown palm civet, rather than a dog.

Two teeth, a left mandibular dp4 from Spit 4 and a molar fragment from Spit 9 were tentatively identified as Javan deer (*Rusa timorensis*). Comparative analysis highlighted the problem of differentiating some skeletal and dental elements of introduced deer from the endemic Anoa (*Bubalus depressicornis*). This was particularly evident in the maxillary and mandibular dp4s, which look remarkably like deer maxillary M1s and mandibular dp4s (Figure 9.18A). The specimens have been subsequently reallocated as the left mandibular dp4 and molar/dp4 fragment of Anoa. The only directly radiometrically dated bone identified as deer is a terminal phalanx from Minanga Sipakko that returned an age of 2810±50 BP or 2789–3059 cal BP (OZE 132) (Bulbeck and Nasruddin 2002). A recent study of c. 2800 bone fragments recovered during the 2004 and 2007 excavations at Minanga Sipakko found just three Anoa teeth (including one confusing maxillary dp4) and no Javan deer skeletal elements (Piper and Campos, unpublished data). Thus, the identification of a single Javan deer basal phalange from Minanga Sipakko should be treated with some caution. Simons and Bulbeck (2004) also noted two fragments of deer previously recorded from Leang Balisao in the Southwest Sulawesi highlands, while Simons (1997) identified six from Leang Karassak and one or two pieces from Leang Burung 1 in the Maros karsts. None of the actual identified specimens are reported. From these results and associated radiocarbon dates, Simons and Bulbeck (2004) argued that the deer was likely introduced to Sulawesi by c. 4000 BP. Although a 4000 BP introduction of deer to Sulawesi is certainly possible, direct dates on clearly identified deer bones/teeth are required to confirm the antiquity for the translocation of this large ungulate from the Sundaic biogeographic region to Sulawesi.

These two examples illustrate the difficulty the analyst often faces when attempting to differentiate between related taxa in the zooarchaeological record, especially in the absence of sufficient comparative collections. Confidence in distinguishing between taxa becomes all that more important when making critical identifications, particularly if the appearance of a domestic or translocated animal in a region where it was previously absent has significant implications for our understanding of human behaviour.

The faunal record from Gua Mo'o hono indicates that humans have been active in and around the rockshelter since at least 6500 cal BP. They primarily hunted babirusa and the Celebes warty pig, and to a lesser extent the Anoa. A variety of other intermediate and small vertebrates were likely captured using a variety of hunting technologies such as traps that would have been effective against nocturnal and diurnal carnivorous and omnivorous mammals and reptiles like the brown palm civet, Sulawesi endemic macaques and monitor lizard. A study of the osseous technologies from Walandawe sites has also indicated that composite projectile technologies might also have been present from the early Holocene onwards (Aplin et al. 2016). The habitat preferences of taxa recorded at Gua Mo'o hono (Burton and Macdonald 2008; Salas et al. 2008) suggest that the occupants foraged within a variety of environments that included dense moist tropical rainforest, along rivers banks, in swamp forest and in more open woodland. Based on the state of preservation of the bone, the concentration of most of the fish (including eel) and bird bones within the uppermost spits is probably a result of preservation bias, rather than reflecting a distinctive change in human subsistence behaviour. From the terminal Pleistocene onwards across Southeast Asia as far east as Palawan (Piper et al. 2011) and Sulawesi (Simons and Bulbeck 2004), a similar focus on the capture of larger mammals (including pigs and primates) was a widespread component of diverse foraging strategies that included the hunting and trapping of a variety of small mammals and reptiles (Piper and Rabett 2009; Barker and Rabett 2010; Rabett et al. 2013). Community participation in foraging and the setting and maintenance of traps was probably one method of offsetting risk from failed large game hunts (Piper and Rabett 2014), as well as adding diversity to the diet.

The bone assemblage for the last c. 2000 years is relatively small, with a total number of fragments of 1715, compared with c. 10,000 and c. 67,000 for the mid and late Holocene, respectively. This has resulted in only 142 taxonomic identifications in the most recent deposits compared with 1081 in earlier phases (Table 9.11). While this may explain the limited taxonomic diversity of the assemblage postdating c. 2000 cal BP, it is notable that many of the obligatory forest dwelling rats (*Taeromys* spp. and *Paruromys dominator*) are absent. The only two identified rat species within this late sequence are the elegant xanthurus rat (*Rattus facetus*) and Andrew's Bunomys (*Bunomys andrewsi*), with the latter known to tolerate disturbance and vegetation modification (Ruedas and Musser 2008). This might tentatively indicate some substantial human modifications to the local environment around Gua Mo'o hono in the latter phases of human frequentation of the rockshelter, even though there is no clear evidence for the introduction of domestic pig or dog.

Several translocated wild animals common in Sulawesi today are also absent from the archaeological record of Gua Mo'o hono, and the timing of their introductions remains enigmatic across the island. This includes the Javan deer (discussed above), common palm civet (*Paradoxurus hermaphroditus*), Malayan civet (*Viverra tangalunga*) and Sunda porcupine (*Hystrix javanica*) (Heinsohn 2002). The common palm civet has been tentatively recorded at Liang Bua on Flores at c. 4000 BP (van den Bergh et al. 2009), and directly dated at Matja Kuru 1 in Timor Leste to 2741±27 BP (Wk-31508; O'Connor 2015). There is currently no confirmed archaeological record of this species on Sulawesi. The recovery of well-stratified and directly dated specimens that have been confidently identified as an introduced species is required before we can clarify the timing of arrival of these invasives.

Bone artefacts

After allowing for fragments from the same original artefact, a total of 49 osseous artefacts were identified from Gua Mo'o hono, distributed though the deposit as follows: c. 6000 to 7000 cal BP (n = 24), 4500 to 6000 cal BP (n = 3), 3400 to 4500 cal BP (n = 8), and <3400 cal BP (n = 14).

The majority of the osseous artefacts can be classified as bone points or point fragments and are made from cortical bone. An example is the attenuate bone point from Spit 7, which shows longitudinal striations from scraping to produce the point and small transverse striations near the midpoint, possibly produced during hafting wear by sand grains trapped in the binding (Figure 9.19A). Points made on dentine are also represented (Figures 9.19B and 9.19D). One unusual example is made on a babirusa mandibular incisor from Spit 28 (Figure 9.19D). It shows sub-parallel transverse and oblique striations, which are most pronounced on the enamel near the tip. This point in unique in terms the assemblage recovered from the Walandawe excavations as it retains the enamel crown, allowing its identification to taxon. Aplin et al. (2016) note that while several of the dentine points are likely suid incisors, none of those examined for that study retained the enamel crown.[3]

---

3   The bone point in Gua Mo'o hono made on a babirusa mandibular incisor from Spit 28 was found amongst the faunal assemblage after that study was completed.

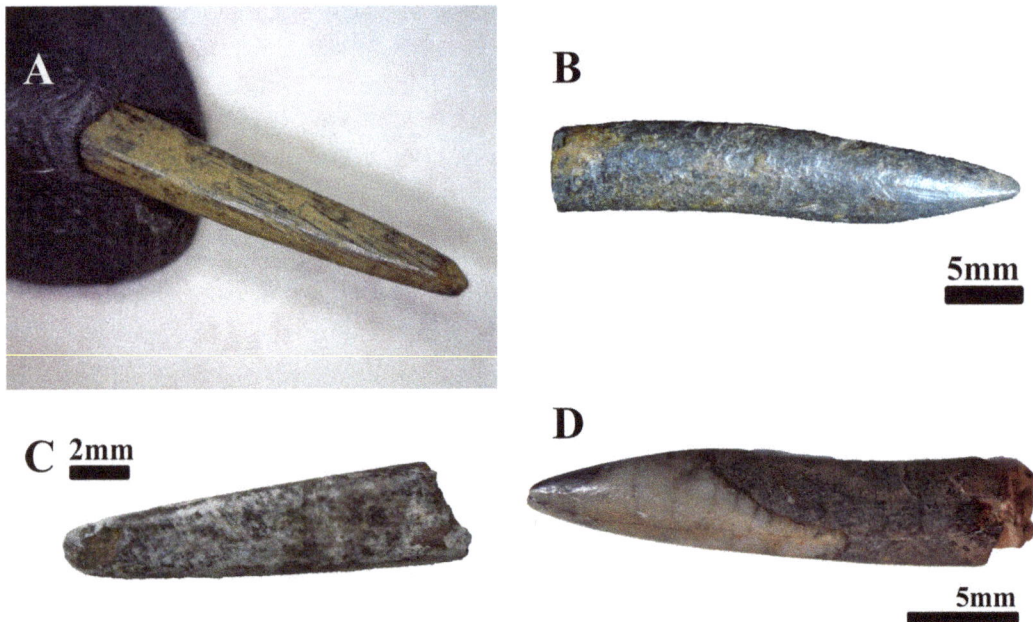

Figure 9.19: A – Attenuate bone unipoint from Gua Mo'o hono Spit 7 made on cortical bone showing longitudinal striations from scraping during manufacture and small parallel transverse striations near the midpoint, which may be from hafting wear. B – Bone point probably made on suid incisor from Spit 24. C – Incidentally calcined bone point made on cortex bone from Gua Mo'o hono Spit 25. D – Bone point made on babirusa mandibular incisor from Gua Mo'o hono Spit 28.

Source: Photographs by Sue O'Connor.

Many are merely fragments and it is difficult to be certain if they are from unipoints or bipoints. Many of the artefacts are also burnt, including some examples burnt to the point of calcination (Figure 9.19C). The calcined artefacts are thought to have been burnt incidentally subsequent to discard, as extreme calcination renders bone very brittle and unsuitable for tool manufacture or use.

One notable expedient bone artefact is a tusk tool from Spit 11 (Aplin et al. 2016), probably dating to c. 3500 cal BP. It is formed from the terminal section of a babirusa lower canine. The basal end is roughly fractured and shows no other modification. The tip is essentially unmodified except through use and some probable resharpening (Figure 9.20A). The Gua Mo'o hono tusk tool was clearly used for cutting. The outer enamel surface has a high gloss and fine oblique striations that are sub-parallel along most of the preserved length. The cutting edge is rounded from use, and relatively blunt except where it has been resharpened (Figures 9.20C and 9.20D). The tip area of the artefact has some bilateral spalling. External spalling is concentrated on the chisel-like end of the tool (Figure 9.20E). It was probably produced in an attempt to resharpen the cutting edge, which may have broken the artefact. Internal spalling on the tip of the artefact is more extensive and extends not only around the tip but back along the blade for c. 10 mm (Figure 9.20F). We suspect the original use was systematic and repetitive, and may have involved the cutting of a plant material that contained siliceous phytoliths. Perhaps due to the blunting of the natural cutting edge of the tooth, spalls were struck from one side and then the other to allow continued use of the artefact, albeit most likely in a different fashion with more focus on the tip than on the cutting edge (Aplin et al. 2016).

Figure 9.20: Tusk tool from Gua Mo'o hono Spit 11.
Source: Photograph by Sue O'Connor.

Four fragments of burnt cortex bone from the upper late Holocene levels of Gua Mo'o hono (Spits 4 and 5) probably represent pieces of a single original artefact manufactured from a long-bone shaft fragment of a large mammal. On each fragment, the outer surface of the bone has at least one flat, glossy facet. The striations on these facets are very fine, suggesting they were ground on a very fine-grained stone. While the original form is uncertain, one fragment 25 mm in length has a narrow grinding facet on the external surface as well as a second facet that descends to what might have been a bevelled tip. If this interpretation is correct, this singular artefact may have originally resembled some of the potential wood-working tools from Pulau Balambangan and other sites categorised by Rabett (2005) as 'edge tools'.

Discussion and conclusion

The Gua Mo'o hono sequence demonstrates that humans were active in and around the rockshelter from at least 6500 cal BP and informs on early to late Holocene subsistence and technology in Southeast Sulawesi. Spits 17 to 32 reflect a period of intensive habitation with high discard rates of flaked stone artefacts during the early 7th millennium BP. Local nodules of high-quality chert were flaked to produce cores, which in turn were extensively reduced in the production of flakes. Only a small proportion of the flakes were retouched, with many of the most extensively retouched pieces being small and steep-angled. These steeply retouched pieces are likely to have functioned as scrapers for a variety of woodworking tasks. Notably, the Maros points and microliths of the Toalean are absent from the assemblage. This non-Toalean tool technology evidently persisted until later times, although associated with lower rates of artefact discard above Spit 8, roughly coinciding with the first appearance of pottery. This is no doubt due to changes in settlement and subsistence following the late movement of agricultural communities into the region and the availability of metal tools (Bulbeck et al. 2016). Bone tools were utilised throughout the sequence and include bone bipoints, unipoints and expedient tools such as the tusk tool that was used for cutting. Small clusters of oblique to transverse striations on the mid-section of the bone tools in the larger Walandawe bone artefact collection are possibly caused by the motion of sediment grains trapped in cordage. In combination with specific crushing and breakage patterns, this suggests that some implements might have been hafted as projectile points for use in hunting (Aplin et al. 2016).

The zooarchaeological record from Gua Mo'o hono provides insights into mid to late Holocene foraging strategies in the north of the southeastern peninsula of Sulawesi. It indicates that, along with encounter hunting, the occupants probably employed a range of techniques to capture a variety of mammal and reptile taxa from a diversity of terrestrial and arboreal habitats within tropical rainforest and swamp forest environments. However, there appears to have been a particular focus on suids, both the babirusa and the Sulawesi warty pig, which might have been common close to the rockshelter during its occupation. Notably, however, there is no evidence for the consumption of the introduced pig *Sus scrofa,* or even the presence of dog in Gua Mo'o hono. Pig and dog have both been identified in West Sulawesi along the Karama River at sites such as Minanga Sipakko and Kamassi, where communities established open-air settlements by c. 3500 cal BP. These settlements also differ from Gua Mo'o hono in that they are often considered to represent colonisation of the island by Malayo-Polynesian-speaking populations and exhibit a variety of associated material culture such as red-slipped pottery, ground-stone technology and stone beads (Anggraeni et al. 2014). Similar types of artefacts are effectively absent from Gua Mo'o hono.

The late appearance of pottery at Gua Mo'o hono also suggests that the inland expansion of agriculturally based populations was a long and drawn-out process, as proposed by Simons and Bulbeck (2004). It not yet possible to determine whether the pottery in Gua Mo'o hono was used by indigenous foragers who had acquired cooking and other vessels from local immigrant farming populations and continued to frequent the site, or whether the shelter was simply utilised on an occasional basis by, say, hunting parties from local villages established nearby. Simons (1997) proposed that late occupation of rockshelters in Southwestern Sulawesi involved indigenous hunter-gatherers who, in the late Holocene, began to engage with the farmers they encountered. A similar argument has been applied to Luzon in the Philippines, where the earliest settled populations introduced a variety of material cultural items, many similar to those recorded along the Karama valley, identified at Dimolit (Peterson 1974) and along the Cagayan River at sites such as Nagsabaran (Hung et al. 2011) and other Lal-lo shell middens (Mijares 2007). Mijares (2007) argued that cave sites within the Peñablanca region of northern Luzon, close to the Cagayan River valley, continued to be frequented by foragers long after the establishment of the first sedentary settlements in lowland valleys. The hunter-gatherers maintained their traditional existence, trading for pottery but little else of the new material culture brought by Neolithic immigrants. On balance, the overall decline in occupational evidence in the upper levels of Gua Mo'o hono shelter might seem to favour the hypothesis of only occasional short-term and/or opportunistic use of the shelter by sedentary populations while exploiting the surrounding forests and nearby river.

Author biographies

Sue O'Connor Department of Archaeology and Natural History, School of Culture, History and Language, College of Asia and the Pacific, The Australian National University, Canberra, Australia; and ARC Centre of Excellence for Australian Biodiversity and Heritage, The Australian National University, Canberra, Australia

David Bulbeck Department of Archaeology and Natural History, School of Culture, History and Language, College of Asia and the Pacific, The Australian National University, Canberra, Australia

Philip J. Piper School of Archaeology and Anthropology, College of Arts and Social Sciences, The Australian National University, Canberra, Australia

Fadhila Aziz Department of Prehistory, Research and Development Agency, Ministry of Education and Culture, National Research Centre of Archaeology, Jakarta, Indonesia

Ben Marwick Department of Anthropology, University of Washington, Seattle, USA

Fredeliza Campos School of Archaeology and Anthropology, College of Arts and Social Sciences, The Australian National University, Canberra, Australia

Jack Fenner Department of Archaeology and Natural History, School of Culture, History and Language, College of Asia and the Pacific, The Australian National University, Canberra, Australia

Ken Aplin Department of Archaeology and Natural History, School of Culture, History and Language, College of Asia and the Pacific, The Australian National University, Canberra, Australia

Fakhri Makassar Archaeology Office, Makassar, South Sulawesi, Indonesia

Suryatman Makassar Archaeology Office, Makassar, South Sulawesi, Indonesia

Tim Maloney Department of Archaeology and Natural History, School of Culture, History and Language, College of Asia and the Pacific, The Australian National University, Canberra, Australia

Budianto Hakim Makassar Archaeology Office, Makassar, South Sulawesi, Indonesia

Rachel Wood Research School of Earth Sciences, The Australian National University, Canberra, Australia

References

Anggraeni, T. Simanjuntak, P. Bellwood and P. Piper. 2014. Neolithic foundations in the Karama valley, West Sulawesi, Indonesia. *Antiquity* 88(341):740–756. doi.org/10.1007/978-94-024-0899-7_13 (accessed 5 June 2018).

Aplin, K.P., S. O'Connor, D. Bulbeck, P.J. Piper, B. Marwick, E.S. Pierre and F. Aziz. 2016. The Walandawe tradition from Southeast Sulawesi and osseous artefact traditions in Island Southeast Asia. In M. Langley (ed.), *Osseous Projectile Technology: Towards an Understanding of Pleistocene Cultural Variability*. Vertebrate Paleobiology and Paleoanthropology Series. Dordrecht: Springer. doi.org/10.1007/978-94-024-0899-7_13 (accessed 5 June 2018).

Aubert, M., A. Brumm, M. Ramli, T. Sutikna, E.W. Saptomo, B. Hakim, M.J. Morwood, G.D. van den Bergh, L. Kinsley and A. Dosseto. 2014. Pleistocene cave art from Sulawesi, Indonesia. *Nature* 514(7521):223–227. doi.org/10.1038/nature13422 (accessed 5 June 2018).

Barker, G. and R.J. Rabett. 2010. Late Pleistocene and early Holocene forager mobility in Southeast Asia. In B. Bellina, E.A. Bacus, T.O. Pryce and J.W. Christie (eds), *50 Years of Archaeology in Southeast Asia: Essays in Honour of Ian Glover*, pp. 66–77. Bangkok: River Books.

Behrensmeyer, A.K., S.M. Kidwell and R.A. Gastaldo. 2000. Taphonomy and paleobiology. *Paleobiology* 26(sp4):103–147. doi.org/10.1666/0094-8373(2000)26[103:TAP]2.0.CO;2 (accessed 5 June 2018).

Bräuer, G. 1988. Osteometrie des Kranialskeletts. In R. Knußman (ed.), *Wesen und Methoden der Anthropologie, 1. Teil, Wissenschafttheorie, Geschichte, Morphologischen Methoden*. Stuttgart: Gustav Fischer Verlag.

Bronk Ramsey, C., T.F.G. Higham, F. Brock, D. Baker and P. Ditchfield. 2009. Radiocarbon dates from the Oxford AMS System: Archaeometry Datelist 33. *Archaeometry* 51(2):323–349. doi.org/10.1111/j.1475-4754.2008.00457.x (accessed 5 June 2018).

Brown, P. 1989. *Coobool Creek*. Terra Australis 13. Canberra: The Australian National University.

Bulbeck, D. 2004. Divided in space, united in time: The Holocene prehistory of South Sulawesi. In S.G. Keates and J.M. Pasveer (eds), *Quaternary Research in Indonesia*, pp. 129–166. Modern Quaternary Research in Southeast Asia, Volume 18. Leiden: A.A. Balkema.

Bulbeck, D. 2004. South Sulawesi in the corridor of island populations along East Asia's Pacific rim. In S. Keates and J.M. Pasveer (eds), *Quaternary Research in Indonesia*, pp. 221–258. Modern Quaternary Research in Southeast, Volume 18. Leiden: A.A. Balkema.

Bulbeck, D., F.A. Aziz, S. O'Connor, A. Calo, J.N. Fenner, B. Marwick, J. Feathers, R. Wood and D. Prastiningtyas. 2016. Mortuary caves and the dammar trade in the Towuti-Routa region, Sulawesi, in an Island Southeast Asian context. *Asian Perspectives* 55(2):148–183. doi.org/10.1353/asi.2016.0017 (accessed 5 June 2018).

Bulbeck, D. and Nasruddin. 2002. Recent insights into the chronology and ceramics of the Kalumpang site complex, South Sulawesi, Indonesia. *Bulletin of The Indo-Pacific Prehistory Association* 22:83–99.

Bulbeck, D., M. Pasqua and A. Di Lello. 2000. Culture history of the Toalean of south Sulawesi, Indonesia. *Asian Perspectives* 39(1–2):71–108. doi.org/10.1353/asi.2000.0004 (accessed 5 June 2018).

Burton, J. and A.A. Macdonald. 2008. *Sus celebensis. The IUCN Red List of Threatened Species*. www.iucnredlist.org/details/41773/0 (accessed 11 August 2014).

Glover, I.C. and G. Presland. 1985. Microliths in Indonesian flaked stone industries. In V.N. Misra and P. Bellwood (eds), *Recent Advances in Indo-Pacific Prehistory*, pp. 185–195. Leiden: E.J. Brill.

Heinsohn, T. 2002. Animal translocation: Long-term human influences on the vertebrate zoogeography of Australasia (natural dispersal versus ethnophoresy). *Australian Zoologist* 32(3):351–376. doi.org/10.7882/AZ.2002.014 (accessed 5 June 2018).

Hillson, S. 1996. *Dental Anthropology*. Cambridge: Cambridge University Press. doi.org/10.1017/CBO 9781139170697 (accessed 5 June 2018).

Hiscock, P. 2015. Making it small in the Palaeolithic: Bipolar stone-working, miniature artefacts and models of core recycling. *World Archaeology* 47(1):158–169. doi.org/10.1080/00438243.2014.991808 (accessed 5 June 2018).

Hogg, A.G., Q. Hua, P. Blackwell, M. Niu, C. Buck, T. Guilderson, T. Heaton, J. Palmer, P. Reimer, R. Reimer, C. Turney and S. Zimmerman. 2013. SHCal13 Southern Hemisphere calibration, 0–50,000 years cal BP. *Radiocarbon* 55(4):1889–1903. doi.org/10.2458/azu_js_rc.55.16783.

Hung, H.-c., M.T. Carson, P. Bellwood, F.Z. Campos, P.J. Piper, E. Dizon, M.J.L.A. Bolunia, M. Oxenham and Z. Chi. 2011. The first settlement of Remote Oceania: The Philippines to the Marianas. *Antiquity* 85(329):909–926.

Larnach, S.L. and N.W.G. Macintosh. 1971. *The Mandible in Eastern Australian Aborigines*. Oceania Monographs 17. Sydney: University of Sydney.

Lyman, R.L. 1994. *Vertebrate Taphonomy*. Cambridge: Cambridge University Press. doi.org/10.1017/CBO9781139878302 (accessed 5 June 2018).

McWilliam, A. and S. Lorenzen. 2009. *Sulawesi Nickel Baseline and Community Relations Project*. Canberra: The Australian National University.

Mijares, A.S.B. 2007. *Unearthing Prehistory: The Archaeology of Northeastern Luzon, Philippine Islands.* BAR International Series 1613. Oxford: John and Erica Hedges Ltd.

Moore, M.W., T. Sutikna, Jatmiko, M.J. Morwood and A. Brumm. 2009. Continuities in stone flaking technology at Liang Bua, Flores, Indonesia. *Journal of Human Evolution* 57(5):503–526. doi.org/10.1016/j.jhevol.2008.10.006 (accessed 5 June 2018).

Morant, G.M. 1923. A first study of the Tibetan skull. *Biometrika* 14(3/4):193–260. doi.org/10.2307/2331812.

O'Connor, S. 2015. Rethinking the Neolithic in island Southeast Asia, with particular reference to the archaeology of Timor-Leste and Sulawesi. *Archipel* 90:15–48. doi.org/10.4000/archipel.362 (accessed 5 June 2018).

Oktaviana, A.A., D. Bulbeck, S. O'Connor, B. Hakim, Suryatman, U.P. Wibowo, E. St Pierre and Fakhri. 2016. Hand stencils with and without narrowed fingers at two new rock art sites in Sulawesi, Indonesia. *Rock Art Research* 33(1):32–48.

Peterson, W. 1974. Summary report of two archaeological sites from north-eastern Luzon. *Archaeology & Physical Anthropology in Oceania* 9(1):26–35.

Piper, P.J., J. Ochoa, E.C. Robles, H. Lewis and V. Paz. 2011. Palaeozoology of Palawan Island, Philippines. *Quaternary International* 233(2):142–158. doi.org/10.1016/j.quaint.2010.07.009 (accessed 5 June 2018).

Piper, P.J. and R.J. Rabett. 2009. Hunting in a tropical rainforest: Evidence from the Terminal Pleistocene at Lobang Hangus, Niah Caves, Sarawak. *International Journal of Osteoarchaeology* 19(4):551–565. doi.org/10.1002/oa.1046 (accessed 5 June 2018).

Piper, P.J. and R.J. Rabett. 2014. Late Pleistocene subsistence strategies in Southeast Asia and their implications for understanding the development of modern human behaviour. In R. Dennell and M. Porr (eds), *Southern Asia, Australasia and the Search for Modern Human Origins*, pp. 118–134. Cambridge: Cambridge University Press.

Rabett, R.J. 2005. The early exploitation of Southeast Asian mangroves: Bone technology from caves and open sites. *Asian Perspectives* 44(1):154–179. doi.org/10.1353/asi.2005.0013 (accessed 5 June 2018).

Rabett, R.J., G. Barker, H. Barton, C. Hunt, L. Lloyd-Smith, V. Paz, P. Piper, R. Premathilake, G. Rushworth, M. Stephens and K. Szabó. 2013. Landscape transformations and human responses c. 11,500-c. 4500 years ago. In G. Barker (ed.), *Rainforest Foraging and Farming in Island Southeast Asia: the Archaeology of the Niah Caves, Sarawak: Volume 1*, pp. 217–253. United Kingdom: McDonald Institute for Archaeological Research.

Ruedas, L. and G. Musser. 2008. *Bunomys andrewsi. The IUCN Red List of Threatened Species.* www.iucnredlist.org/details/3327/0 (accessed 11 August 2014).

Salas, L., C. Dickman, K. Helgen and T. Flannery. 2008. *Ailurops ursinus. The IUCN Red List of Threatened Species.* www.iucnredlist.org/details/40637/0 (accessed 11 August 2014).

Simons, A.G. 1997. The Whole Hog: The Indigenous Response to the Introduction of Farming to South Sulawesi: A Faunal Analysis. Unpublished BA (Hons) thesis, Centre for Prehistory, University of Western Australia, Perth.

Simons, A.G. and D. Bulbeck. 2004. Late Quaternary faunal successions in South Sulawesi, Indonesia. In S.G. Keates and J.M. Pasveer (eds), *Quaternary Research in Indonesia Asia*, pp. 167–189. Quaternary Research in Southeast Asia, Volume 18. Leiden: A.A. Balkema.

Spriggs, M. 1989. The dating of the Island Southeast Asian Neolithic: An attempt at chronometric hygiene and linguistic correlation. *Antiquity* 63(240):587–613. doi.org/10.1017/S0003598X00076560 (accessed 5 June 2018).

Supriatna, J. 2008. *Macaca ochreata. The IUCN Red List of Threatened Species* 2008: e.T12557A3357511. doi.org/10.2305/IUCN.UK.2008.RLTS.T12557A3357511.en (accessed 27 October 2018).

Supriatna, J. and M. Richardson. 2008. *Macaca tonkeana. The IUCN Red List of Threatened Species* 2008: e.T12563A3359793. doi.org/10.2305/IUCN.UK.2008.RLTS.T12563A3359793.en (accessed 27 October 2018).

Tasirin, J., V. Dinets, E. Meijaard, J. Brodie, V. Nijman, T.A.C. Loffeld, H. Hilser, C. Shepherd, A.S. Seymour and J.W. Duckworth. 2015. *Macrogalidia musschenbroekii. The IUCN Red List of Threatened Species* 2015: e.T12592A45198901. doi.org/10.2305/IUCN.UK.2015-4.RLTS.T12592A45198901.en (accessed 27 October 2018).

van den Bergh, G.D., H.J. Meijer, R. Due Awe, M.J. Morwood, K. Szabo, L.W. van den Hoek Ostende, T. Sutikna, E.W. Saptomo, P.J. Piper and K.M. Dobney. 2009. The Liang Bua faunal remains: a 95k. yr. sequence from Flores, East Indonesia. *Journal of Human Evolution* 57(5):527–537. doi.org/10.1016/j. jhevol.2008.08.015 (accessed 5 June 2018).

Appendix A

Table A9.1: Summary of geoarchaeological analyses of sediments from Gua Mo'o hono.

Sample ID (metres)	Average pH	Mean EC	LOI percent organic material average	LOI percent carbonate content average	Average Magnetic Susceptibility	Munsell colour (Dry)
0.05	7.53	973.67	9.67	7.6	957.97	Dark brown
0.1	7	869	7.71	8.89	848.87	Dark brown
0.15	7.73	1135	8.36	7.35	862.65	Dark brown
0.2	7.1	980.33	8.16	9.49	1175.74	Dark brown
0.25	7.6	1009.33	5.51	11.8	1546.51	Brown/dark brown
0.3	7.4	669.33	4.43	15.36	4211.98	Pinkish-grey
0.34	7.73	468	4.49	8.96	931.06	Brown
0.4	7.63	413.33	6.66	12.73	1682.88	Brown/dark brown
0.43	8.03	413	3.75	18.76	2322.91	Pinkish-grey
0.5	7.8	283.33	4.74	16.7	1563.01	Brown
0.54	8.23	323	3.3	21.41	1949.46	Pinkish-grey
0.6	7.8	281.33	4.32	14.37	1315.35	Brown/dark brown
0.65	7.93	299	6.08	15.01	1413.28	Dark brown
0.7	7.57	289.67	5.4	10.43	1484.89	Strong brown
0.75	8.07	281	5.01	9.7	1733	Brown
0.8	7.6	276.33	7.21	11.84	2149.98	Brown
0.85	8	278.33	6.22	12.3	1842.04	Brown/dark brown
0.9	7	276.33	6.41	13.03	1863.44	Strong brown
0.95	8.2	287.33	6.52	12.51	1766.66	Brown/dark brown
1	7.97	280.33	6.74	15.22	1957.29	Brown/dark brown
1.05	7.97	275.67	5.66	16.78	1887.91	Dark brown
1.1	7.33	350	6.42	12.32	2463.29	Brown
1.15	8.03	281.67	6.62	11.78	2001.88	Strong brown
1.2	7.97	266.5	7.8	13.15	2245.07	Brown
1.25	7.9	312	6.23	15.13	2620.18	Brown/dark brown
1.3	7.33	301.67	6.78	13.99	2706.36	Brown/dark brown
1.4	7.8	329.67	7.03	12.42	2167.7	Dark brown
1.45	6.93	312	7.38	13.98	2342.5	Brown/dark brown
1.5	7.67	404.33	7.17	11.97	1725.56	Dark brown

Sample ID (metres)	Average pH	Mean EC	LOI percent organic material average	LOI percent carbonate content average	Average Magnetic Susceptibility	Munsell colour (Dry)
1.55	7.03	367	6.47	11.39	2204.35	Dark brown
1.6	7.87	339.67	7.6	11.31	2559.82	Dark brown
1.65	7.47	311.67	7.55	13.3	2063.82	Brown
1.7	7.73	427	8.08	10.7	2182.47	Dark brown
1.75	7	411.33	7.14	12.37	1877.19	Dark brown
1.8	7.6	582.67	7.21	11.48	2601.33	Strong brown
1.85	7.27	391	7.4	12.2	2404.85	Strong brown
1.9	7.47	449.67	8.31	10.93	2129.32	Brown/dark brown
1.95	6.77	532.67	7.63	11.26	2136.92	Strong brown
2	7.4	501.33	7.31	13.81	2453.27	Brown/dark brown
2.05	7.1	393.67	7.43	10.85	1905.35	Brown
2.1	7.33	439.67	7.68	12.7	2196.72	Strong brown
2.15	6.83	398.33	7.28	11.52	2144.4	Strong brown
2.2	7.8	296.33	5.82	12.68	2383.74	Strong brown
2.3	6.9	308.33	6.06	13.96	2441.48	Brown/dark brown
2.35	7.53	260.33	5.99	3.82	682.31	Strong brown
2.4	7.03	167.33	5.84	3.64	375.62	Strong brown
2.45	7.53	242.33	5.5	3.16	498.6	Brown
2.5	7.03	316.33	4.06	3.52	286.76	Strong brown

Note: EC = electrical conductivity; LOI = loss on ignition.
Source: Ben Marwick's laboratory data.

Appendix B

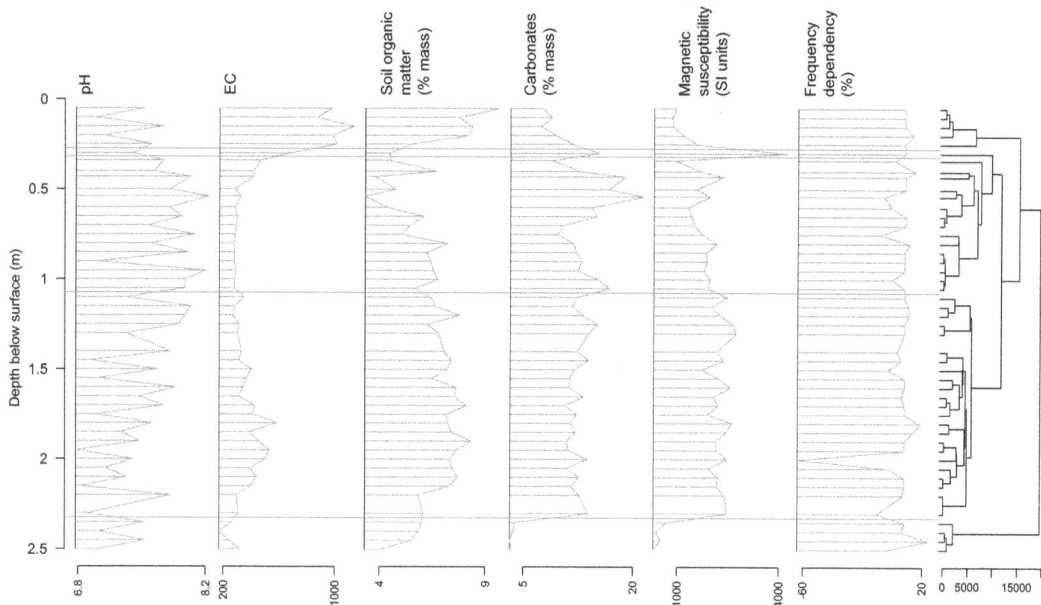

Figure B9.1: Stratigraphic plot of geoarchaeological data from Gua Mo'o hono.
Source: Ben Marwick (based on laboratory observations by archaeology students Ramona Steele and Cheyenne Galindo).

10

Vertebrate fauna from Gua Sambangoala, Southeast Sulawesi

Fakhri

Abstract

The purpose of this paper is to document the variety of fauna that the occupants of the Gua Sambangoala rockshelter interacted with and relied on for subsistence during the period 5500 to 3500 years ago. The faunal sample was recovered during excavation. Taxonomic frequencies and abundance were calculated using NISP (Number of Individual Specimens) and MNI (Minimum Number of Individuals). During the mid-Holocene period, the Sambangoala rockshelter inhabitants shared their environment with many endemic animals, including fish, toads/frogs, lizards, snakes, birds, bear cuscus, Sulawesi dwarf cuscus, bats, monkeys, rats, squirrels, civet cats, pig-deer (babirusa), Sulawesi warty pig (*Sus celebensis*) and Anoa water buffaloes. The larger of these animals were hunted by the forager inhabitants, whereas the smaller animals represented in the assemblage may have been taken by non-human predators. The identified fauna reflects surrounding environmental conditions that included open grasslands, valleys, karstic hills and wet rainforest habitat, suggesting that the mid-Holocene environment near the site was similar to today's.

Keywords: Gua Sambangoala, Southeast Sulawesi, mid-Holocene, faunal variety, faunal associations, environment

Introduction

Research funded by the Australian Research Council and led by Sue O'Connor between 2011 and 2014 documented 30 sites in an area spanning the north of Southeast Sulawesi Province and the northeastern lobe of South Sulawesi Province. The project's objectives included research into the time frame of the colonisation of Sulawesi by anatomically modern humans, their forager technology and adaptation to the environment, and the antiquity of iron technology in Sulawesi (O'Connor et al. 2014). A significant aspect of this research focuses on the interpretation of changing human economic strategies, and the reconstruction of local and regional environments through time. In this respect, the vertebrate fauna from Gua Sambangoala dated approximately 5500–3500 years ago provides useful new insights into human foraging behaviour during the mid-Holocene in Southeast Sulawesi. In addition, study of the small vertebrate remains that had become inadvertently incorporated into the accumulating cave sediments also provides information on local palaeoecology during periods of human occupation of the rockshelter.

Gua Sambangoala

Gua Sambangoala is a rockshelter in Walandawe village, Routa Subdistrict, North Konawe District, Southeast Sulawesi Province. It lies under an overhang in a karst cliff that is long and continuous, and clearly visible from the approach path to the site. The complex surrounding geology includes outcrops of ultramafic ophiolitic rocks, which have been explored for their potential for nickel mining (O'Connor et al. 2014). Gua Sambangoala is located at coordinates 3°1'17.4"S 121°43'12.9"E and an elevation of 344 metres above sea level (m asl). The entrance is 5 m long, 2.4 m high and oriented south. The rockshelter is well illuminated at the entrance but dim towards the rear, where a narrow channel runs. There are no stalactites or stalagmites within the site, and the sediment on the surface is fully dry and rich with freshwater shell remains (Figures 10.1 and 10.2).

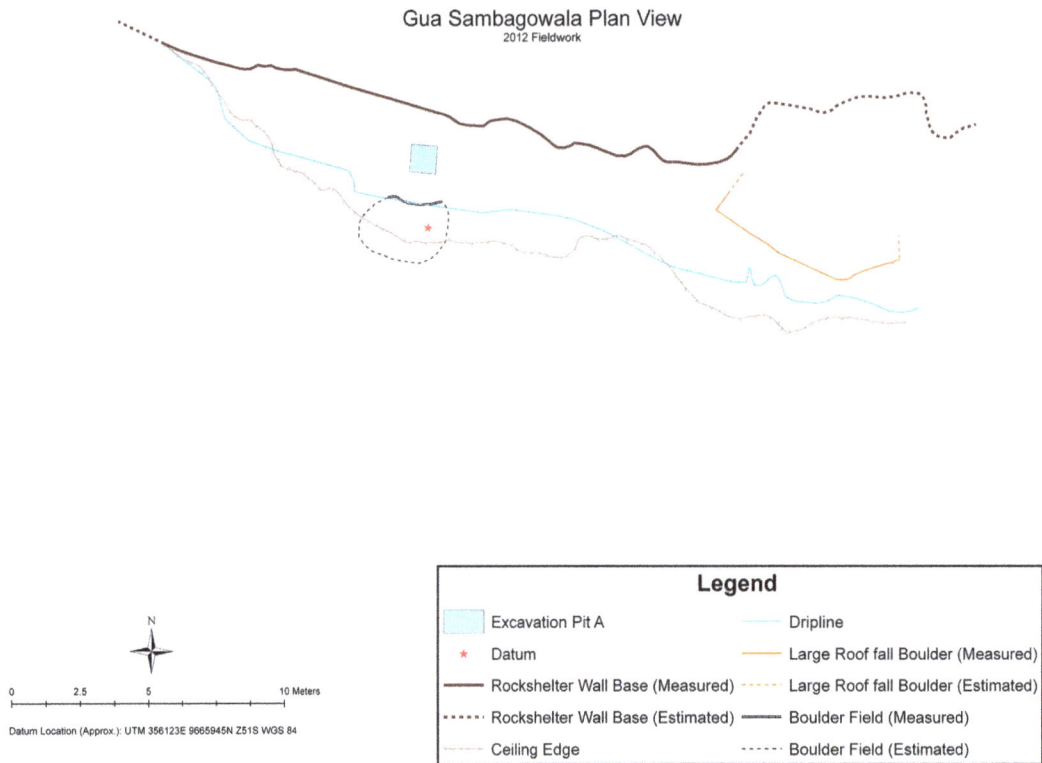

Figure 10.1: Gua Sambangoala site plan.

Source: Original plan by Jack Fenner.

The site is in a valley surrounded by the mountain ranges and hilly karsts of North Konawe. The topography here is predominantly sloping, dissected by steep cliffs. The plants growing in front of and around the rockshelter include scrub (*semak belukar*) and various other sturdy types such as bamboo and teak. A small stream, a tributary of the Wiwirano River which drains southward into the Lasolo River, passes 50 m in front of the rockshelter.

Figure 10.2: Gua Sambangoala site, test pit and approach path.

Source: Photograph by Jack Fenner.

The choice of where to excavate was based on surface-find concentrations of cultural remains. The excavation involved a 1 m² test pit, called square A, excavated to a depth of 2.4 m. The finds from the excavation include porcelain and earthenware sherds, dammar, a metallic lump that resembles iron slag, bone tools, flaked stone artefacts and stone manuports, baked clay fragments, and charcoal (O'Connor et al. 2014). Seven Accelerator Mass Spectrometry (AMS) dates were obtained on charcoal samples (Table 10.1). The earliest dates of around 5500 cal BP were obtained at a depth of 2.3–2.4 m. All of the dates relate to pre-Neolithic occupation, because pottery was restricted to the top 15 cm. In summary, the archaeological record bracketed by the radiocarbon assays consists of just over 2 m of cultural deposit dated to between approximately 3500 and 5500 cal BP (Figure 10.3).

Table 10.1: Gua Sambangoala square A AMS dates, processed by the Accelerator Mass Spectrometry Laboratory (Direct AMS) in Seattle, Washington.

Submitter ID	Approximate Depth	Direct AMS code	Determination	95% calibrated confidence interval*
Sam A_Spit 4	25 cm	D-AMS 001988	3297±29 BP	3453–3586 BP
Sam A_Spit 10	70 cm	D-AMS 001989	3295±29 BP	4248–4438 BP
Sam A_Spit 20	1.3 m	D-AMS 001990	3883±29 BP	4235–4418 BP
Sam A_Spit 25	1.6 m	D-AMS 001991	4766±31 BP	5333–5589 BP
Sam A_Spit 31	2.0 m	D-AMS 001992	4482±28 BP	4983–5290 BP
Sam A_Spit 37	2.3 m	D-AMS 001993	4923±30 BP	5597–5715 BP
Sam A_Spit 38	2.4 m	D-AMS 001994	4802±26 BP	5475–5595 BP

* Calibrated using OxCal 4.2 (Bronk Ramsey 2013).

Source: O'Connor et al. (2014).

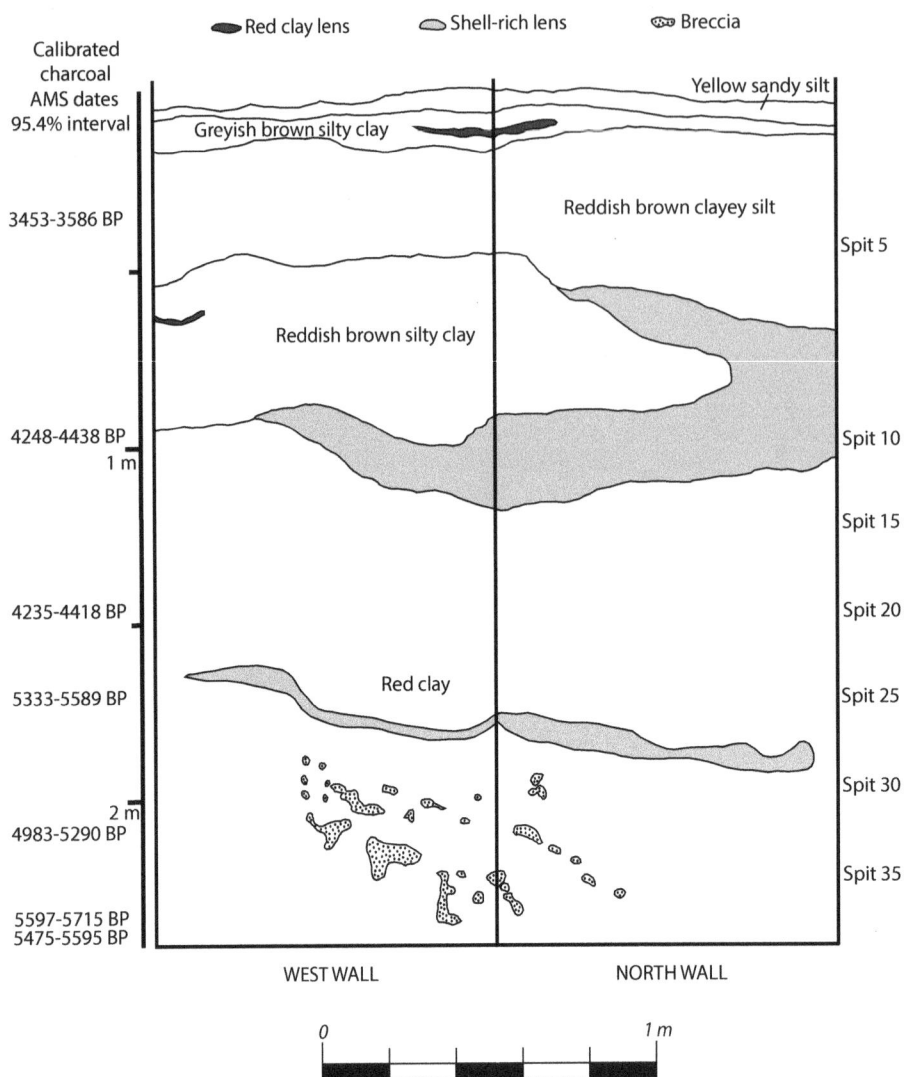

Figure 10.3: Gua Sambangoala stratigraphy and calibrated AMS dates.
Source: Bulbeck et al. (2015).

Background to zooarchaeology in Sulawesi

Ever since the pioneering research into Indonesia's biogeography by Alfred Russel Wallace, Sulawesi has attracted zoological interest for its diversity of endemic fauna. Groves (1976) identified 100 endemic mammalian species in Sulawesi, while Musser (1987) added 23 species to the list to arrive at a total of 123. Whitten et al. (1987) noted that Sulawesi appeared to have been formed by the collision of splinters of land that had respectively drifted eastward and westward from the Caenozoic continents of Sunda (Southeast Asia) and Sahul (Australia/ New Guinea), but its final location close to Borneo allowed Sunda-based species to raft across to Sulawesi in later times. Accordingly, summarising previous studies, Groves (2001) divided the endemic fauna into two main groups. The first involved the 'old endemics', which included Anoa water buffaloes, *Babyroussa* and (the now extinct) *Celebochoerus* suids, *Macrogalidia* civets, *Macaca* monkeys, tarsiers, shrews, squirrels, cuscuses and various Muridae amongst other taxa. The second, the 'new endemics', included (*inter alia*) *Sus celebensis*, *Crocidura nigripes* shrews and some rodent species.

Between the early 19th and mid-20th centuries, there was considerable analysis of faunal remains by archaeologists with the assistance of experts in the natural sciences such as biology, zoology and palaeontology, but this has now evolved into its own methodology, which adds cultural considerations to the natural science foundations (Davis 1987). In the South Sulawesi context, Sarasin and Sarasin (1905) reported on the fauna they had excavated from the Leang Ululeba, Leang Balisao and Leang Cakondo sites, and Hooijer (1950) reported on the faunal assemblages excavated by Dutch colonial archaeologists from the sites of Bola Batu, Panganreang Tudea, Batu Ejjaya and Leang Tomatoa Kacicang. The identified taxa from these assemblages, all undated, included endemic Anoa water buffaloes, and the endemic Sulawesi warty pig (*Sus celebensis*) and *Babyroussa* pig-deer, amongst other taxa, as well as the introduced *Bubalus bubalis* (water buffaloes) and Canidae (dogs).

The subsequent development of radiocarbon allowed South Sulawesi assemblages to be analysed in the context of their chronology. Clason (1976) reported on the mid to late Holocene fauna from the Ulu Leang 1 site, excavated by Ian Glover. It included the Sulawesi warty pig as the taxon most frequently utilised as a probable food source, along with variable quantities of remains from the bear cuscus (*Ailurops ursinus*), dwarf cuscus (*Strigocuscus celebensis*), moor macaque (*Macaca maura*), Anoa (*Bubalus depressicornis*) and various non-mammalian taxa including tortoises (*Coura amboinensis*), large snakes (pythons) and a range of small reptiles. Simons and Bulbeck (2004) reported on the late Holocene faunal assemblages excavated by John Mulvaney and R.P. Soejono from the Leang Burung 1, Leang Karassak, and Batu Ejjaya 1 and 2 sites. The identified taxa from these assemblages were similar to those from Ulu Leang 1, except that the introduced rusa deer (*Cervus timorensis*) replaced Anoa as the identified bovid, and indeed Simons and Bulbeck (2004) developed a hypothesis whereby increased forest disturbance related to human population build-up diminished Anoa numbers but increased the *Sus celebensis* stock over time.

Subsequent archaeozoological research has extended to the provinces surrounding South Sulawesi. Minanga Sipakko and Kamassi in West Sulawesi, which are open-air sites (unlike the South Sulawesi sites, which are all cave sites), have yielded a faunal assemblage firmly associated with Neolithic habitation and dated to approximately 3500–3000 cal BP. *Sus celebensis* were abundant throughout the deposits, along with small numbers of *Babyroussa* remains, but there are also identifications of the introduced *Sus scrofa* pigs and domestic dogs (Anggraeni et al. 2014). In contrast, the fauna excavated from the Gua Mo'o hono cave Southeast Sulawesi, which is dated between approximately 6500 and 500 cal BP, did not include any identified domesticates, although, as in the West Sulawesi sites, endemic suid identifications were common (O'Connor et al., this volume).

Formulation of the issues

The previously discussed research into Sulawesi faunal remains has produced a picture of how foragers adapted to their forested environment prior to becoming settled farmers. Unfortunately, apart from the analysis of the Gua Mo'o hono fauna, research on archaeological bone and tooth remains in the northern part of Southeast Sulawesi is limited. The present study aims to complement the Gua Mo'o hono analysis with a similar analysis for Gua Sambangoala. This research began by identifying the local fauna present during the relevant time periods and examining the ways in which people interacted with the fauna in the remote reaches of the Konawe karst ranges. This gave rise to questions such as which types of fauna were known to the Gua Sambangoala occupants, and what was the area's environmental conditions 5500–3500 years ago? Addressing these questions led to an understanding of the adaptations of the local foragers to the variety of mammals within their foraging range during the mid-Holocene.

Research methods

Data collection

The excavation of Gua Sambangoala proceeded using spits of 5 cm and 10 cm depths within a 1 m x 1 m square (Test Pit A), with the deposit sieved using a 1.5 mm mesh.

Analysis and methods

The excavated osteological remains were identified to the lowest taxonomic level possible; some of these taxa were as broad as classes and others as narrow as species. My principal guide was the notes I had taken on the metrical and morphological attributes of the teeth, jaws and other bones of Sulawesi forest fauna during my participation in the classification of the Gua Mo'o hono excavated fauna (see Acknowledgements). This identifications work was assisted by the comparative collection at the Makassar Archaeology Office, which included skeletal remains of monkey (*Macaca*), bear cuscus (*Ailurops ursinus*), domestic pig (*Sus scrofa*), fruit bats (Pteropodidae) and birds (Aves). Photographs from the vertebrate collection of the Rijksmuseum voor Natuurlijke Historie in Leiden, Holland, were also consulted.

The analysis utilised summation methods for all the counts of dental and bone specimens that could be identified. The methods most frequently used in zooarchaeology are the Number of Individual Specimens (NISP) and Minimum Number of Individuals (MNI). NISP is the principal method utilised in faunal quantification (O'Connor 2000) and the method used here for comparing the faunal classifications.

Bone weights of the Gua Sambangoala assemblage were also recorded. Bone weights are not useful in comparing the abundance of taxa with each other because the bones of large species weigh much more than the bones of small species. On the other hand, bone weights are useful for stratigraphic and taphonomic analysis because the proportional distribution of element weights across the skeleton is similar across taxa (O'Connor 2000), and so are employed here to supplement the NISP analysis.

The surface condition of the bone was classified as either plain (with no difference in colouration from fresh bone) and discoloured (dark brown to black, resembling heavily burnt bone). When bone fragments were covered by limey concretions, or their surface revealed macrosocopically visible striations (especially those that suggested production of bone tools) or tooth marks, this was also recorded. These and other observations were entered into a Microsoft Excel workbook for analysis.

Results

Stratigraphic and taphonomic analysis of the Gua Sambangoala square A fauna

Inspection of the faunal material recorded a count of 7260 fragments weighing 4574.18 g (Table 10.2). In terms of overall abundance, there were two layers, an upper layer (Spits 1–20) with fewer remains and a lower layer (Spits 21–38) with more abundant remains. Total bone weight ranged between 15.18 g and 102.00 g in Spits 1–20 but between 103.56 g and 418.03 g in Spits 21–38. Total NISP indicates a similar division; 34–132 for Spits 1–20 (excluding an outlier of 208) compared with 134–570 for Spits 21–38. The AMS dates (Table 10.1) accordingly indicate a greater quantity of faunal remains deposited between c. 5500–4500 cal BP compared with a smaller quantity between 4500–3500 cal BP. Further, there is little indication that faunal abundance was tapering off towards the base of the excavation. For instance, the Spit 36 and Spit 38 total bone weights were respectively the third and fourth largest recorded for any spit, although admittedly the NISP counts of 196 and 166 were less than any NISP count between Spits 21 and 34 (Table 10.2).

Table 10.2: Stratigraphic and taphonomic data on Gua Sambangoala vertebrate remains.

Spit	Discoloured fragments (NISP)	Plain fragments (NISP)	Total fragments (NISP)	Discoloured weight (grams), slightly weathered	Discoloured weight (grams), other	Plain weight (grams), slightly weathered	Plain weight (grams), other	Total weight (grams)
1	16	44	60	4.36	—	24.91	—	29.27
2	140	17	157	43.88	—	8.22	—	52.10
3	42	7	49	7.90	—	7.28	—	15.18
4	42	7	49	11.10	—	1.67	—	12.77
5	111	7	118	96.96	0.22 (SS)	4.82	—	102.00
6	76	2	78	27.80	—	0.55	—	28.35
7	126	4	130	69.53	—	4.43	—	73.96
8	199	9	208	86.40	—	3.77	—	90.17
9	168	8	176	84.34	0.28 (BT)	3.30	3.34 (CN)	91.26
10	130	2	132	87.10	—	1.46	—	88.56
11	141	1	142	79.90	0.56 (BT) 12.24 (CN)	0.74	—	93.44
12	33	1	34	22.50	—	0.12	—	22.62
13	93	3	96	52.71	—	0.43	—	53.14
14	63	—	63	47.89	0.24 (BT)	—	—	48.13
15	79	1	80	56.20	—	0.08	—	56.28
16	66	6	72	44.50	—	4.19	—	48.69
17	79	—	79	72.44	—	—	—	72.44
18	43	3	46	31.04	0.72 (BT)	11.72	—	43.48
19	75	—	75	43.12	—	—	—	43.12
20	103	5	108	81.22	0.44 (BT)	1.34	—	83.00
21	282	4	286	113.41	2.80 (CN)	0.61	—	116.82
22	564	6	570	221.73	—	0.84	195.46 (CN)	418.03
23	356	4	360	179.75	—	0.90	0.92 (CN)	181.57
24	247	—	247	103.56	—	—	—	103.56
25	435	9	444	167.64	0.60 (BT)	12.64	—	180.88
26	389	1	390	182.40	—	3.00	—	185.40
27	331	1	332	176.71	1.46 (BT)	0.58	—	178.75
28	414	6	420	277.78	15.58 (CN)	0.38	—	293.74
29	277	5	282	140.27	0.28 (SS)	0.98	—	141.53
30	247	2	249	135.59	0.24 (SS) 1.74 (BT)	0.30	—	137.87
31	263	1	264	121.06	—	0.72	—	121.78
32	326	2	328	244.99	0.40 (SS)	3.78	—	249.17
33	213	3	216	132.28	0.26 (SS) 1.90 (BT) 31.40 (CN)	0.42	—	166.26
34	257	2	259	7.14	127.74 (CN)	—	0.64 (SS)	135.52
35	160	5	165	3.61	0.18 (SS) 0.05 (BT) 133.10 (CN)	0.18	10.94 (CN)	148.06
36	190	6	196	25.51	0.62 (BT) 232.00 (CN)	0.82	16.74 (CN)	275.69

Spit	Discoloured fragments (NISP)	Plain fragments (NISP)	Total fragments (NISP)	Discoloured weight (grams), slightly weathered	Discoloured weight (grams), other	Plain weight (grams), slightly weathered	Plain weight (grams), other	Total weight (grams)
37	132	2	134	3.87	0.36 (TM) 122.78 (CN)	—	2.24 (CN)	129.25
38	164	2	166	56.40	205.40 (CN)	0.54	—	262.34
Total	7072	188	7260	3344.59	1.58 (SS) 8.61 (BT) 0.36 (TM) 883.04 (CN)	105.72	0.64 (SS) 229.64 (CN)	4574.18

SS = surface striation; BT = surface striation interpreted as involved in production of bone tool; TM = tooth mark; CN = covered by concretion.

Source: Author's observations.

There was a general tendency for the proportion of discoloured bone to increase with stratigraphic depth (Table 10.2). In terms of NISP counts, this proportion was 27% in Spit 1, increasing to 86–89% in Spits 2–4, 92–100% in Spits 5–20, and 97% or greater in all deeper spits. The corresponding decrease in the proportion of plain bone with depth can also be shown by referring to the weight of slightly weathered but otherwise plain bone as a proportion of total bone weight. This proportion was 85% in Spit 1, 16–48% in Spits 2–3, 0–27% in Spits 4–18, and just 0–7% in Spits 19–38. The increased proportion of discoloured bone corresponds to the change from a thin layer of yellow sediment underlain by another thin layer of greyish-brown sediment at the top of the stratigraphic section, underlain in turn by reddish-brown clay until Spit 10 and red clay beneath Spit 10 (Figure 10.3).

Another depth-related phenomenon was the occurrence of strongly adherent dirt concretions on the bone fragments (Table 10.2). These were not recorded for Spits 1–8, before being recorded sporadically for Spits 9–33, and finally coating the majority of the remains (78–97% by weight) in Spits 34–38.[1] These concretions were predominantly heavy clay, which reflects the clay sedimentary matrix in the excavated sediment below Spit 10 (Figure 10.3). The concretions were included in the recorded bone weights, which accordingly would be somewhat inflated in the lowest spits.

Concretions would also cover over surface modifications, but their comparative rarity in Spits 1–33 implies that they cannot be treated as the cause for the rarity of surface modifications recorded for the Gua Sambangoala assemblage. As shown in Table 10.2, just 2.22 g (six specimens, all taxonomically unidentified) were recorded for surface striations that were not attributed to bone-tool manufacture and that accordingly may be evidence for butchery.

Tables 10.3–10.6 present the weights per taxonomic category by spit including whether a proportion or all of the fragments assigned to that category were discoloured. As shown there, the great proportion of the specimens assigned to the 'unidentified mammal' and 'unidentified' categories were discoloured, even in the uppermost spits where the majority of the other faunal remains were plain. As for the categories for the better identified specimens, most of these tended to transition from plain specimens in the higher spits to discoloured specimens in the lower spits, in line with the general increase in the proportion of discoloured remains with stratigraphic depth. A good example is the rat-sized murid category, recorded in small quantities from all except four of the spits; most of its remains in Spits 1–5 were plain, whereas the majority from Spits 6–38 were discoloured. On the other hand, the small proportion of remains from the lowest spits that were plain could often be assigned to a specific taxon, such as the *Sus celebensis*

1   The predominance of concretions in the lowest spits may well reflect a particularly lengthy period of interment of the remains in the deposit, although the radiocarbon dates (Table 10.1) do not discriminate clearly between Spits 25–33 and Spits 34–38 in terms of antiquity.

fragments from Spits 35 and 36, and the two identified squirrel fragments (Spits 30 and 38). Overall, the discoloured status of most of the faunal assemblage (97% in terms of NISP count) impacted negatively on the identifiability of the specimens and contributed to the situation whereby 'unidentified' fragments constituted the single largest category (79% by weight; 91% by NISP count as detailed below).

Table 10.3: Ungulate identifications from Gua Sambangoala (weight in grams).

Spit	*Babyroussa celebensis*	*Sus celebensis*	Babirusa/Celebes warty pig	Deer or bovid	*Bubalus depressicornis*	Unidentified ungulate
1	—	—	3.24	—	—	—
2	—	—	4.02*	1.30	—	—
3	—	5.52	0.64	—	—	—
4	—	—	2.18*	—	—	—
5	—	—	4.30**	—	—	—
6	—	—	—	—	—	—
7	—	3.32	2.80*	—	—	—
8	—	1.30	4.30**	—	—	—
9	—	3.18**	1.36**	—	—	—
10	—	—	1.52*	—	15.72**	—
11	—	12.24**	1.02*	1.08**	—	2.54**
12	—	—	—	—	—	—
13	—	—	1.34**	—	—	—
14	—	—	2.26**	—	—	—
15	—	3.28**	—	—	—	—
16	—	3.34	2.22**	—	0.72**	—
17	—	0.80**	—	—	—	—
18	—	4.46	—	—	—	26.66*
19	—	—	0.92**	—	—	—
20	—	0.62	0.76*	0.34	—	—
21	—	—	1.40*	0.38	—	10.30**
22	—	—	1.08**	0.44	—	195.46
23	—	—	1.94**	—	—	10.78**
24	—	—	—	—	—	6.12**
25	—	—	2.88*	—	—	16.10*
26	0.28**	—	—	—	20.98**	0.24**
27	—	—	9.52**	—	—	9.42**
28	—	—	30.06**	—	—	—
29	—	—	—	—	2.78**	2.92**
30	—	—	0.48**	—	—	8.92**
31	—	—	0.62**	—	—	—
32	—	—	5.96*	—	—	—
33	—	—	56.18**	—	—	—
34	—	—	1.16**	—	—	—
35	—	10.94	2.26*	—	—	—
36	—	12.34	13.18*	—	—	6.34**
37	—	—	1.66	1.64**	—	—
38	—	32.48**	10.98*	6.74**	2.90**	—
Total	0.28	93.82	172.14	11.92	43.10	295.80

* A proportion discoloured. ** All discoloured.

Source: Author's observations.

Table 10.4: Medium-sized mammal identifications from Gua Sambangoala (weight in grams).

Spit	*Ailurops ursinus*	*Strigocuscus celebensis*	*Macaca* sp(p).	Squirrel	*Macrogalidia musschenbroekii*	Unidentified medium-sized mammal
1	—	—	—	—	—	—
2	—	—	0.32	—	—	—
3	—	—	—	—	—	—
4	—	—	—	—	—	—
5	0.58	—	—	—	—	—
6	—	—	0.52	—	—	—
7	—	—	—	—	—	—
8	0.44	1.22	0.38	—	—	—
9	0.86**	—	0.62*	—	—	—
10	—	—	1.18**	—	—	—
11	—	—	—	—	—	—
12	—	—	—	—	—	—
13	—	0.03	—	—	—	—
14	—	—	—	—	—	—
15	—	0.18**	—	—	—	—
16	0.26	—	0.24**	—	0.27*	—
17	—	0.18**	—	—	—	—
18	—	0.28**	—	—	—	—
19	—	—	—	—	—	—
20	—	—	—	—	—	—
21	—	—	—	—	—	—
22	—	0.33*	—	—	—	—
23	—	—	0.78	—	—	—
24	—	0.16**	—	—	—	—
25	—	0.20**	—	—	—	—
26	—	0.14**	—	—	—	—
27	—	0.15**	—	—	—	—
28	—	0.10**	—	—	0.05	—
29	—	2.02**	—	—	—	—
30	—	0.10	—	0.20	—	—
31	—	0.20**	—	—	—	—
32	—	3.06**	—	—	—	—
33	—	1.38**	—	—	—	—
34	0.40**	1.44**	—	—	—	0.74**
35	—	1.16**	—	—	—	—
36	—	2.40*	8.08*	—	—	—
37	—	0.44**	6.12*	—	—	—
38	0.16**	—	3.20**	0.02	—	—
Total	2.70	15.17	21.44	0.22	0.32	0.74

* A proportion discoloured. ** All discoloured.

Source: Author's observations.

Table 10.5: Other mammal identifications from Gua Sambangoala (weight in grams).

Spit	*Homo*	Old World fruit bat	Insectivorous bat	Unidentified bat	Rat-sized murid	Unidentified small mammal	Unidentified mammal
1	1.34	—	—	—	0.03	—	1.50**
2	2.94	—	—	—	0.14	—	—
3	—	—	0.78	—	0.34	—	0.70**
4	—	—	—	—	0.68*	—	0.20**
5	—	—	—	—	0.62	—	—
6	—	—	—	—	0.06*	—	—
7	—	—	—	0.34**	0.36*	—	0.93*
8	—	—	0.14	—	0.68*	—	1.26*
9	—	—	—	—	0.64**	—	0.50**
10	0.70	—	—	0.14**	0.50**	—	5.50**
11	—	—	—	—	0.51**	—	2.20**
12	—	—	—	—	—	—	1.10**
13	—	—	—	—	1.44*	—	0.50**
14	—	—	—	—	—	—	1.10**
15	—	—	—	—	0.08	—	9.90**
16	—	—	—	—	0.54**	—	1.20**
17	—	—	0.16**	—	-	—	2.50**
18	—	—	—	—	0.58*	—	0.38**
19	—	—	—	—	-	—	—
20	—	—	—	—	0.50*	—	—
21	—	—	—	—	0.65*	—	2.80**
22	—	—	—	—	1.34*	—	5.60**
23	—	0.12	—	—	1.35*	—	1.80**
24	—	—	—	—	0.36**	—	3.40**
25	—	—	0.40**	—	3.44*	—	5.30**
26	—	—	0.38**	—	4.70*	—	5.70**
27	0.58	—	—	—	4.62**	0.40**	8.00**
28	—	0.08	—	—	5.87*	-	9.90**
29	—	—	—	—	3.74*	-	3.08*
30	—	—	0.14**	—	2.38**	-	13.06**
31	—	—	—	—	0.72*	0.42**	1.02**
32	—	—	—	—	1.74**	—	0.40**
33	—	—	—	—	2.86*	—	1.50**
34	—	—	—	—	3.22**	—	0.60**
35	—	—	—	0.05**	0.24*	—	12.90**
36	—	—	—	—	0.24*	—	3.60**
37	—	—	—	—	0.54**	—	2.28**
38	—	—	—	—	0.46**	—	—
Total	5.56	0.20	2.00	0.53	46.17	0.82	110.41

* A proportion discoloured. ** All discoloured.

Source: Author's observation.

Table 10.6: Other identifications from Gua Sambangoala (weight in grams).

Spit	Fish	Frog/toad	Monitor lizard	Snake	Bird	Unidentified
1	—	—	—	1.14	—	22.02*
2	—	1.14	—	—	0.14	42.10*
3	—	—	—	—	—	7.20**
4	—	—	0.03	—	0.38**	9.30**
5	—	—	—	—	0.18**	96.42**
6	—	0.77*	—	0.20**	—	26.80**
7	0.48**	0.61**	—	12.32**	—	52.80**
8	—	0.62**	—	—	0.03	79.80**
9	—	3.50*	—	4.12*	—	76.48*
10	—	—	—	—	—	63.30**
11	0.66**	0.86**	0.03**	8.64**	—	63.66*
12	0.12	0.20**	—	—	—	21.20**
13	—	1.50*	—	0.03**	—	48.30**
14	—	0.78**	—	—	0.05**	43.94**
15	—	0.56**	—	0.38**	—	41.90**
16	—	—	—	—	—	39.90**
17	—	—	—	—	—	68.80**
18	—	—	—	—	—	11.12**
19	—	0.14**	—	—	0.16**	41.90**
20	—	0.64**	—	24.18**	—	55.96**
21	0.16	0.03**	0.08**	1.16**	—	99.86**
22	—	1.47**	—	11.91**	—	200.40**
23	—	0.32**	—	1.20**	—	163.28**
24	—	1.50**	—	—	—	92.02**
25	—	1.26**	—	1.20**	—	150.10**
26	—	0.78**	0.10**	—	—	152.10**
27	—	1.16**	—	26.44**	—	118.46**
28	—	1.42**	—	7.06**	—	239.20**
29	—	1.79**	—	0.60**	—	124.60**
30	—	1.00**	—	—	0.01**	111.58**
31	—	0.38**	—	1.12**	—	117.3**
32	0.74	1.04**	—	0.03**	—	236.20**
33	—	0.58**	—	-	—	103.76**
34	—	—	—	1.82**	—	126.14*
35	—	—	—	5.88*	—	114.63**
36	—	—	—	0.49**	—	229.02**
37	—	0.51**	—	0.10**	—	115.96**
38	—	—	—	—	—	205.40**
Total	2.16	24.56	0.24	110.02	0.95	3612.91

* A proportion discoloured. ** All discoloured.

Source: Author's observations.

Faunal variation at the Gua Sambangoala site, square A

The 7260 fragments bone and tooth fragments included eight fragments (0.1%) identified as human, 528 other fragments (7.3%) classifiable to various taxonomic levels, and a further 126 fragments (1.7%) sufficiently intact to be classified to the 'small mammal', 'medium-sized mammal' and 'mammal' categories (see Figure 10.4). The remaining fragments (90.9%) were too fragmentary for even these high-level classifications to be applied. Mammals (notably rats and suids) dominate the faunal identifications, but small to medium numbers of birds, reptiles, amphibians and fish were also identified (see Table 10.7).

The identified human remains (all plain) were concentrated in the top two spits (Table 10.5), and these subsurface specimens probably derive from ethnohistorical mortuary disposals at the site (see O'Connor et al. 2014). Otherwise, it is very difficult to see any patterning in the stratigraphic distribution of the identifications, particularly when the increased abundance of faunal material below Spit 20 is taken into account. For instance, suid identifications were made for every spit except Spits 6, 12 and 29 (Table 10.3), similar to the identification of rats throughout the sequence. As another example, Sulawesi dwarf cuscus identifications were made for just five of the upper 20 spits, which are characterised by a relatively small faunal assemblage overall, but for 15 of the lower 18 spits (Table 10.4).[2] In summary, the Gua Sambangoala square A faunal assemblage is best treated as stratigraphically unpatterned in terms of taxonomic composition, with the proviso that the low proportion of identifications combined with their diversity hinders stratigraphic discrimination.

The high proportion of discoloured fragments noted above applies virtually across the faunal spectra, including the main microfauna categories of rats (90/145 NISP, 62%) and frogs/toads (77/88 NISP, 87.5%). Accordingly, discoloured compared with plain status is unlikely to reflect cooking of the animal but instead the post-depositional effects. At the Tron Bon Lei site in Alor, the fragments of small vertebrates such as rats revealed traces of owl digestion but were also often blackened, either burnt through incidental exposure to hearth fires and/or manganese-stained (Hawkins et al. 2018). To extend this observation to Gua Sambangoala, its discoloured vertebrate fragments may also have been incorporated within hearths. Although there were no red clay lenses (probable hearth features) in the stratigraphic section below Spit 8 (Figure 10.3), the reddish to red clay matrix at greater depths, combined with the increased proportion of burnt remains, may reflect successive hearth-formation events that made it difficult for the excavators to identify individual hearth features. Alternatively, traces of heavy metal in the sediment (as perhaps reflected in the metallic lump that resembles iron slag, noted above) may have been the main discolouration agent.

The frog/toad, insectivorous bat and an unknown proportion of the rat remains at Gua Sambangoala may reflect non-human rather than human predation, or even the use of the rockshelter as a dwelling place. Naturally occurring predators on Sulawesi include civets, snakes and varanids (all found amongst the faunal remains) as well as various birds of prey. Sulawesi's murids include large forest rats, fully suitable for human consumption, as well as a plethora of small rats (Musser 1987); unfortunately, identification of the Gua Sambangoala rat specimens to species was not possible. Similarly, observations of tooth marks (one fragment) and possible cut marks (six fragments, none taxonomically identified) were too infrequent to provide an insight into the non-human versus the human contribution to the faunal assemblage. Overall, in view of

---

2   Differences between the spits in their quantity of the Sulawesi dwarf cuscus can be largely attributed to the quantity of recovered bone overall, as shown by the Pearson-r correlation coefficients of 0.41 between the dwarf cuscus and total bone weights and 0.37 between the dwarf cuscus and total bone NISP counts.

the distribution of small quantities of microfauna throughout the assemblage (Tables 10.5 and 10.6), it is likely that the human denizens alternated their presence with non-human predators throughout the recorded occupation sequence.

In addition to rats and anurans, the faunal remains that were represented at the site include snakes, middle-sized mammals (e.g. cuscus and macaques) and suids, as well as various other types of fauna that have a tropical rainforest habitat (Figure 10.4; Table 10.7). The local suids, the babirusa and the Sulawesi warty pig, made up the major portion of the large mammals included in the Gua Sambangoala diet. Their remains were often difficult to tell apart, which may explain why babirusa was much less frequently identified than *Sus celebensis* at Gua Sambangoala, whereas it was more frequently identified than *Sus celebensis* at Gua Mo'o hono (O'Connor et al., this volume). In any case, suids may have had larger population numbers in the Walandawe region than any other large mammal (notably the Anoa) at the time. While the variety of faunal identifications associated with the Gua Sambangoala foragers indicates a broad-spectrum hunting strategy, ranging from forest rats (potentially) to Anoa, the large size of the suids compared with most of the other identified animals suggests that they constituted the major source of animal protein.

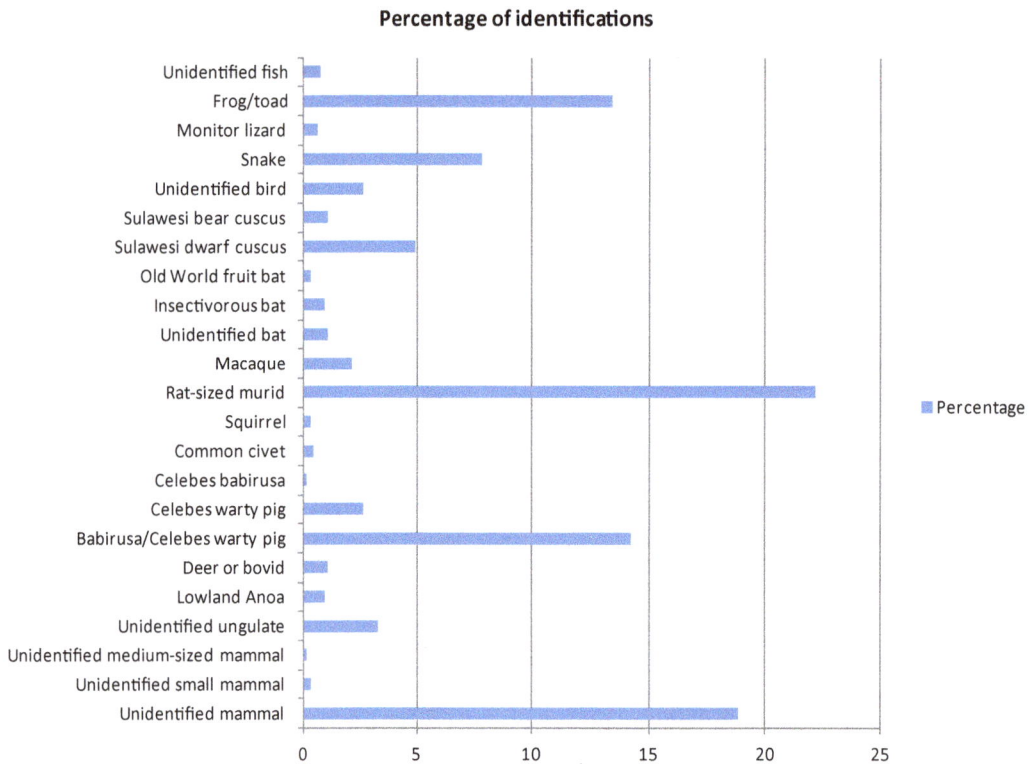

Figure 10.4: Percentages of the NISP identification at Gua Sambangoala.

Source: Author's analysis.

Table 10.7: Counts of taxonomic identifications from the bone fragments and teeth from the Gua Sambangoala excavation.

Class	Order	Family	Taxon	Common name	NISP	MNI
Osteichthyes				Fish	5	1
Amphibia	Anura			Frog/Toad	88	15
Reptiles	Squamata	Varanidae	*Varanus* sp(p).	Monitor lizard	4	1
		Serpentes (suborder)		Snake	51	1
Aves				Unidentified bird	17	1
Mammalia	Diprotodontia	Phalangeridae	*Ailurops ursinus*	Sulawesi bear cuscus	7	1
			Strigocuscus celebensis	Sulawesi dwarf cuscus	32	9
		Pteropodidae		Old World fruit bat	2	1
		Yangochiroptera (suborder)		Insectivorous bat	6	2
	Chiroptera			Unidentified bat	7	1
	Primates	Cercopithecidae	*Macaca* sp(p).	Macaque	14	2
	Rodentia	Muridae		Rat-sized murid	145	24
		Sciuridae		Squirrel	2	1
	Carnivora	Viverridae	*Macrogalidia musschenbroekii*	Sulawesi palm civet	3	3
	Artiodactyla	Suidae	*Babyroussa celebensis*	Sulawesi babirusa	1	1
			Sus celebensis	Celebes warty pig	17	7
		Suidae		Babirusa/Celebes warty pig	93	22
		Bovinae		Deer or bovid	7	1
			Bubalus depressicornis	Lowland Anoa	6	2
				Unidentified ungulate	21	–
				Unidentified medium-sized mammal	1	–
				Unidentified small mammal	2	–
				Unidentified mammal	123	–
TOTAL					**654**	**96**

Source: Author's analysis.

Condition of the Gua Sambangoala environment at 5500–3500 BP

There are unlikely to have been significant changes in the limestone karst and surrounding environments of Gua Sambangoala between the mid-Holocene and the present. The types of fauna identified from the site suggest an environment with a mosaic of open grasslands, woodland and rainforest. While we cannot be specific about which of these components would have been the focus of the Gua Sambangoala occupants, it can nonetheless be inferred that their protein data included terrestrial resources and aquatic resources in the form of fish, probably from local nearby rivers and streams. The site also contained significant quantities of freshwater shellfish, which do not form part of the present study. Identification of the rat remains to species level, which may be possible in the future, may provide a better insight into the diversity of habitat catchments near the site, as well as environmental change over time.

Conclusion

The Gua Sambangoala square A faunal assemblage was predominantly deposited between c. 5500–4500 cal BP (Spits 21–38) and a minor proportion between c. 4500–3500 cal BP (Spits 1–20). Taphonomic alterations to the bone, however, varied according to a different pattern. Only in Spit 1 did the quantity of plain bone exceed the quantity of discoloured bone, and by Spit 5 (and below) the proportion of plain bone was almost negligible. The predominance of discoloured bone, which can be attributed to incidental exposure to heat and/or metallic staining rather than cooking practices, contributed to the high proportion of the assemblage (91% by NISP count) being classified as 'unidentified'. Another taphonomic phenomenon, the incidence of concretions on the bone remains, was recorded sporadically between Spits 9 and 33 but coated the majority of the remains in Spits 34 to 38.

During the period covered by the radiocarbon dates the fauna available to the rockshelter occupants included fish, anurans, lizards, snakes, birds, bear cuscus and Sulawesi dwarf cuscus, bats, monkeys, rats, squirrels, civet cats, pig-deer (babirusa), Sulawesi warty pig (*Sus celebensis*) and Anoa. No clear evidence could be found for change in the composition of the fauna over time, notwithstanding the caveat that the great majority of the remains could not be identified with any specificity. One apparent feature of the assemblage is a greater representation of suids than Anoa; this may reflect greater ease of hunting in more open habitats, which are attractive to suids, rather than the thickly forested habitats preferred by Anoa (Simons and Bulbeck 2004). Accordingly, the environment of the Gua Sambangoala site between 5500 and 3500 years ago was probably not very different from the present environment.

Acknowledgements

The author acknowledges funding assistance from the Australian Research Council for its Discovery Project grant DP110101357 'The Archaeology of Sulawesi: A strategic island for understanding modern human colonization and interactions across our region' (awarded to Sue O'Connor, Jack Fenner, Janelle Stevenson and Ben Marwick). This assistance funded the author's participation in the classification of the Gua Mo'o hono excavated faunal assistance at The Australian National University in Canberra (under the supervision of Ken Aplin) and the Makassar Archaeology Office (under the supervision of Philip Piper, who also assisted the author with access to photographs from the Risksmuseum voor Natuurlijke Historie vertebrate collection). This assistance also funded classificatory work on the Gua Sambangoala fauna by the author (assisted by Jamil, then an archaeology student at Hasanuddin University in Makassar). The valuable comments by two anonymous referees are also gratefully acknowledged.

Author biography

Fakhri Makassar Archaeology Office, Makassar, South Sulawesi, Indonesia

References

Anggraeni, T. Simanjuntak, P. Bellwood and P. Piper. 2014. Neolithic foundations in the Karama valley, West Sulawesi, Indonesia. *Antiquity* 88:740–756. doi.org/10.1017/S0003598X00050663 (accessed 5 June 2018).

Bronk Ramsey, C. 2013. *OxCal 4.2 manual.* c14.arch.ox.ac.uk/oxcal/OxCal.html (accessed 27 October 2018).

Bulbeck, D., S. O'Connor and Fakhri. 2015. Decorated and plain baked clay from the initial to the late Holocene at Gua Talimbue, Southeast Sulawesi, Indonesia. Presentation at the 15th International Conference of the European Association of Southeast Asian Archaeologists, Paris, 6–10 July.

Clason, A.T. 1976. A preliminary note about the animal remains from the Leang 1 cave, South Sulawesi, Indonesia. *Modern Quaternary Research in Southeast Asia*, pp. 53–57. Modern Quaternary Research in Southeast Asia, Volume 2. Rotterdam: A.A. Balkema.

Davis, S.J.M. 1987. *The Archaeology of Animals*. London: B.T. Batsford.

Groves, C.P. 1976. The origin of the mammalian fauna of Sulawesi (Celebes). *Zeitschrift für Säugetierkunde* 41:201–216.

Groves, C.P. 2001. Mammals in Sulawesi: Where did they come from and when, and what happened to them when they got there? In I. Metcalfe, J. Smith, M. Morwood and I. Davidson (eds), *Faunal and Floral Migrations and Evolution in SE Asia-Australasia*, pp. 332–342. Lisse: A. A. Balkema.

Hawkins, S., S.C. Samper Carro, J. Louys, K. Aplin, S. O'Connor and Mahirta. 2018. Human palaeoecological interactions and owl roosting at Tron Bon Lei, Alor Island, eastern Indonesia. *The Journal of Island and Coastal Archaeology* 13(3):371–387. doi.org/10.1080/15564894.2017.128 5834 (accessed 5 June 2018).

Hooijer, D.A. 1950. *Man and Other Mammals from Toalian Sites in south-western Celebes*. Verhandelingen der Koninklijke Nederlandse Akademie van Wetenschappen, Afd. Natuurkunde. Amsterdam: North-Holland Publishing Co.

Musser, G. 1987. The mammals of Sulawesi. In T.C. Whitmore (ed.), *Biogeographical Evolution of the Malay Archipelago*, pp. 73–93. Oxford: Clarendon Press.

O'Connor, S., F.A. Aziz, B. Marwick, J. Fenner, B. Prasetyo, D. Bulbeck, T. Maloney, E.S. Pierre, R. Whitau, U.P. Wibowo, B. Hakim, A. Calo, Fakhri, M. Husni, Hasanuddin, A.A. Oktaviana, D. Prastiningtyas, F.Z. Campos, and P.J. Piper with an appendix by A.A. Oktaviana and Suryatman. 2014. *The Archaeology of Sulawesi: A Strategic Island for Understanding Modern Human Colonization and Interactions Across our Region*. Final Report to Indonesia's Bureau of Research and Technology, Department of Archaeology and Natural History, The Australian National University, Canberra and Department of Prehistory, Indonesia's National Centre for Archaeological Research and Development, Jakarta.

O'Connor, S., D. Bulbeck, P.J. Piper, F. Aziz, B. Marwick, F. Campos, J.N. Fenner, K. Aplin, Fakhri, Suryatman, T. Maloney, B. Hakim and R. Wood. 2018. The human occupation record of Gua Mo'o hono shelter, Towuti-Routa region of Southeastern Sulawesi. In S. O'Connor, D. Bulbeck and J. Meyer (eds), *The Archaeology of Sulawesi: Current Research on the Pleistocene to the Historic Period*, pp. 117–152. Canberra: ANU Press.

O'Connor, T. 2000. *The Archaeology of Animal Bones*. Stroud, Gloucestershire: Sutton Publishing.

Sarasin, P. and F. Sarasin. 1905. *Versuch einer Anthopologie der Insel Celebes. Erster Teil: Die Toála-höhlen von Lamontjong*. (Materialien zur Naturgeschichte der insel Celebes, V Band, 1 Teil). Wiesbaden: C.W. Kriedel's Verlag.

Simons, A.G. and D. Bulbeck. 2004. Late Quaternary faunal successions in South Sulawesi, Indonesia. In S.G. Keates and J.M. Pasveer (eds), *Quaternary Research in Indonesia Asia*, pp. 167–189. Quaternary Research in Southeast Asia, Volume 18. Leiden: A.A. Balkema.

Whitten, A.J., M. Mustafa and G.S. Henderson. 1987. *The Ecology of Sulawesi*. Yogyakarta: Gadjah Mada University Press.

11

Prehistoric sites in Kabupaten Enrekang, South Sulawesi

Hasanuddin

Abstract

Research on the prehistory of Enrekang, South Sulawesi, was conducted to find evidence of early human occupation in the region from the artefactual evidence preserved at various sites. A series of surveys was undertaken in sites at Mendatte, Buntu Banua and Buttu Batu, where there are traces of prehistoric habitation such as earthenware sherds, flaked stone artefacts, grindstones, hammerstones, barkcloth beaters and metal fragments. Test pits were excavated in the Buttu Batu rockshelter and revealed a basal habitation deposit that lacked earthenware pottery and an upper layer with abundant earthenware pottery. These results indicate a variety of activities suggestive of long-term settlement in the region from prior to the Neolithic and continuing to the Metal Age.

Keywords: prehistory, habitation, Buttu Batu, South Sulawesi, Enrekang

Introduction

The island of Sulawesi is located centrally within Indonesia, making it a strategic location for investigating cultural movements and developments. Its landscapes and seascapes have the potential to inform on the process of human migration and the introduction of domestic animals and crops, as well as human adaptation to the varying environmental and geological conditions within Sulawesi. South Sulawesi, in particular, has been shown to have a rich archaeological record from prehistoric to recent times (Simanjuntak and Widianto 2012).

Bulbeck (2004), writing on the survey and excavation results from Holocene sites in the South Sulawesi peninsula, synthesises the evidence into five phases from the early Holocene through to the Early Metal Phase as follows:

(a) the early Holocene, pre-7500 BP, characterised by stone tools of undistinguished quality across South Sulawesi

(b) the Early Toalean phase, between 7500–5500 BP, with the emergence of bone points and (in the southwest corner of Sulawesi) microliths

(c) the Late Preceramic Toalean phase, dating to 5500–3500 BP, marked by the appearance of Maros Points, also in the southwest corner of Sulawesi

(d) the Ceramic Toalean phase, from 3500–2000 BP, which saw the first Neolithic cultural traces emerging

(e) the Early Metal Phase, between 2000–1000 BP, when evidence of kampongs and agricultural activities arose, associated with handicrafts and trade. This phase also saw the development of social classes which are clearly visible in the early history of South Sulawesi beginning at around 600 BP.

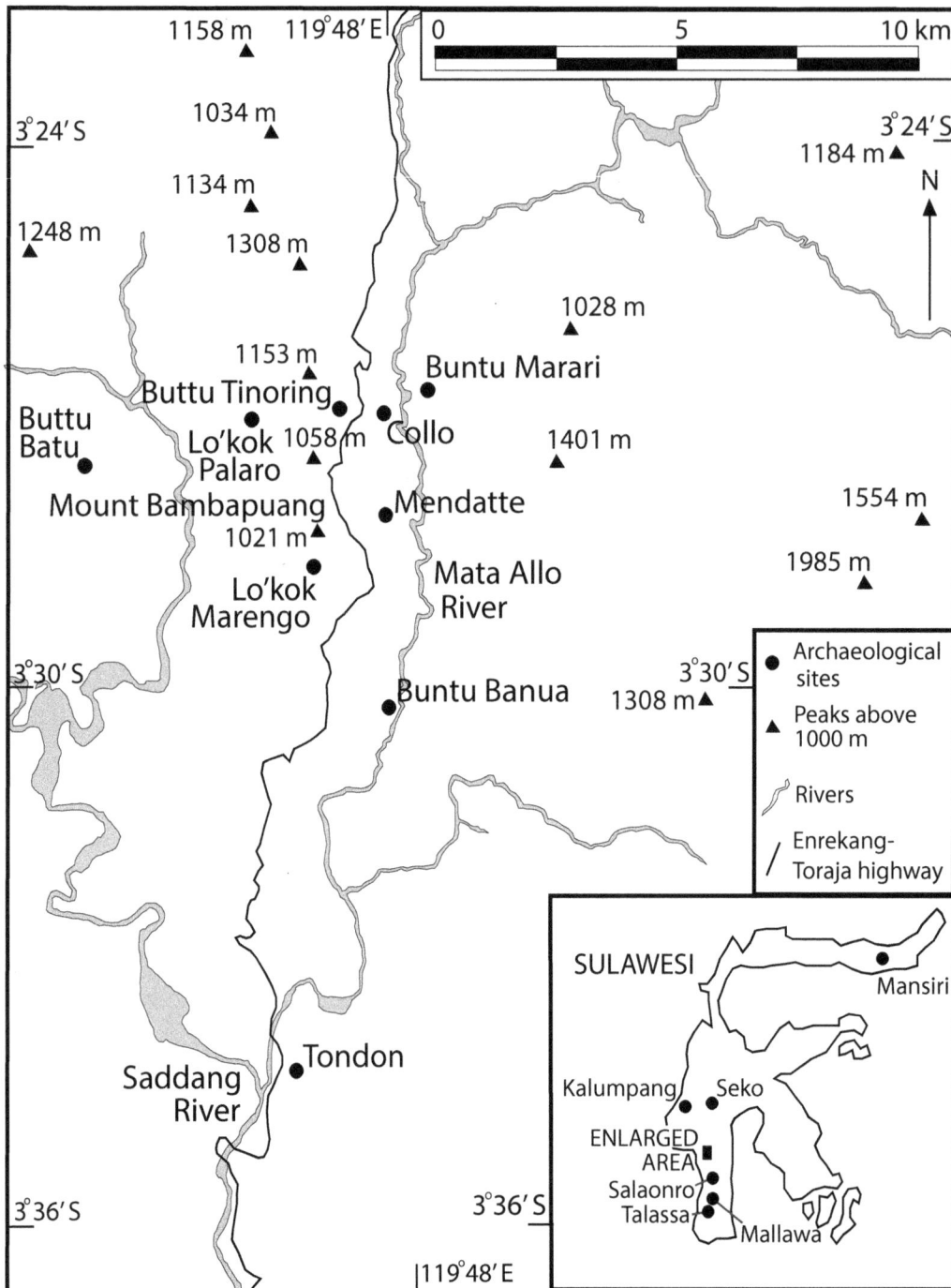

Figure 11.1: Sites and topographic features mentioned in the text.

Source: Base map from Duli (2013).

Kabupaten (District) Enrekang is of relevance to this schema as it lies directly north of the South Sulawesi peninsula, whose archaeology was synthesised by Bulbeck. It is also of relevance for its intermediate location between the Neolithic settlements at Minanga Sipakko and Kamassi, Kalumpang, in West Sulawesi and Mallawa in the Maros hinterland of South Sulawesi (Figure 11.1). Neolithic radiocarbon dates for Minanga Sipakko range between 3690±160 BP (P3G-05) and 2570±110 BP (P3G-97) (Simanjuntak et al. 2008); for Kamassi they range between 3345±40 BP (ANU 36406) and 2700±150 BP (Geolabs-411) (Anggraeni et al. 2014) and for Mallawa the range is 3580±130 BP (P3G-06) to 2281±46 BP (Wk-20380) (Mahmud 2008a; Hakim et al. 2009). These results point to the presence of Neolithic occupation sites in South and West Sulawesi between approximately 3500 and 2000 BP. Research undertaken in Enrekang between 2006 and 2011 by the Makassar Archaeology Office recovered a range of materials from prehistoric times through to the first influences of Islam (Somba 2009, 2011), but none of the habitation sites have been directly dated. Accordingly, this paper aims for indirect dating of these sites by comparing the archaeological finds from Enrekang with those from directly dated contexts elsewhere in Sulawesi.

Background: Kabupaten Enrekang and overview of survey

Enrekang District covers around 1,786 km² or 2.83% of the total extent of South Sulawesi province. Much of the district is mountainous (about 85%), with only small areas of rolling and flat landscapes. The mountainous regions are mostly in the north and central parts of Enrekang. The highest mountains are within the Latimojong and Bambapuang ranges. Mount Latimojong, also known as Mount Rantemario, has the highest peak in Sulawesi reaching 3478 metres above sea level (m asl). The flat lowlands are found in the south near the Tempe (Bila) and Malino rivers, on the border with Sidrap District. The main river systems are the Saddang, Mata Allo, Maula and Tabang rivers, which wind their way across much of Enrekang; Saddang being the largest of these waterways extending over roughly 150 km. All of these systems have been, and still are, integral to the lifeways of the region's inhabitants for drinking water as well as irrigation for their crops.

In 2006 and 2007, archaeological survey was undertaken near Mount Bambapuang (Figure 11.1) as well as an excavation at Collo where the survey had found earthenware pottery (Balar Makassar 2007). Two of the new sites discovered were the burial caves of Lo'kok Palaro and Lo'kok Marengo, and a third site was the open-air artefact scatter at Buttu Tinoring (Somba 2011). Collo is likely to be the oldest of these sites, possibly as old as Minanga Sipakko, based on its association of red-slipped pottery with coarse decorated pottery (incised triangles and impressed wavy designs) as well as flaked stone artefacts (Mahmud 2008b).

Additional field survey in 2008 resulted in investigation of the region's megalithic heritage at several sites, including Buntu Marari and Tondon (Figure 11.1). The range of recorded stone features (following the terminology defined by Hasanuddin 2015) included mortars, altars, stepped terraces, menhirs, *dakon* stones (with their chequerboard of circular depressions) and incised stones, demonstrating that the Enrekang area possesses a variety of megalithic styles (Hasanuddin 2011).

Although there are not yet any Carbon-14 dates for the sites described above, the material culture can be compared between sites in order to construct a relative chronology of the lifeways of the region's inhabitants. This approach is particularly useful when examining the stone artefacts from the Buttu Batu and Buntu Banua sites (see below). Also, absolute age determinations have been obtained on boat-shaped coffins with side planks and domed lids, known as *duni* or *mandu*, from Enrekang. In his research, Duli (2013) published Carbon-14 dates between 790±50 BP

(Beta-274731, 659–893 cal BP) and 470±40 BP (Beta-274734, 343–622 cal BP) taken from the wood of the coffins in six burial caves (*lo'kok*). Combining these results with the investigations into the prehistoric occupation of the Enrekang caves, we may infer that the original use of these caves as habitation sites changed to the storage of mortuary coffins prior to 700 BP.

2014 fieldwork overview

In 2014, several sites were surveyed in an attempt to locate early human occupation sites in the Enrekang region. Three sites were chosen for further investigation—Mendatte open site, Buntu Banua cave and the Buttu Batu rockshelter. After reviewing the survey results from these sites, it was apparent that Buttu Batu, with its considerable variety in surface finds as well as its favourable location in the Mount Bambapuang landscape, had the greatest potential for multi-phase occupation (Balar Makassar 2014).

Mendatte open site

Mendatte is located in the village (*desa*) of Rura in Kecamatan (Subdistrict) Anggeraja. The coordinates for the site are 03°28'13.0"S 119°47'37.7"E, with an altitude of 389 m asl (Figure 11.2). The topographic conditions within the survey area are mostly steep slopes. The archaeological finds included stone artefacts and earthenware sherds. Ten limestone boulders that had been purposefully shaped into rough cubes were also found at or near the site. These stones were not arranged in an obvious pattern; however, they were evidently brought up from the river and shaped. It is possible that they had previously been placed beneath houses as pile supports or flagstones.

Figure 11.2: Mandatte open site located to the east of Mount Bambapuang.
Source: Balar Makassar (2014).

Buntu Banua cave

Buntu Banua cave is located in the village (*desa*) of Kotu in Kecamatan Anggeraja with coordinates 03°30'10.3"S 119°47'23"E, at 606 m asl. This cave is located on a hilltop and features two interconnected openings, one oriented to the northwest and the other to the east (Figure 11.3). The first of these openings is about 80 cm high and 7 m wide, while the second is 1.2 m high and 2.5 m wide. In front of the second entrance is a narrow depression about 34 m long that ends in a flat bottom between 0.5 m and 4 m deep. The cave floor is scattered with stones that are covered by limestone gravel and sediment. Geologically, the cave is no longer active and is void of any speleothems.

The surface materials collected during the 2014 survey included human remains (tibia, rib and femur fragments), animal bones, a barkcloth beater (*batu ike*), earthenware pottery fragments, river cobbles and midden material. These materials are consistent with the assemblage recovered from the site during previous fieldwork (Mahmud 2008b), which included a polished stone axe with round cross-section, a barkcloth beater and earthenware sherds that sometimes show the use of a slow potter's wheel. The pottery vessel forms had open to everted rims, variably with flat and curved lips, and some featured carinated bodies. Rim decorations included parallel diagonal incisions bracketed by rectangular panels or vertical lines, while the decorations on the vessel bodies included impressed fishnet patterns and impressed parallel lines.

Figure 11.3: Entrances to Buntu Banua cave.
Source: Hasanuddin, Makassar Archaeology Office.

Buttu Batu rockshelter

Buttu Batu rockshelter is located near the village of Buttu Batu in Kabupaten Enrekang, 16.5 km from the regional capital of Enrekang, and northwest of Mount Bambapuang (Figure 11.4). The shelter is situated on a hilltop approximately 1.4 km east of and 280 m higher than the Saddang River. Two open-air 'sectors' to the southeast of the rockshelter were also surveyed for surface finds, and these are described here before describing the excavation of the rockshelter.

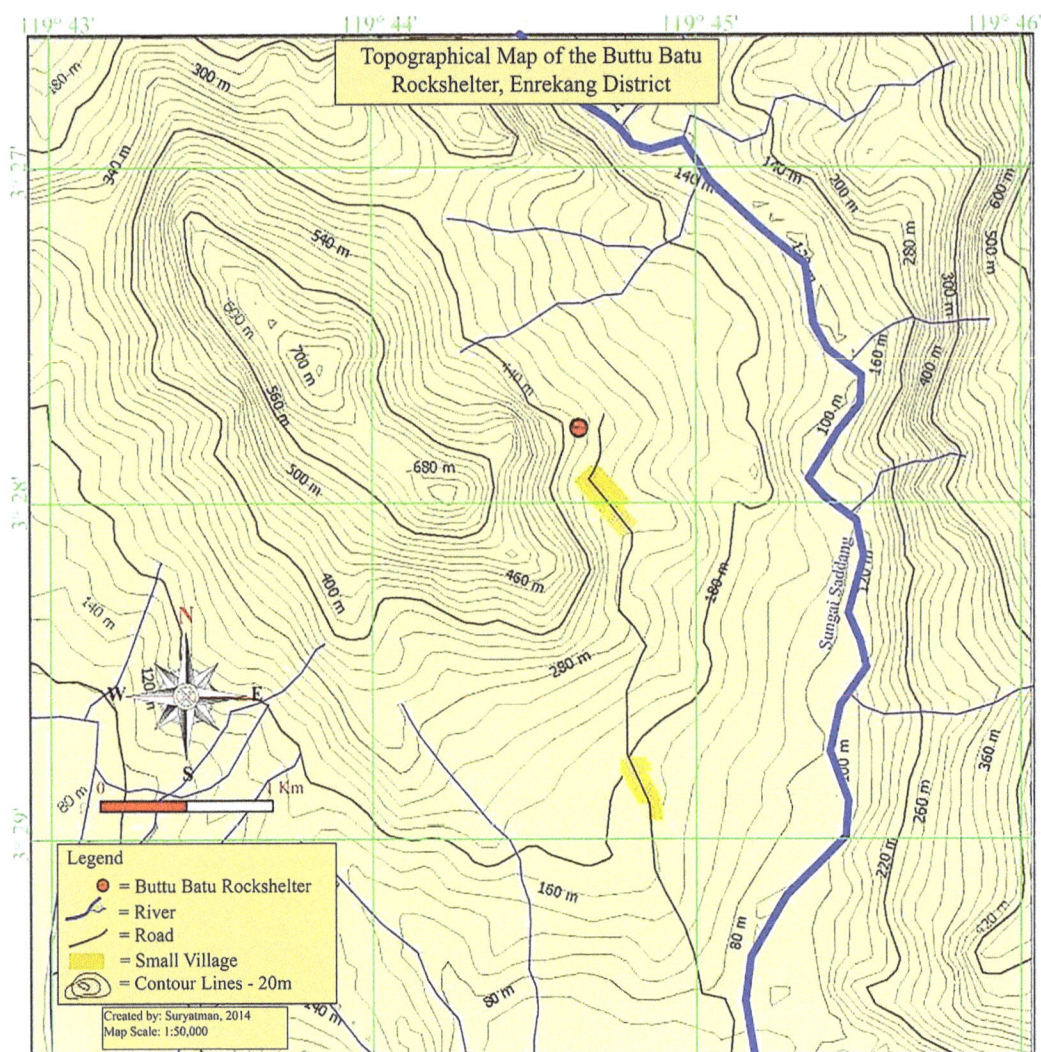

Figure 11.4: Topographic map with location of Buttu Batu Rockshelter.

Source: Suryatman, Makassar Archaeology Office.

Sector 1 has coordinates 03°27'58.2"S 119°44'44.9"E. It is situated on the mountainous slopes in an area near the road that has been previously used as gardens by the inhabitants of the Buttu Batu village to the south. The ground surface is overgrown by grass and littered with limestone blocks. Archaeological materials found in this sector included earthenware pottery sherds, river cobbles, flaked stone artefacts and a barkcloth beater.

Sector 2 of the surveyed area was located a short distance northwest of Sector 1 with coordinates 03°27'46.9"S 119°44'38.7"E and an elevation of 383 m asl. This sector lies within a limestone outcrop on a steep slope and includes a cleft in the stone that is roughly 90 cm in width. The inhabitants use this area for growing teak (*Tectona* sp.) and kemiri trees (*Aleurites moluccana*, or candlenut). The recorded archaeological materials included stone artefacts, earthenware sherds (some coarse, some decorated and some with a red or a black slip), river cobbles, animal bones and teeth, shell midden material and corroded metal fragments.

Buttu Batu excavation data

Overview

An excavation was opened at Buttu Batu site to document the cultural sequence and chronology. The excavation area, which was selected as it promised the greatest potential for the oldest habitation, was located about one metre behind the rockshelter opening, at the highest point inside the dripline (Figure 11.5a). Three contiguous 1 m x 1 m squares were measured out with a west to east orientation. They were labelled U1-T1, U1-T2 and U1-T3 (Figure 11.5). The surface sloped where the excavation took place, with U1-T1 at the highest point and U1-T3 at the lowest.

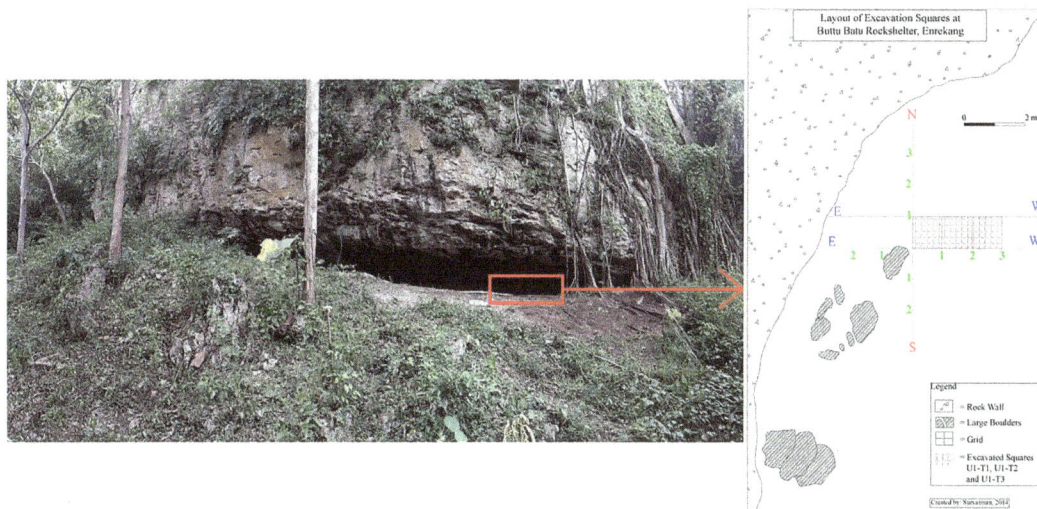

Figure 11.5: Photograph of Buttu Batu Rockshelter at Enrekang (left); A map of the excavated squares (right).
Source: Suryatman, Makassar Archaeology Office.

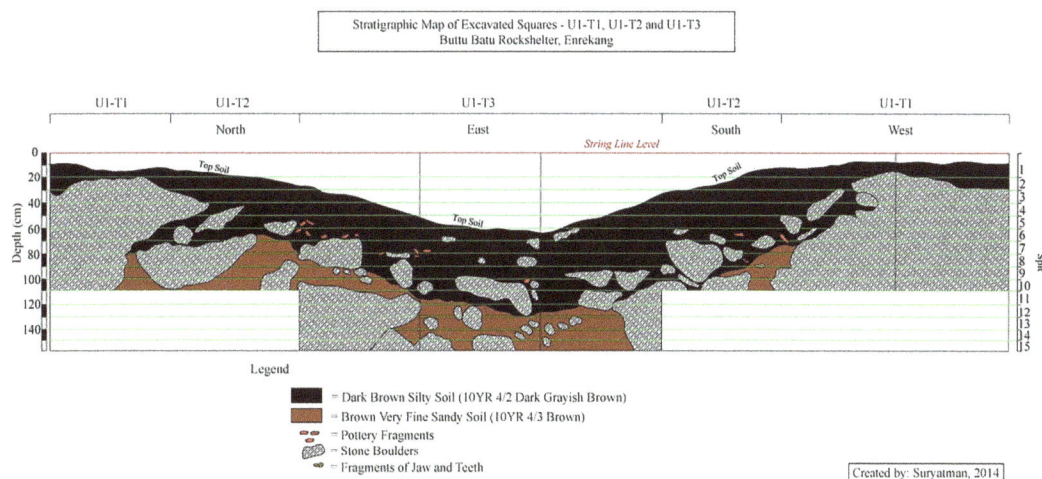

Figure 11.6: Stratigraphic map of U1-T1, U1-T3 and U1-T3 squares.
Source: Suryatman, Makassar Archaeology Office.

The excavation strategy was to remove sediment in 10 cm spits within the three 1 m² squares. Spits were counted below a common datum, hence the first U1-T3 spit was recorded as Spit 3 along the western margin of U1-T3 but as Spit 5 along the test pit's eastern margin (see Figure 11.6). Considerable rock fall was uncovered in the excavation, particularly in U1-T1 and U1-T2, precluding excavation of the lower levels (Spits 11–15). The roof and the floor slope towards each other moving from U1-T3 (where there is sufficient room for standing erect) to U1-T1 (where space is cramped). These squares had a maximum depth of 110 cm, whereas it was possible to excavate down to 160 cm beneath the datum in U1-T3. The excavation revealed two distinct cultural layers that are described below, and illustrated in Figure 11.6.

Stratigraphic analysis and vertical distribution of the excavated materials

The upper layer (Layer 1) consisted of dark brown silt (10 YR 4/2 dark greyish brown in Munsell chart terminology). The depth of this layer beneath the datum ranged between 10 cm to the west and 130 cm to the east, demonstrating a slope descending towards the east (as well as to the north and south). Boulders made up a large portion of the west wall and some of the north wall. Earthenware pottery sherds were common in the upper layer (Figure 11.6). Metal fragments were recovered from the surface of the upper layer but not from the excavated sediment; this may be due to unfavourable circumstances for long-term preservation of metal rather than an antiquity of the entire upper layer predating the Early Metal Phase.

The lower layer (Layer 2) was a very fine brown sand (10 YR 4/3 brown). Its uppermost extent occurred at 65 cm along the northern wall and it continued to the base of the excavation. Earthenware sherd quantities decreased as depth increased, where a transition occurred to flaked stone artefacts dominating the deposits. Midden materials including vertebrate (bone and tooth) fragments and shellfish were recovered from the excavation. Tables 11.1 and 11.2 below present the total weights of these excavated materials from U1-T1/U1-T2 (combined, to increase sample sizes) and U1-T3, respectively.

Table 11.1: Combined weights (grams) of earthenware sherds, flaked stone artefacts, bone and shellfish by spit for U1-T1 and U1-T2, Buttu Batu.

Spit	Layer	Earthenware sherds	Flaked stone artefacts	Bone and tooth fragments	Shellfish
1	1	3049	42	101	38
2	1	2752	56	223	92
3	1	2680	22	311	40
4	1	2214	22	213	5
5	1	7755	91	414	23
6	1	4865	289	402	62
7	1/2 transition	933	31	258	15
8	1/2 transition	757	243	943	175
9	1/2 transition	82	608	260	589
10	2	0	484	193	110
Total		25,087	1888	3318	1149

Source: Suryatman, Balai Arkeologi Makassar.

Table 11.2: Weights (grams) of earthenware sherds, flaked stone artefacts, bone and shellfish by spit for U1-T3, Buttu Batu.

Spit	Layer	Earthenware sherds	Flaked stone artefacts	Bone and tooth fragments	Shellfish
1	—	—	—	—	—
2	—	—	—	—	—
3	1	286	0	7	0
4	1	707	13	62	0
5	1	1082	0	168	0
6	1	1775	4	260	0
7	1	2427	43	208	10
8	1	3102	121	79	0
9	1	2792	381	101	77
10	1/2 transition	857	0	62	142
11	1/2 transition	76	115	76	67
12	2	0	193	80	83
13	2	0	108	55	50
14	2	0	210	77	8
15	2	0	46	148	32
Total		13,104	1234	1383	469

Source: Suryatman, Balai Arkeologi Makassar.

Earthenware sherds (Figure 11.7) were found through the deposit in U1-T1/U1-T2, with gradually decreasing weights from Spits 1 to 4, then a marked increase in Spit 5, followed by a decline that continued into Spit 10 (Layer 2, where no pottery was recovered). In the lower-lying U1-T3, sherds began in Spit 3 and increased to a maximum in Spit 8. Quantities then decreased, and no pottery was recovered from Spits 12–15 (corresponding to Layer 2). Overall, pottery was most prevalent at the middle depths (Spit 5 in U1-T1 and U1-T2, Spits 8 and 9 in U1-T3), before decreasing in subsequent spits and disappearing all together by 100 cm beneath the surface of the deposit.

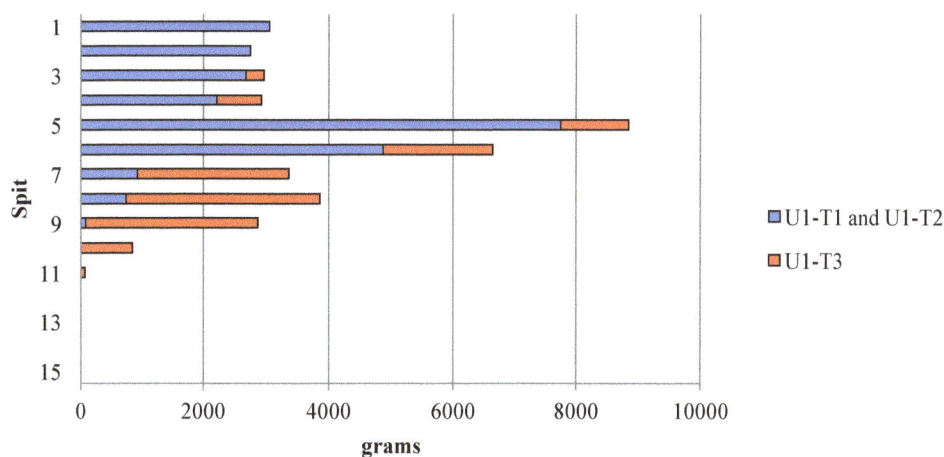

Figure 11.7: Bar graph showing the weights of the excavated pottery sherds by spit from Buttu Batu squares U1-T1, U1-T2 (blue) and U1-T3 (red).
Source: Data from Tables 11.1 and 11.2.

The weights of flaked stone artefacts, osseous remains and shellfish in U1-T1/U1-T2 are presented in Figure 11.8. All are variably present within the deposit with larger quantities of each towards the basal spits, despite the decreased volume of excavated sediment owing to the increasing density of roof fall. Flaked stone was present in the uppermost spits but became more abundant in Spit 6. Spit 7 saw a sharp drop in stone artefacts followed by an increase again in Spits 8–10, corresponding to the transition to Layer 2, with the largest quantity recovered from Spit 9. Bones and teeth were found throughout, but with the highest weights recorded in Spit 8. Shell was found in each spit and, like the stone artefacts, was most abundant towards the base of these squares, peaking in Spit 9.

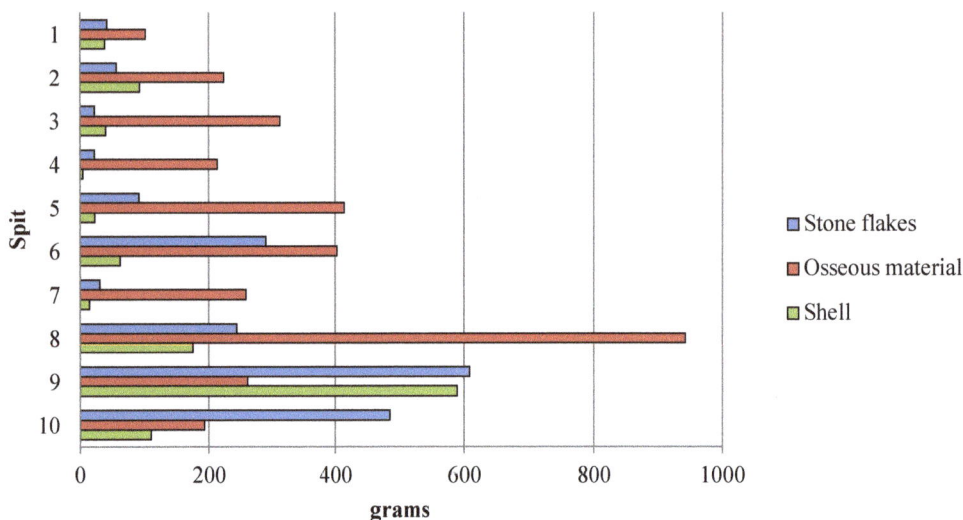

Figure 11.8: Bar graph showing the weights of flaked stone artefacts, osseous remains and shellfish in U1-T1 and U1-T2, Buttu Batu.

Source: Data from Table 11.1.

In square U1-T3 (Figure 11.9), flaked stone artefacts and osseous remains began appearing in Spits 3 and 4, reflecting the lack of excavated deposit above Spit 3 (Figure 11.6). Only small quantities of stone artefacts were retrieved from the upper levels before an increase in Spit 7 that peaked in Spit 9. No stone artefacts were recovered from Spit 10; however, they returned in subsequent spits (corresponding to Layer 2) with fair regularity. Osseous materials outweighed the stone artefacts in the upper spits of this square with the maximum amount in Spit 6 and then a return to steady abundance in lower spits. Shells did not appear until Spit 7 with none recovered again until Spit 9. Their prevalence in the deposit continued downwards with the greatest quantity of shell recovered from Spit 10.

Of particular interest were the barkcloth beater (*batu ike*), polished stone axe fragment and bone artefacts, all from U1-T1 and U1-T2 (Table 11.3). The first two of these were found in the pottery-bearing spits. As for the bone artefacts, two were found in Spit 3 and so may not be very old, whereas the third (from Spit 9) may be older than any of the pottery deposited at the site.

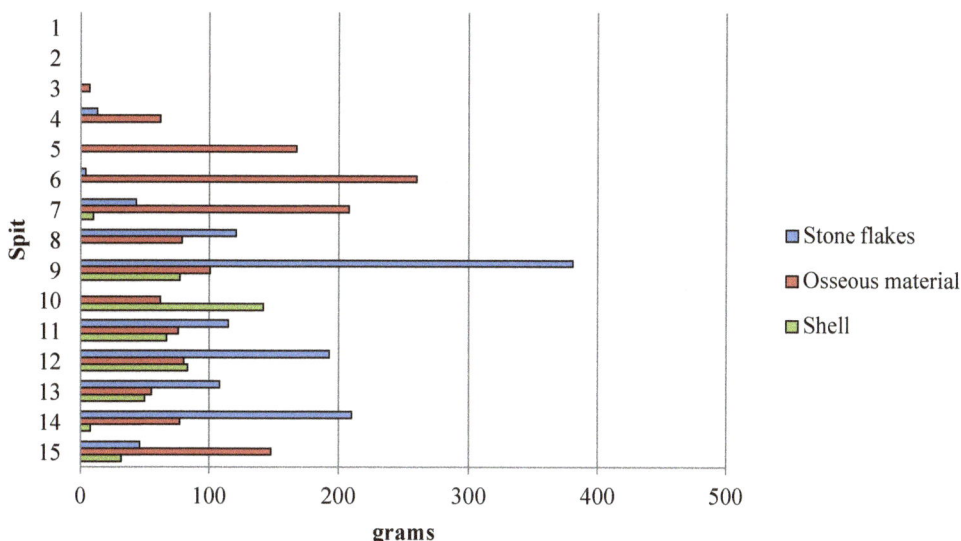

Figure 11.9: Bar graph showing the weights of flaked stone, osseous remains and shellfish in U1-T3, Buttu Batu.

Source: Data from Table 11.2.

Table 11.3: Spit Locations of the barkcloth beater (*batu ike*), stone axe fragments and bone artefacts in the U1-T1 and U1-T2 Squares (combined), Buttu Batu.

Spit	Layer	Barkcloth beater	Stone axe	Bone artefacts
1	1	0	0	0
2	1	0	0	0
3	1	0	0	2
4	1	0	0	0
5	1	1	0	0
6	1	0	0	0
7	1/2 transition	0	0	0
8	1/2 transition	0	1	0
9	1/2 transition	0	0	1
10	2	0	0	0
Total		1	1	3

Source: Suryatman, Balai Arkeologi Makassar.

Analysis of the earthenware pottery

A total of 7527 earthenware sherds were analysed, including 5523 plain sherds (73%) with no discernible decoration and 2004 decorated sherds (27%). This proportion of decorated sherds is high. By way of comparison, the recorded proportion of decorated sherds in the Kalumpang sites is less than 10%, and usually between 0–5% in all of the spits in Minanga Sipakko Trench III and Kamassi square K1 (Anggraeni et al. 2014); at the Neolithic site of Mansiri in North Sulawesi it is less than 1% (Azis et al., this volume).

The Buttu Batu motifs were divided into eight simple motifs and seven combination or complex motifs. The simple motifs included sets of parallel depressions and wavy incisions, overlapping zigzags, translations of circular depressions, scalloped rims, scored rims, lug holes (Figures 11.10–11.12) and parallel vertical incisions (Figure 11.13). The complex motifs included combinations of circles, parallel horizontal and vertical lines, dentate (punctate) dots aligned in parallel format or inside triangles, zigzag incisions, lattice patterns filling rectangular panels, triangles filled with slanting lines, scored rims with a central furrow, and corrugated carinations (Figures 11.10 and 11.12). These motifs show some similarities to the Buntu Banua pottery decorations as described by Mahmud (2008b), such as parallel diagonal incisions, rectangular panels, fishnet (lattice) patterns and impressed parallel lines. On the other hand, similarities with the decorations on the Kalumpang Neolithic pottery are less clear. For instance, of the motifs listed in Table 11.4, both Buttu Batu and Kamassi have 15 motifs in their recorded repertoire, but only seven (47%) in common.

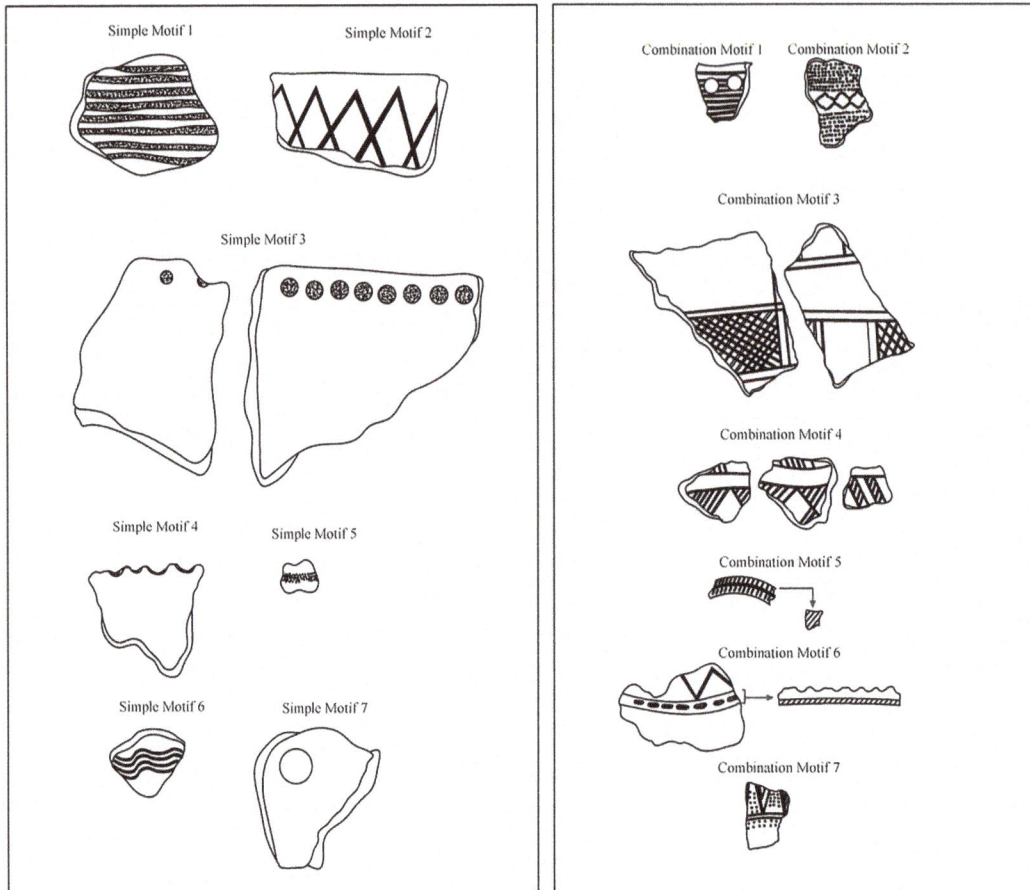

Figure 11.10: Varieties of simple and combination motifs on the pottery from Buttu Batu.
Source: Hasanuddin, Makassar Archaeology Office.

Figure 11.11: Simple Buttu Batu motifs 1 (left) and 4 (right).
Source: Hasanuddin, Makassar Archaeology Office.

Figure 11.12: Simple Buttu Batu motif 2 (left) and combination Buttu Batu motifs 2 (centre) and 3 (right).
Source: Hasanuddin, Makassar Archaeology Office.

2cm

Figure 11.13: Examples of the rim sherds from pottery found at Buttu Batu.
Source: Hasanuddin, Makassar Archaeology Office.

Table 11.4: Comparison of the Buttu Batu motifs with the Kalumpang (Minanga Sipakko and Kamassi) motifs.

Motif	Buttu Batu	Minanga Sipakko	Kamassi
Diagonal cross-hatching	√	√	x
Standalone diagonal incisions	x	√	√
Open circles	√	√	x
Filled circles	√	x	√
Double-stamped circles	x	√	√
Semi-circles	x	√	√
Parallel zigzags with vertical incised lines	x	√	x
Other zigzag incisions	√	√	x
Zigzag lines of punctate points	x	√	x
Lines of punctate points	√	√	√
Triangular punctations	x	√	x
Triangles filled with punctations	√	√	√
Triangles with incised infill	√	√	√
Right-angled triangles	x	√	x
Parallel vertical incisions	√	√	x
Parallel horizontal incisions	√	√	x

Motif	Buttu Batu	Minanga Sipakko	Kamassi
Parallel slanting incisions	√	√	√
Bone-shaped stamp	x	√	x
Lunates	x	√	√
Arca shell impressions	x	√	√
Square/rectangular mazes	x	√	√
Waves	√	√	√
Leaf designs	x	x	√
Incised stylised human figures	x	x	√
Pierced holes	√	√	x
Scalloped rims	√	√	√
Scored rims	√	x	x
Rectangular panels	√	x	x

Source: Figures 11.10–11.13 (this chapter); Prasetyo (2008).

The rims (Figure 11.13) were examined to investigate the vessel forms. Only rims that had more than 10% of the orifice preserved (n=134) were considered complete enough to infer the shape of the whole pot and its type and potential use.

The dominant vessel form was cooking pots (*periuk*), with 80 identified (60% of the analysed rims). The next most commonly identified forms were bowls or *mangkuk* (33% of the sample, n=45; Figure 11.14) and vases or *jambangan* (seven sherds or 5% of the sample). A cup (*cawan*) fragment and a fragment from a covered jar (*tempayan tertutup*) were also distinguishable.

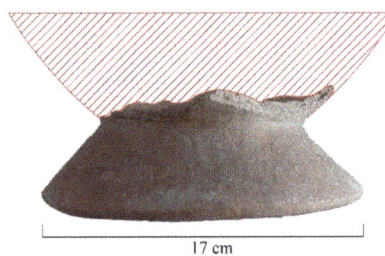

Figure 11.14: Reconstruction of a Buttu Batu bowl represented by its base.

Source: Hasanuddin, Makassar Archaeology Office.

Analysis of the stone artefacts

The excavation at Buttu Batu uncovered a number of stone artefacts produced using various technologies. Limestone, basalt and chert were the most common raw materials used to produce tools at the site. The artefacts recovered included cores, retouched and unretouched flakes, blades, polished axes and a fragment of a barkcloth beater (*batu ike*).

The term *batu ike* comes from the Kulawi and Biromaru communities in Central Sulawesi and describes a tool with deep parallel grooves that was used to turn the inner bark of the paper mulberry tree *Broussonetia papyrifia* into barkcloth (Bellwood 1978:139; Aragon 1990). The barkcloth beater fragment excavated at Buttu Batu was made from andesite and was 3.9 cm x 3.3 cm x 2.3 cm (Figure 11.15b). Its shape suggests it is of the Kalumpang type, one of the two barkcloth beater forms found in the region. Kalumpang barkcloth beaters generally have a squat cuboid shape with two main faces in the shape of shallow concave surface. There are grooves on one of the concave surfaces that is used to tether a rope connected to the butt of the stone. This type is very common in Sulawesi and Kalimantan (Indonesian Borneo). The other barkcloth beater form, the Philippine or horned type, has only one concave surface, which is striated, and a stone handle connected to the butt. This type is common in the Philippines (Soejono 1984) and also in Malaysian Borneo, such as the examples from Bukit Tengkorak (Chia 2003:62, 2015:46).

There were four axe blanks and fragments found at the site that reveal a process of manufacture through the two steps of hammer dressing followed by polishing. Two of the axes had physical evidence of the hammer-dressing phase; the other two had polishing on one face. Two of the axes were made of andesite. The first was 4.5 cm x 2.6 cm x 0.7 cm and the other was 7.6 cm x 4.1 cm x 1.2 cm. The other two axes were basalt. One measured 7.2 cm x 5.7 cm x 1.6 cm and the final piece (Figure 11.15a) was 6 cm x 4.5 cm x 1.3 cm.

Flaked stone artefacts at this site were abundant. Flaking debitage dominates the flaked stone assemblage at Buttu Batu, which is a common feature of stone tool industries in eastern Indonesia (e.g. Simanjuntak and Widianto 2012:178). As well as 44 unretouched flakes in a range of shapes (Figures 11.15c and 11.16a–d), ventrally retouched flakes were recovered, one from Spit 3 and two from Spit 4 (Figure 11.15d–e), as well as edge-trimmed flakes (Figure 11.17). Hammer stones with scarring on one surface were found in Spits 4 and 6, and a grindstone was recovered from Spit 5. The site also contained the waste products from tool manufacturing such as debitage and cores (Figure 11.16e).

Figure 11.15: Stone artefacts found during excavation at Buttu Batu: (a) stone axe blank, (b) barkcloth beater fragment (Spit 5), (c) abruptly-backed blade and (d–e) stone flakes with ventral retouch.

Source: Hasanuddin, Makassar Archaeology Office.

Figure 11.16: Stone artefacts found during excavation at Buttu Batu: (a–b) pointed flakes, (c–d) blade-like flakes and (e) core.

Source: Hasanuddin, Makassar Archaeology Office.

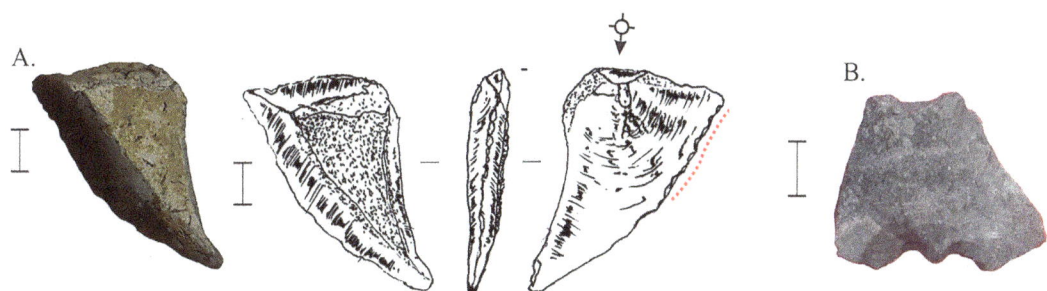

Figure 11.17: Edge-trimmed flakes from Buttu Batu of chert (A) and limestone (B).

Source: Hasanuddin, Makassar Archaeology Office.

The barkcloth beater (*batu ike*) and polished stone tools such as the axe blanks and fragments reflect a more complex use of stone artefacts during the Neolithic than during pre-pottery times. The Kalumpang type of barkcloth beater found at the Buttu Batu site is the usual form found in South Sulawesi, not only at Buntu Banua (Enrekang District) but also the Salaonro site (Soppeng District). It has also been recorded ethnographically as still in use at Seko in the northern part of Luwu, amongst other places.

Discussion

The survey results of several sites in Enrekang District in South Sulawesi indicate a settled Neolithic lifestyle with artefactual evidence in the form of earthenware fragments, flaked stone artefacts, grindstones, river cobbles, stone axe fragments and barkcloth beaters. The Buttu Batu rockshelter is an occupation site with evidence of this kind on its surface. Excavation of the site revealed two occupation layers with abundant archaeological finds. For the most part, the upper layer contained artefactual finds similar to those on the surface, such as earthenware fragments, axe fragments and a barkcloth beater, which together reflect a prehistoric occupation with a Neolithic aspect.

On the other hand, the lower layer at Buttu Batu is a pre-pottery occupation level as there was an absence of sherds in Spits 12–15 in the U1-T3 square, as well as a marked decrease in the presence of sherds below Spit 6 in the U1-T1/U1-T2 squares. Remains of shellfish, bone and flaked stone remained plentiful throughout the excavation of the lower layer, even though the quantity of excavated deposit from each spit decreased due to the increase in boulders from past roof falls. These data indicate a late pre-pottery 'Mesolithic' habitation phase (Bulbeck et al. 2000) equating approximately to Spit 10 and below, despite the lack of any recovered Maros points (which are associated with the Mesolithic phase of the southwest of Sulawesi).

Remains of bone and, to a lesser degree, flaked stone and shell were recovered from the upper layer, along with large quantities of earthenware sherds, a barkcloth beater and a stone axe fragment. If we remember that there was little or no excavated deposit in the top two spits recognised for U1-T3, we can appreciate that the main classes of finds, notably the earthenware sherds (which constitute the dominant finds), are distributed throughout the layer. From the analysis of the stratigraphy of this upper layer and its artefact distribution, it is reasonable to suggest that it is a single assemblage, reflecting a single pattern of social behaviour (Deetz 1967:105–106). The set of activities reflected by the finds include making and using stone tools both in flaked and axe forms, using earthenware pottery, and making barkcloth—all of which suggest a settled lifestyle at or within the vicinity of the rockshelter.

However, in view of its isolated location and spatial constraints, the Buttu Batu rockshelter itself may not have hosted a settled population during the Neolithic. Instead, it may have served as a rockshelter for foragers who traded forest produce for pottery and other Neolithic items produced by their settled neighbours, or as a temporary camp for parties travelling out from settlements nearby (cf. Bulbeck 2004). Both uses of the site are possible, including a transition over time from the former to the latter, as suggested by the general decline in flaked stone artefacts and rise in earthenware sherds moving from the lower to the upper spits in Layer 1 (Tables 11.1 and 11.2).

The information from Buttu Batu presents a new perspective for our understanding of a Neolithic site on a high plateau of South Sulawesi. Although there are not yet any Carbon-14 dates to provide absolute dating, comparisons with sites that have produced technological and artefactual remains of the same kind (Simanjuntak 2008) suggest that the people who successfully occupied the Enrekang region partook of the same Neolithic culture as found at the open sites of Mallawa and Talassa in Maros, South Sulawesi, and those at Kalumpang in West Sulawesi. An initial date of ~3500 BP has been proposed for the Neolithic in South Sulawesi and West Sulawesi, based on the dates associated with early pottery (Simanjuntak 2008), although whether this chronology would be applicable to the strongly decorated pottery from Buttu Batu may be a matter of contention. In any case, the Buttu Batu rockshelter also preserves deposits that reflect pre-Neolithic habitation prior to the appearance of pottery. This provides valuable information on the activities undertaken in the highlands of the northern part of South Sulawesi prior to the incursion into Sulawesi of Austronesian speakers with their Neolithic culture at around 3500 BP (Simanjuntak 2008).

For the most part, Enrekang is an area dominated by hills and mountains that favour the development of agriculture. Mountain runoff and the large flowing rivers of the Saddang, Mata Allo, Maula and Tabang are integral for agricultural irrigation as well as providing fresh water to the region. The geographic situation of Enrekang works to create a dynamic and variable lifestyle, with its peaks interlaced by large flowing rivers that provide a laneway for interconnections and interactions with the outside world.

The Saddang River, which is navigable as far as Enrekang, in particular opened a vast area of the region to travelling peoples. Foot traffic through the hills along the Saddang River provided access to the Toraja highlands to the north of Enrekang, while river traffic connected Enrekang with the lowlands towards the south as far as the coast where the Saddang and its anabranches debouch. Along the coast, river entrances could be used for mooring boats, even in marshy areas, and as routes through the mangrove forest barriers (Pelras 1996:6). Indeed, the linguist Roger Mills proposed that the first speakers of South Sulawesi languages arrived by sea, not in a single migration but in a series of movements from an island nearby, attracted to the mouth of the Saddang River for the access it provided to trade routes into the hinterland (Pelras 1996:42). Pelras (1996:43) set the scenario proposed by Mills to the Early Metal Phase, shortly after 2000 BP, which would be too recent to apply to the Neolithic. Nonetheless, the major rivers of Sulawesi such as the Saddang may also have served as transport routes for the Austronesian-speaking immigrants arriving in the region (Azis et al., this volume).

Conclusion

The upper occupation layer at the Buttu Batu site produced finds (e.g. earthenware pottery, barkcloth beater, stone axes and flakes) similar to those associated with early Austronesian speakers in the Philippines and West Sulawesi (Anggraeni et al. 2014). The onset of this occupation phase may be comparable to the ~3500 BP dating recorded for the Sulawesi Neolithic sites of Kalumpang and Mallawa. Importantly, the Buttu Batu sequence demonstrates that occupation in the Bambapuang area occurred prior to the introduction of pottery, as found widely elsewhere across the Indonesian Archipelago (Bulbeck et al. 2000). In the future, excavation should be extended deeper through the lower deposits with limestone boulders as far down as the earliest habitation deposit. In addition, absolute dating techniques should be applied in order to establish the chronology of pre-Neolithic and Neolithic settlement at the site, and the relationship with early occupation and the Neolithic transition as recorded at other sites in Sulawesi.

Acknowledgements

The author gratefully acknowledges the assistance of his colleague Suryatman at the Makassar Archaeology Office, who has provided tables and illustrative material with permission for their presentation here, and the helpful comments of two anonymous referees on an earlier draft of this contribution.

Author biography

Hasanuddin Makassar Archaeology Office, Makassar, South Sulawesi, Indonesia

References

Anggraeni, T. Simanjuntak, P. Bellwood and P. Piper. 2014. Neolithic foundations in the Karama valley, West Sulawesi, Indonesia. *Antiquity* 88(341):740–756. doi: 10.1017/S0003598X00050663 (accessed 5 June 2018).

Aragon, L.V. 1990. Barkcloth production in Central Sulawesi. *Expedition* 32(1):33–48. anthropology.unc. edu/files/2018/02/Aragon-barkcloth-in-Sulawesi-color-Expedition-1990.pdf (accessed 9 March 2017).

Azis, N., C. Reepmeyer, G. Clark, Sriwigati and D.A. Tanudirjo. 2018. Mansiri in North Sulawesi: A new dentate-stamped pottery site in Island Southeast Asia. In S. O'Connor, D. Bulbeck and J. Meyer (eds), *The Archaeology of Sulawesi: Current Research on the Pleistocene to the Historic Period*, pp. 191–206. Canberra: ANU Press.

Balar Makassar. 2007. Laporan Survei dan Ekskavasi di Kawasan Bambapuang Kabupaten Enrekang. Unpublished report. Makassar: Makassar Archaeological Office.

Balar Makassar. 2014. Laporan Penelitian Arkeologi di Kabupaten Enrekang. Unpublished report. Makassar: Balai Arkeologi.

Bellwood, P. 1978. *Man's Conquest of the Pacific.* Sydney: Collins.

Bulbeck, D. 2004. Divided in space, united in time: The Holocene prehistory of South Sulawesi. In S. Keates and J.M. Pasveer (eds), *Quaternary Research in Indonesia*, pp. 129–166. Modern Quaternary Research in Southeast Asia, Volume 18. Leiden: A.A. Balkema.

Bulbeck, D., M. Pasqua and A. Di Lello. 2000. Culture history of the Toalean of South Sulawesi, Indonesia. *Asian Perspectives* 39(1–2):71–108. doi.org/10.1353/asi.2000.0004 (accessed 5 June 2018).

Chia, S.M.S. 2003. *The Prehistory of Bukit Tengkorak as a Major Pottery Making Site in Southeast Asia.* Kota Kinabalu: Department of Sabah Museum.

Chia, S.M.S. 2015. *Arkeologi Bukit Tengkorak, Sabah.* Pulau Pinang: Universiti Sains Malaysia.

Deetz, J. 1967. *Invitation to Archaeology.* New York: Natural History Press.

Duli, A. 2013. The mandu coffin: A boat symbol of ancestral spirits among the Enrekang people of South Sulawesi. *Review of Indonesian and Malaysian Affairs* 47(1):115–138.

Hakim, B., M. Nur and Rustam. 2009. The sites of Gua Pasaung (Rammang-Rammang) and Mallawa: Indicators of cultural contact between the Toalian and Neolithic complexes in South Sulawesi. *Bulletin of The Indo-Pacific Prehistory Association* 29:45–52. doi.org/10.7152/bippa.v29i0.9476 (accessed 5 June 2018).

Hasanuddin. 2011. Temuan megalitik dan penataan ruang permukiman di Kabupaten Enrekang, Sulawesi Selatan. *Walennae* 13(2):159–168.

Hasanuddin. 2015. Kebudayaan Megalitik di Sulawesi Selatan dan Hubungannya dengan Asia Tenggara. Unpublished PhD thesis, Centre for Archaeological Research Malaysia, Universiti Sains Malaysia, Kuala Lumpur. www.oxis.org/theses/hasanuddin-2015.pdf (accessed 5 June 2018).

Mahmud, I. 2008a. The Neolithic site of Mallawa. In T. Simanjuntak (ed.), *Austronesian in Sulawesi*, pp. 119–127. Jakarta: Center for Prehistoric and Austronesian Studies.

Mahmud, I. 2008b. The Neolithic and the ethnogenesis process of Enrekang. In T. Simanjuntak (ed.), *Austronesian in Sulawesi*, pp. 105–118. Jakarta: Center for Prehistoric and Austronesian Studies.

Pelras, C. 1996. *The Bugis.* Oxford: Blackwell.

Prasetyo, B. 2008. Pottery from the Neolithic sites at the banks of Karama River. In T. Simanjuntak (ed.), *Austronesian in Sulawesi*, pp. 77–92. Jakarta: Center for Prehistoric and Austronesian Studies.

Simanjuntak, T. 2008. Austronesian in Sulawesi: Its origin, diaspora, and living tradition. In T. Simanjuntak (ed.), *Austronesian in Sulawesi*, pp. 215–251. Jakarta: Center for Prehistoric and Austronesian Studies.

Simanjuntak, T., M.J. Morwood, F.S. Intan, I. Mahmud, K. Grant, N. Somba, B. Akw and D.W. Utomo. 2008. Minanga Sipakko and the Neolithic of the Karama River. In T. Simanjuntak (ed.), *Austronesian in Sulawesi*, pp. 57–75. Jakarta: Center for Prehistoric and Austronesian Studies.

Simanjuntak, T., and Widianto, H. (eds). 2012. *Indonesia dalam Arus Sejarah: Prasejarah*. Jakarta: PT Ichtiar Baru van Hoeve.

Soejono, R. P. 1984. *Sejarah Nasional Indonesia, Vol. 1. Jaman Prasejarah*. Jakarta: Balai Pustaka.

Somba, N. 2009. Jejak-jejak arkeologis di kaki Gunung Bambapuang Kabupaten Enrekang, Sulawesi Selatan. *Walennae* 11(2):107–124.

Somba, N. 2011. Ciri budaya Austronesia di kawasan Enrekang Sulawesi Selatan. *Walennae* 12(1):1–10.

12

Mansiri in North Sulawesi: A new dentate-stamped pottery site in Island Southeast Asia

Naszrullah Azis, Christian Reepmeyer, Geoffrey Clark, Sriwigati and Daud A. Tanudirjo

Abstract

This report outlines new results from the Mansiri site, close to Toraut village, in North Sulawesi. A series of small excavations in 2015 recovered red-slipped pottery with decorations including dentate stamping, most commonly in straight or curved lines, circle impression and red painting including horizontal lines sometimes associated with dentate-stamped borders. These are decorative similarities shared with middle Lapita assemblages from the southwest Pacific, but the Mansiri assemblage also shows notable differences from the highly ornate Lapita pottery. Initial radiocarbon dating from the excavation shows evidence of a possible pre-3000 BP deposit at the site.

Keywords: North Sulawesi, Neolithic dating, Neolithic pottery, red slipping, dentate stamping

Introduction

Early Neolithic open sites in Island Southeast Asia (ISEA) are exceptionally rare with only around 20 sites dated to 3000 cal BP or older, and several have significant disturbance leading to doubt about the association of their cultural deposits with an early Austronesian occupation (Spriggs 2003, 2007, 2011). Despite decades of archaeological research, it remains unclear whether conclusive ceramic evidence has been recovered for a direct connection between the Lapita culture in the West Pacific and any Neolithic culture in ISEA, although there are claims to the contrary (Hung et al. 2011; Spriggs 2011; Carson and Kurashina 2012). Recently, Specht et al. (2014), in 'deconstructing' the Lapita Cultural Complex in the Bismarck Archipelago, noted the absence of an ancestral 'homeland' for the distinctive Lapita dentate-stamped pottery. Nonetheless, eastern Indonesia and the north coast of New Guinea were likely routes through which population movement occurred during the Neolithic, but these areas have received only modest amounts of archaeological research.

In this paper, we report a new site containing dentate-stamped, circle impressed, red-slipped and red-painted pottery in North Sulawesi. The small amount of decorated pottery at Mansiri parallels some of the techniques and designs identified in Lapita and ISEA assemblages, but Mansiri also contains vessel forms that have not been identified in any Lapita assemblage. The initial and tentative dating of Mansiri indicates the beginning of the ceramic phaseat the site around 3300–2700 cal BP and the ceramics might represent two-way movement between ISEA and the West Pacific after the initial occurrence of Far Western Lapita in the Bismarck Archipelago (Denham et al. 2012; Specht et al. 2014). This hypothesis would also support the simultaneous westward transportation of Kutau/Bao obsidian from New Britain in the Bismarck Archipelago, as seen in Neolithic levels of Bukit Tengkorak, Sabah, at around 3200–2900 cal BP (Bellwood and Koon 1989; Chia 2003) and its occurrence on Cebu, Philippines (Reepmeyer et al. 2011), albeit undated.

Location

The Mansiri site (0°32'42"N 123°52'3"E) is in the Bogani Nani Wartabone National Park, Bolaang Mongondow District of North Sulawesi, approximately 50 km west of Kotamobagu City (Figure 12.1). Situated in an upland region of North Sulawesi, the site location follows a similar settlement pattern to sites in the Karama Valley in Western Sulawesi (Anggraeni et al. 2014), being associated with a main inland river system. The closest distance to the sea is to the south, 25 km in straight line. The large river system of the Sungai Dumoga, however, drains in a west–east direction from the Central Mountains of North Sulawesi to the northeast, where it meets the sea at the Lombagin village, approximately 60 km away. The Mansiri site is located at 273 metres above sea level (m asl) at the western end of the Dumoga valley in the foothills of the Central Mountain range. The site experiences an equatorial climate and used to be covered by tropical rainforest. Unfortunately, in recent times, the area has been subject to uncontrolled logging and forest clearing and is now used as farmland for sweet corn agriculture.

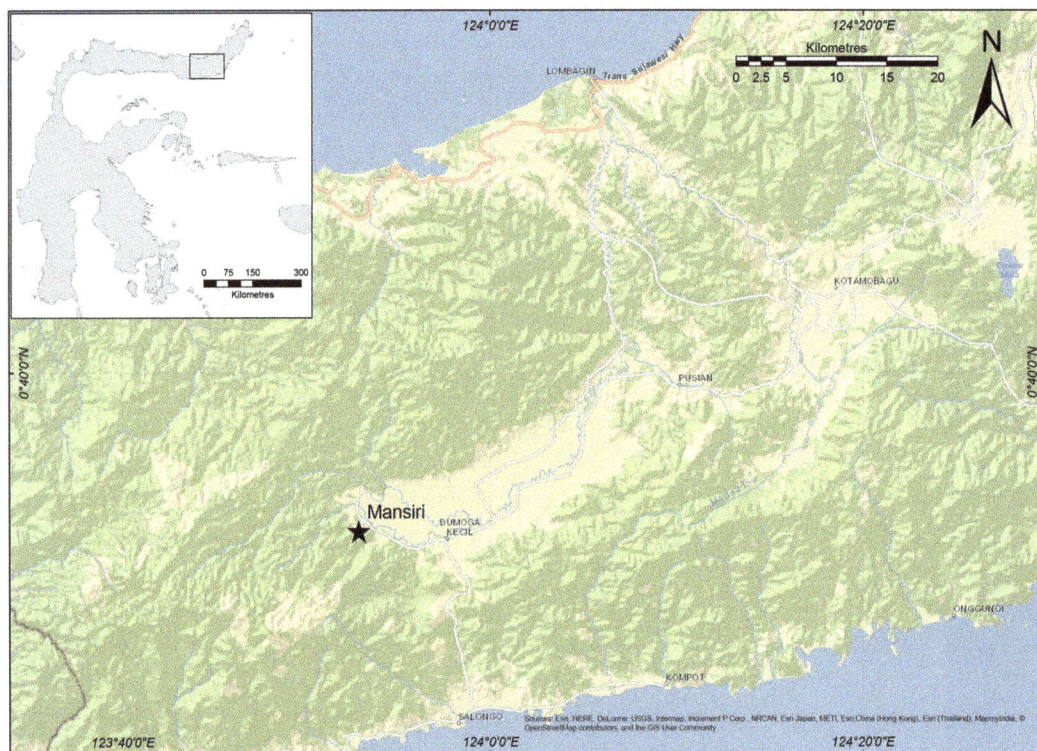

Figure 12.1: Map of the location of Mansiri site.
Source: Manado Archaeology Office.

Survey and excavation

Initially discovered during survey activities in the early 1990s by Dr Joko Siswanto of the Manado Archaeology Office, the Mansiri site had not been a focus of archaeological activities until a revisit to the area by the Manado Archaeology Office in 2011, and a surface survey of the surrounding area detected additional artefactual material. Previous excavations conducted by the Manado Archaeology Office in 2011–13 uncovered large numbers of decorated ceramic sherds indicative of an early Neolithic site.

Fieldwork in 2015 was conducted on 13 days between the 9–12 of April (Figure 12.2). During this time, activities included excavation of four test pits (Trenches A–D) and a north–south auger test drilling transect (16 samples, spaced at 2 m, total length of 32 m), to identify the extent of the site, as well as digital mapping of the general topography of the area (Figure 12.3).

Figure 12.2: (a) Panorama (facing north) of the site and (b) location at the foot of hill slope.
Source: Christian Reepmeyer.

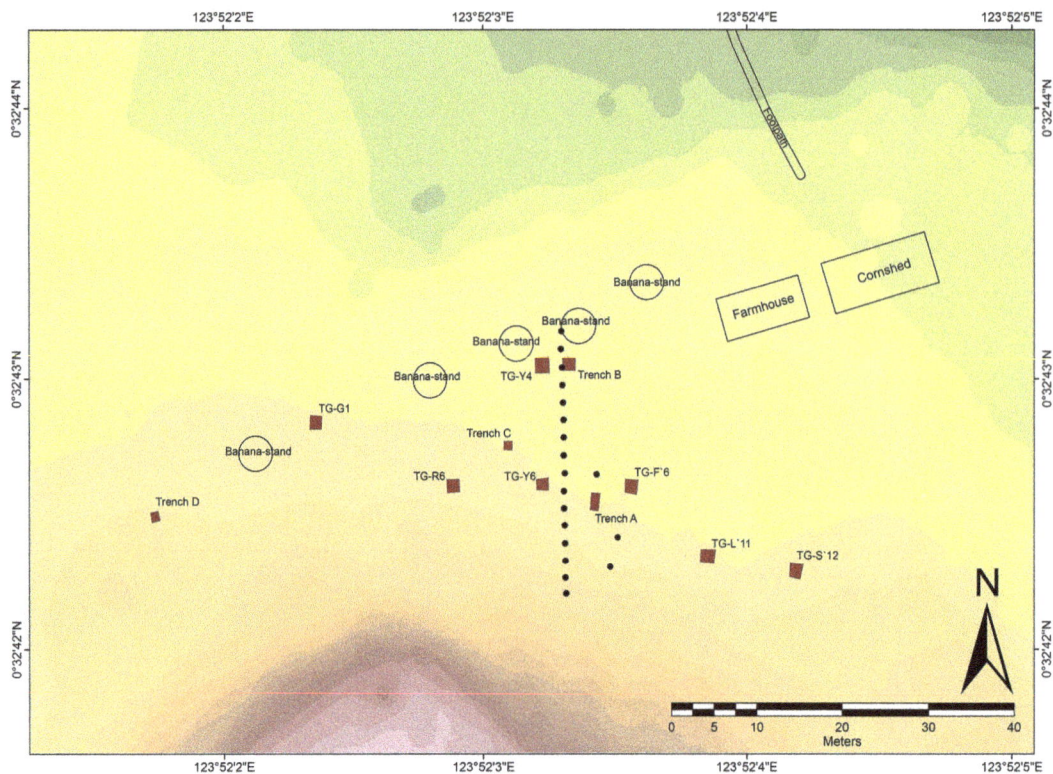

Figure 12.3: Digital elevation (green colour represents low areas and lavender high areas) and site plan of the Mansiri site with the location of previous excavation by Balai Arkeologi Manado (TG-G1 to TG-S`12) and 2015 excavations (Trenches A–D).

Source: Christian Reepmeyer.

The Mansiri site is an elevated, relatively level area of approximately 100 m x 40 m extent, situated to the south of an old creek bed (now dry) on a gentle rise. Currently, the area is only used for intermittent cattle grazing, with no sweet corn planted on the site location. Artefact density in prior excavations of the Manado office was found to be highest in the central area and to decline significantly to the north (Trench TG-G1) and east (TG-S`12). The northern boundary of the site is demarcated by an old creek bed and large banana stands; however, pottery was found in all of the auger drill holes to the north, indicating that the site extent most likely reaches still further north. The southern border is the steeper part of the slope of a hill that rises to about 400 m asl. It appears that the southern site boundary does not extend further up the hill slope as indicated by the lack of artefactual material in the southern auger drill holes and the lack of artefacts or structures on the hill top. Significant erosion is occurring due to logging/burning of vegetation on the hill slope.

Trenches A, C and D[1]

Trench A (Figure 12.4) is a 1 m x 2 m excavation in north–south alignment, whereas both Trenches C and D were 1 m x 1 m test units to the north of the site. The deposit was excavated in natural (stratigraphic) layers, or arbitrary 10 cm units if finer stratigraphic units could not be detected during digging, until a sterile layer was reached at ~160 cm (Table 12.1).

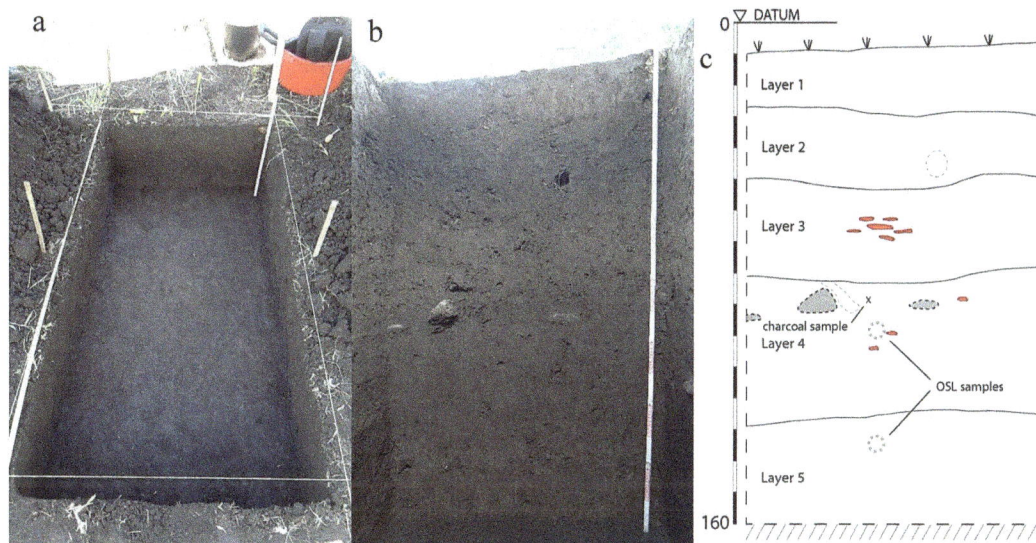

Figure 12.4: Trench A in plan (a) and section (b) view of the south section. Section drawing (c) of the south section of Trench A.

Source: Christian Reepmeyer.

Table 12.1: Stratigraphy of Trenches A and C at Mansiri.

Layer 1 (5 – 27 cm uD):	Topsoil, lighter brown sandy silt with frequent tree roots. Some rat burrows.
Layer 2 (27 – 50 cm uD):	Topsoil, very humic, loose, dark sandy silt, loamy. Some large rat burrows. Frequent tree roots.
Layer 3 (50 cm – 80 cm uD):	Lighter grey-brown sandy silt. Some tree roots. One pottery concentration, most likely 16th century. Some rat burrows.
Layer 4 (80 cm – 125 cm uD):	Main cultural layer until 102 cm uD. Below 105 cm only rarely ceramics. Grey (slightly darker than Layer 3) sandy silt with some clay content. Rare rat burrows and other bioturbations (mainly in top part of layer).
Layer 5 (125 cm – 160 cm uD):	Sterile yellow-brown mottled soil. Medium sand with some clay content. Most likely top part of weathered bedrock.

Note: uD = under Datum.

Source: Excavators' field notes.

Trench B

Trench B (Figure 12.5) is located around 10 m to the north of Trench A and in the same alignment as TG-Y4 trench excavated in 2014 by the lead author and his team. Trench dimensions were 1.5 m x 1.5 m to a maximum depth of 210 cm where either bedrock or a terrace of large water-rolled boulders was reached (Table 12.2). The trench was excavated in 10 cm units below 100 cm. The top 100 cm were excavated in one unit by shovel.

---

1   Trench D shows the same stratigraphic sequence as Trenches A and C, but is slightly deeper. The radiocarbon date at 143 cm is associated with the main cultural Layer 4, as described in Table 12.1.

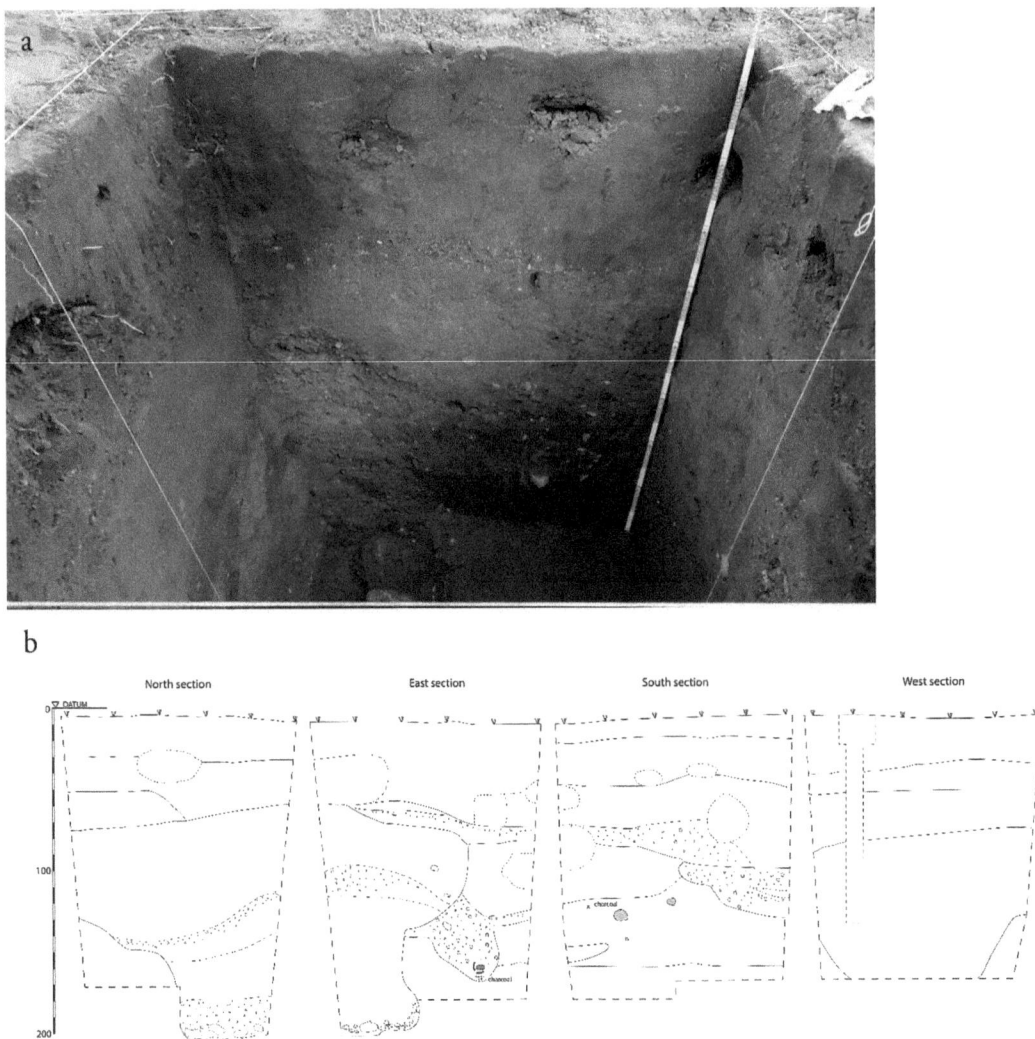

Figure 12.5: (a) View of east section of Trench B, drainage channel in the northern part, which cuts through cultural layers at around 180 cm; (b) Section drawing of all sections of Trench B.

Source: Christian Reepmeyer.

Table 12.2: Stratigraphy of Trench B at Mansiri.

Layer 1 (10 cm – 25 cm uD):	Topsoil, light grey humic silt. Frequent rat burrows and tree roots.
Layer 2 (25 cm – 55 cm uD):	Topsoil. Dark grey humic soil. Frequent roots and bioturbation, relatively loose material.
Layer 3a (55 cm – 65 cm uD):	Compacted grey silt with clay content. Frequent eroded gravel and white specks, most likely weathered dolomite (or sandstone) pieces.
Layer 3b (65 cm – ~80 cm uD):	Compacted grey silt, sandy with frequent angular or river-rounded gravel. Weathered white specks continue.
Layer 4 (80 cm – 200 cm uD):	Sandy layer. Frequent river-rolled gravel. Relative soft material in the top part. Alternating between finer sand layers and compacted gravelly sand. In the lower part increasingly banded, frequent iron and black layered concretions. To the sides particularly in the base part gravelly, mostly rounded. This layer cuts through all subsequent layers. In the base of the layer large boulders, some angular and some river-rolled. Frequently eroded sandstone gravel. There is a clear border between this layer and the silt/clay layers to the south. Most likely old drainage channel.
Layer 5 (85 cm – 127 cm uD):	Very compacted silt/clay layer. Light grey-brown. Frequent burned tree roots. A large moist patch (east section) appears to be an old tree root.

Layer 6 (127 cm – 168 cm uD):	Very compacted silty sand with frequent river-rolled gravel. Larger pieces of rock, partly angular. Frequent pottery, main layer with cultural material. Only specks of charcoal, most likely from only small tree roots. Frequent iron concretions.
Layer 7 (135 cm – 160 cm uD):	Very compacted grey-brown silt/clay with frequent white specks (weathered dolomite or sandstone?). Mottled with some fine sand content.
Layer 8 (below 160 cm uD):	Sterile compacted mottled yellow-brown silt.

Note: uD = under Datum.

Source: Excavators' field notes.

Trench B shows significant disturbance from a drainage channel that cut through earlier deposits, including pottery-containing layers. It appears that these drainage channels are not recent as there is a substantial amount of sediment accumulated (~70 cm) on top of them. Ceramics were found in a pit feature filled with compacted silt/fine sand deposit with some clay content; the southern boundary of this pit feature is unclear. The sediment is concreted by iron aggregations. Charcoal samples were collected from the pit feature (unfortunately, these samples might have been contaminated by tree root disturbances) and the surrounding sediment.

Results

Stratigraphy and age

Only a limited amount of bioturbation (specifically, rats burrows) could be detected, which might have brought in sediment from higher layers. One charcoal sample recovered from the upper part of the pottery layer dates to 3355–3084 cal BP, while two additional samples from Trenches A (in the highest sections of the ceramic layer that might overlie the ceramic deposition) and D (in direct association with ceramic) showed slightly younger ages of 2720–2480 cal BP and 2720–2430 cal BP, respectively (Table 12.3 and Figure 12.4). Charcoal was scarce in the highly acidic soil, limiting the potential for radiocarbon dating of the site and encouraging the use of alternative dating methods.

Table 12.3: Summary of radiocarbon dates from Mansiri Trench TG7'6, Trenches A and D.

Radiocarbon Date						
Lab. code #	Trench	Burial depth (cm)	d13C	D14C	¹⁴C age	cal BP (95.4%)
S-ANU 40031[1]	TG-F'6	90–100	-28.58±1.0	-314.6±2.6	3035±35	3355–3084
Wk44605[2]	A1	80–90	-28.0±0.4	-266.9±1.8	2494±20	2720–2480
Wk44610[2]	D	143	-26.7±0.4	-264.6±1.8	2469±20	2720–2430

Sources:

1. ANU Radiocarbon Dating Centre. For experimental setup, see Fallon et al. (2010).

2. Waikato Radiocarbon Dating Laboratories.

It was decided to employ Optical Stimulated Luminescence (OSL) dating at the Oxford University Luminescence Dating Laboratory to investigate the radiocarbon ages. OSL results are based on luminescence measurements of sand-sized quartz (180–255 μm) extracted from the samples using standard preparation techniques including, wet sieving, HCl (10%) treatment to remove carbonates, HF treatment (48%) to dissolve feldspathic minerals and heavy mineral separation with sodium polytungstate. Measurements were performed in an automated luminescence reader (Risø DA15 upgraded to Risø DA20) made by Risø (Bøtter-Jensen 1988, 1997; Bøtter-Jensen et al. 2000) using a SAR post-IR blue OSL measurement protocol (Murray and Wintle 2000; Banerjee et al. 2001; Wintle and Murray 2006). A preheat combination of 220°C for the main OSL signal and 200°C for the test dose signal were adopted following the outcome of a dose recovery test on four of the samples (X6836 – X6839). Dose rate calculations are based on Aitken (1985) and are derived from the concentration of radioactive elements (potassium, thorium and uranium) within the samples. These were derived from elemental analysis by ICP-MS/AES using a fusion sample preparation technique. The final OSL age estimates include an additional 4% systematic error to account for uncertainties in source calibration and measurement reproducibility. These incorporated beta attenuation factors (Mejdahl 1979), dose rate conversion factors (Guérin et al. 2011) and an absorption coefficient for the water content (Zimmerman 1971). The contribution of cosmic radiation to the total dose rate was calculated as a function of latitude, altitude, burial depth and average over-burden density based on data by Prescott and Hutton (1994).

Unfortunately, OSL dating of the sediments resulted in anomalous dating of the pottery layer to a maximum of 1400 BP with underlying sterile deposition at a maximum of approximately 2900 BP (Table 12.4). At this stage, the discrepancy between the radiocarbon and OSL dates is unexplained; however, it is possible that this either evidences significant disturbances of sediment deposition or that water content in the sediment resulted in incomplete bleaching, degrading the accuracy of the OSL readings from the site (Murray and Olley 2002; Rhodes 2011). Furthermore, sampling of sediment cores for OSL dating was not ideal, as only improvised sampling containers (PVC pipe with 7 cm diameter, cut into 25 cm long sections) were used.

Table 12.4: Summary of OSL dates from Mansiri Trench A.

OSL Dates					
Lab. code #	Burial depth (cm)	Water content (%)	Palaeodose (Gy)	Dose rate (Gy/ka)	OSL age estimate (years before 2015)
X6839	98	18.87	1.27±0.17	0.98±0.07	1290±195
X6841	135	21.39	2.94±0.38	1.21±0.09	2430±380

Source: Oxford University Luminescence Dating Laboratory.

Pottery

In total, 2146 pottery fragments were excavated in 2015. Due to the high acidic content of the soil, the pottery is poorly preserved and highly fragmented, making the pot forms difficult to reconstruct. Identified pot forms include small flat bottom dishes, ring-foot dishes and globular pots with everted and thickened rims (Figures 12.6 and 12.7).

Figure 12.6: Example of a dentate-stamped ring-foot stand.
Source: Naszrullah Azis.

Figure 12.7: Examples of rim shapes.
Source: Christian Reepmeyer.

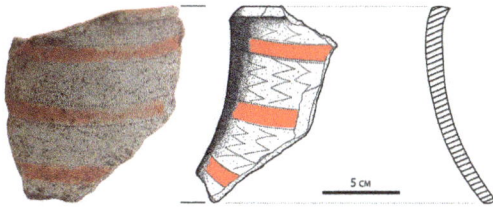

Figure 12.8: Selected example of red-painted and dentate-stamp decorated ceramic.

Source: Naszrullah Azis.

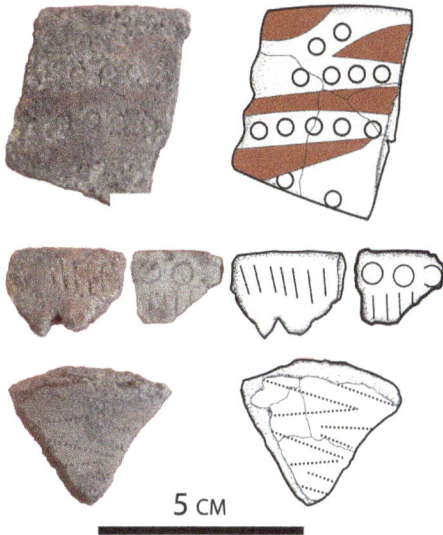

Figure 12.9: Selected examples of red-painted, circle-stamped and dentate-stamped decorated ceramics.

Source: Naszrullah Azis.

Figure 12.10: Selected examples of red-painted, circle-stamped and dentate-stamped decorated ceramics.

Source: Naszrullah Azis.

Pottery fragments with decoration are exceptionally rare and account for less than 1% of the assemblage (Figures 12.8–10). Decorations include dentate stamping, most commonly in straight or curved lines. Zigzag patterns and rhombic motifs are common. Single lines of circular bamboo stamps bordered by dentate-stamped lines have been recorded. There are two instances where bamboo stamps were noted, both as part of a joint composition with red paint, again with a rhombic pattern. Most of the decorated pottery shows red painting, including horizontal lines associated with dentate-stamped borders on several sherds. One sample showed white incrustation associated with dentate stamping, albeit it is unclear whether this is a weathering product or intentional addition of lime or other carbonate film. At this stage, identified incision is extremely rare as only one sherd with possible incision was found. Instances of rim-notching have been detected.

A red slip, which has substantially exfoliated, was frequently applied. Of the 1019 wall sherds analysed, 150 (14.7%) retained red slip or red paint on the inside surface and 165 (16.2%) on the outside. This high percentage (24.6%, taking both inside and outside surfaces into account) of applied slip would be further enhanced by only considering the 611 sherds with non-eroded surfaces, which would result in 41% of the sample displaying red-slipped surfaces.

Discussion

The location of the Mansiri site follows a similar settlement pattern to the sites of the Karama valley, Kalumpang in West Sulawesi (van Heekeren 1957; Anggraeni et al. 2014), both being associated with main inland river systems. The distance from the coast along the river system of the Mansiri site is comparable with Pantara'an 1, whereas the sites at Minanga Sipakko and Kamassi are twice that distance. Mansiri appears to be slightly younger than the Neolithic deposits at Minanga Sipakko, which have been dated from c. 3500 cal BP ranging to 3000 cal BP

(Anggraeni et al. 2014:745, Table 1). Anggraeni et al. (2014:746) state that the dates from Kamassi confirm that the transition to pottery making was completed by 1500 BC in the Karama valley at Minanga Sipakko; however, the Kamassi early dates derive from uncalibrated freshwater molluscs for which no local calibration curve was adopted (see Keaveney and Reimer (2012) and Philippsen (2013) for discussions of significant in-built ages in freshwater molluscs). The only published charcoal date for Kamassi suggests a later deposition at around 3175–2365 cal BP; however, this sample derives from higher levels than the freshwater mollusc dates. Similarities in the vertical distribution of different types of ceramics at Kamassi and Minanga Sipakko might indicate that the earlier dates at both sites are outliers and an initial transition to pottery use might have occurred a few hundred years later than inferred by Anggraeni et al. (2014). This is also reflected in the ceramics found at Mansiri, which show some similarities such as circular stamping with the pottery from Minanga Sipakko and Kamassi as well as those from Nagsabaran in Luzon (Hung et al. 2011). However, incisions that are common at these latter sites are virtually absent from Mansiri. The lack of incisions in association with missing curvy-linear decoration patterns, and rectangular, instead of circular or triangular stamping, also excludes a comparison with later Iron Age Sa-Huynh Kalanay ceramics (Solheim 2006).

Dentate stamped red-painted pottery is exceptionally rare in ISEA and its occurrence in a possible 3000-year-old site in North Sulawesi invites a comparison with Lapita assemblages in Near Oceania. A detailed analysis of the decoration is ongoing and will be presented at a later stage. Initial similarities between the Mansiri dentate-stamping, infilled and red-painted horizontal lines can be detected with middle Lapita assemblages from Vanuatu (Bedford 2006), but the Mansiri assemblage also shows significant differences from the highly ornate Lapita pottery, and so significant additional research is necessary to determine the nature of any connections.

The ambiguous status of the Mansiri radiocarbon dates is not unique for ISEA where the transition to the Neolithic is not very well dated. The earliest radiocarbon dates of initial pottery occurrence overlap at the 2-sigma 95.4% confidence interval (Table 12.5). Almost none of these dates have been unambiguously accepted (for example, Spriggs 2003, 2007, 2011), particularly as only in rare cases in ISEA are local correction curves available for marine shell dates, and there are suggestions that the Neolithic transition might have occurred significantly later at each of the sites (Spriggs 2011; Carson and Kurashina 2012; Gaffney et al. 2015).

The hypothesis of a multi-directional backward and forward movement of goods and people has long been accepted further east in the Lapita distribution (Sheppard 2011), as exemplified by the flow of obsidian raw material (Green 1987; Sheppard 1993; Reepmeyer 2009). If we accept the later proposed dates for the appearance of Lapita in the Bismarck Archipelago (post-3200 cal BP; Specht et al. 2014) and the earlier age range of both Mansiri and the Karama valley sites (pre-3300 cal BP), then the Mansiri site might be viewed as an archaeological precursor to Lapita in ISEA, which would support earlier claims for direct connections between ISEA and the Western Pacific (Hung et al. 2011; Carson et al. 2014). This proposal, admittedly, is tenuous at best, and instead cultural influences in the reverse direction might have been at play.

However, the Lapita culture has been associated with highly mobile settlement patterns and a distinct maritime focus (Kirch 2000; Bedford et al. 2007). This adaptation does not accord well with the site location of Mansiri, which is as far away from the coast as the river system allows. Mansiri's location is unexplained at this stage, but would fit with the hypothesis that agricultural expansion followed an opportunistic pattern whereby arable land along large freshwater systems provided the primary targets for farming communities after an initial maritime spread of people and innovations (Bellwood 2005).

Table 12.5: Summary of radiocarbon dates from selected early Neolithic sites in Island Southeast Asia.

Region	Site	Lab-number	Age (calibrated) (95.4%)	Shell dates	Reference
Batanes Islands	Torongan Cave	OZH 771	4510–4085 cal BP		Bellwood and Dizon 2013
		Wk 14642	3640–3452 cal BP		
Philippines	Nagsabaran	WK-23397	4517–4248 cal BP		Hung et al. 2011
		ANU 13016	3867–3697 cal BP		
		NTU-3799		3450±40 uncalibrated	
	Dimolit	GaK 2937	4815–3930 cal BP		Peterson 1974
	Andarayan	N.G.	3975–3380 cal BP		Snow et al. 1986
	Edjek	Beta-1117	4421–3183 cal BP		Hutterer 1982
Talaud Islands	Leang Tuwo Mane'e	ANU 1515	4821–4295 cal BP		Bellwood 1976
		ANU 10209		3690±70 uncalibrated	Tanudirjo 2001
Sarawak	Gua Sireh	CAMS-725	4962–3581 cal BP		Datan and Bellwood 1991
		ANU 7047	3921–2953 cal BP		
	Niah Cave	Gm-7204	3915–3410 cal BP		Harrisson 1975
Northern Papua New Guinea	Wañelek	Wk-22060	4146–3929 cal BP		Gaffney et al. 2015
		GX-3326	4226–3253 cal BP		

Source: See Reference column.

On the other hand, recent research has shown that social interaction between distant communities, including maritime transportation of raw materials in ISEA, can be traced back into the early Holocene period and might be associated with sea-level changes following the Late Glacial Maximum (Torrence and Swadling 2008; Neri et al. 2015; Pawlik et al. 2015). Considering the intensification of forest management evidenced at Niah Cave in Sabah (Barker et al. 2011) and early independent domestication of tuber crops in highland Papua New Guinea (Denham et al. 2003), it seems that the transition to pottery production and agricultural systems in ISEA was indeed complex and most likely a process that involved multiple migrations (Tumonggor et al. 2013), as well as staggered acceptance and discard of innovations by local communities over hundreds of years.

Conclusions

The new dentate-stamped ceramic site of Mansiri adds new information to the Neolithic transformations in ISEA. Radiocarbon and OSL dating show a level of uncertainty about the true age, and occupation length, of the site. Based on the acquired preliminary age determinations, we propose that there might be a Neolithic presence at the site of a few hundred years, which started just prior to 3000 cal BP. At this stage of investigation, it might be tentatively inferred that the new-found pottery indicates links with the emergence of highly decorated dentate-stamped pottery of the Lapita Cultural Complex in the Bismarck Archipelago. However, the probability of a slightly later date of occupation at Mansiri makes it an unlikely precursor to Lapita. We propose here that the Mansiri site might show a backflow of ideas and people to the west, as would accord with the appearance of Kutau/Bao obsidian in ISEA at a similar time frame.

A more detailed analysis of the ceramics, combining results from the 2012–14 excavation and the 2015 excavation is forthcoming. These analyses will include typological assessment of rim shapes, a detailed study of the decorative motifs and technological analysis of manufacturing by examining direction of pores, geochemical and petrographic analysis of clay, temper and red-slip types, and compound specific radiocarbon analysis (CSRA) to obtain direct dates on the pottery manufacture.

Acknowledgements

This research was funded through an ARC Discovery Early Career Researcher Award (DECRA, DE130100046) to Christian Reepmeyer.

Author biographies

Naszrullah Azis Manado Archaeology Office, Manado, North Sulawesi, Indonesia

Christian Reepmeyer College of Arts, Society and Education, Cairns Campus, James Cook University, Cairns, Australia; and Department of Archaeology and Natural History, School of Culture, History and Language, College of Asia and the Pacific, The Australian National University, Canberra, Australia

Geoffrey Clark Department of Archaeology and Natural History, School of Culture, History and Language, College of Asia and the Pacific, The Australian National University, Canberra, Australia

Sriwigati Manado Archaeology Office, Manado, North Sulawesi, Indonesia

Daud A. Tanudirjo Department of Archaeology, Gadjah Mada University, Yogyakarta, Indonesia

References

Aitken, M.J. 1985. *Thermoluminescence Dating*. London: Academic Press.

Anggraeni, T. Simanjuntak, P. Bellwood and P. Piper. 2014. Neolithic foundations in the Karama valley, West Sulawesi, Indonesia. *Antiquity* 88(341):740–756. doi.org/10.1017/S0003598X00050663 (accessed 5 June 2018).

Banerjee, D., A.S. Murray, L. Bøtter-Jensen and A. Lang. 2001. Equivalent dose estimation using a single aliquot of polymineral fine grains. *Radiation Measurements* 33(1):73–94. doi.org/10.1016/S1350-4487(00)00101-3 (accessed 5 June 2018).

Barker, G., L. Lloyd-Smith, H. Barton, F. Cole, C. Hunt, Philip J. Piper, R. Rabett, V. Paz and K. Szabó. 2011. Foraging-farming transitions at the Niah Caves, Sarawak, Borneo. *Antiquity* 85(328):492–509. doi.org/10.1017/S0003598X00067909 (accessed 5 June 2018).

Bedford, S. 2006. The Pacific's earliest painted pottery: An added layer of intrigue to the Lapita debate and beyond. *Antiquity* 80(309):544–557. doi.org/10.1017/S0003598X00094023 (accessed 5 June 2018).

Bedford, S., C. Sand and S.P. Connaughton. 2007. *Oceanic Exploration: Lapita and Western Pacific Settlement*. Canberra: ANU E Press.

Bellwood, P. 1976. Archaeological Research in Minahasa and the Talaud Islands, Northeastern Indonesia. *Asian Perspectives* 19(2):240–288.

Bellwood, P. 2005. *First Farmers: The Origins of Agricultural Societies*. Malden, MA: Blackwell Publishing.

Bellwood, P. and E. Dizon. 2013. The Chronology of Batanes prehistory. In P. Bellwood and E. Dizon (eds), *4000 Years of Migration and Cultural Exchange: The Archaeology of the Batanes Islands, Northern Philippines*, pp.67–76. Terra Australis 40. Canberra: ANU E Press. doi.org/10.22459/TA40.12.2013.05 (accessed 5 June 2018).

Bellwood, P. and P. Koon. 1989. 'Lapita colonists leave boats unburned!' The question of Lapita links with Island Southeast Asia. *Antiquity* 63(240):613–622. doi.org/10.1017/S0003598X00076572 (accessed 5 June 2018).

Bøtter-Jensen, L. 1988. The automated Risø TL dating reader system. *International Journal of Radiation Applications and Instrumentation. Part D. Nuclear Tracks and Radiation Measurements* 14(1):177–180. doi.org/10.1016/1359-0189(88)90060-X (accessed 5 June 2018).

Bøtter-Jensen, L. 1997. Luminescence techniques: Instrumentation and methods. *Radiation Measurements* 27(5–6):749–768. doi.org/10.1016/S1350-4487(97)00206-0 (accessed 5 June 2018).

Bøtter-Jensen, L., E. Bulur, G.A.T. Duller and A.S. Murray. 2000. Advances in luminescence instrument systems. *Radiation Measurements* 32(5–6):523–528. doi.org/10.1016/S1350-4487(00)00039-1 (accessed 5 June 2018).

Carson, M.T., H.-c. Hung, G. Summerhayes and P. Bellwood. 2014. The pottery trail from Southeast Asia to Remote Oceania. *Journal of Coastal and Island Archaeology* 8(1):17–36. doi.org/10.1080/15564894.2012.726941 (accessed 5 June 2018).

Carson, M.T. and H. Kurashina. 2012. Re-envisioning long-distance Oceanic migration: Early dates in the Mariana Islands. *World Archaeology* 44(3):409–435. doi.org/10.1080/00438243.2012.727342 (accessed 5 June 2018).

Chia, S.M.S. 2003. *The Prehistory of Bukit Tengkorak as a Major Pottery Making Site in Southeast Asia*. Kota Kinabalu: Department of Sabah Museum.

Datan, I. and P. Bellwood. 1991. Recent Research at Gua Sireh (Serian) and Lubang Angin (Gunung Mulu National Park). *Bulletin of The Indo-Pacific Prehistory Association* 10:386–405. doi.org/10.7152/bippa.v10i0.11328 (accessed 5 June 2018).

Denham, T., C.B. Ramsey and J. Specht. 2012. Dating the appearance of Lapita pottery in the Bismarck Archipelago and its dispersal to Remote Oceania. *Archaeology in Oceania* 47(1):39–46. doi.org/10.1002/j.1834-4453.2012.tb00113.x (accessed 5 June 2018).

Denham, T.P., S.G. Haberle, C. Lentfer, R. Fullagar, J. Field, M. Therin, N. Porch and B. Winsborough. 2003. Origins of agriculture at Kuk Swamp in the Highlands of New Guinea. *Science* 301(5630):189–193. doi.org/10.1126/science.1085255 (accessed 5 June 2018).

Fallon, S.J., L.K. Fifield and J.M. Chappell. 2010. The next chapter in radiocarbon dating at the Australian National University: Status report on the single stage AMS. *Nuclear Instruments and Methods in Physics Research Section B: Beam Interactions with Materials and Atoms* 268(7–8):898–901. doi.org/10.1016/j.nimb.2009.10.059 (accessed 5 June 2018).

Gaffney, D., G.R. Summerhayes, A. Ford, J.M. Scott, T. Denham, J. Field and W.R. Dickinson. 2015. Earliest pottery on New Guinea Mainland reveals Austronesian influences in Highland environments 3000 years ago. *PLoS ONE* 10(9):e0134497. doi.org/10.1371/journal.pone.0134497 (accessed 5 June 2018).

Green, R.C. 1987. Obsidian results from the Lapita sites of the Reef/Santa Cruz Islands. In W.R. Ambrose and J.M.J. Mummery (eds), *Archaeometry: Further Australasian studies*, pp. 239–249. Canberra: Research School of Pacific and Asian Studies, The Australia National University.

Guérin, G., N. Mercier and G. Adamiec. 2011. Dose-rate conversion factors: Update. *Ancient TL* 29(1):5–8.

Harrisson, T. 1975. Early dates for 'seated' burials and burial matting at Niah Caves, Sarawak (Borneo). *Asian Perspectives* 18:161–165.

Hung, H.-c., M.T. Carson, P. Bellwood, F.Z. Campos, P.J. Piper, E. Dizon, M.J.L.A. Bolunia, M. Oxenham and Z. Chi. 2011. The first settlement of Remote Oceania: The Philippines to the Marianas. *Antiquity* 85(329):909–926. doi.org/10.1017/S0003598X00068393 (accessed 5 June 2018).

Hutterer, K.L. 1982. Test excavations at the Edjek site (T V 161A) Tanjay, Negros Oriental. In K.L. Hutterer and W.K. Macdonald (eds), *Houses built on scattered Poles: Prehistory and Ecology in Negros Oriental, Philippines*, pp. 209–226. Cebu City: University of Santo Carlos.

Keaveney, E.M. and P.J. Reimer. 2012. Understanding the variability in freshwater radiocarbon reservoir offsets: a cautionary tale. *Journal of Archaeological Science* 39(5):1306–1316. doi.org/10.1016/j.jas.2011.12.025 (accessed 5 June 2018).

Kirch, P.V. 2000. *On the Road of the Winds: An Archaeological History of the Pacific Islands before European Contact*. Berkeley, CA: University of California Press.

Mejdahl, V. 1979. Thermoluminescence dating: Beta-dose attenuation in quartz grains. *Archaeometry* 21(1):61–72. doi.org/10.1111/j.1475-4754.1979.tb00241.x (accessed 5 June 2018).

Murray, A.S. and J.M. Olley. 2002. Precision and accuracy in the Optically Stimulated Luminescence dating of sedimentary quartz: A status review. *Geochronometria* 21:1–16.

Murray, A.S. and A.G. Wintle. 2000. Luminescence dating of quartz using an improved single-aliquot regenerative-dose protocol. *Radiation measurements* 32(1):57–73. doi.org/10.1016/S1350-4487(99)00253-X (accessed 5 June 2018).

Neri, L.A.M., A.F. Pawlik, C. Reepmeyer, A.S.B. Mijares and V.J. Paz. 2015. Mobility of early islanders in the Philippines during the terminal Pleistocene/early Holocene boundary: pXRF-analysis of obsidian artefacts. *Journal of Archaeological Science* 61:149–157. doi.org/10.1016/j.jas.2015.05.005 (accessed 5 June 2018).

Pawlik, A.F., P.J. Piper, R.E. Wood, K.K.A. Lim, M.G.P.G. Faylona, A.S.B. Mijares and M. Porr. 2015. Shell tool technology in Island Southeast Asia: An early Middle Holocene Tridacna adze from Ilin Island, Mindoro, Philippines. *Antiquity* 89(344):292–308. doi.org/10.15184/aqy.2015.3 (accessed 5 June 2018).

Peterson, W. 1974. Summary report of two archaeological sites from north-eastern Luzon. *Archaeology & Physical Anthropology in Oceania* 9(1):26–35.

Philippsen, B. 2013. The freshwater reservoir effect in radiocarbon dating. *Heritage Science* 1(1):24–43. doi.org/10.1186/2050-7445-1-24 (accessed 5 June 2018).

Prescott, J. and J.T. Hutton. 1994. Cosmic ray contributions to dose rates for luminescence and ESR dating: Large depths and long-term time variations. *Radiation Measurements* 23(2–3):497–500. doi.org/10.1016/1350-4487(94)90086-8 (accessed 5 June 2018).

Reepmeyer, C. 2009. Obsidian Sources and Distribution systems emanating from Gaua and Vanua Lava in the Banks Islands of Vanuatu. Unpublished PhD thesis, Centre for Asia and the Pacific, The Australian National University, Canberra.

Reepmeyer, C., M. Spriggs, Anggraeni, P. Lape, L. Neri, W.P. Ronquillo, T. Simanjuntak, G. Summerhayes, D. Tanudirjo and A. Tiauzon. 2011. Obsidian sources and distribution systems in Island Southeast Asia: New results and implications from geochemical research using LA-ICPMS. *Journal of Archaeological Science* 38(11):2995–3005. doi.org/10.1016/j.jas.2011.06.023 (accessed 5 June 2018).

Rhodes, E.J. 2011. Optically Stimulated Luminescence dating of sediments over the past 200,000 years. *Annual Review of Earth and Planetary Sciences* 39(1):461–488. doi.org/10.1146/annurev-earth-040610-133425 (accessed 5 June 2018).

Sheppard, P.J. 1993. Lapita lithics: trade/exchange and technology. A view from the Reefs/Santa Cruz. *Archaeology in Oceania* 28(3):121–137. doi.org/10.1002/j.1834-4453.1993.tb00303.x (accessed 5 June 2018).

Sheppard, P.J. 2011. Lapita colonization across the Near/Remote Oceania Boundary. *Current Anthropology* 52(6):799–840. doi.org/10.1086/662201 (accessed 5 June 2018).

Snow, B.E., R. Shutler, D.E. Nelson, J.S. Vogel and J.R. Southon. 1986. Evidence of early rice cultivation in the Philippines. *Philippine Quarterly of Culture and Society* 14(1):3–11.

Solheim, W.G. II. 2006. *Archaeology and Culture in Southeast Asia: Unraveling the Nusantao*. Manila: The University of the Philippines Press.

Specht, J., T. Denham, J. Goff and J.E. Terrell. 2014. Deconstructing the Lapita Cultural Complex in the Bismarck Archipelago. *Journal of Archaeological Research* 22(2):89–140. doi.org/10.1007/s10814-013-9070-4 (accessed 5 June 2018).

Spriggs, M. 2003. Chronology of the Neolithic Transition in Island Southeast Asia and the Western Pacific: A View from 2003. *The Review of Archaeology* 24(2):57–80.

Spriggs, M. 2007. The Neolithic and Austronesian expansion within Island Southeast Asia and into the Pacific. In S. Chiu and C. Sand (eds), *From Southeast Asia to the Pacific: Archaeological Perspectives on the Austronesian Expansion and the Lapita Cultural Complex*, pp. 104–139. Taipei Academia Sinica: Research Center for Humanities and Social Sciences. doi.org/10.1017/S0003598X00067910 (accessed 5 June 2018).

Spriggs, M. 2011. Archaeology and the Austronesian expansion: Where are we now? *Antiquity* 85(328):510–528, doi.org/10.1017/S0003598X00067910 (accessed 5 June 2018).

Tanudirjo, D.A. 2001. Islands in Between: Prehistory of the Northeastern Indonesian Archipelago. Unpublished PhD thesis, School of Archaeology and Anthropology, The Australian National University, Canberra.

Torrence, R. and P. Swadling. 2008. Social networks and the spread of Lapita. *Antiquity* 82(317):600–616. doi.org/10.1017/S0003598X00097258 (accessed 5 June 2018).

Tumonggor, M.K., T.M. Karafet, B. Hallmark, J.S. Lansing, H. Sudoyo, M.F. Hammer and M.P. Cox. 2013. The Indonesian archipelago: An ancient genetic highway linking Asia and the Pacific. *Journal of Human Genetics* 58(3):165–173. doi.org/10.1038/jhg.2012.154 (accessed 5 June 2018).

van Heekeren, H.R. 1957. *The Stone Age of Indonesia*. Verhandelingen van het Koninklijk Instituut voor Taal-, Land- en Volkenkunde 21. The Hague: Martinus Nijhoff.

Wintle, A.G. and A.S. Murray. 2006. A review of quartz optically stimulated luminescence characteristics and their relevance in single-aliquot regeneration dating protocols. *Radiation Measurements* 41(4):369–391. doi.org/10.1016/j.radmeas.2005.11.001 (accessed 5 June 2018).

Zimmerman, D.W. 1971. Thermoluminescent dating using fine grains from pottery. *Archaeometry* 13(1):29–52. doi.org/10.1111/j.1475-4754.1971.tb00028.x (accessed 5 June 2018).

13

The Sakkarra site: New data on prehistoric occupation from the Metal Phase (2000 BP) along the Karama drainage, West Sulawesi

Suryatman, Budianto Hakim and Fakhri

Abstract

The Karama drainage supported the lifeways of prehistoric Austronesian speakers following their first arrival in Sulawesi. Beginning in 1935, early research along the Karama River brought to light various occupation phases related to the founding lineages and dispersal of Austronesian speakers within Southeast Asia's borders. More recent research indicates a Neolithic occupation phase between 3500 and 2500 years ago, after which time the Metal Phase began. The Metal Phase is fully demonstrated in the deposits of the Sakkarra site, on the Bonehau River in the southern Karama drainage, as described in this paper. Cultural developments associated with the Neolithic continued unabated into the Early Metal Phase, including the technology of polishing stone artefacts, which indeed appears to have been practised with enhanced skill.

Keywords: Karama drainage, Sakkara site, cultural development, Early Metal Phase

Introduction

Recent archaeological research confirms the scenario, originally developed from historical linguistics, that the Austronesian languages spoken almost universally by the indigenous inhabitants of Island Southeast Asia (ISEA) have their origins in mid-Holocene Taiwan. Austronesian speakers evidently migrated southward into the Philippines at around 4000 cal BP and further south into Borneo and Sulawesi by 3500 cal BP, as reflected at occupation and burial sites with a Neolithic technology that included earthenware pottery and polished stone adzes. Between 2500 and 2000 cal BP (the exact timing depending on area), the Early Metal Phase began, marked by the appearance of exotic items (especially from India) and the incorporation of metallurgy to complement the technologies introduced with the Neolithic (Bellwood 2017). As explained below, the Karama drainage opens an important window on this cultural sequence as it contains major habitation sites from both the Neolithic and Early Metal Phase.

The Karama drainage covers a large area that extends for a distance of 150 km from the highlands of West Sulawesi (Sulawesi Barat). Two main rivers mark the Karama drainage: the upper Karama, which originates from the east near the western range of Tanah Toraja Regency and flows past Kalumpang village; and the Bonehua, which runs for 43 km from the southern part of Mamuju Regency before draining into the Karama. These two rivers meet at a distance of 29 km from the Karama mouth, which lies on the Makassar Strait in the area of Sikendeng, Tarailu, Mamuju District (Figure 13.1). Research shows that the Karama drainage played a major role in the livelihoods of Austronesian speakers during their early occupation of the island of Sulawesi. This research, undertaken between 1935 and the present, has brought to light several sites with evidence relating to the occupation, dispersal and foundations of Austronesian speakers in the ISEA region.

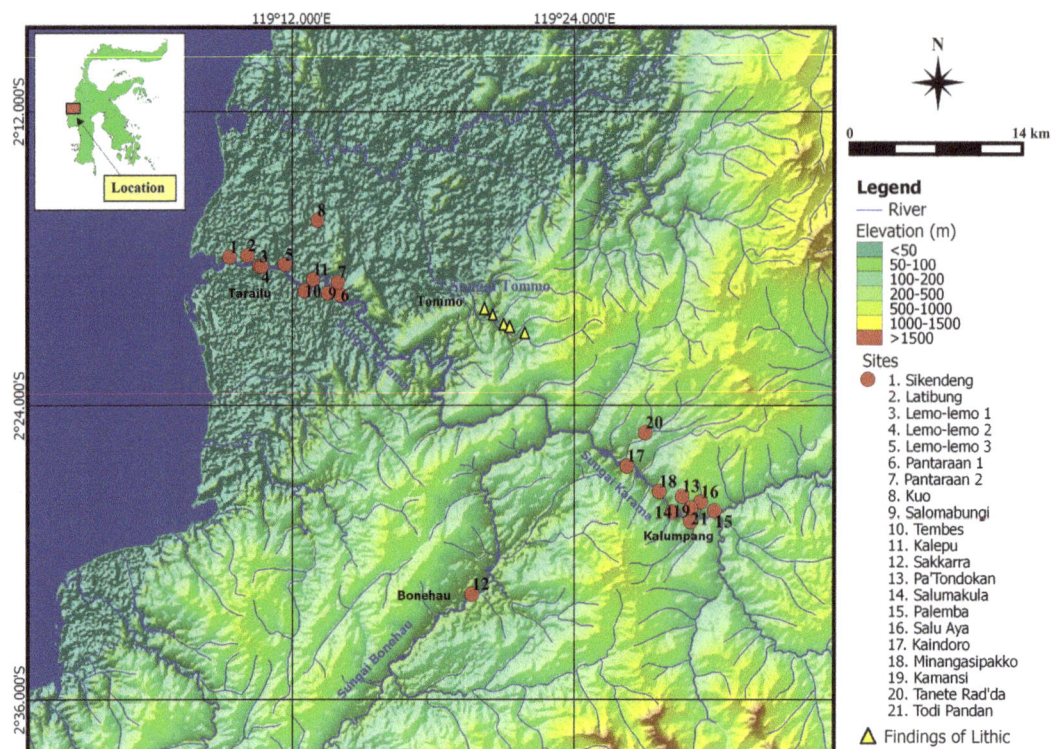

Figure 13.1: Map of the sectors and site locations along the Karama River drainage.
Source: Fakhri et al. (2015:Figure 1).

Kamansi (Kamassi) is a site on the upper Karama River, near Kalumpang. It was first excavated in 1937 by van Stein Callenfels, who recognised three occupation phases (van Stein Callenfels 1951). The first was the Proto-Neolithic phase, marked by edge-trimmed adzes, prototype shouldered adzes, Hoabinhian tools and primitive pottery. The second, Neolithic phase was marked by smoothly polished adzes and plain pottery. Finally, the third phase, the late Neolithic, was characterised by highly polished adzes, chisels and arrowheads, and decorated pottery. Van Stein Callenfels surmised that the first and third waves of occupants came from the Philippines, with Manchuria as the ultimate source in the case of the third wave. His work has led to a great amount of further research in the area, seeking to clarify these findings.

One such research effort was undertaken by Truman Simanjuntak in the Kalumpang region over multiple years (1994, 1995, 2004, 2007 and 2008), which also involved joint research projects with Australian archaeologists beginning in 2004 (Simanjuntak 1994; Morwood et al. 2007; Simanjuntak et al. 2007, 2008). Simanjuntak concluded that there were two Neolithic cultural phases at Kalumpang, particularly apparent at the Minanga Sipakko site. He described the first occupation phase, 3800–3000 cal BP, as being marked by red-slipped pottery and bone points. The following occupation phase, 3000–2500 cal BP, was marked by a change from red-slipped pottery to low-fired decorated pottery and the use of obsidian for making tools. The excavated deposits from both occupation phases also produced rectangular adzes and faunal remains (Simanjuntak 2015; Simanjuntak et al. 2007, 2008, 2016).

In 2011 and 2012, a team from the Makassar Archaeology Office returned to the Kamansi site to undertake excavations. This fieldwork indicated that the distribution of finds in the Kamansi and Minanga Sipakko sites were not very different. The basal layer produced red-slipped pottery associated with shell artefacts, adzes, stone bracelets and a decorated green-coloured stone. The upper layer produced coarse decorated pottery along with some obsidian flakes. The substantial increase in the quantity of pottery in the upper layer suggested a growing need for earthenware vessels (Hakim and Suryatman 2012).

Further research was performed by Anggraeni in 2012, including her excavation of the Pantara'an 1 site in the downstream stretches of the Karama drainage region. The available dates from char on potsherds were inferred to reflect Neolithic occupation from approximately 3000 to 2500 cal BP. Interpretation of the archaeological sequence was complicated by the recovery of a jar, apparently associated with or used for holding a burial, placed in a hole dug through the habitation deposit into the sterile gravel below. Metal artefacts, beads and a bracelet of glass had been deposited in the burial jar, which accordingly would date to after 2500 BP, even though the metal and glass were recovered from a greater depth than the Neolithic habitation deposit (Anggraeni 2012; Anggraeni et al. 2014).

In 2014, a team funded by The Anthony F. Granucci Fund for Archaeological Research in Indonesia and Timor Leste returned to the Karama River drainage to collect further archaeological data (Fakhri et al. 2015). The surveyed area was divided into four sectors (Figure 13.1). The Tarailu sector was based near the mouth of the Karama, and data were collected from the Sikendeng, Latibung, Lemo-Lemo 1, 2 and 3, Kuo, Pantara'an 1 and 2, Salo Mabongi, Tembes and Kalipu sites. The Tommo sector along the north of the Karama drainage yielded various stone artefacts of limestone and chert. The Kalumpang sector to the east included various sites including Pattondokan, Salu Makula, Palemba, Kaindoro, Kamansi and Minanga Sipakko. Finally, an area along the southern border of the Karama drainage was labelled the Bonehau sector after a site with a high potential for prehistoric occupation was found there. This site, Sakkarra, is the focus of the present contribution.

Description of the Sakkarra site

The Sakkarra site is located in Bonehau village, Bonehau District, Mamuju Regency, West Sulawesi, Indonesia. The geographic coordinates are 02°31'42.0"S 119°19'40.1"E, and the elevation is 84 metres above sea level. The distance of the Sakkarra Site from Bonehau River is only 20 m, whereas the Karama River lies 13 km away. It is an open site located about 1.3 km from the Talondo settlement and 1 km from the Mamuju–Kalumpang asphalt road. The land around the site is highly disturbed as it has been contracted as a gold mining area for five years. The land at the site is covered by shrubs and other secondary forest. A large portion of the site has been mined but operations have stopped because only a small quantity of gold was extracted.

The Sakkarra site (Figure 13.2) was found by the team in 2014 while surveying the Bonehau District, following local information of deposits rich with earthenware pottery uncovered during mining operations two years previously (Figure 13.3). About 20% of the site's surface had not been mined, and the parts that had been mined produced a thick coverage of earthenware sherds. Other finds on the surface include various adze fragments, glass beads, stone barkcloth beater fragments and various flaked stone artefacts (Figures 13.4 and 13.5a). Additionally, a stone adze was found by a local resident at the edge of a stream not far from the site (Figure 13.5b).

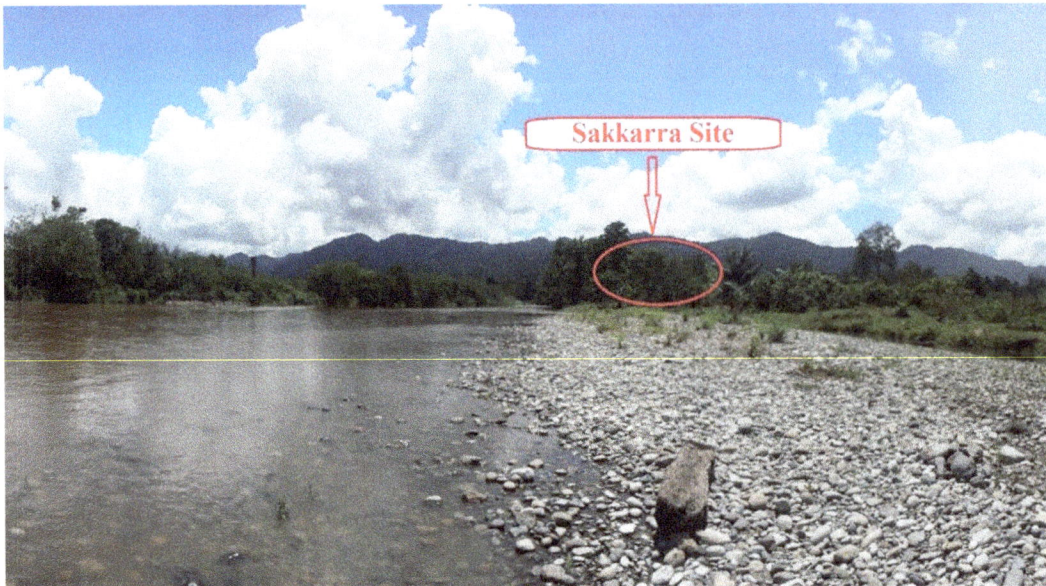

Figure 13.2: The Sakkarra site location on a hillock along the bank of the Bonehau River.
Source: Fakhri et al. (2015:Figure 6).

Figure 13.3: Exposure to a depth of 3 metres by mining activity (left), and an example of the earthenware sherds carpeting the mined area (right).
Source: The authors.

Figure 13.4: A barkcloth beater fragment (left) and glass beads (right) recovered from the surface of the Sakkarra site.
Source: Fakhri et al. (2015:Figures 8 and 9).

a)

b)

Figure 13.5: (a) Stone adze fragment found on the Sakkarra site surface, and (b) a stone adze found along the Bonehau River not far from the Sakkarra site.

Source: Fakhri et al. (2015:Figure 10).

Excavation

Excavation took place in 2014, three months after the discovery of the site. There were two excavation teams: a Makassar Archaeology Office team and a team funded by The Anthony F. Granucci Fund. Two test excavations were opened at a location that had not previously been disturbed through mining. The first excavation pit measuring 1 m x 1 m was labelled *kotak* (square) T2S1, while the second excavation pit measuring 2 m x 1 m contained *kotak* (squares) B2S1 and B3S1. Excavation proceeded using 10 cm spit depths; the deposit was removed, wet sieved in the adjacent stream and sorted on site (Figures 13.6–13.7).

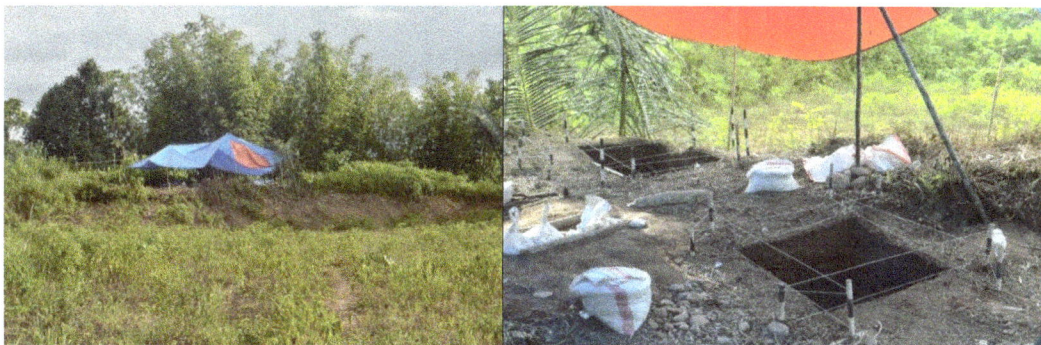

Figure 13.6: Location of the excavation squares at Sakkarra site.

Source: The authors.

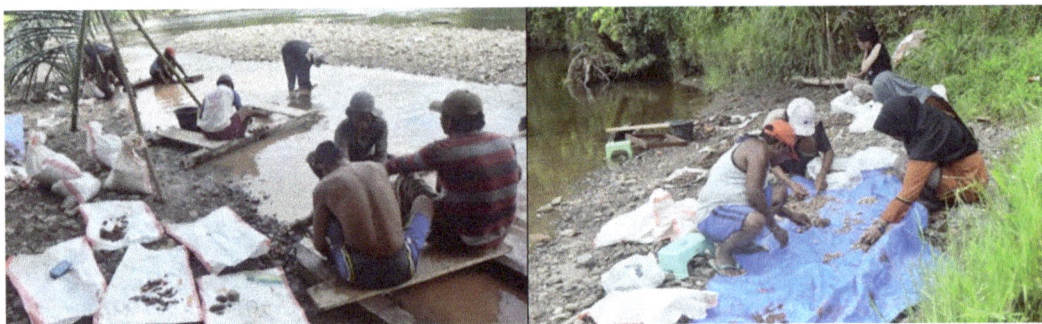

Figure 13.7: Wet sieving (left) and sorting (right) on site during the excavation of the Sakkarra site.
Source: The authors.

The T2S1 square was excavated to a depth of 2 m below the string line level, revealing a stratigraphy of four distinct layers (Figure 13.8). The top layer (Layer 1) was a very fine sand coloured dark brown (7.5YR 3/4). This top soil layer measured between 10 and 20 cm thickness with a maximum depth below the string line of 40 cm along the eastern wall. Layer 2 was a sandy clay that was dark yellowish-brown (10YR 4/6) in colour. It had a thickness of about 40 cm to almost 70 cm at its thickest part, which occurred on the north wall with a maximum depth of 86 cm below the string line. Layer 3 was a dark olive-brown silt (2.5Y 3/3) that measured between 35 cm and 60 cm thick, reaching 125 cm below the string line on the north wall. The bottom layer (Layer 4) was a clay of olive-yellow colour (2.5Y 6/8), which continued through to the maximum excavated depth of 2 m.

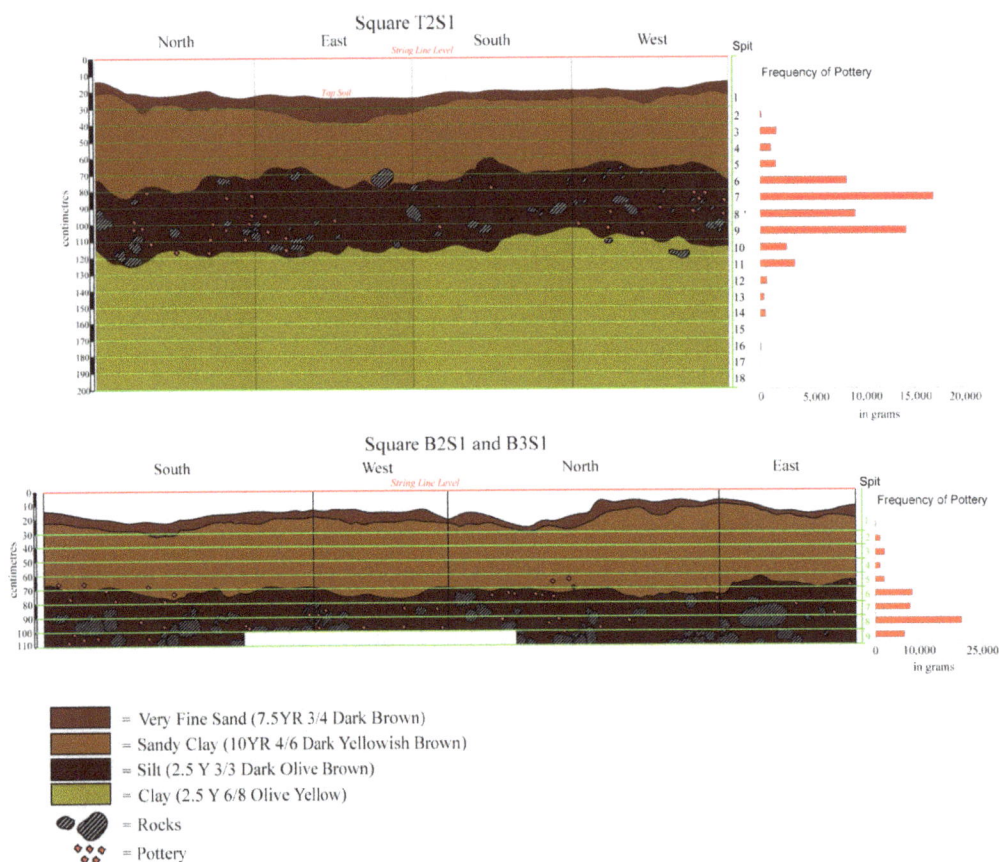

Figure 13.8: Stratigraphy of the excavated squares: T2S1 (above) and B2S1 and B3S1 (below).
Source: The authors.

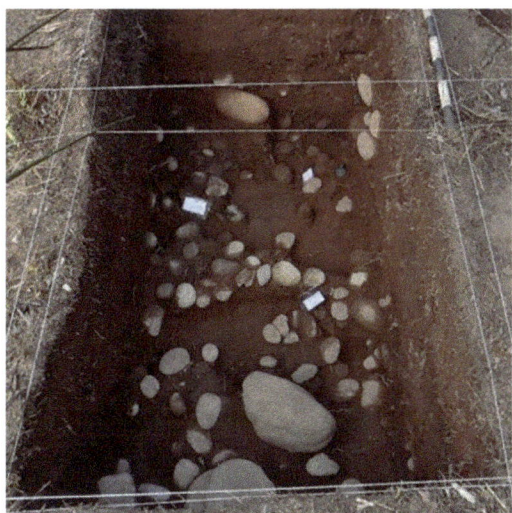

Figure 13.9: Layer of river boulders and cobbles at the floor of the B2S1 and B3S1 excavation squares.
Source: The authors.

The B2S1 and B3S1 squares were excavated to the base of the Spit 9 at a depth of 110 cm below the string line level. The stratigraphy to that depth consisted of three layers with the same sedimentary characteristics as Layers 1–3 in T2S1 and similar layer thicknesses (Figure 13.8). The excavators decided to stop excavation at this level when they came upon a layer of river boulders and cobbles of volcanic stone that impeded further progress. This is an interesting finding as the stones are arranged like a pavement (Figure 13.9). Since the stones cover the clay-rich sediment lying beneath, perhaps they had been set in place to provide a walking surface on top of the underlying slippery sediment.

Site analysis

Evidence of occupation

Pottery sherds were recovered from most spits although, as shown in Figure 13.8, the highest concentrations of pottery fragments were found in the spits within stratigraphic Layer 3. In T2S1, the sherd weight was highest between Spit 6 (8454 g) and Spit 9 (14,218 g), with its peak at Spit 7 (16,857 g). In B2S1 and B3S1, the sherd quantity also increased markedly at Spit 6 (8531 g) before peaking at Spit 9 (20,090 g). Other finds also show that Layer 3 is the main occupation layer even though imported stoneware sherds were restricted to Layer 2 (Tables 13.1 and 13.2). Layer 3 cultural materials include iron slag (Figure 13.10), glass beads and glass bracelet fragments (Figure 13.11), a metal artefact, grindstones, stone adzes and a stone barkcloth beater fragment (Figure 13.12). Accelerator Mass Spectrometry (AMS) dates from charcoal samples taken from Layer 3 demonstrate that the period of occupation dates to approximately 2000 cal BP (Table 13.3). Fragments of bone were not recovered but this can be attributed to the strongly acidic nature of the deposit at the Sakkarra site (pH=4).

Table 13.1: Distribution of the excavated finds in the T2S1 square.

Spit	Earthenware pottery (grams)	Iron slag (grams)	Glass beads (count)	Stoneware sherds (count)	Glass bracelet fragments (count)	Ground stone artefacts (count)
1	0	0	0	0	0	0
2	120	56	0	0	0	0
3	1618	0	0	2	0	0
4	1031	0	0	1	0	0
5	1549	0	0	0	0	0
6	8454	145	0	0	0	0
7	16,857	0	4	0	1	0
8	9295	0	2	0	0	0
9	14,218	428	1	0	0	0
10	2590	86.5	0	0	0	5
11	3400	0	0	0	0	5

Spit	Earthenware pottery (grams)	Iron slag (grams)	Glass beads (count)	Stoneware sherds (count)	Glass bracelet fragments (count)	Ground stone artefacts (count)
12	654	0	0	0	0	0
13	328	0	0	0	0	0
14	486	0	0	0	0	0
15	0	0	0	0	0	0
16	31	0	0	0	0	0
17	0	0	0	0	0	0
18	0	0	0	0	0	0
Total	60,631	715	7	3	1	10

Source: Fakhri et al. (2015:Table 3).

Table 13.2: Distribution of the excavated finds in the B2S1 and B3S1 squares.

Spit	Earthenware (grams)	Iron slag (grams)	Glass beads count)	Stone barkcloth beater fragments (count)	Glass bracelet fragments (count)	Metal artefacts (count)
1	20	0	0	0	0	0
2	1057	0	0	1	0	0
3	2110	0	0	0	0	1
4	1051	0	0	0	0	0
5	2060	0	0	0	0	0
6	8531	254.3	9	0	2	0
7	8069	0	6	0	0	0
8	20,090	0	1	0	0	0
9	6750	0	0	0	0	0
Total	49,738.7	254.3	16	1	2	1

Source: Analysis by Makassar Archaeology Office in 2014.

Figure 13.10: Iron slag found in Spit 9 in the T2S1 square.

Source: The authors.

Figure 13.12: Stone adze fragment found in Spit 10 in the T2S1 square (left), and stone barkcloth beater fragment found in Spit 2 in the B3S1 square (right).

Source: Left: Fakhri et al. (2015:Figure 16); Right: The authors.

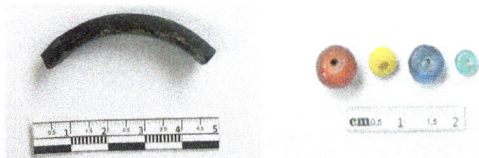

Figure 13.11: Glass bracelet fragment found in Spit 7 in the T2S1 square (left), and glass beads found in Spit 6 in the B2S1 square (right).

Source: Left: Fakhri et al. (2015:Figure 15): Right: The authors.

Table 13.3: AMS ^{14}C dates from the T2S1 square at the Sakkarra site (The ANU Radiocarbon Dating Centre).

Sample code	Dated material	Spit/depth	^{14}C age	Calibrated dates BP
S-ANU 39336	Charcoal	Spit 8 (90–100 cm)	2000 BP	2062–1867
S-ANU 39337	Charcoal	Spit 9 (100–110 cm)	2040 BP	2123–1895

Note: Calibration based on Fallon et al. (2010).

Source: Fakhri et al. (2015:Table 4).

Metal and glass artefacts

Figure 13.13: Metal artefact in the shape of a fish hook from Spit 3 in the B3S1 square (left) and river pebble with two parallel incisions from Spit 4 in the B2S1 square (right).

Source: The authors.

The metallic artefact found in Spit 3 in the B3S1 square is shaped like a fish hook. It has a maximum length of 2.1 cm including its corroded surface (see Figure 13.13). In other aspects, Sakkarra appears to resemble the Pantara'an 1 site on the lower Karama River, even though the data have not yet been collected to allow a complete comparison. Anggraeni (2012) notes that the glass beads from Pantara'an 1 are of the 'Indo-Pacific' variety and coloured blue, yellow, green and reddish-brown, similar to the range of colours of the Sakkarra glass beads (Figures 13.4 and 13.11 (right)). She further describes fragments from green glass bracelets and four iron slag fragments excavated at Pantara'an 1, which are artefact categories matched at Sakkarra (Figures 13.10 and 13.11 (left)).

Stone artefacts

Figure 13.14: Polished stone cog with teeth along its perimeter (square T2S1, Spit 11).

Source: Fakhri et al. (2015:Figure 17).

A river pebble from Spit 4 in the B2S1 square has two parallel incisions on one of its faces. The diameter of this pebble is 8 cm (see Figure 13.13). A similar pebble was excavated at Minanga Sipakko (Simanjuntak et al. 2008:Figures 6–14). The two barkcloth beater fragments from Sakkarra, one from the surface and the second from the T2S1 square (Figures 13.4 and 13.12), indicate a rectangular shape and deep grooves on the working surface, as recorded for the Karama River barkcloth beaters (Hasanuddin, this volume).

The majority of the excavated ground stone artefacts are adze fragments (e.g. Figure 13.12). An exception is the sandstone artefact from Spit 11 in T2S1, which is shaped like a mace head (Figure 13.14). This artefact has a diameter of about 9.5 cm and is a cog stone with seven symmetrical teeth around its perimeter. There is a central hole of 2.3 cm diameter, and a central boss on one face that looks like it could have held a rod for manipulating the cog stone. The complex symmetry of this sandstone artefact points to an advanced ability in grinding stone. Its function is not yet clearly determined, but one possibility is its use in smelting metal.

Pottery

The total quantity of earthenware from the two test excavations amounted to 8488 sherds. These were predominantly body sherds (n=7415, 87.4%), supplemented by rim sherds (n=1027, 12.1%), carination sherds (n=25, 0.3%), cover sherds (n=7, 0.1%), foot-ring sherds (n=6, 0.1%), base sherds (n=3, <0.1%), crucible sherds (n=2, <0.1%) and a single handle sherd.

Only 82 of the excavated sherds (1.0%) are decorated, contrasting with the 99.0% (n=8406) that are plain. This indicates a low cultural propensity for decorating pottery. Further, just nine sherds show traces of a red slip (0.1%), contrasting with the 99.9% (n=8479) that are unslipped. These characteristics also apply to the very late Neolithic pottery at Minanga Sipakko, where over 95% of the pottery in the uppermost habitation spits was plain and unslipped, and only a small percentage either decorated or red-slipped (Anggraeni et al. 2014:Figure 3).

At Sakkarra, only body sherds appear to have been decorated. The observed motifs include stamped concentric circles, vertically oriented parallel incisions, commas, incised squares (sometimes punctate filled) and diagonal cross-hatching (Figure 13.15). Most of these motifs are broadly matched by motifs recorded for the Minanga Sipakko pottery, less so the motifs recorded at the sites of Latibung (near the mouth of the Karama River) and Kamansi (Table 13.4). However, it is unclear which of the highly diverse Minanga Sipakko decorative elements, which included various zigzag, triangular, lunate, arca shell and curvilinear motifs (Prasetyo 2008), persisted through to the late Neolithic, and so the comparisons of individual motifs in Table 13.4 is probably of limited diagnostic value.

Figure 13.15: Decorated earthenware pottery from the Sakkarra site.

Source: The authors.

Table 13.4: Comparison of Sakkara and Karama River pottery decorations.

Motif	Sakkara	Kamansi	Minanga Sipakko	Latibung
Stamped concentric circles	Triple circles	Double circles	Double circles	Single circles only
Vertical parallel incisions	Present	Absent	Present	Absent
Commas	Present	Absent	Present	Absent
Unfilled squares	Present	Square maze	Absent	Absent
Filled square(/rectangle) motifs	Vertical incisions; punctate dots	Punctate dots	Vertical incisions	Diagonal incisions with punctate dots
Diagonal cross-hatching	Present	Absent	Present	Present

Note: Latibung is undated but appears to be an Early Metal Phase site (Anggraeni 2012).

Sources: Sakkara (this chapter); Kamansi, Minanga Sipakko, Latibung (Prasetyo 2008).

A total of 651 sherds could be assigned to a vessel form (Figure 13.16). Cooking pots (*periuk*) are dominant, accounting for 79.1% of the identified vessels (n=515). Bowls (*mangkuk*) accounted for 15.5% (n=101), *jambangan* jars for 3.4% (n=22), large open jars (*tempayan*) for 1.7% and kendis for 0.3% (n=2). Statistical analysis of the rim diameters (Figure 13.17) indicates that the cooking pots were the most heterogeneous. Their diameters averaged out at 17.7 cm (SD=3.8) with a range between 8 and 28 cm. The average rim diameter of the bowls was 20.0 cm (SD=3.1) and the range was 12 to 24 cm. The *jambangan* jars had an average rim diameter of 27.4 cm (SD=2.2), ranging between 26 and 34 cm. The *tempayan* jars had the largest diameters overall, with an average of 33.3 cm (SD=4.7) and a range between 28 cm and 40 cm. The kendis had the smallest rim diameters, with an average of just 4 cm.

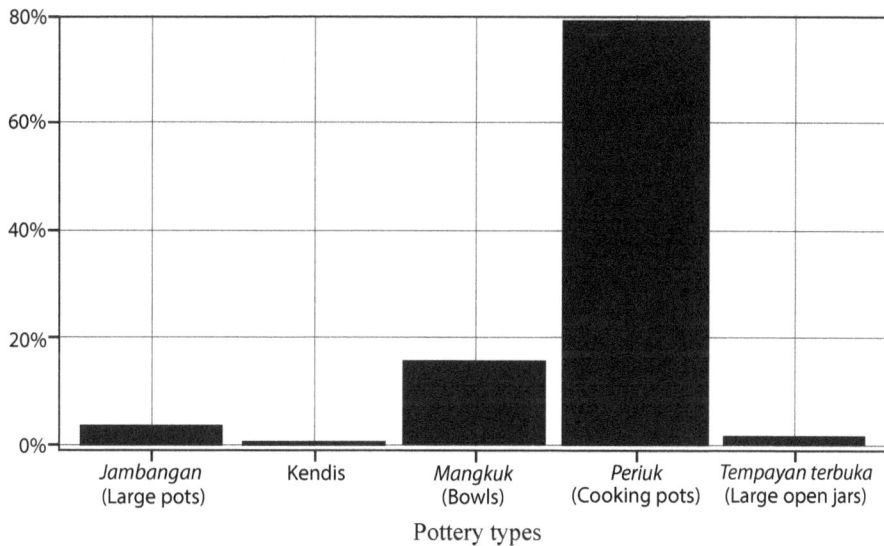

Figure 13.16: Percentages of pottery vessel form based on analysis of rim sherds.
Source: The authors.

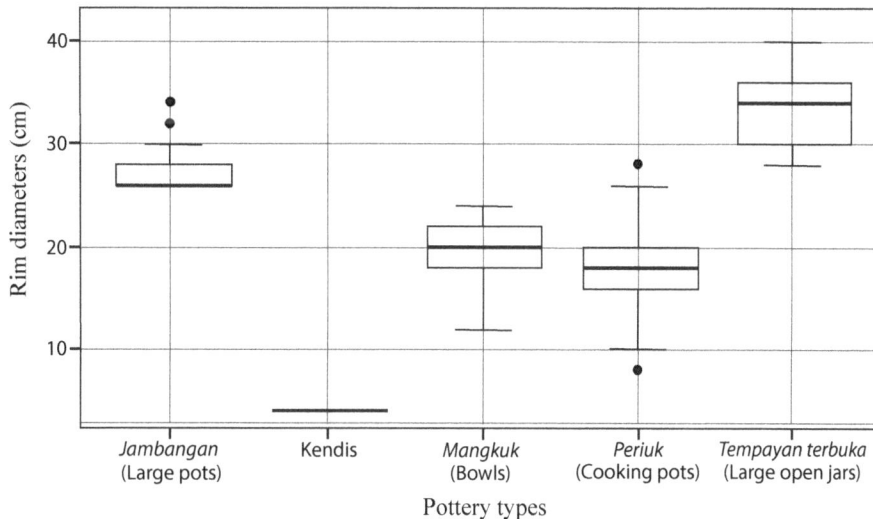

Figure 13.17: Box plot diagram of the distribution of the vessels' rim diameters.
Source: The authors.

The cooking pots showed the greatest variety of rim types. Figure 13.18 illustrates the six rim types observed for cooking pots and the three rim types observed for bowls. Type A cooking pots were the most frequently recorded type (n=398, 77.3% of cooking pots). Type B cooking pots accounted for 17.7% (n=91), Type C for 0.2% (n=1), Type D for 1.6% (n=8), Type E for 2.5% (n=13) and Type F for 0.8% (n=4). As for the bowls, the Type A variant was the most frequently recorded, accounting for 90.1% of bowls (n=91). The rarer variants were the Type B (n=8, 7.9%) and Type C bowls (n=2, 2.0%).

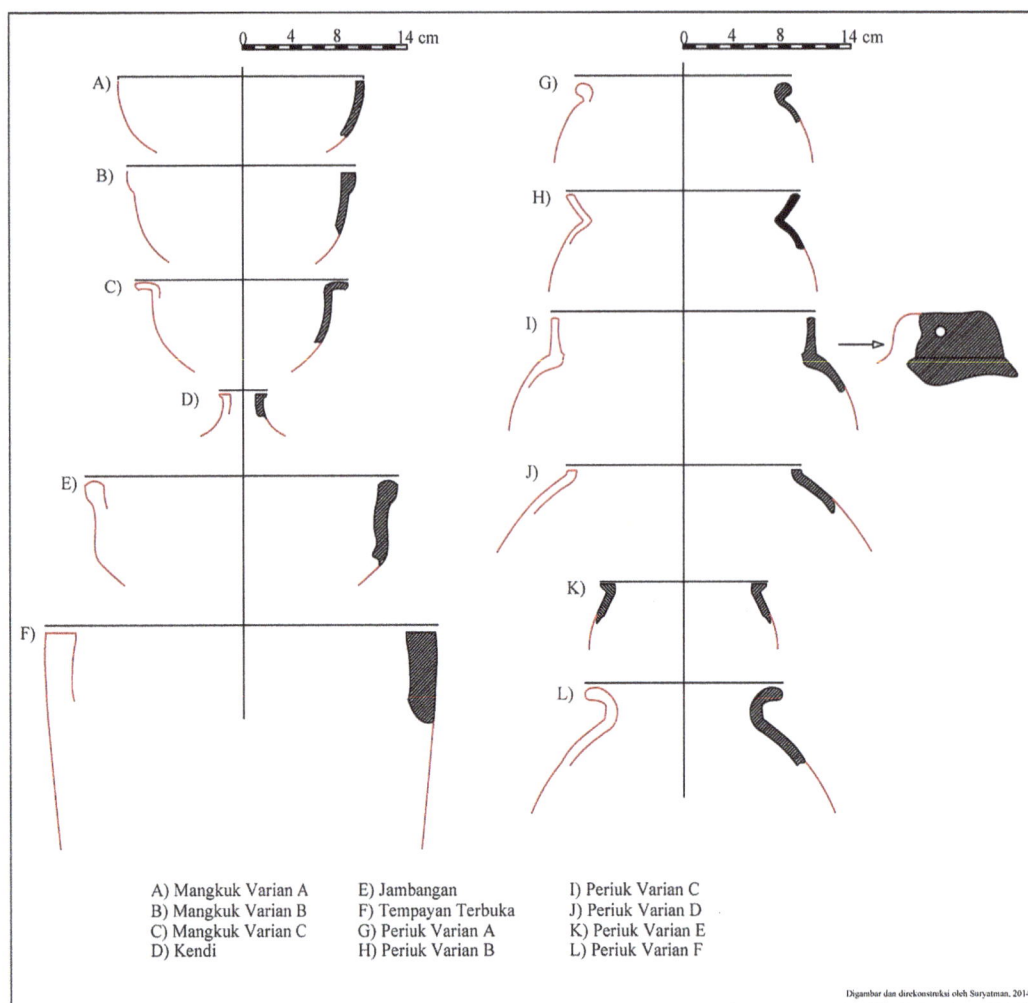

Figure 13.18: Reconstruction of the earthenware vessel forms at the Sakkarra site based on rim analysis. The vessel types are scaled to each other based on their average recorded diameters.

Source: Fakhri et al. (2015:Figure 18).

The Sakkarra rim shapes show few similarities with the rim shapes from Kamansi, Minanga Sipakko and Pantara'an 1 (Anggraeni et al. 2014:Figures 13.5 and 13.6). Only the Sakkarra 'Cooking Pot Type E' rim shape (K in Figure 13.18) is also documented for all of Kamansi, Minanga Sipakko and Pantara'an 1. The only other apparent similarities are between the Sakkarra 'Bowl Type A' and 'Cooking Pot Type C' rim shapes (A and I in Figure 13.18), which are respectively matched by early Neolithic rims from Minanga Sipakko and Kamansi.

Discussion and comparisons

The ability to use and manipulate metals is one of the major technological advances for prehistoric human societies, and Sulawesi has much to contribute to the understanding of the technological transition from the Neolithic to the Metal Phase. The research findings from the Sakkarra site show that the Karama drainage region was already occupied by prehistoric Austronesian speakers when the practice of metal smelting came to the region at around 2000 BP.

The results of research undertaken to date show that there were four phases of occupation by Austronesian speakers in the Karama drainage area. The first phase is believed to have begun at least 3500 BP, when Austronesian speakers began to colonise the Sulawesi interior via the Karama drainage and introduce their early Neolithic traditions. Fine, red-slipped pottery was the signature of this phase in the Kalumpang area, associated with bone points, adzes (some pierced), haematite, grindstones, whetstones, ornamental pendants of green stone (but not nephrite), fragments of limestone bracelets and various shell artefacts (Hakim and Suryatman 2012; Simanjuntak et al. 2007, 2016). Similarly, several other sites contain red-slipped pottery in their early settlement phases, including the Dimolit site in the Philippines, which, probably dating to 4500–3500 BP, may be the earliest in ISEA (Bellwood 2000). Also, the Bukit Tengkorak site in Sabah contained red-slipped pottery during its initial occupation (Chia 2003).

The second phase in the Kalumpang area began at around 3000 BP. The fine pottery of the first phase was replaced by coarse, low-fired ware and dwindling application of a red slip. Some of the vessels were found to be decorated at this time, although the proportion of decorated sherds (at Minanga Sipakko) also dwindled during the late Neolithic. The research by Simanjuntak et al. (2007) at Minanga Sipakko and by Hakim and Suryatman (2012) at Kamansi shows that obsidian artefacts belong to this second phase. The Kamansi excavations also indicate a notable increase in the quantity of pottery during the second phase, reflecting an increase in the use of pottery vessels and perhaps as well in the population size in the Kalumpang area. Population pressure may also have resulted in the establishment of new settlements in the Karama area. Occupation at the Pantara'an 1 site, which lies closer to the coast, evidently commenced during this second phase (Anggraeni et al. 2014).

The third phase, denoting the transition from the Neolithic to the Metal Phase, is thought to have commenced before 2000 BP. This phase might be represented by Pantara'an 1 with its earthenware sherds and associated metal artefacts, iron slag and glass beads, dating to after 2500 BP, some but not all of which can be related to jar burials at the site (Anggraeni 2012). Neolithic technology did not disappear with the early use of metals. This can be seen in the various polished stone artefacts from Pantara'an 1 such as adzes (one from the main jar burial), which perhaps were still important for agricultural activities.

The fourth phase is thought to have already been underway by 2000 BP. The fieldwork at the Sakkara site recovered traces of this fourth occupation phase in the southern hinterland of the Karama drainage area. The technology of smelting metals was established by then, but Neolithic traditions still persisted. This is demonstrated by the various stone adze fragments excavated at Sakkarra, the fragments of barkcloth beaters similar to the Karama River barkcloth beaters, and in particular the symmetrically toothed cog stone, which displays remarkably adept skills in polishing stone. Its function is not clear, but it may have been used in smelting metal. The earthenware pottery was generally undistinguished, as shown by the low proportion of sherds with decorations (1.0%) or a red slip (0.1%), similar to the very late Neolithic pottery at Minanga Sipakko. However, rim comparisons tend to distinguish the Sakkara pottery from the pottery at Minanga Sipakko as well as other Karama Rivers sites.

Investigations into the prehistory of the Karama drainage portray a picture of cultural development between the Neolithic (3500 BP) and the Metal Phase (2000 BP). The development of metallurgy did not lead to the loss of polished stone technology in the Karama drainage area, which was still present 2000 years ago, as shown at the Sakkara site.

Unfortunately, the Sakkarra site is currently under considerable threat from the potential of further gold mining. Though mining has ceased for the time being, there is still a contractual mining period of a further five years. The second threat is erosion by the Bonehau River, which is slowly eroding away the bank and the contained site deposits. Further research incorporating a combination of scientific disciplines and techniques at the Sakkarra site is necessary in order to gain a more comprehensive picture of the cultural developments of its prehistoric inhabitants.

Conclusions

The Sakkarra site plays an important role in reconstructing the cultural developments of prehistoric Austronesian speakers during the Early Metal Phase both in Sulawesi and in ISEA more generally. Colonisation of the Sakkarra site can be reasonably traced back to the Neolithic occupation of the Karama River, which lies a short distance to the north. Cultural continuity is reflected in the maintenance of Neolithic technological traditions such as the manufacture of earthenware pottery and polished stone tools. On the other hand, the appearance of glass and iron artefacts (at Pantara'an 1 as well Sakkarra) heralds the introduction of new cultural influences on the Karama drainage inhabitants. The pottery rim shapes at Sakkarra are dissimilar from those at the Karama River Neolithic sites, but, in the current state of research, it is unclear whether these dissimilarities reflect introduced, Early Metal Phase cultural influences or local cultural change. Certainly, the polished cog stone is difficult to ascribe to external influence because examples of this tool type do not appear to have been documented from other sites. Thus, the example of Sakkarra suggests that the Neolithic to Metal Phase transition involved continuity of Neolithic technology but with scope for local innovation, along with the capacity to absorb metallurgy and participate in the growing trade in glass and other exotic items.

Author biographies

Suryatman Makassar Archaeology Office, Makassar, South Sulawesi, Indonesia

Budianto Hakim Makassar Archaeology Office, Makassar, South Sulawesi, Indonesia

Fakhri Makassar Archaeology Office, Makassar, South Sulawesi, Indonesia

References

Anggraeni. 2012. The Austronesian Migration Hypothesis as seen from Prehistoric Settlements on the Karama River, Mamuju, West Sulawesi. Unpublished PhD thesis, School of Archaeology and Anthropology, The Australian National University, Canberra.

Anggraeni, T. Simanjuntak, P. Bellwood and P. Piper. 2014. Neolithic foundations in the Karama valley, West Sulawesi, Indonesia. *Antiquity* 88(341):740-756, doi.org/10.1017/S0003598X00050663 (accessed 5 June 2018).

Bellwood, P. 2000. *Prasejarah Kepulauan Indo-Malaysia (Prehistory of the Indo-Malaysian Archipelago).* (Translated by D. Tanudirjo). Jakarta: PT Gramedia Pustaka Utama.

Bellwood, P. 2017. *First Islanders: Prehistory and Human Migration in Island Southeast Asia.* Oxford: Wiley Blackwell. doi.org/10.1002/9781119251583 (accessed 5 June 2018).

Chia, S.M.S. 2003. *The Prehistory of Bukit Tengkorak as a Major Pottery Making Site in Southeast Asia.* Kota Kinabalu: Department of Sabah Museum.

Fakhri, Suryatman, B. Hakim and R. Sardi. 2015. Exploration of prehistoric sites in the Karama watershed, West Sulawesi, Indonesia. *Journal of Indo-Pacific Archaeology* 39:18–25. journals.lib.washington.edu/index.php/JIPA/article/view/14786/12489 (accessed 5 June 2018).

Fallon, S.J., L.K. Fifield and J.M. Chappell. 2010. The next chapter in radiocarbon dating at The Australian National University: Status report on the single stage AMS. *Nuclear Instruments and Methods in Physics Research Section B: Beam Interactions with Materials and Atoms* 268(7–8):898-901. doi.org/10.1016/j.nimb.2009.10.059 (accessed 5 June 2018).

Hakim, B. and Suryatman. 2012. Eksistensi Penutur Austronesia di Situs Kamansi. Unpublished Report. Makassar: Balai Arkeologi Makassar.

Hasanuddin. 2018. Prehistoric sites in Enrekang Kabupaten, South Sulawesi. In S. O'Connor, D. Bulbeck and J. Meyer (eds), *The Archaeology of Sulawesi: Current Research on the Pleistocene to the Historic Period*, pp. 171–190. Canberra: ANU Press.

Morwood, M., I. Mahmud and T. Simanjuntak. 2007. Penelitian situs Minanga Sipakko dan sekitarnya. In T. Simanjuntak, F.S. Intan and I. Mahmud (eds), *Kalumpang: Arkeologi dan Etnografi*, pp. 46–53. Jakarta: Pusat Penelitian dan Pengembangan Arkeologi Nasional.

Prasetyo, B. 2008. Pottery from the Neolithic sites at the banks of Karama River. In T. Simanjuntak (ed.), *Austronesian in Sulawesi*, pp. 77–92. Jakarta: Center for Prehistoric and Austronesian Studies.

Simanjuntak, T. 1994. *Kalumpang: Hunian tepi Sungai bercorak Neolitik-Paleometalik di Pedalaman Sulawesi Selatan.* Aspek-aspek Arkeologi Indonesia No. 17. Jakarta: Pusat Penelitian dan Pengembangan Arkeologi Nasional.

Simanjuntak, T. 2015. Progres penelitian Austronesia di Nusantara. *Jurnal Amerta* 33 (1):1–76. doi.org/10.24832/amt.v33i1.211 (accessed 5 June 2018).

Simanjuntak, T., F.S. Intan and I. Mahmud (eds). 2007. *Kalumpang: Arkeologi dan Etnografi*. Jakarta: Pusat Penelitian dan Pengembangan Arkeologi Nasional.

Simanjuntak, T., M.J. Morwood, F.S. Intan, I. Mahmud, K. Grant, N. Somba, B. Akw and D.W. Utomo. 2008. Minanga Sipakko and the Neolithic of the Karama River. In T. Simanjuntak (ed.), *Austronesian in Sulawesi*, pp. 57–75. Jakarta: Center for Prehistoric and Austronesian Studies.

Simanjuntak, T., A.A Oktaviana and R. Handini. 2016. Updated views on the Austronesian studies in Indonesia. In B. Prasetyo, T.S. Nastiti and T. Simanjuntak (eds), *Austonesian Diaspora: A New Perspective*, pp. 207–222. Yogyakarta: Gadjah Mada University Press.

van Stein Callenfels, P.V. 1951. Prehistoric sites on the Karama River. *Journal of East Asiatic Studies* 1(1):82–93.

14

Neolithic dispersal implications of murids from late Holocene archaeological and modern natural deposits in the Talaud Islands, northern Sulawesi

Julien Louys, Michael Herrera, Stuart Hawkins, Ken Aplin,
Christian Reepmeyer, Felicitas Hopf, Stephen C. Donnellan,
Sue O'Connor and Daud A. Tanudirjo

Abstract

The Sangihe-Talaud Archipelago represents a group of 77 remote islands located between the Philippines and North Sulawesi, in the northern sector of Wallacea. The Talaud Islands have a rich and significant archaeological record going back to the Pleistocene and are instrumental in understanding Pleistocene colonisation of small islands and later models of Austronesian language dispersal. Here we report on vertebrate material excavated from Leang Mande'et, a late Holocene rockshelter on Karakelang, the main island in the Talaud group. The site represents a periodically occupied shelter used for gardening. Fauna recovered predominately comprises murid elements, with at least four taxa (*Rattus rattus, Rattus exulans* and two *Melomys* species) found. The rodents show clear signs of being deposited by raptors rather than humans, unlike the small number of fish remains also recovered. DNA sequences from several *Rattus rattus* specimens are referrable to *Rattus rattus* complex lineage IV, a lineage with a southern Indochinese origins and broad modern representation through Indonesia and the Philippines. The lack of any *Rattus rattus* complex lineage II from Leang Mande'et suggests that the first agricultural inhabitants of this island did not come from Taiwan or northern Indochina, but rather that they either originated from the south or that, once established in the Talauds, opened up significant trade networks to the south and in the process acquired a significant pest.

Keywords: Black rat, Austronesian migration, Karakelang, ancient DNA

Introduction

Commensal rodents represent a strong proxy for the distribution of human settlements and the spread of agricultural practices (Matisoo-Smith and Robins 2004; Aplin et al. 2011; Thomson et al. 2014). Of the various commensal rodents, the Black rat (*Rattus rattus sensu lato*) is the most widely distributed and arguably the species with greatest past and present impact on human livelihoods. It occurs in disturbed and human-modified landscapes throughout much of the world, typically occupying villages, field complexes and disturbed forests (Aplin et al. 2011). Recent studies of mitochondrial DNA (mtDNA) diversity within the Black rat found multiple, deeply divergent lineages (some of it corresponding with known chromosomal variants; Yosida 1980), particularly within its likely ancestral source area on mainland Asia (Pagés et al. 2010; Aplin et al. 2011). This diversity probably arose through allopatric divergence among populations occupying discrete geographic areas (Aplin et al. 2011) and most likely commenced around 0.18–0.27 Ma (Robins et al. 2008). Aplin et al. (2011) coined the term '*Rattus rattus* Complex' (RrC) for the evolutionary unit that includes the various geographic lineages of 'typical' Black rats, as well as two other closely related species. The deep and complex genetic structuring of the RrC provides excellent opportunities to track patterns of human dispersals and contacts, particularly in response to the emergence and spread of agricultural communities and the operation of maritime trade networks (Aplin et al. 2011).

Two lineages of *R. rattus* are of particular interest in Wallacea, namely the RrC lineages II and IV. RrC lineage II rats are thought to have originated in northern Indochina to East Asia, with highest haplotype diversity observed in Myanmar, Laos, northern Vietnam and southern China (Aplin et al. 2011). Population expansion analysis of this lineage indicates a relatively recent population increase, beginning during the terminal Pleistocene to early Holocene, while haplotype network analyses indicate a likely dispersal out of Taiwan and flowing through the Philippines and Japan, and from the former into Wallacea and Micronesia (Aplin et al. 2011). RrC lineage IV rats, on the other hand, had a more southern origin, probably around the lower catchment of the Mekong River and potentially on the Sundaic Shelf (Aplin et al. 2011). Population expansion of RrC lineage IV rats may have been slightly later than that of RrC lineage II, with dispersal principally through the Sundaic and Wallacean islands but extending to the Philippines in the north and Sri Lanka in the west.

The Sangihe-Talaud Archipelago, a group of 77 tiny and remote islands located between the Philippines and North Sulawesi (Figure 14.1), sits in a strategic geographical location relevant to models describing the initial dispersal routes of Neolithic innovations, and has thus received considerable archaeological attention. In the Blust–Bellwood model of migration dispersal (Blust 1995; Bellwood 2011), the Leang Tuwo Mane'e rockshelter in the Talaud Islands (Bellwood 2007; Tanudirjo 2001) in particular has played a crucial role in determining the age of initial spread of red-slipped pottery and related agricultural groups southwards from northern Island Southeast Asia (ISEA), connecting the Philippines chronologically with later Neolithic sites in Sulawesi, the Moluccas and the Western Pacific (Spriggs 2011).

During the course of new surveys and excavations in the Talaud Islands, we recovered well-preserved faunal assemblages that included specimens referred to *Rattus rattus*. Here we describe the stratigraphic context and age of these specimens and present the results of genetic analysis that sheds light on the likely route and timing of dispersal of the commensal Black rat to the Talaud Islands. We discuss the broader implications of the results for understanding Neolithic population movements in the region.

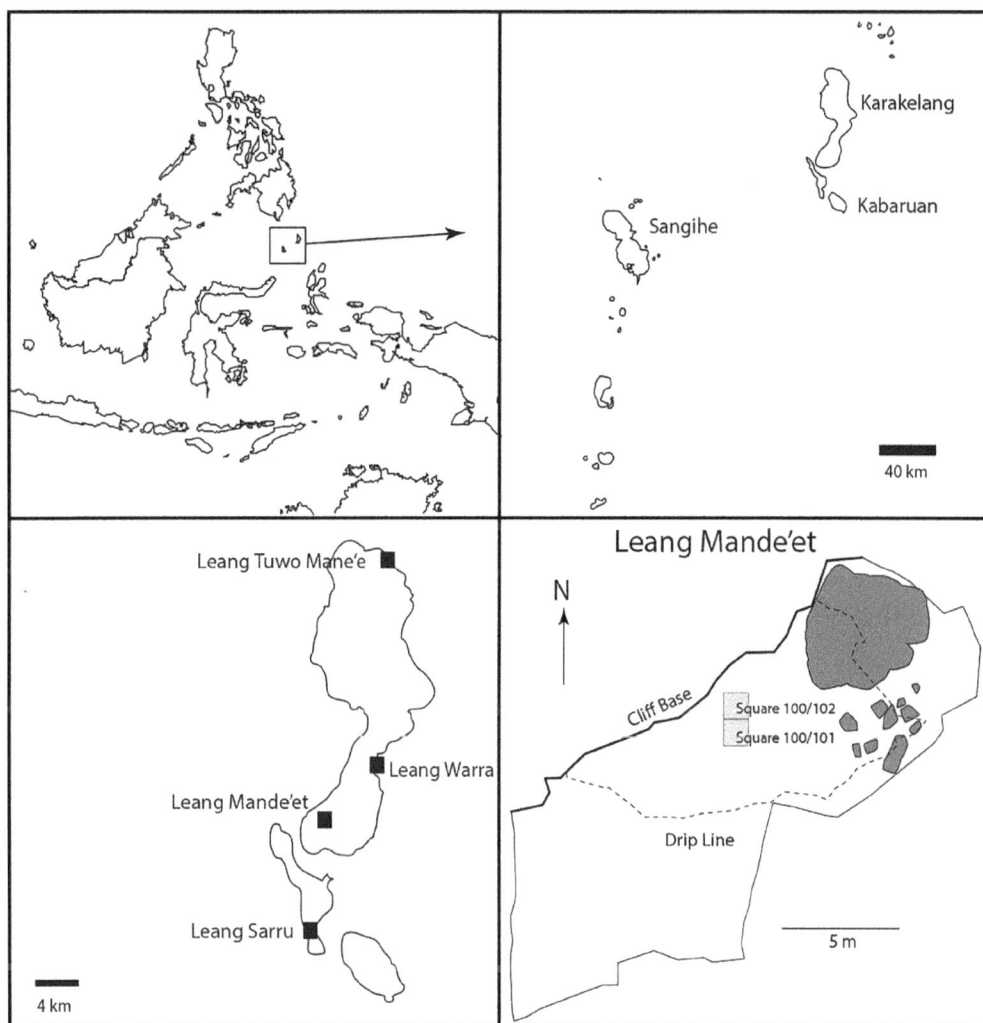

Figure 14.1: Location of the Sangihe-Talaud Archipelago, the major Talaud Islands, and the sites discussed in the text.

Source: Maps prepared by Julien Louys.

Methods

Archaeological excavation

The Mande'et rockshelter (Leang Mande'et; LMD) is situated on the western side of Karakelang Island, the main island of the Talaud group, about a 45-minute walk upslope of Pampalu village (4°04'32"N 126°42'23"E). It is a fairly large overhang with a 12 m opening, depth of 5.5 m and height at dripline of about 6.5–8 m. It is located at approximately 130 m elevation with a southeastern aspect. The surface of the shelter is a level, slightly outward sloping area with steep access beyond the shelter. There are recent fire traces on the rock fall and the shelter is currently in use as a resting area for local people. A 2 m x 1 m test pit was excavated to a depth of 140 cm below the datum (uD). Excavations were conducted by trowelling in 10 cm spits until 140 cm uD in square 100/101 and in 5 cm spits until 30 cm uD in square 100/102, and all sediments were wet sieved through a 1.5 mm mesh sieve. Here, we focus predominantly on the faunal remains from this site.

Zooarchaeology and taphonomy

The vertebrate skeletal material recovered from LMD was identified by comparison with modern and archaeological reference specimens housed at The Australian National University (ANU) Osteology Collections in the Department of Archaeology and Natural History. Where possible, murid taxonomic identification was supplemented by aDNA results. Skeletal material was identified to element at the lowest taxonomic classification possible. Small lizards (Lacertilia) and snakes (Serpentes) could be identified only to order. Pacific fishbone studies usually only include family-level identifications of the five paired jaw bones due to difficulties reconciling morphological variability with high species diversity within tropical family groups, compounded by incomplete reference collections (Dye and Longenecker 2004), and this approach was followed here. The small amount of bird material was too fragmented for taxonomic determination, so this was recorded only by skeletal element.

The taphonomic history of bone deposition was investigated by measuring relative taxonomic abundance, taxonomic diversity, skeletal element representation, bone breakages and bone surface modifications. Since the sample represents a very limited temporal deposit, the assemblage was aggregated into one unit. Relative abundance was quantified by Number of Individual Specimens (NISP). Diversity was measured by simply counting the number of taxa present while the Shannon–Wiener diversity index (Keylock 2005) was calculated using PAST (Hammer et al. 2001) to measure the evenness of taxonomic representation. Evenness values close to 0 indicate faunal abundance is concentrated on a few taxa, whereas values close to 1 indicate a more even spread. This was applied to the lowest taxonomic level possible, with the highest taxonomic level excluded to reduce overlapping levels of diversity. In the case of murids these were aggregated regardless of taxonomy due to the uncertainty of identifications.

Skeletal elements were quantified by the Minimum Number of Elements (MNE) present. This was calculated by quantifying the most frequent side and portion of each skeletal element, recorded by distinctive morphological features, and fraction summation of long bone epiphyses and shafts. Murid skeletal element representation was calculated following Fernández et al. (2012) where the percentage of bone survivorship was estimated using the following formula: MNEi/(Ei x MNI) x 100 (where E = element, MNI = Minimum Number of Individuals). Murid bone breakage was investigated by calculating the proportions of complete, proximal, distal and shaft long bones, as well as the degree of skull breakage, following Andrews (1990).

Bone surface modifications recorded include coloration from a scale of 0–4, with 0 = no colour, 1 = light brown, 2 = dark brown, 3 = black, 4 = grey white. A select group of postcranial murid bones (humerus, radius, ulna, pelvis, femur, tibia) were observed under a high-powered microscope for signs of predator digestion on a scale of 0–4, whereby 0 = no digestion, 1 = light digestion, 2 = moderate, 3 = heavy, and 4 = extreme as described by Andrews (1990). Tooth punctures from predators were also recorded.

Pollen

Sediment samples from each spit were thoroughly homogenised and 10 cc subsamples taken for pollen processing, which followed standard HCl, KOH and acetolysis methods (Faegri and Iversen 1989) and included addition of *Lycopodium* marker grains to calculate concentrations of pollen, spores and microscopic charcoal (Stockmarr 1971). Lithium polytungstate was used at a specific gravity of 2.0 to further concentrate pollen in the samples (Caffrey and Horn 2013). Pollen, spores and microscopic charcoal (>10 μm) were counted at 400 x magnification using a Zeiss Axiophot microscope and identifications made using the reference collection held at the Department of Archaeology and Natural History, ANU, and the Australian Pollen and Spore Atlas (APSA Members 2007). Pollen diagrams were produced using Tilia v. 2.0.33 (Grimm 2013).

Sediment analysis

Particle size analysis of the sediment was carried out by laser diffraction using a Malvern Mastersizer 2000 with Hydro MU attachment housed at the Fenner School of Environment and Society, ANU. Pre-treatment of 2.5 cc subsamples included 10% HCl to remove carbonates, 30% H_2O_2 to remove organic matter, addition of calgon to disperse aggregates and an additional 30 seconds of ultrasonic dispersal just prior to measurement. Organic matter content of the sediment was determined by loss on ignition (Dean 1974) using 2.5 cc subsamples.

Ancient DNA extraction, amplification and sequencing

The DNA analysis included specimens recovered from the excavated deposits as well as several naturally deposited specimens. Two surface skeletons of *Rattus rattus* were collected during surveys. These remains were observed on the forest floor less than 2 km from LMD. Several additional faunal remains submitted for analysis were collected from the surface of Leang Warra, a small limestone cave situated on the eastern side of the island (Figure 14.1).

The samples were extracted, and PCR amplified in a specialised ancient DNA laboratory at the Australian Centre for Ancient DNA (ACAD) at the University of Adelaide, South Australia. These samples comprised incisor fragments. Preparation of samples for DNA extraction was carried out using a DNA extraction protocol based on a standard silica-based extraction (Brotherton et al. 2013). The incisors, ranging between 0.03 g to 0.07 g, were each incubated for 1 hour under constant rotation at 37°C in 1.6 mL of 0.5M EDTA (Ethylenediaminetetraacetic acid), then replaced with fresh 0.5M EDTA and left to incubate for 24 hours. After decalcification, 40 μL Proteinase K (20 mg/mL) was added, and incubation continued for 2 hours at 55°C. After lysis, the samples were centrifuged at 4,500 rpm for 2 minutes to pellet undigested material. The supernatant was transferred to a 15 mL tube containing 100 μL silica suspension and 3 mL of in-house binding buffer (4.0 mL QG buffer (Qiagen), 0.06 mL of 1X Triton, 20 mM NaCl, 0.2 M acetic acid (all Sigma-Aldrich)) and left to bind to silica for 1 hour at room temperature under slow and constant rotation. The samples were centrifuged for 3 minutes at 4,500 rpm to pellet silica particles and the supernatant was poured off. The pellet was transferred to a 1.5 mL tube and washed three times by resuspension in 1 mL 80% ethanol, centrifuged for 1 minute at 14,000 rpm and the supernatant removed. The pellet was left to dry for 30 minutes and subsequently re-suspended in 200 μL of pre-warmed (to 50°C) TE buffer (10 mM Tris, 1 mM EDTA) and incubated for 10 minutes. After pelleting for 1 minute at 13,000 rpm, the supernatant was collected, aliquoted and stored at −18°C until further use.

PCRs were done using primer sets that amplify two overlapping fragments and another short fragment of the mitochondrial *cytochrome b* (*cyt b*) gene. The sequences of the primers are: A1872 (5'-CCCCATCCAACATCTCATCA3')/A1873 (5'-TACGTCTCGGCAGATGTG-3'), A838 (5'-TAACAGCATTCTCATCAGT-3')/A839 (5'-TCCAATGTTTCATGTTTC-3'), and A1936 (5'-GGTTATGTACTCCCATGAGG-3')/A1937 (5'-GTTGCTTTGTCTACTGAGAA-3'). PCR reactions (25 μL final volume) contained a final concentration of 1 x HiFi PCR buffer (Invitrogen), 200 μM each dNTP, 3 mM MgSO$_4$, 1 mg.mL-1 Rabbit Serum Albumin (Sigma), 200 μM of each primer and 1 Unit of Platinum *Taq*HiFi DNA polymerase (Invitrogen). Thermocycling included initial denaturation and enzyme activation at 94°C for 2 minutes, then 55 cycles of denaturing at 94°C for 30 seconds, primer annealing at 55°C for 30 seconds and extension at 68°C for 30 seconds, and a final extension 68°C for 10 minutes. Amplifications of extractions and PCR blank controls were also performed in all experiments to monitor for contamination. Amplicons were separated by electrophoresis on a 2.5% agarose gel. Confirmatory re-amplification and re-sequencing was also performed for each PCR product for each specimen. PCR clean-up, Sanger sequencing and capillary electrophoresis were conducted at the Australian Genome Research Facility Ltd (Australia).

The forward and reverse sequence chromatograms were assembled, visually inspected and edited manually using Geneious v.7.1.2 (Biomatters) to obtain a consensus sequence. The newly generated sequences were aligned with published *Rattus rattus* Complex sequences of known lineage affinity (from Aplin et al. 2011) using the Muscle alignment algorithm (Edgar 2004) and refined by eye to form a 367 bp alignment.

To ascertain the lineage identity of the Talaud *Rattus* specimens, and to demonstrate their evolutionary relationships with other rat sequences in Southeast Asia, we generated a haplotype network using Haplotype Viewer (www.cibiv.at/~greg/haploviewer). The input Neighbour-Joining tree for the program was generated using the Juke-Cantor model of nucleotide substitution in Genius v.7.1.2 (Biomatters).

Results

Archaeological excavation and dating

The stratigraphy at LMD was as follows (Figure 14.2): Layer 1 (0–20 cm uD (under Datum), 10YR 5/5) was found only in the northern part of 100/102 and consisted of light yellow-brown, very loose sandy silt. There was significant bioturbation by an earth wasp nest with particularly loose soil in the top 5 cm. Layer 2 (~10–25 cm uD, 10YR 5/4) comprised a loose sandy silt, yellow-brown, slightly darker and slightly more compacted layer than Layer 1. Frequent shell fragments and fine charcoal particles, some ceramics and stone artefacts were found. This was the main cultural layer at the site. Roots were observed frequently in the southern section of the square. Layer 3a (~25–~60 cm uD, 10YR 5/5) comprised a compacted sandy silt with frequent clay concretions and tree roots. Only a few charcoal fragments and rare shell fragments were detected. No cultural artefacts were found in this layer. In the eastern section (square 100/102) bioturbation from an earth wasp nest was recorded up to 25 cm uD. Layer 3b (~60–~85–100 cm uD, 10YR 5/6) was similar in structure and texture to Layer 3a, but more yellowish. It was slightly more compacted and sloping downward to the back of the shelter. No cultural artefacts were found in this layer. Layer 4 (~85–140 cm uD, Munsell GLEY 5/10Y) comprised very compacted clay concretions in a silt-clay matrix with frequent limestone gravel. The deposit was increasingly gravelly to the base of the excavation. No cultural material was found in this layer and excavation was discontinued at this point, although sediment continues to an unknown depth.

Animal burrows at the back of the shelter were detected, which displaced fine material from lower deposits. While it is unclear whether cultural layers were disturbed, no artefacts were detected in this sediment. Stronger sloping deposits at the back of the shelter derived from the recent animal burrows. The sediment comprised predominantly silt and fine sand, and contained a low amount of organic matter (8.4–13.5%), with frequent tree roots. Also on the southern side, there was significant rock fall, which appeared to be relatively recent. The excavation uncovered only a small archaeological assemblage comprising several stone artefacts and pottery fragments. The artefacts were archived at the Manado Archaeology Office and the technological analysis is pending. Due to the excavation methodology, a significant microfaunal assemblage was recovered (see below). A maximum age of 340 cal BP using OxCal 4.2 (ANU 37037, 225±25, on kenari seed (*Canarium* sp.)) was determined for the cultural layer (Layer 2 in square 100/102). In square 100/101, a charred kenari nut husk from Spit 10 at the base of Layer 3 gave a modern age (ANU 37036, modern age, on charred kenari nut). On the basis of the radiocarbon dates, significant disturbance of the site is considered highly likely.

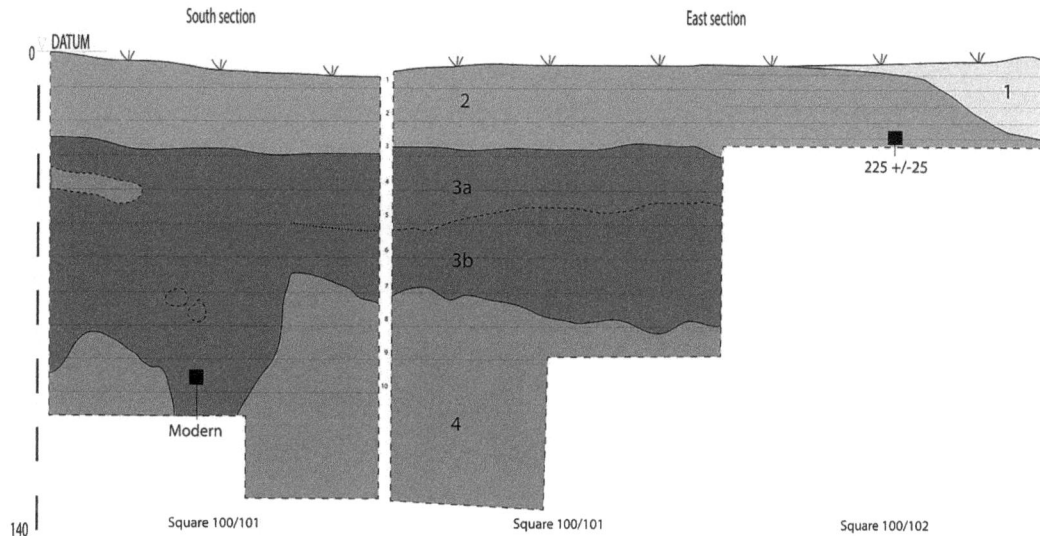

Figure 14.2: Stratigraphy of Leang Mande'et showing the location of the two dates recovered (black squares). Layers are indicated by numbers on the section; spits are indicated by horizontal lines within the sections and numbers listed between the south and east profiles.

Source: Section prepared by Julien Louys.

Zooarchaeology and taphonomy

A total of 784 vertebrate remains were recovered, with most of these concentrated in Spits 1 and 2, and as deep as Spit 6. At least 16 distinct taxa were recorded. These include five mammal species with four small murids (two *Melomys* spp., *R. rattus*, *R. exulans*), pig (*Sus* cf. *scrofa*), human (*Homo sapiens*) and an unidentified bat (Chiroptera). Six distinct fish families were identified, including triggerfishes (Balistidae), surgeonfishes, tangs and unicornfishes (Acanthuridae), snappers (Lutjanidae), sea basses and groupers (Serranidae), parrotfishes (Scaridae), and probably shark catfishes (cf. Pangasiidae). At least two reptile taxa, snakes (Serpentes) and small lizards (Lacertilia), and one bird taxon were present.

Small murids dominated the assemblage by NISP (56.1%), with the remains of two native species of *Melomys* (*M. talaudium* and *M. caurinus*) outnumbering the remains of the two commensal *Rattus* species (*R. rattus* and *R. exulans*) (Table 14.1). Other mammals present include pig (1.3%), human (0.6%) and bat (0.1%). Fish bones were present in significant numbers (18.9%), with much smaller proportions of reptiles (4.1%) and birds (1.4%). These results are reflected in a skewed Shannon–Wiener diversity index (0.59) towards small murids relative to fish and small reptiles, with an equitability J value of 0.23 (Taxa = 13; Muridae, *Sus*, Chiroptera, *Homo sapiens*, Balistidae, Acanthuridae, Lutjanidae, Serranidae, Scaridae, cf. Pangasiidae, Aves, Lacertilia, Serpentes).

Table 14.1: Number of Individual Specimens (NISP) for each spit from Leang Mande'et.

Spit	1	2	3	4	5	6	Total
Mammalia	NISP	NISP	NISP	NISP	NISP	NISP	NISP
Muridae	190	93	25	1	6	11	326
Melomys sp.	41	8	1	0	0	1	51
cf. *Melomys* sp.	2	4	0	0	0	0	6
Rattus rattus	13	5	2	0	0	1	21
Rattus cf. *rattus*	11	6	0	1	1	0	19
Rattus exulans	2	0	0	0	0	0	2
Rattus cf. *exulans*	2	1	0	0	0	0	3
Rattus sp.	2	0	0	0	0	0	2
cf. *Rattus* sp.	0	1	0	0	0	0	1
Muridae gen. et sp. Indet.	3	6	0	0	0	0	9
Sus cf. *scrofa*	2	3	4	0	0	1	10
Chiroptera	0	1	0	0	0	0	1
Homo sapiens	1	1	0	2	0	0	4
cf. *Homo sapiens*	0	1	0	0	0	0	1
medium mammal	5	14	13	7	0	0	39
Osteichthyes							
Unidentified	38	35	31	12	11	6	133
Balistidae	0	1	1	2	1	1	6
Acanthuridae	0	1	0	0	0	0	1
Lutjanidae	0	1	0	0	0	0	1
Serranidae	3	1	0	0	0	0	4
Scaridae	2	0	0	0	0	0	2
cfPangasiidae	0	0	0	0	0	1	1
Aves							
Unidentified Aves	3	5	1	0	0	0	9
cf. Aves	2	0	0	0	0	0	2
Reptilia							
Lacertilia	3	6	3	0	0	0	12
Serpentes	0	1	0	2	1	0	4
Unidentified reptile	3	5	2	1	0	1	12
cf. Reptile	1	2	1	0	0	0	4
Unidentified Vertebrate	33	24	17	9	1	14	98
Total	362	226	101	37	21	37	784

Source: Stuart Hawkins' laboratory data.

The murids and small lizards were clearly deposited naturally as signs of non-human predation were prevalent amongst the terrestrial vertebrate specimens. Small puncture marks on murid lower limb bones (femora and tibiae) and caudal vertebra were frequently observed. In addition, high rates of moderate to extreme digestion patterns (Table 14.2) were noted on many of the murid and lizard bones, indicating predation by a raptor or possibly a larger varanid. The amount of digestion is far too high for a Barn owl (*Tyto alba*), which are often responsible for the deposition of small mammals in caves worldwide, and another owl species with a more powerful digestive tract may be responsible (see Andrews 1990). This indicates the site was not occupied permanently and saw periods of short cultural use, followed by periods of abandonment, as it is unlikely that avian or large lizard predators would cohabitate so closely to permanent human occupation. Skeletal element survivorship (Table 14.3) and bone breakage (Table 14.4) data indicate high loss of many skeletal elements and significant bone breakages, more so than that recorded for typical avian predation (Andrews 1990). Since recovery was fairly complete given the use of fine-meshed sieves, this was probably due to trampling and other site disturbances occurring during short periods of human occupation. Small numbers of murid bones appeared black or grey/blue/white, and this was likely due to burning (see Nicholson 1993). This most likely occurred as incidental burning in hearth fires of microfaunal remains already present within the deposit.

Table 14.2: Extent of digestion on murid postcranial elements.

Element	Absent		Light		Moderate		Heavy		Extreme		Total NISP
	N	%	N	%	N	%	N	%	N	%	
Humerus	8	61.54	3	23.08	1	7.69	1	7.69	0	0	13
Ulna	3	30	2	20	1	10	3	30	1	10	10
Radius	7	77.78	1	11.11	0	0	1	11.11	0	0	9
Pelvis	5	50	0	0	2	20	1	10	2	20	10
Femur	14	45.16	5	16.13	5	16.13	5	16.13	2	6.45	31
Tibia	15	53.57	7	25	4	14.29	1	3.57	1	3.57	28

Source: Stuart Hawkins' laboratory data.

Table 14.3: Murid element survivorship.

Element	%MNE survivorship
Maxilla	38.1
Mandible	35.71
Incisors	80.95
Atlas	14.29
Axis	19.05
Cervical	3.81
Thoracic	1.1
Rib	1.28
Lumbar	3.97
Sacrum	4.76
Caudal	6.12
Scapula	11.91
Humerus	19.05
Ulna	19.05
Radius	21.43
Pelvis	16.67
Femur	35.71
Tibia	30.95
Metapodial	12.17
Calcaneus	21.43
Astragalus	2.38
Phalange	3.04

Source: Stuart Hawkins' laboratory data.

Table 14.4: Murid skeletal element breakages.

Skeletal element	N	%
Skull		
Complete	0	0
Maxillary with zygomatic	2	15.39
Maxillary without zygomatic	11	84.62
Mandible		
Complete	0	0
Ascendingramus broken	3	13.64
Without ascending ramus	5	22.73
Without ascending ramus, inferior edge broken	14	63.64
Postcrania		
Humerus		
Complete	1	8.33
Proximal	1	8.33
Shaft	5	41.67
Distal	5	41.67
Ulna		
Complete	0	0
Proximal	5	41.67
Shaft	5	41.67
Distal	2	16.67
Femur		
Complete	0	0
Proximal	14	42.42
Shaft	7	21.21
Distal	12	36.36
Tibia		
Complete	3	9.68
Proximal	6	19.35
Shaft	6	19.35
Distal	16	51.61

Source: Stuart Hawkins' laboratory data.

Pollen

No pollen, spores or microscopic charcoal were observed in Spit 10, and only very low concentrations were present in Spits 6–9. With the exception of Spit 9, the total terrestrial pollen count was very low for these spits and the data presented as presence/absence of taxa only (Figure 14.3). There was a notable lack of observed forest taxa with palms, Euphorbiaceae and herbs predominating. Spit 9 contained almost exclusively *Cocos nucifera* pollen. Pollen concentrations improved in Spits 4–5 and were highest in Spits 1–3. After Spit 4, there was a reduction in other palm taxa and Euphorbiaceae and an increase in the diversity of identified forest taxa and *Cocos nucifera*. Only a small amount of fern spores was observed and microscopic charcoal particle concentrations were highest in Spits 1–4.

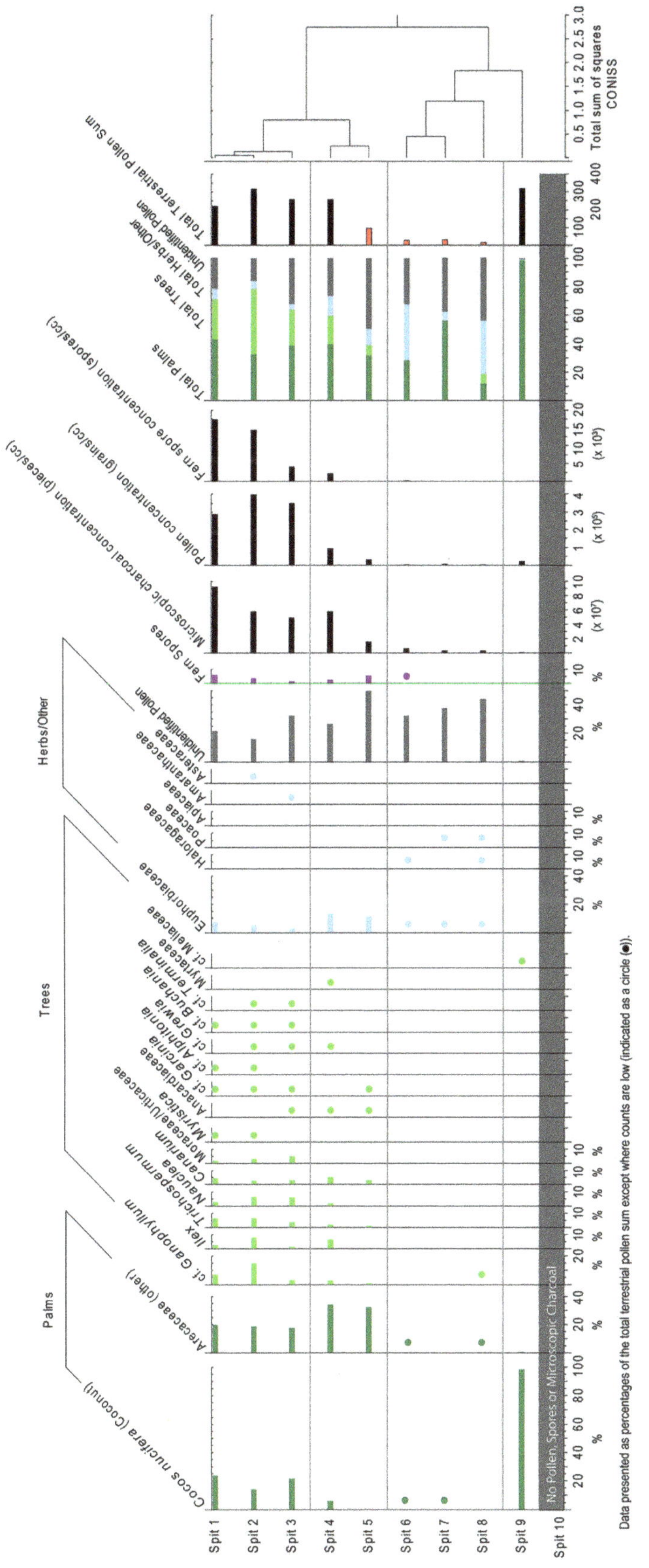

Figure 14.3: Summary diagram of pollen recovered from each spit of Leang Mande'et.

Source: Felicitas Hopf's laboratory data.

Taxonomy and aDNA

Three *cytb* haplotypes were found in the *R. rattus* samples from Talaud, all belonging to RrC lineage IV (Figure 14.4; Appendix A). The Talaud haplotypes formed a discrete sub-lineage that is not known from elsewhere in the region and adds to the known diversity of RrC lineage IV in ISEA. The central haplotype of the Talaud sub-lineage differed by two substitutions from a haplotype that is common in both Indonesia and the Philippines. A maximum of four substitutions were observed between the two most divergent of the Talaud haplotypes. The basal position of the Talaud samples within lineage IV, relative to the other lineages of the RrC was a product of the relatively short (356 bp) segment of *cytb* used in computation of this network. Analysis of longer segments of *cytb* placed the common Indonesian/Philippine network in a peripheral position relative to the central diversity observed among samples from Indochinese localities (Aplin et al. 2011).

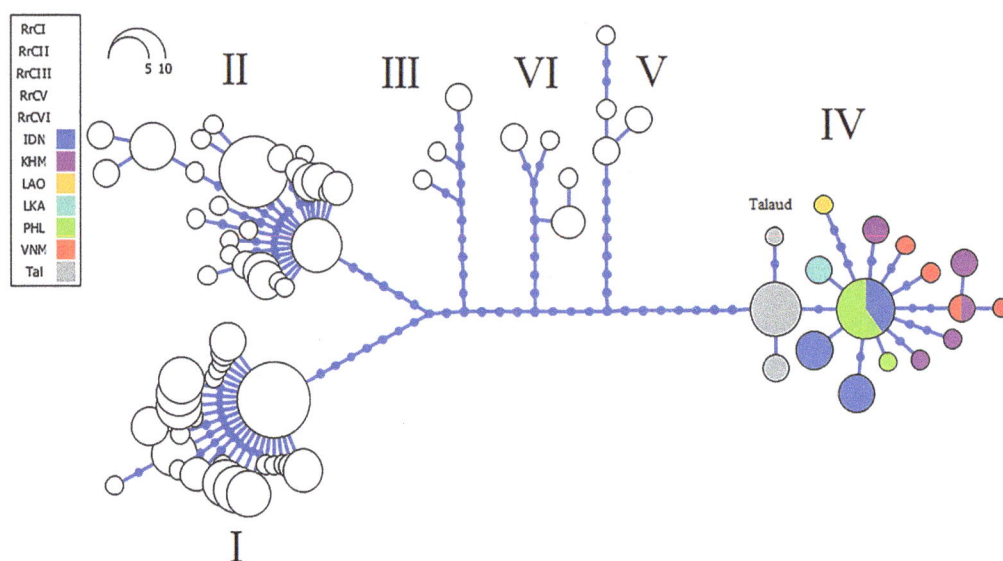

Figure 14.4: Haplotype network of *cytochrome b* dataset comprising 367 bp across *Rattus rattus* complex lineages. Colours of RrC lineage IV haplotypes are blue (IDN–Indonesia), purple (KHM–Cambodia), orange (LAO–Laos), light blue (LKA–Sri Lanka), green (PHL–Philippines), red (VNM–Vietnam), grey (Tal-Talaud). Blue dots represent the number of mutations leading to a haplotype.

Source: Michael Herrera and Stephen Donnellan's laboratory data.

Discussion

The site shows significant disturbance, with a modern date produced from Spit 9, and bioturbation observed during excavation. Despite the disturbed nature of the sediments, it's evident that during the short periods when humans recently occupied LMD, their subsistence practices were focused on agriculture of the surrounding hill slopes. Active gardens were observed during fieldwork, with lowland tropical moist forest dominating local conditions near the site, interspersed gardens on the hillslope leading up to LMD and coconut plantations at sea level. In the deposit, coconut (*Cocos nucifera*) dominates Spit 9, although it is present in most other spits in lower amounts other than Spits 5 and 8. While long distance transport of coconut pollen can't be ruled out (Maloney 1993), it is thought to be predominantly dispersed by insects (Anderson et al. 1988) and, as a result, an indicator of the local presence of coconut palms. Wind dispersal of coconut pollen through forests is limited to about 180 m from a coconut plantation

(Manthriratna 1965). Coconut palms are not found inland unless planted (Harries 1978), thus the significant proportions of coconut pollen in the LMD record suggest coconut trees were agricultural in nature. Interestingly, coconuts may not have been widespread on Talaud during the pre-colonial period. Historical records indicate that:

> Until about 1885 there were said to be 'almost no coconut trees' on the Talaud Islands. Possibly this was because the Sangirese kingdoms to which they were subject had succeeded up to that point in discouraging the export of oil or copra. Thereafter the crop spread rapidly, and Talaud participated in the copra boom. In 1920, nevertheless, it was still 'only the lower parts' of the larger islands which were occupied by coconut gardens, while timber, including valuable ebony, remained plentiful elsewhere (Henley 2005:512).

Thus, the pollen data suggests that deposition of the site was predominately post-colonial. It further suggests that gardening activities at LMD focused, at least in part, on coconut, a low-maintenance crop. During irregular gardening activities, fish were evidently brought to the rockshelter for consumption. These were mostly marine herbivorous and carnivorous reef fishes that could have been caught by people using nets, spears, traps and baited hooks and lines (e.g. Ono 2010) from the adjacent bay. However, the tentative shark catfish bone identification indicates possible utilisation of brackish freshwater environments, such as nearby rivers and streams or the nearby river mouth. Adult pig remains were present from Spit 1 to Spit 6 and include teeth, phalanges, sesamoids and vertebra elements. The mandibular canine showed signs of percussion and may indicate removal of these for ceremonial items. This suggests pigs were also brought to the site and could indicate that small ceremonial feasts were conducted at the shelter. The human teeth recovered may be intrusive from a potential burial adjacent to the excavation pits or lost by individuals at the site during the course of their lifetime.

All the small murid remains recovered from LMD were deposited evidently by non-human predators. The dominance of the endemic *Melomys* species over the introduced commensal species of *Rattus* is noteworthy. These species are known from few modern specimens, and their current status and ecology are poorly documented (Corbet and Hill 1992; Flannery 1995; Riley 2002). *Melomys caurinus* is thought to be terrestrial on account of its relatively short tail, and *M. talaudium* to be arboreal. Both are ranked Endangered in the IUCN Red List, although Riley (2002) considered them to be present in both primary and secondary forests, and to be secure (Riley 2002). We recovered the remains of a minimum of 17 individuals of *Melomys* spp. (NISP=51), including representatives of both endemic species. Some of these are currently being sampled for DNA, and the results will be reported elsewhere. The abundance of the *Melomys* species in the deposit suggests that they were not displaced as a result of the introduction of the commensal rodents (*R. rattus* and *R. exulans*) and were able to thrive in a landscape that has been anthropogenically disturbed and irregularly used for gardening for at least several hundred years. Given this apparent resilience, it would seem likely that they may be under less severe threat than suggested by current IUCN ranking.

The genetic data from the archaeological specimens provides the first evidence for the lineage identity of *R. rattus* on the Talaud Islands. The fact that the samples produced a total of three closely related haplotypes of RrC lineage IV is significant for several reasons. In the first place, the recovery of a unique sub-lineage thus far known only from the Talaud Islands points to a potentially early introduction followed by the *in situ* production of genetic diversity through local mutation within the Talaud Archipelago. However, the alternative possibility that the diversity was created elsewhere and imported through separate dispersal events cannot be discounted altogether, even though it seems unlikely. The notion that lineage IV *R. rattus* reached the Talaud Islands at a relatively early date can be tested by the discovery of new sites that extend the record of murids back even a few thousand years.

The second point of great interest is the occurrence of lineage IV rather than lineage II in the Talaud Islands. At face value, this appears to favour a southern route of colonisation into the Talaud Archipelago, presumably from somewhere in Wallacea and most likely from northern Sulawesi. However, it must be noted that the widespread haplotype that appears to be the ancestral haplotype for the Talaud sub-lineage is present also in the Philippines—strictly speaking, the Talaud population might have come from either direction. However, given that Indonesia was clearly occupied by lineage IV from early times (Aplin et al. 2011), to postulate that they came to the Talaud Islands from the north would require an initial dispersal from Wallacea to the Philippines followed by a back-dispersal to the Talaud Islands. Until such time as there is independent evidence to support this more complex history, we will assume that the simpler version is correct—i.e. that the Talaud Islands population was introduced in ancient times from the south. To pinpoint the place of origin more closely, further sampling of RrC lineage IV Black rats is needed for Sundaland, especially Borneo, as well as the various Moluccan island groups, and Sulawesi.

A southern rather than northern origin of the Talaud Black rat population appears to be contrary to more general thinking concerning the pattern of dispersal of agricultural practices (and presumably their associated commensal pest rodents) through this region. The Talaud Archipelago has a relatively ancient record of occupation, represented by the Pleistocene-aged site of Leang Sarru. This site preserves evidence of episodic occupation during the Pleistocene and early Holocene: between c. 35 and 32 cal BP, between c. 21 and 18 cal BP, and again between 10 and 8 cal BP (Ono et al. 2009; Tanudirjo 2001, 2005), but none of these early phases provide any clue as to the direction of human dispersals. By contrast, the Neolithic-aged site of Leang Tuwo Mane'e, situated on Karakelang Island, has resulted in the island group featuring heavily in models describing the initial dispersal routes of Neolithic innovations, exemplified by the Blust–Bellwood model of Austronesian expansion (Bellwood 2007). This model is predicated on the similarities observed between the sub-grouping structure of the Austronesian language family tree and the patterns of distributions of cultural materials such as stone adzes, red-slipped pottery, rock art, domesticated animals and certain kinds of shell ornament. In this model, Taiwan is regarded as the point of origin for Proto-Austronesian peoples, from which agricultural groups migrated rapidly after about 4,000 cal BP into the Philippines, then the Moluccas, Sulawesi, Micronesia and further into the Western Pacific. While this longstanding colonisation model is accepted by many researchers working in Southeast Asia and Oceania, a number of recent discoveries and new analyses (Barker and Richards 2013), including those regarding the translocation of domesticated animals (Piper 2017) and the distribution and origin of the 'Austronesian Painting Tradition' (O'Connor et al. 2015), suggest that the origins and dispersal history of the Austronesians may not be as clear-cut as the Blust–Bellwood model predicts.

If commensal rats moved around as part of a complete 'package' of agricultural innovations and associated problems, the Blust–Bellwood model would predict the occurrence of lineage II of the RrC on the Talaud Islands, as there would seem to be quite strong genetic evidence to postulate an early dispersal of one or more sub-lineages of lineage II out of Taiwan and into areas subsequently occupied by Austronesian speaking peoples (Aplin et al. 2011). The lack of RrC lineage II rats in the LMD assemblage thus generates a number of competing scenarios that are testable by recovery of further data. Foremost is the possibility that the earliest dispersal of agricultural peoples and/or practices was not accompanied by commensal rodents, but that these were introduced subsequently and potentially from a different direction to the original dispersal of agriculture. Failure to find commensal rodent remains in the earliest agricultural sites on the Talaud Islands would support this notion, especially if the sites did yield remains of the native murids *Melomys* spp. Another possibility is that an initial population of lineage II

Black rats, introduced from the north, was later replaced by a secondary southern immigrant of lineage IV, or if not replaced then at least heavily introgressed by lineage IV mtDNA. This notion is testable through the discovery, DNA testing and direct dating of *R. rattus* remains from earlier archaeological sites.

Other groups of organisms might also provide independent clues concerning the ancient human and biotic dispersal routes. The Sangihe-Talaud Archipelago complex represents a natural stepping stone for an initial Austronesian expansion south from Taiwan, into the Philippines and thence into the Moluccas and Sulawesi. However, biogeographical data from other organisms, specifically the herpetofauna, strongly suggest that the Talaud Islands themselves may never have served as a natural waypoint between the Philippines and northern Sulawesi, with a route through the Sangihe Islands considered more likely (Koch et al. 2009). The herpetofauna instead hint at strong biogeographical connections between the Talaud Archipelago and the Moluccas, with only weaker links evident between the Talaud Islands and the Philippines and Sulawesi (Koch et al. 2009). Meanwhile, the common presence of several mammalian taxa on the Philippines, Sangihe and northern Sulawesi but not Talaud, such as stegodons, squirrels and, for the latter two islands, tarsiers, suggests strong biogeographic connections between these island groups. While all such dispersals are likely to have been stochastic and considerably more ancient than the Austronesian expansion, the biogeographical record, underpinned by movement dictated by oceanic currents, nevertheless suggests that a route through Sangihe might have been more likely for seafaring Neolithic peoples. Unfortunately, and despite surveys over considerable parts of the island, neither natural nor archaeological deposits have been identified on Sangihe.

Conclusions

The significant Neolithic human migration that occurred throughout ISEA, suggested by the occurrence of red-slipped ceramics, ground stone tools, a rock art tradition focusing on the depiction of boats and anthropogenic figures on cliff faces, and remains of cereal plants and domesticated animals is thought to be strongly linked to the spread of Austronesian languages from Taiwan. Attempts to trace this Austronesian movement have traditionally relied on the recovery of these types of evidence from the archaeological record. The absence of such evidence makes it difficult to accurately trace directions and timings of movements of Neolithic peoples. The Talaud Islands had been no exception to this, and little evidence of the direction of origin of Austronesians exists in the archipelago. However, the recovery of significant numbers of DNA-producing rodents from the Talaud Islands allows us to make inferences on the origins and number of independent colonisation events of the islands by people who brought with them rats (i.e. probably agriculturalists). All Black rats recovered from Karakelang Island belong to RrC lineage IV, a group with origins in southern Indochina with subsequent dispersals, coincident with the spread of human agricultural communities, into eastern Indonesia and the Philippines. Significantly, our analyses failed to recover any RrC lineage II rats, which are characteristic of similar movements between northern Indochina, South Asia and Taiwan. Furthermore, our genetic data strongly suggests that there was only one dispersal event of Black rats into the Talaud Islands, and that this represents an early migration for the group. While Talaud's rat record does not provide clues as to the identity of the island's first agriculturalists, it does suggest that they either originated from the south; or that, once established in Talaud, the Neolithic communities in Talaud opened up significant trade networks to the south and, in the process, acquired a significant pest whilst helping to write genetic history.

Acknowledgements

This research was funded through an ARC Laureate Fellowship to Professor Sue O'Connor (FL120100156), a Discovery Project Award (DP140103650) to Stephen Donnellan, Ken Aplin and Phil Piper, and a Discovery Early Career Researcher Award (DECRA, DE130100046) to Christian Reepmeyer. We thank the staff from the Manado Archaeology Office, particularly Drs Bonny A. Tooy, S.S. Sriwigati and S. Si. Paulina E.H. Nugrahini, for their help organising the fieldwork, the Australian Centre for Ancient DNA, University of Adelaide, for facilities and technical support, and Vicki Thomson for designing the PCR primers for the DNA analysis.

Author biographies

Julien Louys Department of Archaeology and Natural History, School of Culture, History and Language, College of Asia and the Pacific, The Australian National University, Canberra, Australia

Michael Herrera School of Biological Sciences, the University of Adelaide, Adelaide, Australia

Stuart Hawkins Department of Archaeology and Natural History, School of Culture, History and Language, College of Asia and the Pacific, The Australian National University, Canberra, Australia

Ken Aplin Department of Archaeology and Natural History, School of Culture, History and Language, College of Asia and the Pacific, The Australian National University, Canberra, Australia

Christian Reepmeyer Department of Archaeology and Natural History, School of Culture, History and Language, College of Asia and the Pacific, The Australian National University, Canberra, Australia; and College of Arts, Society and Education, Cairns Campus, James Cook University, Cairns, Australia

Felicitas Hopf Department of Archaeology and Natural History, School of Culture, History and Language, College of Asia and the Pacific, The Australian National University, Canberra, Australia; and ARC Centre of Excellence for Australian Biodiversity and Heritage, The Australian National University, Canberra, Australia

Stephen C. Donnellan South Australia Museum and School of Biological Sciences, University of Adelaide, Adelaide, Australia

Sue O'Connor Department of Archaeology and Natural History, School of Culture, History and Language, College of Asia and the Pacific, The Australian National University, Canberra, Australia; and ARC Centre of Excellence for Australian Biodiversity and Heritage, The Australian National University, Canberra, Australia

Daud A. Tanudirjo Department of Archaeology, Gadjah Mada University, Yogyakarta, Indonesia

References

Anderson, A.B., W.L. Overal and A. Henderson. 1988. Pollination ecology of a forest-dominant palm (*Orbignya phalerata* Mart.) in northern Brazil. *Biotropica* 20(3):192–205. doi.org/10.2307/2388234 (accessed 5 June 2018).

Andrews, P. 1990. *Owls, Caves and Fossils: Predation, Preservation and Accumulation of Small Mammal Bones in Caves, with an Analysis of the Pleistocene Cave Faunas From Westbury-Sub-Mendip.* Somerset: University of Chicago Press.

Aplin, K.P., H. Suzuki, A.A. Chinen, R.T. Chesser, J. ten Have, S.C. Donnellan, J. Austin, A. Frost, J.P. Gonzalez, V. Herbreteau, F. Catzeflis, J. Soubrier, Y.-P. Fang, J. Robins, E. Matisoo-Smith, A.D.S. Bastos, I. Maryanto, M.H. Sinaga, C. Denys, R.A. Van Den Bussche, C. Conroy, K. Rowe and A. Cooper. 2011. Multiple geographic origins of commensalism and complex dispersal history of black rats. *PLoS ONE* 6(11):e26357. doi.org/10.1371/journal.pone.0026357 (accessed 5 June 2018).

APSA Members. 2007. *The Australasian Pollen and Spore Atlas V1.0.* The Australian National University. apsa.anu.edu.au/ (accessed 5 June 2018).

Barker, G. and M.B. Richards. 2013. Foraging–farming transitions in Island Southeast Asia. *Journal of Archaeological Method and Theory* 20(2):256–280. doi.org/10.1007/s10816-012-9150-7 (accessed 5 June 2018).

Bellwood, P. 2007. *Prehistory of the Indo-Malaysian Archipelago.* Revised edition. Canberra: ANU E Press, doi.org/10.26530/OAPEN_459472 (accessed 5 June 2018).

Bellwood, P. 2011. Holocene population history in the Pacific Region as a model for worldwide food producer dispersals. *Current Anthropology* 52(S4):S363–S378. doi.org/10.1086/658181 (accessed 5 June 2018).

Blust, R. 1995. The prehistory of the Austronesian-speaking peoples: A view from language. *Journal of World Prehistory* 9(4):453–510. doi.org/10.1007/BF02221119 (accessed 5 June 2018).

Brotherton, P., W. Haak, J. Templeton, G. Brandt, J. Soubrier, C.J. Adler, S.M. Richards, C. Der Sarkissian, R. Ganslmeier and S. Friederich. 2013. Neolithic mitochondrial haplogroup H genomes and the genetic origins of Europeans. *Nature Communications* 4(1764). doi.org/10.1038/ncomms2656 (accessed 5 June 2018).

Caffrey, M.A. and S.P. Horn. 2013. The use of lithium heteropolytungstate in the heavy liquid separation of samples which are sparse in pollen. *Palynology* 37(1):143–150. doi.org/10.1080/01916122.2012.736417 (accessed 5 June 2018).

Corbet, G.B. and J.E. Hill. 1992. *The Mammals of the Indomalayan Region: A Systematic Review.* Oxford: Oxford University Press.

Dean, W.E. 1974. Determination of carbonate and organic matter in calcareous sediments and sedimentary rocks by loss on ignition; comparison with other methods. *Journal of Sedimentary Research* 44(1):242–248. doi.org/10.1306/74d729d2-2b21-11d7-8648000102c1865d (accessed 5 June 2018).

Dye, T. and K.R. Longenecker. 2004. *Manual of Hawaiian Fish Remains Identification Based on the Skeletal Reference Collection of Alan C. Ziegler and including Otoliths.* Hawai'i: Society for Hawaiian Archaeology (in English).

Edgar, R.C. 2004. MUSCLE: Multiple sequence alignment with high accuracy and high throughput. *Nucleic Acids Research* 32(5):1792–1797. doi.org/10.1093/nar/gkh340 (accessed 5 June 2018).

Fægri, K. and J. Iversen. 1989. *Textbook of Pollen Analysis.* Chichester: John Wiley and Sons.

Fernández, F.J., P. Teta, R. Barberena and U.F.J. Pardiñas. 2012. Small mammal remains from Cueva Huenul 1, northern Patagonia, Argentina: Taphonomy and paleoenvironments since the Late Pleistocene. *Quaternary International* 278:22–31. doi.org/10.1016/j.quaint.2012.01.005 (accessed 5 June 2018).

Flannery, T.F. 1995. *Mammals of the South-West Pacific & Moluccan Islands.* Ithaca, N.Y.: Cornell University Press.

Grimm, E.C. 2013. Tilia v2.0.33. Springfield: Illinois State Museum.

Hammer, Ø., D.A.T. Harper and P.D. Ryan. 2001. PAST: Paleontological statistics software package for education and data analysis. *Palaeontologia Electronica* 4(1):1–9.

Harries, H.C. 1978. The evolution, dissemination and classification of *Cocos nucifera* L. *The Botanical Review* 44(3):265–319. doi.org/10.1007/bf02957852 (accessed 5 June 2018).

Henley, D. 2005. *Fertility, Food and Fever: Population, Economy and Environment in North and Central Sulawesi, 1600–1930*. Leiden: KITLV Press.

Keylock, C.J. 2005. Simpson diversity and the Shannon–Wiener index as special cases of a generalized entropy. *Oikos* 109(1):203–207. doi: 10.1111/j.0030-1299.2005.13735.x (accessed 5 June 2018).

Koch, A., E. Arida, A. Riyanto and W. Böhme. 2009. Islands between the realms: A revised checklist of the herpetofauna of the Talaud Archipelago, Indonesia, with a discussion about its biogeographic affinities. *Bonner Zoologische Beiträge* 56(1/2):107–129.

Maloney, B.K. 1993. Palaeoecology and the origin of the coconut. *GeoJournal* 31(4):355–362.

Manthriratna, M. 1965. Coconut pollen. *Ceylon Coconut Quarterly* 16:102–110.

Matisoo-Smith, E. and J.H. Robins. 2004. Origins and dispersals of Pacific peoples: Evidence from mtDNA phylogenies of the Pacific rat. *Proceedings of the National Academy of Sciences of the United States of America* 101(24):9167–9172. doi.org/10.1073/pnas.0403120101 (accessed 5 June 2018).

Nicholson, R.A. 1993. A morphological investigation of burnt animal bone and an evaluation of its utility in archaeology. *Journal of Archaeological Science* 20(4):411–428. doi.org/10.1006/jasc.1993.1025 (accessed 5 June 2018).

O'Connor, S., J. Louys, S. Kealy and Mahirta. 2015. First record of painted rock art in Kupang, West Timor, Indonesia and the origins and distribution of the Austronesian Painting Tradition. *Rock Art Research* 32(2):193–201.

Ono, R. 2010. Ethno-archaeology and early Austronesian fishing strategies in near-shore environments. *The Journal of the Polynesian Society* 119(3):269–314.

Ono, R., S. Soegondho and M. Yoneda. 2009. Changing marine exploitation during Late Pleistocene in Northern Wallacea: Shell remains from Leang Sarru Rockshelter in Talaud Islands. *Asian Perspectives* 48(2):318–341. doi.org/10.1353/asi.2009.0002 (accessed 5 June 2018).

Pagès, M., Y. Chaval, V. Herbreteau, S. Waengsothorn, J.-F. Cosson, J.-P. Hugot, S. Morand and J. Michaux. 2010. Revisiting the taxonomy of the Rattini tribe: A phylogeny-based delimitation of species boundaries. *BMC Evolutionary Biology* 10(184):1–27. doi.org/10.1186/1471-2148-10-184 (accessed 5 June 2018).

Piper, P.J. 2017. The origins and arrival of the earliest domestic animals in Mainland and Island Southeast Asia: A developing story of complexity. In P.J. Piper, H. Matsumura and D. Bulbeck (eds), *New Perspectives in Southeast Asian and Pacific Prehistory*, pp. 251–274. Canberra: ANU Press. doi.org/10.22459/TA45.03.2017.15 (accessed 5 June 2018).

Riley, J. 2002. Mammals on the Sangihe and Talaud Islands, Indonesia, and the impact of hunting and habitat loss. *Oryx* 36(3):288–296. doi.org/10.1017/S0030605302000510 (accessed 5 June 2018).

Robins, J.H., P.A. McLenachan, M.J. Phillips, L. Craig, H.A. Ross and E. Matisoo-Smith. 2008. Dating of divergences within the Rattus genus phylogeny using whole mitochondrial genomes. *Molecular Phylogenetics and Evolution* 49(2):460-466. doi.org/10.1016/j.ympev.2008.08.001 (accessed 5 June 2018).

Spriggs, M. 2011. Archaeology and the Austronesian expansion: Where are we now? *Antiquity* 85(328):510–528. doi.org/10.1017/S0003598X00067910 (accessed 5 June 2018).

Stockmarr, J. 1971. Tablets with spores used in absolute pollen analysis. *Pollen Spores* 13:615–621.

Tanudirjo, D.A. 2001. Islands in Between: Prehistory of the Northeastern Indonesian Archipelago. Unpublished PhD thesis, School of Archaeology and Anthropology, The Australian National University, Canberra.

Tanudirjo, D.A. 2005. Long-continuous or short-occasional occupation? The human use of Leang Sarru rockshelter in the Talaud Islands, northeastern Indonesia. *Bulletin of The Indo-Pacific Prehistory Association* 25(3):15–19.

Thomson, V., K.P. Aplin, A. Cooper, S. Hisheh, H. Suzuki, I. Maryanto, G. Yap and S.C. Donnellan. 2014. Molecular genetic evidence for the place of origin of the Pacific rat, *Rattus exulans*. *PLoS ONE* 9(3):e91356. doi.org/10.1371/journal.pone.0091356 (accessed 5 June 2018).

Yosida, T.H. 1980. *Cytogenetics of the Black Rat: Karyotype Evolution and Species Differentiation.* Tokyo: University of Tokyo Press.

Appendix A

The sequences of the Talaud haplotype 1, 2, and 3. Sequence for the overlapping fragments 1 and 2 is situated between base positions 14,220 and 14,480 based on the *Rattus novergicus* whole mitochondrial genome sequence with GenBank accession number AJ428514. Fragment 3 is situated between positions 14,519 and 14,624 of the same sequence.

Fragments 1 and 2

Talaud Haplotype 1

TGATGAAATTTTGGCTCTTTACTAGGAGTATGCCTCATAGTCCAAATTATC
ACAGGCCTATTCCTAGCAATACACTACACATCCGACACTTTAACAGCATTC
TCATCAGTTACCCACATCTGCCGAGACGTAAACTACGGCTGACTAATCCGA
TACTTACACGCCAACGGAGCTTCAATATTCTTTATCTGCCTATTCCTTCATG
TAGGACGAGGGATATACTACGGATCCTATACTTTCCTAGAAACATGAAACATTGGA

Talaud Haplotype 2

TGATGAAATTTTGGCTCTTTACTAGGAGTATGCCTCATAGTCCAAATTATC
ACAGGCCTATTCCTAGCAATACACTACACATCCGACACTTTAACAGCATTC
TCATCAGTTACCCACATCTGCCGAGACGTAAACTACGGCTGACTAATCCGA
TACTTACACGCCAACGGAGCTTCAATATTCTTTATCTGCCTATTCCTTCATG
TAGGGCGAGGGATATACTACGGATCCTATACTTTCCTAGAAACATGAAACATTGGA

Talaud Haplotype 3

TGATGAAATTTTGGCTCTTTACTAGGAGTATGCCTCATAGTCCAAATTATC
ACAGGCCTATTCCTAGCAATACACTACACATCCGACACTTTAACAGCATTC
TCATCAGTTACCCACATCTGCCGAGACGTAAACTACGGCTGACTAATCCGAT
ACTTACACGCCAACGGAGCTTCAATATTCTTTATCTGCCTATTCCTCCATGTAGG
GCGAGGGATATACTACGGATCCTATACTTTCCTAGAAACATGAAACATTGGA

Fragment 3

Talaud Haplotype 1

AGGTTATGTACTCCCATGAGGACAAATATCATTCTGAGGGGCCACAGTAATTACAA
ACCTATTATCAGCCATCCCCTATATTGGCACCACTCTAGTCGAATGAATC

Talaud Haplotype 2

AGGTTATGTACTCCCATGAGGACAAATATCATTCTGAGGGGCCACAGTAATTACAA
ACCTATTATCAGCCATCCCCTATATTGGCACCACCCTAGTCGAATGAATC

Talaud Haplotype 3

AGGTTATGTACTCCCATGAGGACAAATATCATTCTGAGGGGCCACAGTAATTACAA
ACCTATTATCAGCCATCCCCTATATTGGCACCACCCTAGTCGAATGAATC

15

Development of marine and terrestrial resource use in the Talaud Islands AD 1000–1800, northern Sulawesi region

Rintaro Ono, Sriwigati and Joko Siswanto

Abstract

This chapter reviews the excavation results from the Leang Buida and Bukit Tiwing sites in the Talaud Islands of North Sulawesi, with a focus on the faunal remains and likely fishing tools. The available Carbon-14 determinations date the occupation of Leang Buida on Kabaruan Island to around AD 1000–1600 and Bukit Tiwing on Salibabu Island to around AD 1500–1800. From comparing the excavation results to data from other sites in Southeast Asia, East Asia and the Pacific, we outline the possible development of marine and terrestrial use of the remote Talaud Islands during the Metal Age and historic times.

Keywords: marine exploitation, fishing technology, animal use, Talaud Islands

Introduction

This chapter deals with the excavated remains from two sites in the remote Talaud Islands of North Sulawesi in the context of the development of inter-island maritime networks in Island Southeast Asia (ISEA) during the Metal Age. The Metal Age refers to the time of availability of metal goods and tools, notably copper or bronze and iron, which in ISEA evidently appeared together in the last centuries BC, along with a range of exotic imports (Bellwood 2017). Characteristic pottery (e.g. Solheim 2006; Ono et al. 2013; Yamagata et al. 2013), precious and rare materials such as metal, glass and nephrite (e.g. Francis 2002; Bellina 2003; Bulbeck 2010; Dussubieux and Gratuze 2010; Hung and Bellwood 2010; Hung et al. 2013), and trade ceramics can be some of the best archaeological indicators for the establishment of ISEA inter-island maritime network systems. Other potential archaeological indicators include the appearance of plant and terrestrial animal resources in remote islands where no such resources naturally existed before their evident introduction by humans. Also, the appearance of new fishing tools associated with the development of fishing technology and marine exploitation can be another indicator.

Based on these understandings, we conducted archaeological excavations of sites dating to around AD 1000 to 1800 in the Sangihe-Talaud Islands, Eastern Indonesia, during 2003 to 2005. In this chapter, we introduce the excavated fish and other animal remains along with possible capture tools in the Talaud Islands as a platform for discussing the possible development of inter-island maritime networks and the associated marine and terrestrial resource use.

Talaud Islands and associated archaeological sites

The Talaud Islands form part of the small island group of the Sangihe and Talaud chain, geopolitically located in Indonesia (Figure 15.1), between the northern Sulawesi mainland and Mindanao in the Philippines. The Sangihe Islands extend north from Minahasa (North Sulawesi) for about 230 km, and include the two main islands of Siau and Sangir. The Talaud Islands are located about 120 km northeast of the Sangihe group. The Talaud group is basically composed of three large islands (see Figure 15.2), including Karakelang (976 km²), Salibabu (about 95 km²) and Kabaruan (about 200 km²), along with eight small (about 10–18 km² each) uplifted coral islands in the north called the Nanusa Islands. The Talaud Islands have no active volcanos and are low-lying (the highest point being the summit of Mount Manuk in Karakelang at 648 metres above sea level (m asl)).

Figure 15.1: Location of Sulawesi Sea and Talaud Islands.

Source: Jennifer Sheehan, CartoGIS, College of Asia and the Pacific, The Australian National University; based on original by Rintaro Ono.

Figure 15.2: Location of archaeological sites in the Talaud Islands.

Source: Jennifer Sheehan, CartoGIS, College of Asia and the Pacific, The Australian National University; based on original by Rintaro Ono.

The isolated location of the Talaud Islands, more than 100 km from any adjacent islands, was also the case during Pleistocene times, even though the Talauds boast the oldest archaeological site in the Sulawesi Sea—Leang Sarru (see Figure 15.2). The original excavation of Leang Sarru by Tanudirjo (2001, 2005) and our re-excavation (Ono and Soegondho 2004; Ono et al. 2009, 2015) found a large number of flaked stone artefacts, mainly chert, along with a variety of marine and land shell remains dating to between 35,000 years ago and the early Holocene (around 8000 years ago). However, there are no known archaeological sites dating to between c. 8000 and 5500 years ago, and so it is unclear whether the early inhabitants who migrated to the Talaud Islands during the Late Pleistocene continually inhabited these islands or not.

The next oldest traces of human habitation in the Talaud Islands derive from the Leang Tuwo Mane'e site located at the northern tip of Karakelang Island (see Figure 15.2). The original excavation by Bellwood (1976) and the re-excavation by Tanudirjo (2001) found a Neolithic layer with pottery including red-slipped sherds dating back to around 1500 BC, and an older layer with some flaked stone but no pottery dating back to around 5500 years ago. It is unclear whether the pre-pottery layer represents habitation by descendants of the Leang Sarru occupants or other immigrants to the Talauds. However, Leang Tuwo Mane'e had possibly been used continually from Neolithic to recent times at around AD 1700,[1] considering also the current village located next to the site, including a 'Late Phase' with Chinese trade ceramics and Rarangunusa-style pottery, which Bellwood (1976) dates to the 2nd millennium AD.

All other archaeological sites in the Talauds are post-Neolithic and date entirely to the centuries AD. Among them, Leang Buidane on Salibabu Island is a secondary burial cave site with a large number of human bones, burial jars, bronze and iron fragments, and accessories including glass, shell and various carnelian and other stone beads. Based on a thermoluminescence date from an excavated baked clay mould of around AD 1000 and a radiocarbon date of 510±80 BP (ANU 1516) on charcoal excavated from the top layer above the jar burials, Bellwood (1976:278) estimated the date of the burials to between AD 700 and 1200. Leang Arandangana on Kabaruan Island is another Metal Age site, and its lower layer is dated to around AD 1200 from marine shell samples. The site also yielded a number of Rarangunusa-style potsherds from its two layers and two pieces of Chinese trade ceramics from the upper layer (Tanudirjo 2001).

Leang Buida on Kabaruan Island, one of the sites we report on here, is dated to around AD 1000 in its lower layers, making these layers contemporary with the Leang Buidane burials, even though Leang Buida is mainly a habitation site. The upper layers of the site date to around AD 1600, while another site on Salibabu Island, Bukit Tiwing, dates to around AD 1500–1800. Both sites produced large numbers of potsherds, possible fishing gear and other tools, along with a large quantity of marine and terrestrial faunal remains. The earthenware pottery and its motifs from these two sites seem to have similarities with their Leang Buidane counterparts, while Leang Buida also has a number of Rarangunusa-style potsherds, mainly from the upper layers but also from the bottom layer.

The Rarangunusa style has a widespread distribution, especially within the southern Philippines, including Mindanao, Davao, Cotabato and Samar (Spoehr 1973; Solheim et al. 1979) and in Eastern Indonesia including Haruku Island in Northern Maluku (Soegondho 1996) and the Sangihe-Talaud Islands (see Bellwood 1976, 1980; Tanudirjo 2001; Ono 2004; Ono et al. 2013). Bellwood (1976:282) suggests that the Rarangunusa decoration style might have originated in Mindanao and spread through intermarriage and the movement of potters (rather than by mass population movement) in early historic times, mainly under European or Islamic influence.

Based on this background, we summarise the excavation results from Leang Buida and Bukit Tiwing, and discuss the possible development of their marine and terrestrial resource use and also inter-island networks during AD 1000–1800.

Excavation of Leang Buida

Leang Buida site is a limestone cave (*leang*) site along the western coast of Kabaruan Island (Figure 15.2). The cave mouth is about 8 m in length and 4 m in height, and the length of the inner area expands to about 10 m to form a tight sheltered area (Figure 15.3A). Fragments of shells and potsherds were scattered on the surface. Most of these potsherds are plain with some Rarangunusa. The site was first excavated by the Manado Archaeology Office and Ono in 2005, and a further 10 m² area was later excavated by the Manado Archaeology Office in 2007 and 2008.

---

1   There are three Carbon-14 dates from Layer 2, which is considered Early Metal to historic, and these are 990±100 BP (ANU 1715) on *Turbo* shell from the lower part of Layer 2, and 410±60 BP (ANU 1514) and 250±70 BP (ANU 1513) on charcoal from the upper part of Layer 2 (Bellwood 1976:261).

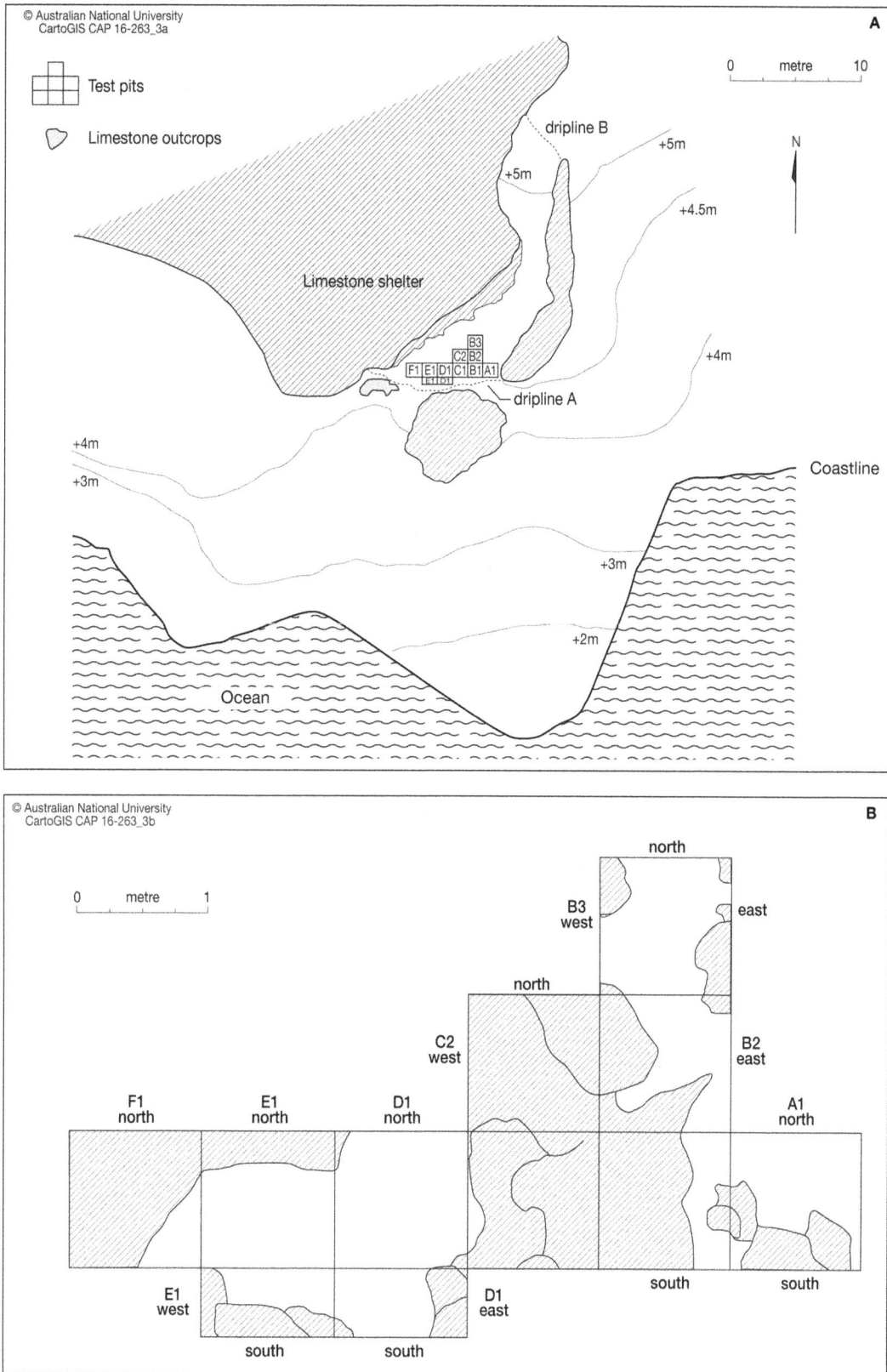

Figure 15.3: Leang Buida (A) and the excavated area in 2005 (B).

Note the contour breaks in A at places where the rocky cliffs of the coastline drops precipitously into the sea.

Source: Jennifer Sheehan, CartoGIS, College of Asia and the Pacific, The Australian National University; based on original by Manado Archaeology Office.

We opened a 10 m² excavated area around the mouth of the shelter in our 2005 excavation (Figure 15.3B) using spit depths of 10 cm. During the excavation, we first used both 5 mm and 3 mm sized mesh for dry screening, but owing to the wetness of the excavated sediment, we gave up on trying to use the 3 mm sized mesh. Our excavation indicated three cultural layers down to 130 cm (at the maximum depth from the surface): Layer 1 as top soil; Layer 2 as a blackish organic soil containing lots of shells, potsherds and animal bones; and Layer 3 as a sticky yellowish soil containing a lower concentration of habitation debris.

All seven Accelerator Mass Spectrometry (AMS) dates available for the site are consistent in indicating a difference of about 600 years between Layer 3 and Layer 2 (Table 15.1). However, the AMS dates on marine shell are about 300 years older than the AMS dates on charcoal from the same layer, apparently reflecting marine reservoir effects, hence we here refer to the AMS dates from charcoal samples. Thus, in terms of cultural layers and AMS dates, Leang Buida registers two occupation phases respectively dated to around AD 1600 (Layer 2) and AD 1000 (Layer 3). It should be added, however, that there may also have been earlier habitation at the site, which has not been preserved due to scouring out of older deposit through exceptionally high tides, as can occur at coastal sites such as Leang Buida.

Table 15.1: AMS Dates from Leang Buida.

Lab. Code	Sample	Layer	Depth	Date (BP)	Age (cal AD)[a]
TERRA-070407a06	*Turbo* sp.	3	E1/120cm	1358±31	—
TERRA-070407a07	*Turbo* sp.	3	E1/70cm	1312±34	—
TERRA-070407a08	*Turbo* sp.	2	E1/30cm	708±33	—
TERRA-070407a17	Charcoal	3	F1/100cm	998±32	983-1152
TERRA-070407a18	Charcoal	3	D1/90cm	965±32	1017-1155
TERRA-070407a19	Charcoal	2	D1/70cm	348±33	1460-1636
TERRA-070407a20	Charcoal	2	D1/40cm	316±36	1475-1648

(a) 95% calibrated range from Intcal13 (Bronk Ramsey 2016).
Source: Rintaro Ono.

Our excavation unearthed thousands of shellfish (n=21,487), fish and animal remains with potsherds including both decorated (n=409) and plain sherds (n=8100), chert flakes (n=297), stone adzes (n=2), stone tools identified as nutcrackers (n=37), and fragments of iron (n=14) and two trade ceramic sherds (Table 15.2). As for macro-plant remains, *Canarium* nut shells (n=176) were excavated. Iron fragments were recovered only from Layer 1, while the two trade ceramic sherds (origin yet unknown) were excavated from Layer 3.

Table 15.2: Excavated cultural remains (counts) in each grid unit at Leang Buida in 2005.

Unit	Decorated potsherds	Plain potsherds	Imported ceramic sherds	Stone flakes	Stone adzes	Nut crackers	Iron tools	Fishnet sinkers	Shells	Animal bones	Canarium nuts
A1	36	658	0	52	0	0	1	0	2441	119	5
B1	16	216	0	4	0	3	0	0	855	2	8
B2	16	200	0	28	0	0	0	0	1319	0	24
B3	8	145	0	4	0	0	0	0	1009	11	0
C1	19	240	0	15	0	1	0	0	1268	7	4
C2	6	147	0	8	0	0	0	0	411	0	6
D1N	33	1431	1	55	0	3	2	2	3591	416	32
D1S	30	541	1	8	1	4	0	0	1373	380	0
E1N	91	1808	0	84	0	11	9	2	3927	599	54

Unit	Decorated potsherds	Plain potsherds	Imported ceramic sherds	Stone flakes	Stone adzes	Nut crackers	Iron tools	Fishnet sinkers	Shells	Animal bones	Canarium nuts
E1S	46	1317	0	30	0	4	0	0	2720	512	7
F1	108	1397	0	9	1	11	2	1	2573	841	36
Total	409	8100	2	297	2	37	14	5	21,487	2887	176

Source: The authors.

Most of the decorated potsherds from Leang Buida can be classified with the Rarangunusa type. Rarangunusa pottery mainly comprises restricted vessels with everted rims, globular or carinated bodies and round bases (Tanudirjo 2001). Rims are generally rounded and tapering (Figure 15.4). Some rims have notched lips or are inflected outside the lip. The most distinctive characteristic of this pottery are the parallel incisions mostly made by two- or three-pronged tools, arranged in vertical zones (Figures 15.4A and 15.4C) on the outer wall of the vessel, generally from a carination or point of vertical tangency up to the lip. Among the popular motifs are paired vertical lines, vertical and horizontal zigzags, and paired notches lined in a vertical row. As described in the Introduction to this chapter, this pottery type has been dated to the 2nd millennium AD (Bellwood 1976; Tanudirjo 2001).

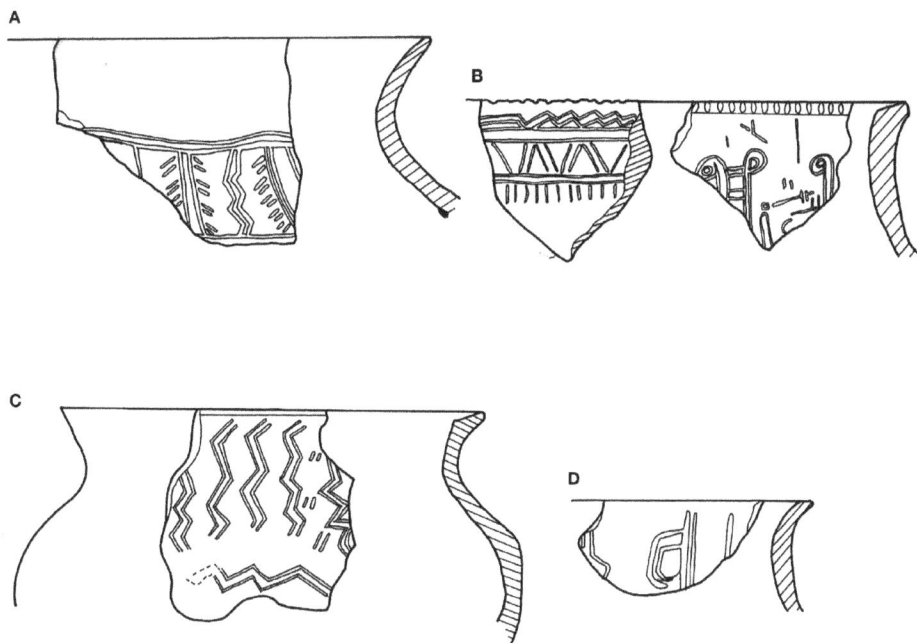

Figure 15.4: Decorated pottery from Leang Buida.

A: Decorated neck from square F1 Spit 11. B: Decorated rims from square F1 Spit 7. C: Decorated rim and shoulder from square F1 Spit 7. D: Decorated rim from square F1 Spit 7.

Source: Manado Archaeology Office.

However, our excavation at Leang Buida indicates that the Rarangunusa pottery prototype had already appeared by AD 1000, possibly developed from Metal Age pottery styles and decorated motifs. For example, one of the decorated lip sherds from Layer 3 (Figure 15.4B) has a horizontal translation of paired zigzags on its inner lip, more simplified than the horizontal triangular mazes illustrated for Leang Buidane (Bellwood 1976:Figure 11) but different in orientation from the vertical translation of paired zigzags typical of Rarangunusa decorations (Bellwood 1976: Plate IIc). Considering also the excavation results at Liang Arandangana by Tanudirjo (2001), we may infer that the Rarangunusa motifs do not show any spatial patterning and persisted without radical changes for hundreds of years. Bellwood (1976) proposed that the Rarangunusa style might have survived until as recently as the mid-20th century. While not disagreeing with this proposal, we add the possibility that the designs may have become more simple and functional over time.

Fishing tools from Leang Buida

One class of special finds from Leang Buida involves variably sized clay tools with two punched holes, which are probably fishnet sinkers (n=5). They can be classified into two main types: the rounded type (n=2; Figure 15.5C, Figure 15.6B) and the disc-shaped type (n=3; Figures 15.5B and 15.5D; Figures 15.6C–E). Among these, the smallest disc-shaped sinker and the larger of the rounded sinkers were excavated from Layer 3 (respectively 130 cm and 110 cm in depth), while the others were from Layer 2 (70 cm in depth). To judge from their excavated context, these clay sinkers appeared by AD 1000 and their use continued to at least AD 1600.

Figure 15.5: Photographs of clay net sinkers from Leang Buida.

Source: Rintaro Ono.

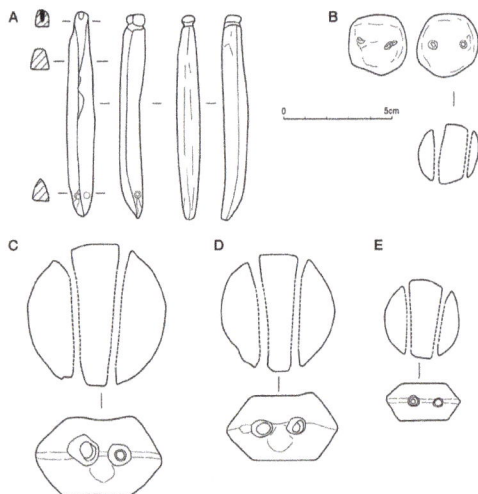

Net sinkers of clay or stone are common fishing tools in East Asia, including Japan, back to 8000 years ago. The older sinkers were mainly simple, for instance using fragments of potsherds or pebble stones, while the more sophisticated sinkers with a single furrow or double furrows appeared after the Middle to Late Jomon age dated to around 2–1000 years BC. After the Yayoi period around 500–0 BC, the tubular type of clay sinker with a single hole become common widely across East Asia as far south as Taiwan (e.g. Li 1997, 2002). However, so far no net sinkers have been found or excavated in ISEA, including Eastern Indonesia, and so our finding in Leang Buida may be the first archaeological evidence of clay net sinkers anywhere in Indonesia, including the Sulawesi region. Interestingly, all of the Leang Buida net sinkers have two holes in them. In East Asia, stick-shaped net sinker of various sizes with two holes appeared in Western Japan after around AD 400 and were commonly used until around AD 1200. These sinkers are not similar in shape to those from Leang Buida, but bolster the case for inferring that clay artefacts with two holes could be net sinkers.

Figure 15.6: Illustrations of Leang Buida fishing tools.

A: Suspected lure shanks, B: rounded clay net sinker; C–E: disc-shaped clay net sinker.

Source: Jennifer Sheehan, CartoGIS, College of Asia and the Pacific, The Australian National University; based on sketches by Rintaro Ono.

Another important finding related to fishing involves two possible lure shanks made from *Tridacna* shell (Figure 15.6A, Figure 15.7). Both were excavated from the middle to upper layers by the Manado Archaeology Office in 2007. Both lure shanks have a notch possibly for attaching a line at one end, while the other end is slightly bent upward and has a pierced hole. Interestingly, the surface pierced by the hole is broad and flat on one specimen but raised and bevelled on the other specimen. Since they were unearthed from Leang Buida's middle to upper layers, they would date to around AD 1600. However, no such artefacts have yet been found in ISEA, including Eastern Indonesia, hence they may be the first archaeological evidence for the use of shell lure shanks in the region.

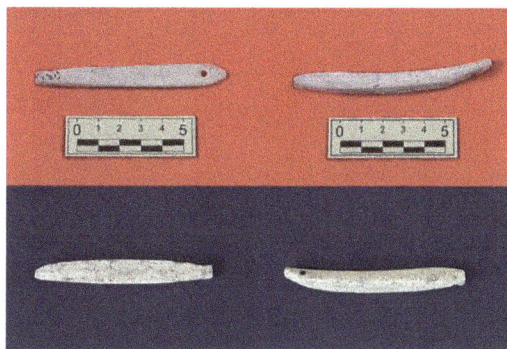

Figure 15.7: Suspected lure shanks made from *Tridacna* shell, with hole from front to back sides (top) and from right to left sides (bottom).
Source: Rintaro Ono.

In southern Wallacea and Near Oceania, fish hooks made of *Trochus* date back to the Late Pleistocene in Alor (Samper Carro et al. 2016) and Timor (O'Connor et al. 2011). In Remote Oceania, a variety of one-piece rotating or trolling fish hooks made of *Trochus* and *Turbo* shell appeared on early Lapita sites in Melanesia dated to 1300–800 BC (e.g. Kirch 1997; Szabó 2010), while one-piece rotating fish hooks of *Isognomon* and rarely *Turbo* shell appeared with early human settlement in the Marianas Islands, Micronesia dated to 1500–1000 BC (e.g. Hung et al. 2011). After around AD 100–

400, pearl-shell lure shanks become common in Melanesia and some islands in Micronesia, while compound or two-piece hooks and trolling shanks appeared mainly after AD 1000 in the Marianas.

However, there have been no discoveries of shell-made fish hooks and trolling gear in northern Wallacea including the Sangihe-Talaud Islands prior to our finding of an apparent trolling shank used in the Talaud Islands by AD 1600. Interestingly, one of the Remote Oceanic islands closest to the Talauds, Tobi Island in the southwestern Palau group, has produced a number of *Tridacna* trolling shanks, and the earliest dates for prehistoric sites in Tobi now register to around AD 1700 (Intoh and Ono 2006:Figure 6). The Tobi *Tridaca* shanks are not exactly the same as the Talaud ones, but there are similarities between them, and cultural influence or human interaction between the Talauds and Tobi Islands would be plausible. However, it should also be noted that the only other suggestion of shared material culture between these islands involves *Tridacna* shell adzes (moreover, represented only as surface finds in the Talauds).

Excavation of Bukit Tiwing

Bukit Tiwing is an open site located on a hill (*bukit*) called 'Tiwing' about 1 km inland from the village of Ballang, on the western coast of Salibabu Island. The site is situated in secondary forest on the flat top of a small limestone hill surrounded by cliffs (Figure 15.8). The flat area covers about 15 m x 20 m. Fragments of imported ceramics, probably from China are scattered on the surface. Local potsherds were also found quite abundantly and some of them are of the Rarangunusa type. The site was excavated by the Manado Archaeology Office and Ono in 2004.

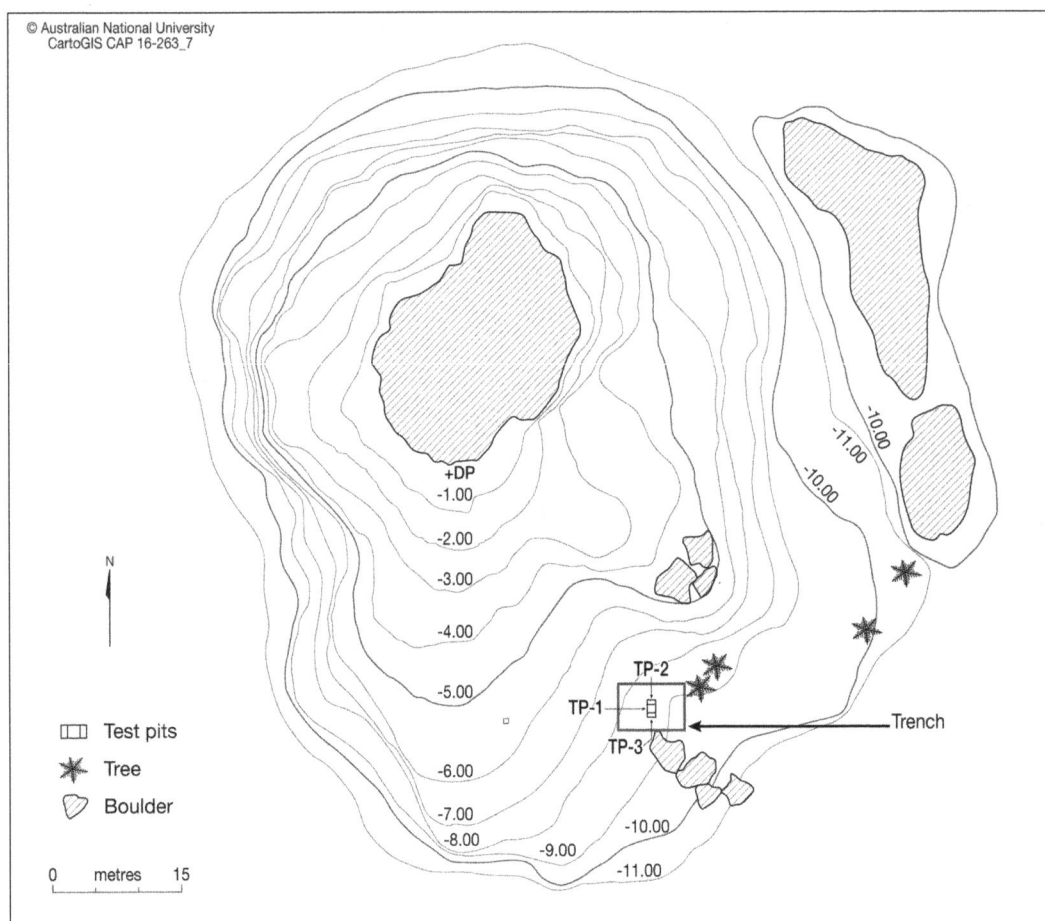

Figure 15.8: Bukit Tiwing and the excavated test pits.

Source: Jennifer Sheehan, CartoGIS, College of Asia and the Pacific, The Australian National University; based on original by Manado Archaeology Office.

We first opened a 1 m x 1 m test pit (TP1), then later we expanded the test pit to excavate the northern and southern sides of TP1 by 50 cm, to produce a 2 m x 1 m test trench. The smaller test pits are named TP2 (north) and TP3 (south). Excavation was undertaken with 10 cm spits to a maximum depth of 1 m below the surface. During the excavation, we first applied dry screening through both the 5 mm and 3 mm size meshes, but owing to the wetness of the excavated sediment, we later desisted from using the 3 mm size mesh. Our excavation identified three cultural layers: Layer 1 as top soil; Layer 2 as blackish organic soil containing lots of shells, potsherds and animal bones; and Layer 3 as a sticky yellowish soil containing only small quantities of potsherds.

Charcoal samples were collected from all of the test pits down to Spit 7 and some were also collected from Spit 8. A total of four AMS dates were obtained from charcoal, while two radiocarbon dates were taken from marine shells (Table 15.3). The AMS determinations from charcoal are c. 300 BP from Layer 2, and c. 350–550 BP from Layer 3. On the other hand, the radiocarbon dates from marine shell, around 700 BP from Layer 2 at 50 cm depth, are at least 300 years older than the corresponding AMS determinations from charcoal.

Table 15.3: Radiocarbon and AMS dates from Bukit Tiwing.

Lab. Code	Sample	Layer	Location	Date (BP)	Age (cal AD)[a]
TERRA-070407a10	Marine shell	2	TP2/Spit 5	688±33	–
TERRA-070407a13	Marine shell	2	TP3/Spit 5	700±33	–
Wk-15740	Charcoal	3	TP3/Spit 7	539±81	1276–1615
TERRA-070407a23	Charcoal	3	TP2/Spit 7	343±30	1466–1639
Wk-15741	Charcoal	3	TP3/Spit 6	371±31	1446–1634
TERRA-070407a24	Charcoal	2	TP2/Spit 4	294±33	1489–1661

(a) 95% calibrated range from Intcal13 (Bronk Ramsey 2016).
Source: Rintaro Ono.

Our Carbon-14 dates from Leang Buida and Bukit Tiwing clearly show that marine shell dates carry a marine reservoir effect that usually makes these dates appear hundreds of years older than their counterpart dates on charcoal (e.g. Nakamura 2003; Yoneda et al. 2004). Accordingly, we endorse the charcoal dates rather than the unreliable marine shell dates, and date the main occupation of Bukit Tiwing to around AD 1500–1600 or the 16th–17th centuries.

The cultural artefacts excavated from the site include 3178 potsherds including the Rarangunusa type, 70 imported ceramic sherds, six fragments of iron, two bone tools, 19 lithic waste flakes, 20 stone tools including nuts cracker or hammerstones, seven coral tools (mainly pestles) and a piece of baked clay spindle whorl (Table 15.4). Fragment of iron were excavated only down to Spit 4 (Layer 2), while imported ceramics were excavated down to Spit 6 (upper Layer 3). Animal bones and marine shells together with stone and coral tools were mainly collected from Layer 2 (Spits 3–5) and decreased in frequency in Layer 3 (Spits 6–10). Earthenware potsherds are the only item collected from all of the spits.

Table 15.4: Excavated cultural artefacts from Bukit Tiwing.

TP1, 2, 3	L1		L2			L3					Total
Category	Spit 1	Spit 2	Spit 3	Spit 4	Spit 5	Spit 6	Spit 7	Spit 8	Spit 9	Spit 10	
Potsherd	169	692	1025	352	382	282	107	116	49	4	3178
Ceramic	2	20	30	10	5	3					70
Iron			1	5							6
Stone waste		3		2	6	6	1		1		19
Stone tool	4	3	2	2	2	5	1			1	20
Coral pestle	1		2		3	1					7
Bone tool			1	1							2
Spindle whorl				1							1
Total	176	718	1061	373	398	297	109	116	50	5	3303

Source: Authors' data.

Most of the decorated sherds can be identified as Rarangunusa-style pottery characterised by parallel wavy incisions possibly made by two-pronged tools, without other incisions or decorations on their surface (see Ono et al. 2013). Most of the imported ceramics are blue-and-white wares from the Qing Dynasty (late 17th to 19th centuries) that represent cheap mass productions (Figure 15.9), some of them possibly made in Zhangzhou, Fujian Province in China. However, the imported ceramics also include older celadon sherds with fish and flower designs.

Figure 15.9: Excavated Qing Dynasty sherds from Bukit Tiwing.

Source: Rintaro Ono.

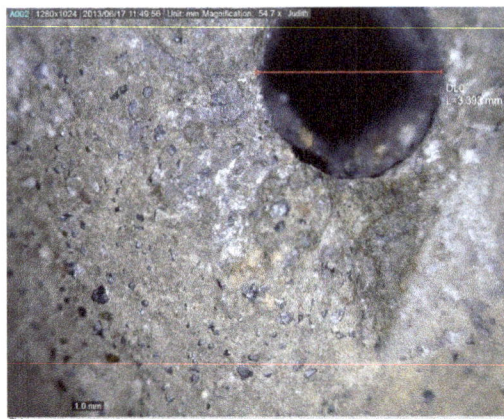

Figure 15.10: Excavated spindle whorl from Bukit Tiwing and possible use-wear marks beside the central perforation.

Source: Judith Cameron, with permission.

Besides the pottery, a piece of baked clay spindle whorl (Figure 15.10) was excavated from the bottom of Layer 2 (TP3/Spit5). Its height is 17 mm, its maximum width is 20 mm, and it has a single hole with a diameter of 2.5–4 mm in its middle (Ono et al. 2013). A spindle whorl is a tool used for spinning and twisting fibres into yarn; many kinds of spindle whorl made of clay, wood and other materials have been found in archaeological sites around the world. Clay spindle whorls are a common feature of Neolithic and Bronze Age levels in Mainland Southeast Asian sites (Bellwood 2017; Cameron 2005, 2011). They are less common in ISEA sites (e.g. Oliver 1989; Cameron and Mijares 2006), although the Sunget site on Batan and the Savidug Dune site on Sabtang, in the Batanes Islands at the far north of the Philippines, produced some clay spindle whorls by 1200 BC (Cameron 2013). Compared with these spindle whorls, the Bukit Tiwing specimen is much younger, but it is so far the first excavated case of a clay spindle whorl in the Sangihe-Talaud Islands.

Marine resource use in Leang Buida and Bukit Tiwing

Fish and shell remains were excavated from both Leang Buida and Bukit Tiwing. Leang Buida produced the larger Numbers of Individual Specimens (NISP): 21,487 NISP of shell remains (about 50 kg) and 356 NISP of fish remains. Bukit Tiwing produced only 3,301 NISP of shell remains and 121 NISP of fish remains. We first report on shell exploitation at Leang Buida and Bukit Tiwing, and then focus on the fish remains.

Shellfish exploitation

Table 15.5 shows the NISP of each family by layer for the 23 families (and 117 taxa) of shell excavated and identified at Leang Buida. Excluding the Ellobiidae land snail species, which was possibly a natural inclusion (especially in the upper layers), Neritidae, Turbinidae, Chitonidae and Cypraeanidae were the major shell families exploited at Leang Buida. Since a large number and variety of shells were recovered from the site, we show detailed identifications only for Neritidae and Turbinidae, the two main marine shell families (Table 15.6). *Nerita undata* and *Nerita albicilla* were the two main species for the Neritidae, and *Turbo stenogyrus* and *Turbo argyrostoms* for the Turbinidae. However, the site also produced a number of opercula belonging to Turbo malmoratus shells, which is a larger species and so might also have been important for human subsistence as its larger size would indicate a relatively high meat value.

Table 15.5: List of invertebrate remains from Leang Buida (NISP).

Taxa/Family	L1	L2	L3	Total
(Gastropoda)				
Neritidae	2720	4805	1794	9319
Turbinidae	608	1729	572	2909
Cypraenidae	26	193	61	280
Vasidae	28	91	34	153
Fissurellidae	60	43	44	147
Trochidae	17	45	19	81
Conidae	7	30	45	82
Haliotidae	5	13	17	35
Patellidae	6	11	1	18
Nassariidae	0	3	0	3
Cassididae	1	1	0	2
Fasciolariidae	2	0	0	2
Tonnidae	0	1	0	1
Hipponicidae	1	0	0	1
Harpidae	1	0	0	1
Pylanidellidae	0	1	0	1
Strombidae	1	0	0	1
Sub-total	3483	6966	2587	13036

Taxa/Family	L1	L2	L3	Total
(Bivalvia)				
Arcidae	0	48	15	63
Tridacnidae	16	21	8	45
Veneridae	1	15	3	19
Mitridae	0	1	0	1
(Polyplacophora)				
Chitonidae	123	249	4	376
(Echinoidea)				
Sea urchin	2	12	2	14
(Malacostraca)				
Crab	22	13	2	37
(Ellobiidae)				
Land snail	3962	1985	340	6287
Sub-total	4126	2344	374	6844

Source: Rintaro Ono.

Table 15.6: List of excavated species of Neritidae and Turbinidae, Leang Buida (NISP).

Family	Species	L1	L2	L3	Total
Neritidae		2720	4805	1794	9319
	Nerita undata	1209	1769	667	3645
	Nerita albicilla	645	1246	537	2428
	Nerita lineata	367	961	283	1611
	Ritena costana	449	703	266	1418
	Septaria porcellana	5	67	36	108
	Neritopsts radula	27	42	5	74
	?	16	17	0	33
	?	1	0	0	1
	?	1	0	0	1
Turbinidae		608	1729	572	2909
	Turbo stenogyrus	210	875	415	1500
	Turbo argyrostoms	168	429	74	671
	Turbo marmoratus	50	141	14	205
	Turbo marmoratus (o)*	38	68	2	108
	Turbo sp.	94	130	1	225
	Turbo sp.	19	46	0	65
	Turbo stosus	29	40	66	135

(o)* = operculum.

Source: Rintaro Ono.

Tables 15.7 and 15.8 show the NISP by layer for the 20 families and 43 taxa of shell excavated and identified at Bukit Tiwing. *Turbo*, principally *Turbo* sp., *Turbo chrysostomus* and *Turbo stosus* is the most frequently identified family at Bukit Tiwing, followed by Neritidae including *Nerita undata* and *Nerita albicilla*. The Chitonidae are also a major shell family exploited at Bukit Tiwing. As for the *Turbo* shells, it should be noted that some species with large NISP number are not yet identified to species level. In terms of meat value, however, *Turbo* and *Trochus* sp. shells could be the most important at the site.

Table 15.7: List of invertebrate remains from Bukit Tiwing (NISP).

Family	Species	L1		L2			L3			Total
		1	2	3	4	5	6	7	8	
Gastropoda										
Turbinidae	See Table 15.8	102	109	440	397	503	248	19	0	1818
Neritidae	See Table 15.8	0	0	40	44	295	78	21	0	478
Muricidae	*Muricidae* sp.	2	2	21	43	81	35	1	0	185
Trochidae	See Table 15.8	0	2	18	19	21	35	5	0	100
Conidae	*Conidae* sp.	1	1	15	17	18	13	0	0	65
Terebridae	?	1	0	1	1	22	30	4	0	59
Strombidae	See Table 15.8	4	0	4	8	17	3	0	0	36
Fasciolariidae	See Table 15.8	0	0	2	6	4	4	2	0	18
Cypraeidae	See Table 15.8	0	0	3	4	5	5	0	0	17
Tridacnidae	See Table 15.8	0	1	2	5	4	0	0	0	12
Veneridae?	?	0	0	1	3	0	2	0	0	6
Ranellidae?	?	0	2	1	0	0	2	0	0	5
Acmaeidae	*Patelloida saccharina*	0	0	0	0	1	3	1	0	5
Rapidaea	*Latiaxis armatus*?	0	0	0	1	2	1	0	0	4
Psammobiidae	*Asaphis deflorata*	0	0	1	0	1	2	0	0	4
Mactridae?	?	0	0	0	1	0	1	1	0	3
Mitridae	?	0	0	0	0	1	0	0	0	1
Unknown	?	0	0	1	0	0	0	0	0	1
Polyplacophora										
Chitonidae	*Acanthopleura/Liolophura*	0	0	4	22	187	134	6	0	353
Land snail										
Ellobiidae	*Pythia panthrina*	12	3	0	5	0	1	0	0	21
Land snail	?	1	0	0	0	0	0	0	0	1
Total		123	120	554	576	1162	597	60	0	3192

Source: Rintaro Ono.

Table 15.8: List of identified marine gastropod species from Bukit Tiwing (NISP).

Family	Species	L1		L2			L3			Total
		1	2	3	4	5	6	7	8	
Turbinidae	*Turbo* sp.	102	98	303	216	302	159	12	0	1192
	Turbo chrysostomus	0	6	70	64	65	24	4	0	233
	Turbo stosus	0	2	28	61	74	40	3	0	208
	Turbo sp.	0	3	36	30	28	25	0	0	122
	Turbo stengyrus	0	0	2	24	34	0	0	0	60
	Turbo marmoratus	0	0	0	2	0	0	0	0	2
	Turbo sp.	0	0	1	0	0	0	0	0	1
		102	109	440	397	503	248	19	0	1818

Family	Species	L1		L2			L3			Total
		1	2	3	4	5	6	7	8	
Neritidae	Nerita undata	0	0	20	11	249	57	12	0	349
	Nerita albicilla	0	0	20	33	46	19	9	0	127
	Ritena costana	0	0	0	0	0	1	0	0	1
	Ritena squamulta	0	0	0	0	0	1	0	0	1
		0	0	40	44	295	78	21	0	478
Trochidae	Trochus maculatus	0	1	1	17	7	13	3	0	42
	Trochus niloticus maximus	0	1	17	2	13	9	1	0	43
	Umbonium sp.	0	0	0	0	1	7	1	0	9
	Tectus pyramis	0	0	0	0	0	6	0	0	6
		0	2	18	19	21	35	5	0	100
Strombidae	Lambis lambis	4	0	3	3	3	0	0	0	13
	Storombus decorus	0	0	1	4	14	3	0	0	22
	(Totals include 1?)	4	0	4	8	17	3	0	0	36
Fasciolariidae	Fusinus undatus	0	0	0	3	2	0	0	0	5
	Latirus nagasakiensis	0	0	0	3	2	4	2	0	11
	(Totals include 2?)	0	0	2	6	4	4	2	0	18
Cypraeidae	Cypraea caputserpentis	0	0	3	2	2	2	0	0	9
	Cypraea lynx	0	0	0	1	2	0	0	0	3
	Cypraea tigris	0	0	0	1	0	0	0	0	1
	(Totals include 4?)	0	0	3	4	5	5	0	0	17
Tridacnidae	Tridacna crocea	0	0	0	5	3	0	0	0	8
	Hippopus hippopus	0	1	0	0	0	0	0	0	1
	Tridacna gigas	0	0	1	0	0	0	0	0	1
	Tridacna maxima	0	0	1	0	1	0	0	0	2
		0	1	2	5	4	0	0	0	12

Source: Rintaro Ono.

Fish exploitation

At Leang Buida, 356 NISP of identified fish bones (246 Minimum Number of Individuals (MNI)) were excavated. They were identified into 16 fish families (all marine species) including Scaridae, Serranidae, Labridae, Lethrinidae, Lutjanidae, Acanthuridae, Balistidae, Diodontidae, Holocentridae, Scombridae, Muraenidae, Siganidae, Carangidae, Sphyraenidae, and Sharks, mainly Carcharhinidae (see Table 15.9). As for the inshore fish species, the Serranids (groupers) and Lutjanids (snappers) are the two most frequent families. These are more commonly captured by angling rather than netting and spearing, based on ethno-archaeological studies in ISEA and the tropical Pacific. Holocentrids and Labrids are also commonly captured by angling, while Lethrinids and Balistids are usually captured by both angling and netting, depending on size and species. Other inshore fish species such as the Scarids, Diodontids and Acanthurids are mainly omnivorous fishes in shallow coral reef habitat, and are commonly captured by netting and spearing (Kirch and Dickinson 1976; Kirch and Dye 1979; Dye 1983; Goto 1986, 1990; Masse 1986, 1989; Rolett 1989; Ono 2010, 2011).

Table 15.9: Identified fish remains from Leang Buida (MNI).

Family	Habitation	L1		L2					L3				Total
		1	2	3	4	5	6	7	8	9	10	11	MNI
(Inshore)													
Serranidae	Inshore/bottom	2	11	10	13	10	7	6	5	5	0	1	70
Lutjanidae	Inshore/reef	0	3	4	6	4	1	3	4	1	0	0	26
Scaridae	Inshore/reef	0	4	0	2	1	3	5	0	3	1	0	19
Diodontidae	Inshore/reef	0	1	1	0	1	3	4	4	3	1	1	19
Labridae	Inshore/bottom	1	1	4	5	3	0	2	1	1	0	0	18
Balistidae	Inshore/bottom	0	1	2	5	2	0	4	4	0	0	0	18
Lethrinidae	Inshore/reef	0	1	3	3	2	2	1	4	1	0	0	17
Acanthuridae	Inshore/reef	0	0	1	3	2	0	4	1	0	0	0	11
Holocentridae	Inshore	0	0	2	0	2	2	1	0	1	0	0	8
?		0	0	2	2	1	0	2	0	0	0	0	7
Muraenidae	Inshore/bottom	0	0	0	1	2	0	1	0	0	0	0	4
Siganidae	Inshore/reef	0	0	0	1	1	0	1	0	0	0	0	3
(Inshore–Pelagic)													
Sharks/Carcharhinidae	Inshore-Pelagic	0	0	0	0	1	2	1	1	1	2	1	9
Carangidae	Inshore-Pelagic	1	2	0	4	1	0	0	0	0	0	0	8
Scombridae	Pelagic	0	1	2	2	1	0	0	0	0	0	0	6
Sphyraenidae	Inshore-Pelagic	0	0	1	1	0	0	1	0	0	0	0	3
Total		4	25	32	48	34	20	36	24	16	4	3	246

Source: Rintaro Ono.

It is also important to note that Leang Buida produced pelagic species including Scombrids (tunas), Carangids (trevallies) and Sphyraenids (barracudas), as well as sharks, all of which are commonly captured by angling or trolling. Except sharks, however, no pelagic fish were excavated from Layer 3, which dates to around AD 1000. Layer 2 produced the highest number and greatest variety of fish bones, suggesting that more active fishing possibly with various kinds of fishing methods was practised after AD 1600 by the Leang Buida occupants.

Compared with Leang Buida, far fewer identified fish bones were recovered from Bukit Tiwing (40 NISP; 25 MNI) but they include the 10 fish families of Scaridae, Serranidae, Lethrinidae, Lutjanidae, Acanthuridae, Balistidae, Diodontidae, Scombridae, Tetradontidae and Holocentridae (Table 15.10). Most of these are inshore fish species, which inhabit shallow reef or reef edge and are captured mainly by netting, angling and spearing. Lethrinids, especially *Monotaxis* species with their large jaws, Lutjanids, Serranids, Holocentrids and Labrids are commonly captured by angling, while Scarids, Acanthurids and Diodontids are mainly captured by netting and spearing. Muraenids (moray eels) are usually captured by spearing. As for pelagic species, some Scombrid bones were excavated from Layer 2.

Table 15.10: Identified fish remains from Bukit Tiwing (NISP, MNI in brackets).

Rank	Taxa/Spit	L1		L2			L3			Total
		1	2	3	4	5	6	7	8	
1	Lethrinidae	0	0	3 (2)	1	0	0	0	0	4 (3)
	Monotaxis grandoculis	0	0	2 (1)	0	0	0	0	0	2 (1)
1	Scaridae	0	2 (1)	4 (2)	0	1	0	0	0	7 (4)
3	Acanthridae	0	0	2 (1)	0	1	1	0	0	4 (3)
3	Lutjanidae	0	0	0	1	2 (1)	1	0	0	4 (3)
3	Serranidae	1	0	1	1	0	0	0	0	3 (3)

Rank	Taxa/Spit	L1		L2			L3			Total
		1	2	3	4	5	6	7	8	
6	Diodontidae	0	0	4 (1)	2 (1)	0	0	0	0	6 (2)
6	Balistidae	0	0	1	0	1	0	0	0	2 (2)
8	Scombridae	0	0	4 (1)	0	0	0	0	0	4 (1)
8	Muraenidae	0	0	0	0	1	0	0	0	1
8	Holocentridae	0	0	0	1	0	0	0	0	1
8	Labridae	0	0	0	0	0	1	0	0	1
	Total	1	2	21	6	6	3	0	0	39 (25)

Source: Rintaro Ono.

Terrestrial resource use at Leang Buida and Bukit Tiwing

Leang Buida produced 409 NISP of mammal, bird and sea turtle remains, and over 80% of them were unearthed from Layers 2 and 3 (Table 15.11). Although the total number and volume of animal remains is limited, the available identifications indicate that at least four taxa—pig (*Sus scrofa*), goat (*Capra hircus*), rat (Murids) and sea turtles—were exploited at the site. A significant finding involves the goat teeth and bones from Layer 3 dated to around AD 1000, which indicate that goats were introduced to the Talaud Islands by at least the 11th century AD. The earliest securely dated goats in ISEA (Bali) date back to 200 BC in association with rouletted ware imported from India (Calo et al. 2015); thus, these goats could have been introduced from India. However, goats possibly became popular as food meat after the expansion of Islam, notably in Western Indonesia. Goats are also a popular domesticated animal in the Philippine Islands and in remote island ecosystems as they can thrive in grassland. The earliest ISEA goat remains of possible Chinese origin have been identified at a couple of sites on the Batanes Islands after AD 1000 (Piper et al. 2013). Similarly, our excavations provide archaeological evidence for the introduction of goats to the Talaud Islands by around AD 1000. Although the origin of the Talaud goats is as yet unknown, they could be of Chinese origin in view of the proximity of the Talauds to the Philippines Islands.

Table 15.11: Identified taxon and unidentified animal bones from Leang Buida.

Taxa	L1		L2					L3				NISP (MNI)
	1	2	3	4	5	6	7	8	9	10	11	
Pig	0	3	0	2	3	1	1	4	2	0	0	16 (4)
Goat	6	3	2	1	0	0	0	0	1	0	0	13 (4)
Rat	0	0	1	11	0	0	0	0	0	0	0	12 (1)
Bird	0	1	1	0	1	1	1	0	0	0	0	5 (2)
Sea turtle	0	2	3	1	1	1	0	0	0	0	0	8 (2)
Unidentified	12	17	33	46	52	100	24	32	24	12	3	355
Total	18	26	40	61	57	103	26	36	27	12	20	409 (13)

Source: The authors.

Bukit Tiwing produce 1448 NISP (3128 g) of mammal and sea turtle remains, with 77% of the faunal remains unearthed from Layer 2 (Table 15.12). The identified animals are domesticated pig (*Sus scrofa*), sea turtle (*Chelonioidea* sp.), dog (*Canis familiaris*), goat (*Capra hircus*) and rat (Muridae). Among these, pigs are the leading species with 101 NISP and 12 MNI, followed by sea turtles with 81 NISP and 5 MNI. Two dog mandible fragments (MNI=1), one goat tooth and one rat tooth were also identified. Nine mandibles/fragments (MNI=6), tentatively identified as primate remains (*Macaca* sp. or *Tarsius* sp.), were also unearthed.[2] Anatomical elements other than teeth and mandibles are not yet analysed and identified to taxa; although impressionistically, pig seems to account for a larger number and volume than any other species.

The Bukit Tiwing identifications point to pig as the major source of animal protein followed by sea turtle and monkey. Detailed analysis of the excavated pig teeth indicates that most of the pigs were killed at a young age of around 6–20 months old. Many of pig femur bones have bite marks from dogs. Also, the dog mandible fragments have some cut marks, which suggest that dogs were also eaten in the Talauds in times past. Another interesting finding is the goat tooth, derived from domesticated goats in the Talaud Islands or goat meat imported from some other location during the 16th or 17th century AD.

Table 15.12: Identified taxon and unidentified animal bones from Bukit Tiwing.

Taxon	L1		L2			L3			Total
	1	2	3	4	5	6	7	8	
Pig (tooth)	5	13	15	29	10	3	0	0	75
Pig (mandible)	0	4	2	16	4	0	0	0	26
Pig (total)	5	17	17	45	14	3	0	0	101 (12)*
Sea Turtle	0	3	22	41	10	5	0	0	81 (5)*
Macaca/Tarsius? (mandible)	1	0	4	1	2	1	0	0	9 (6)*
Dog (mandible)	0	0	0	1	1	0	0	0	2 (1)*
Goat (tooth)	0	0	1	0	0	0	0	0	1
Rat (tooth)	0	0	1	0	0	0	0	0	1
Unidentified bones									
Tooth	1	3	9	14	8	1	0	0	36
Vertebra	0	0	2	1	0	1	0	0	4
Others	29	174	361	385	184	76	4	0	1213
Total	36	197	417	488	219	87	4	0	1448

( )* = MNI number.

Source: The authors.

All of the larger terrestrial animals were clearly introduced to the Talaud Islands by humans because the only terrestrial mammals native to the Talaud Islands (e.g. Riley 2002) were four species of flying fox (*Pteropus* spp.), 14 other species of bat, five species of rat and two species of cuscus (*Ailurops ursinus* and *Strigocuscus celebensis*). The rat tooth is not identified to species level and we are not sure if it represents a wild species or one that arrived with humans in the past.

Discussion

Based on our excavation results at Leang Buida and Bukit Tiwing in the Talaud Islands, we now discuss the possible development of marine and terrestrial resource use as well as regional maritime networks in the Sulawesi Sea during the 2nd millennium AD. The lower layer of Leang Buida is dated to around AD 1000, while the upper layers of Leang Buida and Bukit Tiwing date to around AD 1500–1700, hence these sites can provide archaeological evidence on the

2   The literature on Talaud Island mammals does not include any references to the human introduction of tarsiers (including *Tarsius sangirensis*, native to the Sangihe Islands) or monkeys. However, in 2004, the authors saw a few monkeys (species not clear) along the coast of Salibabu Island. According to the villagers, they used to be pet monkeys kept for collecting coconuts, though our interviews with other Talaud islanders indicated that any such use of monkey is not common and this could be a very recent and exceptional case. Owing to the lack of *Macaca* and *Tarsius* specimens in the reference collections available to us, we retain the identification of these Bukit Tiwing mandibles as uncertain and are continuing our efforts to identify them.

use of shellfish, fish and other animals at these two intervals. The detail of developments during AD 1100–1500 is unclear, but we can at least compare certain changes between AD 1000 and the interval after AD 1500 in the Talauds.

Development of marine and terrestrial use

In terms of marine resource use, Leang Buida clearly suggests a heightened dependence on inshore fish species at about AD 1000 in the Talaud Islands. However, it should be noted that angling could have been the most important fishing technique in the Talauds where the extent of shallow reef is very limited. High proportions of carnivorous fish species identified as Serranids, Lutjanids and Holocentrids, all of which are captured mainly by angling, confirms this possibility. On the other hand, no fish hooks were recovered from Layer 3 at Leang Buida, which instead yielded a piece of bone-made fish spear and two clay net sinkers, indicating that spear fishing and netting were also actively practised at around AD 1000. This possibility is further supported by the recovery of reef-dwelling omnivorous fish species including Scarids, Diodontids and Acanthurids. The clay net sinkers offer a clear picture on past netting practices in the Talauds and also suggest influence from the north as they have some similarity with the clay and stone net sinkers in the East Asian region dated to AD 500–1200, whereas no evidence of such net sinkers in Eastern Indonesia or the Pacific dated back before AD 1000 has so far been reported.

After around AD 1600, two types of the clay net sinker with more variety in size were used at Leang Buida. Also, evidence for the use of shell-made lure shanks appeared at this time. The remains of fast-swimming pelagic fish species such as tunas (Scombrids) in Layer 2 further support the proposition that the fishing practices after AD 1600 included trolling on the outer reef. Although it is unclear when trolling on the outer reef started in the Talauds, this fishing technique and shell-made lures could reflect influence from the Pacific region, and in particular the Palau Islands in Micronesia, given that a similar type of shell lure shank was produced in Tobi Island after AD 1700, and that the southwest Palau Islands where Tobi is located are the closest Pacific Island group to the Talauds.

Evidence for offshore fishing with trolling lure shanks could date back to 2000 BC in southern Taiwan (e.g. Li 1997, 2002), 1300 BC at early Lapita sites in Melanesia (e.g. Kirch 1997) and possibly from 500 BC in the Marianas (Hung et al. 2011), but no comparable evidence has been found in the northern part of Wallacea including the Talaud Islands and Sulawesi. The reason for this region's widespread absence of fishing gear such as simple one-piece shell-made fish hooks and more complicated two-piece hooks and trolling lures is not yet known, but our finding qualifies as the earliest evidence of fishing with shell-made trolling lures in the Talaud Islands, dating to around AD 1600.

Bukit Tiwing also produced both inshore and pelagic species, including a wide variety of fish species after around AD 1600, which shows a similar pattern to the Leang Buida upper layers. Although the Bukit Tiwing excavation produced no fishing tools and marine faunal remains are more limited at the site, possibly because of its location on a hill side, the high proportions of Lethrinids including *Monotaxis* sp., Lutjanids and Serranids indicate the use of angling.

When the analytical results from both Leang Buida and Bukit Tiwing are combined, it is apparent that basic fishing methods such as angling, netting and spearing were already practised at around AD 1000, but that a wider variety of fishing methods and gear appeared after AD 1600. Lure fishing with shell-made lure shanks appear to be one of the new fishing techniques in the Talauds, as confirmed by the appearance of pelagic fish species in both sites after AD 1600. Capture of sea turtles was also practised after AD 1600.

In terms of shellfish exploitation, a greater variety of species were exploited at Leang Buida than Bukit Tiwing, though the status of Neritidae and Turbinidae as the main exploited families is similar at both sites.[3] A similar pattern of shellfish use is also found at Leang Sarru on Salibabu Island, dating back to 35,000 years ago (Tanudirjo 2005; Ono et al. 2009), indicating that Turbinidae and Neritidae had been the most commonly exploited shells for over 30,000 years up to AD 1800 in the Talaud Islands. Other molluscs recovered in quantity from both Leang Sarru and Leang Buida include Trochidae, Chitonidae and Ellobiidae. On the other hand, some shellfish families such as Cypraenidae, Vasidae and Fissurellidae are common at Leang Buida but not Leang Sarru, and differences like these could be affected by the sites' location and surrounding coastal environment. Temporal changes in shell exploitation are not very clear at either site, although a larger number and variety of shellfish were exploited at Leang Buida after AD 1600.

Turning next to the exploitation of terrestrial resources, we note that our excavation at Leang Buida indicates the introduction and use of goats and pigs by AD 1000. Since no such domesticated animals were recorded at previous excavations of earlier sites in the Talaud Islands, the Leang Buida finds stand as the earliest evidence for the introduction of domesticated animals to the Talauds. In general, the major domesticated animals including pig, dog and chicken were introduced into ISEA and the Pacific after Neolithic times from around 1500–1000 BC. However, no such animal bones were recovered from the single site in the Talaud Islands with Neolithic occupation (Leang Tuwo Mane'e), and so the date for the earliest introduction of domesticated animals into the Talaud group is still unclear.

Bukit Tiwing produced dog bones as well as pig, goat and rat bones dated to after AD 1500. Dogs and rats are also identified in the Talaud faunal record after AD 1500, but possibly introduced to the islands earlier since goats and pigs were already in evidence by at least AD 1000 at Leang Buida. The number of identifications of pig far exceeds any other mammal at Bukit Tiwing, with at least 12 pigs accounted for at the site. Most of the pig mandibles reflect an age at death of less than two years, and it is highly likely that pigs were slaughtered for food. The rats are not yet identified to the family or species level, and it is uncertain whether they were exploited by humans as food or died naturally at the site. Overall, it appears that a greater variety of terrestrial animals appeared after AD 1500 and most of them were exploited by humans for food.

In terms of plant remains, both sites produced nut shells and stone artefacts identified as nut crackers. Canarium nut is nowadays a very popular and common food in the Sangihe-Talaud Islands and elsewhere in North Sulawesi. Our excavation in Leang Buida demonstrates the use of Canarium back to AD 1000, though it could have a longer history of human use and possibly cultivation in the region.

Development of regional maritime networks

When we consider archaeological evidence for the possible development of inter-island maritime networks, earthenware pottery and imported ceramics can be just as important as introduced fauna and botanical remains. In the Talaud Islands, located at the eastern margin of the Sulawesi Sea, most of the excavated trade ceramics are late Ming and Qing wares, and their numbers are limited. So far, the oldest possible ceramics in the Talaud Islands are two thick fragments of stoneware from the lowest layer of Leang Buida dating to around AD 1000. Although the origin and age of these stoneware fragments are as yet unknown, they appear different from Ming and Qing wares or indeed Thai and Vietnamese tradewares, and could be much older as indicated by the associated Carbon-14 dates.

---

3   To be sure, there were more Neritidae than Turbinidae at Leang Buida, but the Neritidae shells are generally small, and so it is clear that the Turbinidae were the more important food source.

Bellwood (1976:266) reported that the top layer of Leang Tuwo Mane'e site produced a small number of Chinese wares dating back to the Tang or Song Dynasty, around 1000 years ago. Tanudirjo's re-excavation of the site also collected a blue-and-white porcelain sherd and a light green celadon sherd from the top layer, but they were too small to be identified. Although no Carbon-14 dates were obtained from this top layer, the dates obtained from Layer 2 (see footnote 1 above) include two dates on charcoal between approximately AD 1400 and 1700, and an older determination on *Turbo* shell, which is unreliable in view of the marine reservoir effect on dates from marine shell. Accordingly, Layer 1 could date to no earlier than the 15th–18th centuries AD, and so it is unclear whether the Tang or Song ceramics reported by Bellwood had been imported to the Talaud Islands at around the time of their manufacture or much later as antique goods. Indeed, these ceramics might date to after the Song Dynasty, because there are no photographs, drawings or detailed descriptions of these excavated trade ceramics in Bellwood (1976).

The only tradewares identified from younger sites including Leang Arandangana (Tanudirjo 2001) and Bukit Tiwing are represented by late Ming to Qing sherds recovered from the upper layers. The numbers of these trade ceramics are much larger than older ceramic types, which might suggest that long-distance maritime trade networks were established at around the late 14th or 15th century in the Talaud Islands. However, Bellwood (1976:282) also collected some possible Tang and Yuan sherds as well as Rarangunusa-style potsherds as surface finds at Leang Timpalo on Sangir Island. We were also shown possible Song and Yuan trade ceramics by local antique dealers during our surveys of Sangir Island. According to them, these ceramics were illegally excavated or collected in the Sangihe Islands. Based on this information, the establishment of long-distance maritime trade networks to the Sangihe Islands possibly dates to around the 13th century.

Turning our review to the eastern coast of Borneo, we observe that the upper layers of the Madai caves, located about 30 km inland from the coast, produced sherds of Ming wares along with a few Thailand and Vietnamese tradewares (Bellwood 1988). Also, the old port site of Bukit Silam on Borneo's eastern coast yielded a large number of trade ceramics along with gold and glass ornaments. The excavated ceramics are mainly Ming wares, supplemented by a minority of Yuan wares, along with Thailand and Vietnamese tradewares (Aoyagi 1992). While no Carbon-14 determinations were obtained, the Bukit Silam site suggests that the eastern coast of Borneo was connected to long-distance maritime trade networks by around the late 13th or 14th century.

Beside the trade ceramics, earthenware pottery motifs and styles can be an indicator of local inter-island interaction. In the Talaud Islands, both Leang Buida and Bukit Tiwing produced Rarangunusa-style potteries after AD 1500, while Leang Buida produced possible prototype Rarangunusa pottery dated to around AD 1000. Leang Arandangana also produced Rarangunusa pottery, possibly after AD 1500 (Tanudirjo 2001). Across the wider area, Rarangunsa-style pottery was also excavated from the De Arce House site in southern Mindanao and possibly dated back to around the 15th century (Solheim et al. 1979:Figure 29b), while the Bungao rockshelter in south-western Mindanao also produced a potsherd with similar decoration (Spoehr 1973:164). Such evidence possibly indicates more frequent contacts between the Talaud Islands and Mindanao after AD 1400. The centre of origin of Rarangunusa pottery is uncertain, but the Talaud sites have produced the largest quantities of this type of pottery so far (Ono et al. 2013).

When we combine the ceramic and earthenware pottery evidence with the archaeological evidence for marine and terrestrial resource exploitation in the Talauds during AD 1000–1800, we concur with Bellwood (1976:283–284) that the Talaud Island inhabitants had connections with surrounding regions including the Sangihe Islands and Mindanao by at least AD 1000, succeeded by more frequent human movement and interactions after AD 1500. However, we can expand on Bellwood's proposed geographical range of connections by suggesting the inclusion of Tobi Island in Palau. Further, the Sangihe-Talaud Islands evidently fell in a gap between Spanish rule affecting the main Philippine islands (including Mindanao) and Islamic influences in the Sulu archipelago to the north, and the commercial and ideological contests in the Moluccas to the south (Watson Andaya 1992), without major change to the nature of Sangihe-Talaud Island society until the 19th century (Bellwood 1976; Henley 2005). It is true that the Portuguese, with their particular interest in Moluccan spices, were sufficiently aware of the Sangihe Islands to record the establishment of its four local chiefdoms by 1521 (Bellwood 1976:284), but the Dutch (who supplanted the Portuguese) did not recognise any particular commercial attractions in the Sangihe-Talaud Islands before establishing their initial presence there in the late 17th century (Ricklefs 2008:75). The Talaud Islands remained free from foreign intervention for many centuries, but this did not prevent their beneficial participation in exchange networks with neighbouring islands, notably the Philippines, as described here. This development of maritime inter-island networks promoted the development of fishing techniques employing a variety of gear and terrestrial resource use including the husbandry of domesticated animals in the Talaud Islands.

Acknowledgements

We would like to acknowledge Lembaga Ilmu Pengetahuan Indonesia, RISTEK and Pusat Arkeologi Nasional Indonesia for their administrative and moral support to our research. We are also greatly indebted to Dr Boony Tooy, the head of Balai Arkeologi Manado, for his kind support and assistance. The research and analysis were funded to Ono by the Japan Society of Promotion for Science (JSPS) 2003–2005, and also 2011–2012.

Author biographies

Rintaro Ono School of Marine Science and Technology, Tokai University, Japan; and Department of Archaeology and Natural History, School of Culture, History and Language, College of Asia and the Pacific, The Australian National University, Canberra, Australia

Sriwigati Manado Archaeology Office, Manado, North Sulawesi, Indonesia

Joko Siswanto Manado Archaeology Office, Manado, North Sulawesi, Indonesia

References

Aoyagi, Y. 1992. Asian trade ceramics in the Philippines: Ninth to Sixteenth Centuries. *Journal of Sophia Asian Studies* 10:144–176.

Bellina, B. 2003. Beads, social change and interaction between India and South-east Asia. *Antiquity* 77(296):285–297. doi.org/10.1017/S0003598X00092279 (accessed 5 June 2018).

Bellwood, P. 1976. Archaeological research in Minahasa and the Talaud Islands, Northeastern Indonesia. *Asian Perspectives* 19(2):240–288.

Bellwood, P. 1980. The Buidane culture of the Talaud Islands, north-eastern Indonesia. *Bulletin of The Indo-Pacific Prehistory Association* 2:69–127.

Bellwood, P. (ed.). 1988. *Archaeological Research in South-Eastern Sabah*. Sabah Museum Monograph 2. Kota Kinabalu: Sabah Museum.

Bellwood, P. 2017. *First Islanders: Prehistory and Human Migration in Island Southeast Asia*. Oxford: Wiley Blackwell. doi.org/10.1002/9781119251583 (accessed 5 June 2018).

Bronk Ramsey, C. 2013. *OxCal 4.2 manual.* c14.arch.ox.ac.uk/oxcal/OxCal.html (accessed 27 October 2018).

Bulbeck, D. 2010. Uneven development in Southwest Sulawesi, Indonesia during the Early Metal Phase. In B. Bellina, E.A. Bacus, T.O. Pryce and J.W. Christie (eds), *50 Years of Archaeology in Southeast Asia: Essays in Honour of Ian Glover*, pp. 153–169. Bangkok: River Books.

Calo, A., B. Prasetyo, P. Bellwood, J.W. Lankton, B. Gratuze, T.O. Pryce, A. Reinecke, V. Leusch, H. Schenk, R. Wood, R.A. Bawono, I.D.K. Gede, N.L.K.C. Yuliati, J. Fenner, C. Reepmeyer, C. Castillo and A.K. Carter. 2015. Sembiran and Pacung on the north coast of Bali: a strategic crossroads for early trans-Asiatic exchange. *Antiquity* 89:378–396. doi.org/10.15184/aqy.2014.45 (accessed 5 June 2018).

Cameron, J. 2005. Spindle whorls. In C.F.W. Higham (ed.), *The Origins of the Civilization of Angkor: The Excavation of Ban Lum Khao*, pp. 211–216. Bangkok: Fine Arts Department.

Cameron, J. 2011. The spinning tools. In C.F.W. Higham and A. Kijngam (eds), *The Origins of the Civilizations of Angkor, Volume Five: The Excavation of Ban Non Wat Part III. The Bronze Age*, pp. 492–500. Bangkok: Fine Arts Department.

Cameron, J. 2013. The spinning tools from Sunget, Anaro and Savidug. In P. Bellwood and E. Dizon (eds), *4000 Years of Migration and Cultural Exchange: The Archaeology of the Batanes Islands, Northern Philippines*, pp. 115–121. Terra Australis 40. Canberra: ANU E Press.

Cameron, J. and A.S.B. Mijares. 2006. Report on an analysis of spindle whorl from Callao Cave, Peñablanca, Northern Luzon Philippines. *Hukay* 9:5–13.

Dussubieux, L. and B. Gratuze. 2010. Glass in Southeast Asia. In B. Bellina, E.A. Bacus, T.O. Pryce and J.W. Christie (eds), *50 Years of Archaeology in Southeast Asia: Essays in Honour of Ian Glover*, pp. 246–259. Bangkok: River Books.

Dye, T. 1983. Fish and fishing on Niuatoputapu, Tonga. *Oceania* 53(3):242–271. doi.org/10.1002/j.1834-4461.1983.tb01983.x (accessed 5 June 2018).

Francis, P. 2002. *Asia's Maritime Bead Trade: 300 B.C. to the Present.* Honolulu: University of Hawai'i Press.

Goto, A. 1986. Prehistoric Ecology and Economy of Fishing in Hawaii: An Ethnoarchaeological Approach. Unpublished PhD thesis, Department of Anthropology, University of Hawai'i, Manoa.

Goto, A. 1990. Prehistoric Hawaiian fishing lore: An integrated approach. *Man and Culture in Oceania* 6:1–34.

Henley, D. 2005. *Fertility, Food and Fever: Population, Economy and Environment in North and Central Sulawesi, 1600–1930.* Leiden: KITLV Press.

Hung, H.-c. and P. Bellwood. 2010. Movement of raw materials and manufactured goods across the South China Sea after 500 BCE: From Taiwan to Thailand, and back. In B. Bellina, E.A. Bacus, T.O. Pryce and J.W. Christie (eds), *50 Years of Archaeology in Southeast Asia: Essays in Honour of Ian Glover*, pp. 235–245. Bangkok: River Books.

Hung, H.-c., M.T. Carson, P. Bellwood, F.Z. Campos, P.J. Piper, E. Dizon, M.J.L.A. Bolunia, M. Oxenham and Z. Chi. 2011. The first settlement of Remote Oceania: The Philippines to the Marianas. *Antiquity* 85(329):909–926. doi.org/10.1017/S0003598X00068393 (accessed 5 June 2018).

Hung, H.-c., K.D. Nguyen, P. Bellwood and M.T. Carson. 2013. Coastal connectivity: Long-term trading networks across the South China Sea. *The Journal of Island and Coastal Archaeology* 8(3):384–404. doi.org/10.1080/15564894.2013.781085 (accessed 5 June 2018).

Intoh, M. and R. Ono. 2006. Reconnaissance archaeological research on Tobi Island, Hatohobei State, Palau. *People and Culture in Oceania* 22:53–82.

Kirch, P.V. 1997. *The Lapita Peoples: Ancestors of the Oceanic World*. Oxford: Blackwell.

Kirch, P.V. and W.R. Dickinson. 1976. Ethno-archaeological investigations in Futuna and Uvea (Western Polynesia): A preliminary report. *The Journal of the Polynesian Society* 85(1):27–69.

Kirch, P.V. and T.S. Dye. 1979. Ethno-archaeology and the development of Polynesian fishing strategies. *The Journal of the Polynesian Society* 88:53–76.

Li, K.C. 1997. Change and Stability in the Dietary System of a Prehistoric Coastal Population in Southern Taiwan. Unpublished PhD thesis, School of Anthropology, Arizona State University, Tucson.

Li, K.C. 2002. Prehistoric marine fishing adaptation in southern Taiwan. *Journal of East Asian Archaeology* 3(1–2):47–74.

Masse, W.B. 1986. A millennium of fishing in the Palau Islands, Micronesia. In A. Anderson (ed.), *Traditional Fishing in the Pacific: Ethnographic and Archaeological Papers from the 15th Pacific Science Congress*, pp. 85–117. Pacific Anthropological Records 37. Honolulu: Bernice P. Bishop Museum.

Masse, W.B. 1989. The Archaeology and Ecology of Fishing in the Belau Islands, Micronesia. Unpublished PhD thesis, Department of Anthropology, Southern Illinois University, Carbondale.

Nakamura, T. 2003. *Calibration of radiocarbon ages for marine samples*. Proceedings of the 16th Symposium on Researches Using the Tandetron AMS System, Nagoya University.

O'Connor, S., R. Ono and C. Clarkson. 2011. Pelagic Fishing at 42,000 Years Before the Present and the Maritime Skills of Modern Humans. *Science* 334(6059):1117–1121. doi.org/10.1126/science.1207703 (accessed 5 June 2018).

Oliver, D.L. 1989. *Oceania: The Native Cultures of Australia and the Pacific Islands*. Honolulu: University of Hawai'i Press.

Ono, R. 2004. *An archaeological and ethno-archaeological Research on Settlement and Subsistence Patterns at Sangihe-Talaud Islands, North Sulawesi Province*. Quarterly report submitted to Lembaga Ilmu Pengetahuan Indonesia, Jakarta.

Ono, R. 2010. Ethno-archaeology and early Austronesian fishing strategies in near-shore environments. *The Journal of the Polynesian Society* 119(3):269–314.

Ono, R. 2011. *Marine Exploitation and Fishing Strategies in Celebes Sea: Area Studies in Maritime Southeast Asia*. Kyoto: Kyoto University Press (in Japanese).

Ono, R., N. Nakajima, H. Nishizawa, S. Oda and S. Soegondho. 2015. Maritime migration and lithic assemblage on the Talaud Islands in northern Wallacea during the Late Pleistocene to the early Holocene. In Y. Kaifu, M. Izuho, T. Goebel, H. Sato and A. Ono (eds), *Emergence and Diversity of Modern Human Behavior in Paleolithic Asia*, pp. 201–213. College Station: Texas A&M University Press.

Ono, R. and S. Soegondho. 2004. A short report for the re-excavation at Leang Sarru site, Talaud Islands. *Jejak-Jejak Arkeologi* 4:37–50.

Ono, R., S. Soegondho and J. Siswanto. 2013. Possible development of regional maritime networks during the 16th to 19th centuries: An excavation report of the Bukit Tiwing site in the Talaud Islands, eastern Indonesia. *People and Culture in Oceania* 29:1–33.

Ono, R., S. Soegondho and M. Yoneda. 2009. Changing marine exploitation during Late Pleistocene in Northern Wallacea: Shell remains from Leang Sarru Rockshelter in Talaud Islands. *Asian Perspectives* 48(2):318–341. doi.org/10.1353/asi.2009.0002 (accessed 5 June 2018).

Piper, P., N. Amano Jr., S. H.-Y. Yang and T. O'Connor. 2013. The terrestrial vertebrate remains. In P. Bellwood and E. Dizon (eds), *4000 Years of Migration and Cultural Exchange: The Archaeology of the Batanes Islands, Northern Philippines*, pp. 169–200. Terra Australis 40. Canberra: ANU E Press. doi.org/10.22459/TA40.12.2013.10 (accessed 5 June 2018).

Ricklefs, M. 2008. *A History of Modern Indonesia since c. 1200*. New York: Palgrave MacMillan.

Riley, J. 2002. Mammals on the Sangihe and Talaud Islands, Indonesia, and the impact of hunting and habitat loss. *Oryx* 36(3):288–296. doi.org/10.1017/S0030605302000510.

Rolett, B.V. 1989. Hanamiai: Changing Subsistence and Ecology in the Prehistory of Tahuata, Marquesas Islands, French Polynesia. Unpublished PhD thesis, Department of Anthropology, Yale University, New Haven.

Samper Carro, S.C., S. O'Connor, J. Louys, S. Hawkins and M. Mahirta. 2016. Human maritime subsistence strategies in the Lesser Sunda Islands during the terminal Pleistocene–early Holocene: New evidence from Alor, Indonesia. *Quaternary International* 416:64–79. doi.org/10.1016/j.quaint. 2015.07.068 (accessed 5 June 2018).

Soegondho, S. 1996. *Penelitian Lepurbakalaan di Desa Aboru, Kacamatan Pulau Haruku, Maluku Utara*. Unpublished report. Ambon: Proyek Penelitian Purbakala Maluku.

Solheim, W.G. II. 2006. *Archaeology and Culture in Southeast Asia: Unraveling the Nusantao*. Quezon City: The University of the Philippines Press.

Solheim, W.G. II, A.M. Legaspi and J.S. Neri. 1979. *Archaeological Survey in Southern Mindanao*. Monograph 8. Manila: National Museum of the Philippines and the University of Hawai'i.

Spoehr, A. 1973. *Zamboanga and Sulu: An Archaeological Approach to Ethnic Diversity*. Ethnology Monographs No. 1. Pittsburgh: University of Pittsburgh.

Szabó, K. 2010. Shell artefacts and shell-working within the Lapita Cultural Complex. *Journal of Pacific Archaeology* 1(2):115–127.

Tanudirjo, D.A. 2001. Islands in Between: Prehistory of the Northeastern Indonesian Archipelago. Unpublished PhD thesis, School of Archaeology and Anthropology, The Australian National University, Canberra.

Tanudirjo, D.A. 2005. Long-continuous or short-occasional occupation? The human use of Leang Sarru rockshelter in the Talaud Islands, northeastern Indonesia. *Bulletin of The Indo-Pacific Prehistory Association* 25(3):15–19.

Watson Andaya, B. 1992. Religious developments in Southeast Asia c. 1500–1800. In N. Tarling (ed.), *The Cambridge History of Southeast Asia: Volume 1, From Early Times to c. 1800*, pp. 508–571. Cambridge: Cambridge University Press.

Yamagata, M., C.H. Bui and K.D. Nguyen (eds). 2013. *The Excavation of Hoa Diem in Central Vietnam*. Showa Women's University Institute of International Culture Bulletin 17. Setagaya, Tokyo: Showa Women's University Institute of International Culture.

Yoneda, M., R. Suzuki, Y. Shibata, M. Morita, T. Sukegawa, N. Shigehara and T. Akazawa. 2004. Isotopic evidence of inland-water fishing by a Jomon population excavated from the Boji site, Nagano, Japan. *Journal of Archaeological Science* 31(1):97–107. doi.org/10.1016/S0305-4403(03)00103-1 (accessed 5 June 2018).

16

Imported tradeware ceramics and their relevance for dating socio-political developments in South Sulawesi, with special reference to the Allangkanangnge ri Latanete site

David Bulbeck, Ian Caldwell, Stephen Druce, Budianto Hakim and Campbell Macknight

Abstract

Imported high-fired ceramics (tradewares) are critical for dating early South Sulawesi historical sites between the 13th/14th and 16th/17th centuries AD. The Allangkanangnge ri Latanete site is of great importance in the South Sulawesi context because of its large tradeware assemblage of more than 2000 sherds and its radiometric chronology that confirms the 13th/14th–16th/17th-century dating assigned by ceramic specialists to the tradeware classes. The site is also of major importance in its local identification with the palace centre of Cina, an early Bugis kingdom. The combined chronological evidence from tradewares and chronometric determinations demonstrates a 14th-century antiquity for the deepest examples of the abundant rice phytoliths recovered from the site. Allangkanangnge ri Latanete exemplifies the major role of rice in the economy of the early Bugis agrarian kingdoms as their subsistence basis and as a source of surplus produce to trade for ceramics and other exotic imports.

Keywords: tradewares, South Sulawesi early history, Allangkanangnge ri Latanete, Cina, Bugis pre-Islamic kingdoms

Introduction

Remarkable quantities of stonewares and porcelains were imported to South Sulawesi throughout the 2nd millennium AD. In an early study, a grand total of 14,611 imported ceramics classified by the local Archaeological Service includes five Tang identifications (AD 618–907), and about 10% of the total identified as Song (AD 960–1279) and 1% as Yuan (AD 1271–1368), with the remainder identified as post-Yuan Chinese, Thai, Vietnamese, Korean, Japanese and European. Possible Tang wares have also been identified in other South Sulawesi contexts, but the much larger volume of identifications of Song wares inspires more confidence in their status as a substantive category of imports (Hadimuljono and

Macknight 1983). Review of the classificatory system applied by the local Archaeological Service, however, suggests that hardly any of the ceramics imported to South Sulawesi are of 12th-century or earlier antiquity, including the early Chinese whitewares and celadon-like monochromes that are best dated to the 13th/14th centuries, and black-on-white 'Jizhou' stoneware jars (Figure 16.1), which may date to as late as the 15th century (Bulbeck 1992).

Figure 16.1: Jizhou sherd recovered during surface survey of the Pattimang Tua site immediately to the northwest of Utti Batue in Luwu.

Source: Photograph by David Bulbeck.

Historical records and archaeological inspections point to the use of large imported urns for burying the cremated remains of the deceased amongst the lowland Bugis of areas including Sawitto, Soppeng, Sengkang and its vicinity, and Bone (Lamuru to Watampone) between the 14th century and the conversion of South Sulawesi lowlanders to Islam in the early 17th century (Bulbeck 1996–97:1035). On the other hand, Makasar and Selayar speakers evidently interred a range of imported ceramics with extended burials in late pre-Islamic times, before turning to the curation of tradewares as cherished household possessions during Islamic times (Hadimuljono and Macknight 1983). A combination of the central Bugis and Makasar/Selayar traditions was followed by the pre-Islamic Luwu Bugis and their Lemolang neighbours, who buried the ashes of the deceased in large jars but also accompanied the departed with a wealth of other ceramics (Caldwell 1994; Bulbeck 1996–97).

The 13th/14th-century dating for the earliest bulk importation of ceramics to South Sulawesi coincides with the zenith of the Majapahit Empire based in Java. The *Desawanana*, a Javanese poem written in 1365, claims four identifiable South Sulawesi places in the list of lands purportedly ruled by Majapahit: Makassar, Bantaeng, Luwu and Selayar (Robson 1995:34). The Makassar, Selayar and (in the vicinity of Utti Batue) Luwu archaeological programs encountered the greatest concentrations of sites with 13th/14th-century ceramics in South Sulawesi (Figure 16.2); these programs aimed to exhaustively document pre-Islamic burial grounds in the study region (Naniek 1983; Wibisono 1985; Bulbeck 1992; Bulbeck and Caldwell 2000). The lighter concentration of these sites recorded during the Bantaeng survey is because its survey methodology relied predominantly on summarising looters' general accounts of the antiques they had unearthed (Bougas 1998). Subsequent research in Bantaeng recovered hundreds of tradewares including sherds from six sites dated to the 13th/14th centuries (no more closely identified; Nayati 2005:Table 6) and Song[1] and Yuan ceramics (Hajramurni 2011); unfortunately, details of the archaeological work have not yet been published. The overall interpretation recommended for Figure 16.2 is that 13th/14th-century ceramics reached widely across the South Sulawesi lowlands.

---

1   Presumably Southern rather than Northern Song.

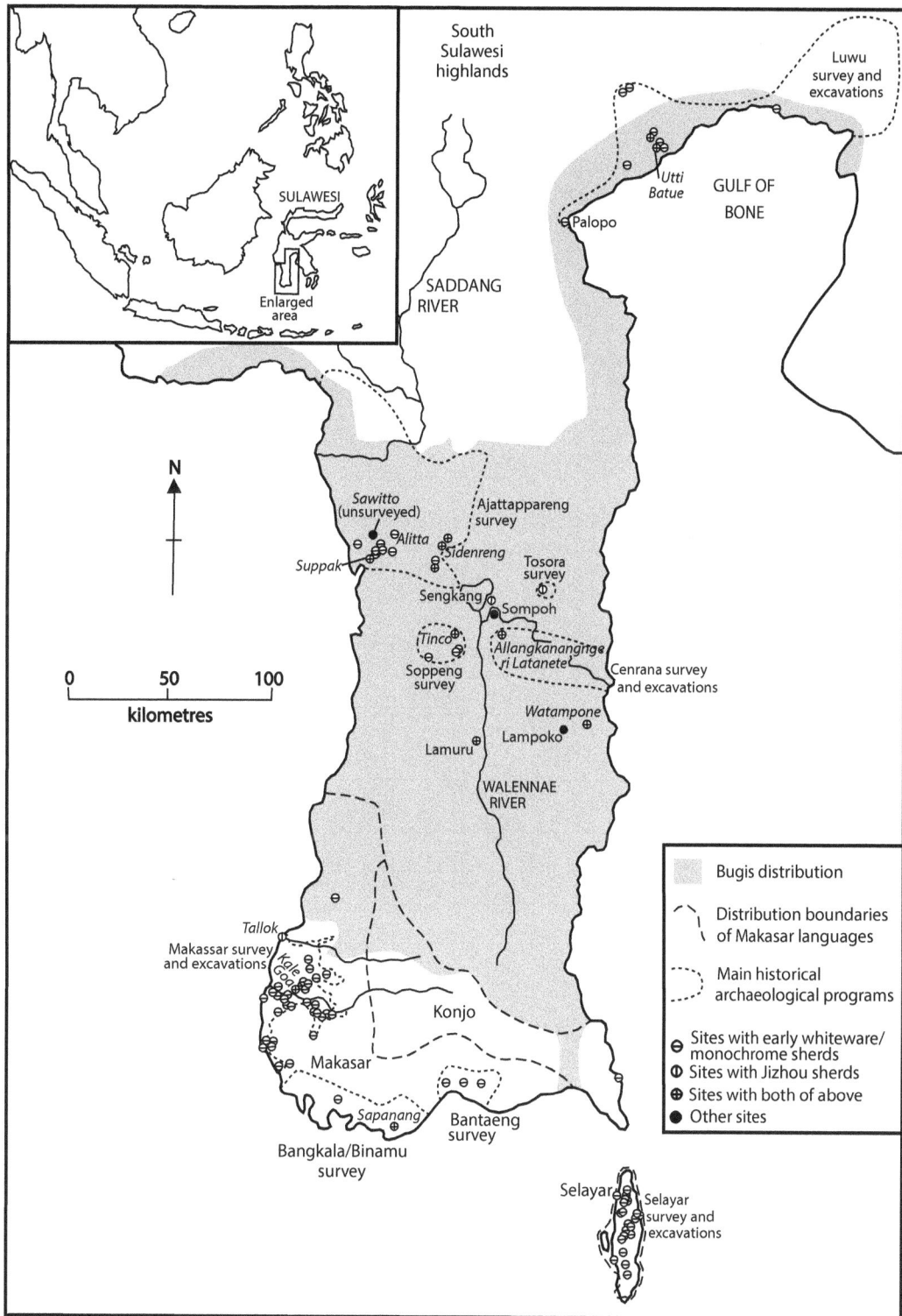

Figure 16.2: South Sulawesi with places discussed in the text (suspected pre-Islamic palace centres italicised) and sites with early whiteware/monochrome and Jizhou sherds.

Sources: Oudheidkundige Dienst in Indonesia (1949:12–13); Naniek (1983); Wibisono (1985); Kallupa et al. (1989); Bulbeck (1992); Bulbeck (1996–97); Bougas (1998); Bulbeck and Caldwell (2000); Caldwell and Bougas (2004); Druce (2009); Bulbeck laboratory notes for Tosora, Sengkang and Lamuru.

Sources on early Bugis history include indigenous texts that derive from the development of a Bugis script at around AD 1400 (Caldwell 1995) and European sources dating from the 16th century. In the 17th century, the main Makasar and Bugis kingdoms initiated a tradition of compiling 'chronicles' that typically covered the kingdom's mythological foundations, the sequence of rulers and their family relationships, and the major achievements and developments associated with particular reigns. Macknight (1983) recognised the value of the chronicle of Bone for its documentation of the expansion of centrally sponsored wet-rice production, after AD 1400, across the coastal belt that constituted the heartland of this Bugis kingdom in later centuries. Kallupa et al. (1989) developed on Macknight's approach through archaeological survey of the major toponyms cited in the origin tradition of the Bugis kingdom of Soppeng. The identifications of the collected tradewares, combined with chronological reckoning of the genealogical records, led Kallupa et al. (1989:83) to propose the establishment of Soppeng as a centralised agrarian kingdom by the 13th century. In a similar vein, identifications of collected tradewares formed the basis for a c. AD 1300 estimate for the origins of concerted wet-rice production in the southern Ajattappareng region (Druce 2009) and in the vicinity of Kale Goa, the heartland of the Makasar-speaking kingdom of Goa (Bulbeck 1992).

A further step in this general research program was undertaken by the Origin of Complex Society in South Sulawesi (OXIS) project (Bulbeck and Caldwell 2000). The OXIS project targeted the legendary origins of Bugis kingship through its investigation of sites associated with the Luwu and Cina polities that figure in the cycle of Bugis stories associated with the name La Galigo. The aim was to resolve the discrepancy between the 11th to 13th century dating for the 'Age of La Galigo', as believed by many scholars of South Sulawesi history (e.g. Zainal Abidin 1974; Pelras 1996), and the lack of solid historical evidence for these polities' existence prior to the 14th century (Caldwell 1988).

The investigation that constitutes the focus of this contribution was carried out in June and July 2005 at Allangkanangnge ri Latanete, 'The Palace Site on the Hill' (hereafter, Allangkanangnge), in the western Cenrana valley. Allangkanangnge is a hilltop site in the village of Sarapao, Kabupaten Wajo, 6 km southeast of the regional capital Sengkang (Figure 16.2). The hill, which rises some metres above the rice fields to its east, forms part of a low molasse ridge that runs north–south through Sengkang. The hill is identified locally as the palace site of Cina, an important kingdom in the La Galigo stories. This cycle, which covers seven generations of a semi-divine ruling family, is believed to contain a collective memory of the early development of complex chiefdoms (Pelras 1996). Cina is portrayed as a large and powerful kingdom that dominated the central rice-growing lands of the South Sulawesi peninsula and controlled trade with the outside world. Indeed, based on their review of the historical and archaeological evidence for the Cenrana valley, Caldwell and Wellen (2017) propose that it can be identified with Uda, the fifth South Sulawesi toponym mentioned in the *Desawanana*, which previously had not been matched to a particular location.

Allangkanangnge survey and surface collections

The Allangkanangnge hill extends approximately 550 m north–south by 400 m east–west (Figure 16.3). Today it is free of permanent dwellings and is planted with vegetables, tobacco, cacao, maize and other cash crops. It includes a raised earth platform of around 1000 m² (35 m x 30 m) on its northeastern shoulder. On this platform are a dozen substantial stone graves, built in a variety of Islamic styles; these are claimed to be the graves of the rulers of Cina. The earth platform is edged with stone retaining walls that appear to be original and largely undisturbed. This platform, which is visited daily by people seeking blessings and favours, was likely the location of the palace from which the hill obtains its name.

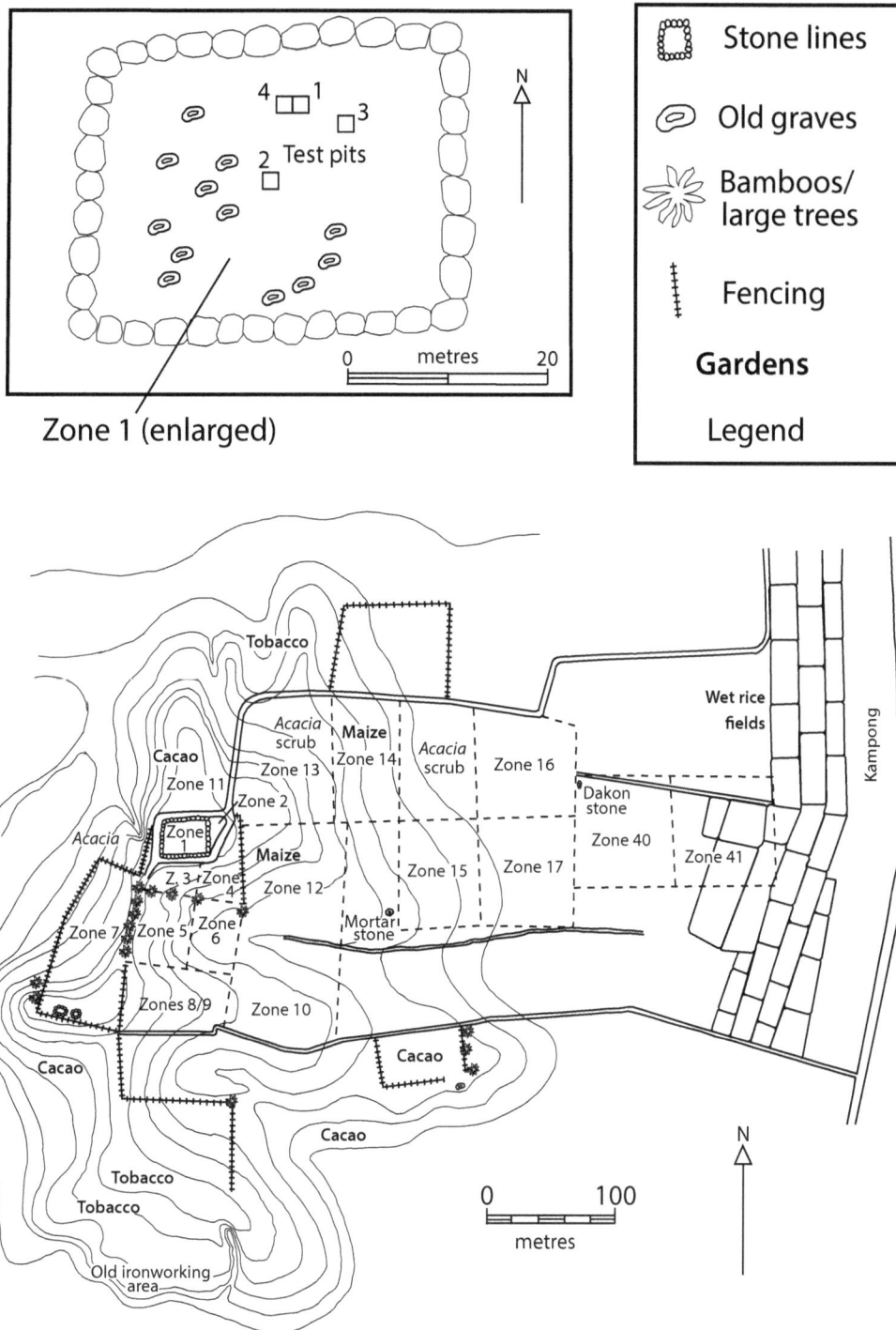

Figure 16.3: Theodolite survey of Allangkanangnge ri Latanete and collection zones (2005).
Source: Pak Mansur, Makassar Archaeology Office.

Early work at the Allangkanangnge site resulted in the recovery of 58 tradeware sherds, which Orsoy de Flines, the ceramics expert working for the Dutch colonial archaeological service, dated to between the 15th and 17th centuries (Bulbeck 1996–97:1047). Later, Kaharuddin (1994) sketched the location of a royal installation stone, stone graves and old wells, and made a surface collection of earthenware and 151 tradeware sherds. Nearly half of the imported ceramics were classified as 'yellow and brown' (Jizhou?) and half of the remainder as 'blue' (blue and white), followed by small percentages of celadons, whitewares, blackwares and brownwares. Kaharuddin further classified 34 of the sherds by vessel form: 11 martavans (large stoneware jars), 10 plates, seven bowls and six jars.

In July 1999, the OXIS project mapped five locales on the hilltop and opened a 1 m x 1 m test pit on the raised earth platform (Bulbeck and Caldwell 2000). Archaeological work was resumed by an international team of researchers over five days in June and July 2005. The hill and flats to the east were mapped using a theodolite and the 1999 excavations were extended (see below).[2] The site was divided into 41 zones, including 19 where surface materials were collected, assisted by the recent clearing of the hill surface for planting crops (Figure 16.3). The available surface collection of tradewares includes 251 collected in 1999 and 1869 collected in 2005, making a total of 2120 sherds (Table 16.1). Several of the earlier classes, notably the *Dehua* and *Qingbai* whiteware classes and the Jizhou class, had long histories of production prior to the earliest examples reaching South Sulawesi (Bulbeck 1992:Appendix B). The ceramic class age estimates used here are taken from Bulbeck and Caldwell (2000).

Table 16.1 and Figure 16.4 show that tradewares of all ages, from the 13th/14th to the 19th/20th centuries, were distributed widely across the site. Around 95% of the sherdage is 17th century or earlier in age and reflects the residential occupation of the site from the 13th century to the mid-17th century. Thereafter, Allangkanangnge appears to have been abandoned, probably as a result of the harrowing of Wajo in 1670 by La Tenritatta, the ruler of Bone (Andaya 1981). The remaining 5% of the collected sherdage reflects the site's subsequent use for dryland gardening and the veneration of ancestral stone graves, notably along the southern ridge (see below).

Table 16.1: Imported ceramics collected from the Allangkanangnge surface in 1999 and 2005.

Ceramic type	Centuries AD	Hilltop summit[a]	Southern ridge[b]	Slopes[c]	Eastern flats[d]	Total
Dehua whiteware	13–14	30	7	28	14	79
Qingbai whiteware	13–14	—	1	2	—	3
Yuan celadon	13–14	2	1	6	—	9
Chinese martavan	13–17	227	227	198	54	706
Yuan overglaze enamelled	14	—	—	1	—	1
Jizhou iron-painted martavan	14–15	19	10	19	5	53
Jizhou iron-painted bowl	14–15	2	—	—	—	2
Yuan/Ming celadon	14–15	3	—	—	—	3
Ming whiteware	14–16	1	2	5	—	8
Vietnamese monochrome	14–16	6	9	21	4	40
Vietnamese martavan	14–17	46	113	76	28	263
Sancai lead-glazed vases	15	2	1	14	—	17
Sukothai plate	15–16	—	—	1	1	2
Vietnamese blue-and-white/overglaze red	15–16	3	2	14	2	21
Sawankhalok celadon/monochrome	15–16	51	43	48	18	160
Thai jar/martavan	15–16	11	3	7	5	26
Ming celadon	15–17	16	13	36	6	71
Sawankhalok black-and-white	16	1	—	1	—	2
Ming blue-and-white	16	44	32	77	56	209

2   Ali Fadillah, then Director of the Makassar Archaeology Office, directed the 1999 survey and excavations, assisted by Ian Caldwell and Budianto Hakim. Ian Caldwell, Steven Druce and Campbell Macknight directed the 2005 survey, and Budianto Hakim directed the 2005 excavations. The imported ceramic sherds were identified by Karaeng Demmanari, a Makassar expert in tradewares, assisted by David Bulbeck. Ceramic textbooks were used to assist the identifications, e.g. Guy (1986) and Harrisson (1990).

Ceramic type	Centuries AD	Hilltop summit[a]	Southern ridge[b]	Slopes[c]	Eastern flats[d]	Total
Ming red/green overglaze enamelled	16	1	2	2	—	5
Ming Swatow	16	5	8	20	6	39
Wanli whiteware/blue-and-white	Late 16–early 17	2	8	2	2	14
Transitional whiteware/blue-and-white	17	5	2	2	—	9
Swatow	17	40	30	88	78	236
Qing blue-and-white	Late 17–19	12	59	23	10	104
Japanese blue-and-white stamped ware	19–20	—	—	4	1	5
Qing celadon	19–20	—	4	1	1	6
European	19–20	3	9	9	5	26
Qing whiteware	20	1	—	—	—	1
Total		533	586	705	296	2120

(a) Upper Locales 1 and 2 (1999) and Zones 1, 2, 3 and 11 (2005).

(b) Locale 4 (1999) and Zones 7–9 (2005).

(c) Lower Locales 1 and 2, Locales 3 and 5 (1999) and Zones 4-6, 10–12, 14-15 (no tradewares in Zone 13) and 18–20 (2005).

(d) Zones 16, 17, and 40–41 (2005).

Source: David Bulbeck's laboratory notes.

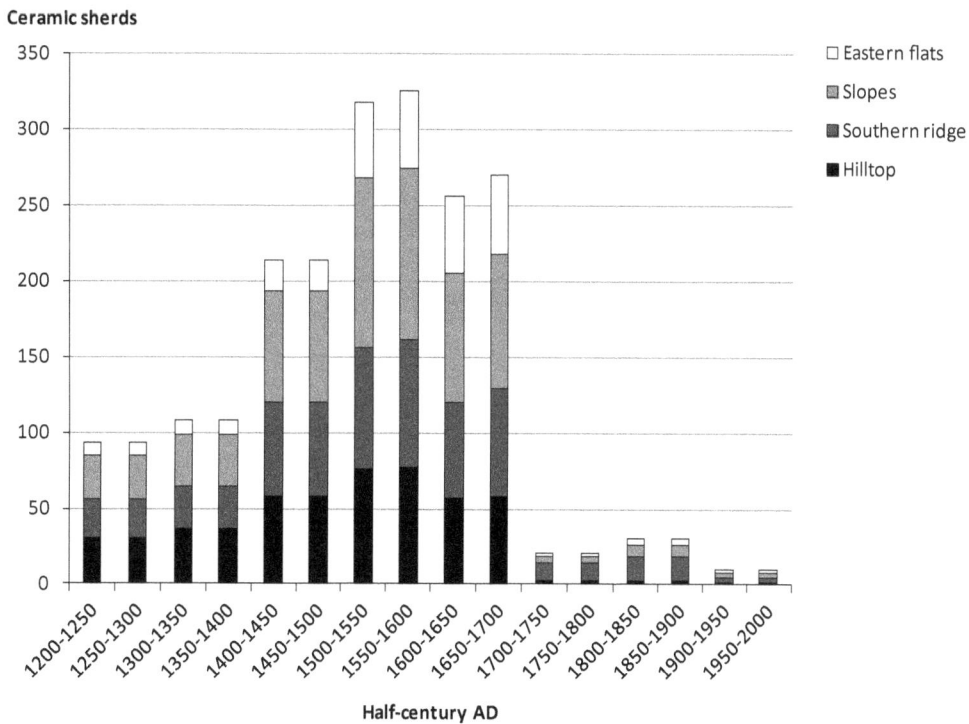

Figure 16.4: Histogram of Allangkanangnge tradeware identifications distributed by half-century AD.
Source: Data from Table 16.1.

Proportionate analysis of the ceramic identifications in terms of their location is presented in Table 16.2. Nearly half of the sherdage (49%) is classified as large martavan jars, with the highest proportion on the hilltop summit (57% of all sherds) and the ridge immediately to its south (60% of all sherds), and the lowest proportion on the eastern flats (31% of all sherds). The distinction between the summit and southern ridge collections lies in the non-martavan identifications. These are earlier for the summit and appreciably younger for the southern ridge (for instance, 6% of the summit collection comprises 13th–14th century non-martavan sherds and just 3% comprises late 17th–20th century non-martavan sherds, compared with 1.5% and 12% respectively for the southern ridge collection). The slope and eastern flats collections are intermediate in this regard, although the eastern flats collection stands out in that nearly half of it dates to between the 16th to early 17th centuries.

Table 16.2: Topographic distribution of the Allangkanangnge tradeware surface collection (%).

Analytical ceramic category	Hilltop summit	Southern ridge	Slopes	Eastern flats	Total
Jizhou martavan	3.9	1.7	2.7	1.7	2.6
Other Chinese martavan (13th–17th centuries)	42.6	38.7	28.1	18.2	33.3
Vietnamese martavan (14th–17th centuries)	8.6	19.3	10.8	9.5	12.4
Thai jar/martavan (15th–16th centuries)	2.1	0.5	1.0	1.7	1.2
Other types 13th–14th centuries	6.0	1.5	5.2	4.7	4.3
Other types 14th–15th centuries	1.9	1.9	3.7	1.4	2.4
Other types 15th–17th centuries	13.5	10.1	16.0	9.1	12.8
Other types 16th to early 17th centuries	18.4	14.0	27.2	48.0	24.2
Other types late 17th–20th centuries	3.0	12.3	5.2	5.7	6.7
Total	100.0	100.0	100.0	100.0	100.0

Note: Percentages may not sum exactly to 100.0% due to rounding.

Source: Compilations of the figures presented in Table 16.1.

Scattered across the southern ridge and in various locations on the lower slopes are some dozens of highly disturbed stone arrangements. Two of the clearer examples were mapped in the southwestern corner of Zone 7 (Figure 16.2), but many examples are now difficult to discern. The pattern of these arrangements is a rectangular platform or enclosure, with a standing stone in the centre. Some of these standing stones are sculpted to show a rudimentary head. These evoke the menhirs at Sompoh and the field of rectangular tumuli at Lampoko, associated with the disturbed remnants of cremated human remains in martavans and with other 15th–17th-century tradeware sherds (van Heekeren 1958:84–85; Bulbeck 1996–97:1035). Thus, the southern ridge appears to have been a zone of concentrated burial of cremated human remains, as recorded widely for lowland Bugis in the South Sulawesi peninsula. This interpretation would explain the high proportion of martavan sherds in the southern ridge collection, as well as its paucity of 13th/14th-century tradeware sherdage (if the main focus of the Bugis tradition of pre-Islamic cremations spanned the 15th and 16th centuries), and its relatively high proportion of Islamic-period tradewares (brought to the graves as offerings to the ancestors).

In summary, while imported sherdage of all types and all ages were found distributed across the site, martavan sherds were most concentrated on the hilltop summit and southern ridge, and the older ceramic classes most concentrated on the hilltop summit.

Site excavation and chronology

Four 1 m² test pits (TP) were excavated on the raised earth platform within the walled area containing old graves (Zone 1). TP1 was placed near the north stone wall, TP2 near the centre of the platform, TP3 towards the east stone wall, and TP4 extended TP1 1 m to the west (Figure 16.3). TP1 had been excavated in 1999 to a depth of around 0.4 m and then backfilled (Bulbeck and Caldwell 2008). This backfill was removed in 2005 and four further spits were excavated to sterile soil at a depth of 0.85 m. The other three test pits were excavated in 10–20 cm spits to sterile soil. A single unit of 40 cm was removed below the lowest spit of TP4 to include a distinctive feature that descended into the sterile soil.

The stratigraphy in each of the test pits included deposit recorded during excavation as dark silty sand in the upper spits and yellowish silty sand in the lower spits.[3] The dark sand contained the denser remains of habitation, whereas the yellow sand extended between deposit with light evidence for occupation higher up and sterile deposit at the base. TP4 was unusual in having a hole filled with black sand at the base of the excavation. All test pits produced one or more tradeware sherds, with their identifications provided in Table 16.3. Their estimated age in relation to stratigraphic depth and radiometrically dated samples (calibrated using Oxcal 4.2; Bronk Ramsey 2016) are illustrated in Figures 16.5–16.8.

Table 16.3: Tradewares excavated from Allangkanangnge.

Ceramic identification	TP1	TP2	TP3	TP4
C11–12 Vietnam/Guangdong brownware	Spit 6	—	—	—
C12–14 'Yueh' olive-greenware	Spit 4 (2)	—	Spit 3	—
C13–14 *Dehua* whiteware	-	—	Spit 3	—
C13–14 Yuan celadon	Spit 6	—	-	—
C14 *Dehua* whiteware	Spit 7	—	-	—
C14–15 *Dehua* whiteware	Spit 5	—	Spit 3	—
C14–15 Ming celadon	Spit 5	—	—	—
C15 Sancai	—	—	Spit 1	—
C15 Ming whiteware	—	—	Spit 2	—
C15 Ming celadon	—	—	Spit 1	Spit 3
C15–16 Sawankhalok *tempayan*	Spit 5	—	—	—
C15–16 Thai coarse brownware *tempayan*	Spit 1	—	—	—
C15–16 Guangdong brownware *tempayan*	Spit 4; Spit 5 (2)	—	—	Spit 3
C15–16 Go Sanh *tempayan*	Spit 4 (2)	—	—	Spit 2
C15–16 Ming celadon	Spits 2, 3, 4	—	—	—
C16 Sawankhalok black-and-white	Spit 2	—	—	—
C16 Ming blue-and-white	-	Spit 1	—	—
C16 Ming Swatow blue-and-white	Spits 1, 2	—	—	—
C16–17 Ming Wanli blue-and-white	Spit 3	—	—	—
C15–17 Guangdong brownware *tempayan*	Surface (2), Spit 1, Spit 3 (3)	—	Spit 1	—
C16–17 Coarse red *tempayan*	—	—	Spit 1	Spit 5

Source: David Bulbeck's laboratory notes.

---

3   Munsell colour readings were taken only for the sediment in Spits 1–6 of TP1, which was consistently very dark grey (Hakim et al., this volume). For consistency's sake, the sediment colours in Figures 16.5–16.8 are field descriptions.

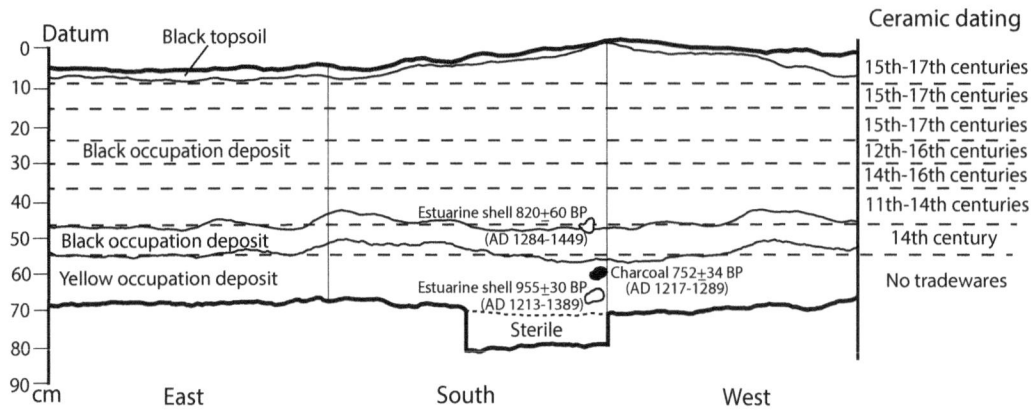

Figure 16.5: East, south and west stratigraphic sections of TP1, Allangkanangnge ri Latanete, with tradeware datings.

The figure is a composite of the 1999 and 2005 excavations. The lower black excavation deposit relates to the resumption of excavation in 2005.

Source: Budianto Hakim's fieldwork records.

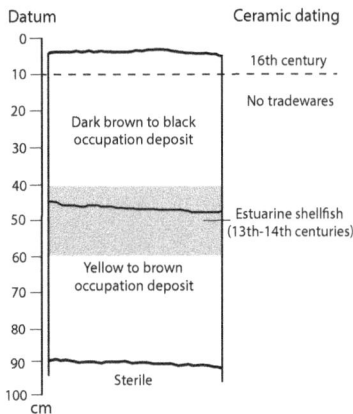

Figure 16.6: Stratigraphic section of northwest wall of TP2, Allangkanangnge ri Latanete, with tradeware dating.

Source: Budianto Hakim's fieldwork records.

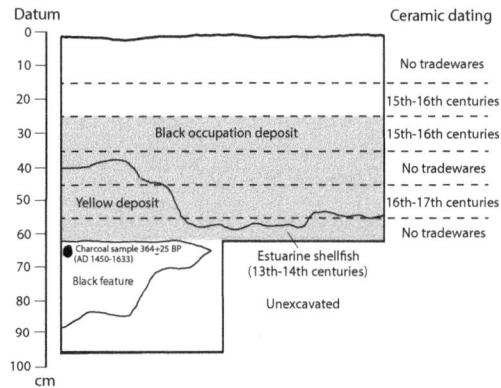

Figure 16.7: Stratigraphic section of west wall of TP3, Allangkanangnge ri Latanete, with tradeware datings.

Source: Budianto Hakim's fieldwork records.

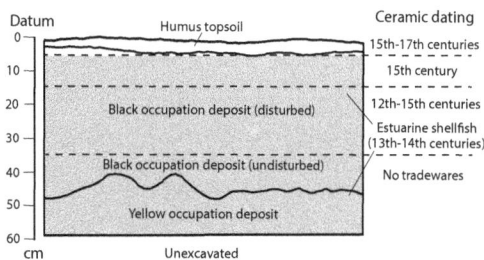

Figure 16.8: Stratigraphic section of west wall of TP4, Allangkanangnge ri Latanete, with tradeware datings.

Source: Budianto Hakim's fieldwork records.

Field records from the 1999 and 2005 excavations of TP1 were combined for analysis and the result is presented here as a single excavation. The most consistent interpretation of depth and age is obtained by focusing on the upper limit of the range of tradeware date estimates (Figure 16.5). This would imply a dating of around the 17th century for Spits 1–3, the 16th century for Spits 4 and 5, and the 14th century for Spits 6 and 7. This chronological interpretation indicates increasing age of the recovered ceramics with increasing stratigraphic depth.

The three radiometrically dated samples support this chronology. After allowing for the marine reservoir effect, the upper estuarine shell sample recovered from the base of Spit 6 and dated to 820±60 BP (ANU-11352) has a median calibrated date in the 14th century. This corresponds to the 14th-century dating for Spits 6 and 7 inferred from the tradewares. The two radiometrically obtained dates from Spit 8, which produced no tradewares, suggest initial occupation in the 13th century: one date spans the 13th–14th centuries and one lies squarely in the 13th century.[4]

The excavation of TP2 produced only a modest quantity of remains (Hakim et al., this volume). Nonetheless, the 16th-century dating for its single tradeware, from Spit 1 (Figure 16.6), is consistent with the inferred dating of the late occupation of the site to the 16th/17th centuries, and with a 13th/14th-century dating for the estuarine shellfish (as indicated by the radiometric dates on the TP1 shellfish) from the interface between the dark and yellow occupation deposit at Spit 4, three spits beneath Spit 1.

TP3 produced a small number of sherds from the top three spits, which include a topsoil layer and a disturbed deposit in the second and third spits. The topsoil and underlying disturbed deposit would be respectively dated to the 17th and 15th centuries, with reference to the upper limit of the range of ceramic datings (Figure 16.7). The presence of estuarine shellfish throughout most of the deposit is consistent with a 13th/14th-century onset of occupation corresponding to the undisturbed deposit at excavated depths beneath 35 cm, and the incorporation of some of these shellfish remains within the overlying disturbed occupation deposit.

TP4 is more problematic in terms of its chronological implications. The simplest interpretation is a 16th-century dating throughout the deposit, including the median calibrated date of the charcoal sample (364±25 BP, Wk-29737) recovered from the black sandy feature towards the base of the excavation. However, there is a suggestion of an inverted stratigraphy in that 13th/14th-century estuarine shellfish (predominantly *Telescopium telescopium*) was recovered throughout much of the deposit that lies above the black sandy feature (Figure 16.8). As discussed elsewhere (Hakim et al., this volume), this stratigraphic inversion would be consistent with the burial of human cremated remains within the black feature to produce the sample submitted for Carbon-14 dating.

An important finding from the 1999 OXIS excavation was the recovery of large numbers of rice phytoliths (approximately 500 to 1700) from each of the 5 g sediment samples in TP1 Spits 1 to 6. The phytoliths reflect the pounding and final winnowing of rice that had been cultivated and harvested elsewhere. It is not possible to say whether the rice was from dryland or wetland fields, but they provide a record of rice cultivation between the 14th and 16th/17th centuries (Bulbeck and Caldwell 2008). Sediment samples were not collected during the 2005 excavations and we are unable to report on phytolith evidence from any of the other excavated spits. We are, however, able to infer occupation at Allangkanangnge by the 13th century.

Imported ceramics analysis

Initial occupation of Allangkanangnge can be securely dated to the 13th century based on the two deepest radiometric dates obtained from TP1 (Figure 16.5). The only suggestion of earlier occupation derives from the c. 12th-century dating proposed for the Vietnam/Guangdong brownware sherd from Spit 6 in TP1 and the 'Yueh' olive-greenware sherds in TP1 and TP3 (Table 16.3). However, there are two reasons why this 12th-century dating should not be taken

---

4   With regard to the radiometrically dated samples of marine shellfish, the upper sample was the *Telescopium telescopium* gastropod and the lower sample was the *Pinctada margaritifera* oyster (Hakim et al., this volume, where the uncertainties of the resulting dates are discussed).

at face value. First, small tradeware sherds can be difficult to identify; second, tradewares may have remained in use long after the time of their manufacture (Fenner and Bulbeck 2013).[5] The c. 13th-century basal dating for a substantial number of Allangkanangnge tradewares (Table 16.1) agrees with the site's earliest radiometric dates, pointing to initial occupation during that century.

Occupation of Allangkanangnge until the 16th/17th centuries is indicated by the most recent of the excavated tradeware sherds (Table 16.3), and by the charcoal date from TP4, even if the sample suffers from stratigraphic inversion (Figure 16.8). The final date for the main period of occupation can be further narrowed to the 17th century based on the 17th-century dating of a large number of sherds from the surface collection (Table 16.1).

The ceramic evidence from Allangkanangnge corresponds with that from Tinco, an early Bugis pre-Islamic palace centre in the Walennae valley. A survey in 1986 yielded a large surface collection of 2180 imported ceramic sherds (Kallupa et al. 1989) and recent work by Hasanuddin (2015) has produced Carbon-14 dates. Both sites now have Carbon-14 dates between the 13th and 16th/17th centuries AD and a corresponding preponderance of 13th/14th–17th-century imported ceramics (Table 16.4). The site of Talaborong in Gowa, with its potentially pre-13th-century date and ceramics dating back to the 12th century, hints at an even earlier onset for the arrival of imported ceramics into South Sulawesi, but may be more prudently interpreted as consistent with the Allangkanangnge/Tinco chronology. This is certainly the case for the Salabu and Pinanto sites in Luwu, whose 15th–17th-century ceramics correspond well with their median 15th–17th-century Carbon-14 dates. In summary, where Carbon-14 determinations can be related to imported ceramics at Allangkanangnge and other South Sulawesi sites, their dating is in good agreement.

Table 16.4: Carbon-14 dates on charcoal and bone from South Sulawesi sites with imported ceramics.

Site	Date	Laboratory code	Dated material	95% calibrated range[a]	Main ceramics dating	Reference(s)
Talaborong, Gowa[b]	920±70 BP	ANU 5924	Burnt bone collected from site surface	AD 720–1392	12th–14th centuries	Bulbeck 1992
Tinco, Soppeng	760±30 BP	Beta-324215	Excavated charcoal	AD 1218–1283	13th/14th–17th centuries	Hasanuddin 2015; Kallupa et al. 1989
Allangkanangnge	752±34 BP	Wk-17818	Excavated charcoal	AD 1217–1289	13th/14th–17th centuries	This paper
Salabu, Luwu	400±60 BP	Wk-7336	Excavated pig tooth	AD 1424–1637	15th–17th centuries	Bulbeck and Caldwell 2000
Pinanto, Luwu	390±90 BP	ANU 11355	Excavated charcoal	AD 1323–1796	15th–17th centuries	Bulbeck and Caldwell 2000
Tinco, Soppeng	380±30 BP	Beta-324216	Excavated charcoal	AD 1440–1630	13th/14th–17th centuries	Hasanuddin 2015; Kallupa et al. 1989
Allangkanangnge	364±25 BP	Wk-29737	Suspected human ashes	AD 1450–1633	13th/14th–17th centuries	This paper
Tinco, Soppeng	320±30 BP	Beta-324217	Excavated charcoal	AD 1481–1644	13th/14th–17th centuries	Hasanuddin 2015; Kallupa et al. 1989

(a) Calibrated using Oxcal 4.2 (Bronk Ramsey 2016).

(b) Recorded during the Makassar survey. The date was obtained from the apatite fraction of the bone, which reduces the date's reliability (Bulbeck, this volume).

---

5   Indeed, the lowest occupation level in TP1, from which the early radiometric dates come, yielded no identifiable tradewares, only earthenwares.

The excavated tradeware sherds from Allangkanangnge include a strong representation of *tempayan* or large stoneware jars (17 of 39 sherds, 44%), mainly from production centres in China or Vietnam (Table 16.3). A similar ratio (1048 of 2120 sherds, 49%) was noted for the surface collection (Table 16.1). Despite dating to a similar time frame, in other ways the excavated and surface assemblages are dissimilar. For instance, Swatow, Ming blue-and-white and Sawankhalok monochromes, the three most frequent non-*tempayan* classes from the surface collection, are represented by none, or at most one, of the excavated sherds. One reason for this discrepancy may be the small size of the excavated assemblage, compared to the much larger (and hence more reliable) sample obtained during the surface survey.

Two remarkable features of the Allangkanangnge tradewares are the high frequencies of early whitewares and Jizhou iron-painted wares, coupled with relatively low concentrations of early monochromes and 16th-century Chinese blue-and-white sherds. Table 16.5 shows that, in the context of all surveyed Bugis sites known to the authors, 53% of early whitewares and 64% of Jizhou sherds were obtained at Allangkanangnge, compared with just 7% of early monochromes and 16th-century Chinese blue-and-white. Allangkanangnge's high proportion of early whitewares may be attributed to the importance of Cina as an early Bugis kingdom (Bulbeck and Caldwell 2000), while its high proportion of Jizhou sherds reflects the frequent association of Jizhou wares with pre-Islamic palace centres (Caldwell and Bougas 2004). In terms of relatively high proportions of pre-Ming compared to 16th-century sherdage, the only other potentially comparable collection from a Bugis site is a small collection from Watampone (the historical capital of the major Bugis kingdom of Bone) studied by Orsoy de Flines (Table 16.5). Based on age estimates from the Bugis chronicle of Bone, its first rulers would date to the 14th century (Macknight and Mukhlis n.d.; Bulbeck 1992:Figure 13-13); regrettably, the archaeological circumstances of the Watampone sherd collection and how it may relate to the establishment of Bone are unknown.

Table 16.5: Comparison of selected Allangkanangnge tradeware classes with other Bugis collections.

Site/s	Early white-wares[a]	Early mono-chromes[b]	Jizhou	16th-century Ming[c]
Allangkanangnge[d]	84	13	55	256
Other Cenrana suspected palace centres[e]	0	0	0	142
Tosora/Sengkang[f]	0	0	2	39
Watampone[f]	9	13	2	1
Other Bone sites[f]	0	2	1	92
Utti Batue suspected palace centre[e]	1	0	3	271
Palopo tumuli[f]	0	2	0	12
Other Luwu Bugis sites[e]	10	4	6	94
Tinco palace centre[g]	13	79	3	284
Other Soppeng sites[g]	3	18	0	153
Sidrap suspected palace centres[h]	13	10	5	781
Other Sidrap sites[h]	25	39	9	1525
Total Bugis sites	158	180	86	3650
Percentages				
Allangkanangnge	53.2	7.2	64.0	7.0
Other Cenrana suspected palace centres	0.0	0.0	0.0	3.9
Tosora/Sengkang	0.0	0.0	2.3	1.1
Watampone	5.7	7.2	2.3	0.3
Other Bone sites	0.0	1.1	1.2	2.5
Utti Batue suspected palace centre	0.6	0.0	3.5	7.4

Site/s	Early white-wares[a]	Early mono-chromes[b]	Jizhou	16th-century Ming[c]
Palopo tumuli	0.0	1.1	0.0	0.3
Other Luwu Bugis sites	6.3	2.2	7.0	2.6
Tinco suspected palace centre	8.2	43.9	3.5	7.8
Other Soppeng sites	1.9	10.0	0.0	4.2
Sidrap suspected palace centres	8.2	5.6	5.8	21.4
Other Sidrap sites	15.8	21.7	10.5	41.8
Total Bugis sites	100.0	100.0	100.0	100.0

(a) Includes *Dehua* and *Qingbai* whitewares.

(b) Includes 'Yueh' olive-greenwares and Yuan celadons.

(c) Includes Ming blue-and-white, Ming overglaze enamelled and Ming Swatow (combined).

(d) Tables 16.1 and 16.3 (this paper).

(e) Bulbeck and Caldwell (2000).

(f) Oudheidkundige Dienst in Indonesia (1949:12–13); Bulbeck (1996–97).

(g) Kallupa et al. (1989).

(h) Druce (2009); suspected palace centres include Suppak pre-Islamic centre/Makaraié/Indok Lompoa, Watang Sidenreng and Alitta.

Table 16.5 also provides a context for interpreting the histogram of tradeware datings in Figure 16.3. As documented by Kallupa et al. (1989) for Soppeng, and Bulbeck (1992) for Makassar, the available quantities of imported ceramics in South Sulawesi evidently increased continuously from the 13th/14th centuries to the 17th century, which would offer a sufficient explanation for the increase over time in the tradewares recorded for Allangkanangnge during its pre-Islamic period. That is, Figure 16.3 suggests continual occupation of at an intensive level throughout the 13th (or 14th) to 16th centuries, followed by a 17th-century decline.

Historical interpretation

The sherdage from Allangkanangnge provides clear, unequivocal evidence that the process of social complexification (state formation) in Bugis-speaking areas of South Sulawesi was underway by the 13th century AD. This process was closely linked to the availability of foreign prestige goods, of which sherds of Chinese and Southeast Asian ceramics have persisted in the archaeological records. The bulk of the exotic imports at Allangkanangnge would likely have been cloth, including Gujarati blockprint cloths, of which there are several examples from South Sulawesi highlands dated to the 14th–16th centuries (Guy 1998). Bulbeck and Caldwell (2000) have argued that trade and agriculture were two sides of the same economic coin, and that the development of complex society in South Sulawesi was a continuous process from the 13th century onwards. The two-stage 'Age of La Galigo' model of early trade-based kingdoms and post-1400 agricultural kingdoms proposed by Pelras (1996) finds no support in the historical or archaeological record. Neither does his suggestion of an intervening 'Age of Chaos' as one political economy replaced another.

The control of prestige goods imported from Java and Sumatra, and perhaps through the southern Philippines as well, and paid for by the export of rice to the Moluccas and Malacca, drove the development of Bugis political hierarchies in the 13th–17th centuries. The first driving force was symbolic, in that luxury or prestige goods articulated and promoted social hierarchy and political control. The second was the means by which these goods were paid for: with its relatively small population and extensive fertile lowlands, South Sulawesi has in most years produced more rice than its inhabitants can consume (Caldwell and Bougas 2004). When the Dutch admiral

Cornelis Speelman sailed into the harbour at Bantaeng in 1667, he seized 800 tons of rice laden on ships for export to other parts of the archipelago (Andaya 1981:78); even today, South Sulawesi is a net exporter of rice (Hajramurni 2015). The numerous rice phytoliths recovered from TP1 in 1999 shows that rice cultivation was established at or near Allangkanangnge from the 14th century onwards.

Estuarine shell dating from 13th/14th century was recovered from all of the test pits, implying that the coast then lay considerably closer to Allangkanangnge than is currently the case (Hakim et al., this volume). Allangkanangnge lay on a hill overlooking a shallow valley leading to the Cenrana River, providing access to the central South Sulawesi lowlands and the coast. The valley has a flat alluvial floor, and the northern end, which abuts the Cenrana River, floods regularly in the wet season. It is possible that the valley floor as far as Allangkanangnge was once flooded, which would have made the hill an ideal location to control both the trade of imported goods into the central Bugis lowlands in return for surplus rice cultivation (Kallupa et al. 1989). Excavations around the swamps on the northern side of the Cenrana river (Nur and Hakim 2010) also indicate early wet-rice cultivation. Providing enough rice could be harvested to generate a surplus as well as meet local demand, the trade of exotic prestige goods in return for exported rice would have been lucrative for a controlling elite. The retreat of the sea, as measured by retreating estuarine influences (Gremmen 1990) could have been caused by a combination of tectonic uplift, falling sea levels during the Little Ice Age, and the accumulation of riverine silts from agriculture as lowlands and hill slopes were cleared for agriculture. These silts would over time have improved the fertility of the soils surrounding Allangkanangnge and encouraged rice production. The stratigraphically secure 14th-century dating for the deepest rice phytoliths documented for Allangkanangnge is the oldest direct evidence for intensive rice cultivation in South Sulawesi. However, it seems probable that rice was cultivated at Allangkanangnge from initial occupation in the 13th century onwards.

Conclusions

Research on the historical archaeology of South Sulawesi's pre-Islamic polities (e.g. Kallupa et al. 1989; Bulbeck 1992; Bulbeck and Caldwell 2000; Druce 2009) has relied primarily on tradeware identifications for dating the recorded sites. Recent excavations at the Bugis palace centres of Allangkanangnge and Tinco have produced Carbon-14 determinations that match the 13th/14th–16th/17th-century dating for the bulk of the imported ceramics documented at these sites and, by extrapolation, confirm the tradeware identifications proposed for other historical sites in South Sulawesi. Allangkanangnge is of particular interest for its large assemblages of early Chinese whitewares and cream and brown Jizhou jars, especially the latter, which are predominantly associated with pre-Islamic palace centres. This site is of major importance for understanding political developments during South Sulawesi's pre-Islamic period, including the role of rice production as an economic and political staple.

Acknowledgements

The Australian Research Council funded the 1999 fieldwork by OXIS at the Allangkanangnge site and paid for one of the radiocarbon dates. The British Academy funded the 2005 fieldwork season at the site. The Centre for Archaeological Research (The Australian National University) funded two of the radiocarbon dates, and the University of Hull paid for one radiocarbon date. The Australia-Indonesia Institute funded the laboratory work on the surveyed and excavated remains. The reviews by two anonymous referees are gratefully acknowledged.

Author biographies

David Bulbeck Department of Archaeology and Natural History, School of Culture, History and Language, College of Asia and the Pacific, The Australian National University, Canberra, Australia

Ian Caldwell Archaeological Studies Program, University of the Philippines Diliman, Republic of the Philippines

Stephen Druce Academy of Brunei Studies, Universiti Brunei Darussalam, Brunei Darussalam

Budianto Hakim Makassar Archaeology Office, Makassar, South Sulawesi, Indonesia

Campbell Macknight College of Asia and the Pacific, The Australian National University, Canberra, Australia

References

Andaya, L.Y. 1981. *The Heritage of Arung Palakka: A History of South Sulawesi (Celebes) in the Seventeenth Century*. Verhandelingen van het Koninklijk Instituut voor Taal-, Land- en Volkenkunde 91. The Hague: Martinus Nijhoff.

Bougas, W.A. 1998. Bantayan: An early Makassarese kingdom, 1200-1600 AD. *Archipel* 55(1):83–123. doi.org/10.3406/arch.1998.3444 (accessed 5 June 2018).

Bronk Ramsey, C. 2013. *OxCal 4.2 manual*. c14.arch.ox.ac.uk/oxcal/OxCal.html (accessed 27 October 2018).

Bulbeck, F.D. 1992. A Tale of Two Kingdoms: The Historical Archaeology of Gowa and Tallok, South Sulawesi, Indonesia. Unpublished PhD thesis, School of Archaeology and Anthropology, The Australian National University, Canberra. www.oxis.org/theses/bulbeck-1992.pdf (accessed 5 June 2018).

Bulbeck, D. 1996–97. The Bronze-Iron Age of South Sulawesi, Indonesia: Mortuary traditions, metallurgy and trade. In D. Bulbeck and N. Barnard (eds), *Ancient Chinese and Southeast Asian Bronze Age Cultures, Vol. II*, pp. 1007–1076. Taipei: Southern Materials Center Inc.

Bulbeck, D. 2018. Holocene site occupancy in Sulawesi. In S. O'Connor, D. Bulbeck and J. Meyer (eds), *The Archaeology of Sulawesi: Current Research on the Pleistocene to the Historic Period*, pp. 93–116. Canberra: ANU Press.

Bulbeck, D. and I. Caldwell. 2000. *Land of Iron: The Historical Archaeology of Luwu and the Cenrana Valley. Results of the Origin of Complex Society in South Sulawesi Project (OXIS)*. Hull: Centre for South-East Asian Studies, University of Hull. www.oxis.org/books/land-of-iron.pdf (accessed 5 June 2018).

Bulbeck, D. and I. Caldwell. 2008. *Oryza sativa* and the origins of kingdoms in South Sulawesi, Indonesia: Evidence from rice husk phytoliths. *Indonesia and the Malay World* 36(104):1–20. doi.org/10.1080/13639810802016117 (accessed 5 June 2018).

Caldwell, I. 1988. South Sulawesi A.D. 1300–1600: Ten Bugis Texts. Unpublished PhD thesis, Department of History, The Australian National University, Canberra. www.oxis.org/theses/caldwell-1988.pdf (accessed 5 June 2018).

Caldwell, I. 1994. A report on fieldwork in Luwu with Bahru Kallupa and Iwan Sumantri in August 1994. *Baruga* 10:9–10.

Caldwell, I. 1995. Power, state and society among the pre-Islamic Bugis. *Bijdragen tot de Taal-, Land- en Volkenkunde* 151(3):394-421. doi.org/10.1163/22134379-90003038 (accessed 5 June 2018).

Caldwell, I. and W.A. Bougas. 2004. The early history of Binamu and Bangkala, South Sulawesi. *Bijdragen tot de Taal-, Land- en Volkenkunde* 160(4):456–510. doi.org/10.1163/22134379-90003720 (accessed 5 June 2018).

Caldwell, I. and K. Wellen. 2017. Finding Cina: A new paradigm for early Bugis history. *Bijdragen tot de Taal-, Land- en Volkenkunde* 173(2/3):296–324. doi.org/10.1163/22134379-17302004 (accessed 5 June 2018).

Druce, S.C. 2009. *The Lands West of the Lakes: A History of the Ajattappareng Kingdoms of South Sulawesi, 1200 to 1600 CE*. Verhandelingen van het Koninklijk Instituut voor Taal-, Land- en Volkenkunde 261. Leiden: Martinus Nijhoff. doi.org/10.1163/9789004253827 (accessed 5 June 2018).

Fenner, J.N. and D. Bulbeck. 2013. Two clocks: A comparison of ceramic and radiocarbon dates at Macapainara, East Timor. *Asian Perspectives* 52(1):143–156. doi.org/10.1353/asi.2013.0005 (accessed 5 June 2018).

Gremmen, W.H.E. 1990. Palynological investigations in the Danau Tempe depression, southwest Sulawesi (Celebes), Indonesia. *Modern Quaternary Research in Southeast Asia*, pp. 123–134. Modern Quaternary Research in Southeast Asia, Volume 11. Rotterdam: A.A. Balkema.

Guy, J. 1986. *Oriental Trade Ceramics in South-East Asia, Ninth to Sixteenth Centuries*. Oxford: Oxford University Press.

Guy, J. 1998. *Woven Cargoes: Indian Textiles in the East*. London: Thames and Hudson.

Hadimuljono and C.C. Macknight. 1983. Imported ceramics in South Sulawesi. *Review of Indonesian and Malaysian Affairs* 17:66–91.

Hajramurni, A. 2011. Hundreds of artifacts unearthed in S. Sulawesi. *The Jakarta Post*, 4 April. www.pressreader.com/indonesia/the-jakarta-post/20110401/281621006867797 (accessed 24 December 2017).

Hajramurni, A. 2015. South Sulawesi hopes to export surplus rice production. *The Jakarta Post*, 23 January. www.thejakartapost.com/news/2015/01/23/south-sulawesi-hopes-export-surplus-rice-production.html (accessed 24 December 2017).

Hakim, B., S. Hawkins, D. Bulbeck, I. Caldwell, S. Druce and C. Macknight. 2018. Material culture at Allangkanangnge ri Latanete in relation to the origins of Bugis kingdoms. In S. O'Connor, D. Bulbeck and J. Meyer (eds), *The Archaeology of Sulawesi: Current Research on the Pleistocene to the Historic Period*, pp. 287–312. Canberra: ANU Press.

Harrisson, B.V. 1990. *Pusaka: Heirloom Jars of Borneo*. Singapore: Oxford University Press.

Hasanuddin. 2015. Kebudayaan Megalitik di Sulawesi Selatan dan Hubungannya dengan Asia Tenggara. Unpublished PhD thesis, Centre for Archaeological Research Malaysia, Universiti Sains Malaysia, Kuala Lumpur. www.oxis.org/theses/hasanuddin-2015.pdf (accessed 5 June 2018).

Kaharuddin. 1994. Permukiman Kuno Allangkanangnge ri Latanete Kecamatan Pammana Kabupaten Wajo. Unpublished Bachelor of Arts thesis, Hasanuddin University, Makassar.

Kallupa, B., D. Bulbeck, I. Caldwell, I. Sumantri and K. Demmanari. 1989. *Survey Pusat Kerajaan Soppeng 1100-1986 [Survey of the Capital of Soppeng Kingdom 1100–1986]*. Final Report to the Australian Myer Foundation, Privately published in Canberra, ACT. www.oxis.org/books/soppeng-1986.pdf (accessed 5 June 2018).

Macknight, C.C. 1983. The rise of agriculture in South Sulawesi before 1600. *Review of Indonesian and Malaysian Affairs* 17:92–116.

Macknight, C.C. and P. Mukhlis. n.d. The Chronicle of Bone. Unpublished typescript.

Naniek, H.M.T. 1983. *Ceramics from Selayar: A preliminary study.* SPAFA Final Report, Workshop to Standardize Studies of Ceramics of East and Southeast Asia, pp. 75–92, Southeast Asian Ministers of Education, Project in Archaeology and Fine Arts, Cebu City, Philippines.

Nayati, W. 2005. Social Dynamics and Local Trading Patterns in the Bantaeng Region, South Sulawesi (Indonesia) circa 17th Century. Unpublished PhD thesis, The Southeast Asian Studies Programme, National University of Singapore, Singapore. www.oxis.org/theses/widiya-nayati-2005.pdf (accessed 5 June 2018).

Nur, M. and B. Hakim. 2010. Telaah awal tembikar Wajo. *Walennae* 12(2):189–194.

Oudheidkundige Dienst in Indonesia. 1949. *Oudheidkundig Verslag 1948.* Bandung: A.C. Nix & Co.

Pelras, C. 1996. *The Bugis.* Oxford: Basil Blackwell.

Robson, S. (translator). 1995. *Désawanana (Nagarakrtagamana) by Mpu Prapañca.* Leiden: KITLV Press.

van Heekeren, H.R. 1958. *The Bronze-Iron Age of Indonesia.* Verhandelingen van het Koninklijk Instituut voor Taal-, Land- en Volkenkunde 22. The Hague: Martinus Nijhoff.

Wibisono, C.S. 1985. *Sebaran situs kubur sebagai studi awal pola pemukiman di Pulau Selayar.* Rapat Evaluasi Hasil Penelitian Arkeologi II, pp. 370–383, Pusat Penelitian Arkeologi Nasional, Jakarta.

Zainal Abidin, A. 1974. The I La Galigo epic cycle of South Celebes and its diffusion. *Indonesia* 17:160–169. doi.org/10.2307/3350778 (accessed 5 June 2018).

17

Material culture at Allangkanangnge ri Latanete in relation to the origins of Bugis kingdoms

Budianto Hakim, Stuart Hawkins, David Bulbeck, Ian Caldwell, Stephen Druce and Campbell Macknight

Abstract

The early historical South Sulawesi site Allangkanangnge ri Latanete is reputed to be the location of the palace of the legendary Bugis kingdom of Cina. This vanished kingdom arose in the 13th century AD and disappeared in the 16th century. The Allangkanangnge ri Latanete site is dated to between the 13th and 17th centuries based on Carbon-14 determinations and imported stoneware and porcelain sherds recovered through survey and excavation. The material cultural remains excavated at the site are dominated by earthenware sherds: their frequencies indicate light occupation during the 13th century, a main period of habitation between the 14th and 16th centuries, and a decline during the 17th century. Excavated earthenware vessel forms reflect a range of functions including food preparation and storage. There is evidence of ironworking from iron slag debris, earthenware sherds identified as crucibles rims and local oral history. The excavated area near the summit of the hill is characterised by old Islamic graves, said to be those of the rulers of Cina. However, there is no evidence here for burials older than the 16th century; in earlier centuries, the area on the summit, which is protected by a low stone wall, may have been the location of a wooden palace. Some dozens of stone arrangements scattered over the eastern slope may possibly be associated with marking the burials of cremated remains in jars. The site displays a partially coastal orientation, both in terms of physical proximity and subsistence debris during the 13th and 14th centuries followed by a greater focus on wet-rice production during the 14th to 17th centuries.

Keywords: Allangkanangnge ri Latanete, Cina, Wajo, Bugis kingdoms, pre-Islamic history

Introduction

This article sets out a descriptive analysis of elite Bugis pre-Islamic material culture from the remains obtained through survey and excavation of the hilltop site of Allangkanangnge ri Latanete in the village of Sarapao, 6 km southeast of the regional capital of Sengkang in Wajo, South Sulawesi (Figure 17.1). This hilltop (hereafter, Allangkanangnge) is believed by local people to have been the palace site of Cina, one of the oldest kingdoms in South Sulawesi (Bulbeck and Caldwell 2000). Cina is also an important kingdom in the stories known as the La Galigo cycle.

The date of these stories and the extent to which they reflect a memory of real events have been much debated (Pelras 1996; Nurhayati et al. 2003). The kingdom is rarely mentioned by name in Bugis chronicles, the sources of which date back to around 1400. Instead, the term 'Galigo' is used to refer to a period before the rise of the historical kingdoms.

Caldwell and Wellen (2017) have shown that Cina can be traced in genealogical sources from a group of three settlements in the western Cenrana Valley around 1300 to a peninsula-wide power in the 14th and 15th centuries. During the latter century, Cina founded at least two new palace centres at Baringeng in Soppeng and Amali in Bone. In the 16th century, Cina was attacked by Wajo, which seized its northern lands, and was later attacked in the east by Soppeng and in the south by Bone. By 1600, it had been dissolved and its ruling family vanquished, except for a branch in Luwu. As the origin story of Soppeng puts it, 'Those whose ancestry could be traced to the age of Galigo were no more' (Caldwell 1988:109). It is clear from the 'Chronicle of Bone', however, that Cina was remembered by successor kingdoms as the source of political order and diplomacy. The chronicle states that 'the earlier kings who went back to Galigo had already organized [the conduct of] negotiations as well as of giving orders' (Caldwell and Wellen 2017:310).

Despite its apparent importance in the emergence of stratified society, it is difficult to envisage Cina as a centralised kingdom of the type familiar to 16th- and 17th-century European visitors. According to Bugis genealogies, Cina's lands stretched across the central peninsula, encompassing both lowland and highland areas, making it approximately the combined size of the three kingdoms—Wajo, Soppeng and Bone—that succeeded it (Figure 17.1). These kingdoms used highland areas as boundaries: La Ummasak, a mid to late 15th-century ruler of Bone, is recorded in the 'Chronicle of Bone' as having entered into treaties with hill chiefdoms instead of conquering them (Macknight and Mukhlis n.d.).

Only an echo of an apparently once powerful kingdom of Cina can be found in Bugis historical records. The most important source is a collection of nine related genealogies that record the relationships of a large elite group associated with Cina, and the names of places where they married and ruled. Other than these genealogies, there is little apart from an apocryphal tradition that Cina's name was changed to Pammana at the request of a late 16th-century ruler (Zainal Abidin 1983). Considering that the historical sources on Cina are almost all genealogical, it might be sensible to consider the kingdom of Cina as a reference to an extended, elite family that ruled at places across the central peninsula before about 1500 (Caldwell and Wellen 2017:316).[1] The legitimising claim of this elite to rule was descent from an archetypal, heavenly ancestor (*to manurung*), Simpurusia, who descended at Lompo near Sengkang. Following this line of argument, 'Cina' is perhaps best interpreted as a metaphor for an age comprising the 13th to 15th centuries, as well as an actual kingdom of this name.

---

1   Caldwell (1988:171) sets out evidence that writing in the Bugis script was developed around 1400. Caldwell and Wellen (2016) have argued that for the first 200 years writing was used simply for recording elite genealogies, and perhaps the occasional treaty.

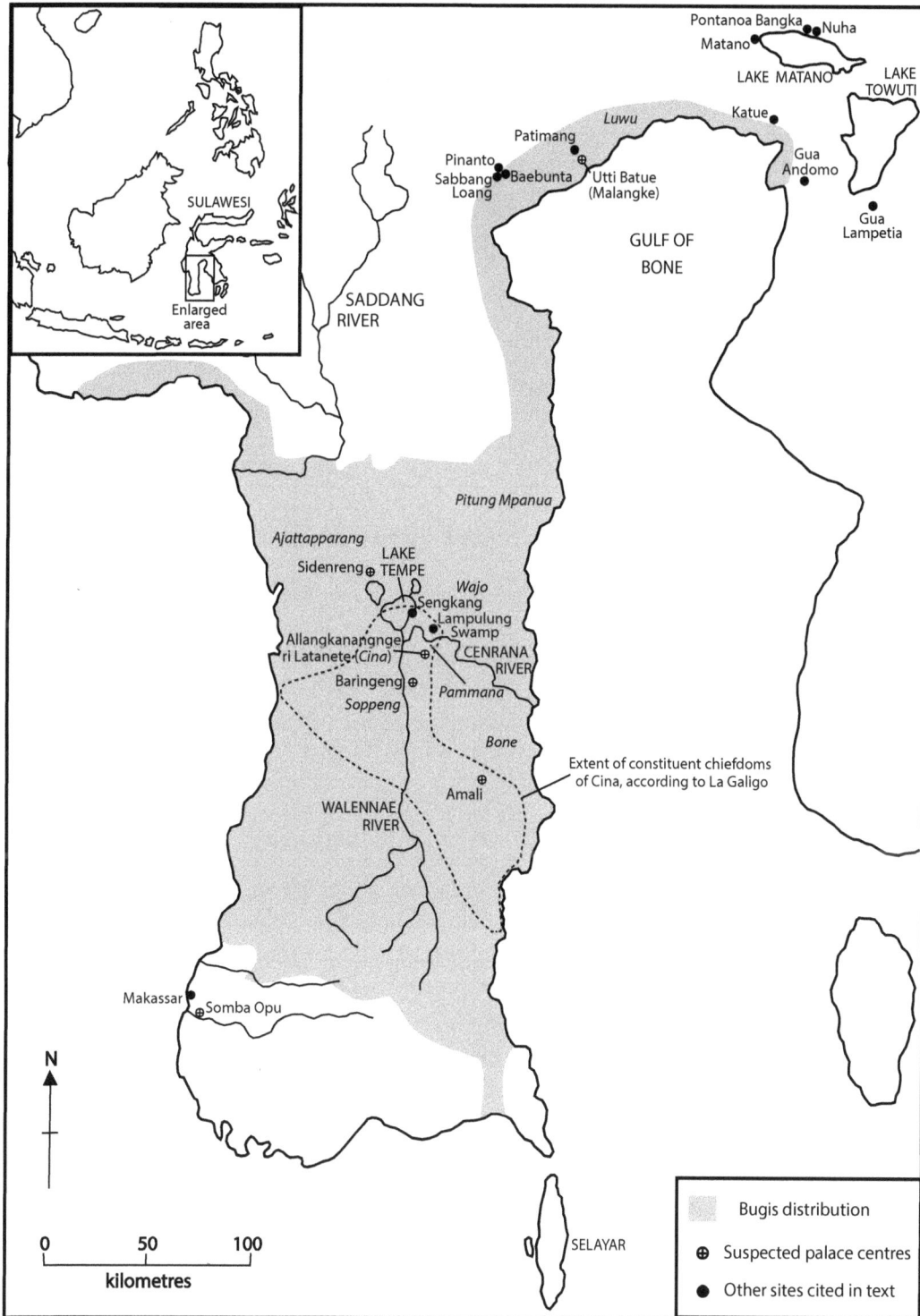

Figure 17.1: Southern Sulawesi with kingdoms and locations mentioned in the text.

Sources: Gremmen (1990); Bulbeck and Caldwell (2000); Bulbeck et al. (2016); Caldwell and Wellen (2017); Bulbeck et al. (this volume).

This is not to deny that there may have been a powerful kingdom called Cina, the name of which became synonymous with the Bugis of the central peninsula. Agrarian kingdoms (or complex chiefdoms) first emerged in the Cenrana and Walennae valleys in the 13th century (Figure 17.1).[2] Their rulers sponsored the expansion of wet-rice agriculture to produce a growing subsistence base and to extract a surplus for trade. The central role of wet-rice cultivation in these kingdoms' economies is clear from Bugis historical texts (Macknight 1983). Allangkanangnge's location in the western Cenrana valley, and the wealth of ceramics recovered from the summit, suggests that the hilltop was an early palace site occupied by members of an elite ruling family involved in this agricultural expansion. Ceramic sherdage from Allangkanangngne dates from the 13th century, and two 13th-century radiocarbon dates have also been obtained from the summit (Bulbeck et al., this volume). The hill itself is the largest in the chain of low hills that runs through Sengkang and southwards from the city (see Bulbeck 1992:Photo 1–2). These hills provide the natural points of control for trade and agriculture in the region south and west of Lake Tempe. It seems reasonable to hypothesise that Allangkanangnge may at one time have been a palace centre of a kingdom called Cina.

The structure of Bugis historical agrarian kingdoms

Bugis agrarian kingdoms were formed from groupings of *wanua*, the smallest Bugis political unit, which ranged in size from a single large settlement to a cluster of neighbouring settlements (Pelras 1996). A *wanua* could have under it several *anaq banua* (child *wanua*) while being at the same time subject to a more powerful *wanua*, making for a hierarchical confederation. Pelras (2010:233–234) argues that this was the basic system on which the Bugis kingdoms rested: 'All of them had been constituted around a core wanua (*watang mpanua*, 'trunk wanua') which, from the 15th century on, had progressively concluded treaties (*uluada*) with surrounding ones, henceforth called *wanua paliliq* ('satellite wanua').'

Wanua were headed by *arung* or chiefs, selected from a noble class whose members claimed descent in varying degrees from the rulers of the upper and lower worlds (Caldwell and Wellen 2016). *Arung* were embedded in networks of kin relations and obligations; power was executed though these networks, arranged and expressed as traditional allegiances. Large *wanua* groupings were structured around a *primus inter pares*, who, as *arung* of the central settlement, drew revenues from its lands, administered by *matoa* or district headmen.[3] Above the level of headman, the Bugis political system was founded on a metaphysical claim to high status: *arung* were noble and had ancestors in the upper and lower worlds; *matoa* were commoners, and did not. The rulers of these kingdoms are recorded in historical sources as having encouraged and directed the expansion of wet-rice agriculture. They married their children to the children of tributary *arung*, and in times of conflict raised armies from tributary *wanua*. Treaty, marriage and war were the three key strategies used in the expansion of kingdoms.

By the 16th century, Bugis *wanua* groupings had grown to considerable size. The size and degree of centralisation of kingdoms varied according to geographic constraints. In some kingdoms, such as Bone, which lay on extensive agricultural lowlands, power was held by a ruler, advised by a small council of nobles. Kingdoms such as Wajo, which lay on a fragmented landscape of hills, valleys and marshlands, were less centralised. Wajo was led by an Arung Matoa ('lord headman'),

---

2   Contemporary written sources date back to about 1400, beyond which lie undatable oral traditions. The associated archaeological record stretches back a further century or two, in the form of imported Chinese and Southeast Asian ceramics (Bulbeck et al., this volume).

3   Rulers could hold lands in other areas of the kingdom and these appanages could be granted as fiefs.

selected and advised by a council of 40 nobles. The office does not appear to have been easy: one Arung Matoa is recorded as having twice declined it, and for three years after his death the kingdom was ruled by his ashes (Zainal Abidin 1985:276).

Kingdoms, as well as smaller political units, could ally to form larger political groupings that allowed for corporate political decision-making. A well-known example is Ajattapparang, an alliance of five kingdoms northwest of Lake Sidenreng led by the ruler of Sidenreng (Druce 2009). An example of an alliance on a smaller scale is the Pitung Mpanua, a confederation of seven *wanua* on the northern borders of Wajo. Large or small, all political structures followed the same principles of alliance and hierarchy, and were headed by a recognised leader. As a result, it is not always easy to separate the idea of *wanua* groupings from those of kingdoms and alliances: the Bugis language has no single word for 'kingdom' or 'alliance', these terms reflect scholars' attempts to classify things by size and importance. An example of this problem is Lamuru, which formed part of Soppeng, and later Bone. Yet Lamuru had the structure of a kingdom, with an eponymous central place, appanage lands, tributary chiefdoms from which the ruler raised armies, and settlements or *wanua* groupings that were subject to these chiefs. The ruler of Lamuru held the title of Datu, as did the ruler of the Soppeng, as well as a number of his tributary chiefs, who were effectively heads of smaller *wanua* groupings. In short, the system was like a series of nesting boxes: the rulers of large kingdoms had tributary *arung* who were themselves rulers of smaller kingdoms who had tributary *arung* beneath them (Caldwell 1995).

Site survey and excavation

Allangkananngnge lies south of the Cenrana River, and east of the lower reaches of the Walennae River that drains the inland watershed of South Sulawesi's major cordilleras (Figure 17.1).[4] The hill forms part of a low ridge that runs north–south through Sengkang. Geologically, this ridge, which separates the two watersheds, is composed of 'Celebes morasse' consisting of late Miocene to Pliocene conglomerate, sandstone, claystone and marl, interbedded with limestone and lignite (Sukamto 1975). The Allangkananngngne hill, which sits on the eastern side of the ridge, is currently uninhabited and planted with a variety of cash crops such as vegetables, tobacco, maize and cacao. The hill rises some 20 m above a shallow valley, the floor of which is laid out with wet-rice fields; the foot of the valley abuts the Cenrana River and floods when the river is high. Palynological records from Lampulung swamp, a short distance northeast of Allangkananngnge, indicate mangrove conditions at the head of the Cenrana as recently as 2600 years ago (Gremmen 1990). Until the 14th century, estuarine swamps lay within the foraging range of the Allangkananngnge's inhabitants, receding in later centuries as a result of the eastward progradation of the lower Cenrana (see below).

A survey of the summit of Allangkananngnge was carried out by a team funded by the Origin of Complex Society in South Sulawesi (OXIS) project[5] in 1999 and a 1 m x 1 m test pit was dug to approximately the 14th-century level (Bulbeck et al., this volume). Ali Fadillah, then director of the Makassar Archaeology Office, directed the 1999 survey and excavations, assisted by Ian Caldwell and Budianto Hakim. Allangkananngnge was surveyed again by an international team in 2005 directed by Ian Caldwell, Steven Druce and Campbell Macknight, when the site

---

4   In most years, the western and eastern cordilleras experience separate monsoonal events, approximately six months apart, resulting in two flooding events along the lower Walennae. The waters from the Walennae drain into the Cenrana River; as they rise they block the exit of the Bila River, which flows from the north. To meet the height of the swollen Walennae, the Bila River also has to rise, creating a floodplain called Lake Tempe (Caldwell and Lillie 2004).

5   The OXIS project was designed to combine archaeological data and local historical accounts in Luwu and along the Cenrana River for the purpose of investigating the roles of rice cultivation, iron metallurgy and organised trade as major economic factors in the establishment of the early Bugis kingdoms (Bulbeck and Caldwell 2000; Fadillah and Sumantri 2000).

was divided into 41 zones including 19 where surface materials were collected (Figure 17.2). Collecting conditions were excellent as the hill had recently been cleared in preparation for the planting of cash crops. Zone 1, where the 2005 test pits were excavated (under Budianto Hakim's direction), is the reputed palace site of We Cudaiq, princess of Cina in the La Galigo stories. The zone is bounded by a 35 m x 30 m rectangular wall enclosing old Islamic graves. This wall contains the only stratified deposit on the site; outside this area, collected material lay directly on the surface, which may even have been slightly eroded.

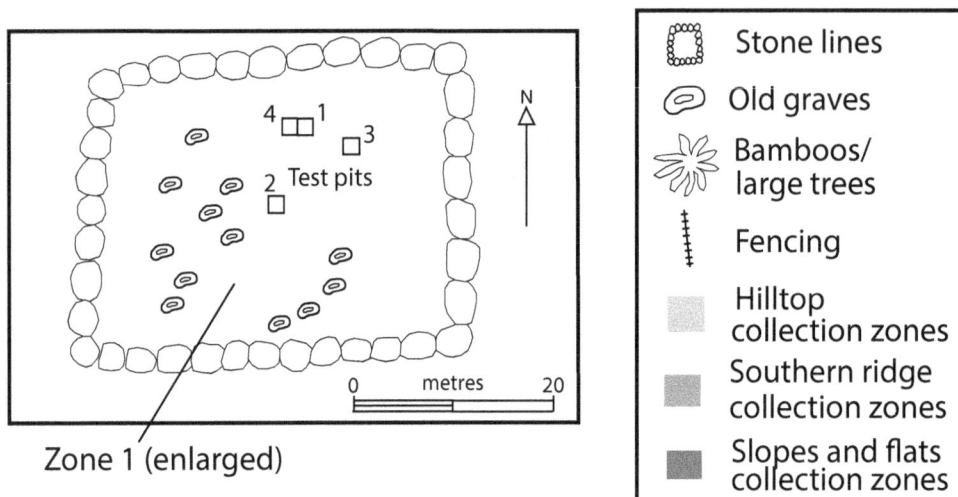

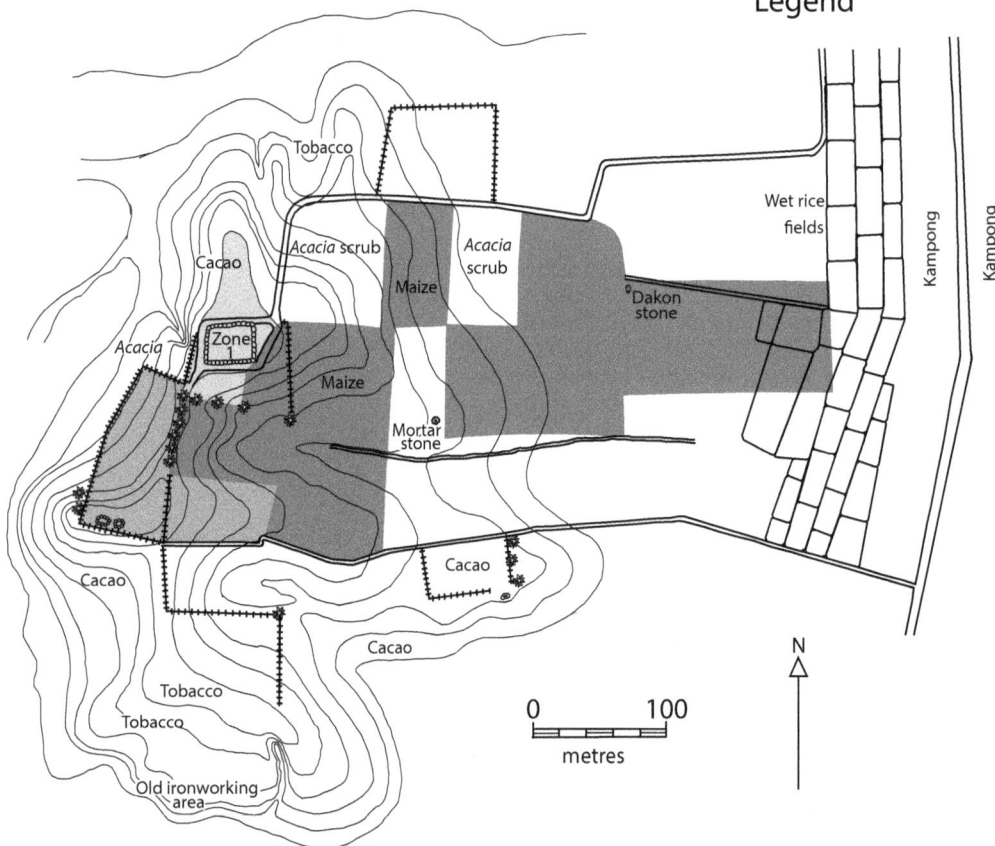

Figure 17.2: Theodolite survey of Allangkanangnge ri Latanete and grouped collection zones (2005).

Source: Pak Mansur, Makassar Archaeology Office.

Other stone features include a mortar stone and *dakon* stone (with indentations for playing a game similar to Malay *congklak*) at the eastern corner, and two stone arrangements at the southwest corner. The latter are two of the best-preserved examples of the dozens of stone arrangements (most of which are now very disturbed) with a standing stone in their centre, often sculpted to show a rudimentary human head. Their main area of occurrence is the ridge line south of the summit, although other examples are distributed across the slopes to the east. Finally, Zone 20 (on the southern slopes) is locally known as Panré Bessié (Bugis for 'the iron smith') and is remembered as an old ironworking area.

A combined surface assemblage of 2120 tradeware sherds[6] was collected by the current project during the 1999 and 2005 surveys. Around 95% of the sherdage is 13th–17th century in age and reflects the occupation of the site from the 13th century to South Sulawesi's internecine wars of the mid-17th century. The remaining 5% of more recent sherdage relates to the site's subsequent use for dryland gardening, as well as the spiritual potency of the site, which attracts pilgrims to the site to this day (Bulbeck et al., this volume).

Four 1 m² test pits (TP) were excavated, generally using spits of around 5–10 cm depth. TP1 was initially excavated in six spits to a depth of around 40 cm in 1999. The test pit was re-opened in 2005 and four further spits were excavated to sterile soil at a depth of 85 cm. TP1 was placed near the north stone wall, TP2 near the centre of Zone 1, TP3 towards the east stone wall, and TP4 extended TP1 1 m to the west. The other three pits were excavated down to sterile soil in 2005. TP4 revealed a 40 cm depression for a distinctive feature at the base into sterile soil, which was removed as a single unit. Apart from this feature, the stratigraphy of the test pits appeared generally featureless, although some layering could be observed when the sections were drawn. Plans were drawn at the completion of each spit and the location of any finds noticed by the excavators was plotted.

Sediment samples were not collected during the 2005 excavations, and we are unable to report on phytolith evidence from any of the spits excavated in 2005. We are, however, able to place the evidence for pre-Islamic rice processing at Allangkanangnge (Bulbeck and Caldwell 2008) in a more complete chronological and environmental context through the context of the 2005 excavations, and the five radiocarbon dates now available, all calibrated using Oxcal 4.2 (Bronk Ramsey 2016).

The stratigraphy in all of the test pits included deposit recorded during excavation as black silty sand in the upper spits and yellow silty sand in the lower spits. Topsoil development was also recorded for TP1, 2 and 3. The black sand contained the denser remains of habitation whereas the yellow sand extended between deposit, with light evidence for occupation higher up and sterile deposit at the base. This change in occupation debris would not appear related to preservation conditions because the alkalinity of the sediment, wherever tested, fell in the pH range of 7–7.5, which is neutral to slightly alkaline (Bulbeck 2000). TP4 was unusual in having a hole filled with black sand that plunged at an angle into the yellow sand and exited the western wall of the test pit as a feature encased by yellow sand. Stratigraphic sections of the test pits are presented in (Bulbeck et al., this volume).

Excavated contents

The main occupation phase in TP1 extends between Spits 1 and 7, which yielded more than 150 earthenware sherds per spit and all of the tradeware sherds excavated from this test pit (Table 17.1). With reference to the most recent of the tradeware sherds, Spits 1–3 would be dated to the 17th century, Spits 4–5 to the 16th century and Spits 6–7 to the 14th century. This last dating is confirmed by the Carbon-14 determination (ANU 11352) obtained from the marine

---

6   Identified by Karaeng Demmanari, a Makassar expert in tradewares, and David Bulbeck.

(estuarine) shell sample from Spit 6, which is the stratigraphically highest marine shell sample in the test pit. Although the c. 14th-century dating for this sample is not secure, relying as it does on an estimate of the proportion of the 'marine reservoir effect' to allow for the delta R value to use in offsetting the date for the marine reservoir effect (footnote d to Table 17.1), it is nonetheless consistent with the tradeware dating.

Table 17.1: Test pit 1 excavation summary.

Spit	Basal depth	Sediment colour (wet)[a]	Burnt sediment	Earthenware sherds	Imported ceramics[b]	Other finds	Vertebrate fragments[c]	Charcoal (grams)	Shell
1	5-10 cm	Very dark grey	2 grams	361	3 (15th-17th centuries)	Iron rod, bronze fragment	52 (50 grams)	1.5	3 fragments, 2.0 grams (terrestrial)
2	10-15 cm	Very dark grey	20 grams	162	3 (15th-16th centuries)	—	22 (17 grams)	7.6	—
3	20-25 cm	Very dark grey	18 grams	718	5 (15th-17th centuries)	Glass bead (0.2 grams)	79 (137 grams)	8.0 (+ 0.1 gram wood)	—
4	25-30 cm	Very dark grey	—	212	6 (12th-16th centuries)	—	32	0.8	—
5	30-35 cm	Very dark grey	—	308	5 (14th-16th centuries)	—	31	0.9	—
6	38-43 cm	Very dark grey	—	207	2 (11th-14th centuries)	—	49	3.5	3 fragments, 29.6 grams[d]
7	48-53 cm	Yellow	5.1 grams	512	1 (14th century)	—	88	—	12 fragments, 83.7 grams[e]
8	58-63 cm	Yellow	30.8 grams	134	—	2 joining iron fragments	30 (89.6 grams)	6.0(f)	21 fragments, 15.0 grams[e]
9	68-74 cm	Yellow	40.4 grams	53	—	—	9 (42.4 grams)	3.7(g)	4 fragments, 47.7 grams[h]
10	85 cm	Yellow	—	—	—	—	—	—	—
Total	—	—	116 grams	2,667	25	—	392	32.0	70 fragments

(a) Munsell colour readings for Spits 1-6 (Bulbeck 2000); field descriptions for the lower spits.

(b) Summarised from Bulbeck et al. (this volume).

(c) Identifications in Makassar by David Bulbeck include two rodent teeth from Spit 4, a bovid molar from Spit 6 and a bovid proximal femur from Spit 7. In addition, 74 fragments from Spits 7-9 were sent to Canberra for specialist identification by Stuart Hawkins.

(d) *Telescopium telescopium* (estuarine), radiocarbon dated to 820+60 BP (ANU-11352), which calibrates to AD 1284-1449 (2 sigma), assuming 50% marine content and delta R value of 89+70 (Sa Bui Bay, South Kalimantan).

(e) *Telescopium telescopium* (estuarine).

(f) Radiocarbon dated to 752+34 BP (Wk-17818), which calibrates to AD 1217-1289 (2 sigma).

(g) Radiocarbon dated as modern (Wk-17743), so the sample presumably resulted from contamination during the excavation.

(h) *Telescopium telescopium* (32.5 g), estuarine; *Pinctada margaritifera* (10.8 g), intertidal and subtidal; *Saccostrea mytiloides* (4.4 g), estuarine and intertidal. *Pinctada margaritifera* radiocarbon dated to 955+30 BP (Wk-19966), calibrates to AD 1213-1389 (2 sigma) assuming 50% marine content and delta R value of 89+70 (Sa Bui Bay, South Kalimantan).

Source: Budianto Hakim and David Bulbeck's laboratory data.

Early occupation of the site as reflected in TP1 (Spits 8–9) would appear to have been less intensive than during the main occupation phase (Table 17.1). Spit 8 is similar to Spit 2 (the sparsest of the spits from the main occupation phase) in its earthenware sherd count, vertebrate fragment count and charcoal quantity. Spit 9, which registers the evidence for initial occupation, is poorer than Spits 2 and 8 in all of these aspects. The distinguishing feature of Spit 9 is its evidence for the collection of intertidal and subtidal shellfish as well as estuarine shellfish. Chronometrically, the Spit 8 charcoal is securely dated to the 13th century, consistent with the 14th century and later datings for the stratigraphically higher spits, whereas the Spit 9 shellfish is estimated to date to the 13th or 14th century. In view of the uncertainties of Carbon-14 determinations on marine shellfish noted above, the most reasonable course would be to infer a 13th-century antiquity as indicated on stratigraphic grounds.

A notable feature of Spits 7–9 was their concentration of burnt sediment, which was absent from Spits 4–6 (Table 17.1). The surface of the burnt sediment from Spit 7 had in places a metallic sheen, suggesting the sediment derived from ironworking or other local metallurgical activities. The burnt sediment from Spit 8 contained very little charcoal, although it did contain comminuted shellfish fragments (around 3% by weight), whereas the Spit 9 burnt sediment contained a greater density of carbon specks but no faunal material (David Bulbeck, laboratory notes, held privately). The Spit 7–9 samples may respectively represent the remnants of the surface, body and base of a hearth.

Only five spits were excavated in TP2 (Table 17.2), and the fifth spit was extended across just one quarter of the test pit because Hakim observed that its presence of habitation debris was minimal. Generally speaking, the density of habitation debris in TP2 was light throughout the sequence, as reflected by earthenware sherd and vertebrate fragment counts similar to or less than those recorded for Spit 9 in TP1. The marine shell from Spit 4, at the intersection between the upper black deposit and the lower yellow deposit, can be reasonably dated to the 13th–14th centuries (see below). Accordingly, there does appear to be an orderly stratigraphic sequence from c. 16th-century deposits at the top of TP2 to c. 13th-century deposits towards its base.

Table 17.2: Test pit 2 excavation summary.

Spit	Basal depth	Earthenware sherds	Imported ceramics[a]	Vertebrate fragments	Charcoal (grams)	Marine shell
1	10 cm	60	1 (16th century)	2	—	—
2	20 cm	59	—	6	—	—
3	40 cm	7	—	—	—	—
4	60 cm	15	—	—	1	4 (20 grams)[b]
5	85 cm	1	—	1	—	—
Total	—	142	1	9	1	4 fragments

(a) Bulbeck et al. (this volume).

(b) One fragment each of *Telescopium telescopium* (estuarine), *Anadara* (intertidal), *Terebralia sulcata* (mangroves) and Ostreidae. Source: Budianto Hakim and David Bulbeck's laboratory data.

The black deposit in TP3 extended from Spit 1 to Spit 4, where it interfaced with the underlying yellow deposit. Tradeware sherds were recovered from the upper spits and their datings suggest an orderly chronological sequence from c. 16th-century antiquity in Spit 1 to c. 14th-century antiquity in Spit 3 (Table 17.3). Unfortunately, the black layer in TP3 was notably disturbed, as recorded by the excavators, which would appear to account for how 13th–14th-century marine shellfish (see below) could have been recovered from every spit below Spit 1. Nonetheless, a substantial assemblage of earthenware pottery was recovered from Spits 2 and 3, even if its chronological status can be no more precisely described than probably predating the 16th century.

Table 17.3: Test pit 3 excavation summary.

Spit	Basal depth	Earthenware sherds	Imported ceramics[a]	Vertebrate fragments[b]	Charcoal	Marine shell[c]
1	5 cm	20	4 (15th–17th centuries)	6	—	—
2	15 cm	212	1 (15th century)	16	3 grams	4 fragments
3	35 cm	499	3 (12th–15th centuries)	62	Wood fragment	8 fragments
4	45 cm	23	—	2	3 grams	3 fragments
5[d]	60 cm	16	—	1	—	2 fragments
Total	—	770	8	87	6 grams	17 fragments

(a) Summarised from Bulbeck et al. (this volume).

(b) Identifications in Makassar by David Bulbeck include a bovid molar from each of Spit 1 and Spit 3 and a bovid incisor from Spit 3.

(c) Collection includes 12 fragments of *Telescopium telescopium* (estuarine), three fragments of Veneridae (marine), and one fragment each of *Anadara* (intertidal) and *Pinctada margaritifera* (intertidal/subtidal).

(d) Finds restricted to upper part of spit.

Source: Budianto Hakim and David Bulbeck's laboratory data.

TP4, which abuts TP1, produced a similar concentration of habitation debris to TP1 in Spits 1–4 (Table 17.4). In Spit 5, the deposit was observed to be sterile across most of the square, but Hakim noted a dark feature plunging into the sterile yellow deposit in the southwest corner. Excavation of the feature (Spit 6) yielded iron slag along with charcoal of more than 200 g. A sample of 20 g was dated, yielding a calibrated age of AD 1450–1633.

Table 17.4: Test pit 4 excavation summary.

Spit	Basal depth	Earthenware sherds	Imported ceramics[a]	Other finds	Vertebrate fragments[b]	Charcoal (grams)	Shellfish fragments
1	15 cm	190	—	—	7	—	—
2	25 cm	255	1 (15th–16th centuries)	—	32	16	—
3	35 cm	74	2 (15th–16th centuries)	—	10 (207.5 g)	10	3 (20.4 g)[c]
4	45 cm	282	—	—	26 (175.6 g)	15	8 (70.6 g)[d]
5	55 cm	37	1 (16th–17th centuries)	—	11 (144.2 g)	—	11 (64.0 g)[e]
6	95 cm	30	—	Iron slag	11 (48.3 g)	207[f]	4 (27.5 g)[g]
Total	—	868	4	—	97 fragments	248	26 fragments

(a) Summarised from Bulbeck et al. (this volume).

(b) Identifications in Makassar by David Bulbeck include a bovid molar from Spit 2 and six pig molars from Spits 3–5. In addition, 58 fragments from Spits 3–6 were sent to Canberra for specialist identification by Stuart Hawkins.

(c) *Telescopium telescopium* (9.4 g) (estuarine); *Anadara granosa* (1.6 g) (intertidal).

(d) *Telescopium telescopium* (49.8 g) (estuarine); *Polymesoda coaxans* (12.4 g) and *Terebralia sulcata* (8.4 g) (mangroves).

(e) *Telescopium telescopium* (58.0 g) (estuarine); *Batissa violacea* (3.4 g) (coastal streams); *Anadara* sp. (2.0 g) (intertidal); Ostreidae (0.6 g).

(f) Radiocarbon dated to 364 ±25 BP (Wk-29737), which calibrates to AD 1450–1633 (2 sigma).

(g) *Telescopium telescopium* (25.4 g) (estuarine); *Batissa violacea* (2.1 g) (coastal streams).

Source: Budianto Hakim and David Bulbeck's laboratory data.

This basal date is inconsistent with the probable 13th–14th-century antiquity of the marine shellfish recovered from Spits 3–5 as well as Spit 6 (see below). The presence of a crucible fragment (Table 17.5 below) together with iron slag in the TP4 Spit 6 feature suggests that they were redeposited in the feature from higher in the profile when a hole was dug deep into sterile deposit. However, this would not explain the much larger concentration of charcoal in Spit 6 compared with the higher spits. Accordingly, this charcoal is inferred to represent the remains of a cremation burial, the traditional burial mode amongst the Bugis in pre-Islamic times (Druce et al. 2005). This interpretation would explain the large amount of charcoal in this sample compared to elsewhere in the site, and its relatively young age of AD 1450–1633 (barely within the pre-Islamic period) relative to its depth.

Description of the inorganic excavated remains

High-fired ceramics and glass beads

The small excavated assemblage of high-fired ceramics and the large surface assemblage are similar in predominantly dating to the same 13th–17th-century time frame. Compared with tradeware assemblages from other Bugis sites, the remarkable features of the Allangkanangnge tradewares are their high frequencies of large martavan jars (about half of the sherdage) including Jizhou iron-painted wares, and early (13th–14th century) whitewares, coupled with a relatively low concentration of 16th-century Chinese blue-and-white sherds. In particular, the tradeware assemblage from the Allangkanangnge hilltop collection zones (Figure 17.2) is distinguished from the assemblage from the site's slopes and flats by having a higher proportion of Jizhou and other martavan sherdage, as well as a larger proportion of the older ceramic categories (13th–14th centuries, compared to the 15th–17th centuries). The tradeware assemblage from the southern ridge, where the rectangular stone arrangements are concentrated, resembles the hilltop assemblage in its high proportion of martavan sherds, but not in the antiquity of the sherdage, which instead resembles the slopes and flats assemblage. In summary, while imported ceramics of all types and all ages were found widely distributed across the site, martavans (mainly from production centres in China and Vietnam) and older ceramic classes were most concentrated on the hilltop (Bulbeck et al., this volume).

The glass bead from Spit 3 of TP1 is oblate in Horace Beck's (1936) terminology. It is of moderate size with a length of 6.6 mm, maximum diameter of 7.6 mm, and stringing-hole diameter of 2.1 mm. The colour is dark greenish-grey (Munsell 5GY 4/1). The size, shape and colour fall comfortably within the range recorded for late 2nd millennium AD glass beads excavated from Gua Andomo and Gua Lampetia in southeastern Sulawesi (Bulbeck et al. 2016). However, the single glass bead from Allangkanangnge, compared with its excavated earthenware count of 4447 sherds (Tables 17.1–4), contrasts with the much higher number of 283 glass beads from Gua Andomo and Gua Lampetia and their much lower number of 1066 earthenware sherds (19.35 kg). Instead, Allangkanangnge is similar to the 15th–16th-century Bugis suspected palace centre of Utti Batue in Luwu, where a single glass bead (weighing 0.1 g) was excavated in association with a large earthenware assemblage of nearly 20 kg (Bulbeck et al. 2007). This comparison suggests that glass beads constituted a minimal component of the material culture at Bugis palace centres, in contrast with their importance for adornment and as status symbols in other parts of Indonesia such as Kalimantan, Nusa Tenggara and West Papua until ethnographic times (Adhyatman and Arifin 1996:3).

Metallic remains

The only available documentation on the iron rod and bronze fragment from Spit 1 in TP1 is their collective weight of 4 g. The two iron fragments from Spit 8 in TP1 together constitute what may be the terminal blade and tip of a knife or dagger. The blade is wavy and the tip is off-centre, suggesting this may have been part of a *keris* dagger. Their weight, including the corrosion product, is 11.3 g; combined length is 60 mm, and the blade inside the corrosion product would have had a maximum width of 18 mm and maximum thickness of 6 mm. The iron slag from the Spit 6 feature in TP4 is a small, amorphous fragment weighing 8 g and coloured dark grey.

Evidence for iron metallurgy in South Sulawesi dates back to the 1st millennium AD in Luwu, in the form of small quantities of iron slag/gangue from Katue and Sabbang Loang, and abundant ironstone at Pontanoa Bangka (Bulbeck and Caldwell 2000; Do 2013). This was followed by the establishment of industrial sites for smelting the local iron ore fortified with nickel and especially chromium at the Lake Matano sites of Nuha (11th–13th centuries) and Matano (15th–18th centuries) (Do 2013). Evidence for local ironworking (iron slag, ironstone) is a regular feature of Luwu sites dating to approximately the 16th century, including Pinanto (Do 2013), Baebunta, Pattimang (Bulbeck and Prasetyo 2000) and Utti Batue (Bulbeck et al. 2007). South of Luwu, oxidised iron fragments have frequently been recovered from the excavation of open-air sites (e.g. Nayati 2005), but the 16th–17th-century fortified palace of Somba Opu is one of the few sites where the excavators felt confident in identifying iron slag (Tim 1992:59).

The salience of the kingdom of Luwu until the early 17th century is attributed to its export of high-quality iron weapons and tools prior to the widespread availability of imported steel by the 18th century, which led to a proliferation of local iron-puddling workshops (Bulbeck and Caldwell 2000; Do 2013). The excavated, pre-Islamic samples from Allangkanangnge provide the opportunity for future chemical testing for a 'Luwu signature'.

Earthenware pottery

The earthenware pottery was analysed by Budianto Hakim. It accounts for the bulk of the excavated material from Allangkanangnge, similar to the situation at Uttie Batue where earthenware pottery also accounted for the bulk of the inorganic remains. The 4447 excavated earthenware sherds at Allangkanangnge dwarfs the 38 excavated tradeware sherds (Tables 17.1–17.4), producing a ratio of approximately 1:120, which resembles the excavated tradeware/earthenware (by weight) of approximately 1:50 at Utti Batue (Bulbeck et al. 2007). A relatively small number of earthenware sherds (not covered in this contribution) were also collected from the surface of Allangkanangnge, consisting of visibly decorated sherds and/or sherds with a rim or base.

By dint of its abundance, compared with the other classes of excavated finds, earthenware pottery may be the most reliable indicator of occupation intensity. On that basis, the small earthenware assemblage in TP1 assignable to the 13th century (Spits 8 and 9), compared with the 14th–17th-century spits, would point to light occupation prior to the 14th century (Table 17.1). As for the TP1 spits for which excavated sediment weights were recorded (Bulbeck and Caldwell 2008:Table 17.2), these suggest more intensive occupation in Spits 5–6 (14th–16th centuries) than the overlying spits (16th–17th centuries). Similarly, the TP3 earthenware counts suggest a reduced occupation intensity after the 15th century (Tables 17.3).[7]

---

7   TP2 and TP4 (Tables 17.2 and 17.4) appear to reflect occupation intensity during the 16th and 17th centuries at a similar level to the 15th century, but their excavated contents are respectively slight and disturbed.

Most of the Allangkanangnge earthenware appears to represent a single fabric type, described as coarse and variable in its density, and with Munsell hues ranging between 2.5YR and 10YR (predominantly brown, reddish-brown and greyish-brown). Five sherds in TP1 and three sherds in TP4 stood apart from the rest of the assemblage. Two sherds (TP1 Spit 3) resemble kaolin-rich fine 'white pottery' found at scattered early historical trading sites across Indonesia, Malaysia and the Philippines (Miksic and Yap 1990; Stargardt 2003). Three sherds from TP1 Spits 2 and 3 were identified from their appearance as resembling Luwu 'soft pottery' of 14th–17th-century age (Bulbeck 2009), which corroborates the close links between pre-Islamic Cina and Luwu as indicated by textual evidence (Caldwell and Wellen 2017). Three sherds from Spit 4 of TP4 appeared to be unusually high-fired, with the toughness of stoneware; two of them have red walls and a black core, while the third, possibly a cover, has an unusual shape.

Pottery decorations recorded in Spits 7–9 of the TP1 assemblage, and from the other test pits, are similar to those illustrated in Bulbeck and Caldwell (2008) for TP1 Spits 1–6, consisting predominantly of criss-cross paddle impressions, and otherwise horizontal incisions and punctate lines of dots. Approximately 8% of the studied sherds are decorated (Bulbeck and Caldwell 2008), notably higher than at Utti Batue where a very small number of decorated sherds (with motifs generally different from those at Allangkanangnge) were recorded (Bulbeck et al. 2007). On the other hand, the limited range of motifs at both of these sites suggests this may be a feature of Bugis historical sites, apparently contrasting with historical sites near Makassar with their wide variety of decorations on the pottery collected from surface contexts (Clune and Bulbeck 1999).

Just over 800 earthenware forms at Allangkanangnge could be identified on the basis of sherds that retain diagnostic sections such as rims or feet (Table 17.5; Figure 17.3). The most commonly identified form was standard bowls (Indonesian, *mangkuk*), making up 34% of the identifications, and identified in most of the spits. The other relatively common forms, together accounting for 46% of the identifications, included large bowls (*jambangan*), large pots (*pasu*) and cooking pots (*periuk*). Small numbers of sherds were identified as representing earthenware cooking stoves (*tungku*), large jars (*tempayan* and *buyung*), covers (*tutup*), censers (*pedupaan*) and small serving vessels (cups or *cangkir* and a suspected jarlet or *buli-buli*).

Large jars were restricted to TP1, suggesting a storage function not represented at the other test pits. This aligns with the phytolith evidence for processing and storing rice recovered in abundance from Spits 1–6 in TP1 (Bulbeck and Caldwell 2008). Nonetheless, the earthenware identifications from all four test pits suggest that a range of domestic tasks, including cooking and serving food, had been undertaken across the site.

Possibly the most interesting earthenware form is the crucible (Indonesian, *wadah pelebur logam*) because its identification corroborates oral memories that ironworking formerly occurred at the site. Of particular note is a concentration of 34 crucible fragments in Spits 7–9 of TP1, which accords with the metallic sheen noted on the sediment sample from Spit 8 in suggesting that a portion of the sediment consists of metalworking debris. A second concentration involves the 17 crucible fragments from TP4, although with 16 of them recovered from above the iron slag in Spit 6.

Table 17.5: Earthenware form identifications from the Allangkanangnge excavations.

Artefact	Test pit 1									Test pit 2				Test pit 3					Test pit 4						Total
Spit	1	2	3	4	5	6	7	8	9	1	2	3	4	1	2	3	4	5	1	2	3	4	5	6	
Covers	1	3	1	–	2	1	2	–	–	1	–	–	–	1	5	11	–	–	4	4	4	5	–	1	46 (5.7%)
Large jars	8	4	7	6	1	–	6	1	–	–	–	–	–	–	–	–	–	–	–	–	–	–	–	–	33 (4.0%)
Large bowls	5	–	8	13	7	8	23	7	4	–	2	–	2	1	4	22	–	2	5	3	1	8	2	3	130 (16.1%)
Standard bowls	6	–	5	2	11	2	35	3	5	5	2	–	–	6	22	50	4	3	29	27	6	33	7	8	271 (33.8%)
Large carinated pots	2	–	16	–	1	5	17	3	–	–	3	–	–	1	3	14	1	1	1	10	5	21	7	1	112 (13.9%)
Cooking pots	–	–	25	10	–	–	22	5	3	4	3	1	1	1	8	16	1	–	3	14	2	6	3	–	128 (15.9%)
Stoves	–	1	–	–	1	–	3	1	–	1	–	–	1	–	–	5	–	–	–	6	–	–	–	–	19 (2.4%)
Crucibles	–	–	2	–	–	–	21	8	5	–	–	–	–	–	2	2	–	–	2	2	1	9	2	1	57 (7.1%)
Censers	–	–	–	–	–	–	–	–	–	–	–	–	–	–	–	–	–	1	–	1	1	–	–	–	3 (0.4%)
Small serving vessels	4	–	1	–	–	–	–	–	–	–	–	–	–	–	–	–	–	–	–	–	–	–	–	–	6 (0.7%)
Total	26	8	65	31	23	16	129	28	17	11	10	1	4	10	44	120	6	7	44	67	20	82	21	15	805 (100%)

Source: Budianto Hakim's laboratory data.

Cover rims
TP3 spit 2

Tempayan large jar rims
TP1 spit 4 (left) and
TP1 spit 3 (right)

Bujung
large jar rim
TP1 spit 7

Large bowl rims
TP1 spit 3

Standard bowl rims
TP1 spit 3 (left) and TP1 spit 7 (right)

Large pot rim
TP3 spit 3

Cooking pot rims
TP1 spit 4 (left) and TP2 spit 4 (right)

Stove rim
TP4 spit 2

Crucible rims
TP4 spit 4

0   5
centimetres

Cup rims
TP1 spit 1

Jarlet rim
TP3 spit 5

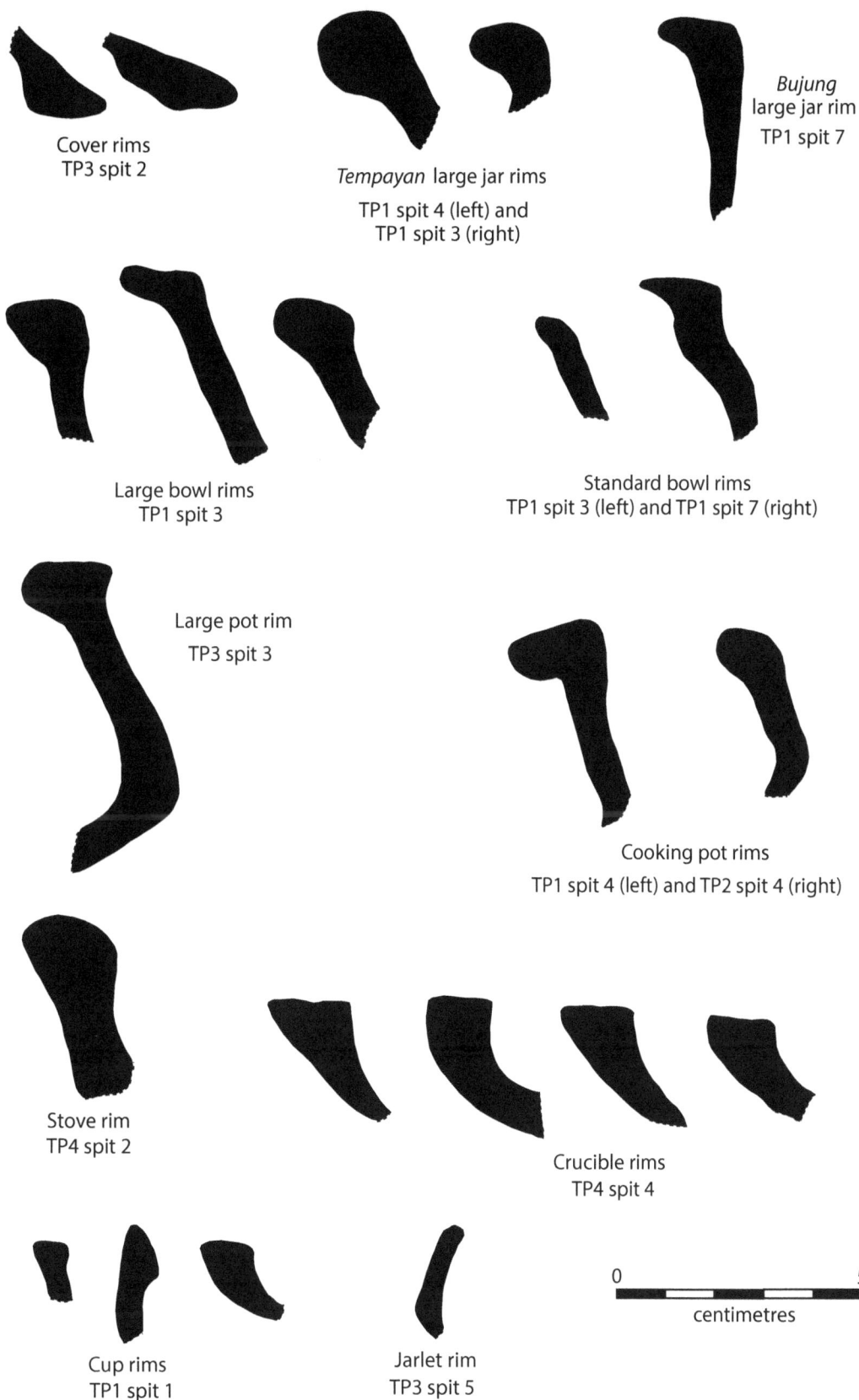

Figure 17.3: Allangkanangnge earthenware pottery rim examples.
Source: Budianto Hakim's laboratory notes.

Description of the organic excavated remains

Shellfish remains

The shellfish were identified by Budianto Hakim and David Bulbeck with reference to an identikit based on complete and semi-complete specimens collected from sites excavated in 1998 and 1999 in Luwu (see Bulbeck and Caldwell 2000). These specimens were sent in 1999 to Ian Loch, then curator of the Malacology Collection at the Australian Museum, who provided identifications to the species or, occasionally, just the genus level. There are two sets of the shell identikit, one in Makassar and one at The Australian National University, and both were used in identifying the Allangkanangnge mollusc remains.

The main collected taxon was *Telescopium telescopium*, an estuarine species, which was represented in every spit with shellfish and accounted for about 80% of the total assemblage (Tables 17.1–17.4). Except for Spits 6–8 in TP1, the shellfish collections also contained other taxa, all represented in small quantities of about 15 g or less. These include the mangrove species *Terebralia sulcata* (Belitong snail) and *Polymesoda coaxans* (mud mussel), the estuarine/intertidal *Saccostrea mytiloides* (tropical black-lipped rock oyster) along with other Ostreidae, the intertidal-dwelling *Anadara granosa* (ark clam), the intertidal/subtidal *Pinctada margaritifera* (black-lipped pearl oyster), marine Veneridae (Venus clams), and *Batissa violacea*, which is a freshwater clam found in coastal streams. *B. violacea* looks out of place in its association with a less brackish hydrology than *T. telescopium*, whereas the other taxa are associated with a mangrove or intertidal environment.

The TP1 sequence, which can be considered the site's 'master sequence', suggests a transition from collecting of both estuarine and intertidal shellfish associated with Spit 9, to purely estuarine collecting of *T. telescopium* associated with Spits 6–8. Direct radiocarbon dates (Table 17.1) suggest a c. 13th-century date for the Spit 9 shellfish and a c. 14th-century date for the Spit 6 shellfish, providing a time frame for this transition. Such a transition is not evident for the other test pits where *T. telescopium* was consistently associated with mangrove or intertidal species (Tables 17.2–17.4), which would recommend a generalised 13th/14th-century dating for these assemblages. In the case of TP2, all of the shellfish were found in a single spit low in the habitation sequence; in the case of TP3, the shellfish were recovered from deposits noted by the excavators to be disturbed. Disturbance, indeed a partially inverted stratigraphy, is particularly evident for TP4 in view of the recovery of the site's only freshwater shellfish from the two basal spits of TP4, as also reflected in the ceramic datings (Bulbeck et al., this volume).

Vertebrate remains

A total of 132 vertebrate specimens excavated from Spits 7–9 of TP1 (176.1 g) and Spits 3–6 of TP4 (575.6 g) were sent to The Australian National University for specialist analysis by Stuart Hawkins. Most identifications were made by comparison with the Archaeology and Natural History osteological reference collection. Two suspected Anoa (pygmy water buffalo) fragments were taken to Paris to check the identification at the Comparative Anatomy Collection at France's National Museum of Natural History (in one case, disproving the suspected identification). The TP1 assemblage is of particular interest in being dated to the period of shellfish foraging during the 13th/14th centuries, whereas the TP4 assemblage unfortunately cannot be dated more closely than to the 13th/14th–16th/17th-century period of main site occupancy.

Only 3% of the faunal remains consisted of complete bones (all foot bones); the rest were highly fragmented. Identifications were made to the lowest taxonomic level possible: family, genus or species (Tables 17.6 and 17.7). But in many cases, depending on the degree of how fragmented and diagnostic a bone was, this could only be narrowed down to sheep/goat, large/medium bovine or even broader and less specific identifications to large/medium mammal, mammal or fish. In some instances, tentative identifications have the prefix cf., which means compare, and this represents a close match. The bones are quantified by Number of Individual Specimens (NISP), but, in some cases, it could be established that more than one Minimum Number of Individuals (MNI) was present. Ages were estimated into juvenile, sub-adult and adult categories based on rates of known epiphyseal fusion for domesticated mammals (Silver 1969; Schmid 1972; Wilson et al. 1982) to understand animal exploitation strategies.

Table 17.6: Allangkanangnge taxa NISP by provenance.

Taxon	TP4 spits				TP1 spits			
	3	4	5	6	7	8	9	Total
Bubalus depressicornis	1	0	0	0	0	0	0	1
Bubalus bubalis	3	3	2	4	0	1	1	14
Medium bovine	0	0	0	0	0	3	0	3
cf. *Capra hircus*	1	0	1	0	3	0	0	5
Suidae	0	2	1	0	0	0	3	6
Canis cf. *familiaris*	1	0	0	0	0	0	1	2
Rattus sp.	0	0	0	0	1	0	0	1
Medium mammal	4	2	1	2	2	2	2	15
Large mammal	0	0	0	0	0	1	1	2
Mammal	0	19	6	5	18	21	0	69
Testudines	0	0	0	0	11	0	0	11
Fish	0	0	0	0	0	2	0	2
Bird	0	0	0	0	0	0	1	1
Total	10	26	11	11	35	30	9	132

Source: Stuart Hawkins' laboratory data.

Bone modifications were recorded including the number of cut marks and their location on the bone, as well as the bone fracture orientation and fracture surfaces according to Sadek-Kooros (1975). The animal remains show signs of intensive butchery with 9.9% of bones displaying cut marks, with several observed parallel cut marks (13 bones with a total of 32 cut marks) indicating intensive meat removal; 9.9% of bones had observed oblique regular fractures, 5.3% observed transverse regular fractures, while 42.4% of the assemblage consists of small bone fragments with fresh breaks of no discernible orientation. Five long bones had regular longitudinal fractures split down the shaft, an indication that bones were split for marrow extraction, while oblique and transverse regular fractures have been associated with human butchery practices (Sadek-Kooros 1975; Shipman et al. 1981; Morales Muniz 1988). A few bones show signs of post-deposition mechanical breakdown, with 3% of bones with transverse irregular breaks, 13.8% of bones with stepped fractures and 2.3% with oblique irregular breaks.

Table 17.7: Allangkanangnge ri Latanete skeletal units (test pit – NISP) by taxon.

Skeletal unit	Anoa	Canid	cf. goat	Bubalus bubalis	Medium bovine	Suidae	Rattus sp.	Medium mammal	Large mammal	Mammal	Testudines	Fish	Bird	Total
Ulna		1 (TP4)												1
Humerus	1 (TP4)	1 (TP1)				3 (TP1)	1 (TP1)							6
Cranium			1 (TP1)		2 (TP1)			2 (TP1)		1 (TP4)				6
Cervical vertebra			1 (TP4)											1
Calcaneus			1 (TP1)											1
Proximal phalanx			1 (TP1) 1 (TP4)	1 (TP1)										3
Scapula				3 (TP4)		1 (TP4)								4
Rib				2 (TP4)				2 (TP4)						4
Tooth fragment				3 (TP4)										3
Long bone				1 (TP4)				2 (TP4)						3
Astragalus				1 (TP4)										1
Intermediate phalanx				1 (TP1) 1 (TP4)										2
2nd & 3rd fused carpal				1 (TP4)										1
Mandible					1 (TP1)	2 (TP4)								3
Thoracic vertebra								1 (TP1)						1
Vertebra								1 (TP4)						1
Femur								1 (TP1)						1
Radius								1 (TP4)						1
Unidentified fragment								2 (TP1) 3 (TP4)	1 (TP1) 1 (TP1)	39 (TP1) 29 (TP4)		2 (TP1)	1 (TP1)	78
Shell											11 (TP1)			11
Total	1	2	5	14	3	6	1	15	2	69	11	2	1	132

Source: Stuart Hawkins' laboratory data.

TP1 Spits 7–9 had concentrations of unidentified mammal bone fragments, while Spit 7 also had a concentration of turtle (Testudines) shell fragments. A single rat humerus was recovered from Spit 7. A water buffalo (*Bubalus bubalis*) proximal phalanx, a Canid (dog) humerus distal shaft fragment with four parallel cut marks, and a Suid (pig) humerus shaft were identified from Spit 9. A few unidentifiable fish bones were present in Spit 8, while an unidentified bird long bone shaft was present in Spit 9. The presence of turtle shell and fish remains restricted to TP1 Spits 7 and 8 suggests a marine component to the diet, in accord with the evidence for marine shellfish collection during the 13th and 14th centuries. However, it should be noted that the presumed turtle shell could have belonged to the Sulawesi forest turtle (*Leucocephalon yuwonoi*).

TP4 had concentrations of unidentified mammal bone fragments from Spit 4. A dog ulna fragment identified from Spit 3 has an oblique regular fracture and three parallel cut marks, indicating butchery for food or materials for manufacture. The dog remains from both TP1 and TP4 most likely belonged to the domesticated *Canis familiaris*. Pig remains (species unknown) were also identified from TP4, including a mandibular deciduous fourth premolar and a permanent mandibular incisor from Spit 4, as well as a partially carbonised scapula with a fused epiphysis from Spit 5. This indicates the remains of at least one pig sub-adult individual. These sparse Suid remains from TP1 and TP4 could represent domestic pig *Sus scrofa* or wild pigs (Sulawesi warty pig (*Sus celebensis*) and Sulawesi babirusa (*Babyrousa celebensis*)). The endemic pygmy water buffalo or Anoa was identified on the basis of a distal shaft humerus fragment from Spit 3, which had been sawn with a sharp implement leaving parallel saw marks.

Common to both units TP1 and TP4 are a range of medium mammal and medium bovine fragments or cf. goat (*Capra hircus*). The cf. *Capra hircus* fragments were too fragmented to tell the difference between sheep and goat using known osteological markers (Boessneck 1969; Prummel and Frisch 1986), but it is likely they are goat *Capra hircus* fragments based on known mammal introductions into South Sulawesi. Some of the medium bovine fragments could also potentially be the introduced rusa deer (*Cervus timorensis*), which has thrived in South Sulawesi since its late Holocene introduction (Simons and Bulbeck 2004) and which the 18th-century chronicle of Wajo records as a mammal once abundant in the landscape:

> Before there were people living in Wajo there were only wide expanses of grass, and thick, pathless forests that were home to animals: wild pigs, deer, buffaloes and birds. There were numerous lakes full of fish, as well as crocodiles (Zainal Abidin 1985:52).

The Anoa fragment in the assemblage can be positively matched with the lowland *Bubalus depressicornis* (Figure 17.4), although no comparative specimens of the mountain *Bubalus quarlesi* were available to rule out that possible identification. These two Anoa species are still present on Sulawesi in very small numbers, with the former confined to retreating forest margins and the latter to mountain ranges (Burton et al. 2005). The endemic buffalo presence in the assemblage probably represents hunting of the lowland Anoa *Bubalus depressicornis* within or on the fringes of extant rainforest that may have been present nearby, although whether early or late during Allangkanangnge's period of occupation is unknown owing to disturbance to the TP4 deposit.

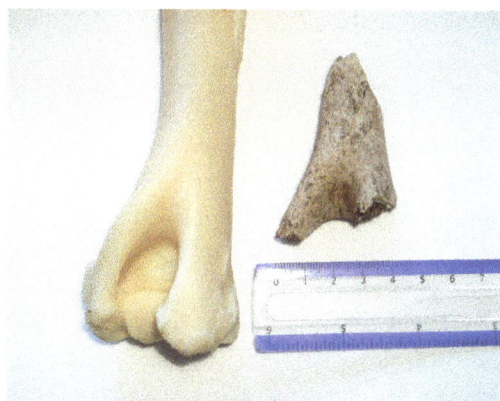

Figure 17.4: Dorsal humerus: comparison of Anoa specimen 1847-354 at left and the TP4 fragment at right.

Source: Anoa specimen courtesy Musée d'histoire naturelle, Paris; photograph by David Bulbeck.

Also, common to both excavation units are a number of large bovine remains, one each from TP1 Spits 8 and 9 and 12 from Spits 3 to 6 in TP4. These are undoubtedly water buffalo (*Bubalus bubalis*) remains as no other large bovines are known to have been introduced to Sulawesi before recent times (Simons and Bulbeck 2004). Water buffalo elements include mostly foot bones (astragalus, second and third fused carpal, intermediate phalanges), as well as ribs and scapula bones. Two of these scapula fragments from TP4 represent two water buffalo individuals with fused epiphyses, while the phalanges' proximal epiphyses were unfused suggesting at least one sub-adult individual present but no juveniles. Four of these large bovine bones from TP4 had a number of parallel cut marks and a long bone was split down the shaft in a fresh fracture (a sign that marrow was extracted).

In summary, the vertebrate identifications reflect a faunal assemblage dominated by domesticated (water buffalo, dog) or potentially domesticated (suid, cf. goat) taxa. The suid and cf. goat taxa can be characterised no more closely than potentially domesticated because, in the former case, an unknown proportion may represent the native Sulawesi warty hog and 'pig-deer' suids rather than the introduced, domesticated *Sus scrofa* pig, and, in the latter case, an unknown proportion may be the remains of deer (introduced to Sulawesi to roam wild) rather than goats. The suid and dog identifications reflect the pre-Islamic character of the vertebrate identifications as both of these are regarded as unclean beasts according to Islamic precepts. Equally importantly, cut marks on the bone fragments reveal a pattern of intensive butchery and meat consumption, which may well reflect feasting activities as would befit a palace centre. Also, water buffaloes are a critical traction animal for traditional wet-rice agriculture, which aligns with the evidence from micro-fossils in the sediment samples in indicating the major role of rice in the subsistence economy at Allangkanangnge (Bulbeck and Caldwell 2008).

Plant remains

Conditions for the preservation of plant material appear to have been far from ideal at Allangkanangnge. The recovered charcoal amounted to 287 g (and just 39 g, if the suspected cremation burial from TP4 is excluded), and just two fragments of wood were preserved (Tables 17.1–17.4). The anaerobic conditions at Utti Batue, in contrast, fostered the preservation of 1.4 kg of charcoal, 13 kg of wood and around 1.7 kg of other plant matter in the excavated test pit. The large quantity of wood at Utti Batue can be attributed to timber houses erected on piles in the traditional Bugis manner (Bulbeck et al. 2007). This had surely occurred at Allangkanangnge too despite the lack of direct archaeological evidence (Bulbeck and Caldwell 2008), and probably involved the construction of a wooden palace on the hilltop summit.

The importance of plant micro-fossils at a site with poor plant-matter preservation, such as Allangkanangnge, is amply shown by the thousands of rice phytoliths identified within the TP1 deposits excavated in 1999. Each 5 g sample from Spits 1–6, which are dated to between the 14th and 17th centuries, yielded approximately 500–1700 rice phytoliths. While unidentifiable as originating from dryland rice or wetland rice, the phytoliths reflect the pounding and final winnowing of rice (Bulbeck and Caldwell 2008). However, the local area under cultivation was probably less extensive when Allangkanangnge was first occupied, with the possibility of primary forest within foraging range as suggested by the analysis of the vertebrate faunal remains described above, and the name of a nearby settlement, Sumpang Alek ('Mouth of the Forest').

Discussion

Zone 1 was selected for excavation because of its retention of stratified deposit, as well as its topographic prominence and the fact that it is bordered by a low stone wall, which appears to be original. However, the evidence for pre-Islamic burials in Zone 1 is weak. Only one of the four test pits (TP4) produced remains that can be reasonably attributed to a pre-Islamic cremation burial, and its direct dating suggests that a pre-16th-century interment is unlikely (Table 17.4). Similarly, prestige goods take a clear second place to quotidian items in the excavated remains, as reflected in the ratio of one tradeware sherd to 120 earthenware sherds, and the absence of gold and scarcity of bronze. Zone 1 may have been the site of a wooden palace and a focus for feasting and related ceremonial activities, consistent with the vertebrate assemblage, rice phytoliths and earthenware assemblage dominated by serving vessels and cooking pots. A change to its predominant use for burials can be dated to the 16th or even the 17th century.

The purpose of the numerous stone arrangements with a central standing stone is not known, but it is possible that they mark the burials of cremated remains in jars (Bulbeck et al., this volume). The concentration of these structures along the southern ridge, where there is a high proportion of martavan sherdage similar to the hilltop, and their further dispersal onto the eastern slopes would go some way to explaining the distribution of imported ceramics over the site.

Both the excavated remains and the surface tradeware collection agree in dating initial settlement of Allangkanangnge to the 13th century, followed by a major occupation phase between the 14th and 16th centuries. The major attraction of the site during the 13th and 14th centuries may have been its status as a raised location closer than it is today to the mouth of the Cenrana River, from where trade could be controlled and taxed. With the subsequent progradation of the lower Cenrana, the opportunities for wet-rice cultivation in the vicinity of the site would have improved, and an emphasis on farming rather than a coastal economy evidently underpinned the site's 14th–16th-century heyday.

In the lead-up phase, during the 13th and 14th centuries, estuarine and coastal conditions apparently lay within the foraging range of the Allangkanangnge inhabitants, as reflected by the excavated shellfish dating to this period as well as the fish and turtle remains from TP1 Spits 7 and 8. This observation implies marked progradation of the lower Cenrana following the 14th century and, following the geomorphological model of Carson (2017), a dramatic expansion of the flanking lands suitable for wet-rice production. The central lakes area, of which Allangkanangnge forms part, is an ideal region in which to develop irrigated wet-rice cultivation due to seasonal inundation. The margins of the lakes and swamps that characterise the landscape form natural rice beds; today, one can witness the speculative planting of wetland rice on the margins of Lake Tempe. The management of these lake edges tends naturally to the construction of artificial bunds and the development of drainage, as well as co-operative forms of hydrological management (Caldwell and Lillie 2004).

Allangkanangnge would have been an ideal place from which to direct the expansion of agrarian settlement and expansion south and east of Lake Tempe during the 15th and 16th centuries. Whoever occupied the hill during this period would have almost certainly have taken a close interest in the central direction of wet-rice cultivation. Analogously, the 'Chronicle of Bone' describes the process of agrarian expansion during the 15th century within a pocket of coastal plain to the south of the Cenrana before extending its zone of direct influence as far north as the Cenrana during the 16th century (Macknight 1983).

It is difficult to directly match Allangkanangnge, which was continuously occupied from the 13th to late 17th centuries, with a kingdom called Cina that originated in the Cenrana Valley to the east in the 13th century, rose to prominence in the 14th and 15th centuries, and vanished in the 16th century. Cina appears to have had more than one palace site; indeed, it is difficult to identify any fixed centre in the historical record of Cina (Caldwell and Wellen 2017). The local tradition that Allangkanangnge was the pre-eminent palace site of Cina cannot be proven by archaeology, nor by historical sources as these do not name it. Certainly, however, Allangkanangnge's location, the richness of the ceramic assemblages on its hilltop, the evidence for elite feasting from the vertebrate identifications, and the persistent oral tradition that the hill was once the palace site of Cina, point to its being the focus of an important polity in the central lakes region.

Conclusion

Survey and excavation of the Allangkanangnge site document light occupation during the 13th century and a more intense phase of occupation between the 14th and 16th centuries. Faunal remains reflect a minor marine component to the diet from initial occupation through to the 14th century. Wet-rice cultivation probably underpinned the subsistence economy throughout the period of occupation although direct evidence for this relates to the 14th century onwards. The large assemblage of excavated earthenware pottery reflects a range of domestic activities including storage and food preparation and serving, as well as iron metallurgy (which is also recorded in local folklore for the site). At the height of its prosperity, the settlement evidently consisted of a major building or palace centre on the summit and rectangular stone arrangements marking the burial sites of cremated remains in jars along the southern ridge and eastern slopes. During the 17th century, occupation declined and there was a greater emphasis on mortuary activities. The site was probably abandoned in 1670 as a result of the harrowing of Wajo by Arung Palakka La Tenritatta (Andaya 1981).

In a landmark paper, Macknight (1983) suggested a date of around AD 1400 for the start of this agrarian expansion, based on the evidence of the Bugis chronicle of the kingdom of Bone, but in later publications this estimate has been revised down to AD 1300, based on new data (Bulbeck and Caldwell 2000; Druce 2009). In this paper, we establish that origins of the agrarian expansion lay in the 13th century, and that the process of centralised expansion of wet-rice agriculture, which today dominates the landscape of lowland South Sulawesi, may have begun in the western Cenrana valley. The complementary economic specialisations of South Sulawesi's late pre-Islamic economy—Luwu's production of ironware for local use and trade (Bulbeck and Caldwell 2000), intensive wet-rice production in the lower Walennae and Cenrana valleys (this paper), and long-distance maritime trade along the south coast (Nayati 2005)—can be confidently traced back to the 13th/14th centuries.

Acknowledgements

The Australian Research Council funded the 1999 fieldwork at the Allangkanangngne site and paid for one of the radiocarbon dates, while the British Academy funded the 2005 fieldwork season. The Centre for Archaeological Research (The Australian National University) funded two radiocarbon dates and the University of Hull paid for one radiocarbon date. The laboratory work on the surveyed and excavated remains was funded by the Australia-Indonesia Institute. The comments from two anonymous referees on an earlier version of this paper are gratefully acknowledged.

Author biographies

Budianto Hakim Makassar Archaeology Office, Makassar, South Sulawesi, Indonesia

Stuart Hawkins Department of Archaeology and Natural History, School of Culture, History and Language, College of Asia and the Pacific, The Australian National University, Canberra, Australia

David Bulbeck Department of Archaeology and Natural History, School of Culture, History and Language, College of Asia and the Pacific, The Australian National University, Canberra, Australia

Ian Caldwell Archaeological Studies Program, University of the Philippines Diliman, Republic of the Philippines

Stephen Druce Academy of Brunei Studies, Universiti Brunei Darussalam, Brunei Darussalam

Campbell Macknight College of Asia and the Pacific, The Australian National University, Canberra, Australia

References

Adhyatman, S. and R. Arifin. 1996. *Manik-Manik di Indonesia Beads in Indonesia*. 2nd edition. Jakarta: Penerbit Djambatan.

Andaya, L.Y. 1981. *The Heritage of Arung Palakka: A History of South Sulawesi (Celebes) in the Seventeenth Century*. Verhandelingen van het Koninklijk Instituut voor Taal-, Land- en Volkenkunde 91. The Hague: Martinus Nijhoff.

Beck, H. 1936. *Beads & Magic*. London: Robert Stockwell.

Boessneck, J. 1969. Osteological differences between sheep (*Ovis aries* Linné) and goat (*Capra hircus* Linné). In D.R. Brothwell and E.S. Higgs (eds), *Science in Archaeology: A Survey of Progress and Research*. London: Thames and Hudson.

Bronk Ramsey, C. 2013. *OxCal 4.2 manual*. c14.arch.ox.ac.uk/oxcal/OxCal.html (accessed 27 October 2018).

Bulbeck, F.D. 1992. A Tale of Two Kingdoms: The Historical Archaeology of Gowa and Tallok, South Sulawesi, Indonesia. Unpublished PhD thesis, School of Archaeology and Anthropology, The Australian National University, Canberra. Available at www.oxis.org/theses/bulbeck-1992.pdf (accessed 5 June 2018).

Bulbeck, D. 2000. *Sediments and Ceramics from Cina and Cenrana*. Report to the Australia-Indonesia Institute, Appendix A. Canberra: The Australian National University.

Bulbeck, D. 2009. The application of Darwinian cultural evolutionary theory to ceramics: the case of 'soft pottery' from Luwu, South Sulawesi, Indonesia. In H.J. Muscio and G.E.J. López (eds), *Theoretical and Methodological Issues in Evolutionary Archaeology: Toward an Unified Darwinian Paradigm Questions théorétiqes et méthodologiques en archéologie évolutive: Vers un paradigme Darwinien unifié*, pp. 3–11. Oxford: BAR International Series 1915.

Bulbeck, D., F.A. Aziz, S. O'Connor, A. Calo, J.N. Fenner, B. Marwick, J. Feathers, R. Wood and D. Prastiningtyas. 2016. Mortuary caves and the dammar trade in the Towuti-Routa region, Sulawesi, in an Island Southeast Asian context. *Asian Perspectives* 55(2):148–183. doi.org/10.1353/asi.2016.0017 (accessed 5 June 2018).

Bulbeck, D., D. Bowdery, J. Field and B. Prasetyo. 2007. The Palace Centre of Sago City: Utti Batue site, Luwu, South Sulawesi, Indonesia. In M. Lillie and S. Ellis (eds), *Wetland Archaeology & Environments: Regional Issues, Global Perspectives*, pp. 119–141. Oxford: Oxbow Books.

Bulbeck, D. and I. Caldwell. 2000. *Land of Iron: The Historical Archaeology of Luwu and the Cenrana Valley. Results of the Origin of Complex Society in South Sulawesi Project (OXIS)*. Hull: Centre for South-East Asian Studies, University of Hull. Available at www.oxis.org/books/land-of-iron.pdf (accessed 5 June 2018).

Bulbeck, D. and I. Caldwell. 2008. Oryza sativa and the origins of kingdoms in South Sulawesi, Indonesia: Evidence from rice husk phytoliths. *Indonesia and the Malay World* 36(104):1–20. doi.org/10.1080/13639810802016117 (accessed 5 June 2018).

Bulbeck, D., I. Caldwell, S. Druce, B. Hakim and C. Macknight. 2018. Imported tradeware ceramics and their relevance for dating socio-political developments in South Sulawesi, with special reference to the Allangkanangnge ri Latanete site. In S. O'Connor, D. Bulbeck and J. Meyer (eds), *The Archaeology of Sulawesi: Current Research on the Pleistocene to the Historic Period*, pp. 269–286. Canberra: ANU Press.

Bulbeck, D. and B. Prasetyo. 2000. Perkembangan masyarakat di Sulawesi Selatan: Hasil penelitian sementara di Luwu. In M.A. Fadillah and I. Sumantri (eds), *Kedatuan Luwu: Perspektif Arkeologi, Sejarah dan Antropologi*, pp. 29–46. Makassar: Lembaga Penerbitan Universitas Hasanuddin/Institut Etnografi Indonesia.

Burton, J.A., S. Hedges and A.H. Mustari. 2005. The taxonomic status, distribution and conservation of the lowland anoa *Bubalus depressicornis* and mountain anoa *Bubalus quarlesi*. *Mammal Review* 35(1):25–50. doi.org/10.1111/j.1365-2907.2005.00048.x (accessed 5 June 2018).

Caldwell, I. 1988. South Sulawesi A.D. 1300–1600: Ten Bugis Texts. Unpublished PhD thesis, Department of History, The Australian National University, Canberra. www.oxis.org/theses/caldwell-1988.pdf (accessed 5 June 2018).

Caldwell, I. 1995. Power, state and society among the pre-Islamic Bugis. *Bijdragen tot de Taal-, Land- en Volkenkunde* 151(3):394–421. doi.org/10.1163/22134379-90003038 (accessed 5 June 2018).

Caldwell, I. and M. Lillie. 2004. Manuel Pinto's inland sea: Using palaeoenvironmental techniques to assess historical evidence from southwest Sulawesi. In S.G. Keates and J.M. Pasveer (eds), *Modern Quaternary Research in Indonesia*, pp. 259–271. Quaternary Research in Southeast Asia, Volume 18. Leiden: A.A. Balkema.

Caldwell, I. and K. Wellen. 2016. Family matters: Bugis genealogies and their contribution to Austronesian studies. In S.C. Druce (ed.), *Orality, Writing and History: The Literature of the Bugis and Makasar of South Sulawesi. International Journal of Asia Pacific Studies* 12(Supplement 1): 119–141. doi.org/10.21315/ijaps2016.12.s1.6.

Caldwell, I. and K. Wellen. 2017. Finding Cina: A new paradigm for early Bugis history. *Bijdragen tot de Taal-, Land- en Volkenkunde* 173(2/3):296–324. doi.org/10.1163/22134379-17302004 (accessed 5 June 2018).

Carson, M. 2017. Coastal palaeo-landscapes of the Neolithic. Invited contribution to P. Bellwood, *First Islanders: Prehistory and Human Migration in Island Southeast Asia*, pp. 240–244. Oxford: Wiley Blackwell.

Clune, G. and D. Bulbeck. 1999. Description and preliminary chronology of Macassar historical earthenware decorations. *Walennae* 3(2):39–60. doi.org/10.24832/wln.v2i1.65 (accessed 5 June 2018).

Do, M. 2013. Iron-Nickel Alloy Smelting Production in Luwu, South Sulawesi during the pre-Islamic Period. Unpublished MSc thesis, Institute of Archaeology, University College London, London. www.oxis.org/theses/misol-2103.pdf.

Druce, S.C. 2009. *The Lands West of the Lakes: A History of the Ajattappareng Kingdoms of South Sulawesi, 1200 to 1600 CE*. Leiden: Verhandelingen van het Koninklijk Instituut voor Taal-, Land- en Volkenkunde 261. doi.org/10.1163/9789004253827 (accessed 5 June 2018).

Druce, S., D. Bulbeck and I. Mahmud. 2005. A transitional Islamic Bugis cremation in Bulubangi, South Sulawesi: Its historical and archaeological context. *Review of Indonesian and Malaysian Affairs* 39(1):1–22.

Fadillah, M.A. and I. Sumantri (eds). 2000. *Kedatuan Luwu: Perspektif Arkeologi, Sejarah dan Antropologi*. Makassar: Lembaga Penerbitan Universitas Hasanuddin/Institut Etnografi Indonesia.

Gremmen, W.H.E. 1990. Palynological investigations in the Danau Tempe depression, southwest Sulawesi (Celebes), Indonesia. *Modern Quaternary Research in Southeast Asia*, pp. 123–134. Quaternary Research in Southeast Asia, Volume 11. Rotterdam: A.A. Balkema.

Macknight, C.C. 1983. The rise of agriculture in South Sulawesi before 1600. *Review of Indonesian and Malaysian Affairs* 17:92–116.

Macknight, C.C. and P. Mukhlis. n.d. The Chronicle of Bone. Unpublished typescript.

Miksic, J.N. and C.T. Yap. 1990. *X-ray fluorescence data on earthenware pottery trade in Sumatra, 12th–14th centuries*. Paper presented at the 14th Indo-Pacific Prehistory Association Congress, Yogyakarta, 25 August – 2 September.

Morales Muniz, A. 1988. On the use of butchering as a paleocultural index: Proposal of a new methodology for the study of bone fracture from archaeological sites. *ArchaeoZoologia* 2(1/2):111–150.

Nayati, W. 2005. Social Dynamics and Local Trading Patterns in the Bantaeng Region, South Sulawesi (Indonesia) circa 17th Century. Unpublished PhD thesis, The Southeast Asian Studies Programme, National University of Singapore, Singapore. www.oxis.org/theses/widiya-nayati-2005.pdf (accessed 5 June 2018).

Nurhayati, R., A. Hukma and I. Anwar (eds). 2003. *La Galigo: Menelusuri jejak Warisan Sastra Dunia*. Makassar: Pusat Studi La Galigo, Hasanuddin University.

Pelras, C. 1996. *The Bugis*. Oxford: Basil Blackwell.

Pelras, C. 2010. *Explorations dans l'univers des Bugis: Un choix de trente-trois rencontres*. Cahiers d'Archipel 39. Paris: Association Archipel.

Prummel, W. and H.-J. Frisch. 1986. A guide for the distinction of species, sex and body side in bones of sheep and goat. *Journal of Archaeological Science* 13(6):567–577. doi.org/10.1016/0305-4403(86)90041-5 (accessed 5 June 2018).

Sadek-Kooros, H. 1975. Intentional fracturing of bone: Description of criteria. In A.T. Clason (ed.), *Archaeozoological Studies*, pp. 139–150. Amsterdam: North Holland Publishing Co.

Schmid, E. 1972. *Atlas of Animal Bones: For Prehistorians, Archaeologists and Quaternary Geologists*. Amsterdam: Elsevier Science Publishers.

Shipman, P., W. Bosler, K.L. Davis, A.K. Behrensmeyer, R.I.M. Dunbar, C.P. Groves, F. Thackeray, J.A.H.V. Couvering and R.K. Stucky. 1981. Butchering of Giant Geladas at an Acheulian Site. *Current Anthropology* 22(3):257–268. doi.org/10.1086/202663 (accessed 5 June 2018).

Silver, I.A. 1969. The ageing of domestic animals. In D.R. Brothwell and E.S. Higgs (eds), *Science in Archaeology: A Survey of Progress and Research*, pp. 283–302. London: Thames and Hudson.

Simons, A.G. and D. Bulbeck. 2004. Late Quaternary faunal successions in South Sulawesi, Indonesia. In S.G. Keates and J.M. Pasveer (eds), *Quaternary Research in Indonesia*, pp. 167–189. Modern Quaternary Research in Southeast Asia, Volume 18. Leiden: A.A. Balkema.

Stargardt, J. 2003. Mapping the mind: Some cultural cargoes of the sea-trade in Southeast Asia, 5th–13th centuries. In A. Karlström and A. Källén (eds), *Fishbones and Glittering Emblems: Southeast Asian Archaeology 2002*, pp. 103–117. Stockholm: Museum of Far Eastern Antiquities.

Sukamto, R. 1975. *Peta Geologi Indonesia, Lembang Ujung Pandang, Benteng dan Sinjai*. Bandung: Geological Research and Development Centre.

Tim Penyusun Laporan Ekskavasi Penyelamatan dan Rekonstruksi Dinding Barat BSO (Tim). 1992. *Ekskavasi Penyelamatan dan Rekonstruksi Dinding Barat Benteng Somba Opu Kabupaten Gowa 14 September S.D 14 Nopember 1992*. Makassar: Suaka Peninggalan Sejarah dan Purbakala Sulawesi Selatan dan Tenggara/Proyek Persiapan Pembangunan Miniatur Sulawesi Pemda Tingkat I Propinsi Sulawesi Selatan.

Wilson, B., C. Grigson and S. Payne (eds). 1982. *Ageing and Sexing Animal Bones from Archaeological Sites*. British Archaeological Reports British Series 109. Oxford: BAR Publishing.

Zainal Abidin, A. 1983. The emergence of early kingdoms in Sulawesi. In A. Zainal Abidin (ed.), *Persepsi Orang Bugis, Makasar tentang Hukum, Negara dan Dunia Luar*, pp. 455–491. Bandung: Penerbit Alumni.

Zainal Abidin, A. 1985. *Wajo' pada Abad XV-XVI: Suatu Penggalian Sejarah terpendam Sulawesi Selatan dari Lontara'*. Bandung: Penerbit Alumni.

Reflections on the social and cultural aspects of the megalithic site of Onto, Bantaeng, South Sulawesi

Akin Duli

Abstract

This paper presents the results from an archaeological survey of the megalithic site of Onto in Bantaeng, South Sulawesi. A variety of archaeological remains were found at this site including menhirs, incised stones, rings of stacked stones, stone tablets including a stone altar, *dakon* stones with circular impressions, royal installation stones, structural stone walls, and pottery (imported and locally made). The surface survey undertaken at Onto documented the boundaries and spatial structure of its cultural remains. The analysis of these remains produced descriptions of each type of artefactual material as well as interpretations of their meaning. This research adds to the available information on the role of Onto in the origins of the early historical kingdom of Bantaeng and to our understanding of settlements attached to megalithic culture in South Sulawesi.

Keywords: South Sulawesi early history, megaliths, Bantaeng, Onto

Introduction

Bantaeng is a small district, covering an area of about 396 km², located along the southern coast of South Sulawesi about 125 km from the capital city of Makassar (Figure 18.1). The majority of its ~180,000 inhabitants belong to the Makasar ethnic group, although many Bugis have immigrated following the defeat of Makassar empire by the United East India Company (VOC) and its Bugis allies in 1667. Both the Makasar and Bugis have adopted Islam following its introduction to the region at the turn of the 17th century. More than 60% of the Bantaeng inhabitants work in the agricultural sector predominately growing rice and maize, along with cash crops such as cloves, cotton, cacao and (at higher elevations) potatoes, carrots and the kapok fibre harvested from forest remnants. Much of the remaining population lives near the sea, practising a maritime lifestyle including fishing (Bougas 1998; Nayati 2005; Wikipedia 2017).

Figure 18.1: Relevant place names in South Sulawesi including district boundaries (dashed).

Sources: Caldwell and Bougas (2004); Nayati (2005); Duli (2008); Hasanuddin University (2013).

Bantaeng is a minor administrative centre today, but was of greater importance during the early history of South Sulawesi. When the VOC targeted Bantaeng during its assault on Makassar, the VOC commander described Bantaeng as a large, prosperous city that was a major rice-producing centre for Makassar (Andaya 1981:75–76). Bantaeng was also known to the eastern Javanese empire of Majapahit in AD 1365, as recorded in a poem that documented its existence alongside four other South Sulawesi places (Robson 1995). This poem specifically linked Bantaeng to the reportedly less prominent places of Luwu (located at the northeast of the peninsula) and 'Uda', which probably was then based along the Cenrana River (Caldwell and Wellen 2017). Local looters have been active in plundering imported ceramics from Bantaeng's pre-Islamic cemeteries, including 13th/14th-century wares from Bantaeng city and the archaeological sites of Benteng Batu Terang, Borong Kapala and Borong Tua to the west of Bantaeng city (Nayati 2005:Table 6).

In an influential text, Bougas (1998) examines the importance of South Sulawesi and Bantaeng's role in the region's pre-Islamic history. He uses a number of sources to produce this work including archaeological surveys in 1995 and 1996, which include maps and descriptions of the Onto site, interviews with local looters who have pilfered grave goods such as high-fired ceramics, ancient texts containing myths and legends of the time, and observations on pre-Islamic rites that have survived to the present day. This paper will develop on Bougas's work by:

(a) incorporating relevant literature postdating 1998

(b) summarising information obtained during interviews on the legends, mythology, toponyms and local beliefs as to the significance of Onto in the origins of the Bantaeng kingdom

(c) describing results from an archaeological survey conducted as part of this research on Onto

(d) discussing the prehistoric origins of the tradition of megaliths documented at Onto and other early historical sites in South Sulawesi.

Description of the Onto site

Location

Onto lies in Balla Tujua *lingkungan* or *kampung* (kampong), Kelurahan (Village) Onto, Kecamatan (Subdistrict) Bantaeng, Kabupaten (District) Bantaeng in South Sulawesi province. It lies in the hills about 12 km north of Bantaeng township at an altitude of 800 metres above sea level (m asl), with geographical coordinates of 5°28'42.8"S 119°58'33.3"E. Access to the site is facilitated by a four-wheel drive track, which connects the site to an asphalt road.

The site is surrounded by a settlement and gardens with field houses. Outside of these maintained areas, the vegetation is a dense mixture of self-generating and agricultural flora. The identified flora includes teak (*jati*), banyan, cacao, kapok, breadfruit, mango and *langsat* trees, coconut and banana palms, rattan, vines and sundry weeds. According to the local community's beliefs, the vegetation may not be cleared because felling the trees could wreak havoc.

The topography of the area is generally undulating with sharp breaks in some places and andesite rock outcrops. The soil is dark brown and generally wet from interspersed springs and streams.

Overview of mythological associations

It became apparent during interviews that Onto is believed to be the source of power of the Bantaeng royal lineage, with pre-Islamic origins. Onto is a traditional law area, and despite the community's formal conversion to Islam, traces of their traditional *patuntung* beliefs persist

(Nayati 2005:268). The *patuntung* belief system emphasises dutiful observation of the traditional customs and precepts bequeathed by the ancestors including reverence for the ancestors (Rössler 1990). According to local community leaders, the *Tomanurung* (heavenly founding figure) of central Bantaeng descended from the sky at Onto to resolve the prevailing social confusion (Ulaen 1978:21–39). There he met the seven brothers who became the *Karaengloe* (great rulers) of Bantaeng, Gantarang Keke (eastern Bantaeng), Kajang, Luwu, Gowa, Bone and Solo in Java (Bougas 1998). The story of the seven *Karaengloe* brothers is commemorated at the site by seven miniature houses, where traditional ceremonies were performed. The *Balla tujua* hamlet, which means 'seven houses', is named for it. The site is also known by the local community as *lalang bata*, which means 'inside the fort'.

Physical description

In general terms, the Onto site runs along a north–south tending ridge top (see Figure 18.2). Surveys have documented a considerable variety of structures including the *lalang bata* fort, *Balla tujua* (seven houses), *Barugayya* festival seat, *Bonto-bontoa* (high point), main stone altar, *Batu Pallantikang* royal installation stones, *Toddo ballanga, batu mentenga* menhirs and graves (pre-Islamic and Islamic). The ceremonial associations of the Onto structures have been noted by previous observers (Ulaen 1978; Bougas 1998; Nayati 2005) as well as during the author's survey, although there has been no direct witnessing of the associated ceremonies in any of these cases.

Lalang bata

The *lalang bata* is a stacked arrangement of andesite stones, around 1 m high, that circumscribes most of the Onto structures (Figure 18.2). It is difficult to determine the original outline of this arrangement as it has collapsed in some places. The shape appears approximately rectangular following the hilltop's north–south contours, although the corners of the construction could not be ascertained during the survey. The estimated diameters are 125 m north–south and 150 m east–west. The stones included in the construction were likely collected from the local andesite outcrops. They have variable dimensions with no evidence of shaping.

Our survey team was informed that the old fort walls are the staging ground for a local ceremony known as the *A'dete Babang*. In this ceremonial offering to the *Karaengloe*, a procession walks around the fort with sacrificial animals and other ceremonial items. The ceremony is usually led by a *dukun* (shaman) who has supernatural powers that enable communication with the magical forces of nature. This shaman is a woman called the *pinati* by the local community.

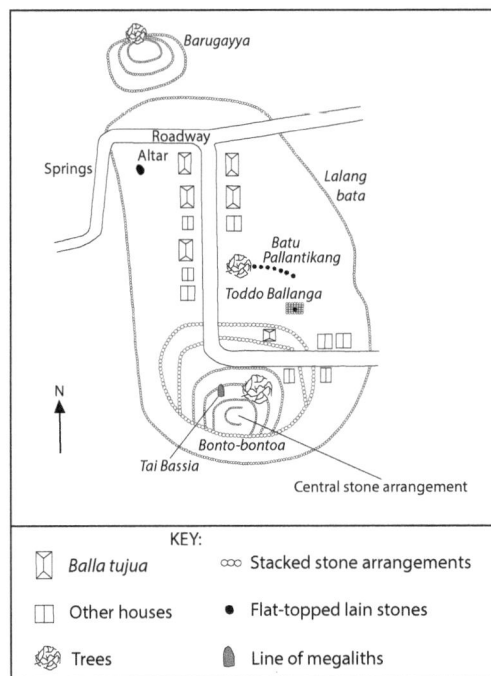

Figure 18.2: Map of Onto site (not to scale).
Source: Adapted from Bougas (1998:104).

Balla tujua

Balla tujua refers to seven miniature stilt houses erected at various times inside the *lalang bata*. These houses had a north–south orientation following the direction of the sea from the mountains. There were three buildings aligned on the east, three others aligned on the west and one in the middle (Ulaen 1978:17; Tuti 1991:23). More recently, six modern houses (along with some other modern houses) were built to replace the *Balla tujua*, but they do not replicate the *Balla tujua* that they replaced.

The function of the *Balla tujua* is to symbolise the houses of the seven brothers who ruled the domain. Accordingly, each house is named for the area that the brother ruled—that is, Balla of the Law of Bantaeng, Balla of the Law of Bone, and so on. The original function of the *Balla tujua* was to be the place of residence for the *pinati* who conducted the sacred ceremonies. According to custom, every house sheltered a family and the head of the household or his wife served as the ceremonial master (Ulaen 1978:17).

Barugayya

The *Barugayya* festival seat is a three-stepped terrace that lies immediately north of the *lalang bata* boundary (Figure 18.2). The top terrace roughly 5.5 m in diameter. The middle terrace is 4.5 m from the edge of the top terrace to its south side and 3.5 m on its east and west sides. The lower terrace is 5.5 m from the edge of the middle terrace at its south end and 3.5 m on the east and west sides. The complex includes a stone altar propped up by stacks of small stones.

The *Barugayya* terraces are built from locally collected andesite stones of various sizes ranging from 17 cm to 1 m in length. These stones have not been altered before being arranged to form the edges of each terrace. The top terrace has a consistent wall height of 65 cm. The arrangement is broken in places where stones have gone missing. At times, members of the local community have carried away stones from the lowest terrace to make garden walls.

The *Barugayya* is used in a series of ceremonial processions for praying to the *Karaengloe*. During our survey in October 2008, remnants of these ceremonies were still visible including coconut shells, wicker baskets and coconut fruits at the eastern side, which marks the entrance gate to the upper terrace of the *Barugayya*.

Bonto-bontoa (Pocci Butta)

Bonto-bontoa refers to the ring-shaped stone arrangements located on the high point of the southern side of the site, in a complementary relationship to the *Barugayya* at the north. There are five of these stone rings, with a similar terrace construction to the *Barugayya*. The southern section of the site is on a steep slope, and the terraces lead to the central part of the site. The breadth of the uppermost stone ring is 3.5 m east–west and 7.5 m north–south. Its distance from the next (fourth) stone ring is 4.2 m and the difference in height is 55 cm. The fourth stone ring has a banyan tree, which is revered as a holy tree by the local populace. The distance from the fourth level and the third stone ring is 4 m with a difference in height of 65 cm. The distance between the third and second stone ring is 7 m with a height difference of 47 cm. The distance from the second to the lowest stone ring is 11 with a difference in height of 26 cm. The base level is roughly 63 m east to west and 37 m from north–south.

As with the *Barugayya*, the *Bonto-bontoa* terraces are constructed with unshaped andesite blocks. On the west side, the natural stones include both rounded and tapered shapes, individually placed or stacked on each other in an irregular way. According to local beliefs, the round stones are female symbols and the tapering stones are male symbols (Bougas 2007).

Figure 18.3: Ring-shaped pile of stones at the *Bonto-bontoa* peak.
Source: Akin Duli.

A considerable portion of these terraces are degraded from use of the stones for the adjacent asphalt road, yards and houses. One feature that remains whole is a ring-shaped arrangement at the peak, which is a centre for *Karaengloe* worship (Figure 18.3). The rocks that make up the circle are sandstone as well as andesite, with dimensions between 10 cm and 30 cm. There is an entrance to the circular feature on the east side. The open space in the centre is 2.5 m wide.

Stone altar

The main stone altar is a natural block of stone with a flattish top located to the west side of the *lalang bata* (Figure 18.2). It is 2.8 m long, 1 m high and 1.8 m wide. Tree roots have penetrated a crack in the altar, widening the split and causing the altar to divide.

Batu Pallantikang

The *Batu Pallantikang*, or royal inauguration stones, consist of seven rocks laid in a row from west to east. They served as the place for the installation of the ruler (*jannang*) of Onto and its six subsidiaries, symbolised by the *Balla tujua*. These seven stones (Figure 18.4) have naturally flat surfaces and are arranged between 25 cm and 37 cm apart. Their breadth varies between 23 cm and 65 cm and their width between 7 cm and 27 cm. The third and sixth stones from the west are *dakon* (pockmarked) stones with 12 regularly spaced shallow indentations on their surface. The sixth stone also has long, irregular incisions across its short axis with a depth of 0.4 cm to 0.9 cm. According to an informant, these incisions symbolise the number of rulers who have been inaugurated. However, this report should be treated with caution because if the incisions did symbolise all the inaugurated *jannang*, a more regular pattern might be expected.

Figure 18.4: *Batu Pallantikang.*
Source: Akin Duli.

Toddo Ballanga

The *Toddo Ballanga* is a stack of andesite stones with a diameter of 97 cm. The size of the stones varies between 20 cm x 10 cm and 30 cm x 20 cm. The stack is surrounded by a rectangular arrangement of stones that is 2 m in breadth and 1.9 m in width. An attached wooden rail with coconut fronds runs around the stone arrangement. The *Toddo Ballanga* is positioned 1 m north of the widest stone circle of the *Bonto-bontoa* (basal stone ring) and 3 m from *Batu Pallantikang* (inauguration stones). A flat-topped stone altar is located in the centre (Figure 18.2).

According to the local community, the *Toddo Ballanga* is where the *Tomanurung* descended from the sky, making it an important monument for *Karaengloe* homage. At the time of our survey, the remains of offerings were present inside the fence, including basket wickers, coconut fruits and flowers.

Batu mentenga

Standing stones (menhirs) are called *batu mentenga* by the local community. There are two locations with menhirs at the site. The first includes a line of six menhirs between the second and third *Bonto-bontoa* stone arrays, and the second consists of a single menhir near the western border of the *lalang bata* (see Figure 18.2). The single megalith, or monolith, serves as the seating place for the series of *Karaengloe* homage ceremonies. Its height is 97 cm and its maximum diameter is 52 cm, becoming thinner towards the top.

Figure 18.5: *Tai Bassia* line of menhirs.
Source: Akin Duli.

The six menhirs in a line, all of which are andesite, have partially fallen over (Figure 18.5). They have their natural shape, and their dimensions are variable. The westernmost is 1 m tall and has a diameter of 46 cm. Proceeding east, we find the other menhirs are respectively 96 cm tall with a diameter of 39 cm, 56 cm tall with a diameter of 38 cm, 86 cm tall with a diameter of 39 cm, 75 cm tall with a diameter of 32 cm, and 68 cm tall with a diameter of 36 cm. The local community calls them *Tai Bassia*, which means iron rust. According to local sources, there used to be seven menhirs (the same number as for the *Balla Tujua*), but one was carried away to help build the road.

Cemetery complex

A cemetery complex containing both Islamic and pre-Islamic graves lies to the south of the *lalang bata*. The characteristic feature of the pre-Islamic graves is their form as a pile of stones with an east–west orientation (Bougas 1998:106; Nayati 2005).

Distribution of surface fragments

The fragments found on the ground surface during the survey are dominated by sherds of earthenware pottery but also include porcelain sherds. The sherds are concentrated within the *lalang bata*, and do not extend up the hill slope to the north nor to the east or the west. They do, however, reach across the south side of the *lalang bata* towards the foot of the hill. Here our survey came upon looter's holes, which still have freshly broken, imported ceramic sherds. This southward-trending distribution of the earthenware and imported ceramic sherds reflects the landscape's morphology. In this area, the slope is gentle and there is closer access to the river. Thus, it appears that the area to the north, east and west of the *lalang bata* was not occupied owing to difficulties of access and freshwater availability.

Preliminary analysis of the Onto earthenware pottery has identified rim, body and base fragments from a range of forms including plates, bowls, cooking pots and barrel-shaped jars. An earlier study on imported ceramics found at Onto dates them to the 16th–17th centuries (Nayati 2005:245). Occupation at Onto clearly spanned the transition to Islam as reflected by its cemetery complex with the presence of both pre-Islamic and early Islamic graves.

Social and cultural aspects of the Onto megaliths

The prominent peak of Mount Lompobattang, which lies at the source of Bantaeng's rivers and is associated with Bantaeng's origin myths (Bougas 1998), is situated to the north of the site. The two largest megalithic structures at Onto, the *Barugayya* and *Bonto-bontoa*, form a pair at the far north and south of the site. The site's layout in general reflects a micro-cosmos oriented north to south between the mountains and sea. According to Mahmud et al. (2007:80), this local conception of the cosmos invokes a parallel with the human head, whose frontal or upper interior part is believed to be the placed to be revered, and the holy place where the ancestors, who have risen to the status of gods, reside. This interpretation reflects the view of Soejono (1984) that the tradition of megaliths in Indonesia is associated with paying homage to the ancestors.

The cosmological analogy extends to the ring-shaped stone arrangement at *Bonto-bontoa*, the centre of local *Karaengloe* worship. The *pinati* would enter the stone arrangement from the east with the procession following from east to west. The direction of the procession thus mimics that of the sun across the sky. This celestial passage of the sun is believed to symbolise the human life cycle from birth (sunrise) to death (sunset), and also the passage of the deceased from the state of recently passed away to the realm of the ancestors (*alam puya*) (Bougas 2007; Mahmud et al. 2007).

Megalithic constructions, varying from single standing stones to more complex structures, are found widely across Indonesia. The oldest megaliths perhaps functioned as grave markers including dolmens (stone tables on upright pillars), stone burial chests and chambers, sarcophagi, *kalamba* burial receptacles (Central Sulawesi), *waruga* (North Sulawesi), stone stalls and circular rings. At these burial places there are usually several other megaliths that venerate the ancestors, such as menhirs, statues of the ancestors, stone mortars (*batu lumpang* and *batu lesung*), *dakon* stones, decked stones, stone walls and stone-lined paths (Hasanuddin 2015). In addition, there are some megaliths that connect the population with the locally venerated ancestors. These include altars that have been used both as thrones by rulers and as a holy place for paying homage to the ancestors through meetings and ceremonies. Other examples are the stone mortars placed on the corners of dry gardens or wet paddy fields that are believed to channel supernatural energy to boost crop production (personal observations).

The following sections discuss some possible purposes of the Onto megaliths, which include stone terraces, ring-shaped stone arrangements, menhirs, stone altars and the royal inauguration stones, which include two *dakon* stones.

Stepped terraces

Stepped terraces are constructions of stones arranged into terraces or steps, usually with three, five or seven levels. They are found at several megalithic sites in South Sulawesi, usually located at the foot of a hill, on a hilltop (e.g. Onto) or on holy peaks (e.g. Bulu Matanre; Kallupa et al. 1989). They mark the transition from the lower, everyday outer levels to the elevated, sacred levels on the inside. Other megaliths associated with the stepped terraces would have had different functions during the ceremonial processions along the stepped terraces. At Onto, the stepped terraces had a communal function for ritual ceremonies involving the mass gathering of all community members reflecting the social strata of the entire community. At another site with stepped terraces on an earthen mound, Karaengloe Burane in Jeneponto (Caldwell and Bougas 2004), the stepped terraces mark the approach to a ring-shaped stone arrangement that circumscribes a square stone arrangement, which is a focus of local *Tomanurung* rites.

Ring-shaped stone arrangements

The function of the ring-shaped arrangement of stones at *Bonto-bontoa* was to provide a place to worship the ancestral spirits. The pairing of round stones (vagina = female) with cylindrical stones (phallus = male) symbolises the meeting between the 'Upperworld' of the sky and celestial bodies and the 'Underworld' of the earth and sea, which gave birth to the 'Middleworld' where humanity resides. This 'Austronesian cosmology' (see Gibson 2005:50–51) aligns with the local belief that the *Bonto-bontoa* (*Pocci Butta*) is the centre of the settlement (*kampung*)—that is, the natural centre of local microcosmic power as a symbol of the macrocosmic world at large. Fittingly, this monument commemorates the *Karaengloe* who became the ancestors of Bantaeng's leaders after meeting with the *Tomanurung*.

Onto's second ring-shaped stone arrangement, the *Barugayya*, functioned as the place for conferences between the community leader and members, where the leader would be positioned inside the circle and the other community members towards the outside.

One of the most important of the ritual sites in western Bantaeng, Borong Kapala, also features stone arrangements, but further details are unavailable because the local inhabitants refused access for archaeological documentation (Nayati 2005:259).

Menhirs

Menhirs are widely distributed across Indonesia. Amongst traditional communities that continue their megalithic culture, menhirs are involved in practical matters such as displays of social status, but this use is still strongly tied to a belief in the megaliths' connections with the spirits of the ancestors (e.g. Bonatz 2002). The menhirs at the Onto site are not well understood by the local community, but their explanations centre around the continuation of the traditional *Karaengloe* ceremonies. The menhirs are also associated with veneration for bygone iron workers (*taka bessia*), their unique ability to work iron symbolised by the peculiar shapes of the assembled menhirs (Bougas 1998). In South Sulawesi, menhirs are far more a feature of archaeological sites in Bugis- than in Makasar-speaking areas (Hasanuddin 2015), although a large menhir originally 2 m high (now lying on its side) was recorded near the royal installation stones of the Kale Gowa rulers of Makassar (Bulbeck 1992).

Stone altars

Stone altars are usually associated with other megaliths and, like menhirs, they are common across Indonesia. They are flat-lain stones, sometimes supported by feet of stacked stones. These raised stone altars have been found widely across the South Sulawesi peninsula (Duli 2008; Hasanuddin University 2013), not only at Onto (within the *Barugayya*) but also at Nek Lumombang and Buntu Pattunuang Asu (Enrekang), Biloka (Sidrap), Sewo, Lawo, Tinco, Umpengngeng, Akkurung, Madenra (Soppeng), Bulu Kaili (Barru), Samaillo, Labuaja, Bulu Garaccing and Sumaling (Bone), Kajuara-Camba (Maros), Gojeng, Karampuang, Caroppo, Bulu Podo, Bulo-Bulo and Bulu Bappejang (Sinjai), Bungung Salapang (Jeneponto), Lembang Gantarang Keke and Gantarang Keke (Bantaeng), Possi Tana, Bulo-Bulo, Batu Datar Salossoe and Anrong Guru Lagoppo (Bulukumba) and Bissorang (Selayar).

In the Tana Toraja regency to the north of the peninsula, raised stone altars functioned as places to present offerings during thanksgiving harvest ceremonies at sites such as Sillanan, Potok Tengan, Ke'pe and Sassak (Duli 1999). At Onto, the stone altar at the *Toddo balanga* served to honour the *Karaengloe*. The stone altars at Lembang Gantarang Keke are associated with various aspects of veneration of the local *Tomanurung*, including the location where he descended from heaven, his seating place and the spot where offerings of sugar palm were prepared for him; while a large stone at Gantarang Keke is believed to mark the site where this *Tomanurung* returned to heaven (Bougas 1998:93–95).

Royal inauguration stones

The other flat stones at Onto form a row of stones for the installation of rulers at the *Batu Pallantikang*. Two of the installation stones are *dakon*, which may have been used for keeping a count of 'days of good fortune' or to confirm predictions made by traditional law leaders. The *dakon* stone with incisions may also have functioned to impart magical power to blades that were sharpened across its surface.

Chronology of the Onto site

Bantaeng has a lengthy occupation history as demonstrated by the cave sequences at Panganreang Tudea and Batu Ejaya. These deposits include a Mesolithic layer dating back to at least the 3rd millennium BC and a Neolithic occupation layer marked by the appearance of earthenware pottery. The Batu Ejaya decorated pottery is associated with a ^{14}C date on charcoal of c. AD 1000. This date coincides with the approximate age of the Bonto-bontoa site in eastern Bantaeng, where similar decorated pottery, metal wares and 21 imported carnelian beads were excavated (Bulbeck 2004). Tuti (1991:50) proposed that the megalithic remains at Onto distinguish it as an ancient monumental site (1st millennium BC) according to Heine Geldern's (1945) classification of Indonesian megaliths into old (Neolithic) and more recent (Metal Age) examples. However, Heine Geldern's schema was problematic as it was not supported by any direct dates (Bellwood 1978; Soejono 1984) and is now disproved with the recent availability of ^{14}C dates associated with megaliths (Hasanuddin 2015).

It is unlikely that initial occupation at Onto preceded the 15th century (Nayati 2005:268). The significance of the Onto site for the origins of the Bantaeng royal line are strongly attested in local legendary accounts, both oral and written (Bougas 1998), but this line includes only six rulers who preceded Bantaeng's 17th-century conversion to Islam, including a probably 16th-century antiquity for the *Tomanurung* who reportedly descended at Onto (Nayati 2005:Table 3). For earlier evidence of chiefly authority in Bantaeng, we would need to turn to Lembang Gantarang Keke and Gantarang Keke in eastern Bantaeng, which were established regional centres in the 11th or 12th century AD, preceding the 13th-century evidence found from looted pre-Islamic graves at these sites, including Chinese porcelain and stoneware of Song Dynasty antiquity (Bougas 1998). Moreover, Lembang Gantarang Keke and Gantarang Keke are also associated with a *Tomanurung* site whose sacred status is more widely acknowledged across Bantaeng than its Onto counterpart (Nayati 2005:243). Certainly, by the 14th century, corresponding to the Javanese reference to Bantaeng noted in the Introduction, Chinese (Yuan Dynasty) imported pottery was widespread across Bantaeng, political centralisation was more developed and Bantaeng appears to have become an important staging post for the trade in spices from the Moluccas to Java, but the participation of Onto/Bantaeng city in this development does not appear to have preceded the 15th century (Bougas 1998:119).

Discussion and Conclusions

When aligned within the overall pattern of Bantaeng's early development (Bougas 1998; Nayati 2005), the Onto site exemplifies the megalithic monuments and *Tomanurung* veneration found at early historical sites in western, central and eastern Bantaeng. Additionally, its porcelain and stoneware surface fragments suggest that it produced commodities to exchange for imported pottery. Indigenous texts and local traditions point to Onto as a point of reference for the traditional agrarian communities residing in central Bantaeng with their belief system based on traditional *patuntung* precepts. In summary, it continued a system for the recognition of chiefly authority first in evidence in eastern Bantaeng, but which expanded in late pre-Islamic times with the integration of western, central and eastern Bantaeng into a single polity (Bougas 1998).

The orientation of the Onto monuments running east–west and north–south reflects a cosmology found more widely across traditional Bugis-Makasar societies. This configuration follows the cosmological conception that the sun's rising in the east symbolises light, happiness, success and the sources of life, whereas the sun's setting in the west represents darkness, grief, difficult matters and death (Bougas 2007). The Onto community associates this east–west orientation with the phases of life, for the sun rises in the east and crosses over the hilltop at its zenith before finishing its journey at dusk, the symbol of death. As for the north–south arrangement, Mount Lompobattang to the north is compared with the human head, the frontal part where people receive adoration, and the holy place where the *Karaengloe* spirit survives as a god. The microcosmic kampong centred at *Bonto-bontoa* (*Pocci Butta*) is the template for the world at large, a model for how the kampong *patuntung* residents should fit within the world's divinely ordained qualities and cosmological design (Mahmud et al. 2007).

Acknowledgements

The constructive comments of two anonymous referees are gratefully acknowledged.

Author biography

Akin Duli Archaeology Program, Faculty of Law and Culture, Hasanuddin University, Makassar, South Sulawesi, Indonesia

References

Andaya, L.Y. 1981. *The Heritage of Arung Palakka: A History of South Sulawesi (Celebes) in the Seventeenth Century*. Verhandelingen van het Koninklijk Instituut voor Taal-, Land- en Volkenkunde 91. The Hague: Martinus Nijhoff.

Bellwood, P. 1978. *Man's Conquest of the Pacific*. Sydney: Collins.

Bonatz, D. 2002. Megaliths on Nias: The retention of identity. *Indonesia and the Malay World* 30(88):253–276. doi.org/10.1080/1363981022000064357 (accessed 5 June 2018).

Bougas, W.A. 1998. Bantayan: An early Makassarese kingdom, 1200-1600 AD. *Archipel* 55(1):83–123. doi.org/10.3406/arch.1998.3444.

Bougas, W.A. 2007. Gold looted and excavated from late (1300 AD-1600 AD) pre-Islamic Makassar graves. *Archipel* 73(1):111–166. doi.org/arch_0044-8613_2007_num_73_1_3877 (accessed 5 June 2018).

Bulbeck, F.D. 1992. A Tale of Two Kingdoms: The Historical Archaeology of Gowa and Tallok, South Sulawesi, Indonesia. Unpublished PhD thesis, School of Archaeology and Anthropology, The Australian National University, Canberra. www.oxis.org/theses/bulbeck-1992.pdf (accessed 5 June 2018).

Bulbeck, D. 2004. Divided in space, united in time: The Holocene prehistory of South Sulawesi. In S. Keates and J.M. Pasveer (eds), *Quaternary Research in Indonesia*, pp. 129–166. Modern Quaternary Research in Southeast Asia, Volume 18. Leiden: A.A. Balkema.

Caldwell, I. and W.A. Bougas. 2004. The early history of Binamu and Bangkala, South Sulawesi. *Bijdragen tot de Taal-, Land- en Volkenkunde* 160(4):456–510. doi.org/10.1163/22134379-90003720 (accessed 5 June 2018).

Caldwell, I. and K. Wellen. 2017. Finding Cina: A new paradigm for early Bugis history. *Bijdragen tot de Taal-, Land- en Volkenkunde* 173(2/3):296–324. doi.org/10.1163/22134379-17302004 (accessed 5 June 2018).

Duli, A. 1999. *Bentuk-bentuk Penguburan Orang Toraja, suatu Studi Etnoarkeologi*. Presentation at the Pengetahuan Ilmiah Arkeologi VIII congress, Yogyakarta.

Duli, A. 2008. Bentuk dan peranan budaya megalitik pada beberapa situs di Kabupaten Bantaeng. *Walennae* 10(14):19–43.

Gibson, T. 2005. *And the Sun Pursued the Moon: Symbolic Knowledge and Traditional Authority among the Makassar*. Honolulu: University of Hawai'i Press.

Hasanuddin. 2015. Kebudayaan Megalitik di Sulawesi Selatan dan Hubungannya dengan Asia Tenggara. Unpublished PhD thesis, Centre for Archaeological Research Malaysia, Universiti Sains Malaysia, Kuala Lumpur. www.oxis.org/theses/hasanuddin-2015.pdf (accessed 5 June 2018).

Hasanuddin University. 2013. *Judul Skripsi Sejarah Arkeologi II*. www.gurusejarah.com/2013/03/judul-skripsi-sejarah-arkeologi-ii.html (accessed 5 June 2018).

Heine Geldern, R. 1945. Prehistoric research in the Netherlands Indies. In P. Honig and F. Verdoorn (eds), *Science and Scientists in the Netherlands Indies*, pp. 129–167. New York: Board for the Netherlands Indies, Surinam and Curaçao.

Kallupa, B., D. Bulbeck, I. Caldwell, I. Sumantri and K. Demmanari. 1989. *Survey Pusat Kerajaan Soppeng 1100-1986 [Survey of the Capital of Soppeng Kingdom 1100-1986]*. Final Report to the Australian Myer Foundation, Privately published in Canberra, ACT. www.oxis.org/books/soppeng-1986.pdf (accessed 5 June 2018).

Mahmud, M.I., A. Duli, M.N.A. Thosibo and B. Hakim. 2007. *Bantaeng, dari Masa Prasejarah ke Masa Islam*. Makassar: Masagena Press.

Nayati, W. 2005. Social Dynamics and Local Trading Patterns in the Bantaeng Region, South Sulawesi (Indonesia) circa 17th Century. Unpublished PhD thesis, The Southeast Asian Studies Programme, National University of Singapore, Singapore. www.oxis.org/theses/widiya-nayati-2005.pdf (accessed 5 June 2018).

Robson, S. (translator). 1995. *Désawanana (Nagarakrtagamana) by Mpu Prapañca*. Leiden: KITLV Press.

Rössler, M. 1990. Striving for modesty: Fundamentals of the religion and social organization of the Makassarese Patuntung. *Bijdragen tot de Taal-, Land- en Volkenkunde* 146(2/3):289–324. doi.org/10.1163/22134379-90003220 (accessed 5 June 2018).

Soejono, R.P. 1984. *Sejarah Nasional Indonesia, vol. 1. Jaman Prasejarah*. Jakarta: Balai Pustaka.

Tuti, D.L.A. 1991. Peninggalan Megalitik Onto di Bantaeng. Unpublished PhD thesis, Arts Faculty, Archaeology Program, Hasanuddin University, Ujung Pandang [Makassar].

Ulaen, A.J. 1978 *Onto di Bantaeng, antara Mitos dan Realitas: Studi Rintisan Antropologis Tentang Struktur Kepemimpinan Tradisional.* Laporan Penelitian. Ujung Pandang [Makassar]: Pusat Latihan Penelitian Ilmu-Ilmu Sosial.

Wikipedia. 2017. *Bantaeng Regency.* en.wikipedia.org/wiki/Bantaeng_Regency (accessed 26 June 2017).

19

Typology and efflorescence of early Islamic tomb and gravestone forms in South Sulawesi and Majene, West Sulawesi

Rosmawati

Abstract

South Sulawesi province and the adjacent district of Majene in West Sulawesi are rich with the historic expressions of Islamic culture, in particular the many ancient tombs that are widespread across the area. The distribution of ancient tombs has had little empirical investigation, limiting our understanding of the cultural meaning of the form and content of these tombs. In order to expand our current knowledge of these memorial sites, as summarised in this paper, the author developed a typology of the tombs and gravestones located in the region with the aim of assisting further studies in the future. In terms of typology, the form of the gravestones in particular indicates influences of Malay culture (the Aceh type of gravestone) and Javanese culture (the Troloyo-Demak type of gravestone), as well as local cultural development (Bugis-Makasar tomb and gravestone types).

Keywords: South Sulawesi, Majene, graves, tombs, gravestones, Islamic culture

Introduction

An important archaeological legacy of early Islam in South Sulawesi is the cemeteries of kings, religious leaders and dukes (local authorities), buried with their relatives, friends, chiefs and closest slaves. These cemeteries are widespread across certain *kabupaten* or districts of South Sulawesi (i.e. former kingdoms whose territorial boundaries have persisted to the present day). These former kingdoms are represented in their cemetery complexes like those of the rulers of Gowa at Kale Gowa in Gowa District, the rulers of Tallok in Makassar city, the rulers of Sanrabone in Takalar District, the rulers of Binamu in Jeneponto District, the cemetery of the rulers of Luwu in Lokkoe (Palopo city), the rulers of Bone at Lala Bata Watampone and Makam Nagauleng, Jera Lompoe royal cemetery in Soppeng District, Tosora royal cemetery in Wajo District, Allakkuang cemetery in Sidrap District, Laiya cemetery in Enrekang District, and cemeteries for local rulers in Barru. Other cemetery complexes for the local elite include Makam Dea Daeng Lita in Bulukumba (18th century and later) and Makam Tandijalling in Enrekang (19th century and later) (Duli et al. 2013). Similar cemeteries have been recorded in Majene District in West Sulawesi (Figure 19.1).

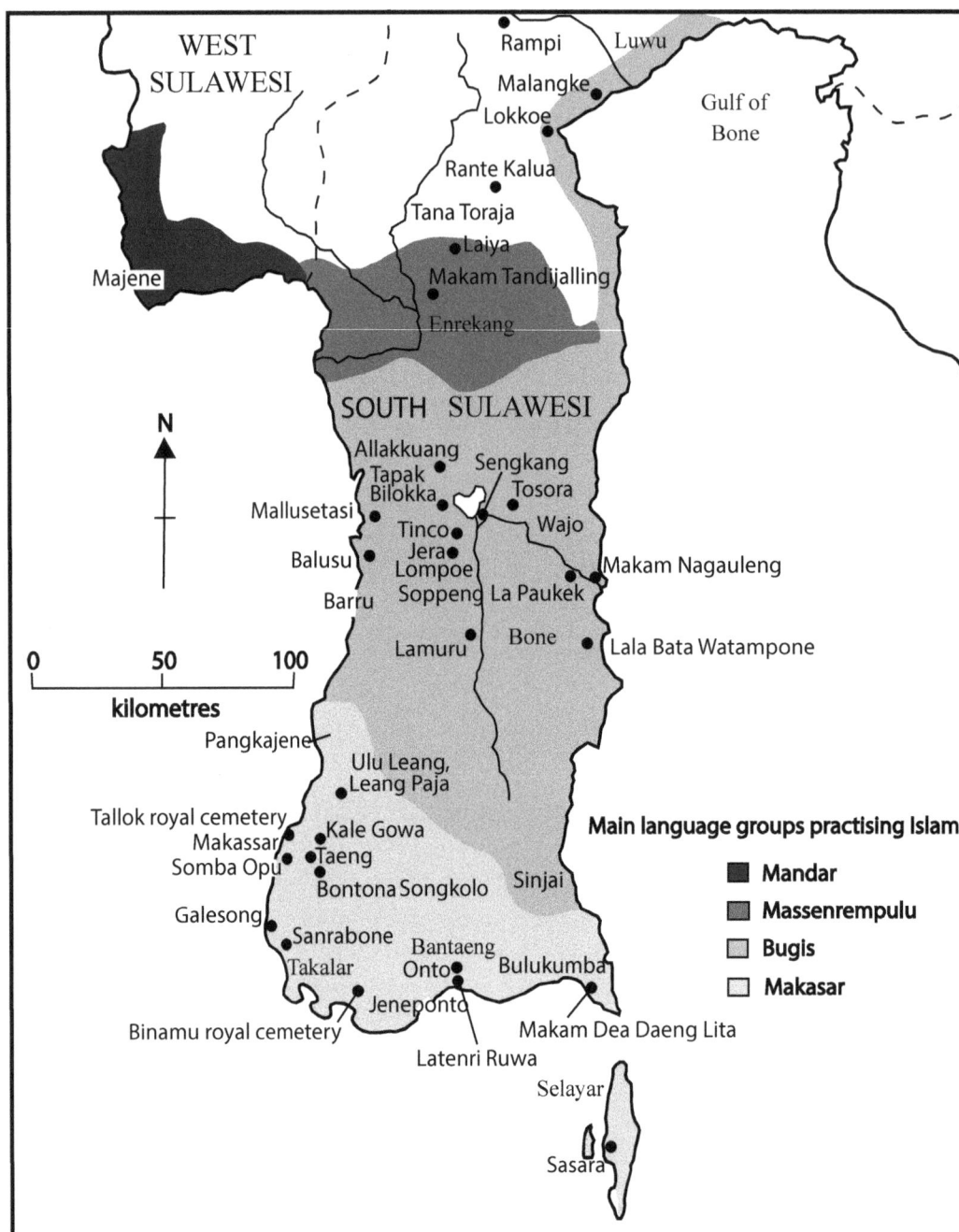

Figure 19.1: South and West Sulawesi—main language groups practising Islam and places mentioned in the text.

Sources: Masdoeki (1984, 1985a); Muttalib (1984); Makkullasse (1986); Bulbeck (1992); Duli et al. (2013); Hasanuddin (2015).

Functional interpretation of the tombs and their components is redundant as the function of tombs from prehistoric to present-day examples is clear. The relevant issues for archaeological study of the headstones and the graves are their style, shape and components, as well as the related geographic distribution both in coastal regions and the interior. In the majority of cases, analysis is restricted to the ornamental dimension, even if the philosophy behind the ornamental patterns cannot be determined (Santosa 1980:486; Marioga 1995:41).

Research into Islamic archaeology in Indonesia is not new, and indeed can be traced back to 1907 in the coastal stretches of northern Aceh (Djajadiningrat 1911; Vink 1912). The development of this research can be seen in Tjandrasamita (2000), who compiled earlier scholars' research under the themes of Indonesian archaeology and history, Indonesian Islamic antiquities and Indonesia's historic sites. Tjandrasamita's (2009) posthumous synthesis structured research into Indonesia's Islamic archaeology in terms of Islam's relationship with cosmopolitan dynamics, local social dynamics in Indonesia, traditions of written works in Indonesia, and the shaping and inheritance of Indonesian cultural traditions. Research specifically directed at the history of Islam in South Sulawesi include Pelras (1985), whose approach integrated his broad knowledge of relevant historical texts with his extensive knowledge of South Sulawesi ethnography accumulated over several decades, and Suriada and Abbas (2003), whose approach focused on sources locally available in South Sulawesi.

A common theme (e.g. Tjandrasamita 2009; Sulistyo 2013) is the incorporation of pre-Islamic beliefs and rituals within Islamic practice during the expansion of Islam across Indonesia, including South Sulawesi after AD 1603. For instance, Pelras (1985) observed that many devout Muslims in South Sulawesi comfortably entertain non-Islamic notions such as beliefs in local spirits and the literal truth of the La Galigo (with its tales of how the world was populated by godly figures and their servants from the heavens and the underworld); they also venerate the regalia that the divine founders of South Sulawesi's historical kingdoms supposedly brought with them to pass onto future rulers, and uphold a tradition of transvestite priests (*bissu*) who have custody over the regalia and related aristocratic ceremonies. The archaeological documentation of syncretist Islam in Indonesia is a particular feature of Ambary's (1998) research. One component of his investigations involved the study of Islamic graveyards associated with historical (17th to early 20th century) aristocracy in South Sulawesi (Ambary 1985), a research program subsequently expanded by Duli et al. (2013).

The work by Duli et al. (2013) forms a basis for the present contribution, which develops on it in the following respects. First, the typology of graves and headstones developed there—which is an essential prerequisite for relating these Islamic mortuary monuments to the development of South Sulawesi's brand of syncretist Islam—is expanded here (see Appendix A). Second, the material culture associated with pre-Islamic mortuary practices and other rituals honouring the ancestors in South Sulawesi is covered, based on currently available evidence. This material culture was associated with a tradition of geometric and curvilinear decorations, which show stylistic overlap with the decorations found on South Sulawesi's gravestones. Third, changes in South Sulawesi graves and gravestones are placed in a historical context with reference to potential influences on South Sulawesi society from other Islamised regions.

Pre-Islamic ritual material culture in South Sulawesi

Anthropomorphic representations

Anthropomorphic representations are of interest for their presence in the 'Type D2' gravestones at some Islamic cemeteries in South and West Sulawesi (Figure A19.5), in apparent abrogation of the general Islamic proscription against portraying human figures as idols. They are a recurrent if not a dominant motif in the South Sulawesi pre-Islamic archaeological record that can be associated with Austronesian speakers, as the following examples show.

Anthropomorphic rock art drawings are a notable component of the 'Austronesian Painting Tradition' documented in the Maros-Pangkep karsts and assumed to date to the last few thousand years (Oktaviana et al. 2016). These anthropomorphs were mainly rendered as stick figures and often in dynamic pose (Sumantri 1996), quite unlike any other pre-Islamic or Islamic anthropomorphic artworks in South Sulawesi.

Stone human statues similar to the Laiya anthropomorphic gravestones (Figure A19.5) are recorded as a feature of the northern highlands of South Sulawesi at Rante Kalua (Tana Toraja) and the Rampi District. These statues resemble the larger statues of the Bada, Besoa and Napu valleys of Central Sulawesi, where a rich tradition of sculpting megaliths (including massive stone jars called *kalamba*) is well documented. Contemporaneity of the Rampi human statues with their Central Sulawesi counterparts is indicated by three Accelerator Mass Spectrometry (AMS) determinations on charcoal, excavated near the base of one of the statues, which date to the early centuries AD (Hasanuddin 2015; Fakhri 2016).

Three bronzes considered to be locally produced during the 1st millennium AD or shortly after include anthropomorphic depictions. One is the unique 'Makassar flask', which is a large, swallowtail bronze axe with a human face similar to that on the human statues mentioned above (van der Hoop 1941:Fig. 54). The other two are seated figures of minor Buddhist deities found at Sasara, Selayar, which are interpreted as local imitations of East Java's Nganjuk style of Buddhist bronze statuettes (Caldwell and Nur 2005). Their Javanese imprint distinguishes them from Sulawesi's other anthropomorphic artworks, including the death masks of beaten gold that have occasionally been found covering the facial skeleton of late pre-Islamic burials in Makasar-speaking areas (Bougas 2007). On the other hand, their seated position marks a specific resemblance to the Binamu anthropomorphic gravestones (Figure A19.5).

Anthropomorphic pottery in mortuary contexts includes a terra cotta human head amongst the 98 kg of pottery associated with mortuary disposals dating to the 1st millennium AD at Ulu Leang 2 in the Maros karsts (Andrews and Glover 1986; Flavel 1997). There are also human figurines of terra cotta looted from cemeteries in Bantaeng and Jeneponto in association with 13th–16th-century imported ceramics. Bougas (1998, 2007) interprets them as ancestor figures and suggests a specific link with the Binamu anthropomorphic gravestones, but more generally they reinforce the impression that, from time to time in the past, Austronesian-speaking artists in South Sulawesi have resorted to the use of human images.

Standing stones

Menhirs (tall standing stones) are often thought of as a major component of the South Sulawesi 'megalithic tradition', as is especially true of Tana Toraja where they were intimately associated with 'animist' mortuary feasts (Hasanuddin 2015). Within the peninsula, single menhirs are documented at Tapak Bilokka in Sidrap (Hasanuddin 2015), various Soppeng sites including Laleng Benteng and Bila (near Jera Lompoe) and Tinco (Kallupa et al. 1989), and at Kale Gowa (Bulbeck 1992). Multiple menhirs have been documented for Wajo sites including Sengkang, Sompoh (near Sengkang) and La Paukek, in the latter two cases associated with disturbed urn-fields and surface scatters of imported ceramics dated between the 15th and 17th centuries (van Heekeren 1950; Bulbeck and Caldwell 2000). A late pre-Islamic antiquity is also indicated by local legends that associate the Kale Gowa menhir with the c. 14th-century foundation of Gowa, and the Laleng Benteng and Tinco examples with the c. 14th-century foundation of Soppeng; in the case of Tinco, supported by an abundance of c. 13th–17th-century ceramics on the site's surface (Kallupa et al. 1989) and three AMS determinations on excavated charcoal dating between the 13th and 15th–17th centuries (Hasanuddin 2015:309). These menhirs with late pre-Islamic credentials were a potential inspiration for the menhir (Type D12) Islamic gravestones so widespread across the South Sulawesi peninsula (see Appendix A), even if menhir production may have 'taken off' with Islamisation. A case in point is the Ujung Islamic cemetery near Jera Lompoe, whose 84 menhir gravestones (plain and decorated), with an estimated age between the 17th and 19th centuries, is the largest concentration recorded for Soppeng (Kallupa et al. 1989).

A similar situation may apply for South Sulawesi's *lingga* or phallic stones, which are often thought to reflect pre-Islamic Hinduist influence (Duli et al. 2013; Hasanuddin 2015). The cylindrical 'uncircumcised' variant, such as the 'male stones' heaped together with round 'female stones' at the Onto pre-Islamic ritual centre in Bantaeng (Bougas 2007), has no clear mortuary association. In contrast, the Type D11, phallic Islamic gravestones reveal a circumcised form (Figure A19.2), consistent with the importance of circumcision as an initiation ceremony for Muslim males.

Mortuary practices

Cremation of the remains of the deceased is suspected to reflect influence from Java where it is associated with the Hindu/Buddhist ideology that held sway prior to the widespread conversion to Islam across Java during the 16th century. Cremation is the only practice for handling corpses documented for the pre-Islamic Bugis who interred the ashes in large jars at cemeteries, such as the urn-fields mentioned above.

In the case of the Makasars, however, there appears to have been a change at around the 14th century from cremation/urn burial to inhumation of the deceased in an extended east–west position, accompanied by grave goods and sometimes placed in boat-shaped coffins. Bougas (2007) discusses the possibility that this change in burial practice reflects influence from the Samar-Bajau sea gypsies of the southern Philippine region, but also emphasises the significance of an east–west orientation in the context of the Makasar pre-Islamic worship of the sun. There is no documentation of any durable markers erected above the ground to mark Makasar pre-Islamic burial locations, but Masdoeki (1985a) and Bulbeck (1992) recorded a large number of graves in early Islamic Makasar graveyards oriented east–west rather than following the north–south orientation, which is orthodox for Indonesian Muslims (with the corpse placed on its side, facing Mecca). These east–west oriented graves could reflect Islamic-inspired marking of the graves of persons who had originally been buried according to the pre-Islamic tradition, or a syncretist blending of indigenous pre-Islamic and introduced Islamic beliefs.

Non-anthropomorphic decorative designs

The non-anthropomorphic component of the 'Austronesian Painting Tradition' (described above) consisted mainly of sketchy abstract compositions, blocky zoomorphs and representations of boats and other wooden material culture (Sumantri 1996). The incised designs recorded for Soppeng megaliths include a deer incorporated in a set of square panels and a composition of spoked wheels interpreted as possible cakras of Hindu/Buddhist inspiration (Hasanuddin 2015). None of these designs can be traced as influences on South and West Sulawesi Islamic art.

More promising is the 'Sa-Huynh Kalanay' earthenware pottery from several sites in the southern peninsula of South Sulawesi, dating approximately to the 1st millennium AD. These remarkably ornate assemblages predominantly involve horizontal translations of a wide variety of punctate and incised motifs along with a smaller component of triangular and rectangular mazes and curvilinear compositions. Most of the sites have mortuary associations, but the particularly ornate pottery at Batu Ejayya in Bantaeng evidently had non-mortuary ritual associations (Flavel 1997). The abstract designs on the Makassar flask may belong to the same decorative tradition, even though they include some motifs not yet recorded for pottery in South Sulawesi.

Various 'Sa-Huynh Kalanay'-related designs can be found on Islamic gravestones in South Sulawesi (Table 19.1), although the floral representations that dominate these gravestones do not appear to have pre-Islamic precedents.

Table 19.1: Decorative designs on Islamic gravestones with Sa-Huynh Kalanay associations, South Sulawesi.

Design	Gravestone type	Pre-Islamic object/assemblage	Reference
Curvilinear maze	Crenulated gravestone (Figure A19.2)[a]	Batu Ejayya	Flavel 1997
Interlocking waves	D1, Jear Lompoe (Figure A19.5)	Leang Paja, Maros	Flavel 1997
Fern tendril scroll	D4, Binamu cemetery (Figure A19.5)	Makassar flask	van der Hoop 1941
Chevron translation	D4, Tosora (Figure A19.5)	Ulu Leang, Maros	Flavel 1997
Fretwork	D7, Jear Lompoe (Figure A19.5)	Leang Paja, Maros	Flavel 1997

(a) A similar design is shown at the entrance to the tomb of Sultan Abdullah Muhiddin, Malangke (Chamshi-Pasha 2008).

Architectural trends of ancient tombs and gravestones and their expansion in South and West Sulawesi

By identifying the types, noting the inscriptions (including names and dates), associating the commemorated deceased with the available historical information from oral and textual sources, and recording the occurrences of the varying styles in the many ancient cemetery complexes of South and West Sulawesi, it is possible to delineate the flux of stylistic trends and the timeline of their appearance. Tables 19.2 and 19.3 present a diagnostic selection of grave and gravestone types for Islamic personages with approximately or exactly known burial date.

Table 19.2: Examples of graves and gravestones associated with Islamic personages of 17th-century burial date.

Personage	Grave type	Gravestone type	Reference
La Tenri Ruwa, 11th Bone ruler, buried at Bantaeng in 1634	D	AA (Othman Type C)	Muttalib 1980
Sultan Abdullah Muhiddin, 2nd Muslim Luwuq ruler, buried at Malangke in 1636	F	D8	Chamshi-Pasha 2008
Sultan Awalul Islam, 7th Tallok ruler, buried at Kale Gowa in 1636	J/D*	AA/AA (both Othman Type C)*	Duli et al. 2013
Sultan Alauddin, 14th Gowa ruler, buried at Kale Gowa in 1639	J/D*	AA/AA (Othman Types H and J)*	Duli et al. 2013
Tumenanga ri To'bana, buried near Sanrabone in early 17th century	E	D10	Masdoeki 1985a
Karaeng Katinting, buried at Tallok in 1650	E	D8	Bulbeck 1992
Sultan Malikussaid, 15th Gowa ruler, buried at Kale Gowa in 1653	J/D*	AA/AA (both Othman Type C)*	Duli et al. 2013
Sultan Mudhaffar, 8th Tallok ruler, buried at Tallok in 1653	B	AA (Othman Type C)	Masdoeki 1985b; Bulbeck 1992
Sultan Mahmud, buried at Kale Gowa in mid-17th century	A	Not recorded	Bulbeck 1992
Sultan Hasanuddin, 16th Gowa ruler, buried at Kale Gowa in 1670	J/D*	AA (Othman Type K)/D8*	Duli et al. 2013
Sultan Amir Hamzah, 17th Gowa ruler, buried at Kale Gowa in 1674	J/D	AA (Othman Type C)	Duli et al. 2013
We Tenri Kawareng, buried at Jera Lompoe in late 17th century	J	AA (Othman Type K)	Duli et al. 2013

Personage	Grave type	Gravestone type	Reference
Addatuang Sidenreng, buried at Jera Lompoe in late 17th century	D	D12	Ambary 1985; Muttalib 1984
Sultan Muhammad Ali, 18th Gowa ruler, buried at Kale Gowa in late 17th century	J/D*	AA (Othman Type K)/D8*	Duli et al. 2013
La Tenri Bali Matinroe ri Datunna, 15th Soppeng ruler, buried at Jera Lompoe in late 17th century	J	D9	Muttalib 1984
Karaeng Bungaya, buried at Taeng in mid-17th century	I	D9	Figure A19.1, this chapter
Karaeng Parang Parang, buried at Tallok in late 17th century	C	Not recorded	Bulbeck 1992; Trip Advisor 2017
Gowa noble, buried at Somba Opu in 1692	D	D8	Bulbeck 1992

* Two paired gravestones: one pair with the grave inside the stepped terrace and the second pair on top of the stepped terrace.

Table 19.3: Examples of graves and gravestones associated with Islamic personages of approximately 18th-century burial date.

Personage	Grave type	Gravestone type	Reference
Syech Yusuf, buried at Kale Gowa in 1705	A	D15	Bulbeck 1992
La Cella, 5th Lamuru ruler, buried at Lamuru in 1710	B	D3	Duli et al. 2013
Sultan Abdul Jalil, 19th Gowa ruler, buried at Kale Gowa in 1711	J/D	Not reported	Duli et al. 2013
Sultan Alimuddin (16th Bone ruler) and two wives, buried at Makam Nagauleng in early 18th century	Not reported	D12	Duli et al. 2013
La Mappa Poleonro Sultan Nuh., 28th Soppeng ruler, buried at Jera Lompoe in late 18th century	C	D11	Muttalib 1984
Datu Mari-Mari Guttu Patalo, buried at Jera Lompoe in late 18th century	G	D10	Muttalib 1984
Sultan Sirajuddin, buried at Tallok in 1756	D	B	Masdoeki 1985b; Bulbeck 1992
La Mappaware Petta Matinroe, 7th Lamuru ruler, buried at Lamuru in 18th century	D	D9	van Romondt 1985
Tumenanga ri Masigini, buried at Sanrabone in 18th century	A	B	Masdoeki 1985a
Karaeng Gosseya Bombang, buried at Binamu in 18th century	D	AA (Othman Type A)/D2	Bougas 2007
Raja Laiya, buried at Laiya in 18th century	F	D8	Duli et al. 2013
Sultan Saifuddin, buried at Tallok in late 18th century	A	AA (Othman Type C)/C	Masdoeki 1985b
Matinroa ri Lanna, buried at Galesong in 1809	D	D8	Masdoeki 1985a

The earliest styles of tombs (Table 19.2) include the terraced style (Type B) and stepped tomb (Type D), first appearing in the early 17th century. These were usually associated with gravestones of the Aceh type (as defined by Othman 1988), reflecting Malay influence from Java. Further tomb styles that appeared by the early to mid-17th century, sometimes associated with Bugis-Makasar style gravestones (e.g. D8 and D10), include the standard (Type J), boat-shaped (Type E), *candi* (Type F) and dome-covered styles (Type A). The *candi*-style tomb at Malangke is specifically linked to Hindu/Buddhist influence from Java by van Romondt (1985) and Chamshi-Pasha (2008). The boat-shaped tombs resemble the pre-Islamic Makasar boat-shaped coffins in concept but not in design, as these Type E Islamic tombs are above-ground structures and also grander and more complex. Note that continuity of pre-Islamic iconography in the Bugis-Makasar gravestone types is probably stronger than indicated in Table 19.2: the kris handle style (D1) is locally associated with the 11th Soppeng ruler La Mata Esso, but he died shortly before Soppeng had accepted Islam (Ambary 1985); and the great majority of the menhir (D12) gravestones were erected for personages whose identities are no longer remembered (e.g. Kallupa et al. 1989).

The Type A dome-covered tomb does not have clear antecedents outside of Sulawesi and may be a local development. However, probably reflecting cultural influence from South Sulawesi, late 17th-century examples of this tomb type also occur on the island of Sumbawa (Noorduyn 1987). These include the graves of the Bima sultans Abdul Khair Sirajuddin (reigned 1640–1682), Nuruddin (reigned 1682–1687) and Jamaluddin (reigned 1687–1696), all of whom entered into marriage relationships during the 17th century with the ruling lineages of Makassar (Bulbeck 1992).

The tomb styles mentioned above continued in use during the late 17th and the 18th centuries (Tables 19.2 and 19.3), but additional styles also began to emerge, such as wooden graves (Type I) and the traditional house style (Type C). Also during the 18th century, utilisation of the Demak-Troloyo gravestone type began, along with continued use of the Aceh and Bugis-Makasar gravestone types (now expanded to include D2, D3, D9, D10, D12 and D15), whereby the latter saw a continuation of pre-Islamic elements. The Demak-Troloyo gravestone type originated with the 15th-century conversion to Islam of the Hindu/Buddhist rulers of Majapahit in East Java (Tjandrasasmita 2009:76–77). Demak became a major centre of mystical Islam thought in the 18th century (Ricklefs 2008:60), which may have been the stimulus for the adoption of this gravestone type in South and West Sulawesi at this time.

Tombs are usually refined in their construction; they often have parallel siding and smooth finishing, and some even resemble the houses of the living. The majority of the tombs and gravestones were made from stone with the exception of two types, those made from wood (Type I) and tombs constructed from mounding dirt (Type L). The tombs were generally carved with a variety of ornamental embellishments during this early period. In later centuries, these tomb and gravestone types continued, but instead of stone, the builders used newer materials such as brick and cement for their construction (e.g. Bulbeck 1992).

The architecture of the graves displays an Islamic art style rooted in Indonesian culture as can be seen from the rich variety of ornaments on the graves, the gravestones and the tomb covers. In some cases, it seems to be in deliberate abrogation of the Islamic prohibition against the display of human or animal forms for worship. In order to retain their cultural artistic expression while conforming to the Islamic influence of the time, the artists included pre-Islamic forms (including the phallus and Hindu pagoda) alongside more acceptable Islamic decoration such as leaf-shaped motifs and calligraphic inscriptions of holy passages from the Koran (Duli et al. 2013). This syncretistic iconography occurs frequently in the ancient cemetery complexes of South and West Sulawesi.

Other common decorative patterns on the gravestones are of single emblems or fields that are rich in Islamic ornamental decorations. Their grave covers often contain various geometric (e.g. cross-hatched, meandering or rhomboid) and floral decorations (e.g. tendrils, leaves and herbs) on the roof and pillars, as well as medallions, spiralling leaves and calligraphy (Duli et al. 2013).

Themes and conclusion

Cultural evolution and changes in traditional customs are highly apparent with the development of and increased variability in the styles of the tombs and gravestones contained in the many ancient cemeteries of the provinces of South and West Sulawesi. The expression of this cultural change was highly variable, which was reflected in the grave markers themselves, producing a plethora of styles within the many types identified in this study. This diversity was likely inspired by the people who lived, worked, reigned, preached and died in each separate society—adding their own ideas and stylistic flare to the place where they laid their deceased relatives to rest.

The most significant influence was, of course, the introduction of Islam to the region. When external contacts came there, bringing with them the Islamic culture to introduce to the local people, a meeting of the two cultures occurred. The developing relationship of these very different cultures resulted in acculturation and the admixture of elements from both to produce each region's unique cultural identity. However, the process did not involve a passive blending of local pre-Islamic and introduced Islamic elements, but also generated new stylistic and religious elements that were not present with the parental cultures. Examples of this include the development of the dome-covered (Type A) tombs and boat-shaped (Type E) tombs as large aboveground structures, as well as certain Bugis-Makasar gravestone types (for instance, the D5, D6 and D10 types), which do not appear to have local pre-Islamic or external Islamic precedents.

Cultural contact and acculturation between the local prehistoric and Islamic cultures, along with influences from the Malays, the Javanese and the Europeans, occurred in stages over a lengthy period (Sulistyo 2013; Bulbeck et al., this volume). It is clear that during this early Islamic period, as part of the process of Islamisation, there were increased tensions and many conflicts between groups. This is common during the early periods of cultural assimilation; however, with the addition of cultural equality and flexibility, success of acculturation in the region between the pre-Islamic and Islamic cultures is demonstrated. This can be witnessed in the construction of the tombs. These new relationships inspired the creativity of the artists to create a new culture, without precedent. And as much as Islam influenced the local people, so too did they enrich local Islamic culture through continuity of the specific characteristics that are unique to the cultures of South and West Sulawesi.

Acknowledgements

The comments of two anonymous referees are gratefully acknowledged.

Author biography

Rosmawati Archaeology Department, Faculty of Law and Culture, Hasanuddin University, Makassar, South Sulawesi, Indonesia

References

Ambary, H.M. 1985. De l'animisme à l'Islam: Le témoignage de quelques monuments funéraires de la région de Bone. *Archipel* 29(1):165–173. doi.org/10.3406/arch.1985.2228 (accessed 5 June 2018).

Ambary, H.M. 1998. *Menemukan Peradaban: Jejak Arkeologis dan Historis Islam Indonesia.* Jakarta: Logos.

Andrews, R.G. and I.C. Glover. 1986. Ulu Leang 2, an Iron Age jar burial cave in South Sulawesi, Indonesia. *Indonesia Circle* 40:47–64. doi.org/10.1080/03062848608729639 (accessed 5 June 2018).

Bougas, W.A. 1998. Bantayan: An early Makassarese kingdom, 1200–1600 AD. *Archipel* 55(1):83–123. doi.org/10.3406/arch.1998.3444.

Bougas, W.A. 2007. Gold looted and excavated from late (1300 AD–1600 AD) pre-Islamic Makassar graves. *Archipel* 73(1):111–166. doi.org/arch_0044-8613_2007_num_73_1_3877 (accessed 5 June 2018).

Bulbeck, F.D. 1992. A Tale of Two Kingdoms: The Historical Archaeology of Gowa and Tallok, South Sulawesi, Indonesia. Unpublished PhD thesis, School of Archaeology and Anthropology, The Australian National University, Canberra. www.oxis.org/theses/bulbeck-1992.pdf (accessed 5 June 2018).

Bulbeck, D. and I. Caldwell. 2000. *Land of Iron: The Historical Archaeology of Luwu and the Cenrana Valley. Results of the Origin of Complex Society in South Sulawesi Project (OXIS)*. Hull: Centre for South-East Asian Studies, University of Hull. www.oxis.org/books/land-of-iron.pdf (accessed 5 June 2018).

Bulbeck, D., I. Caldwell., S. Druce, B. Hakim and C. Macknight. 2018. Imported tradeware ceramics and their relevance for dating socio-political developments in South Sulawesi, with special reference to the Allangkanangnge ri Latanete site. In S. O'Connor, D. Bulbeck and J. Meyer (eds), *The Archaeology of Sulawesi: Current Research on the Pleistocene to the Historic Period*, pp. 269–287. Canberra: ANU Press.

Caldwell, I.A. and M. Nur. 2005. Three locally-made bronzes from South Sulawesi: Possible evidence of cultural transfer from Java about AD 1000. *Review of Indonesian and Malaysian Affairs* 39(1):23–34. www.oxis.org/downloads/caldwell-and-nur.pdf (accessed 5 June 2018).

Chamshi-Pasha, L. 2008. A Study of the Islamisation of South Sulawesi through an Analysis of the Grave of the second Muslim Ruler of Luwuq. Honours thesis. www.oxis.org/theses/chamsi-pasha.pdf (accessed 5 June 2018).

Djajadiningrat, R.A.H. 1911. Critisch overzicht van de in Maleische werken vervatte gegevens over de geschiedenis van het Sultanat van Atjeh. *Bijdragen tot de Taal-, Land- en Volkenkunde* 65:135–260. doi.org/10.1163/22134379-90001836 (accessed 5 June 2018).

Duli, A., Rosmawati and Muhaeminah. 2013. Makam. In A. Duli, A. Rahman, B. Sulistyanto, Muhaeminah, Roadah, Rosmawati and Y. Sumalyo (eds), *Monumen Islam di Sulawesi Selatan*, pp. 109–242. Makassar: Balai Cagar Budaya Makassar. books.google.com.au/books?id=ZKtrCAAAQBAJ&printsec=frontcover &dq=Monumen+Islam+di+Sulawesi+Selatan&hl=en&sa=X&ved=0ahUKEwirmtqchqneAhVjz1QKH dTRD9UQ6AEIKDAA#v=onepage&q=Monumen%20Islam%20di%20Sulawesi%20Selatan&f=false (accessed 27 October 2018).

Fakhri. 2016. Situs Rampi: Masa persebaran arca batu dan hubungannya dengan di wilayah situs terdekat [Rampi sites: The dispersion age of stone statue and the connection between nearest site areas]. *Walennae* 14(1):23–36. walennae.kemdikbud.go.id/index.php/walennae/article/view/38 (accessed 27 October 2018).

Flavel, A. 1997. Sa-Huynh Kalanay? Analysis of the Prehistoric Decorated Earthenware of South Sulawesi in an Island Southeast Asian Context. Unpublished BSc (Hons) thesis, Centre for Prehistory, University of Western Australia, Perth.

Hasanuddin. 2015. Kebudayaan Megalitik di Sulawesi Selatan dan Hubungannya dengan Asia Tenggara. Unpublished PhD thesis, Centre for Archaeological Research Malaysia, Universiti Sains Malaysia, Kuala Lumpur. www.oxis.org/theses/hasanuddin-2015.pdf (accessed 5 June 2018).

Kallupa, B., D. Bulbeck, I. Caldwell, I. Sumantri and K. Demmanari. 1989. *Survey Pusat Kerajaan Soppeng 1100–1986 [Survey of the Capital of Soppeng Kingdom 1100–1986]*. Final Report to the Australian Myer Foundation, Privately published in Canberra, ACT. www.oxis.org/books/soppeng-1986.pdf (accessed 5 June 2018).

Makkullasse, A.H. 1986. *Laporan Pengumpulan Data 'Peninggalan Sejarah dan Purbakala' Kabupaten Enrekang*. Ujung Pandang [Makassar]: Suaka Peninggalan Sejarah dan Purbakala Sulawesi Selatan.

Marioga, N. 1995. Makam Raja-Raja Kutai Kertanegara di Tenggarong Kabupaten Kutai Propinsi Kalimantan Timur. Unpublished B.A. (Hons) thesis, Jurusan Arkeologi, Fakultas Sastra, Universitas Hasanuddin, Makassar.

Masdoeki. 1984. *Laporan Pengumpulan Data Peninggalan Sejarah dan Purbakala di Kabupaten Barru*. Ujung Pandang [Makassar]: Suaka Peninggalan Sejarah dan Purbakala Sulawesi Selatan.

Masdoeki. 1985a. *Laporan Pengumpulan Data Peninggalan Sejarah dan Purbakala di Kabupaten Takalar*. Ujung Pandang [Makassar]: Suaka Peninggalan Sejarah dan Purbakala Sulawesi Selatan.

Masdoeki. 1985b. *Laporan Pengumpulan Data Peninggalan Sejarah di Kotamadia Ujung Pandang*. Ujung Pandang [Makassar]: Suaka Peninggalan Sejarah dan Purbakala Sulawesi Selatan.

McWilliam, A., F.D. Bulbeck, S. Brockwell and S. O'Connor. 2012. The cultural legacy of Makassar stone in East Timor. *The Asia Pacific Journal of Anthropology* 13(3):262–279. doi.org/10.1080/14442213.20 12.674054 (accessed 5 June 2018).

Muttalib, M.A. 1980. *Naskah Studi Kelaykan: Makam La Tenri Ruwa (Raja Bone ke XI) Bantaeng, Sulawesi Selatan*. Ujung Pandang [Makassar]: Proyek Pemuguran dan Pemeliharaan Peninggalan Sejarah dan Purbakala Sulawesi Selatan.

Muttalib, M.A. 1984. *Taman Purbakala Jera Lompoe*. Ujung Pandang [Makassar]: Suaka Peninggalan Sejarah dan Purbakala Sulawesi Selatan.

Noorduyn, J. 1987. *Bima en Sumbawa: Bijdragen tot de Geschiedenis van de Sultanen Bima en Sumbawa door A. Ligtvoet en G.P. Rouffaer*. Dordrecht: Foris Publications.

Oktaviana, A.A., D. Bulbeck, S. O'Connor, B. Hakim, Suryatman, U.P. Wibowo, E. St Pierre and Fakhri. 2016. Hand stencils with and without narrowed fingers at two new rock art sites in Sulawesi, Indonesia. *Rock Art Research* 33(1):32–48.

Othman, M.Y. 1988. *Batu Aceh : Early Islamic Gravestones in Peninsular Malaysia*. Kuala Lumpur: Museum Association of Malaysia.

Pelras, C. 1985. Religion, tradition and the dynamics of Islamization in South Sulawesi. *Archipel* 29:107–135. doi.org/10.3406/arch.1985.2226 (accessed 5 June 2018).

Perret, D. and K.A. Razak. 1999. *Batu Aceh Warisan Sejarah Johor*. Selangor: Yayasan Warisan Johor.

Ricklefs, M.C. 2008. *A History of Modern Indonesia since c. 1200*. London: Palgrave MacMillan.

Santosa, H.B. 1980. *Catatan Tentang Perbandingan Nisan dari beberapa Daerah di Indonesia*. Jakarta: Pusat Penelitian Arkeologi Nasional.

Sulistyo, B. 2013. Islamisasi dan persemaian budaya lokal di Sulawesi Selatan. In A. Duli, A. Rahman, B. Sulistyanto, Muhaeminah, Roadah, Rosmawati and Y. Sumalyo (eds), *Monumen Islam di Sulawesi Selatan*, pp. 3–33. Makassar: Balai Cagar Budaya Makassar. books.google.com.au/books?id=ZKtrCAA AQBAJ&printsec=frontcover&dq=Monumen+Islam+di+Sulawesi+Selatan&hl=en&sa=X&ved=0ahUK EwirmtqchqneAhVjz1QKHdTRD9UQ6AEIKDAA#v=onepage&q=Monumen%20Islam%20di%20 Sulawesi%20Selatan&f=false (accessed 27 October 2018).

Sumantri, I. 1996. Pola Pemukiman Gua-Gua Prasejarah di Biraeng Pangkep, Sulaswesi Selatan. Unpublished MA thesis, Program Studi Arkeologi, University of Indonesia, Jakarta.

Suriada M. and I. Abbas. 2003. *Sejarah Islam di Sulawesi Selatan*. Makassar: Masogena Press.

Tjandrasamita, U. 2000. *Penelitian Arkeologi Islam di Indonesia dar Masa ke Masa*. Kudus: Menara Kudus.

Tjandrasamita, U. 2009. *Arkeologi Islam di Nusantara* (ed. T. Hartimah, A. Chair, Testriono, O. Dahuri and S. Sulaiman). Jakarta: Kepustakaan Populer Gramedia.

Trip Advisor. 2017. Makam Karaeng Parang Parang – Picture of Tallo Kings Cemetery Complex, Makassar. www.tripadvisor.com.au/LocationPhotoDirectLink-g297720-d6538788-i140267287-Tallo_Kings_ Cemetery_Complex-Makassar_South_Sulawesi_Sulawesi.html (accessed 14 January 2017).

van der Hoop, A.N.J. 1941. *Catalogus der Praehistorische Verzameling*. Bandung: A.C. Nix & Co.

van Heekeren, H.R. 1950. De urnenfelden lesung batu en monolithen boven Somph nabij Sengkang, Zuid-Celebes. *Oudheidkundig Verslag 1949*, pp. 17–18. Bandung: A.C. Nix & Co.

van Romondt, V.R. 1985. Makam-makam Islam di Sulawesi Selatan. *Amerta* 1:49–53.

Vink, J.J. de. 1912. Uittreksel uit het verslag over de oudheidkundige werkzaamheden in Pasé. *Oudheidkundig Verslag 1912*, pp. 53–56. Batavia [Jakarta]: Oudheidkundige Dienst in Nederlandsch-Indië. archive.org/ stream/in.ernet.dli.2015.530217/2015.530217.oudheidkundig-verslag_djvu.txt (accessed 5 June 2018).

Appendix A: Typology of ancient tombs and gravestones in South Sulawesi

To facilitate the description and classification of the grave and headstone styles, they can be classified according to the form, size and variety of their ornamentation. The creation of arbitrary labels for the different types provides a shorthand for their unambiguous referencing (Othman 1988), as in the main text here, where the overlapping chronology of the various types is also addressed. The typology presented here is an extension of the less comprehensive typology developed by Duli et al. (2013).

Graves

In order to produce a viable descriptive sequence, the graves are classified into styles based on their manufacturing technology and tomb shape in the following subsections. Photographs and drawings of each type (with the exception of Type I and Type L, illustrations of which are presented immediately after their description) are given as examples in Figure A19.3 at the end of this section.

Type A

The dome-covered style (Type A) consists of a square-footed tomb covered by a dome crowned at the summit with various headstone forms such as cudgels, bubbles, prisms and lotus flowers. The tomb is constructed with brickwork or andesite blocks and plastered with a mixture of sand and lime. There is an entrance on one side from which to view the several graves contained within the tomb. These tombs include both decorated and undecorated examples. The dome shapes vary from semicircular to oval and pyramidal, and there are both large and small examples. The dome-covered style is found at the grave complexes of Kale Gowa (Katangka, Syech Yusuf, Sultan Hasanuddin and Bonto Biraeng), Tinggi Maek near Kale Gowa, the royal Sanrabone cemetery complex in Sanrabone fortress (Bulbeck 1992), Tallok, Lala Bata Watampone (Bone), Lokkoe Palopo and several cemeteries in Barru District. This form of tomb has existed since the mid-17th century in South Sulawesi.

Type B

This style (Type B) has stepped terraces above a rectangular chamber with a single entrance opening on to several graves. The stepped terraces, which are similar to Type D, are made of stacked andesite blocks and have a receding profile. On the topmost level, there are one or two gravestones, sometimes decorated with a variety of motifs. The terraces can have three, five or seven levels. This style of tomb is found in the cemetery complexes of Sultan Hasanuddin, Tallok, Lamuru (interior Bone District), Lokkoe Palopo, Latenri Ruwa (Bantaeng) and in Barru. Its inception and subsequent period of expansion date back to the early 17th century, coinciding with the entry of Islam into South Sulawesi.

Type C

This is a style with a cover shaped like a traditional house (Type C); that is, the top resembles the peaked roofs commonly seen in Indonesian houses. It is built from an arrangement of unworked stones, stone slabs, bricks or timber. The orientation is oblong, the summit consists of a stone replica of a saddled or pyramidal roof, and sometimes the tomb is decorated. On one side, there is an entrance to the interior where several graves are present. This type of tomb is found in the cemetery complexes of Tallok, Katangka, Latenri Ruwa, Barru, Majene, Enrekang and Lokkoe Palopo.

Type D

The stepped terrace style (Type D) is a type of tomb with an undulating outline constructed from a stacked arrangement of stone slabs, unworked stones or bricks. There are between one and five terraces, which may be decorated or plain. The topmost terrace has one or two gravestones, with many variations in their form and dimensions. This type of tomb is found in almost every major cemetery complex in South and West Sulawesi.

Type E

The boat-shaped style (Type E) is built to have the appearance of a boat, consisting of a base, a body and a crowning platform with one or two gravestones. This type of grave is built from stacked stone slabs. It is found in several cemetery complexes in Bulukumba, Enrekang, Barru and Majene. This is also the form of graves documented in the Fataluku-speaking parts of East Timor, where it is referred to as 'Makassar stone'. A similar style was employed for the grave at Tallok of Karaeng Katinting (Table 19.2), brother of the Tallok sultan Mudhaffar Tumammaliang ri Timorok who undertook a successful military expedition to Timor in 1641 (McWilliam et al. 2012).

Type F

The *candi* style (Type F) is a type of tomb shaped like a Hindu/Buddhist temple, consisting of a base, a body and a summit, constructed from a stacked arrangement of non-masoned stones and stone slabs. This style is square at its base with stacked levels and has one gravestone at the summit. Otherwise, it is variable in its form and dimensions. This type of tomb can be seen in various cemetery complexes in Barru, Bulukumba, Enrekang, Malangke and Majene.

Type G

The box style (Type G) is a type of grave shaped like a box or quadrangle, with the same dimensions at its base and its top. It also presents vertical walls that peak at the north and south facings. These tombs are constructed from a stacked arrangement of unworked stones and masonry blocks. There can be one or two gravestones on top of variable dimensions. This type of grave is found in in Jeneponto, Bantaeng, Bulukumba, Enrekang and Majene. Box graves are also common in cemeteries across the Makassar hinterland (Bulbeck 1992).

Type H

Monoliths (Type H) are a type of grave shaped from a single block of quarried stone, including the base, the body and the gravestone components. While the shape and dimensions of these graves vary, they are generally small, and are found in Jeneponto and Majene.

Type I

The wooden variety (Type I) is a grave and gravestones made of certain types of wood such as teak, ironwood and ebony. Usually these graves are richly decorated (Figure A19.1). They are found in various cemetery complexes including Tosora (Wajo), Bone, Barru and Majene.

Figure A19.1: Wooden grave and gravestones (Type I) at Makam Karaengta Bungaya, Taeng, locally associated with Karaeng Bungaya who died in 1640.

Source: Bulbeck (1992:Photo 7-38).

Type J

The standard grave style (Type J) is a grave constructed like a basin, built from unworked stones or stone blocks arranged into a parapet. Sometimes the basin shape peaks at the north and the south, some sort of ornamentation is usual, and there are one or two gravestones inserted at the end(s). This type of grave is found in almost all of the old cemetery complexes of South and West Sulawesi.

Type K

The heaped stone mound (Type K) is a tomb made just from a mound of heaped non-masoned stones, mounded or tapering towards the top, where there are one or two gravestones. This style is found in Sinjai, Soppeng, Barru, Enrekang and Majene.

Type L

The heaped earth mound (Type L) is a tomb made just from a mound of heaped earth, with one or two gravestones on top (Figure A19.2). This type of grave is found in almost all the old cemetery complexes of South and West Sulawesi.

Figure A19.2: Heaped earth mound grave with crenulated masonry gravestone (Type L) at Kuburan Islam Bontona Songkolo, upstream from Kale Gowa, reportedly associated with a local elite.

Source: Bulbeck (1992:Photo 9-38).

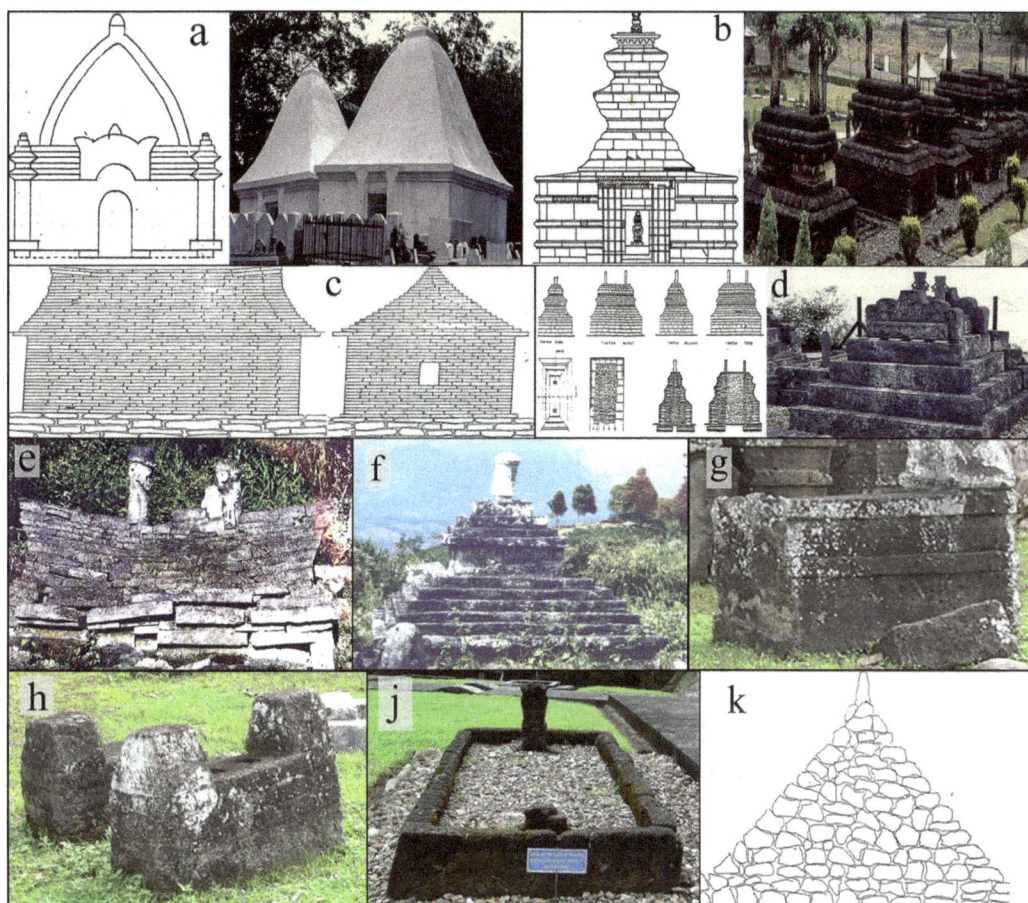

Figure A19.3: Tomb styles in South Sulawesi Islamic cemeteries.

(a) Type A – the dome-covered style, Sultan Hasanuddin complex (left), Katangka (right), Kale Gowa; (b) Type B – style covered with a stepped terrace, Kale Gowa (left), Lamuru (right); (c) Type C – style with a cover shaped like a traditional house, Makam Tandijalling; (d) Type D – stepped terrace style, La Tenri Ruwa (left), Jera Lompoe (right); (e) Type E – boat-shaped style, Makam Laiya; (f) Type F – *candi* style, Makam Laiya; (g) Type G – box style, Binamu royal cemetery; (h) Type H – monoliths, Binamu royal cemetery; (j) Type J – standard grave style, Jera Lompoe; (k) Type K – heaped stone mound (schematic representation).

Sources: Duli et al. (2013); Rosmawati field notes.

Gravestones

The author's classification and typology of gravestones is based on similar work by previous experts. It is apparent that the early Islamic types found in South and West Sulawesi are in many cases also found in Sumatra, the Malay Peninsula and Java, and so we can follow the gravestone classificatory systems of Othman Mohd. Yatim and Hasan Muarif Ambary. Ambary (1998:45) classified the Indonesian Archipelago gravestones under the Aceh, Demak (Troloyo), Ternate-Tidore and Bugis-Makasar types. The Aceh type has been associated with the expansion of Islam in the Indo-Malaysian Archipelago by Othman (1988). He divided the type into 13 styles using an alphabetical coding system (*A, B, C, D, E, F, G, H, J, K, L, M* and *N*), which were supplemented by the *O, P* and *Q* styles by Perret and Razak (1999). In South and West Sulawesi, the Aceh type is common in cemeteries that were founded during the early 17th century when Islam originated in South Sulawesi, and later cemeteries associated with the increasing spread of Islam—cemeteries such as the Sultan Hasanuddin complex in Gowa, the Tallok rulers' complex in Makassar, the Binamu rulers' complex in Jeneponto, the Latenri Ruwa complex in Bantaeng, the Lamuru rulers' complex in Bone, Lokkoe Palopo in Luwu and the Majene aristocrats' cemetery in West Sulawesi.

The Demak (Troloyo) gravestone type includes characteristic influences from Majapahit in the forms of medallions, *kalamakara* decorations, lotuses, water-lily tendrils and other classical designs, such as Javanese inscriptions in the *Jawa* script and tridents. They accompany many 18th-century graves in South and West Sulawesi, probably due to the influence of Eastern Javanese Islamic mysticism (Ricklefs 2008:60) on Sulawesi at the time. The (local) Ternate-Tidore type is characterised by gravestones with the head shaped like a pineapple and Malay inscriptions using the Arabic script, but these are rare in South Sulawesi, except at the Katangka cemetery complex (Kale Gowa). The Bugis-Makasar type is the dominant local type and is rich in floral and anthropomorphic designs, as well as megalithic forms such as statuesque gravestones, kris handles and sculptures of *lontaraq* (Bugis-Makasar script) and Arabic letters, with considerable local variation within this general type. The Bugis-Makasar type is also found in southern Thailand, Brunei and southern Philippines (Ambary 1998:95–104).

The classification applied in this composition is based on the work of previously mentioned experts. The label *A* refers to the Aceh gravestone type, or specifically *AA*. The Demak (Troloyo) type is given the label *B* and the Ternate-Tidore is codified as Type *C*. Type *D* is used for the other style types which flourished in the districts of South Sulawesi. This chapter classifies the local South Sulawesi styles within Type *D*, expanding this type with sequential numbering. For instance, the Bugis-Makasar Type 1 becomes *D1* and so on (*D2, D3* ...).

The various styles of Bugis-Makasar gravestones that occur across South Sulawesi are contained in the following subsections. Figure A19.5 at the end of this subsection represents the styles previously mentioned as well as many of those described below.

Type D1

The kris handle style (Type D1) is shaped like the handle of a kris dagger with some variety in the form, dimensions and decorations and is made from stone or wood. This style is found in the cemetery complexes of Tallok, Binamu, Latenri Ruwa, Jera Lompoe, Tosora, Lamuru, Barru, Allakkuang and Majene.

Type D2

The human figurine style (Type D2) includes anthropomorphic gravestones made of stone whether complex or simple (usually just the head with the eyes, mouth and ears). This style of gravestone is found in the cemetery complexes of Binamu, Latenri Ruwa, some graveyards in the areas of Balusu and Mallusetasi in Barru, Enrekang and Majene.

Type D3

The sword style (Type D3) is a gravestone with a sword in relief and a channel along its midline, or that is shaped like a sword handle. It is made of stone and can be found in most of the old graveyards of South and West Sulawesi.

Type D4

The spear-tip style (Type D4) is shaped like the triangular tip of a spear and is made from stone or wood. It is found in most of the old graveyards of South and West Sulawesi.

Type D5

The Bugis *songkok* style (Type D5) is shaped like a Bugis *songkok* hat, with a cylindrical form and vertical decorative lines. It is made from stone and found in the old cemetery complexes of Wajo, Bone, Sinjai and Soppeng.

Type D6

The half-sphere style (Type D6) has the shape of a semi-sphere and is sometimes accompanied by vertical decorative lines. It is found in various old cemeteries in Wajo such as the Tosora complex.

Type D7

The crown style (Type D7) is shaped like a crown and is made of stone. It is embellished with various designs on four or eight sides. It is found in almost all of the old cemetery complexes of South and West Sulawesi.

Type D8

The block style (Type D8) is made from a single block, and has four identical components and a summit that can be flat, rounded, oval or prismatic. It is made from stone or wood, and can be found in most of the old cemetery complexes of South and West Sulawesi.

Type D9

The cylindrical style (Type D9) has six or eight sides and a peak that can be rounded, oval or prismatic. It is made from stone or wood, and is found in almost all of the old cemetery complexes of South and West Sulawesi.

Type D10

The cudgel style (Type D10) has a tapering rounded shape and is created from masoned stone with varying degrees of preliminary preparation. It can be found in most of the old cemetery complexes of South and West Sulawesi.

Type D11

The phallic style (Type D11) is the gravestone formed like a penis (phallus). It is made from stone or wood and found in most of the old cemetery complexes of South and West Sulawesi.

Type D12

The menhir style (Type D12) is a menhir-shaped gravestone made from non-masoned stone, whether with prior shaping or not, thin or rounded, and found in almost all of the old cemetery complexes of South and West Sulawesi.

Type D13

The cannon style (Type D13) sometimes consists of the rear part of a cannon or is made in a similar shape from stone or wood. It can be found in the cemetery complexes of Tosora, Majene, Enrekang and Barru.

Type D14

The iron helmet style (Type D14) resembles the type of helmet that was used in the army. It is made from stone, and can be found at Tosora and in Enrekang and Majene.

Type D15

The *tempayan* style (Type D15) consists of a large storage jar that is either a high-fired imported ceramic jar from China or a local product made from earthenware. This style is found in Kale Gowa (Figure A19.4), Soppeng, Wajo, Bone and Sinjai.

Figure A19.4: Stoneware jar placed on top of the dome-covered tomb of Syech Yusuf, who was buried at Kale Gowa in 1705.

Source: Bulbeck (1992:Photo 6–25).

Figure A19.5: Gravestone types in South Sulawesi Islamic cemeteries.

(a) Aceh type in the Tallok cemetery complex; (b) Demak-Troloyo type in the Tallok cemetery complex; (c) Type D1 – kris handle style, Jera Lompoe; (d) Type D2 – human figurine style, Binamu royal cemetery (left and centre) and Makam Laiya, Enrekang (right); (e) Type D3 – sword style, Jera Lompoe (left), Makam Nagauleng (right); (f) Type D3 – sword style, Binamu (left), Takalar (centre), Type D4 – spear-tip style, Tosora (right); (g) Type D5 – Bugis *songkok* style, Tosora; (h) Type D6 – half-sphere style, Tosora; (i) Type D7 – crown style, Majene (left), Binamu (right); (j) Type D8 – block style, Makam Dea Daeng Lita (left), Binamu (centre), Tosora (right); (k) Type D9 – cylindrical style, Wajo (left and centre), Kale Gowa (right); between k and l) Type D10 – cudgel style, Takalar; (l) Type D11 – phallic style, Binamu (left), Makam Dae Daeng Lita (centre), unidentified cemetery (right); (m) Type D12 – menhir style, Tosora; (n) Type D13 – cannon style, Tosora (left), Wajo (right); (o) Type D14 – iron helmet style, Laiya.

Sources: Duli et al. (2013); Rosmawati field notes.

20

Typology of early Islamic graves of Mamuju, West Sulawesi

Muhaeminah

Abstract

A survey was performed in Mamuju in order to obtain information on cultural remains from the early Islamic presence in the area. The variety of forms, styles and the distribution of graves and gravestones relating to the early development of Islam was documented. The survey results showed: a) graves were sometimes lined by rectangular stone beams; and b) gravestones came in a large variety of forms, such as cudgel crowns, kris dagger handles and blocks that were occasionally associated with calligraphic inscriptions. The use of calligraphy on grave features might be linked with the introduction of Islam as one of the two gravestones containing calligraphic inscriptions was erected for an individual remembered for the dissemination of Islam in the region. Pre-Islamic elements were maintained as well, depicted in the gravestone types such as kris dagger handles and menhirs. This merging of styles and forms reflects the process of integration of two cultural traditions—pre-Islamic and Islamic—in the larger Mamuju region and the development of the persisting ideological system.

Keywords: Mamuju, Islamic gravestones, decorative patterns, ideological systems

Introduction

The spread of Islam through Indonesia is a significant part of the country's history with each region having its own unique story of integration with this system of beliefs. The process of Islamisation in Indonesia has been thoroughly examined and discussed, yet it is still difficult to make strict observations and conclusions on its initial stages of integration as there are few records of it, and those that are available are often not very informative (Ricklefs 2005). While there is no absolute consensus, Azra (1994) summarises the ongoing debates by describing two probable scenarios by which Islam was introduced to Island Southeast Asia (ISEA). First was via Arab traders in the 7th century AD soon after the birth of Islam in the Middle East. The second, dominant opinion amongst historians is that Islam was introduced through Gujarat traders from India in the 12th and 13th centuries AD (Nurmila 2013).

As for the establishment of Islam as a belief system in Indonesia, Ricklefs (2005) states this was likely due to a combination of factors. First, through contact between these foreign Muslim merchants and the indigenous Indonesians, after which local merchants and others embraced the teachings of Islam that the traders brought with them. Second, through Muslims migrating from the Middle East, India, China and other parts of Asia, assimilating with locals and sharing their faith with their community. Most of the hard evidence of Islamic influence in regions of Indonesia is based on the grave markers that endure even today. Grave markers for Indonesian Muslims first appear in the 13th century AD in the Lamreh cemetery in northern Sumatra where Sultan Sulaiman bin Abdullah bin al-Basir died in 1211 (Ricklefs 2005:3–4).

Tombs and grave markers are a significant resource for documenting the past, not only in observing the cultural trends for burial of the deceased through time, but also for detecting other more complex influences and changes in the region with, conveniently, an associated chronology. This potential is demonstrated in the work of Guillot and Kalus (2008 and numerous articles in *Archipel*) documenting the gravestones of northern Sumatra. This paper addresses the processes of Islamisation through gravestone classification within the Mamuju District in West Sulawesi Province (Sulawesi Barat) during the early Islamic period.

The history of the entry of Islam into Mamuju

It is still not known with certainty when Islam commenced its entry into the domain of the historical Tapalang kingdom. However, it is thought that the seeds of Islam had been sewn across Mandar by the late 17th century, because by this time the *Lanrisang* agreement had become institutionalised (Anon. 2011).[1] An excerpt from the Balanipa Mandar text, describing the *Lanrisang* agreement, follows (author's emphasis):

> Makkedani Arumpone, 'Upappada mua tanae ri Bone tanae ri Menreq usapparanna deceng. Masse ajimuiq sia. <u>Padaniq marola ri petta nabie Muhammad s.a.w</u>, pada pobicaraiq bicaratta, pada porapangngiq rapatta, pada lete ri petawung majekkota, tessi acinnangnge ri abeccukang tessi acinnangngeto ri arajang. Tessi pataqde waram parangngiq, tessipolo tanjengngiq, tessi tato lariwiq. Makkedai Bone nama teppaq Menreq-e, makkedai Menreq nama teppaq Bone. Koniro assituru senna Bone Menreq-e ri lalenna ceppae ri Lanrisang. Inai Arumpone, Torisompae. Inai Maraqdia Balanipa, Idaeng Riosoq.'

Translation:

> The ruler of Bone spoke, 'I treat the lands of Bone and Mandar as equal, our interests are aligned because we are one family. <u>Together we should kneel before the prophet Muhammad (may Allah bless him and give him peace)</u>, we should follow the same rules, equally turn straight to the law and equally use the law to resolve our crises, and not sneer at the other's smaller size nor envy the other's grandeur. We do not deprive each other of wealth, nor exacerbate each other's difficulties or turn to mutual acrimony. What Bone says Mandar believes and what Mandar says Bone believes. This is the *Lanrisang* agreement between Bone and Mandar, between the ruler of Bone, Torisompae and the ruler of Balanipa, Daeng Riosok.'

There is another account for when the Mandar community first became familiar with Islam during the 16th century from contact with Muslim traders, particularly along the coast. At around the same time, Abdurrahim Kamaluddin from Gowa came to meet the leader of Balanipa named Daetta Tommuane to introduce the splendour of Islam. Abdurrahim Kamaluddin propagated Islam by appealing to the grass roots of a populist approach by erecting huts for *pesantren* schools of Islamic studies. The *pesantren* schools and mosques were first built in the Tanggatangga area, within the realm of the historical Balanipa kingdom. Abdurrahim Kamaluddin died and was buried in Binuang, where he is titled the Binuang Master or Master Yusuf. After his death, Islam spread through the areas of Allu, Palili, Binuang and parts of Banggae (Abbas 1999).

---

1   Daeng Riosok, the Balanipa ruler mentioned in the agreement, was deposed in the late 1670s and killed in 1681 during an attempt to retake Balanipa (Andaya 1981:253–254), and so this agreement must date to the 1670s.

Another source states that at a feast in honour of the Kutai kingdom (East Kalimantan, in Indonesian Borneo) in 1608, the Mandar people in attendance abstained from any pig meat offered to them. This can be interpreted as suggesting that the Mandar people were already following the tenets of Islam, which include abstinence from pork, before the 17th century (Poelinggomang 2012:90). During the same period, Raden Suryo Dilogo (a *Kapuang* from Java) and Sayyid Zakariah from Maghreb in North Africa came to Pamboang to meet with the ruler (Mara'dia) of Pamboang whose posthumous title is Tomatindo Diagamana ('the one who died within the Islamic faith'). The acceptance of Islam by Mara'dia Pamboang was immediately followed by the Pamboang community.

In the 17th century (AD 1608), Sukkilan Mara'dia Tondo of the kingdom of Banggae (Majene) was visited by Syekh Abdul Mannan (whose title was Tosalama) whose intention was to spread Islam (Abbas 1999). This visit resulted in the acceptance of Islam by the Mara'dia of Banggae. At the same time, Sendana, Pamboang and Tapalang in the Mamuju area were visited by the Islamic missionaries, Raden Suryo Dilogo and Sayyid Zakariah. Raden Suryo Dilogo was a pupil of Sunan Bonang who also came to Sulawesi (from Kalimantan) and set himself up in Mamuju as his first established residency (Poelinggomang 2012:93; Alimuddin et al. 2013).

Some Mandar texts cite Abdul Rahim Kamaluddin as the first person to disseminate Islam in Mandar, specifically in coastal Tammangalle where he first set foot in Mandar. According to the Pattappingan Mandar text, during the reign of Mara'dia Balanipa Kakanna Ipattang, the Tosalama of Binuang, who was known as Abdul Rahim Kamaluddin, converted the leaders and other people of Balanipa as well as the other large communities of Napo, Samasundu, Mosso and Todatodang (Yasil 1999:60–66). However, the Mandar text itself names Kanne Cunang (Mara'dia Pallis) as the first to embrace Islam, followed by the fourth ruler of Balanipa, Daetta Tommuane, also known as Kakanna Ipattang (Alimuddin et al. 2013). According to a Gowa text, Syekh Yusuf Tuanta Salamaka first brought Islam to Mandar. In 1608, several kingdoms in Mandar, including Balanipa, Pambuang, Binuang, Mamuju, Sendana and Tapalang too, embraced Islam (Hamid 1982:15–16).

Research methods

Fieldwork was based along the coastal lowlands in the west of Mamuju Disrict, namely in the Tapalang Barat and Mamuju subdistricts. Surveys were conducted so as to collect primary data on the early Islamic graves of that region. Survey methods included field observations, photography and recording geographic coordinates of important sites. The equipment used during the survey included measuring tapes, a compass, a GPS and cameras to take photos with a scale and north arrow. Secondary data were also compiled from searching the current literature and reports from previous research. By combining the information from the primary and secondary data, the graves were classified based on the variety of shapes and significant attributes.

Early Islamic graveyards in Mamuju District

During the fieldwork, five early Islamic graveyards were surveyed and recorded in Mamuju District, two of them in West (*Barat*) Tapalang Subdistrict (Dungkait Cemetery and Tosalama Graveyard II) and three in Mamuju Subdistrict (Tosalama Graveyard I, Tonileo Cemetery and Loa Batu Grave). The descriptions of the local sites, exact coordinates of their location and height above sea level are set out in Table 20.1.

Table 20.1: Five early Islamic graveyards recorded by the author in Mamuju District.

Site name	Administrative location				Geographic coordinates		Altitude (metres above sea level)
	Kampong/ Locality	*Desa* (village)	*Kelurahan* (village)	*Kecamatan* (subdistrict)	South	East	
Dungkait Cemetery	Dungkait	Dungkait	—	Tapalang Barat	2°51'09.9"	118°48'09.4"	15
Tosalama I	Timbu	—	Mamuju	Mamuju	2°40'24.1"	118°54'08.7"	22
Tosalama II	Saranga	Pasa'bu	—	Tapalang Barat	2°51'11.1"	118°50'11.8"	8
Tonileo Cemetery	Baru	Mamunyu	—	Mamuju	2°40'10.0"	118°54'00.5"	14
Loda Batu Grave	—	—	Mamunyu	Mamuju	2°40'27.3"	118°54'11.7"	23

Source: Author's data.

Dungkait Cemetery

The Dungkait Cemetery is an early graveyard in the town of Dungkait that is not maintained, and overgrown vegetation encroaches the graves (Figure 20.1). The local people have little to no knowledge of the names or ancestries of the deceased. There are 14 graves in the cemetery, some with large paired gravestones and other early gravestones features, all of which are made from sandstone.

One of the graves has a single standing stone with a second gravestone that has fallen down and subsequently been buried by natural sedimentation processes (far right and back of Figure 20.1). The standing gravestone has a rectangular cross-section and a dome-shaped crown. All four faces have calligraphic bas-relief engravings (Figure 20.2). This gravestone is 90 cm above ground surface and 24 cm at its widest point. Its buried counterpart has sharp features made of sandstone that are slightly visible above the ground surface. According to an informant, this is the grave of Pua Andi Belo who proselytised Islam in Tapalang around the mid-19th century (Abdul Majid Gattung, pers. comm., 12 June 2015). On the other hand, a date at the base of the north face of the gravestone that seems to reads 1226 in the Islamic calendar (AD 1811) suggests an earlier age for this grave.

Figure 20.1: Some of the graves found in Dungkait Cemetery, Tapalang Barat, Mamuju District.

Source: The author.

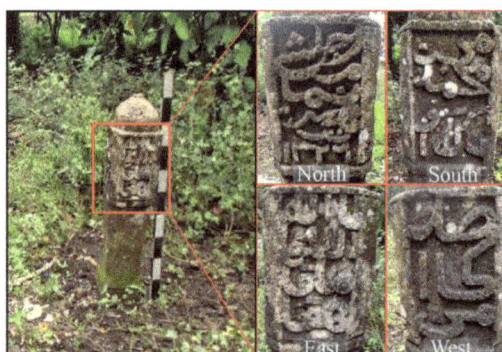

Figure 20.2: Headstone with rectangular cross-section decorated with calligraphic engravings on the upper section of all four faces, Dungkait Cemetery.

Source: The author.

Figure 20.3: Grave with two gravestones, one of them octagonal with a domed top, Dungkait Cemetery.

Source: The author.

Figure 20.4: The third grave with two gravestones mostly buried under the ground surface, Dungkait Cemetery.

Source: The author.

Figure 20.5: The fourth and fifth graves within a retaining wall, Dungkait Cemetery.

Source: The author.

Another grave in the southern part of Dungkait Cemetery also has two gravestones (Figure 20.3). The northern marker is octagonal and is 60 cm high with a diameter of 66 cm. The top is dome shaped, resembling a multiple gyre, and has a variety of ornamental indentations. The southern stone is shaped like the handle of a sharp, bladed weapon (kris dagger) and has little ornamentation. Its dimensions are 44 cm high, 23 cm wide and 9 cm thick.

A third grave in the eastern part of the cemetery has two gravestones that are mostly buried below the ground surface (Figure 20.4). The marker to the north is rectangular that tapers to a pyramid-shaped temple peak with a variety of impressed decorations on its sides. Its height from the ground surface is 29 cm and its width is 21 cm. The southern gravestone has a width of 24 cm and is 7 cm thick.

On the east side of the cemetery is a cluster of graves that include Dungkait Cemetery's fourth and fifth graves (as labelled here) and two other graves. This group of graves is surrounded by a retaining wall that is 20 cm high, built at a later date by the descendants of the deceased, as demonstrated by the cement mortar used to hold the stones together (Figure 20.5). Three of the graves in this group retain both their head- and footstones, whereas the grave markers of the final grave can no longer be seen. The fourth grave's northern marker has a rectangular outline marked with a relief of several hems and impressed bands as well as a dome-shaped top; it measures 71 cm high and 27 cm thick. The southern stone (46 cm high, 28 cm wide and 8 cm thick) is shaped like the handle to a kris dagger and decorated with several spirals. The fifth grave's northern marker has an oval outline and is covered with impressed decorations encircled by calligraphy. It has a dome-shaped top and measures 80 cm high and 49 cm in diameter. The gravestone to the south is rectangular with hems but no calligraphy, and measures 65 cm high and 29 cm thick.

One of the graves has two broken gravestones, round in shape, inside a neighbouring cement retaining wall (far right and behind in Figure 20.5). The gravestone to the north is 44 cm high and 34 cm in diameter, while its counterpart to the south is 38 cm high and 35 cm in diameter. To the east of this grave is another without an enclosing wall, marked by a single gravestone shaped like the handle to a kris dagger. It has spiral and twirled decorations, and measures 52 cm in height, 25 cm in width and 7 cm in thickness.

Approximately 50 m north of the aforementioned group is another cluster of four graves. Two of these are associated with commemorated personages, namely Tumaribawo (also known as Labolong), who proselytised Islam in Tapalang, and his wife, Maddara Takku, also known as Tomapute Darana (person with white (royal) blood). According to information from the head of Dungkait village, Maskur Rahman, and Abdul Majid Gattung, Tomapute Darana was the daughter of a king of Bone (the most powerful of the indigenous Bugis kingdoms whose close relationship with Mandar is reflected in the 17th-century *Lanrisang*

agreement noted previously) who married Labolong (a local Tapalang courageous man) in an act of assistance from the kingdom of Bone (pers. comm., 9 June 2015 and 12 June 2015, respectively). Her memory survives in her grave, which has side walls, crenulated north and south end-markers (*gunongan*) and a gravestone shaped like the handle of a kris dagger (Figure 20.6). The side walls have three levels made from limestone beams. The grave is 179 cm long and 86 cm wide. It is flanked to its east by the grave of Labolong, whose gravestones are broken and have partly collapsed into the grave of Tomapute Darana.

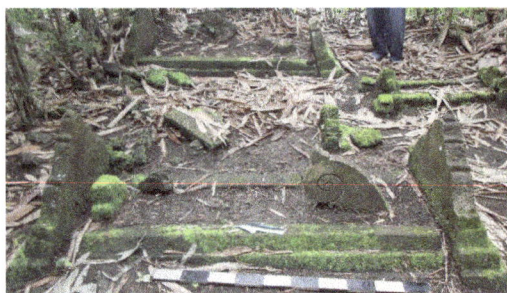

Figure 20.6: The graves of Tomapute Darana, a daughter of a king of Bone, and her husband, Labolong, Dungkait Cemetery.

Source: The author.

The Tosalama of Timbu Graveyard in Timbu (Tosalama I)

The Tosalama of Timbu Graveyard is located on the middle of a hill in Timbu kampong (Figure 20.7). The majority of the graves in this cemetery are degraded, buried in the ground or obscured by vegetation. The only grave that is well looked after is the principal grave belonging to the *Tosalama* of Timbu. The birth name of this person and his community that gave him the title are not exactly known, though it is agreed that he is memorialised for circulating the teachings of Islam in Timbu.

In its present form, the *Tosalama*'s grave enclosure and the two head/foot markers are recent restorations made from cement, but they imitate the original gravestones. The northern marker is shaped like a monolith, measures 70 cm high and 38 cm in diameter, and has several cords around it, which were tied there by pilgrims. The marker at the south, which measures 26 cm high and 18 cm in diameter, has a hexagonal shape and a variety of impressed decorations. The overall shape resembles the gravestones at the Tonileo Cemetery (see below).

Figure 20.7: An example of the graves that are no longer cared for in the Timbu Tosalama graveyard (left); The grave of the *Tosalama* of Timbu, still revered by the local community (right).
Source: The author.

The Tosalama of Labuang Grave at Saranga, Pasu'bu village (Tosalama II)

Another grave dedicated by a local community to a *Tosalama* is located near the coastline in the Saranga locality (Figure 20.8). The grave has deteriorated over time due to water erosion from king tides from the neighbouring shore line (Figure 20.9). The Pasa'bu village community has built a stone wall to act as a levee against this threat from the sea; however, this too is degrading. The stone beams that cover and enclose the grave are displaced, but the grave form and the gravestones are partly preserved. The body of the grave was made from thin, cuboid beams that were once stacked. Just the northern gravestone remains, and its top is broken. It is made of sandstone and has the shape of a cudgel. Its dimensions are 46 cm in height and 43 cm in diameter. The wall is made of course limestone cobbles held together with mortar with an original height of 80 cm and is 9 m long.

Figure 20.8: Arrow points at the grave of the *Tosalama* of Labuang located near the sea at Pasa'bu village.
Source: The author.

Figure 20.9: The *Tosalama* of Labuang's grave in deteriorated condition from beach spray abrasion.
Source: The author.

Tonileo Cemetery

The Tonileo Cemetery includes the grave of a man named Tonileo, as well as other graves on the same hilltop of people whose names and community affiliations are no longer known. According to Muhammad Kasim, who lives in Tambi where the cemetery is located, Tonileo was the father of Lasalaga (see below) and an immigrant from Bali (pers. comm., 10 June 2015). The graves are set in a bamboo clump on a hilltop, which can be reached by a walking path with concrete steps. Tonileo Cemetery is part of a larger cemetery complex with recent graves on the slopes of this same hill.

The walls and gravestones of Tonileo's grave are made of sandstone with a finishing of ceramic tiles along the upper walls, and a ceramic coating holding together the peaked marker at the north largely obscuring its underlying decorations (Figure 20.10). The grave's outer dimensions are 280 cm long and 143 cm wide, and it has two gravestones. The northern gravestone has the shape of an octagonal cudgel with spiralling incised decorations and a dome-shaped top. It is 86 cm high with a diameter of 38 cm. The southern gravestone is buried up to its neck, and the visible part is shaped as the handle of a kris dagger with spiral designs. Its dimensions are 120 cm high, 19 cm wide and 8 cm thick.

Tonileo's grave lies inside a wooden enclosure built by the local community, along with another grave of an unknown person to the immediate northwest. The latter grave includes walls of stacked sandstone arranged in a rectangle. An end-marker in the north protrudes from the wall with another standing marker made of wood.

Outside of the enclosure are 14 graves, most of which are in a poor condition. One of them still retains its side walls and end-markers, although these have disintegrated to the point where their original form is no longer discernible. The grave is 159 cm long and 57 cm wide, while the head marker is 42 cm high, 87 cm wide and 15 cm thick.

Figure 20.10: The grave of Tonileo with its headstone in the shape of an octagonal cudgel and footstone shaped like a weapon handle.

Source: The author.

Further to the east in this cemetery are six graves that still have their side walls and end-markers, though these are collapsed and lack gravestones. Another grave here, located beneath a large tree, has walls made of sandstone beams, and a footstone at the south. This footstone has a flat cross-section, the shape of a handle of a kris dagger and a variety of spiral decorations.

The grave of Lasalaga (Loda Batu)

The grave shown in Figures 20.11 and 20.12 has two names. One is Lasalaga associated with Mamuju nobility, the other is Loda Batu ('atop rock') used generally by the Timbu community. According to a Timbu community member, Muhammad Kasim, the grave is mostly demolished as a result of a large tree falling on it at around 1950 (pers. comm., 10 June 2015). He added that the original grave had a bowed form (with a small top decker mounted by a gravestone) and was made of stacked rectangular stones with a lid shaped like those of the royal graves of Gowa (the most important of the Makasar kingdoms).

Figure 20.11: The Lasalaga (Loda Batu) grave and modern shelter.
Source: The author.

Figure 20.12: The disturbed condition of the Lasalaga (Loda Batu) grave.
Source: The author.

Discussion

Forms of old Islamic Graves in Mamuju

Classification of graves

In Indonesian dictionaries, *makam* (grave) has the same meaning as *kubur* (burial), which means a hole created in the ground for interring a corpse (Pusat Bahasa 2008:827, 970). In general, old graves include an enclosure, gravestones, covering and end-markers, in various forms.

The variables to be used for defining classes include morphological and descriptive variables. They facilitate a preliminary step towards exegesis, because abstract classes are productive for facilitating archaeological analysis (Thomas 1979:213–217). The classification in this study divides the graves into groups based on their shape attributes. This exercise considers that, in general, the graves have several components (e.g. grave cover, enclosure and gravestones) and several graves have one or two end-markers.

To make the classification of graves simpler, the analytical classification of graves in this research is an adaptation of the classificatory model of Rosmawati (this volume), of which the types listed below were observed during the Mamuju survey.

(a) Grave types

    (1) The form covered with a stepped terrace (type B), consisting of stacked terraces ascending to a plateau where one or two gravestones are placed.

    (2) The stone chest form (type E, Rosmawati's type J), which has a long rectangular shape, usually stepped and with raised end markers at the head and foot of the grave.

    (3) The mound form (type F, Rosmawati's types K and L), which is covered by a mound of stones or earth.

(b) Gravestone types

    (1) The kris handle form (type C, Rosmawati's D1 style), which includes gravestones shaped like the handle to a kris dagger.

    (2) The cudgel style (type G, Rosmawati's D10 style), which includes gravestones shaped like cudgels.

(3) The cylindrical form (type H, Rosmawati's D9 style), which includes cylindrical or rounded cylindrical gravestones.

(4) The menhir form (type J, Rosmawati's D12 style), which includes gravestones shaped like monoliths.

(5) The block form (type K, Rosmawati's D8 style), which includes gravestones with a block-shaped or cubic base.

Assignment of the field observations to the grave and gravestone classifications is presented in Table 20.2. This classification is based on 12 graves from five sites.

Table 20.2: Typological classification of the graves and gravestones recorded in Mamuju District.

Grave No.	Site	Grave type	Gravestone type		Raised end-markers		Buried personage
			North	South	North	South	
M1	Dungkait	F	G	C	—	—	Pua Andi Belo
M2	Dungkait	F	H	C	—	—	Unidentified
M3	Dungkait	Unidentified	K	C	—	—	Unidentified
M4	Dungkait	E	K	C	—	—	Unidentified
M5	Dungkait		K	K	—	—	Unidentified
M6	Dungkait	E	Unidentified	C	√	√	Tomapute Darana
M7	Dungkait	E	Unidentified	Unidentified	√	√	Labolong
M8	Tosalama I	E	J	G	√	√	*Tosalama* of Timbu
M9	Tosalama II	Unidentified	G	—	—	—	*Tosalama* of Labuan
M10	Tonileo	E	G	C	√	—	Tonileo
M11	Tonileo	E	Unidentified	C	—	√	Unidentified
M12	Loda Batu	B	Unidentified	Unidentified	—	—	Lasalaga

Source: Author's data.

Of the three types of identified graves, type E was the most widespread, recorded in six graves: three at the Dungkait cemetery, two at Tonileo cemetery and the grave of the *Tosalama* of Timbu. Type F was identified twice at Dungkait cemetery, and type B once, at Loda Batu (the grave of Lasalaga). There are also two collapsed graves whose condition prevented them from being classified (a grave at the Dungkait cemetery, and the *Tosalama* of Labuan grave), but which are included in Table 20.2 because one or both of their gravestones could be classified.

Five gravestone types C, G, H, J and K, were encountered. Type C was the most frequently observed (seven cases), but always placed at the south of the grave, at the M1, M2, M3, M4 and M6 graves of the Dungkait cemetery and two graves at Tonileo cemetery. Type K was also quite frequently observed, at least at the Dungkait cemetery where it was normally placed at the north end of the M3, M4 and M5 graves, and also at the south end of the M5 grave. Four cases of type G were also recorded, erected as the gravestone at the north end of Pua Andi Belo's grave at the Dungkait cemetery (M1), the Tosalama II grave and Tonileo's grave, and as the gravestone at the south end of the Tosalama I grave. Types H and J were both encountered only once, at the north of the M2 grave in the Dungkait Cemetery and the north of the Tosalama I grave, respectively. There were five gravestones whose type could not be identified, namely both gravestones of the M7 grave at Dungkait Cemetery and the Loda Batu grave as well as the north gravestone of the M6 Dungkait Cemetery grave (Table 20.2).

Accordingly, the graves generally have paired gravestones at the north and the south ends, with the exception of the Tosalama II grave with a single gravestone at its north. However, there does not seem to be any clear relationship between grave and gravestone type. For instance, the type C gravestone occurred in association with both E and F type graves.

Rosmawati (this volume) notes the incorporation of traditional Bugis-Makasar iconography into the tomb and gravestone styles of Southwest Sulawesi, including the tombs shaped like a traditional house or like a Hindu pagoda, and the gravestones shaped like a human figurine, phallus or menhir. Of these, the only example recorded during the Mamuju survey was the menhir gravestone at the Tosalama I grave. However, it should be noted that the kris dagger is a traditional Southwest Sulawesi weapon developed into its currently recognised form during the 14th and 15th centuries in Majapahit Java (Frey 1988), and old Islamic gravestones shaped like kris handles are common not only in western coastal Mamuju (this chapter) but also across Southwest Sulawesi more generally (Rosmawati, this volume). Accordingly, kris handles would appear to be a traditional symbol that was particularly important for the development of a syncretist iconography during the early Islamic period in Mamuju.

Chronology and purpose

While it is expected that Islamic graves date back to the 17th century based on the recorded history of the introduction of Islam to Mandar, there is no direct evidence that any of the graves described here date that early. However, the continuity of iconography with pre-Islamic roots in some of the early graves suggests that some could be that early, especially those graves whose associations are no longer remembered. The perpetuation of this iconography into graves dated from oral history to around the 19th century suggests that the entire 17th–19th-century period could be described as the early Islamic period in Mamuju.

Three of the graves recorded during this survey memorialise personages remembered for disseminating Islam. One is the grave of Pua Andi Belo, who proselytised Islam in the 19th century according to local oral history, and the others are the graves of Tumaribawo and the *Tosalama* of Timbu, whose time of proselytising is unrecorded. Significantly, a gravestone of Pua Andi Belo is one of only two recorded examples with calligraphic inscriptions.

Conclusion

The old Islamic graves recorded at Mamuju District include three grave types—the form covered with a stepped terrace, the stone chest form and the mound form. The stone chest form was the most frequent type, found at the Dungkait and Tonileo cemeteries and the Tosalama I grave. Five gravestone types were documented—the kris handle, cudgel, cylindrical, menhir and block forms. As recorded at the Dungkait and Tonileo cemeteries, the kris handle form was the most frequent, albeit apparently not used for the northern gravestone.

This contribution's coverage of the old gravestones of Mamuju District is restricted to the Mamuju and Tapalang subdistricts along the western coastal strip. To obtain a more complete coverage of the old gravestones of Mamuju District, it would be necessary to collect data across a larger area. Follow-up study is required, and then it would be possible to place the information on early Islamic archaeology presented here within its broader context.

Author biography

Muhaeminah Makassar Archaeology Office, Makassar, South Sulawesi, Indonesia

References

Abbas, I. 1999. *Pendekatan Budaya Mandar*. Makassar: UD Hijrah Grafika.

Alimuddin, M.H., S. Yasil and Sulaiman. 2013. *Warisan Salabose: Sejarah dan Tradisi Maulid*. Majene: Kerjasama Pemerintah Kabupaten Majene.

Andaya, L.Y. 1981. *The Heritage of Arung Palakka: A History of South Sulawesi (Celebes) in the Seventeenth Century*. Verhandelingen van het Koninklijk Instituut voor Taal-, Land- en Volkenkunde 91. The Hague: Martinus Nijhoff.

Anon. 2011. *Assitaliang: Sekilas tentang Mandar pada Masa Pemerintahan Tradisional*. budayamandar. blogspot.com/ (accessed 20 November 2015).

Azra, A. 1994. *Jaringan Ulama: Timur Tengah dan Kepulauan Nusantara Abad XVII dan XVIII. Melacak Akar-Akar Pembaruan Pemikiran Islam di Indonesia*. Jakarta: Mizan Publishing.

Frey, E. 1988. *The Kris: Mystic Weapon of the Malay World*. Selangor Darul Ehsan: Oxford University Press.

Guillot, C. and L. Kalus. 2008. *Les Monuments funéraires et l'histoire du Sultanat de Pasai à Sumatra*. Paris: Archipel, Cahiers d'Archipel 37.

Hamid, A. 1982. Selayang Pandang uraian tentang Islam dan kebudayaan orang Bugis-Makassar di Sulawesi Selatan. In A.M. Oesman and A.R. Amir (eds), *Bugis-Makassar dalam Peta Islamisasi Indonesia*. Ujung Pandang [Makassar]: Institut Agama Islam Negeri Alauddin.

Nurmila, N. 2013. The Indonesian Muslim feminist reinterpretation of inheritance. In J. Burhanudin and K. van Dijk (eds), *Islam in Indonesia: Contrasting Images and Interpretations*, pp. 109–122. ICAS Publications Series. Amersterdam: Amsterdam University Press. doi.org/10.2307/j.ctt46mwqt.10 (accessed 5 June 2018).

Poelinggomang, E.L. 2012. *Sejarah dan Budaya Sulawesi Barat*. Makassar: Kerjasama Balai Pelestarian Nilai Budaya Makassar dan De Lamacca.

Pusat Bahasa. 2008. *Kamus Bahasa Indonesia*. Jakarta: Pusat Bahasa.

Ricklefs, M. 2005. *Sejarah Indonesia Modern*. Translated into Indonesian from *A History of Modern Indonesia*. Yogyakarta: Gadjah Mada University Press.

Rosmawati. 2018. Typology and efflorescence of the tomb and gravestone forms of ancient Islamic Graves in South Sulawesi and Majene, West Sulawesi. In S. O'Connor, D. Bulbeck and J. Meyer (eds), *The Archaeology of Sulawesi: Current Research on the Pleistocene to the Historic Period*, pp. 327–344. Canberra: ANU Press.

Thomas, D.H. 1979. *Archaeology*. New York/London: Holt, Rinehart and Winston.

Yasil, S. 1999. *Asal Usul Nama dan Ringkasan Isi Naskah Lontara Pattappingan Mandar dan Kajian Atasnya*. Bulletin Bosara No. 14/VI. Makassar: Balai Kajian Sejarah Nilai Tradisional Makassar.

www.ingramcontent.com/pod-product-compliance
Lightning Source LLC
Chambersburg PA
CBHW041428270326
41932CB00031B/3493